I0820143

The World and Work of Father John J. Burke

Other Books of Interest from St. Augustine's Press

Georg Gänswein with Saverio Gaeta, *Who Believes Is Not Alone: My Life Beside Benedict XVI*

Donald S. Prudlo and Paul J. Voss, *Merchant Saint: The Church, the Market, and the First Lay Canonization*

Predrag Cicovacki, *The Ethic of the Upward Gaze: Essays Inspired by Immanuel Kant and Nicolai Hartmann*

Leo Strauss, *Leo Strauss' Published but Uncollected English Writings*

Jeremy Black, *Defoe's Britain*

Jeremy Black, *In Fielding's Wake*

Jeremy Black, *Smollett's Britain*

Jeremy Black, *The Importance of Being Poirot*

Marvin R. O'Connell, *Telling Stories That Matter: Memoirs and Essays*

George J. Marlin, *Mario Cuomo: The Myth and the Man*

D. Q. McInerny, *Being Philosophical*

Daniel J. Mahoney, *The Other Solzhenitsyn: Telling the Truth about a Misunderstood Writer and Thinker*

Daniel J. Mahoney, *Recovering Politics, Civilization, and the Soul: Essays on Pierre Manent and Roger Scruton*

Gabriel Marcel, *Toward Another Kingdom: Two Dramas of the Darker Years*

Gene Fendt, *Camus' Plague: Myth for Our World*

Gerard V. Bradley, *Unquiet Americans: U.S. Catholics, Moral Truth, and the Preservation of Civil Liberties*

Michael Franz (editor), *Eric Voegelin's Late Meditations and Essays: Critical Commentary Companions*

John von Heyking, *Comprehensive Judgment and Absolute Selflessness: Winston Churchill on Politics as Friendship*

Winston Churchill, *Savrola*

Winston Churchill, *The River War*

Winston Churchill, *My Early Life*

The World and Work of Father John J. Burke

A Mystic in Action

DOUGLAS J. SLAWSON

ST. AUGUSTINE'S PRESS
South Bend, Indiana

Manufactured in the United States of America.

1 2 3 4 5 6 30 29 28 27 26 25

Library of Congress Control Number: 2024940217

Clothbound ISBN: 978-1-58731-914-3

∞ The paper used in this publication meets the minimum requirements of the American National Standard for Information Sciences – Permanence of Paper for Printed Materials, ANSI Z39.48-1984.

St. Augustine's Press
www.staugustine.net

For My Wife and Dearest Friend
Linda M. Lepeirs,
Pilgrim Companion on Life's Journey

Table of Contents

Introduction

Father John J. Burke, C.S.P., is one of the most significant, yet little-known, American Catholic churchmen of the twentieth century. The subtitle of this biography is an underlying theme. Catholicism's most profound influence on Burke was in spirituality. The rich tradition of mysticism within the Church and his own religious community, the Paulist Fathers known formally as the Missionary Society of St. Paul the Apostle, resonated deeply within him. He had a profound sense of the divine in nature and humanity, and an equally profound sense of the love of Christ for him, which drew from him a like response. He lived the "Song of Songs" or the "Song of Solomon": the lover and the beloved. He had a palpable sense of the Church as the Mystical Body of Christ alive in the world. Like Christian mystics of all times, life with and in Christ compelled him to act for others and for society as a whole. His life was a continual sacrifice of himself for others and the Church.

The religious world in which Burke dwelt was a decidedly Catholic one. For him, Catholicism—the ancient faith—was the fullest, truest expression of Christianity. An important mission of the Catholic Church was to convert non-Christians to the faith and to bring Protestant ones back to the fold. Indeed, the Paulist community had as its purpose the conversion of America. Its founder, the convert Father Isaac Hecker, argued that the first principles of the United States were Catholic, rather than Protestant. A key element of his apologetic was to demonstrate that for a Protestant American to be consistent, the person should become Catholic. Moreover, a vibrant Catholic America had a mission to revitalize Catholicism worldwide. American Protestants, who constituted the vast majority of the population, however, considered Catholicism a false, idolatrous religion with a political agenda of subjugating the United States, indeed all nations, to the despotism of Rome. During the 1920s and early 1930s, this anti-Catholicism was a prominent element of the milieu within which Burke functioned.

The secular world in which Burke dwelt was ever changing. He came of age in the industrial era, a time of free-booting capitalism dominated by enterprising men, dubbed by one commentator as "robber barons," who created an aristocracy of wealth. They and the managerial class beneath them amassed fortunes on the back of labor made cheap by hordes of immigrants. It was a time of boom and bust. There followed the Progressive Era, a multifaceted reform movement aimed at redressing the worst evils of the previous age, thereby reducing the lure of socialism and saving the capitalist system. Burke himself was a Catholic of progressive stripe. In 1914, war erupted in Europe, sparked by the assassination of Archduke Franz Ferdinand of the Austro-Hungarian Empire. The United States maintained a pro-Allied neutrality until it entered the fray in 1917, impelling Burke into public life. Following the war came the so-called "Roaring Twenties," an era of prosperity for the upper and middle class, but one that bypassed farmers and wage earners. It was also an era of conformity which sought to maintain the dominance of white, Anglo-Saxon, Protestant culture. Good times for some collapsed into the Great Depression for the many, which Franklin Delano Roosevelt sought to end with a New Deal for the American people.

Burke's work took two forms: first as editor of the Paulist monthly magazine *Catholic World* and then as founder and general secretary (chief administrative officer) of the National Catholic War Council and its successor the National Catholic Welfare Conference, the present-day United States Conference of Catholic Bishops (USCCB). An introverted intellectual with a literary flair, Burke was well suited for and loved publishing, a job he reluctantly relinquished. World War I propelled him onto the public stage. As general secretary of the War Council and Welfare Conference, he engaged heavily with other organizations, both Catholic and non-Catholic, as well as with religious communities, dioceses, and especially the federal government to protect Catholic interests and to inject Catholic principles into public life. Because of his position as general secretary, the biography recounts not only his life but also chronicles, by way of his life, the Church's involvement in national affairs. His post gave him daily oversight of the NCWC headquarters in Washington and immersed him in a myriad of issues. I have tried to select those important to him which I hope general readers and scholars will find interesting: education, particularly the protection of parochial schools against state and federal legislation promoted by anti-Catholic organizations to destroy them; immigration in a time that sought to exclude races and peoples deemed alien and undesirable; motion pictures and their influence on public morality; negotiation for use of wine for sacramental purposes during Prohibition; birth control whose promoters sought legal acceptance of it; the Great Depression and New Deal especially in light of Catholic social justice; and American Catholic international efforts on behalf of Haitians under American occupation and an end to the Church-state conflict in Mexico, a matter that monopolized much of Burke's time and energy in the final decade of his life. Chapters are subdivided by topic and the topics develop along with Burke's life.

Each chapter is headed with a quotation from Burke's book *Christ in Us*. It is a compilation of thoughtful meditations for lay people about how to live in Christ and He in them through all life's ups and downs. That was the life Burke himself lived. The connection of each quotation with the material in the chapter is sometimes obvious, and others will take some thought.

I have chosen to present that life in narrative, chronological form to show the progressive physical toll the work took on Burke, especially his efforts at the War Council and Welfare Conference. The bishops for whom he labored came to depend on him so much that they refused to let him quit. In one sense, they worked him to death; in another sense, his spirituality made him complicit. Throughout the narrative, I have been attentive to Burke's emotional and spiritual life, which comes through most vividly in his memoranda to himself and in his correspondence to beloved friends. He was most forthcoming to the latter about his health and how he felt about the trials and at times joys of his work. My purpose in doing so is to help readers get to know the man personally instead of simply operationally, which is the way most scholars present him, that is, as his work bears on their subject of study. My hope is that when readers finish the book, they will feel that they knew something of John Burke the man.

I have lived with Burke as a historical acquaintance for over forty years through my research and writing on various topics pertaining to the National Catholic Welfare Conference. I have come to know something of the man and along the way incurred many debts to many people. I cannot mention them all because names have fallen from memory over the decades, and it would be unfair to remember some while omitting others. Many of them are archivists who curated sources not directly pertaining to Burke, but which I have used in my writings about the Welfare Conference and which have informed this biography. I do owe special thanks to those who have assisted me over the years with Burke sources directly: Dr. Warren Willis, former archivist of the United States Conference of Catholic Bishops; W. John Shepherd, archivist at the American Catholic Resource Center and University Archives at The Catholic University of America; Dr. Jeffrey Burns, former archivist of the Archdiocese of San Francisco; Father Paul Robichaud, C.S.P., and Denise Eggers at the Paulist Archives.

Last and foremost, I thank my dearest friend and wife Linda M. Lepeirs who has supported and put up with me throughout this project. Often she has felt the widow to it, for which I am deeply sorry. Yet, she has ever been my willing listener, helpmate, and love, to whom and for whom I am most grateful.

Douglas J. Slawson
San Diego, California
March 2024

Abbreviations

AAB-AASMSU	Archives of the Archdiocese of Baltimore–Associated Archives of St. Mary's Seminary and University
AABo	Archives of the Archdiocese of Boston
AASF	Archives of the Archdiocese of San Francisco
AASL	Archives of the Archdiocese of St. Louis
AASUS-AASMSU	Archives of the Associated Sulpicians of the United States, Associated Archives of St. Mary's Seminary and University
AAP	Archives of the Archdiocese of Philadelphia
ACBCCU	Archives of the Central Bureau of the Catholic Central Union
ACUA	American Catholic Resource Center and University Archives at The Catholic University of America
ADA	Archives of the Diocese of Albany
ADCh	Archives of the Diocese of Charleston
ADCl	Archives of the Diocese of Cleveland
ADP	Archives of the Diocese of Portland, Maine
ADR	Archives of the Diocese of Richmond
AFCS	American Federation of Catholic Societies
AGU	Archives of Georgetown University
AKC	Archives of the Knights of Columbus
ANCEA	Archives of the National Catholic Educational Association
AP	Archives of the Paulist Fathers
ASCACL	Archives and Special Collections of Amherst College Library
AUND	Archives of the University of Notre Dame

ASV	*Archivio Segreto del Vaticano*
CMS	Center for Migration Studies
CSWA	Committee on Special War Activities
CTCA	Commission on Training Camp Activities
DAUS	*Delegazione Apostolica Degli Stati Uniti*
FCC	Federal Council of Churches
FDRL	Franklin Delano Roosevelt Library
FULSC	Flinders University Library Special Collections
HLHU	Houghton Library, Harvard University
NA	National Archives
NEA	National Education Association
NCCM	National Council of Catholic Men
NCCW	National Council of Catholic Women
NCWC	National Catholic War/Welfare Council/Conference
NRP	National Revolutionary Party of Mexico
USCCB[1]	United States Conference of Catholic Bishops
YMCA	Young Men's Christian Association
YWCA	Young Women's Christian Association

1 Throughout the endnotes, citations to the USCCB alone refer to papers in the Office of the General Secretary. References to papers in other departments are cited USCCB followed by the department name, for example, USCCB Legal Department.

Part I
From Editor's Chair to Public Stage

Chapter 1
New York Native and Paulist Priest

> Childhood is our only age of innocence. In childhood are planted those seeds which afterwards yield virtue, even as is very necessary, the virtue of penance. When we sin, when we are bound by the habit of sin, we see the hope of recovery in our childhood: in that innocence which was once ours: to which we know we must return if we are ever to be with God again. The years should make us only the stronger, the older children. Thus did our Lord teach when he said unless we become as little children we cannot enter the kingdom of heaven.[1]

Birth and Family

Born to Irish immigrants Patrick and Mary (Regan) Burke, John Joseph Burke entered the world in New York City on 6 June 1875, fourth of eight children to survive infancy. He was preceded in birth by Mary, Thomas, and Anna. When John was two, his parents had James, and later Julia, Elizabeth, and William. There was a ninth sibling who was either stillborn or died in infancy; the child is never named or spoken of in family correspondence.[2]

Patrick was famine Irish and migrated with his parents from Trim, County Meath, in 1850 at age ten. Three years his junior, Mary Regan was from Cork and came to America in 1859 at sixteen. They married in 1868 or 1869. At the time of John's birth, they lived on Manhattan's West Side near new St. Patrick's cathedral, which was then under construction. The nation was in the grip of a depression begun by the Panic of 1873, which hit the city hard. Unemployment climbed as manufacturing and construction sagged, and employees lucky enough to keep jobs found their hours increased and their pay cut by as much as half. Self-employed as a horseshoer, a trade necessary in urban transportation, Patrick was able to weather the storm better than most. Mary supplemented his income by doing needlework for a wealthy clientele. After the depression's end in 1879, Patrick moved the family to a three-story house on 7th Avenue near West 55th Street, four blocks below Central Park. Initially, he rented the home, but at some point purchased it for about $23,000, a substantial sum in those days. His smithy was on the ground floor, the family lived on the second, and rented out the third. Living quarters were not spacious, about 1,300 square feet, but the children had a backyard of equal size in which to play, something rare in Manhattan.[3]

Patrick was a "good looking," hardworking man, who loved his craft and was devoted to Mary and their children. Son James later recalled, "He seemed to think only of work, and the care of his family." Many of his patrons were affluent gentlemen. Serving them was most demanding with the first snowfall, the occasion of a sleigh race through Central Park sponsored by McGowan's Pass Tavern; the prize, a magnum of wine. In preparation, gentlemen brought their horses to have the toes and heels of their shoes sharpened for a better grip. Patrick would work from sunup until nearly midnight without a break, munching sandwiches and drinking coffee Mary sent down.[4] Seeing Patrick's long hours may have influenced John's work ethic because throughout his adult life he labored well into the night until poor health ended the habit. Then, too, his later spirituality provided powerful motive for so spending himself.

John regarded his mother a saint. One of her grandchildren remembered her as considerate, kind, and sympathetic. She could also be strict. James recalled he "often thought her cruel" because she had no hesitation about whipping him to cure his bad temper, an effort that failed miserably. Believing her the essence of sincerity, integrity, and unselfishness, John thought "she possessed something in finite share, yet in reality of the Eternal Divine Life."[5]

Patrick was a good provider, putting plenty of wholesome food on the table. On Saturdays one of his sons would pick up a standing rib roast, sirloin steaks, and pork chops; the family sometimes enjoyed the leftover roast through Tuesday. James recalled that it "didn't make a favorite dish in those days. Nobody seemed to like cold roast beef."[6]

The move to 7th Avenue brought the family into the parish of St. Paul the Apostle, erected by Father Isaac Hecker in 1858 on the northern outskirt of the city, a settlement dominated by truck farms and pocked with crude huts. He dubbed it "Shantyopolis." He also founded the Congregation of the Missionary Priests of St. Paul the Apostle, better known as Paulist Fathers, the first American community of priests established in the U.S. At the time of the Burkes's arrival, the area was a bustling part of town. The family was devout, and their dwelling was later described as "a sanctuary of holiness." Unlike other workingmen who attended the most convenient low Mass on Sunday, Patrick and family always donned their best clothes and went to high Mass at 10:30. John and his brothers became altar boys, and all the siblings attended Sunday catechism in the absence of a parish school.[7] John became acquainted with the Paulists and probably knew Hecker himself, who died there in 1888 when the lad was thirteen.

For elementary education, the Burke children attended Public School 69 a half block from their home. All graduated except James, who quit to work. Both Tom and John attended St. Francis Xavier High School about two miles south of home. Through John's sophomore to senior year, he and James belonged to St. Paul the Apostle Boys Club. Its existence is known through John's minute books as "duplicating secretary," which probably meant he made a second copy of the proceedings. One had to be an altar boy to be a member, and to judge by names in the minutes almost all were Irish. Meetings were held on Sundays, with a temporary adjournment for vespers. They were conducted in parliamentary fashion, and members were referred to as "Mister." Participants wore club "colors," which were purchased with membership dues, and the club had its own "cry." On the solemnity of the Immaculate Conception, for instance, the members donned the colors and gave "the cry in the sacristy after the feast was over." The club bought boxing gloves, baseballs, handballs, lawn-tennis gear, and such board games as checkers and geography. It was John who recommended the last-mentioned and the tennis gear. The club voted down a motion to confine use to members only.[8]

The boys seemed a fractious, unruly bunch. They expelled and fined members for disorderly conduct and non-payment of dues, but no expulsion ever seemed permanent. Shortly before Christmas 1890, the club removed Patrick Hanrahan as president for misconduct, prompting vice-president James O'Brien to resign in protest. When the members elected E. Duffy to replace Hanrahan, Duffy immediately resigned, as did Arthur Lynch after his election. Finally, they chose Joseph Bainton, John's friend, who accepted the post. They then held three consecutive ballots to elect John secretary, and forced his acceptance after he refused to acknowledge the results of the first two. Three weeks later, there was discussion about impeaching Bainton, "but it was settled amicably."[9]

Under Bainton, the club began holding periodic debates. Two of the topics were quite thoughtful: "Have Indians a right to this country" and "Religion should be taught in schools." Others ran truer to interests of a boys club: "Who was the greater general, McClellan or Grant," "Antietam was fiercer than Gettysburg," and "Napoleon versus Wellington." Invariably, John argued the affirmative side. Only once did the minutes indicate who won. John and his team carried the day in arguing McClellan was a better general than Grant, though the minutes also noted the debate over the fierceness of Antietam and Gettysburg "was very good."[10] The Civil War was a subject in which John maintained a lifelong interest.

He had the dubious distinction of being the third president to face impeachment. In May 1891, members elected him to the post and his brother James as secretary. At the next meeting, James's election came under question, but John ruled the balloting valid. When O'Brien moved reconsideration of the matter, the motion failed, and he moved to impeach John. The minutes offer a graphic, if somewhat sanitized, description of what followed:

> During the discussion the President made a short speech to the house which took such an effect on them and on Mr. O'Brien that he immediately got up[,] advanced to the Secretary's table & asked how much he owed, threw down a half a dollar[,] asked for the change[,] resigned[,] and left the room. His resignation was immediately accepted by the President and his motion was dropped. Mr. John Brown excited by the proceedings and nearly beside himself with rage, stood up and delivered a stinging speech about the President's misdemeanors during the past few

> years. But about every ten words cost him five cents and, after his fines had amounted to a half a dollar[,] he disgracefully resigned. His resignation was accepted by the President.

There must have been more disorder than the minutes let on because in addition to Brown's fine of 55 cents, Hanrahan was fined 40, Duffy 10, Lynch 10, and James Burke 8.[11] In 1891, 55 cents was equivalent to almost $19 in 2024 terms.

John's leadership qualities were recognized prior to and after his presidency. During Bainton's term, he conducted meetings in the absence of the president and vice president. After his own term, he was elected vice president. He even sought to formalize procedures by drafting bylaws, which he submitted in January 1892. The record gives no indication of adoption, and the minutes in John's possession ceased the following month.[12] His participation in the club thereafter is unknown.

With the exception of James, the Burke siblings were well educated. Mary, Annie, and Lizzie each became teachers. Mary was the only Burke child eventually to wed and have a family. After teaching as a laywoman, Annie entered the Sisters of Mercy and continued as educator in that order. Tragically, Julia died at age fourteen of unmentioned causes. After high school, Tom, John, and William attended the College of St. Francis Xavier near their former high school. William became an attorney. As for Tom and John, there was "never any question," recalled James, about what they would do with their lives. After graduating from college, Tom entered the Paulist community at St. Thomas College at The Catholic University of America in Washington, D.C. Four years later in 1896, John followed him.[13]

John's was "a virgin soul," remembered Mary G. Hawks, a later coworker and friend who knew him from 1909 until his death. John told her from early youth he saw himself as a priest and hopefully a Paulist, but when it came time to ask for admission to the community, he approached the superior "with great trepidation." He feared he would be rejected and end up "a lonely celibate" for the rest of his life. Perhaps he felt daunted and overshadowed by the special talents of his brother Tom. In fact, the superior received John with the curt statement, "We always expected to take you."[14]

THE PAULIST

Later in life, John acknowledged that Hecker and Father Walter Elliott, one of his first followers, had a profound influence on the person he became. He found Hecker's American spirit and mysticism especially appealing. Hecker was a convert to Catholicism whose spirituality and thought were shaped by Methodism, his time as a transcendentalist, and the millenarian politics of Loco-Foco Democrats in New York City. Yet, he found Catholicism satisfied his deepest thoughts and yearnings. Firmly convinced of the goodness of human nature, he believed the soul was destined for union with God, and its every faculty and power had that union as its end. Rather than mortify or repress human instincts, affections, and desires, the true Christian strove to direct them toward their proper goal. His theology was incarnational: in Jesus, humanity and divinity became one, and humankind was uplifted and transformed. Moreover, Hecker sensed a deep harmony between the Catholic faith and American principles, which led him to develop an apologetic blending Catholicism with Americanism and giving their combination a millenarian thrust, namely, the U.S. was the redeemer nation.[15]

In Hecker's view, the task facing the church was two-fold: to revivify a European Catholicism sapped of vitality by overlong emphasis on structure, authority, and obedience, and to win back the Saxon races lost to the Church in the Protestant Reformation. While accentuation of hierarchical structure had been a necessary reaction to excessive Protestant individualism, Hecker believed the definition of papal infallibility (1870) had secured Church authority. The new age called for emphasis on energetic individualism which would appeal to Saxons and revitalize the European Church. The world would be renewed through interior religious transformation of the individual. Hecker held the U.S. had a providential role to play in bringing this rejuvenation about.[16]

First, however, it must become Catholic. To convert Americans, the Church need not argue doctrine, but should demonstrate how the spirit and institutions of the country were more Catholic than Protestant, by which Hecker meant Calvinist. The Declaration of Independence posited the goodness of human nature, freedom of will, and inalienable rights of persons, which were also tenets of Catholicism. These had spawned a political system based on "a mere naturalism." Given the Catholic axiom that grace built on nature, Hecker saw a "necessary bond and correlation" between principles in the Declaration of Independence and those of the Church because "the truths of the natural order serve as indispensable supports to the body of revealed truths of faith." Protestantism (Calvinism), however, held for total depravity of human nature, loss of free will, and forfeiture of natural rights. To be consistent as an American, therefore, a Protestant had to become a Catholic. "What a Catholic believes as a citizen of the republic," declared Hecker, "he believes as a member of the Catholic Church; and as the natural supports and strengthens the supernatural, this accounts for the universally acknowledged fact that no Catholics are more sincere, ... more loyal to the authority of the Church ... than the Catholic republican citizens of the United States. Catholicity in religion sanctions republicanism in politics, and republicanism in politics favors Catholicity in religion."[17]

For Hecker, the reconciliation of the seeming conflict between Church authority and individual freedom occurred through the Holy Spirit, whose "action ... embodied visibly in the authority of the Church, and ... dwelling invisibly in the soul, form[ed] one inseparable synthesis." Sanctity consisted in the personal struggle to harmonize the internal and external guidance of the Holy Spirit, to make them identical motives. For him, Spirit-filled freedom and individualism were not a threat to the Church, but an asset. An active laity, interiorly transfigured by the Holy Spirit, would take initiative in transforming society by living the gospel in the workplace, marketplace, and recreation place. Hecker expected "a Pentecostal effusion of the Holy Spirit on the Church" in America, whose mission it was to renew the universal Church.[18]

The John Burke who entered St. Thomas College was a twenty-one-year-old, six-foot-three, slender, handsome, blue-eyed, Irish lad. His arrival occurred at the height of the Americanist controversy, a crisis that wracked the American Catholic hierarchy over an attempt by liberal bishops to harmonize Catholicism with values of the nation: individualism, freedom, republicanism, and separation of Church and state. Although Hecker died just as the controversy began, his thought influenced two of its principal protagonists: Archbishop John Ireland of St. Paul and Bishop John Keane, who was forced to resign the rectorate of Catholic University a year before

Burke's arrival. Ireland in particular promoted the idea of a Spirit-filled laity taking initiative in harmonizing the Church with the age by injecting Catholic principles into daily life.[19]

St. Thomas College was the Paulist novitiate and residence, where young men were introduced to the spirit of the community and took courses in the sacred sciences both there and in the University. Burke was a quite studious and scholarly young man, whom his fellows considered brilliant. Though firm of conviction, he was not dogmatic. Because the Americanist controversy was fought in the upper echelons of the Church, students like Burke were probably unaware of the "War of the Prelates," as historian Emmett Curran aptly dubbed the conflict. Though spared the infighting, they were exposed to Americanist ideals because a number of the university's faculty were sympathetic to or supporters of the movement, including Father William Kerby, with whom Burke developed a lifelong friendship. Given Hecker's thinking on the harmony of Church and nation, it would also have been natural for Burke and his fellow Paulists to sympathize with Americanist ideals.[20]

No doubt these were formative years which planted seeds in Burke that later grew to maturity. He absorbed Hecker's conviction that only Catholicism satisfied humanity's deepest longings and that it harmonized best with American principles. Like Hecker, he believed human nature was essentially good. He deplored a too-pronounced distinction between "natural" and "supernatural" virtues. The former were God's gifts in creation to be cultivated, not discounted. They formed the base on which supernatural virtues built. Both were necessary for the formation of a Christian. Through the incarnation of Jesus, the soul's true end was union with God, which began here on earth with the indwelling of the Holy Spirit, the very life of God within the Christian. The Spirit uplifted and sanctified human nature's every faculty, directing each toward love of God and neighbor. A Spirit-filled laity would then bring Christ into workshop, marketplace, and office.[21]

While Paulist students spent the academic year in Washington, a portion of their summer was at the community's retreat on Lake George in the Adirondack Mountains. No doubt it was there Burke developed a love for his favorite sport: canoeing. An introvert by temperament, he probably found it attractive because it afforded him solitude on the water amidst nature. He loved both deeply: water and nature. For him, the latter was a visible expression of the invisible beauty of God. As he later expressed it: "God gives us such times [in the wilderness] that we may learn to know that nature is His own: the moving picture that He grants to earth: the veil of beauty passing before us in time, only to move out and reveal the Beauty of beauty beyond." In autumn, Burke would walk through fallen leaves on the grass because he loved sound of the rustle beneath his feet.[22]

As a student, Burke was known as chief prankster of the community. The record is silent about the jokes he played on his confreres, but not the other way around. The first time fellow-student James Gillis saw him, Burke was walking fully clothed and dripping wet up the hill from the lake to the student house. He either fell into it or more likely was pushed. He put his shoes out to dry on the windowsill of his second-floor room, only to have two of his fellows use a ladder to access them from outside and fill them with water from a pitcher. As Gillis pointed out, Burke gave as good as he got and took payback with equal grace, enjoying a joke on himself as much as perpetrating one on another.[23]

A leader in fun, he was also an accomplished raconteur and mimic. After meals, the priests and students gathered on a porch overlooking the lake. Burke would regale them with jokes and anecdotes, and all would join in repartee. He would have them in stitches with his mimicry. For example, Gillis recalled "one of his popular imitations ... of a candidate for office on the last day of the campaign, haggard, dishevelled [*sic*], so hoarse that his voice seemed to have been torn to shreds, making one last desperate plea to the loyal voters of the 15th precinct to bury the opposition under a landslide, it was we who made the woods and waters resound with laughter."[24] Burke had apparently acquired the Irish art of storytelling.

Just when Burke took up smoking is unknown. Perhaps it was in student days, or maybe after ordination to priesthood. In any case, it became a lifelong habit. He enjoyed both cigars and cigarettes. Of course, the use of tobacco was typical of many men of that time because its hazards were as yet unknown.[25] This habit would have serious ramifications on his later health.

Midway through Burke's last year of study for priesthood, Pope Leo XIII condemned Americanism with his letter *Testem Benevolentiae* (*A Witness of Good Will*). The pontiff was attempting to quiet a controversy that arose in France over the translation of Elliott's biography of Hecker, whose views on spirituality were misunderstood and distorted by French conservatives. Mentioning the book by name, the pope was careful to avoid saying anyone in the U.S. actually held the condemned doctrines. Indeed, the principal promoters of the Americanist movement—Ireland and Keane—assured him the erroneous teachings had never existed in America and it was unfortunate the term "Americanism" was applied to them. Others, however, believed the pope had scotched the snake of heresy. As for the young Burke's view of the condemnation, he left no record at the time. Thirty-three years later, however, when the *Dictionnaire de Spiritualité* identified Hecker as the source of Americanism, he took ferocious exception. Professing "the greatest reverence for the letter of Leo XIII," which gave "warning and instruction on specious and oftentimes unsuspected tendencies," Burke eruditely demonstrated in thirty-three pages those proclivities were not to be found in Hecker.[26]

After three years of study at Catholic University, Burke was scheduled for ordination. As it neared, Father Joseph Searle, superior general, developed qualms about going forward because Burke would turn the minimum canonical age only three days before the event. When Searle decided to defer Burke's ordination, his mother vehemently protested, arguing that since the date was already set, it would be a mistake to make a change. Searle was equally adamant against proceeding. The two went head-to-head until Mary won the fight. In years later, she recalled her surprise at the ferociousness of her own reaction in standing up for her son. Burke was ordained on 9 June 1899 in the chapel of Caldwell Hall at Catholic University by Bishop Alfred Curtis, a former Anglican priest whom the English Catholic-convert Cardinal John Henry Newman had brought into the Church.[27]

Following ordination, Burke remained at Catholic University for two more years to earn a licentiate in theology. A degree higher than a master's, but less than a doctorate, it constituted canonical license for teaching theology in a seminary. Gillis considered the priests whom he and Burke associated with in the licentiate program among the "most mentally alert" he ever knew. They discussed and debated philosophy and theology, all the while keeping a sense of humor and fun. They also kept each other from getting big heads or becoming stuffed shirts, usually through raillery.

"John," bantered one of them, "when you go up for your degree and the examiners propose a theological difficulty, don't imagine you can get by with the answer you make to our best jokes 'Oh, that's an old one!'"[28] This dig was probably as much testimony to his mental ability as a challenge for him to be prepared. Burke received the licentiate 1901.

Very little is known of the next two years. Burke's first pastoral assignment was to parish work in the area of Lake George, news that must have greatly pleased him by affording him the opportunity to canoe in the beauty of nature. After probably less than a year, he was reassigned to give parish missions, which roughly served as the Catholic version of a Protestant revival meeting, though the mission tradition was far older. A mission sought to return the fallen-away parishioners to the fold while deepening the spirituality of regular churchgoers. At its heart was preaching aimed at prompting repentance and conversion to a life of holiness, which would then be strengthened and deepened through reception of the sacraments. As the youngest member of the mission band, it was Burke's duty to keep the alarm clock and wake the others typically at 4:00 A.M. On one occasion, having roused his fellows, they found him "peacefully sleeping with the alarm clock clutched in his arms!" Mission work was rewarding, but exhausting because of daily sermons and long hours spent in the confessional over a period of two to four weeks. In 1903, while Burke was preaching a mission at an Iowa parish, word came of a new assignment, one he was aptly suited for and which would engage him for the next nineteen years.[29]

Endnotes to Chapter 1

1. John J. Burke, C.S.P., *Christ in Us: Meditations* (Philadelphia: The Dolphin Press, 1934), 10.
2. James Burke, Untitled Autobiography, AP, John J. Burke Papers, box 1; Federal Manuscript Census, New York City, 1880; John B. Sheerin, C.S.P., *Never Look Back: The Career and Concerns of John J. Burke* (New York: Paulist Press, 1975), 14–15; Joseph Malloy, C.S.P., "Monsignor John Joseph Burke, Paulist," *Catholic World* 144 (March 1937): 718.
3. James Burke, Untitled Autobiography, AP, Burke Papers, box 1; Thomas Francis Burke, C.S.P., personal information sheet, AP, Thomas Burke Papers; Federal Manuscript Censuses, New York City, 1900, 1910, 1920; Sheerin, *Never Look Back*, 15–16; Malloy, "John Joseph Burke," 718; Carl N. Degler, *The Age of the Economic Revolution: 1876–1900* (Glenview, Ill.: Scott, Foresman

and Company, 1967), 87–88; James E. Bruner, Jr., *Industrialism: The American Experience* (New York: Benziger, Inc., 1972), 119–21.

4. James Burke, Untitled Autobiography, AP, Burke Papers, box 1.
5. Ibid.; John J. Burke to Grace Murray, Eve of S.S. Peter and Paul [29 June 1921], AP, Burke Papers, box 11; Sheerin, *Never Look Back*, 16.
6. James Burke, Untitled Autobiography, AP, Burke Papers, box 1.
7. Ibid.; Walter Elliott, C.S.P., *The Life of Father Hecker* (New York: Book Exchange, 1891), 328–29 ("Shantyopolis" is from here); David J. O'Brien, *Isaac Hecker: An American Catholic* (New York and Mahwah, N.J.: Paulist Press, 1992), 184–85; Edward J. Mullaly, C.S.P., "Eulogy of a Brother Paulist," *Catholic Action* 18 (December 1936): 10 (the quotation is from here); Sheerin, *Never Look Back*, 16; Malloy, "John Joseph Burke," 718.
8. Minutes of the St. Paul the Apostle Boys Club (SPABC), 13 October 1890, 2 and 30 November 1890, 28 December 1890, 11 and 18 January 1891, 22 February 1891, 22 March 1891, 5 April 1891, and 2 and 16 August 1892, AP, Burke Papers, box 2.
9. Minutes of the SPABC, 9 and 23 November 1890 and 21 December 1890, 11 January 1891, AP, Burke Papers, box 2.
10. Minutes of the SPABC, 18 January 1891, 1 and 22 February 1891, 21 June 1891, 19 July 1891, 2 and 16 August 1891, AP, Burke Papers, box 2.
11. Minutes of the SPABC, 24 May 1891 and 7 June 1891, AP, Burke Papers, box 2.
12. Minutes of the SPABC, 19 April 1891, 20 October 1891, 22 November 1891, 1 January 1892, 14 February 1892, AP, Burke Papers, box 2.
13. James Burke, Untitled Autobiography, AP, Burke Papers, box 1(the first quote is here); Mary Dineen Coyle, Memories of the National Catholic War Council: Father John J. Burke,[20 January 1951], ACUA, USCCB 10:72:24 (the second quote is here); Sheerin, *Never Look Back*, 17–19; Malloy, "John Joseph Burke," 718; Kathryn Kish Sklar, "The Historical Foundations of Women's Power in the Creation of the American Welfare State, 1830–1930," in *Mothers of a New World: Maternalist Politics and the Origins of the Welfare State*, eds., Seth Koven and Sonya Michel (New York and London: Routledge, 1993), 62.
14. Mary G. Hawks, "Souvenir of Father John J. Burke, C.S.P.," AP, Burke Papers, box 10.
15. John Farina, *An American Experience of God: The Spirituality of Isaac Hecker* (New York: Paulist Press, 1981), 9–20, 46–83, 101–18; Edward J. Langlois, C.S.P., "Isaac Hecker's Political Thought," in *Hecker Studies: Essays on the Thought of Isaac Hecker*, ed. John Farina (New York: Paulist Press, 1983), 49–62; Joseph F. Gower, "Democracy as a Theological Problem in Isaac Hecker's Apologetics," in *America in Theological Perspective*, ed. Thomas M. McFadden (New York: Seabury Press, 1976), 39–42; David J. O'Brien, "An Evangelical

Imperative: Isaac Hecker, Catholicism, and Modern Society," in Farina, *Hecker Studies*, 102–7, 87–98; O'Brien, *Isaac Hecker*, 339–92; Joseph Chinnici, O.F.M., *Living Stones: The History and Structure of Catholic Spiritual Life in the United States* (New York: Macmillan, 1989), 91–92, 100, 113–18; Martin J. Kirk, O.F.M., *The Spirituality of Isaac Hecker: Reconciling the American Character and the Catholic Faith* (New York: Garland, 1988), 143–74; Margaret Mary Reher, *Catholic Intellectual Life in America: A Historical Study of Persons and Movements* (New York: Macmillan, 1989), 45–47.

16. Isaac T. Hecker, *The Church and the Age: An Exposition of the Catholic Church in View of the Needs and Aspirations of the Present Age* (New York: Catholic Book Exchange, 1896), 7–32.
17. Ibid., 67–87 (quotations are on 75, 79–80); Langlois, "Hecker's Political Thought," 49–86; Gower, "Democracy in Hecker's Apologetics," 42–52; Kirk, *Spirituality of Hecker*, 199–214; Reher, *Catholic Intellectual Life*, 46–49, 57–59.
18. Hecker, *Church and the Age*, 7–57 (quotations are on 33, 34, 37, and 49); Chinnici, *Living Stones*, 107–09; Joseph Chinnici, O.F.M., *Devotion to the Holy Spirit in American Catholicism* (New York: Paulist Press, 1985), 25–34.
19. Thomas Wangler, "Emergence of John J. Keane as a Liberal Catholic and Americanist (1878–1887)," *American Ecclesiastical Review* 166 (September 1972): 457–78; "John Ireland and the Origins of Liberal Catholicism in the United States," *Catholic Historical Review* 56 (January 1971): 617–29; "John Ireland's Emergence as a Liberal Catholic and Americanist: 1875–1887," *Records of the American Catholic Historical Society of Philadelphia* 81 (June 1970): 67–82; "The Birth of Americansim: 'Westward the Apocalyptic Candlestick,'" *Harvard Theological Review* 65 (July 1972): 415–36; James H. Moynihan, *The Life of Archbishop John Ireland* (New York: Harper and Brothers, 1953), 49; John T. Farrell, "Archbishop Ireland and Manifest Destiny," *Catholic Historical Review* 33 (October 1947): 295–301; Patrick Ahern, *The Life of John Keane, 1839–1918* (Milwaukee: Bruce Publishing Company, 1955), 94; Marvin R. O'Connell, *John Ireland and the American Catholic Church* (St. Paul: Minnesota Historical Society Press, 1988), 196–471 *passim*; Thomas McAvoy, C.S.C., *The Great Crisis in American Catholic History, 1895–1900* (Chicago: H. Regnery Co., 1957); Gerald P. Fogarty, S.J., *The Vatican and the Americanist Crisis: Denis J. O'Connell, American Agent in Rome, 1885–1903* (Rome: Universita Gregoriana, 1974), 266–67; Gerald P. Fogarty, S.J., *The Vatican and the American Hierarchy from 1870 to 1965* (Wilmington, Del.: Michael Glazier, 1985), 27–190; Margaret Mary Reher, "The Church and the Kingdom of God in America: The Ecclesiology of the Americanists" (Ph.D. diss., Fordham University, 1972), 48–91, 123–24, 126–29.
20. Robert Emmett Curran, *Michael Augustine Corrigan and the Shaping of Conservative Catholicism in America, 1878–1902* (New York: Arno Press, 1978),

316; Loretto Lawler, *Full Circle: The Story of the National Catholic School of Social Service* (Washington, D.C.: The Catholic University of America Press, 1951), 35–36; Gillis, C.S.P., "Father John J. Burke: Paulist," *Catholic Action* 18 (December 1936): 24; Sheerin, *Never Look Back*, 20—21; Fogarty, *Vatican and American Hierarchy*, 69, 70, 73–75, 109, 153, 158.

21. John J. Burke, C.S.P., "With Our Readers: Father Hecker and the Present Problems," *Catholic World*, 110 (January 1920): 564–75; Hawks, "Souvenir of Burke," AP, Burke Papers, box 10.
22. Burke to Helen Lynch, 14 July 1908, AP, Burke Papers, box 5; Burke to Murray, 25 September 1916, ibid., box 11(the quotation is from here); Coyle, "Memories of War Council, ACUA, NCWC 10:72:24; Gillis, "John J. Burke," 24; R. A. McGowan, "Tribute of a Priest Co-worker," *Catholic Action* 18 (December 1936): 23.
23. Gillis, "John J. Burke," 24.
24. Ibid.; Hawks, "Souvenir of Burke," AP, Burke Papers, box 10.
25. Coyle, Memories of War Council, ACUA, 10:72:24.
26. Burke, untitled response to the article on Americanism in *Dictionnaire de Spiritualité*, 1933, AP, Burke Papers, box 46; Fogarty, *Vatican and American Hierarchy*, 73, 143–84; McAvoy, *Great Crisis*, 155–291; Douglas J. Slawson, *Ambition and Arrogance: Cardinal William O'Connell of Boston and the American Catholic Church* (San Diego: Cobalt Productions, 2007), 5–36; James M. O'Toole, *Militant and Triumphant: William Henry O'Connell and the Catholic Church in Boston, 1859–1944* (Notre Dame: University of Notre Dame Press, 1992), 58–78.
27. James Burke, Untitled Autobiography, AP, Burke Papers, box 1; Sheerin, *Never Look Back*, 20–21.
28. Quoted in Gillis, "John J. Burke," 24; Sheerin, *Never Look Back*, 21–22.
29. Jay P. Dolan, *Catholic Revivalism: The American Experience, 1830–1900* (Notre Dame: University of Notre Dame Press, 1978): 57–112; Douglas J. Slawson, "Catholic Revivalism: The Vincentian Preaching Apostolate in the United States," in Michael J. McClymond, ed., *Embodying the Spirit: New Perspectives on North American Revivalism* (Baltimore: The Johns Hopkins University Press, 2004), 224–38; Douglas J. Slawson, "'To Bring Glad Tidings to the Poor': Vincentian Parish Missions in the United States," in John E. Rybolt, C.M., et al., eds. *The American Vincentians: A Popular History of the Congregation of the Mission in the United States, 1815–1987* (Brooklyn: New City Press, 1988), 163–227; Hawks, "Souvenir of Burke," 4, AP, Burke Papers, box 10 (the quotation is here); Malloy, "John Joseph Burke," 718; McGowan, "Tribute of a Co-worker," 23; Sheerin, *Never Look Back*, 22.

Chapter 2
The Editor

> Our Blessed Lord ever kept before His own soul that one work which he had to do. To every one of us is it likewise given to do one, sole work, and that work is the same in its measure as was given Christ.... One may say that his vocation lies here or there, in religion or in the world, in virginity or in marriage, with his fellows or apart from them. Wheresoever it lies, there is still the one sole work that the individual is to accomplish and his vocation with every phase of it is an integral part thereof. The inspiration, the health of the soul, is to have a work to do, a life to live, come or go what may.[1]

The Appointment

In 1903, twenty-eight-year-old John Burke became assistant editor of *Catholic World*, established in 1865 by Isaac Hecker to spread the Catholic message in America. The assignment placed him close to home because the magazine's office was next to St. Paul the Apostle Church in New York. The editor, Father Alexander Doyle, was nearly twenty years older than his apprentice. Doyle was no Hecker, and under his reign the publication had lost its intellectual edge, becoming a popular, illustrated magazine. Indeed, his interests had recently shifted from publishing to establishing the Apostolic Mission House at Catholic University to train priests in the Paulist method of giving missions. Consequently, he had asked for more help.[2]

Much of Burke's time was devoted, not to *Catholic World*, but to a publication Hecker had established for children: *The Young Catholic*. With what one worker described as "an irrepressible boyishness," Burke completely revamped and renamed it *The Leader*. Under the pseudonym "Uncle Ned," he wrote a monthly letter to its young readers and continued this practice until 1917. The *Leader* became quite popular with Catholic youth.[3]

In 1904, Doyle resigned and Burke assumed the editor's chair which he occupied until 1922. He set out to raise the intellectual caliber of the magazine to what it had been in Hecker's day. As Mary Hawks, who worked at the journal, later recalled, Burke "stressed greatly the service of the mind—'love the Lord thy God with thy whole mind' was a commandment to be filled to the letter." He spared no effort in seeking articles from capable authors both in America and abroad, and he enjoyed cultivating new writers who had something worthwhile to say. There were times when material was hard to get. As Burke told one author who belatedly submitted a manuscript, "Heaven knows ... I would have been glad to have it for November, for I was down to gravel here."[4] The magazine published stories, poetry, and pieces of interest, but for purpose of this study, the articles of most value are those which shed light on the thinking of Burke himself. In this regard, his selection of material did not take shape in a vacuum, but was influenced by trends both in Church and society.

Modernism

In the early twentieth century, American Catholicism enjoyed a budding intellectual life, stimulated by a handful of British and continental Catholic thinkers who became known as Modernists. These intellectuals used tools and methods of contemporary scholarship to defend Church doctrine against challenges from rationalism and liberal Protestantism. They applied historical and literary criticism to scripture and dogma and used a post-Kantian notion of immanence—that is, the presence of, or the need for, the divine implanted within humankind—to balance the exaggerated transcendentalism of neo-Scholasticism, the dominant school of Catholic theology which enshrined medieval thought as the apex of Christian thinking. Although many expressions of Modernism were legitimate and sound, they appeared dangerous to the conventional Catholic mind. During the first decade of the twentieth century, this movement made inroads on American Catholic thought as various Church journals carried articles discussing the latest developments in religious studies.[5]

Sympathetic to the movement, Burke opened the pages of *Catholic World* to this intellectual ferment, if only modestly. He received help from the faculty at St. Thomas College. Three of its members were devotees of Modernism: Father Joseph McSorley, professor of dogmatic theology; Father James Fox, an Irish secular priest and professor of philosophy; and Burke's classmate, Father William Sullivan, professor of moral theology and scripture. As book-review editor for *Catholic World*, Sullivan read voraciously and kept readers abreast of Catholic theological thinking from a Modernist perspective.[6]

A month after becoming editor, Burke gave Fox the idea of writing a six-part series in which a Catholic student at a secular university corresponded with his pastor back home about the Bible, affording Fox the opportunity to expound on higher biblical criticism through fictive letters to the youth whose antagonistic professor highlighted contradictions and scientific errors in scripture. Fox explained that biblical exegesis must be guided by historical and literary criticism and the general laws of discourse. It must also take into account the possibility of mistakes in transcription, the use of implicit and explicit citations by a biblical author who was not affirming their accuracy, and the fact that oral tradition was prone to errors of fact though it preserved an essential truth.[7]

In 1906, Burke published an article by McSorley on a subject that would come to dominate Burke's belief about the Church. Its subject was the Mystical Body of Christ, giving pastoral expression to McSorley's immanentism. Viewing rationalism as the modern enemy of religion, McSorley explained that Darwinian rationalists argued faith was simply a type of animal emotion within humanity that developed from primitive fears and superstitions as humanity evolved. Rationalists of a historical-critical bent argued the Bible was a collection of Middle Eastern tales refashioned by Jewish genius, reflecting the ignorance and errors of the age in which they were written. Finally, rationalist historians viewed Catholicism as a phase in the development of Western civilization—the melding of Jewish hopes, Roman law, and Greek philosophy. McSorley asserted Catholicism accepted the modern conception that viewed the Church "as a living organism marvelously well adapted to its environment, absorbing new elements of growth day after day, drawing upon the best that there is in the external world for its nourishment and its instruments of labor."[8]

He explained one came to know the living Church in the same way as British Modernist George Tyrrell, a Jesuit priest, believed one came to recognize the true faith. Tyrrell argued that primitive revelation was "a concrete religion left by Christ to his Church . . . [and that] devotion and religion existed before theology, in the way that art existed before art-criticism; reasoning, before logic; speech, before grammar." Religious truth was rooted in the immanent experience of transcendent reality. This experienced truth gave rise to and recognized theological truth.[9] Similarly, McSorley held one came to know the Church as Mystical Body of Christ only "by becoming in our own little measure like unto the Christ whose body is the Church." "We see the Church, in very truth," he wrote, "only after we have received and corresponded with the energetic grace of Christ; for only after *doing* the truth may we hope for the light. Religion, then, is a spiritual life; and Christianity is a divine love; and Catholicity is a knitting fast of the soul to God—it is that, or it is nothing." In other words, the person who lived the life of Christ, united with God, would recognize the living Christ in the Church. Lived and experienced truth, would recognize truth. The Church itself was a sacrament through which all could come to know and experience God. It was the visible presence of the invisible Christ. "The Church is not the embodiment of a dead past," declared McSorley, "but the Mystical Body of Christ, living with his life, and working his works among men, yesterday and to-day, and the same forever."[10] For Burke, the Mystical Body was Hecker's incarnational theology taken a step further. As friend Mary Hawks later explained, "The Mystical Body of Christ . . . mastered him [Burke]."[11]

McSorley corresponded with Tyrrell, who used him as go-between to submit to Burke manuscripts for publication. In 1905, he published a probing article wherein Tyrrell argued that John Henry Newman's Anglican theory of development of doctrine was closer to Modernism than his later Catholic formulation of it. Before conversion, Newman had asserted that objects of revelation—the Trinity, the Incarnation, etc.—remained present for Christians to experience, and this religious experience constituted the real touchstone of authenticity for development of doctrine, not the linguistic formulations of the early Church. This conception was virtually identical with liberal Protestantism. When Newman became a Catholic, he squared his theory of development with the neo-Scholastic understanding of it: that documents of tradition were timeless formulations of eternal truths and development of doctrine was essentially propositional, the logical deduction of one truth from another. As helpful as Newman's volte face was for Catholicism, it left unaddressed the issue of knowledge itself. Tyrrell pointed out that as knowledge in various disciplines and aspects of life grew, "knowledge *as a whole* [grew] into something qualitatively different; it is not only *more*, it is *other*.... A building may grow, but if the building materials also grow, the results will be like those of the croquet-party in *Alice's Adventures* [in Wonderland]."[12]

Tyrrell explained that Catholic thinkers were caught between Scylla and Charybdis. If thought grew deductively, as the Catholic Newman argued, and if infallible definitions of the Church bound people to "categories and thought-forms of the age in which they were framed," the Church must show that the formulations of different times were consistent with each other and that all were still valid. It must furnish a rule by which modern secular thought could be corrected, bringing it into line with the deposit of faith. If, on the other hand, thought grew organically, then Church tradition was obsolete and there was no way to defend against liberal Protestantism. Tyrrell noted, however, that a difficulty stated was a difficulty solved. "A reconciliation of an unchangeable body of primitive beliefs with a theory of development in no way prejudicial, either to unity of faith or to the laws of mental growth," he explained, "is to be looked for close at hand in elementary principles common to all Christians, in the recognition that the Gospel was preached to the poor, to the non-scientific."[13]

This was dangerous stuff. Tyrrell was skirting the edge of what was then Catholic orthodoxy and was about to discard Newman's revised theory as unhelpful because it was as propositional and deductive as neo-Scholasticism. Tyrrell had previously hinted that revelation and its theological expression in the deposit of faith were not identical, and twice in this article made passing references to that difference, subtly indicating his belief that personal religious experience should be the starting point of theology. He concluded by suggesting the essence of Christian doctrine was far simpler and more immediately experiential than neo-Scholastics imagined. It was bold of Burke to publish the piece.

In January 1906, Burke began publication of Tyrell's three-part article entitled "The Prayer of Christ," a historical-spiritual disquisition on the Lord's Prayer. In sending the first installment to Burke, McSorley pronounced it "fine stuff if I can judge."[14] Fine it was. The piece represented

Tyrrell at his mystical best. Yet at the very moment of its printing, he was embroiled in controversy. A Milanese newspaper had published an article quoting an unsigned letter Tyrrell had written earlier in which he made explicit the same arguments as in the article above: the essence of Christianity was elemental and experiential. If Catholicism was neo-Scholastic theology, it should be abandoned. Tyrrell summed up Christianity as living the Lord's Prayer, which he saw as the *lex orandi* and *lex credendi*—the rule of praying and the rule of believing—merged into an inseparable unity.[15]

When Tyrrell admitted his authorship of the letter, without repudiating its contents, the superior general of the Jesuits expelled him from the order. Informed by Tyrell of his expulsion, McSorley notified Burke: "I fancy that he wanted to give you a chance to decline to continue the series." Burke had just published the second installment and had no intention of ceasing to present something of such quality. By mid-March McSorley managed to get a copy of Tyrrell's controversial letter and sent it to Burke. "But it is on the condition that you do not pass it around," he wrote. "My advice—almost my precept—to you is this. Read it carefully: wait a week & think, & then read it again."[16] No doubt, McSorley was concerned about its dismissive tone toward contemporary Catholic theology, which Tyrrell had derisively described as a clerical "class interest." McSorley could have had no objection to what Tyrrell had written about the living faith and life of the Church because he himself had said essentially the same thing in his own article on the Mystical Body of Christ. Ten days later he advised Burke to end Tyrell's series with the March issue. Burke, however, had already published the final segment in the April number.[17] With that issue, he ceased using Tyrrell, partly because the latter sent no new manuscripts and partly because he was too hot to handle. *Catholic World* was the last American journal to carry an article by him.

Less controversial than higher criticism was the issue of religious indifferentism discussed by Modernist Maude Petre, Tyrrell's devoted friend and defender. As a young woman, she studied theology in Rome and astonished her professors by her competence.[18] Whether her article on indifferentism shaped Burke's thought or reflected a position he had already reached, is an open question. That he would echo its theme in the future is certain. Petre cogently distinguished between religious tolerance and religious indifference. Her argument rested on the quality of truth. "Any truth which has direct bearing on life, which is not purely scientific or logical, which is practical and human, as opposed to purely speculative truth, must enlist the heart and the feelings as well as the mind." Only persons committed to truth in this larger sense had the capability of being tolerant, for tolerance meant their being "above the narrowness of mere controversy, ... difference of [religious] conviction will not close their hearrs [*sic* for hearts] to any who may need their help, ... their own faith will never make them crush the beliefs of others." In fine, Petre saw religious indifference as the absence of conviction. "To be undenominational and tolerant is nothing"; she wrote, "but to be denominational in the best sense, and likewise tolerant, is much."[19] Such thinking struck a chord in Burke, who deeply believed Catholicism alone embodied the truth that satisfied the human spirit and would solve the problems of society. He would speak that truth boldly and with conviction, without forcing it on others.

Modernism provoked a strong reaction from conservative churchmen, indeed the strongest. Describing it as the synthesis of all heresies, Pope Pius X condemned the movement in September 1907 in the encyclical *Pascendi Dominici Gregis* (*Feeding the Lord's Flock*). He systematized the errors, portraying Modernism as an organized, unified attempt (which it was not) to undermine the faith carried out by theological sappers in the Church's own bosom, men driven by pride. "'Modernism,'" concludes historian Nicholas Sagovsky, "was, in effect, created by Pius X through the encyclical *Pascendi*." The letter, moreover, contained a section on discipline which ordered the establishment of vigilance committees in each diocese to ferret out every vestige of the evil. The encyclical fixed a siege mentality on the Church and thrust it into a defensive posture against modern thought.[20]

With the condemnation and the witch hunt that followed, Burke beat a hasty retreat, publishing a series of articles, one by his brother Thomas, which echoed the papal position. This editorial about-face was not the only such to occur; other Catholic journals lapsed into rigid orthodoxy. In fact, most practitioners of Modernism found it easier to conform than resist.[21] Burke brought closure to *Catholic World*'s involvement by publishing a refutation of Tyrrell's article about development of doctrine carried earlier.[22]

He probably found retreat into orthodoxy less personally costly than to others for several reasons. He was never in the trenches himself defending higher criticism. More important, his consuming interest was in the spiritual life, which in reality was the essence of Christianity, a point made explicitly by McSorley in his article on the Mystical Body and implicitly by Tyrrell when he suggested that the Christian message was accessible to the poor and unscientific. The essence of Christianity—divinely motivated love of God and neighbor—was the end to which Burke devoted his life, as will be seen in the next chapter.

The Editor and Catholic Life

While the condemnation of Modernism scaled back intellectualism in one area, there was plenty going on in Catholic life and secular society to provide Burke with progressive articles in areas other than scripture and theology. The American Catholic Church was beginning a new phase in its organizational life. At the official level, it remained in the words of historian David O'Brien "a states' rights church, dominated by the local bishops."[23] Yet at the grass-roots, a movement was afoot to unite Catholics nationwide. In 1901 the American Federation of Catholic Societies (AFCS) was formed to Catholicize America and to reestablish the nation on Catholic principles through the constitutional exercise of citizenship.[24] Three years later, three major Catholic educational bodies federated to form the Catholic Educational Association in order to promote and safeguard Catholic schools and inject Catholic principles into American academic life.[25] American Catholicism was beginning to coalesce into a national, self-conscious subculture, a movement wherein Burke would play an important part.

American society itself was experiencing socioeconomic turmoil as large corporations amalgamated into massive trusts or monopolies, contributing to expanding urbanization and concentration of wealth. Vast numbers of laborers—men, women, and children, many of them immigrants—lived either in crowded tenement slums or in the "zone," the area bounding slums where an emerging lower-middle class dwelt in fear of relapsing into poverty. Work hours were long, wages low, benefits nonexistent, and working conditions harsh.[26]

This situation gave rise in 1901 to formation of the American Socialist Party, committed to a cooperative commonwealth (the end of private property) through the electoral process and parliamentary action—not violent revolution. By 1910, socialists had gained enough strength to win municipal elections around the country and send a few representatives to Congress. Socialism was "in the air."[27] Partly in response to the socialist challenge but mainly to correct the byproducts of urban-industrial society, a widespread reform movement called Progressivism sprang into being, which accepted the inevitability of modern industrialism and the wage system and sought to ameliorate their worst effects.[28]

As editor, Burke published articles that promoted Catholicism and Catholic social reform, while countering socialism. Indeed, he had been deeply influenced as a student at Catholic University by Father William Kerby, a social and political scientist interested in reform whose articles Burke published. He also solicited writings from Father John A. Ryan, foremost Catholic social ethicist in the first half of the twentieth century. Ryan brought the attention of readers of *Catholic World* to the numerous American laborers whose wages failed to provide their families with a reasonable standard of living. Acknowledging that the focus of bishops and priests had hitherto been on the building of churches and schools, Ryan challenged clergymen to spend their energies on implementing the socio-economic teachings enunciated by Leo XIII in the encyclical *Rerum Novarum* (*Of New Things*, 1891).[29]

In 1909 Ryan set forth in *Catholic World* a comprehensive program of economic reform aimed at taking the wind out of socialist sails by improving the lot of laborers and consumers. His plan advocated legislation for the following: a living wage to provide working-class families with a decent standard of living; an eight-hour work day, instead of the nearly ten-hour average; prohibition of child labor; regulation of women's work; legal recognition of the right to strike; unemployment relief; workman's compensation and pensions; low-cost, government-built housing for working families; income and inheritance taxes; public ownership of utilities, mines, and forests; government regulation of monopolies; and the taxation of the future increase of land values. As the "golden mean between individualism and Socialism," Ryan finally called for the establishment of economic democracy, that is, workers' cooperatives wherein laborers themselves owned and operated industry. In his view, such a system differed radically from socialism, for in it "the workers' ownership of capital would be collective not private, general not specific," and their control of the means of production would be shared with the general public. In Ryan's scheme, the workers of an industry would actually own some, or ideally all, of the stock of a company and thereby share directly in the decision-making and the profits, resulting in both a more equitable distribution of wealth and a citizenry with a higher sense of self-worth.[30] Burke's publication of such thought placed *Catholic World* in the left wing of the Progressive Movement.

The catalyst stimulating Burke's thought about the role of Catholicism in national life came from his mentor Kerby. In late 1906, Burke published Kerby's article analyzing the problem of leakage of Catholic professionals from the Church. "Business, locality ... similar pursuits or ambitions are usually final in fixing our associations," observed Kerby. "There is consequently a tendency to indifference concerning a man's religion." Faith became privatized and a Catholic received no reinforcement for his distinctive beliefs. As remedy, the Church needed to foster group consciousness outside of worship. Kerby averred that participation in a group's government was "a powerful stimulant of group consciousness and spirit." Admitting Church governance was of divine origin and independent of the laity, he added that lay participation in it "was not unknown in the past." He simply called attention to this fact "because the age was democratic" and all prominent social groups relied on shared governance to foster interest and loyalty. "Identity of interest in all that touches faith and Church," concluded Kerby, "massing of the Catholic laity in Catholic interests, the development of a trusted leadership, independent of the clergy though in co-operation, and all such natural phases of social group development, are of the highest value in reinforcing the faith."[31] In effect, the article was a plea to further the movement already afoot for the establishment of organizations to protect and promote Catholic interests in various fields. There was a subtle Americanist flare in the article, not just in its mention of democracy, but in its call for the development of lay leadership independent of the hierarchy.

Deeming the article "wise and courageous," Burke thought "it should be studied ... not read." In his view, the structure of the Church made the lay person "almost a complete extern." The lack of group consciousness, therefore, was not the fault of lay people, but the direct result of "the manner in which ecclesiastical authority has prevented them from sharing in that which is a fundamental necessity for group consciousness, namely: an active, personal part in the organization." While recognizing that some priests would find the idea of lay involvement "galling," Burke believed that the clergy had to become more reliant on the expertise of lay professionals. The office of the priest was, "above all else, one of spiritualizing, of inspiring, and of directing, things of which in themselves he may not be master, to God." Indeed, the priest "should find the material for decisions, not out of his own head—as so often happens—but from specialists and authorities in particular fields in which he is to decide."[32]

Kerby's thinking about the laity and lay spirituality complemented the thought of Isaac Hecker. Shortly before the appearance of Kerby's articles, Burke published newly recovered correspondence Hecker had carried on in the early 1860s with Richard Simpson, a convert from the Oxford Movement and editor of the *Rambler*, an English Catholic lay journal. Their letters dated from a time when Hecker's work as a pastor brought him face-to-face with how lay people might seek perfection apart from entering religious life. In 1861, Hecker told Simpson he was thinking of writing a book on the subject, but lacked the time. "My object is to show that the ordinary duties of life are the highroads to sanctity," he explained. "There is no other way of perfection for the great Mass of Christians than the performance of the common duties of life with an eye to God. The highest, noblest, most perfect life is in the fulfilment of those daily duties imposed upon us by Almighty God. This is devotion."[33]

A corollary to this idea of lay spiritual perfection was the goodness of the natural order, indeed the goodness of human nature. "I think a larger playground may be given to the action of our natural faculties and instincts without displeasing their Author," Hecker told Simpson. "I wish to reconcile the idea of sanctity with the completeness of the natural man. Faith does not demand the depression or mutilation of our nature, or its instincts. Religion gives completeness to character." Because God was the ground of all being, genuine piety called people to praise Him with all within them and all outside them. "A religion, therefore, that does not accord with man's instincts and all nature, is essentially defective," concluded Hecker. "Sanctity is not the destruction of our nature, but is restoration. The world is to be redeemed, not by abandoning it, and giving it over to the devil; but by charity and apostolic zeal."[34] Such thinking about human nature, the world, and religion deeply shaped Burke's own spirituality and how he would spiritually mold others. True piety was not to be found in the suppression of one's nature, but in living that nature to the fullest under God's grace.

Spirituality was not the negation of natural instincts, but their elevation through the Holy Spirit into something nobler and divine.

Until October 1909, Burke had relied on publication of others' words. In that issue of *Catholic World*, he found his own voice in a new column called "With Our Readers." Not surprisingly, his first editorial dealt with the laity. A recent report of the Census Bureau showed Catholics the majority of church-goers in sixteen states. Burke wondered aloud if his co-religionists were "at all proportionately true" regarding their responsibilities to their families and also "to their obligation to present worthily the faith and to lead to the true Church the non-Catholics who are our fellow-countrymen." Here was a Paulist's call to convert America. Burke urged Catholics to become well educated in their religion and take an active part in Church life. Even more, he challenged them to get involved as Catholics in society. "Of Catholic public action many Catholics know nothing, nor do they seek to know anything of these works," lamented Burke. Yet only through her members could the Church meet the pressing problems facing America. The most efficacious means of increasing "individual and corporate worth and power" was Catholic literature. Through publications and pronouncements, the Church should be "the leader—and the leader recognized by all—in the religious, moral, and social life of America." To that end, *Catholic World* had labored for forty-five years. Burke asked the help of all Catholics to put the magazine in every public library and in every home.[35]

This editorial was more than boosterism for the journal; it contained three important elements in Burke's thought. First, like Hecker, he believed only Catholic truth could satisfy personal and national needs and this truth must be communicated by an active laity. Second, he had tremendous respect for the influence of the written word—publicity. Finally, he here first articulated, in inchoate form, his notion of the Mystical Body, that the Church (Christ) was alive in the world through the actions and words of the faithful.

Scarcely a year later he wrote another editorial on lay action that subtly wove together strands of his own thought with those of McSorley, Kerby, and Petre. Burke saw the need for Catholic men and women of conviction, people who had not privatized their religion but who would "courageously and intelligently, in public and in private, stand for the principles of the Catholic faith." A courageous stance, however, did not equate with an intolerant one. "To live happily with others does not mean that we must never speak of those things which ought to be most important and most sacred to all," wrote Burke. "We need not argue; we need not intrude where evidently we are not wanted; we need not seek to oppose. But there is a kinder and more effective way apparent when the opportunity comes to the Catholic layman whose faith is his very life." That way might not be through words at all, especially for the "stammerers" and "tongue-tied." All Catholics had within their reach "that powerful attraction of duty performed, of principle faithfully adhered to, which must make its impress even upon the most callous." Burke then expressed a profound sense of the oneness of all, of the impact of each on the other:

> We do not and we cannot live alone. Matters which we believe are known only to God and ourselves, that we persuade ourselves affect only ourselves, actions that apparently begin and end with ourselves, really reach out and, in their measure, affect all humanity. Every thought, every aspiration, every design, every act of ours, is like a pebble dropped in the great ocean, which inevitably but surely affects the farthest shores. If we but bring the consciousness of our Catholic faith, our Christian responsibility, into the whole of our life, and really make ourselves new men in the sight of God, if we but do even this, we are surely and eloquently preaching the Gospel of Christ and extending Christ's kingdom among men.[36]

This editorial called for lay people to live their religion in their daily lives within the home, workplace, and public forum. By doing so, they would fulfill Hecker's vision of a lay piety which would be redemptive of the world through charity and apostolic zeal.

In 1910 Burke believed that America, indeed the world, was ripe for harvest by the Catholic Church.[37] In line with Petre's thinking, he welcomed every effort by Protestants to live with conviction the principles of their own religion. His concern here was not ecumenical. "It is easier to bring to the true Fold a Christian who conscientiously believes in dogmatic religion than one who has no definite belief," explained Burke. "In truth the stronger his convictions, the more ardent his positive belief, the more likely is it that he may be led to accept the whole of Christ's revelation."

The missionary endeavor of conversion could be extended not only by bringing those led by grace directly into the Church but also by encouraging Protestants to make a dogmatic profession of their own creed and live that to the fullest. Indifferentism was the real enemy of Christianity.[38]

When, in 1916, major Protestant denominations held a conference in New York to prepare for a World Congress aimed at reunion,[39] a sympathetic Burke wished them well and took the occasion for his first full articulation of the Catholic Church as the Mystical Body of Christ in opposition to a fragmented Protestantism. "An organic body is a body in which there is the one principle of life, and that principle of life directs all its members," he wrote. "In the Church, Christ is the Head and we are the members. And that Mystical Body of Christ must have its true and exact representation before men. Christ must live sensibly before men as He lived once in His human body, and walked among them and preached and did the works which no other man ever did.... This is essentially the Christian and Catholic view of the Church of Christ. Unity visible because of unity invisible." That unity was based on the truth revealed by Christ and kept undefiled by his representative on earth. Christian faith was the acceptance of that revealed truth which Christ entrusted to his Church authoritatively. "The authority is humanly real to us: it is visible; it is active; it is independent of us ... else it would be our servant rather than our master," declared Burke. The human representation of that unity and authority was the Pope, "the successor of St. Peter, who speaks with the authority of [the invisible] Christ." The Christian who accepted that "this Voice alone has the words of eternal truth ... renews the life of faith in Christ and is made a member of that Body of which Christ himself is the Head."[40] This vision of organic unity, of the invisible Christ remaining visible in the world through his vicar and the members of his Church committed to his authoritative truth, served not only as the touchstone that proved for Burke the incompleteness of Protestantism but also as the image that would enable him to see the Catholic Church and all those in it as a whole rather than as localized parts.

In coming to this vision, Burke applauded or fostered Catholic movements to make that organic unity effective through organization. As already noted, his friend Kerby had called for the massing of Catholics in particular interests. In 1910 Kerby himself took the lead in bringing together Catholic social reformers into the National Conference of Catholic Charities.

Because local needs and resources varied from place to place, the conference was not to be an instrument of uniformity, but, as Kerby expressed it, a forum "through which the national consciousness of our Catholic charities may come to expression," to get "at whole views of things," to take a step back and "place all things in their relations to catch their meaning." The conference was to be a vehicle through which the whole policy of Catholic charity might be clarified.[41] Viewing the new Conference as a counterbalance to the Socialist Party of America, Burke welcomed its foundation and declared that it "had been organized not a moment too soon." In the face of the Socialist challenge, it appeared to him "as if the appeal for Catholics to join in the work of social reform were an imperative summons to perform a duty too long deferred."[42]

Similarly, Burke hailed the formation of the Catholic Press Association in 1911 as a great step forward. A member of its executive board and chairman of its literature bureau, he believed the welfare of the Church in any country was "inextricably bound up" with the health of Catholic literature. In those places where the Church was persecuted, he argued, where nuns and brothers were proscribed, "where Catholicism as a vitalizing, national force [was] absent … long before these things could be, the Catholic Press had died." Though the work of the CPA would take time to unfold, Burke was sure it would eventually result in "an efficient Catholic Press that will command a hearing from all of our fellow-citizens, vitalize our national life with Catholic truth, and lead our country to the feet of Christ."[43]

While Burke helped found and guide the CPA, he improved the Paulist Press. As editor he learned all the mechanical aspects of printing. He replaced handset type with modern Linotype machines. In 1907, he remodeled the offices, expanding the press room and replacing the old presses with new ones. The effort was not without its inconveniences for the introverted editor: the hammering, the stripping of the walls, the repainting. "Really, the work of moving and the upset have been more than I reckoned on," confessed Burke. In order to pay for the upgrades, the operation of Paulist Press had to be expanded by increasing the volume of books and pamphlets produced. Finally, and in keeping with Catholic social ethics, Burke unionized the shop.[44] Physical improvements at *Catholic World* were not the only ones he undertook. He also engaged in the spiritual improvement of the personnel closest to him.

ENDNOTES TO CHAPTER 2

1. Burke, *Christ in Us*, 64–65.
2. [James Gillis, C.S.P.], "Right Reverend Monsignor John J. Burke, C.S.P.," *Catholic World* 144 (December 1936): 268; Malloy, "John Joseph Burke," 718–19; Hawks, "Souvenir of Burke," 2–3, AP, Burke Papers, box 10; Sheerin, *Never Look Back*, 22.
3. Mary G. Hawks, "Father Burke: Editor, Author, Critic," *Catholic Action* 18 (December 1936): 27 (the quotation is from here); Malloy, "John Joseph Burke," 719.
4. Burke to James Fox, 18 October 1904, AP, Catholic World Correspondence Early 1900s, Ferry-Hurley; Hawks, "Father Burke," 27.
5. Bernard M. G. Reardon, ed., *Roman Catholic Modernism* (Stanford: Stanford University Press, 1970), 9–63; Gabriel Daly, O.S.A., *Transcendence and Immanence: A Study in Catholic Modernism and Integralism* (Oxford: Oxford University Press, 1980), chapters 1–7; Michael V. Gannon, "Before and After Modernism: The Intellectual Isolation of the American Priest," in John Tracy Ellis, *The Catholic Priest in the United States: Historical Investigations* (Collegeville, Minn.: St. John's University Press, 1971), 326–31; Gerald P. Fogarty, S.J., *American Catholic Biblical Scholarship: A History from the Early Republic to Vatican II* (San Francisco: Harper and Row, 1989), 51–55, 78–95, 120–32; R. Scott Appleby, *"Church and Age Unite!": The Modernist Impulse in American Catholicism* (Notre Dame: University of Notre Dame Press, 1992), 55–69, 121–28; William L. Portier, *Divided Friends: Portraits of the Roman Catholic Modernist Crisis in the United States* (Washington, D.C.: The Catholic University of America Press, 2013), 199–227; Paul G. Robichaud, C.S.P., "Modernist Ghosts in the Halls of St. Thomas," *Paulist Studies* 1 (1992): 42–50; Reher, *Catholic Intellectual Life*, 91–93; Reher, "Kingdom of God in America," 255–71.
6. Michael J. Connolly, "The 'Grave Emergency' of 1909: Modernism and the Paulist Fathers," *U.S. Catholic Historian* 20 (Summer 2002): 51–60; R. Scott Appleby, "Modernism as the Final Phase of Americanism: William L. Sullivan, American Catholic Apologist, 1899–1910," *Harvard Theological Review* 81 (April 1988): 171–92; Appleby, *"Church and Age Unite!"* 121–26; Michael McGarry, C.S.P., "Modernism in the United States: William Laurence Sullivan, 1872–1935," *Records of the American Catholic Historical Society* 90 (March-December 1979): 33–52; Warren E. Duclos, "Crisis of an American Catholic Modernist: Toward the Moral Absolutism of William L. Sullivan," *Church History* 41 (1972): 369–84; Portier, *Divided Friends*, 235–37, 259–95; Reher, "Kingdom of God in America," 277–94.
7. Burke to Fox, 18 October 1904, AP, Catholic World Correspondence Early

1900s, Ferry-Hurley; Burke to Fox, 22 September 1905, ibid.; Fox to Burke, [September or October 1905], ibid.; James J. Fox, "A Catholic and the Bible: III," *Catholic World* 81 (April 1905): 72–83, and "A Catholic and the Bible: IV," ibid. (May 1905): 185–98; Connolly, "'Grave Emergency,'" 59–60.

8. Joseph McSorley, C.S.P., "The Mystical Body of Christ," *Catholic World* 81 (June 1905): 307–09 (the quotation on 309).
9. Quoted in Daly, *Transcendence and Immanence*, 140–64 (the quotation is on 143).
10. McSorley, "Mystical Body of Christ," 307–14 (quotations on 309, 310, 311, 312–13, emphasis added).
11. Hawks, "Souvenir of Burke," 7, AP, Burke Papers, box 10.
12. George Tyrrell, S.J., "The Limits of the Development Theory," *Catholic World* 81 (September 1905): 730–43, (quotations are on 742–43, emphasis in original); Portier, *Divided Friends*, 235–37, 252; Daly, *Transcendence and Immanence*, chapter 7; Nicholas Sagovsky, *"On God's Side": A Life of George Tyrrell* (Oxford: Clarendon Press, 1990); Patrick Allit, *Catholic Converts: British and American Intellectuals Turn to Rome* (Ithaca and London: Cornell University Press, 1997), 118–26; William Portier, "George Tyrrell in America," *U.S. Catholic Historian* 20 (Summer 2002): 69–77, 90; Allan Savage, "George Tyrrell: Modernist Theologian (1861–1909): What He Said He Said," *Quodlibet Journal* 4 (Winter 2002), http://www.quodlibet.net/articles/savage-tyrrell.shtml (accessed 4 July 2011). 734–43.
13. Tyrrell, "Limits of Development Theory," 743–44.
14. George Tyrrell, S.J., "The Prayer of Christ, I and II," *Catholic World* 82 (January and March 1906): 446–58, 796–806, and "The Prayer of Christ, III," ibid. 83 (April 1906): 54–64; McSorley to Burke, 16 November 1905, AP, *Catholic World* Correspondence Early 1900s, Mahon–Meadows.
15. George Tyrrell, *A Much Abused Letter* (London: Longman, Green, and Co., 1906), 37–91 (quotations are on 51–52 and 66–67); Portier, "Tyrrell in America," 89–91; Sagovsky, *"On God's Side,"* 171–202.
16. McSorley to Burke, 7 March 1906, AP, *Catholic World* Correspondence Early 1900s, Mahon–Meadows (the first quotation is here); McSorley to Burke, 16 March 1906, second letter of this date, ibid. (the second quotation is here); Sagovsky, *"On God's Side,"* 194–206; Portier, "Tyrrell in America," 91; Connolly, "'Grave Emergency'" 61; Portier, *Divided Friends*, 252–54.
17. McSorley to Burke, 26 March 1906, AP, *Catholic World* Correspondence Early 1900s, Mahon-Meadows; McSorley to Burke, 29 March 1906, ibid. (the quotation is here).
18. Sagovsky, *"On God's Side,"* 56–57.
19. M. D. Petre, "The Fallacy of Undenominationalism," *Catholic World* 84 (February 1907): 640–46 (quotations are on 641, 643, and 646).
20. Roger Aubert, *The Church in the Industrial Age*, vol. 9 of Hubert Jedin, ed.,

History of the Church (New York: Crossroad, 1981), 3840–93, 455–59; Daly, *Transcendence and Immanence*, chapter nine.

21. Joseph Mooney, "The Rights of the Supreme Pontiff"; Thomas F. Burke, C.S.P., "The Errors Condemned"; and Joseph Daily, C.SS.R., "The Causes of Modernism"—all in *Catholic World* 86 (January and February 1908): 519–31, 645–50; Gannon, "Before and After Modernism," 348–50; Fogarty, *Catholic Biblical Scholarship*, 96–116, 132–39, 174–79; John Tracy Ellis, *The Life and Times of Cardinal James Gibbons, Archbishop of Baltimore, 1834–1921*, 2 vols. (Milwaukee: Bruce Publishing Company, 1952), 2:171–82; Kauffman, *Tradition and Transformation*, 230–34; Reher, *Catholic Intellectual Life*, 95–98.
22. Sagovsky, *"On God's Side,"* 223–30. Connolly, "'Grave Emergency,'" 55–57, 61; Duclos, "Crisis of an American Catholic Modernist," 370–71; John Salter, S.J., "Father Tyrrell's View of Revealed Truth," *Catholic World* 89 (April 1909): 27–40.
23. David J. O'Brien, *Public Catholicism* (New York: Macmillan, 1988), 128–29.
24. Alfred J. Ede, *The Lay Crusade for a Christian America: A Study of the American Federation of Catholic Societies, 1900–1919* (New York: Garland, 1988), 57–240.
25. *Catholic Educational Association, Report of the Proceedings and Addresses of the First Annual Meeting, Saint Louis, Missouri, 14–12 July 1904*, 9–38, 185–91.
26. Degler, *Age of Economic Revolution*, chapters 1–3; Thomas Cochran and William Miller, *The Age of Enterprise: A Social History of Industrial America*, 2d ed. rev. (New York: Harper Torchbooks, 1961), chapters 8–12; Alan Trachtenberg, *The Incorporation of America: Culture & Society in the Gilded Age* (New York: Hill and Wang, 1982), chapters 2–3; Alfred D. Chandler, "The Beginnings of 'Big Business' in American Industry," in *Essays on the Age of Enterprise: 1870–1900*, ed. David Brody (Hinsdale, Ill.: Dryden Press, 1974), 32–56; Arthur F. Bently, "The Condition of the Western Farmer," in ibid., 74–90; Zane L. Miller, *The Urbanization of Modern America: A Brief History* (New York: Harcourt Brace Jovanovich, Inc., 1973), chapter 3.
27. David A. Shannon, *The Socialist Party of America: A History* (New York: Macmillan, 1955), 1–80; Ira Kipnis, *The American Socialist Movement, 1897–1912* (New York: Columbia University Press, 1952), 80–429.
28. Arthur S. Link and Richard L. McCormick, *Progressivism* (Arlington Heights, Ill.: Harlan Davidson, 1983). For an opposite view, namely, that big business initiated and dominated the reform movement for its own interests, see Gabriel Kolko, *The Triumph of Conservatism* (New York: Free Press, 1963), and also Samuel P. Hays, "The Politics of Reform in Municipal Government in the Progressive Era," *Pacific Northwest Quarterly* 55 (October 1964): 157–69.
29. John A. Ryan, "The Underpaid Laborers of America: Their Number and Prospects," *Catholic World* 81 (May 1905): 143–56.

30. John A. Ryan, "A Programme of Social Reform by Legislation," *Catholic World* 89 (July and August 1909): 434–44, 608–14; Ryan, "The Church and the Workingman," ibid. (September 1909): 776–82; Ryan, "Coöperation a Partial Solvent of Capitalism," ibid. 101 (May and June 1915): 157–65, 343–51 (quotations are on 349); Charles E. Curran, *American Catholic Social Ethics: Twentieth-Century Approaches* (Notre Dame, Ind.: University of Notre Dame Press, 1982), 26–56; Francis L. Broderick, *Right Reverend New Dealer: John A. Ryan* (New York: The Macmillan Company, 1963), 26–75.
31. William J. Kerby, "Reinforcement of the Bonds of Faith," *Catholic World* 84 (January and February 1907): 508–22, 591–606 (quotations are on 515, 516, and 603); Elizabeth K. McKeown, "Catholic Identity in America," in *America in Theological Perspective*, 56–57.
32. Burke to Kerby, 7 November 1906 and 7 January 1907, ACUA, 58:4:3 (quotations are taken from both letters); McKeown, *War and Welfare*, 18–19.
33. Hecker to Richard Simpson, 22 February 1861, in Abbot Gasquet, O.S.B., ed., "Some Letters of Father Hecker," *Catholic World* 83 (June 1906): 356–57; Farina, *American Experience of God*, 126–29; Allitt, *Catholic Converts*, 88–97.
34. Hecker to Simpson, 22 February 1861, in "Letters of Hecker," 356–57.
35. "With Our Readers," *Catholic World* 90 (October 1909): 140–2.
36. "With Our Readers," *Catholic World* 91 (July 1910): 571–72. For more on this point, see Burke, "Skeleton of a Retreat the General Subject of Which Is '*The Communion of Saints*,'" Exhibit C of Hawks, "Souvenir of Burke," AP, Burke Papers, box 10.
37. "With Our Readers," *Catholic World* 91 (September 1910): 862.
38. "With Our Readers," *Catholic World* 97 (May 1913): 281–83. See also "With Our Readers," ibid. 96 (December 1912): 425–26.
39. Tissington Tatlow, "The World Conference on Faith and Order," in Ruth Rouse and Stephen Charles Neill, eds., *A History of the Ecumenical Movement* 2 vols., 2nd ed. (Philadelphia: Westminster Press, 1967), 1:405–14; "With Our Readers," *Catholic World* 102 (February 1916): 714.
40. "With Our Readers," *Catholic World* 102 (February 1916): 715–19. For a similar argument based on organic unity regarding the truth of Catholicism and the falsity of Protestantism, see "With Our Readers," ibid. 105 (April 1917): 138–39.
41. Kerby, "The National Conference of Catholic Charities: An Interpretation," *Catholic World* 92 (November 1910): 145–56 (quotations are on 147); Donald P. Gavin, *The National Conference of Catholic Charities, 1910–1960* (Milwaukee: Bruce Press, 1962), 1–52.
42. "With Our Readers," *Catholic World* 92 (December 1910): 427. Regarding social reform, Burke believed that priests had a duty to involve themselves in it. Because preparation for that duty had to begin in the formation process,

he advocated the appointment of a specialist in social sciences to every seminary faculty ("With Our Readers," ibid. 91 [May 1910]: 283; Joseph Seliger, "Is Social Reform Work a Duty of the Parish Clergy," *Ecclesiastical Review* 42 [April 1910]: 452–58).

43. Burke, "The Convention of Catholic Editors," *Catholic World* 94 (October 1911): 81–86 (quotations are on 81 and 86).
44. Burke to Helen Lynch, 8 August 1907, AP, Burke Papers, box 5; [Gillis], "John J. Burke," 268; Malloy, "John Joseph Burke," 719.

Chapter 3
The Cloister

> Friendship may be one of the strongest or one of the weakest of human relations.... When friendship is spiritually fruitless, it is but selfishness and no true friendship at all.... Jesus Christ was the true, the truest friend to His disciples. To all He gave the highest and the best of which with His grace they were capable. He looked upon them not only as they actually were, but also as every one of them might be through His favor and power—a worthier, greater self. His friendship, true to itself, and therefore true to them determined every one of them would be that greater self and gave them the power to be such.[1]

The Spiritual Life and Love

Spirituality defined John Burke. It permeated his life and informed his actions. He was a man possessed by love of God. An introvert and lover of solitude, he was temperamentally predisposed toward the interior life. As a novice, Burke was introduced to Hecker's spirituality and also that of the mystic St. Teresa of Avila, patroness of Paulists, whom he highly regarded. His later secretary Mary Coyle remarked that Burke's "piercing blue eyes could look through granite—seemed like he could see the soul of the one spoken to."[2] Mary Hawks at *Catholic World*, who became his spiritual directee, recalled that "even more painstaking, perhaps, than his cultivation of contributors [to the magazine] was his spiritual cultivation of the personnel engaged with him in the work."[3] James Gillis, Burke's successor as editor, concurred: "The driving force in all Father Burke's contacts was the apostle's greed for souls. He drew to him every worker in the establishment, talked with them personally, and taking them as he found them, by example, by counsel and command, nerved them to the realization of their powers in a spirit of devotion second only to his own."[4] Perhaps better than "greed" would be to say Burke was a man ablaze with love for God and desired to ignite that flame in others. To trusted souls, he spoke the language of biblical mysticism: the lover and the beloved of the Song of Songs. His first pupil in "the cloister," as he called the editorial sanctum, was Helen Lynch.[5]

A New Zealander of Irish ancestry, Lynch immigrated to New York City with her mother in 1902 at age fifteen. On an August day in 1905, she called at *Catholic World* looking for work. She was taken with Burke, and he with her. She became his secretary shortly before the feast of the Assumption of Mary. An incident that became memorable for both occurred the following Easter. He asked her to buy him seasonal cards to send family and friends. He expected her to purchase religious ones, but she returned with sentimental greetings featuring bluebirds. He took one look at them and dropped them on the floor. His reaction made him appear mean and inconsiderate. It was a character flaw of which he was aware. He blamed the trait on a quick mind which immediately grasped an idea or purpose he assumed must be equally evident to others. When misunderstood, he became irritated by their apparent obtuseness, but the fault was his for not explaining clearly his wish. Lynch avenged his ingratitude by sending him one of the offensive cards for Easter.[6] She was a spunky young woman, who felt comfortable enough with their relationship to push back.

In August 1906, the first anniversary of her employment, Lynch wrote Burke from the Green Mountains where she was vacationing to remind him of the occasion and request greater responsibility. The letter arrived on the eve of the Assumption. Burke had come to sense in her a kindred spirit: a soul sensitive to God and willing to be formed. His reply, he later explained, "was in great measure then a matter of hope."[7]

Taking her mention of responsibility as an opening, Burke responded with a long discourse on the Virgin Mary. The notion of responsibility had been much on his mind, especially with regard to the following feast day. He viewed Mary as a "type" in the sense used by fathers of the Church: she exemplified what a Christian ought to be. Like all people, Mary had to work out her salvation, and she had done it through faithfulness to God. Jesus made clear this was the source of her specialness when a woman in the crowd called, "Blessed is the womb that carried you and the breasts at which you nursed." His reply, "Rather, blessed are those who hear the word of God and keep it [Luke 11:27–28]." Mary's greatness lay not in the fact that she was Jesus's mother, but in "her realization of her personal responsibility to God and willingness to accept it and to fulfill it with the utmost perfection." Though none could equal Mary, each could "gain courage from her and strive to imitate her." She was human, too. "She had to resign herself to God as the instrument of God," the first step of every Christian for whom she was the type. She labored with and for her son, was separated from him, suffered at his crucifixion, and endured the long wait for her own death after his resurrection. So too, the Christian worked with and for Jesus, was often separated from him by spiritual dryness or depression, indeed crucified him again by his or her own sins, and endured in resignation the wait for His coming at death.[8]

Christian responsibility was actually a labor of love. Christians, Burke told her, often forgot that God called them to be collaborators in the work of salvation. He sent his son to show his love for humankind so that people would respond in kind with love. "Our sense of responsibility ought to be deep, and pleasant and welcome on account of this," he wrote, "and we ought to thank God for making us his co-operators, for giving us the chance to serve Him, for so honoring us, for so exalting us." God loved Christians enough to invite them as equals in the work of salvation, confident to leave them free, trusting their intelligence and faithfulness. The realization of this should make them eager to cooperate, wrote Burke: "To do that little which unless we do it will never be done. Which wonder of wonders, God Himself could not do: which will have its effect for all eternity not only on ourselves but also on the glory of God! The thought is vast and far reaching." Moved by the grace of God's love, the Christian would see opportunities for loving service to which he or she was previously blind.[9]

Burke's concern for Lynch touched her. "Joyfully bearing its many pages I went far away from the one human habitation in that heavenly place [Green Mountains] and read and reread your message for the Feast," she later confided to him. "That day something happened in my soul." She became conscious of Burke's care for her: "How you were giving time and thought to my spiritual growth and enlightenment, how you were holding up ideals and giving me the hope that I could dare reach toward them." She was struck with "wonder" that despite her sense of unworthiness to receive special attention, Burke had taken an interest in her development. Though Lynch felt powerless to accomplish spiritual things, she felt Mary could do them for her. "So that Assumption I gave her your letter, so to speak," she told him, "and begged her to make it the seed of fruit in my soul."[10]

Thereafter, Burke took Lynch under his wing. He increased her responsibility at *Catholic World*, entrusting her with the *Leader*. He initiated a custom of celebrating the end of business on New Year's Eve by reviewing with her their efforts of the previous year and planning for the new. Yet, most of all, he schooled her in spirituality.[11]

In August 1907, Lynch was away caring for her mother. She had written Burke a letter which confirmed in him the belief that God had gifted her with "a heart full of spiritual discernment: a mind of taste and of modesty and a soul that ought to do faithful and steadfast service for Him." This was no small thing to say, he wrote. Unfortunately many people tasted "only the froth of devotion and of faith and of love." Their lives were good, but never got to the meat of Christianity, the painful striving for the greatest measure of service to God, the self-immolating love of lover for the beloved. That measure was unique to each, and one need only live to his or her own best and fullest. "God has created us individually and particularly," explained Burke.

> We are in a measure nothing: we are in our own measure, everything.... God would have his glory fulfilled on earth in an infinite number of ways and each one of us may fulfill it in our own way, in a way that no one else can fulfill it. He hath sent forth His glory in us that a ray might be taken up by each one of us and shine forth, perhaps brighter here than there, but clear and distinct and perfect in each one of us. And the converse of this is also true: that each one of us in his own full measure will receive the full and perfect love of God: that in his presence nothing will be wanting to us, that we will be surfited [*sic*] with His Grace: that it will make no difference to us that star differeth from star in glory, for we shall be so filled and taken up with the love of God that we will be inattentive to all things else or

> rather that we shall so love God, as to see things as He sees them and therefore to see the glory and justice of it all.

This passage rhapsodized Burke's understanding of the divine plan for humankind, that each person was a singular, unrepeatable expression of the deity, sharing in a particular way the divine life and glory. Burke thought that an understanding of this reality ought to appeal to everyone, effectively moving each to love of God.[12]

This understanding launched him into a discourse on how divine love overwhelmed and invited the beloved to return love in kind. God loved humans as if they had never sinned; more precisely, he loved people because they had and he was unwilling to let sin separate them from him. "It is comforting: it is inspiring: it is exalting," rejoiced Burke.

> It is all in all—to the soul[,] and in the light of it the soul reaches out for means whereby it may serve God and show its own love. Love has bound us about, ensnared us, caught us and it will not let us go. And the achievement of love in our own souls is to do all things, to bear all things, to rejoice in all things with our Beloved. Our Beloved is the Lord Jesus who has borne our sins and our iniquities … who has endured the heat of the day: the sweat of toil: the anxiety of home: the criticisms of others: the failure of friends: the disappointments of men. Therefore will we His loved ones bear our own work, our own toil with its trials of patience, of care, of foresight, of delinquence [*sic*] … even with the joy of love. Our Beloved Jesus bore pain and suffering and death: therefore will we gladly, enthusiastically, bear and accept the pain that He may ask us to accept … glad that in these great things He has deigned to ask us to be His co-sufferers. For the test of love is in great measure what we ask of the beloved, and of them whom we love surely and strongly we are not afraid to ask burdens and cares and sympathy and the sharing of our sorrows. So is it with the love of Our Lord, Jesus, and ourselves. And all this is practical and sure and real: not simply devotional: not simply sensible or a matter of feeling. For Jesus

> Christ has actually and really borne these things. In Himself he has centered the universe of human beings: and directed it to God.

Burke concluded by telling Lynch that for him life was to live in thoughtfulness and self-control in love for his brother Jesus. "And death has this for me," he concluded, "that it is but the call of my Beloved to see Him and be with Him in another place, to see Him face to face, and to be with Him in inexpressible union of heavenly love."[13]

While Lynch cared for her mother, Burke himself supervised publication of the *Leader*. On seeing the August edition, she wrote "Uncle Ned" a letter from an anonymous niece in which she impishly criticized his selection of illustrations. "Uncle Ned in his great wisdom," responded Burke, "shrewdly suspects that that letter from a devoted niece comes from a devoted daughter who knows something of the inside working of things." Considering her stricture too severe, he defended his choice of pictures. He then turned to spirituality. Burke wrote, "In the diary of a child, which diary I am permitted to read," he found her to be a person of abiding joy with a "thirst for purer waters." He detected in early passages a tendency toward despair over sins and failings. He said he had spoken to her about how the great love and sacrifice of Christ for the sinner converted such despair into hope, "so with the saint of God there is never a long face, nor an over weighted heart or brain in the presence of problems and uncertain questions." In later entries there was "a solid practice and real sense of Christian faith and love." He complimented her on the progress she had made over the last year and counseled, "We must take ourselves neither too seriously nor too frivolously."[14]

Clearly, the relationship between them had developed considerably on both the human and the spiritual levels. There was genuine affection between them. They bantered with each other through the guise of uncle and niece. Lynch had opened her diary to Burke, and he had assumed the role of spiritual father. Yet, he felt comfortable enough to treat her as an equal in sharing his own spiritual journey with her.

At some point in fall of 1907, Burke was hospitalized and then went for rest to Point Pleasant, New Jersey. It seems he had been pushing himself too hard spiritually and perhaps also at work, which led to a physical breakdown. He would suffer these bouts periodically the rest of his life. Ironically, despite the exertions that landed him in the hospital, he considered their results of little account. He hoped that coming days "may be more fruitful than the idle and indifferent years that have passed." He shared with Lynch the lesson learned from this experience: patience and peace in God. Burke explained that God followed in the supernatural order his manner of acting in the natural. "The plant does not flower at once," he told her, "it must grow to blade and stem and branch and blossom, first: ... it is long and only by patient, invisible growth that we reach our full physical stature. So is it with the soul: ... There must be waiting and patience and trust, with the most diligent and ceaseless labor." Burke cautioned, however, that strength must be husbanded and controlled lest one overreach. "We must often forego heights that seem enviable, yet which are not for us as yet," he told her. "We who would have all love and perfection—must, even with a certain peace, be content to look into ourselves and view what imperfect and sinful creatures we are. What very earthly vessels, that dare to contain the Lord of Heaven and earth." The ability to see oneself and the horror of one's sins and imperfections, and yet do so in patience and peace with the knowledge that one has been purified by the blood of Christ, called for true spiritual balance. "Our falls and our sins should stir us to greater effort: but they should never disturb our confidence," advised Burke. "The deceitful voice of the evil one telling us we are unworthy because of past sins or present faults should never lead us to mistrust ourselves: but rather should make us the stronger and more earnest lovers[,] for Christ has accepted us once more: and we are Christ's: and neither tribulation nor storm nor distress, as the apostle says, will ever separate me from the love of Christ [cf. Romans 8:36]." God would bring forth fruit in his own time. Throughout Burke's entire stay in the hospital, he told Lynch, Jesus's words to his disciples, "Possess your souls in patience [Luke 21:19]," ran through his head.[15]

Probably at Easter in 1908, the two declared a truce about the bluebird cards. Still needling Burke over his initial ingratitude, Lynch had sent him one for Easter in 1907 and yet another now in 1908. When he received this last, he burst out laughing, knowing that he was going to keep getting them until he acknowledged his fault.[16] Later in life, the cards became an endearing memory commemorated at Easter.

Although Burke believed that union with God would be complete only in heaven, it began here really on earth. He declared, "But there is no hereafter; there is but one 'here' and that is with Christ Jesus Our Lord."[17] Like all Catholics, he believed Jesus was mystically, physically present in the Eucharist. Burke's sense of the real presence deepened as did his spirituality. This deepening began in his first years at *Catholic World*. One morning, he overslept and then hurried through Mass. Over breakfast with an older Paulist, one not known for piety, he noticed the man was "grouchy" and had nothing to say. So, Burke asked him what was the matter. "Well, John Burke," came the reply, "I never expected to see you offer Mass as you did today." The rebuke struck him hard. He never rushed through Mass again.[18] In 1907, he told Lynch: "I have ever thanked God for this supreme joy that He has permitted me to offer up the Holy Mass, to call Him to earth, to hold Him in my hands and to offer Him to His Father." And not just to hold him, but to receive Jesus into his own body and soul and offer himself with Jesus to his Father.[19] As Burke's sense of the real presence became more profound, he celebrated the Eucharist with ever increasing intensity so that it eventually took a physical toll.

BRITISH INTERLUDES

In summer 1908, Lynch vacationed in Ireland where her grandparents lived. On her birthday, Burke sent her greetings reminding her it was not just natural life that God had given her, but life forever bound to him in love: "May our good Lord bless the child whom He brought into the world this day, and not alone into this world but into eternity and for Himself always." Burke realized that the letter would reach her "long after the day but 'within the octave,'" that is, the eight-day period of celebration by the Catholic Church after Christmas and Easter.[20] Burke was a great one for keeping octaves. If the anniversary itself was missed, the octave would do.

Four days later, he wrote that her absence seemed weeks, rather than days. He said he managed to get away on weekends "for a taste of the sea or river," but not for his favorite sport, canoeing. Burke confided he was often frequenting "the bungalow," a secret, day-dream retreat of inner solitude deep in a wood. He reached it by canoe, a red-roofed, white-walled place nestled by a stream among trees bathed with golden light of sunset, the sun's rays off the roof seeming a halo. Inside was a sparsely furnished sitting room. Over the entrance to the library was a picture of St. John, the beloved disciple, and within were familiar books which needed "no introduction." Across the hall and next to his bedroom was the chapel, "the dearest place of the whole house," where he often said Mass. "There I have seen and heard what one can never see or hear elsewhere," he wrote. "It is eternity, and outside is time. It is peace and outside is that which tries peace. And at the chapel I stop, for the thought recalls me to the fact that I am selfishly indulging myself in pleasant dreams. And life is not a dream at all."[21]

Burke turned this self-indulgent daydream into grist for a lesson. The Christian life was not for weaklings. "We were not born for the shade and the quiet, but for the sun's heat the day's work," he explained. "But how foolish those who will never rest when they can (and one may, if he wishes, very often) under the great quiet shadow of God's love which is like the great restful shadow thrown by a huge rock in a desert waste. God has sent us to work, and yet we can never work without him." Burke's message was that balance must be struck between contemplation and action. The love of God must be the source of Christian activity, and so the Christian must often rest in the shadow of God's love in order to be renewed for the strenuous life of love. As Lynch later recalled, Burke's favorite passage from scripture was, "I sat down under His Shadow Whom I desired and His fruit was sweet to my palate [Song of Sol., 2:3]."[22]

Yet, Burke cautioned there can be selfishness in spiritual things, "particularly when we look therein only for our own peace and joy." The vision of Jesus in glory on Mount Tabor had to be balanced by Christ on the cross. Again, Mary embodied the type of the Christian. "I think one of the greatest characteristics of our dear Mother Mary," he told Lynch, "was her utter selflessness; an absolute abandonment to God; a willingness to do her utmost and yet no selfish strain to please self; no selfish fear that perhaps she might not do as well as she would like to do—but constant vision of God, and utter service, not to self, but to Him, and of abandoning self, not worrying about self, but with a whole heart seeking the things of God, always living true to the highest inspirations of God irrespective of selfish pleasure or vanity or human respect in the fear of offending and antagonizing." If the Christian lived in this fashion, he or she would "find that wonderful self God has stored up for us in Himself." This passage about Mary so impressed Lynch that she highlighted it in the margin of the letter.[23]

In his final letter to Ireland, Burke explained his purpose in sending Lynch these missives: "I want you to enjoy your trip to the full: and these letters are sent that they may give you happy and gracious thoughts." He reminded her that the closer God led the soul to him, the more difficult it was for the soul to find satisfaction without him. This desire for God led ultimately to "the 'sacrificial' things of life" on his behalf, which "to the trained, delicate soul," were "synonymous with God." Burke said they would continue this conversation when she returned.[24]

In late September 1908, Burke himself went to England and Ireland. He had apparently been suffering for more than a year an abscess that refused to heal, wearing him down physically. The trip was probably meant for convalescence and vacation. Burke would also be mindful of securing articles for *Catholic World.* On her own trip, Lynch had kept a running letter chronicling the crossing, which she sent him on her arrival, so Burke did likewise. He sailed on the S.S. *Minneapolis* with bon-voyage gifts of fruit and cigars enough to last six months. Because there were only twenty-eight passengers aboard, the chief steward, a Catholic named John Martin, upgraded him to a deluxe suite and assigned him a private table with his own waiter. The first three days were calm though the weather was "very foggy." Burke slept and felt well, and days passed quickly: rise at 7:00 A.M., coffee at 7:15, breakfast 8:30, a walk on deck, shuffleboard, "then [divine] office, prayer, and a little writing." He had chicken broth at 11:00 and lunch at 1:30 P.M., after which he conversed with passengers and then a nap. After that, he walked and read for the remainder of the afternoon. At 6:30, the bugle summoned all to supper.[25]

The ship hit strong winds and heavy seas which made the vessel pitch "its nose down—and its toes up and vice versa." Some became seasick, but not Burke, who continued to walk the deck despite swells and the fact he left his topcoat at home. The wind and the rolling continued for a second day, but the nights were clear. The stars seemed so low he could touch them. The aurora borealis "came and went, flashing from East to West like some great electric search light," Burke wrote Lynch. "To think that they are the sun's rays reflected from the icebergs far to the north of us"—a remark that bespoke either the bad science of the day or misinformation he had received. Next morning, the ocean's expanse filled Burke with the "presence and power" of God. "To him were you commended by a sinner," he told

Lynch. "May He not heed the one who asks but listen only to the prayer and give you abiding grace and goodness and love."[26]

During the voyage, Burke and Martin talked religion for hours. They also discussed countries that the well traveled steward had seen. Thinking of Lynch, Burke mentioned her birthplace. Martin declared, "New Zealand is God's own land." One day, Burke toured the boiler and engine rooms, "a marvelous sight—these bowels of the ship." A day or two later he visited the "Marconi room" (radio telegraph room) to see this relatively new invention in operation. "The wonderful Marconi, and the thought of the mariner's compass that made our journey possible has led me to a thought," he wrote to Lynch, "—that after all, the magnetic power of the North and the sound waves of the air are the long ago creations of an all wise God, and ignorant man is but finding out little by little what the good God has made and formed. Instead of priding himself on his knowledge he should be awfully humiliated at his former ignorance."[27]

The ship made landfall at Cornwall on 4 October and reached port the following day. The highlights of Burke's time in the British Isles had to do with things Catholic. After a stay with the Benedictines at Ealing outside London, he traveled to Oxford where he hoped to meet the recusant poet Louise Imogen Guiney at the train station. They had been writing and wiring each other, but Burke was unsure she would be there, and in any case neither knew what the other looked like. He walked through the station twice in search of a woman who might herself appear to be searching for someone. The two almost passed each other when both turned: "Miss Guiney!" "Father Burke!" He found her a down-to-earth woman possessed of a sense of humor and humility. "She it was who made Oxford delightful to me," he wrote Lynch, "for without a guide one would see great buildings but would not see their soul." The soul of the place was the spirit of John Henry Newman. Guiney took Burke to see the lodgings where he had lived as an undergraduate at Oxford University and those he dwelt in while studying there for the Anglican ministry. They went to the church in Littlemore where Newman served as pastor before his conversion to Catholicism. Burke felt privileged to be in the rooms where he slept, worked, prayed, and "was received into the true fold and for the first time went to Holy Communion." The next morning, he and Guiney walked to the well of St. Margaret in Binsey, where they sat and talked for hours, getting so lost in conversation that "we were forced to make an unholy show of ourselves in hurrying back to Oxford," where Burke almost missed his afternoon train to Downside Abbey near Bath.[28]

There, he spent almost two weeks with the Benedictines, the first days pleasurably alone. Because the monks were busy men, Burke had to find "his own occupation and his own enjoyment." The time away from work was doing wonders for his health. The abscess had given him only the "the least trouble." A small flare-up had occurred during the Atlantic crossing, but since then it felt "as if it had never been." "I haven't felt so well in a year as I do now," he reported to Lynch. "May God continue it."[29]

Burke viewed England through Paulist eyes, those that saw potential for a religious harvest in a land of desiccated faith. "Religion among the people—there is none," he explained. In his two weeks there, he came to the opinion that the country needed "a rebirth—a resurrection." The dominant Anglican Church was lifeless and inert. He told Lynch the words of British social commentator John Ruskin were truer at present than when he uttered them: "You might sooner get lightning out of incense smoke than true action or passion out of your modern English religion." Nor was it just the Anglicans. Two and a half centuries of persecution had left Catholics quiescent. Their nobles were "faithful and upright, but … content to remain in their own beautiful castle of faith." The rest were "so under the spell of caste and of class that they have no initiative." Burke spoke to several Benedictines about this situation. He believed their religious order was ideally suited for the task of regeneration, "their spirit" being "nearest to the Paulists," he wrote. They were learned men and some were eloquent, perfectly fit for the work of converting a country strewn with reminders of its Catholic past. If four to six monks were assigned to it, "the effect would be wonderful." Even if England were not converted, the effort would inject new life into English Catholicism.[30]

A monk took Burke on a tour of formerly Catholic sites in Somerset. They visited the old churches, all in Anglican hands. As they approached the ruins of Glastonbury Abbey, Burke saw the hill where Richard Whiting, the last abbot, was hanged. "In one way all these visits are very, very sad to me," he told Lynch. "And I have often asked myself, 'In the eternal justice of an all-knowing God who was to blame for it all.' And there comes at least this salutary answer, 'That every action of our own though we think it not, has its abiding and enduring value.' So let me attend to my own heart, and see that everything is right there." Throughout the day, the weather was dreary, and when Burke returned to Downside, so were his spirits. "I seemed to have wandered through a land that had been laid waste by a ruthless army," he remarked, "whose people had been actually wiped off the earth by their invaders for in all the territory I visited there was not a mark of present Catholicism."[31]

His mood was lifted by a letter from Lynch, who informed him that she had read the life of Hecker. This gladdened Burke because his experience of England had confirmed in him "that Hecker in spite of his limitations was nothing less than a heroic leader raised up by God." He told Lynch he would explain to her why Hecker was so great, but the explanation would take a year. He lamented that people did not yet appreciate the man, nor would they for some time to come. "But some day the vision will dawn." As for Britain, that land awaited its own Hecker. "There is need here of some great preacher in Israel," said Burke, "and some saintly man is yet to arise who will do this for England."[32]

In his final week at Downside, he had little time to himself "as there was always a monk to come in and see me." When he was not conversing with a Benedictine, he was out visiting churches in the surrounding countryside. He spent much time in the company of Maud Quinlan, a contributor to *Catholic World* and sister of one of the monks. The two spent four days together between Quinlan's home in Clevedon and the abbey at Downside. Their conversations "were personal and spiritual, strange to say, and not editorial," remarked Burke to Lynch. This line evoked from Lynch the comment, "Not strange, I say!"[33]

After departing the abbey, Burke crossed into Wales and went through Cardiff to Swansea where he visited more Benedictines, and thence to Fishguard on the Irish Sea to board the *St. Patrick* for the Emerald Isle. He planned to spend two weeks there, where there were "many people to see, and many questions to study." He intended to "strike" retired Lieutenant General Sir William Butler for some articles.[34]

Burke spent a day or two in Dublin, taking a day-trip to Trim to see the village of his father's birth and early life. Dr. John Robert O'Connell, a descendant of Irish liberator Daniel O'Connell, invited Burke to stay with him and his wife in Killiney just below Dublin. Burke was given a good room, and each morning a young maid awakened him, brought him hot water, and opened the shades. "What, oh what will I do when I get back to New York?" he exclaimed. Each evening, he and the doctor talked into the wee hours of the morning.[35]

While in Killiney, Burke sought out Protestant Irish Unionist Horace Plunkett. In early November, Plunkett "got up a little dinner at his home" to which he invited Burke. Plunkett picked him up by car and the two men spent an hour before supper walking and talking in the dusk about Home Rule and other Irish matters. "We didn't altogether agree," noted Burke. The dinner party was a who's who of the Irish agricultural-cooperative movement: Plunkett; Thomas Spring-Rice, second baron Monteagle; his daughter Mary; Father Thomas Finlay, an Irish Jesuit; Robert Andrew Anderson; and George William Russell, described by Burke as "a queer and eccentric poet," who signed his verse *AE*. "It was a mixed up company," commented the American, "but it was entertaining." Of Monteagle, he remarked, "A Lord is a very human person after all."[36]

Burke found Ireland and its people much to his liking. He told Lynch it would be impossible for him to write his impressions of the country. Suffice it to say that the Irish were "excellent" and "I certainly do love them."[37] He wrote to his sister Lizzie that Irish manners included the custom of dressing up for supper. The women always did, and the men did only slightly less often. "My dressing consists generally in 'combing' my hair," he said, "for I've gone about with little baggage, and with great efforts to keep my linen clean." After meals, the women withdrew, leaving the men to smoke and talk awhile before rejoining the ladies.[38]

On 7 November, Burke left Dublin for Bansha Castle in Tipperary to see Butler. His "heart quaked at the word 'castle.'" He was surprised when the general showed up at the station in a pony cart for the five-mile ride home. The castle turned out to be "quite an ordinary house," a small stone dwelling with turreted rooms on one side. Butler, Lady Elizabeth, and their daughter Eileen were gracious and in minutes made him feel at ease. Burke and Butler had many discussions during their days together, but no articles would be forthcoming. So hospitable were the Butlers, they pressed Burke to stay a day beyond his intended departure, and he acquiesced.[39]

He hoped to pay a surprise visit to Lynch's grandparents in Cork City, but his travel plans went awry. He was there only about an hour, part of which he spent persuading Dr. Bertram Windle, president of Queen's College, to write an article. He then had to catch the train back to Dublin. He spent his last night in Ireland again with the O'Connells. Burke and the doctor talked until 2:30 in the morning when his wife came down and turned the lights out on them.[40]

Burke sailed back to England to visit friends in Southbourne for a day or two before returning to Ealing where he remained until he sailed home. Lynch met him at the dock in New York. A beaming Burke descended the gangplank carrying a package. "For you!" he smiled. "The boy in the man," she recalled. Its content, a fifteen-by-thirty-inch reproduction of Leonardo da Vinci's *Virgin of the Rocks*.[41]

Back in the Sanctum

Back in the sanctum, things returned to normal. Close-of-business reviews of the day's events with Lynch resumed as well as talks of spirituality. Burke placed considerable trust in and relied on her. When she was away with her mother on Holy Thursday in 1909, he told her how much he depended on her. "In the work and the questions that come up," he wrote, "I feel that you have grown so close to me that you take a place here which no one ever can. What has been can never be undone. You have been with me through my hardest—except for the first hard—days here and your own enthusiasm, your own zeal your own trustworthy and generous soul have been the greatest sort of help." Lynch treasured these lines through life. She wrote them in her notebook, emphasizing in capital letters the words "WHAT HAS BEEN CAN NEVER BE UNDONE."[42]

Burke's remark was probably prompted by something he read in her diary: her realization of what it meant to have trust placed in her. "It is a signal blessing," he wrote, "to have one soul who can ever be trusted to whom temptation is not a temptation but a glorious incentive to do the right thing." He told Lynch that he had placed every trust in her, and she had always answered it well. He knew her soul and knew it could endure all, ever abiding in faith and peace. Holy Thursday made Burke think of the faith and trust Jesus must have had in his disciples, even after their desertion in his final hour. Real love, true charity, explained Burke, did not overlook or make excuses for failings of others, but enabled the lover to be steadfast in spite of them. "Charity does not force us to blind our eyes," he told Lynch. "Charity is not falsehood. Charity is the clear light of day—and he that has it will have the greater courage because he has the light. Charity is courage to assent and to love God in all things from the highest to the lowest." Real love enabled one to weather shock and disappointment with steadfastness. It enabled one to recognize and affirm the kingdom of God within oneself and in others too. His point seemed to be that Jesus's steadfast love enabled him to withstand the desertion of his disciples and enabled his disciples to repent their action. "Be your best, most zealous self," Burke urged Lynch; "be the most emphatic pronouncement you can be of the intimate, personal, definite love of God."[43]

He concluded the letter by saying he was tempted to ask her to let him read it to her aloud later "that I may stir myself at times and try in myself to live up to what at times my eyes see."[44] This was no idle comment. Burke was indeed self-effacing and humble about his own spiritual life. He told Lynch many times God has "given me at least the vision of the higher truer and eternal things," the ability to view "the mountains," the heights of Christian life and spirituality. Yet, he confessed that as much as he could speak of "the beauties of the summit," he had never "succeeded in more than skirting the base of them," which made him "but a poor guide." "You see my life needs reform in many ways!" he had written to her from Downside. "I am one of those who see, but do not perform." His letters to her in which he waxed eloquent about love, peace, patience, sacrifice, and other matters were really "little short sermons" or meditations meant as much for himself as for her. "But I believe the best correspondence is on the best things, is it not?" he asked. "If letter-writing to you doesn't make me good, then it's my own fault." Although he lamented his example was "not the highest nor best," he hoped and expected "the pupil to outdo, by far, her master."[45]

Within months, Burke began addressing Lynch in correspondence as "Dear Child," rather than by her given name. This salutation emerged gradually over time and seems to have had both personal and theological roots. In his "Uncle Ned" letter, he had called her a "devoted daughter," whom five times he referred to as his child. While convalescing in New Jersey, he concluded his letter about the spiritual lessons of his illness, "Which all leads, my dear child, to the worth of that saying of Our dear Lord … [']In your patience possess your souls.'" Burke recognized she was more truly the daughter of God, Jesus, and Mary than of himself. In April 1908, he begged divine blessing for her that she "may grow to the fullness of a child of Christ." Three months later, while she was away in Ireland, Burke had sent her spiritual encouragement to make her "a still stronger child of God and co-heir with His Son." A year later, he reminded her that she had always been a daughter to Mary, who "has had your soul in care … you are her child and as her child receive her protection and her guidance."[46]

What seems to have started as a whimsical ruse—the interaction between niece/daughter and Uncle Ned—became an endearing and enduring appellation. Burke certainly considered himself Lynch's spiritual father. As much as the term child seemed to infantilize her, it must be kept in mind that in that day, the Church was firmly hierarchical and patriarchal. That patriarchy reached into the home through a Catholic version of the cult of domesticity wherein wife and daughters (sons too) were subjects of the father of the family. The priesthood was a spiritual office which called for respect as the representation of Christ on earth. Burke insisted even his priest friends call him "Father." To be sure, there was ample theological and biblical precedent for referring to a Christian as a child of God. To be sure, Burke and Lynch had grown close, and one can hardly doubt they loved each other, especially in light of his understanding that spiritual love built on natural love. Burke was unlikely to have intended the word child in a demeaning way, and Lynch never rebelled against it. He probably used it as a means of enhancing the warmth and intimacy of their connection, while introducing formal distance through invocation of a paternal relationship, with its concomitant acknowledgment of authority and respect. Even to the time of his death, Burke always addressed Lynch as "Dear Child," and she, him as "Dear Father." Indeed, he addressed all women who came under his spiritual tutelage as "Dear Child."[47]

As another spiritual daughter, Mary Hawks, reminisced, Burke seemed to have "a special gift" for directing the spiritual life of women. "He had no attitude of condescension toward the 'weaker sex,'" she recalled. "He believed in their equality of ability, mental and spiritual; he wanted them to be feminine but he expected them to be *virile* souls." He felt that women had not been given a true "opportunity to prove themselves," something he would change when occasion presented itself.[48]

Burke's concern about his own spiritual performance came to the fore in strange fashion in 1910, prompted by, of all things, the Civil War. For three years, Walter Elliott had importuned him to join other Paulists in touring the battlefield at Gettysburg. "Come down here & go with us." Elliott told him. "I will show you how we licked old man Lee. You need rest, sure."[49] The offer was undoubtedly appealing to Civil War-buff Burke. Finally, in 1910, he accepted. For a day, Elliott, who had fought with the Fifth Ohio Regiment, guided the little troop through all the action. Burke found it immensely interesting and learned many things about the battle he had not previously known. "To stand where they stood," he told Lynch, "to know as Lincoln said 'what they did there,' was wonderfully inspiring." At the spot where the Fifth Ohio had fought, Elliott "jumped out of the carriage saying 'Boys I must make a speech' and he did make it. He told us what happened there and how it happened, and just think—47 years after. It makes a man feel that he ought to be up and doing something," declared Burke.[50]

This notion of doing something worked on his psyche and soul and pressed itself to the fore seven weeks later, while Burke stayed with friends Mary and Mildred Merrick at Linnwood, their family's estate in Maryland. A paraplegic since age fourteen, Mary was foundress of the Christ Child Society, a charitable organization for poor children in Washington. Her sister Mildred cared for her after their parents' deaths. Burke had probably come to know them through William Kerby as a student at Catholic University. It was Mary who in 1909 had insisted her dear friend Mary Hawks place herself under Burke's spiritual care. Thus it was that Hawks became another of his daughters in Christ.[51]

On this September night at Linnwood in 1910, Burke had a dream in which he saw himself in a beautiful garden, whose details he felt rather than perceived. There was a path through it, and he viewed himself walking alongside the Virgin Mary. He felt eager to speak with her about her thoughts and the events in her life from Nazareth through Calvary to her final years with the apostle John in Ephesus. "My heart seemed to overflow with an unspeakable joy and my soul with a love that words cannot express," he wrote. But, his lips were sealed and he could not talk. "Suddenly," he continued, "a sense of absolute unworthiness took possession of me. And a voice said: Go forth and purify thyself. Do something that will make thee worthy to hold converse with the Mother of God and the Queen of Heaven. And my dream had gone: but the sweetness of it had not."[52]

This dream was significant enough for Burke to write it down. He left no record of any other. He dreamt it shortly after his exclamation about doing something at Gettysburg. His work as editor immersed him in the world of words and ideas. In his spiritual life, Burke considered himself blessed with vision, but lacking performance. Evidence suggests he felt the need to act on two levels: to live more spiritually and to do something worthwhile and important. And do he would, though not in the near term.

Rather curiously for a Paulist, Burke first mentioned the Holy Spirit in 1911. He did so in a letter to Lynch wherein he wrote eloquently about the soul's union with God in heaven. It was the mystery of the beatific vision which led him to speak of the Spirit and the Spirit's relation to the individual. Theologians, he wrote, considered Jesus's ascension into heaven as necessary because of sin. Burke thought, however, that even without sin, it would have been necessary. Unless Jesus took flesh and returned to his Father in human form, how could any mortal be in the presence of the intense, burning love of God without being consumed, absorbed by it, and fused with it. The wonder was that, because the humanity of Jesus remained intact before God, other humans could experience the bliss of heavenly love and retain their own identities while doing so. Through the Holy Spirit, humans were swept up into the life of the Trinity.[53]

Burke gave rapturous expression to this mystery. The ascension, he explained, was "a most merciful, loving act" of God. Only by divine acceptance of the human soul as being forever without sin,

> Could it, finite, limited, imperfect as it must be, could it dare to enter the presence of the August Trinity—to look upon Light Uncreated; Love Infinite and Eternal, absolutely Perfect and Transcending Beauty, Unspeakable Joy, Surpassing Harmony of the Three in One, Father, Son and Holy Ghost? Would not even the holiest of souls draw back, and urge another soul to go first. The more one realized of the August Trinity, this Power beyond all power, this Love that burns more intensely than any fire on earth, Wisdom that consumes and overwhelms, the more it would fear that in such an Eternal Furnace poor humanity

> would be taken up, blotted out as a wax candle might be if brought near to the source—lose its own existence, its own personality, and be glad, helpless in the fearful ecstacy [sic] that would seize it to abandon itself, to know itself no more, but to be taken up into God.[54]

The power that enabled one to possess oneself in the presence of God was the Holy Spirit, "the secret so to speak of the Trinity's life." The Spirit was the "Font of love," the union among persons of the Trinity poured out upon Christians to make them "partakers of the Divine Nature."[55] Burke later expressed it thus: "This love of heaven, or rather heaven's love, is the Holy Spirit. He is the Love of God the Father for God the Son. He is the Love that has created all things and sustains all things." Just as the Spirit enlivened and sustained Jesus, "by the same Holy Spirit are we sustained and empowered to be as other Christs in Christ himself."[56] In this earthly life and in heaven, through the gift of the Holy Spirit, the Christian would know himself as himself and as one with God. Moreover, the Holy Spirit was "the invisible soul of the Church," which was "the Visible ... the Body of Christ."[57]

Burke's spiritual friendship and love for Lynch bore fruit. At some point, probably in 1912, she decided to become a sister of the Cenacle, a French religious community with a spirit and mission similar to the Paulists'. Like Mary and the apostles who waited in the Cenacle for the coming of the Holy Spirit after the ascension, so the sisters of the Cenacle prayerfully awaited inspiration from the Spirit to help them make Christianity relevant to people of their time and place. In January 1913, Lynch entered the Cenacle of St. Regis in Harlem. Her decision came as no surprise to Burke. He had recognized for years a hunger in her. Yet the commitment was still difficult. "It was not so pleasant when God showed you that He loved you so much that He wanted you to consecrate yourself to Him," Burke recalled. "There were tears and hours of agony." He commended her for having "chosen the better part [Luke 10:42]" and reminded her of words he had often spoken to her, words that were among his own favorites: "Let no man who has put his hands to plough turn back [Luke 9:62]."[58]

He also explained that total dedication to God did not mean killing one's affections or the "natural bonds of the human heart." Rather, it meant giving God primacy of place in them so that they might be perfected. Burke had previously counseled that Jesus had not condemned human affections, "as many spiritual writers would almost have us believe." Jesus looked "with a true and keen sympathy and love upon human relations"; he blessed them and made them "lead to himself." A true son of Hecker, Burke believed human desires and emotions were not to be repressed or obliterated, but uplifted and directed toward God. "We lovers of Christ are not stoics," he told Lynch. In ministering to people, one's feelings and love for them must be genuine. "Human affection brought to Our Lord and consecrated to him will have more real worth because it is warmed so closely by His love," averred Burke. Jesus desired "the complete living offering of our dearest self to Him"—mind, soul, and heart—"that He may hold us dear: and hold dear all who are dear to us." On 24 December 1915, Burke reminded Lynch: "Christmas is given to us, just as the Incarnation was given to us, to know the beauty and worth of human affections. In His sacred humanity Our Lord has sanctified all human affection." He made this point to her many times over.[59] It was an article of faith for him. So, Lynch's entry into the convent was but a change of situation; their friendship and love would continue to the end.

Within two months of her departure for the Cenacle, Burke found a new assistant, a young woman named Grace Murray, who had been referred to him by a worker at *Catholic World*. He hired her in mid-March and she began on St. Patrick's Day. Burke treasured the memory of her arrival that Monday morning. She rushed up to greet him on 60th Street, "happy: trustful: beaming with hope … as a child would run to the arms of her father." "It seemed to me then and it seems to me now," he later recalled, "as God's own introduction."[60] He told her he was giving her more than a job at *Catholic World*. Obviously, there was the immediate purpose of the work, which was publication of the magazine. Yet, there was "a larger and greater end": "the improvement of yourself for our Lord's sake and the use of all your powers for His service and glory."[61]

Her first month there must have been less than stellar. After four weeks, Burke confided to Lynch that Murray was doing better, and he thought that with time she would improve in the position. Spiritually, she was rougher material to work with than her predecessor had been. Murray lacked self-esteem, was self-critical and fearful, traits that were apparently complicated by physical conditions. "Do pray that I may have the patience to accept this work given me by the Lord," Burke wrote to Lynch; "and if I can[,] prepare this soul for His service."[62]

Within a year, Burke credited Murray with having made great strides spiritually. Yet, her self-doubt and fearfulness caused her to feel that he was angry with her. Far from it, he was quite pleased with her progress and explained to her that with improvement came the desire for even greater improvement, which, unless she was careful, might lead her to feel upset and disturbed with herself for not living up to her ever increasing standards. "You must not only desire to improve still further," he told her, "but you must also find consolation and joy in the improvement you have made." He assured her that if he ever became angry with her, he would tell her so and explain why. Thus far she had bravely fought against her fears, and he encouraged her to continue the struggle heroically.[63]

Perhaps it was this same phenomenon which explained Burke's own self-deprecation about his spirituality: the more he improved, the more he saw need for improvement. Or, as he usually explained it, he had the vision of spiritual heights, but the inability to attain them. While making his annual retreat in 1916, he wrote Murray: "My days are days of immersion in things spiritual: days that show me very plainly what I have not done and what I have not reached. In many ways they are not happy days." On the other hand, when he reflected on all God had done for him, he felt encouraged and hopeful.[64] To Lynch, he remarked he had been reading St. Teresa during the retreat, "and at times it almost makes one despair. What a difference between what one ought to be and what one is." Yet, as Teresa said, ideals were worth clinging to, and the retreat filled him with a surfeit of fitting thoughts. "I have put some of them at least on paper that may some day be helpful to others," he told her. "I hope I have written others into my soul."[65] At the end of the retreat, Burke was sorry to see it go. "Sometimes I think I would make a good hermit," he confided to Murray. "I find it no difficulty to be alone.... But you don't think I'd make a hermit at all."[66] Nor was the hermit's life for him. Soon Burke would depart the cloister for the public stage, and perform there he would.

On 5 March 1915, Burke's seventy-five-year-old father Patrick died. The exact circumstances of his passing are unknown, but it seems there must have been some seriously debilitating ailment, perhaps a severe stroke which left him immobile, because Burke told Mary Merrick that his father's death was "a blessed solution of what was growing insolvable." Hawks reported to Merrick that Burke "felt this first great sorrow by death deeply," the more so because of its effect on his mother and sister, Lizzie. It cost him dearly to see their grief. Hawks thought Lizzie looked "very delicate." Mary missed, "as a wife must," noted Hawks, "the faults as well as the virtues of her husband. It was all a part of him to her—and there is a great blank. Her children idolize her and rightly."[67] Indeed, they did.

A year and a half later, in August 1916, an accident occurred which sent a shudder through Burke's soul and caused him to upbraid Murray for her manner of dealing with it. Burke's seventy-one-year-old mother apparently took a tumble and injured herself while Murray was with her. When Murray blamed herself for the fall, Burke rebuked her for being so quick to put herself down. Rather than a sign of humility, he considered it a serious "fault" and "weakness." He could be blunt and stern when he felt the situation called for it. For his part, he thanked God that Murray was with his mother and told her to get down on her knees and thank Him too that she was there and able to help. "For our dear Lord's sake don't be so willing to put yourself in bad [light]: don't think there is merit or worth in being willing to blame yourself," he chided her. "There's no merit in it: but there is demerit." He encouraged her to look at the situation as an opportunity for doing good. "And if all things are not as good and as pleasant as you wish," he wrote, "smile with the saints, and make the very best of them. Thankful not only they are not worse but thankful they are so good." The incident filled Burke with foreboding at the thought of his mother's death. "If I can write you this way to whom the news is such a blow, what ought you to do," he concluded. "… God is with my mother always: she is in heaven now. When she is taken visibly it will be a horrible pain to me—but I'll be the last one to begrudge her the reward that God has stored up for her."[68] A horrible pain it would be several years hence when his mother would pass away.

A month later, all was forgotten, and Burke was encouraging Murray to drink deeply of God's creation as she vacationed on Raquette Lake in the Adirondacks. She had written to him of the glories of the place. He hoped they would grow upon her soul. "God gives us such times," Burke told her, "that we may learn to know that nature is His own," revealing "the

Beauty of beauty beyond." He reminded her that uncreated beauty dwelt within her—God Himself—enabling her forever to lift her soul to His actual presence and bear with all things of earth. "So may the great mountains lift you up," concluded Burke: "and the wide spaces speak of the liberty of God: and the trees and the forest of the delightful intimacy of his majesty, the welcoming embrace of His mysteries: and under the great blue sky of what the earth seems but a part may your soul be wholly with and in God. So would I think and be silent if I were there for there are thoughts too big for words."[69] The peace and beauty of this scene was soon to be shattered, however, as war which had been raging in Europe for two years was about to break upon America.

ENDNOTES TO CHAPTER 3

1. Burke, *Christ in Us*, 73–74.
2. Coyle, Memories of War Council, ACUA, USCCB 10:72:24. For Teresa of Avila, see Burke to Lynch, undated, [early November 1908], AP, Burke Papers, box 5; Burke to Grace Murray, 15 October 1930, ibid., box 12; Malloy, "John Joseph Burke," 720.
3. Hawks, "Father Burke," 27.
4. "Editorial Comment," *Catholic World* 116 (October 1922): 135.
5. Burke to Lynch, from Point Pleasant, New Jersey, n.d. 1907, AP, Burke Papers, box 5 (the quotation is from here); Malloy, "John Joseph Burke," 719.
6. Sheerin, *Never Look Back*, 219. Regarding Burke's temper and impatience, see Burke to Grace Murray, 10 July 1919, AP, Burke Papers, box 11.
7. Burke to Lynch, 14 August 1906, AP, Burke Papers, box 5; Burke to Lynch, 14 August 1909, ibid. (the quotation is from here).
8. Burke to Lynch, 14 August 1906, AP, Burke Papers, box 5.
9. Ibid.
10. Lynch to Burke, 14 August 1920, copy, AP, Burke Papers, box 5.
11. Ibid.
12. Burke to Lynch, 8 August 1907, AP, Burke Papers, box 5.
13. Ibid.
14. Burke to Lynch, n.d. August 1907, AP, Burke Papers, box 5.
15. Burke to Lynch, from Point Pleasant, [fall 1907], AP, Burke Papers, box 5. For dating this letter, see Burke to Lynch, 16 October 1908, ibid., wherein he indicates that he had been suffering from an abscess since October of 1907.
16. Sheerin, *Never Look Back*, 219.
17. Burke to Lynch, To Ireland, [July] 1908, AP, Burke Papers, box 5.

18. Unattributed Reminiscence about Burke's Intensity at Mass, 1935, AP, Burke Papers, box 1; Hawks, "Souvenir of Burke," ibid., box 10.
19. Burke to Lynch, 8 August 1907, AP, Burke Papers, box 5.
20. Burke to Lynch, 10 July 1908, AP, Burke Papers, box 5.
21. Burke to Lynch, 14 July 1908, AP, Burke Papers, box 5.
22. Ibid. (the first quote is from here); Helen Lynch, Notebook, AP, Burke Papers, box 6 (the second quote is from here).
23. Burke to Lynch, 14 July 1908, AP, Burke Papers, box 5.
24. Burke to Lynch, n.d., n.m. 1908, AP, Burke Papers, box 5.
25. Burke to Lynch, 28 September 1908, AP, Burke Papers, box 5.
26. Ibid.
27. Ibid.
28. Burke to Lynch, 16 October 1908, AP, Burke Papers, box 5.
29. Ibid. (quotes about his health are here); Burke to Lynch, 21 October 1908, AP, Burke Papers, box 5 (the first quote is here).
30. Burke to Lynch 21 October 1908, AP, Burke Papers, box 5.
31. Ibid.
32. Ibid.
33. Burke to Lynch, 29 October 1908, AP, Burke Papers, box 5 (the first quote is here); Lynch, Notebook, ibid., box 6 (the second quote is here).
34. Burke to Lynch, 29 October 1908, AP, Burke Papers, box 5; *Sir William Butler: An Autobiography* (London: Constable and Company, 1911).
35. Burke to Lynch, 29 October 1908, AP, Burke Papers, box 5; Burke to Lynch, undated [November 1908], ibid. (the quote is here).
36. Burke to Elizabeth Burke, 13 November 1908, AP, Burke Papers, box 3 (all but the second quote are from here); Burke to Lynch, undated [November 1908], AP, Burke Papers, box 5 (the second quote is here); Donald Harman Akenson, *Conor: A Biography of Conor Cruise O'Brien* (Ithaca, N.Y.: Cornell University Press, 1994), 41–44, 76–77.
37. Burke to Lynch, undated [November 1908], AP, Burke Papers, box 5.
38. Burke to E. Burke, 13 November 1908, AP, Burke Papers, box 3.
39. Burke to Lynch, 14 November 1908, AP, Burke Papers, box 5 (the first quote is here); Burke to E. Burke, 13 November 1908, ibid., box 3 (the second quote is here).
40. Burke to Lynch, 14 November 1908, AP, Burke Papers, box 5; Burke to E. Burke, 13 November 1908, ibid., box 3.
41. Burke to E. Burke, 13 November 1908, AP, Burke Papers, box 3; Burke to Lynch, 14 November 1908, ibid., box 5; Lynch, Notebook, ibid., box 6 (the quotes are from here).
42. Burke to Lynch, 8 April 1909, AP, Burke Papers, box 5; Lynch, Notebook, ibid., box 6.
43. Burke to Lynch, 8 April 1909, AP, Burke Papers, box 5.

44. Ibid.
45. Burke to Lynch, from Point Pleasant, [1907], AP, Burke Papers, box 5; Burke to Helen Lynch, from Lake George, date lost, ibid.; Burke to Lynch, August 1907, ibid.; Burke to Lynch, 21 October 1908, ibid.; Burke to Lynch, 29 October 1908, ibid. The quotes have been cobbled together from these various letters into a coherent whole.
46. Burke to Lynch, 14 August 1909, AP, Burke Papers, box 5; Burke to Lynch, n.d. August 1907, ibid.; Burke to Lynch, [fall] 1907, ibid.; Burke to Lynch, 12 April 1908, ibid.; Burke to Lynch, 10 July 1908, ibid.; Burke to Lynch, [Greenwich, Connecticut, about 1909], ibid.
47. [Gillis], "Monsignor John J. Burke," 268; Colleen McDannell, "Catholic Domesticity, 1860–1960" in Karen Kennelly, C.S.J., *American Catholic Women: A Historical Exploration* (New York: Macmillan Publishing Company, 1989), 48–65. There is extant a copy of only one letter from Lynch to Burke, and she addresses him as "Dear Father" (14 August 1920, AP, Burke Papers, box 5). It was written seven years after her entry into the convent. Given Gillis's comment about Burke's insistence on being called Father by his friends, there is no reason to question that Lynch called him anything else. Burke also addressed Grace Murray, Mary Hawks, and Iona McNulty as "Dear Child."
48. Hawks, "Souvenir of Burke," AP, Burke Papers, box 10.
49. Walter Elliott to Burke, 26 May 1909, AP, Burke Papers, box 20; Elliott to Burke, 28 August 1907, ibid.; Hawks, "Souvenir of Burke," ibid., box 10.
50. Burke to Lynch, 6 August 1910, AP, Burke Papers, box 5.
51. Burke, Memorandum, 26 September 1910, AP, Burke Papers, box 5; Mary Merrick to Hawks, 3 May 1909, ibid., box 10; Hawks, "Souvenir of Burke," 1; "Causes of Saints," *Catholic Historical Review* 89 (July 2003): 585; Mildred Marrick, "The Early Years of the Christ Child Society" (Washington: The Christ Child Society of Washington, D.C., 1960), 1–32.
52. Burke, Memorandum, 26 September 1910, AP, Burke Papers, box 5.
53. Burke to Lynch, 2 August 1911, AP, Burke Papers, box 5.
54. Ibid.
55. Ibid.
56. Burke, Thoughts on the Holy Spirit for Lent, 2–4, AP, Burke Papers, box 35.
57. Burke, Meditation Book, undated [ca. 1918], AP, Burke Papers, box 35.
58. Burke to Lynch, 12 October 1919, AP, Burke Papers, box 5 (the first two quotes are here); Burke to Lynch, 14 January 1913, ibid. (the last two quotes are here); Sheerin, *Never Look Back*, 222.
59. Burke to Lynch, 14 January 1913, AP, Burke Papers, box 5 (the first quote is here); Burke to Lynch, date lost, from "away," ibid. (the second, third, and fourth quotes are here); Burke to Lynch, 24 April 1913, ibid. (the fifth quote is here); Burke to Lynch, 7 December 1913, ibid.; Burke to Lynch, the Assumption [15 August] 1914, ibid.; Burke to Lynch, 24 December 1915, ibid.

(the final quote is here). See also Burke, Thoughts on the Holy Spirit for Lent, 22, AP, Burke Papers, box 35.

60. Burke to Murray, 14 March 1913, AP, Burke Papers, box 11; Burke to Murray, 10 July 1919, ibid. (the quotations are here); Murray to Marie Murtaugh, 18 April 1918, ACUA, War Council 10:13:26; Sheerin, *Never Look Back*, 226.
61. Burke to Murray, [late August 1914], AP, Burke Papers, box 11.
62. Burke to Lynch, 24 April 1913, AP, Burke Papers, box 5. Regarding Murray's traits and ailments, cf. Burke to Murray, [late August 1914], 10 July 1919, [29 July 1919], 16 September 1920—all in AP, Burke Papers, box 11.
63. Burke to Murray, [late August 1914], AP, Burke Papers, box 11.
64. Burke to Murray, 29 May 1916, AP, Burke Papers, box 11.
65. Burke to Lynch, n.d. May 1916, AP, Burke Papers, box 5.
66. Burke to Murray, 1 June 1916, AP, Burke Papers, box 11. A year earlier Burke had made a similar remark to Lynch: "I am sailing north to Prince Rupert. Being on the Ocean I am happy. I have an inclination to be a maritime anchorite. I've often noticed that the old contemplatives often lived near the sea. Wise children of the light!" (Burke to Lynch, 15 August 1915, AP, Burke Papers, box 5).
67. Mary Merrick to Hawks, 5 March 1915, AP, Burke Papers, box 10; Hawks to Merrick, Sunday [7 March 1915], ibid.
68. Burke to Murray, 16 August 1916, AP, Burke Papers, box 11; Burke to Lynch, 24 December 1915, ibid., box 5.
69. Burke to Murray, 25 September 1916, AP, Burke Papers, box 11.

Chapter 4
A "Vision" Realized but Unshared

> We are all members of Christ and therefore members of one another. My fellow-Christian is a member of Christ.... The Christian faith shows forth the dignity of the Christian: the supreme worth of the person—for that person is incorporated in our Lord Jesus.... We are subject, therefore, one to another because we are in Christ, and we must honor and forever bear in memory that in every one of us Christ dwells, as every one of us dwells in Christ.[1]

The Vision

As early as 1905, John Burke began engaging in a "'free time' dream" about the American Catholic Church, a dream that became "the magnet of his hopes and vision." Using Helen Lynch as "a sort of sounding board," he outlined how he believed the Church ought to be unified and coordinated. He "prayed, worked, even *agonized* at intervals" developing a diagram illustrating his vision of an organization to serve as a "unified Voice that would facilitate discussion of policies affecting the interests and activities of the Church in the United States." The diagram was always on his desk to keep the vision before his eyes. He often discussed it with Lynch and her successor Grace Murray. The year before the U.S. entered World War I, he frequently visited Father Joseph Malloy, his neighbor in the Paulist residence. Malloy listened as Burke paced back and forth, talking of how this organization would unify Catholic efforts in wartime, particularly in support of military chaplains.[2]

It is no coincidence that the vision took shape the same year Burke published Joseph McSorley's article on the Mystical Body of Christ. It began to fill his thoughts. "Creation is the work of the Holy Spirit," he jotted in his meditation book. "The Incarnation is the work of the Holy Ghost. 'He was conceived of the Holy Ghost.' H. Ghost rested in His plenitude upon Christ and through Christ upon the Church. The Church as the Visible Organization is the Body of Christ. See Ephesians 4th Chapter. The invisible soul of the Church is the Holy Spirit."[3] Burke shared Isaac Hecker's belief that the principles underlying democracy were Catholic and that a Catholic America had a special role in the world. "If the principles and teaching of Christ guide not the national life of America, America will not live," wrote Burke. "… All in one, one in Christ, every part of the Church and the country in touch with the whole. Thus will you perfect your labors for God and country."[4] American Catholics, the body of Christ, must act in unity.

Unfortunately, Burke's diagram is lost, so its contents are a matter of conjecture. Evidence suggests it outlined coordinating Catholic activities in the areas of social action, publication, lay organization, military chaplains, and support for them. Excepting the last two, the rest were things about which Burke had written in *Catholic World*. The exact role he had in mind for the hierarchy is unclear. Lynch later wrote he envisioned that the bishops would meet once or twice a year to pool information and statistics and "discuss policies affecting the interests and activities of the Church in the United States." She may, however, have read into the plan the reality of the organization that eventually evolved. Burke intended the diagram for presentation to the federal government in the event of a national emergency to show how Catholic strength could be marshaled for service, both spiritual and temporal.[5]

The occasion that propelled him onto the public stage was World War I, raging in Europe since 1914, with the U.S. maintaining a pro-British neutrality since hostilities began. German resumption of unrestricted submarine warfare in 1917 brought America into the conflict. President Woodrow Wilson's war message articulated ideals which resonated with Burke. The U.S. would fight without rancor or passion, but selflessly in defense of representative government, liberty, and human rights. "The world must be made safe for democracy," declared Wilson. "Its peace must be planted upon the tested foundations of political liberty. We have no selfish ends to serve. We desire no conquest, no dominion. We seek … no material compensation for the sacrifices we shall freely make. We are but one of the champions of the rights of mankind."[6]

The Catholic hierarchy answered the call to arms at once. Cardinal James Gibbons of Baltimore said it behooved "every American citizen to do his duty ... loyalty to country ... manifested more by act than by words." Cardinal John Farley of New York urged Catholics to "rally round the flag with the completest fullness of devotion [as] true Americans, true children of our Church."[7] The Board of Archbishops pledged full support "that the great and holy cause of liberty may triumph.... Our people now, as ever, will rise as one man to serve the nation."[8]

In short, Catholics would fight, not just to make the world safe for democracy, but to do their duty and serve their nation, thereby proving to those who believed their commitment to the pope trumped their loyalty to country, that they were true Americans willing to spill their blood for the cause. Their bishops agreed the fight was just, that Americanism and Christianity were virtually synonymous, and Catholics had, not just a patriotic, but a religious duty to serve the nation in the hour of need. Though comprising about 16 percent of the nation's population, Catholics made up nearly 21 percent of the armed services. During the war they developed a crusading mentality.[9]

Their hearty response faced the Church with the task of caring for the spiritual and social welfare of Catholic servicemen. At the time, the armed forces had only twenty-eight Catholic chaplains, a number inadequate to meet the needs of those soon to swell the ranks. Something must also be done to safeguard Catholic soldiers from moral dangers surrounding camp life, particularly liquor and loose women.[10]

Lynch and Malloy noted that when America went to war, Burke quickly founded the Chaplains' Aid Association. Writing in 1955, Lynch reported Burke then presented his diagram to Gibbons. After studying the plan and questioning him, Gibbons declared, "This is from God, John." Writing in 1937, however, Malloy asserted that after Burke had formed Chaplains' Aid, he saw there was much larger work to be done. He showed his diagram to Farley, who encouraged him to lay it before Gibbons. When Burke did so, Gibbons authorized the calling of a meeting at Catholic University to establish a national organization to unify the Catholic war effort.[11]

Yet, evidence from 1917 indicates Burke's vision was realized more haphazardly. Shortly after America mobilized, Secretary of War Newton Baker appointed the Commission on Training Camp Activities (CTCA) under

Raymond Fosdick, a prominent municipal reformer, to oversee the recreational activity of servicemen in America and abroad. When Father William Kerby saw the list of commissioners, not a Catholic was among them. He approached Father Lewis O'Hern at the Paulist Apostolic Mission House, who was liaison between the Church and federal government for appointment of Catholic chaplains. O'Hern had Burke see Archbishop John Ireland, who was then in New York City. Ireland, Burke, Kerby, and O'Hern then lobbied the government for a Catholic commissioner, only to learn there already was one, Dr. Charles Neill, whose surname was mistakenly published as "Mills."[12]

Burke, O'Hern, Kerby, and Neill met several times to discuss how to provide spiritual care to Catholic soldiers and sailors. "The more we talked," recalled Kerby, "the more staggering appeared the problems that confronted the Church. . . . The situation seized our very souls." Reports of rampant immorality among soldiers on the Mexican border in pursuit of Francisco "Pancho" Villa sent shudders through the three priests. If such conditions prevailed in that relatively small force, what might be expected in the massive mobilization underway? Their remaining "indifferent to this situation would have been treason to our priesthood." Most critical was an adequate supply of equipped chaplains. Kerby and Burke repeatedly conferred about this with Gibbons, Bishop Thomas Shahan, rector of Catholic University, and Farley's two vicars general Monsignors Joseph Mooney and Michael Lavelle. The upshot was Burke's establishment of Chaplains' Aid in New York City, soon replicated in chapters around the country.[13]

In mid-May, Shahan saw Gibbons about accrediting O'Hern as Catholic intermediary with the government for care of military personnel. The cardinal sent O'Hern a letter appointing him the hierarchy's "official representative in all that pertains to the spiritual care of the Catholic soldiers in the National Army, the provision of halls for services, and all similar matters." O'Hern wired Father John Hughes, Paulist superior general, urging him to telegraph approval of the assignment. When Hughes delayed, O'Hern begged Burke to pressure him. Hughes agreed, but Burke advised against publishing Gibbons's letter until he could get similar ones from Farley and Cardinal William O'Connell of Boston. If the three were published together, counseled Burke: "The effect will be magnificent. Everything points to the wisdom of our action in trying to nationalize the work."

Though the letters were never published, the important point here is that Burke took Gibbons's action as sanction for the national idea.[14]

At that moment, the Knights of Columbus, the premier Catholic lay society, was mobilizing to safeguard Catholic soldiers from moral dangers surrounding camp life and to protect them from being proselytized by the Young Men's Christian Association (YMCA), which was hosting recreation centers on military posts. In spring 1917, Supreme Knight James Flaherty received government recognition of the Knights as the official Catholic service agency for war work. They established a War Activities Committee under Patrick Henry Callahan, a Kentucky "Colonel" of independent mind, to establish Catholic recreation centers staffed by volunteer "secretaries"—the YMCA's term—and live-in priests unattached to the military. By August, the Knights had a drive underway for $3 million.[15]

When O'Hern learned of this, he sent Callahan a copy of Gibbons's letter. Callahan forwarded a copy to Daniel Callahan, a member of the War Activities Committee, with the comment it was "very evident that [O'Hern] is going to represent the Hierarchy in our particular work … which thought may be father to the wish, as we could not have a better man to work with."[16] Colonel Callahan clearly viewed O'Hern as the hierarchy's envoy to the Knights for appointment of priests in recreation centers. This situation did not bode well. Both Callahan and Burke saw O'Hern's portfolio as endorsing their respective views of Catholic action: the one national, the other particular to the Knights.

Meanwhile, Burke, Kerby, Neill, and O'Hern forged ahead with nationalizing the Catholic war effort. Either Burke's diagram was more nebulous than admirers admitted or he was diffident about presenting it to his colleagues, because Kerby wrote "we drifted into the conviction that an attempt at a national meeting of some kind should be made in order to find a national body in the Church that could master the situation or to create one if we had none such." Burke approached Gibbons with the idea of a nationwide convention. If indeed Burke showed his diagram to the cardinal, this was probably the moment. Gibbons approved a national meeting, provided Farley and O'Connell concurred. Burke visited each and both agreed.[17]

On 9 July, Burke and J. C. Walsh attended the initial meeting of the Knights' War Activities Committee. Walsh was secretary of the Catholic Interests Committee of New York, nearly a hundred wealthy laymen whom the Knights dubbed "Wall Street Catholics." Burke explained his plan for a national meeting to coordinate the Church's efforts behind the war. His purpose was to mobilize the activities of all other Catholic societies in support of the Knights' work with soldiers and sailors. He asked the committeemen to attend his convention and "help him carry out his large undertaking." Colonel Callahan and his colleagues agreed "it was a splendid idea," but gave Burke no definite answer.[18]

Apparently the "splendid" part was that other societies would support the work of the Knights, who felt no need of a new organization. They saw themselves as the national coordinating body for Catholic war work. They had government recognition and were ready to accept the help of any other Catholic society, be it through fundraising or taking up some special aspect of the work. "It should be understood by all that this is not a Knights of Columbus movement either in its character or its end," reported Callahan. "We feel that we are but the trustees and agents of the Catholic people."[19] This self-understanding missed the point of Burke's vision that the Catholic body as a whole must be stimulated to act.

In mid-July, Burke wrote to each bishop and every Catholic society urging they send representatives to a meeting at Catholic University in August to coordinate how the Church would provide its soldiers with recreation halls, complete with chapels and non-military chaplains. "Measures have already been initiated to meet this problem effectively," acknowledged Burke, "and in support and completion of these measures all the Catholics of the country and all Catholic societies must stand as one body doing their best for the common cause. The work is not the work of one man, nor of one society, but of every Catholic and of every Catholic society in the United States." Without mentioning the Knights by name, Burke credited them with taking initiative in the effort, but saw it as the responsibility of the Church as a whole. He explained that the induction of hundreds of thousands of Catholics into the military would not only change their lives but also "affect the life of the entire Catholic body," creating novel and extraordinary problems. "We must take them up as one body and solve them with one mind and one heart," said Burke. "For the problem is a national, not a local one."[20]

While such reasoning might make sense to a priest whose thinking about the Mystical Body enabled him to see the Church as a whole, it placed Burke on a collision course with the Knights. Their War Activities Committee headquartered itself in the Woodward Building in Washington and gave O'Hern an office there so he could coordinate closely with the Knights in securing volunteer chaplains for their recreation centers. Because he was the hierarchy's representative for appointment of military chaplains, and the Knights were the War Department's Catholic agency for work with the services, Callahan believed, "We are all working in conjunction together, with practically the last word of approval from both the ecclesiastical and the civil authorities."[21]

Despite the bravado of this assertion, the Knights worried about what Burke's meeting portended. Just days before it, the Supreme Board of Directors met in Chicago. In attendance were Knights who were either delegates of bishops or representatives of other Catholic societies to Burke's convention. Many wondered about its purpose and if it would interfere with their war program. Some feared it would thrust the Knights aside. Others thought nothing would happen other "than … adopting some resolutions." Still others believed it would create a new agency, attracting every lay and clerical critic of the Knights while attempting "to divide the war work in such a way as to create confusion and duplication." Worse, the Knights claimed to have received no formal invitation to attend the convention.[22]

Thomas Burke telegraphed from Chicago to alert his brother of the Knights' displeasure and advised him to invite them to the meeting. So, John Burke wired a second invitation, reminding the Knights that in July he had personally invited their War Activities Committee to attend. Nonetheless, the Supreme Board decided to "hold aloof" from the convention because its preparation had occurred without the Knights' participation. The order, after all, had taken the initiative in war work, was raising the money for it, and was beginning to shoulder the task. Although it sent no official deputy, it would have representation in the person of Colonel Callahan, who attended as lay delegate of the bishop of Louisville.[23]

On 11 August, 115 Catholics representing twenty-seven lay societies and sixty-eight of one hundred dioceses met at Catholic University. Misunderstanding, confusion, and rivalry charged the atmosphere. Burke was elected chairman and tried to bring order out of chaos in his opening address. Following Wilson's lead, he pictured the war as a struggle for defense of democracy, the very heart of American life. He rooted his remarks in

Hecker's thinking. "We [Catholics] have constantly and rightly maintained," he declared, "that the basis of a nation's life is spiritual; that our Catholic faith … is the only key that opens the right principles of that national life." The Church had reconciled authority with individual liberty. Catholics had long argued American democracy could not maintain itself unless each person treasured "his free and glorious duty to respect authority, to honor the law, to love his country as he loves himself." True Americanism and Catholicism were thus interchangeable. By doing his patriotic duty, a Catholic would prove the justice of the Church's claims.[24]

Alluding to the Mystical Body, Burke explained: "The individual, the parish, the society, the diocese, must emphasize and sacrifice itself unto that larger Catholic unity of which each is a reflection and from which each borrows its title. That Catholic unity must in turn be employed in the solution of national problems." The Church must respond to the crisis "as a Catholic body." Because most soldiers would train in southeastern states, Burke thought bishops, priests, and people elsewhere around the country might consider spiritual care of recruits the problem of southeastern bishops, a task for which those had neither the personnel nor financial resources. Catholic enlistees would come from everywhere. "The problem belongs to us all," argued Burke. "The problem of one is of all, and it will not be solved unless we recognize that we are the common stewards." For the unity of war work to be organic and authoritative, it must be established on the authority of the hierarchy. Burke asked the assembly to create an organization composed of diocesan committees under their local bishops, who would send representatives to a national board that would operate through an executive committee.[25]

He explained such organization would help Catholics ensure their military chaplains were fully equipped. It also meant gathering statistics on Catholic servicemen to ensure an adequate supply of priests. Those men would also need places of wholesome, intellectually stimulating recreation. Housing must be erected wherein young Catholic women could visit with soldiers under proper supervision. Finally, the Church must take united steps to care for families of absent soldiers as well as for the wounded and maimed who would return.[26]

Callahan later recalled there was tremendous anti-Knight feeling at the convention, especially among prominent, eastern Catholics who felt the order should not "pretend to act for the Church." They considered the Knights a quasi-secret society "not altogether in harmony with the Church authorities in all dioceses," a situation which a "newly formed organization would be able to remedy by taking over in its entirety the control of all Catholic War Work." Several delegates claimed that nothing was being done for soldiers within their communities, insinuating the Knights were laggards, even though Callahan knew that work in those areas was well underway.[27]

To craft a national structure, Burke appointed a committee on resolutions including Callahan and eight other delegates. The convention insisted that the committee's report be unanimous. The committeemen proceeded on the theory that whatever organization eventuated was to be "the sole agency of the Church to direct and supervise all Catholic War Work" and that the Knights should be subsidiary to it. One of them claimed the Knights had no right "to do this work in the name of the Church." Another argued, "The Knights should not be allowed to pursue a policy where other Catholic Societies would not have the same privileges." On the defensive, Callahan exploded, showing himself, as he reported later, "in poor form, lacking the usual tact and diplomacy the situation demanded."[28]

At that point, Burke summoned him back to the convention floor to explain what the Knights had already done and were proposing to do. The colonel detailed their plans, thoroughly delineating their scope and ramifications. He did so hoping the convention would opt not to interfere with them. He explained the Knights "naturally expected all Catholics to support and stand behind [their] work, so as to make the K. of. C. synonomous [*sic*] for Catholic War Activity."[29]

As Callahan recalled, his explanation "did not have a very conciliatory effect on the Resolutions Committee." Several motions prepared in advance were introduced. These called for creation of an organization known as the National Catholic War Council to coordinate and unify the Church's war work. They further called for formation of diocesan councils consisting of at least the bishop and his delegates at the present conference; each bishop was to appoint a member of the diocesan council as his representative to a national council. The overall structure would be presided over by an executive committee of fourteen members, each appointed by one of the nation's fourteen archbishops.[30]

Callahan considered the proposed agency "an ideal organization if perfected under the Hierarchy," but absent direct subordination to the bishops, it would simply be "another organization within the Church." Experience convinced him that it would take months to get it off the ground. In his view the Knights were already nationally structured, with the knowhow to organize the war effort and welcome other Catholic societies to participate. His earlier outburst, however, had gained him the reputation of "being both a 'bull and a bear' having nothing in sight but the Order itself." So, he decided not to oppose the motions in belief that "nothing more would come from a meeting of this kind than the passing of some resolutions." He neglected to note that one of the motions entrusted the Knights with the work they had already begun. The convention accepted and endorsed the resolutions unanimously and ordered the formation of the National Catholic War Council without need of any report back to the assembly.[31]

The convention elected Burke president of the new organization and chairman of its executive committee. Bishop Shahan placed the premises of Catholic University at the disposal of the War Council and assured it assistance. Thus, the university became its original headquarters and meeting place. Burke oversaw the War Council from Manhattan and traveled to Washington for meetings of the executive committee, which presided over six standing ones for the following matters: chaplains, legislation and bylaws, finance, historical records of war activities, recreation halls, and women's organizations. A hallmark of the early days was collaboration. Although Burke was president, he preferred to work with and through committees both permanent and ad hoc. This may have owed to insecurity on his part, novice that he was in the public forum.[32]

With regard to the founding of the War Council, several points are worth mention. Callahan and his War Activities Committee admitted Burke's plan was ideal, though perhaps incomplete unless the hierarchy took actual charge of the new organization. For his part, Burke had no intention of taking over work begun by the Knights. He had explained to Callahan his intention to mobilize the national Catholic community in support of them and to undertake additional works. While Callahan was correct in noting the Knights already had a national structure which could carry out their war plans, he missed the key difference between what the Knights proposed and what Burke proposed. The Knights were willing to welcome help of other Catholic organizations; they had no intention of stimulating support. Burke intended to mobilize the entire national Catholic community behind the war effort. The Mystical Body needed to be roused in national Catholic action.

JOUSTING WITH THE KNIGHTS

At the executive committee's first meeting on 2 September, Burke appointed a subcommittee under himself to coordinate with the supreme officers of the Knights. Days later, Burke, Walsh, Lavelle, and John Agar, treasurer of both the War Council and the Catholic Interests Committee, met with Flaherty, Colonel Callahan, William McGinley, and William Larkin. They reached agreement on two points: the War Council would cooperate with the War Activities Committee, and the latter would furnish a written statement of the work the government entrusted to the Knights. Callahan recommended establishment of an advisory committee to coordinate collaboration between the two organizations. He also urged the War Council and the Catholic Interests Committee to begin a campaign in New York City to raise $1 million for the Knights' budget of $3 million. Everyone but Agar and Walsh, two Wall Street Catholics, agreed. As Callahan saw it, Agar wanted the Knights to submit their war plans to the Catholic Interests Committee first.[33]

After the meeting, McGinley informed Callahan that Wall Street Catholics had initiated fund-raising for the Knights back in July, but had garnered only $20,000, while the Red Cross and YMCA had raised one-third of their total funds there. Moreover, the Knights had yet to receive the $20,000 collected. To McGinley, it seemed the War Council, as represented by Wall Street Catholics, was going to be less than cooperative, creating confusion and interfering with the order's plans.[34]

Several days later, Callahan invited Burke to Washington to discuss matters. He was especially interested in appointment of an advisory committee to interface between the two organizations. The next day, he sent a follow-up letter about fund-raising in New York where the Knights hoped to collect as much as the Red Cross and the YMCA, but Wall Street Catholics, according to McGinley, had managed to raise only a pittance. Callahan explained "it was the fear of something of this kind" that had prompted his remarks at the convention. He expressed hope that "you will get down here very soon so we can talk over these and other matters." Welcoming the invitation, Burke looked forward to meeting with him at the end of the week. Unfortunately, plans fell through, and the situation worsened.[35]

While Callahan believed meeting with Burke would do good, he had no confidence in Wall Street Catholics from whom he was ready to break at the proper moment. The War Activities Committee instructed him to send Burke a brief account of the Knights' war work and inform him that it was being done under the control of the War Department, and the only thing the Knights needed from the War Council was money.[36] Thus did the order serve notice that it wanted nothing to do with the new organization except fund-raising.

Callahan wrote to Agar requesting that Wall Street Catholics do so for the Knights. Agar replied that though the Knights had promised to build recreation halls, appoint secretaries, and provide chaplains, the public believed they had done nothing and were "unable" to do anything. Though not sharing that distrust, Agar challenged the Knights to meet their promise with performance. In light of public perception, he thought it fruitless to attempt a fund-raising campaign.[37]

When the executive committee met, Burke reported that the Knights initially had agreed to cooperate through a joint advisory committee and promised a statement of the work the government entrusted to them. They since, however, "intimated their unwillingness to proceed in regard to either of the items of understanding." After discussion, the committee directed Burke and four others—three appointees of the three American cardinals—to secure from those prelates recognition that the War Council was the official representative of the hierarchy for war work, with which all Catholic organizations must cooperate.[38]

The five left immediately for Baltimore and met with Gibbons. Burke argued that the power and authority of the War Council must be made explicit to all Catholics in the country and that it "must be understood that the Knights of Columbus should work in cooperation with the Nat. Cath. War Council." The group explained that the Knights refused to specify the matters entrusted to them and in some instances performed their work unsatisfactorily. They must be brought under some national Catholic authority like the War Council to ensure they carried out their responsibilities. Gibbons said he considered the council the representative of the hierarchy. He would summon Supreme Knight Flaherty and tell him to expedite the Knights' war work and to cooperate with the War Council via an advisory committee.[39]

Through Gibbons's good offices, the Knights agreed to meet with representatives of the War Council. In October, Colonel Callahan and Daniel Callahan met with Burke and two members of the executive committee. Burke discussed the war needs facing the Church beyond those which the Knights were to fulfill and spoke of the necessity of enlisting all Catholic associations behind the effort. He presented the Callahans with a four-part agreement whereby the Knights (1) recognized the War Council as the official representative of the hierarchy, (2) promised a statement of the war work they intended to do, (3) pledged to appoint a representative to the executive committee of the War Council, and (4) agreed to confer with the council's finance committee "for the purpose of having harmonious and unified action" in the raising of funds. The two Knights "verbally accepted" the authority of the War Council, but said the order's Supreme Board of Directors would have to give final approval. They recommended that Burke meet with it, which he agreed to do.[40]

At this point, the Knights realized they would have to cooperate. The next day, Colonel Callahan attended the War Council's executive committee whereat Burke reported on the previous day's conference. The committee directed him to arrange a meeting with the Supreme Board. Callahan explained the Knights' plans for war work and admitted the task had grown larger than expected. The Knights would need support of the hierarchy and the entire Catholic body, especially in raising funds. In response, the executive committee authorized appointment of a permanent special finance committee of three to cooperate with the Knights' finance committee and elected Supreme Knight Flaherty to membership on the War Council's executive board.[41]

Before these last measures were adopted, Burke left the meeting to report to Gibbons on the previous day's conference. Gibbons encouraged him to meet with the Supreme Board, which he believed would accept the conditions stipulated in the proposed agreement. Furthermore, he directed the council to proceed with its planned work "and let it always be understood that the Executive Board of the National Catholic War Council is the representative of the hierarchy of the United States."[42]

As it turned out, the matter of cooperation resolved itself quietly. In late October, Shahan wired Burke that in light of Colonel Callahan's admission of the need for help and the executive committee's response, the Supreme Board felt no need to meet with Burke. The latter then notified Flaherty of his election to the executive committee, with assurance that "the National Catholic War Council wishes in every way possible to help the Knights in the great work they have in hand." Flaherty accepted the proffered seat on the executive committee.[43]

Burke's report to the executive committee on this settlement led to discussion about the two organizations and war work in general. Monsignor Michael Splaine of Boston said Cardinal O'Connell thought the Knights must continue the work entrusted to them, but should have nothing to do with chaplains. That issue belonged to the hierarchy. Nor did O'Connell believe the War Council had yet been able to command confidence of the bishops or Catholic people. For that to happen, Gibbons would have to be placed at its head. Monsignor Lavelle of New York pointed out that many dioceses had yet to form a local war council. He recommended this issue be laid before the bishops of the Board of Trustees of Catholic University when they met the following day. "We must know whether or not the Council commands the confidence of the Hierarchy," agreed Agar. "We are here as their representatives, and if they are not back of us we must desist." Father John Fenlon of Baltimore seconded that the hierarchy must ensure that the council got the proper recognition it deserved.[44]

Agar and Lavelle had something to do with how matters worked out. Both attended the meeting of the university's trustees. Also present were Cardinals Gibbons and Farley, Archbishops Henry Moeller of Cincinnati, James Keane of Dubuque, John Glennon of St. Louis, along with Bishop Shahan and others. After conducting normal university business, the board summoned Burke. There followed a discussion about the Knights, the relation of the War Council to the hierarchy, war work in general, and the cost of undertaking it. The trustees unanimously decided that the Board of Archbishops, established in 1890, should become the National Catholic War Council and the present War Council would become the executive board of the new one. Gibbons was to communicate this resolution to the hierarchy.[45]

A week later he sent a circular to the bishops of the country, submitting the matter for approval. Adding a new dimension, Gibbons suggested the Board of Archbishops appoint a subcommittee of bishops to direct the actual work. He also asked advice about several issues, including the status and scope of the work of the Knights.[46] Seventy of one hundred bishops replied. The vast majority vigorously supported the plan, and a few hoped the new organization would become permanent.[47] While favoring the proposal, several bishops were concerned about the welfare of the Knights and thought they should be encouraged in their war efforts.[48] Only three opposed or expressed reservations about the plan, and a fourth was noncommittal. The major reservation was about the archbishops involving themselves in war work.[49]

CHAPLAINS

While the War Council jousted with the Knights, the scope and urgency of the chaplaincy problem became clear. Current law provided one chaplain per regiment. With the war, the government tripled regimental size from 1,200 to 3,600 men, without a commensurate increase of ministers. The result, Burke pointed out, was actually a two-thirds reduction in them. Congress sought to remedy the situation through the Chamberlain-Schallenberger bill, amending the law to require one chaplain for every 1,200 men. The Senate passed it in September 1917, and the War Council executive committee went on record in its favor. Unfortunately, the bill stalled in the House because Secretary of War Baker opposed it, believing two chaplains per regiment sufficient.[50]

There was also the matter of morality in military camps both at home and abroad. By June 1917, some 40,000 soldiers in the American Expeditionary Force (AEF) had arrived in France. A government investigation of conditions there raised concern about moral laxity.[51]

The need for chaplains and the promotion of morality was not just a Catholic issue. The religious welfare of all soldiers was urgent. Given Burke's belief that the essence of national life was spiritual and that denominationalism was preferable to indifferentism, he thought the matter called for united action by the various denominations and took it in hand. In early October, he saw Farley about forming an interfaith committee to impress upon the government the spiritual welfare of servicemen. With Farley's permission, Burke gathered the strongest group he could: John R. Mott of the YMCA; Colonel Harry Cutler, chairman of the Jewish Welfare Board; Dr. William Adams Brown of the Federal Council of Churches (FCC); and Bishop James DeWolf Perry of the Episcopal Church. They elected Burke chairman of their ad hoc group and discussed morality among soldiers for two hours. They commissioned Burke to draw up resolutions and send them to Fosdick. The latter invited the committee to meet with him in Washington. During a long interview, the group made three requests: demand that commanders in France maintain the same moral standards there as at home; send an investigator to Europe to ensure this was done; and urge the French government to improve moral conditions there. Fosdick thought the committee should make its wishes known directly to Baker, who was then out of town.[52]

After the interview, the committee discussed the inadequate number of chaplains in the military and unanimously decided to petition the government to permit appointment of volunteer ministers to be maintained by their respective denominations. The group left it to Burke to formulate details. Accordingly, he drafted a memorandum requesting permission for volunteer chaplains in camps both at home and abroad as well as on transports. They would serve without government pay or rank at the ratio of one per 1,200 troops lacking a military chaplain. The committee itself would nominate them and apportion them among the troops according to religious belief, "thus relieving the Government of the embarrassment of decision."[53]

Several days later, Baker met with Burke, Brown, Cutler, and Perry to report he had ordered American commanders in Europe to ensure clean living in and around encampments. Moreover, the government made strong representations to both the British and French governments about the need to improve moral conditions. Baker said an inspector would be sent to France to ensure these matters were carried out. Although Burke had already prepared the memo on volunteer chaplains, he did not present it at this time.[54]

On Halloween, the group met again with Burke, Brown, Cutler, and Perry present. They elected to membership Robert Speer of the FCC, giving that organization a second representative. They thought Fosdick should make them an "advisory commission on religious and moral activities in the United States Army and Navy," with Burke as chairman. It should be known as the Committee of Six. Fosdick agreed it might "be a very useful piece of machinery" and urged Burke to "hold [it] together as a sort of informal advisory committee" with which the government could consult. The committee might be particularly helpful in securing an increased number of military chaplains and in gaining recognition for volunteer chaplains.[55]

Fosdick's request for the committee's continuance came just as the hierarchy was taking steps to assume control of the War Council, placing Burke in a quandary about whether he could remain on the committee. He sent Gibbons a brief history of the group and Fosdick's desire that it endure. Burke said his advisors told him to do nothing without direct permission of the hierarchy. The cardinal instructed Burke to remain on the Committee of Six, assuring that "the National Catholic War Council will not go out of existence completely, but will continue its activities under the council as organized by the Hierarchy."[56]

Burke met with the Committee of Six in December, and members agreed unanimously to extend its existence. Their focus remained an increased number of chaplains, but with the added purpose of improving the efficiency of the army chaplaincy service itself through oversight by either a committee of chaplains or a chaplain general. Burke and Brown were to meet with Baker about these issues and present the memorandum prepared by Burke on volunteer chaplains. Burke's duties at *Catholic World*, however, kept him away. So, Brown and Methodist Bishop William McDowell saw Baker. Though still opposed to the chaplain bill, Baker did not object to the Committee of Six's advocating its passage. With regard to the chaplain service, he inclined toward a chief of chaplains rather than an oversight committee. Baker said he would appoint whoever the Committee of Six proposed.[57]

The committee accepted Baker's idea. It was also determined to change his mind about the chaplain bill. It asked Burke to arrange a meeting with Baker and Representative Hubert Dent, chairman of the House Committee on Military Affairs, so they could argue the urgency of the matter. Brown asked the committee to elect McDowell to membership. Thus far, care had been taken about the balance of denominational representation. There was a Catholic, a Jew, and four Protestants, a mix approximating the various religions in society. Catholics and Jews, however, were religious odd fellows in America's Protestant culture, which Burke and Cutler understood. The two had apparently agreed no more Protestants be added. Burke later informed the absent Cutler that Brown's motion "brought up immediately the question that you and I discussed together and on which we are of one mind." When no one seconded Brown's motion, Mott broke the silence, arguing the inadvisability of adding another Protestant to the group. "He spoke strongly on the point," noted Burke. Brown withdrew the nomination.[58] This incident may have been part of a plan Burke later described as Brown's attempt "to have me deposed as Chairman because the Prot[estant]. bodies back of him taunted him with the fact that four Protestants and a Jew allowed the only Catholic on the Com. to be elected Chairman."[59] The committee did not meet again until after the reorganization of the War Council.

The Bishops Take Charge

Given the favorable response to Gibbons's letter about the hierarchy's takeover of the War Council, he proceeded with it. The Board of Archbishops became the National Catholic War Council and established an Administrative Committee to handle its business. Gibbons asked Bishops Peter Muldoon of Rockford (chairman), William Russell of Charleston, Joseph Schrembs of Toledo, and Patrick Hayes, auxiliary of New York, to serve as the committee. Each of the four was well suited for the task. Both Muldoon and Schrembs had experience with national Catholic action through their work with the AFCS. Before becoming a bishop, Russell, a long-time friend of Gibbons, had served for eight years as a pastor in Washington and also as the cardinal's personal representative to the government. Hayes had recently been appointed bishop of American Catholic servicemen, including chaplains, which constituted a military diocese without borders. Gibbons instructed the four to meet at Catholic University with Burke's executive committee and representatives from the Knights to reorganize the War Council.[60]

The meeting took place in January 1918. For two days, the bishops heard reports by Burke and his people as well as by the Knights. Toward the end of the second day, the four prelates decided to bring Burke's operation and that of the Knights under one organization, permitting each to continue its own work. In order to promote harmony between the Knights and Burke's organization, the bishops formed an advisory board known as the executive committee, composed of the six supreme officers of the Knights and six members of the old War Council, including Burke. The establishment of recreation facilities fell to the Knights' Committee on War Activities, already recognized by the government for that purpose. All other matters were entrusted to the Committee on Special War Activities (CSWA), headed by Burke and composed of the chairmen of the various committees of the original War Council. The two entities were each to report directly to the Administrative Committee. Bishop Muldoon assured the Knights that the new War Council had no intention of reducing the order's independent identity, but wanted only to bring it under the authoritative structure of the Church's united war effort. "This was accepted and the K of C were most agreeable," Muldoon noted in his diary, "and with the devotedness of true sons said, 'All we have belongs to the Church and we give it over cheerfully to your direction & control.'"[61]

It is impossible to say how closely the new War Council may have resembled the vision of Burke's original diagram. Indeed, the original council seems to have evolved in haphazard fashion rather than in any planned way. That is not to say that Burke had nothing in mind as he, Kerby, Neill, and O'Hern groped their way forward. The notion of the Church as the Mystical Body—the Catholic community enlivened by the Holy Spirit and functioning as a unified organism—drove Burke's thinking. Indeed as Lynch suggested, his vision was something of a work in progress over which he labored. Clearly, the overriding concern that gave rise to the War Council was the spiritual welfare of Catholic soldiers and sailors and the concomitant need for chaplains. The role of the hierarchy in the original War Council was tenuous at best. Each archbishop was to appoint someone to the executive committee, and every bishop and archbishop was to establish a diocesan war council. Not all did; in fact many did not. Effective hierarchical control came as a result of the jostling between the Knights and the old War Council. To bring peace and order to the Catholic household, the Board of Archbishops assumed general control with immediate supervision supplied by the Administrative Committee. This reorganization would mitigate, but not halt friction between the two contenders.

Endnotes to Chapter 4

1. Burke, *Christ in Us*, 112–13.
2. Lynch to Michael Ready, n.d. August 1943, copy, AP, Burke Papers, box 6 (quotes in the first sentence are here); Lynch to Loretto Lawler, 29 August 1948, ibid., (the quote in the second sentence is here, emphasis in original); Lynch to Vincent Holden, C.S.P., 3 November 1955), ibid. (the remaining quotes are here); Burke to Murray, [19 December] 1920, ibid., box 11; Malloy, "John Joseph Burke," 721.
3. Burke, undated meditation book, ca. 1918, AP, Burke Papers, box 35.
4. Quoted in Lawler, *Full Circle*, 7; [Burke], "Hecker and Present Problems," 564–72.
5. Lynch to Holden, 3 November 1955, AP, Burke Papers, box 6.
6. Woodrow Wilson, *War Messages*, 65th Cong., 1st Sess. Senate Doc. No. 5, Serial No. 7264, Washington, D.C., 1917, pp. 3–8; Daniel M. Smith, *The Great Departure: The United States and World War I, 1914–1920* (New York: John Wiley and Sons, Inc., 1965), 1–82; August Heckshher, *Woodrow Wilson* (New York: Charles Scribner's Sons, 1992), 359–439; Thomas J. Knock, *To End All Wars: Woodrow Wilson and the Quest for a New World Order* (New York and Oxford: Oxford University Press, 1992), 48–122; George C. Herring, *From Colony to Superpower: U.S. Foreign Relations Since 1776* (Oxford and New York: Oxford University Press, 2008), 398–410.
7. Quoted in "Chronicle," *America* 17 (21 April 1917): 25–26.
8. Minutes of the Board of Archbishops, 18 April 1917, AASL, RG 9, U.S.A. hierarchy.
9. William M. Halsey, *The Survival of American Innocence: Catholicism in an Era of Disillusionment, 1920–1940* (Notre Dame: University of Notre Dame Press, 1980), 45; Bureau of the Census, *Historical Statistics of the United States: Colonial Times to 1957* (Washington, D.C.: U.S. Government Printing Office, 1961), 7, 228; McKeown, *War and Welfare*, 45–59; James Hennesey, S.J., *American Catholics: A History of the Roman Catholic Community in the United States* (Oxford and New York: Oxford University Press, 1983), 225–26; Douglas J. Slawson, *The Foundation and First Decade of the National Catholic Welfare Council* (Washington, D.C.: The Catholic University of America Press, 1992), 16.
10. Sheerin, *Never Look Back*, 38; Michael Williams, *American Catholics in the War: National Catholic War Council, 1917–1921* (New York: Macmillan Company, 1921), 110–12; Christopher J. Kauffman, *Faith and Fraternalism: The History of the Knights of Columbus, 1882–1982* (New York: Harper & Row, Publishers, 1982), 190–97.
11. Lynch to Holden, 3 November 1955, AP, Burke Papers, box 6; Malloy, "John Joseph Burke," 721.

12. Kerby to J. T. O'Connell, 17 August 1917, copy, ACUA, NCWC 10:1:1; Stefani Manowski, "Paulists in the Military," http://www.paulist.org/history/notes_military_manowski.php; Sheerin, *Never Look Back*, 38; McKeown, *War and Welfare*, 75; Thomas T. McAvoy, C.S.C., *A History of the Catholic Church in the United States* (Notre Dame: University of Notre Dame Press, 1969), 364–65; Allan M. Brandt, *No Magic Bullet: A Social History of Venereal Disease in the United States since 1880* (Oxford and New York: Oxford University Press, 1987), 52–61.
13. Kerby to O'Connell, 17 August 1917, copy, ACUA, NCWC 10:1:1; Williams, *Catholics in the War*, 100–04; Malloy, "John Joseph Burke," 721; Brandt, *No Magic Bullet*, 52–57; Arthur S. Link, *Woodrow Wilson and the Progressive Era, 1910–1917* (New York: Harper & Row, 1954), 136–44; Herring, *Colony to Superpower*, 394–98.
14. James Gibbons to Lewis O'Hern, 19 May 1919, copy, AKC, SC–16–1–0007; O'Hern to Burke, 21 May 1917, ACUA, NCWC 10:4:54; Burke to O'Hern, 24 May, 1917, copy, ibid.
15. Kerby to O'Connell, 17 August 1917, copy, ACUA, NCWC 10:1:1; Patrick H. Callahan, "The K.C. War Activities: Part IX," *Good of the Order* 14 (15 June 1919): 5–7, 13–15, in AKC; Patrick H. Callahan, "Report of Committee on War Activities," *Columbiad* 24 (September 1919):16; Williams, *Catholics in War*, 110–12; Kauffman, *Faith and Fraternalism*, 190–200; McKeown, *War and Welfare*, 72–73; William E. Ellis, "Catholicism and the Southern Ethos: The Role of Patrick Henry Callahan," *Catholic Historical Review* 69 (January 1983): 41–50.
16. Gibbons to O'Hern, 19 May 1919, copy, AKC, SC–16–1–0007 (Colonel Callahan's comment is a postscript on this copy).
17. Kerby to O'Connell, 17 August 1917, copy, ACUA, NCWC 10:1:1; Williams, *Catholics in War*, 110–12; McKeown, *War and Welfare*, 72–73; Sheerin, *Never Look Back*, 39–41.
18. Callahan, "K.C. War Activities: IX," 6, in AKC.
19. Ibid., 13; Callahan, "Report of Committee on War Activities," 16–17.
20. Burke circular to the hierarchy, 17 July 1917, with enclosure (quotes are from here), ACUA, NCWC 10:4:31; Burke circular to Catholic societies, [undated], ibid., 10:1:1; Williams, *Catholics in War*, 107–13.
21. Callahan, "Report of Committee on War Activities," 16.
22. Callahan, "K.C. War Activities: IX," 14–15, in AKC.
23. Thomas Burke to Burke, telegram, 7 August 1917, ACUA, NCWC 10:1:1; Callahan, "K.C. War Activities: IX," 14–15, in AKC; Kauffman, *Faith and Fraternalism*, 201.
24. Burke, *War Problems and American Catholics: Chairman's Address, National Catholic War Council* (Washington, D.C.: Executive Committee of War Council, 1917), 3–4; Williams, *Catholics in War*, 117–18.

25. Burke, *War Problems and Catholics*, 4 and 8; Williams, *Catholics in War*, 119 and 125.
26. Burke, *War Problems and Catholics*, 5–14; Williams, *Catholics in War*, 120–33.
27. Callahan, "K.C. War Activities: IX," 5, in AKC; Patrick H. Callahan, "The K.C. War Activities: X," *Good of the Order* 14 (July 1919):5, in ibid.
28. Williams, *Catholics in War*, 134; Callahan, "K.C. War Activities: X," 6.
29. Callahan, "K.C. War Activities: X," 6–7, in AKC; Kauffman, *Faith and Fraternalism*, 201.
30. Callahan, "K.C. War Activities: X," 7, 14–15, in AKC; Williams, *Catholics in War*, 135–36.
31. Callahan, "K.C. War Activities: X," 7, 14–15, in AKC; Williams, *Catholics in War*, 134–37.
32. Minutes of the Executive Committee of the War Council, 2 September 1917, ACUA, NCWC 10:6:7; Williams, *Catholics in War*, 137.
33. Minutes of the Executive Committee of the War Council, 2 and 29 September 1917, ACUA, NCWC 10:6:7; Callahan to John Agar, 10 September 1917, AKC, SC–16–1–0025; Callahan to Pelletier, 10 September 1917, copy, ibid.; Callahan to Luke Hart, 20 September 1917, ibid., SC–16–1–0027.
34. Circular Fund-Raising letter from Adrian Iselin et al., 23 July 1917, copy, ACUA, NCWC 10:6:26; Callahan to Agar, 10 September 1917, AKC, SC–16–1–0025; Callahan to Pelletier, 10 September 1917, copy, ibid.; Callahan to Hart, 20 September 1917, ibid., SC–16–1–0027.
35. Callahan to Burke, 10 September 1917, ACUA, NCWC 10:6:26; Callahan to Burke, 11 September 1917, ibid.; Burke to Callahan, 12 September 1917, copy, ibid.; Callahan to Pelletier, 13 September 1917, AKC, SC–16–1–0026.
36. Callahan to Pelletier, 13 September 1917, AKC, SC–16–1–0026; Memorandum regarding Meeting Committee on War Activities, Supreme Board of Directors, Washington, 16 and 17 September 1917, ibid.
37. Agar to Callahan, 18 September 1917, AKC, SC160–1–0026.
38. Minutes of the Executive Committee of the War Council, 29 September 1917, ACUA, NCWC 10:6:7.
39. Burke, Memorandum on the Meeting with Cardinal Gibbons, 29 September 1917, ACUA, NCWC 10:6:7.
40. Burke, Report on Meeting with Knights of Columbus, 26 October 1917, exhibit 1 of the Minutes of the Executive Committee of the War Council, 13 November 1917, ACUA, NCWC 10:6:7; Burke to Callahan and Pelletier, 22 October 1917, copy, ACUA, NCWC 10:6:27; Pelletier to Burke, 2 October 1917, ibid.; James Flaherty to Gibbons, 9 October 1917, copy, AKC, SC–16–1–0028.
41. Minutes of the Executive Committee of the War Council, 27 October 1917, ACUA, NCWC 10:6:7.

42. Burke, Report on Meeting with Knights of Columbus, 26 October 1917, exhibit 1 of the Minutes of the Executive Committee of the War Council, 13 November 1917, ACUA, NCWC 10:6:7.
43. Ibid.; Burke to Flaherty, 30 October 1917, copy, AKC, SC–16–1–0030–2.
44. Memorandum of Discussion on Report Presented by the Chairman, Rev. John J. Burke, C.S.P., Concerning Conferences with Knights of Columbus, Interviews with Cardinal Gibbons, etc., exhibit 3 of Minutes of the Executive Committee of the War Council, 13 November 1917, ACUA, NCWC 10:6:7.
45. Minutes of the Executive Committee of the War Council, 14 November 1917, ACUA, NCWC 10:6:7; Minutes of the Board of Trustees of The Catholic University of America, 14 November 1917, ACUA, Board Minutes; John Glennon to Gibbons, 21 November 1917, AASL, RG 1E5.1; Burke to Peter Muldoon, 6 March 1918, ACUA, NCWC 10:3:35; Robert Trisco, "An Extracanonical Institution: The Annual Meetings of The American Archbishops, 1890–1919," *The Jurist* 68 (2008): 53–64. The resolution is quoted in the minutes of the War Council; the board minutes contain the names of those present and report on university matters only.
46. Circular from Gibbons to the hierarchy, 21 November 1917, copy, AASMS, RG 13, box 7; Ellis, *Gibbons*, 2:294–95; Elizabeth K. McKeown, "The National Bishops' Conference: An Analysis of Its Origins," *Catholic Historical Review* 66 (October 1980): 569–70; McKeown, *War and Welfare*, 83; Slawson, *Foundation of NCWC*, 30.
47. Joseph Busch to Gibbons, 26 November 1917, AASMS, RG 13, box 7; Joseph Conroy to Gibbons, 27 November 1917, ibid.; Slawson, *Foundation of NCWC*, 30–32.
48. Michael Curley to Gibbons, 25 November 1917, AASMS, RG 13, box 7; Joseph Rice to Gibbons, 27 November 1917, ibid.; Regis Canevin to Gibbons, 25 November 1917, ibid.
49. Thomas Cusack to Gibbons, 24 November 1917; Benjamin Keiley to Gibbons, 28 November 1917; Edmond Prendergast to Gibbons, 27 November 1917; Sebastian Messmer to Gibbons, 30 December 1917—all in AASMS, RG 13, box 7.
50. Report Submitted by Burke to Executive Committee, 27 October 1917, ACUA, NCWC 10:5:10; O'Hern, to Gibbons, 14 November 1917, copy, AKC, SC–16–1–0031–2; *Congressional Record*, 65th Congress, 1st Sess., 55, pt. 7, 7497; Minutes of the Executive Committee of the War Council, 29 September, 1917, ACUA, NCWC 10:6:7; Williams, *Catholics in War*, 141–43, 236–37; Earl F. Stover, *Up from Handyman, 1865–1920* (Washington, D.C.: Office of the Chief of Chaplains, Department of the Army, 1977), 209, vol 3 of *The United States Army Chaplaincy*, 7 vols.; McKeown, *War and Welfare*, 134–35.

51. Minutes of the Executive Committee of the War Council, 27 October 1917, ACUA, NCWC 10:6:7; Burke to Prendergast, 10 November 1917, copy, ibid. 10:5:5.
52. Burke to Prendergast, 10 November 1917, copy, ACUA, NCWC 10:5:5; [Burke], Report No. 2 Made at Meeting of Executive Committee War Council, ibid.; Williams, *Catholics in War*, 140–42.
53. Report Submitted by Burke to Executive Committee, 27 October 1917, in Minutes of the Executive Committee of the War Council, 27 October 1917, ACUA, NCWC 10:5:17; Williams, *Catholics in War*, 141–43; McKeown, *War and Welfare*, 132.
54. Burke to Prendergast, 10 November 1917, copy, ACUA, NCWC 10:5:5; [Burke], Report No. 2 Made at Meeting of Executive Committee War Council, ibid.
55. Minutes of the Committee of Six, 31 October 1917, ACUA, NCWC 10:5:10 (first quote is here); Raymond Fosdick to Burke 3 November 1917, ibid., 10:8:1 (the remaining quotes are here); Burke to Gibbons, 23 November 1917, copy, ibid., 10:5:34; McKeown, *War and Welfare*, 88–89, 132–33; Thomas C. Mackey, *Pursuing Johns: Criminal Law Reform, Defending Character, and New York City's Committee of Fourteen* (Columbus: Ohio State University Press, 2005), 1–34, 223 n. 23.
56. Burke to Gibbons, 23 November 1917, copy, ACUA, NCWC, 10:5:34; Eugene J. Connelly to Burke, 26 November 1917, ibid.
57. Minutes of the Committee of Six, 5 December 1917, ACUA, NCWC 10:5:10; Burke to Harry Cutler, 2 January 1918, copy, ibid.; Stover, *Up from Handyman*, 218–19.
58. Minutes of the Committee of Six, 27 December 1917, ACUA, NCWC 10:5:10; Burke to Cutler, 2 January 1918, copy, ACUA, NCWC 10:5:9.
59. Burke, Diary of 1933 Trip to Rome, AP, Burke Papers, box 72.
60. McKeown, *War and Welfare*, 84–85; Williams, *Catholics in War*, 146–51.
61. Meeting of the National Catholic War Council, 16–18 January 1918, ACUA, NCWC 10:1:19; Diary of Bishop Peter Muldoon, 16 and 17 January 1918, ACUA, microfilm; Williams, *Catholics in War*, 152–53; McKeown, *War and Welfare*, 86–88; Kauffman, *Faith and Fraternalism*, 218.

Chapter 5

An Anchorite in a World at War

> Prayer is the index of our life in Christ. We need not pray audibly: we need not pray explicitly. There are the special times when we go apart and hold communion with our Blessed Lord. There are other times when we must needs put all we have into the integrity of our work: give unstintedly of our time, of all our powers: exhaust ourselves in the service of men. Prayer trains us to do all this in the spirit of prayer.[1]

The Reorganized War Council

John Burke left no record of how he felt about reorganization of the War Council, though he seems to have been relieved to have guidance from the bishops now over him. After all, he was a forty-two-year-old editor inclined to introversion and contemplation, with experience only in publication. During reorganization, Bishop Peter Muldoon seemed to have greatly impressed him. Priests who knew Muldoon considered him balanced and decisive, "one of the most level headed of the whole crowd [of bishops] and there is no yellow streak in him." He and Burke developed a smooth working relationship and became fast friends. Burke acknowledged Muldoon's importance to him in one of his first letters: "Much as I wish it for my help and direction, I will not ask you to come to Washington unless it is absolutely necessary."[2]

The Administrative Committee opened an office in Manhattan, while the CSWA remained in Washington. Burke headed the CSWA consisting of seven committees, one of which he chaired: the Committee on Chaplains' Aid and Literature, two issues dear to his heart. The other committees covered National Catholic Interests, Men's Activities, Women's Activities, Historical Records, Finance, and Reconstruction and After War Activities.[3]

William Kerby found office space and hired secretarial help for the new CSWA headquarters in Washington on 14th Street N.W. He rented two floors above a tire store that faced on Franklin Square. The "unassuming but centrally located" structure, just blocks from the White House, was infested with rats, drawing squeals and shrieks from the secretaries. The pest-control company hired to exterminate the vermin used weasels to do so. "The squeals continued to come," recalled Burke's secretary Mary Dineen Coyle, "as one could be just as frightened to open a desk or a closet and see a weazel [*sic*] as well as a rat. Oh, those were the days." She considered Burke "the greatest and kindest man" she had ever met.[4]

Burke's office at the back of the third floor spanned the width of the building, "a bleak large room—with huge windows almost from floor to ceiling—looking out on a black brick wall." The one in front of Burke belonged to Lewis O'Hern, who left his office with the Knights for one with the CSWA. Burke was known as "the Lion" because his voice carried so; when he spoke forcefully, all listened. Gone was the prankster of earlier years. Weighed down by cares of editorship and the concerns of war, he "seldom laughed but when he did it was a ROAR." He now divided his time between the CSWA and *Catholic World*, spending three days in Washington and four in Manhattan one week, and then vice versa the next. "No one had any hours," recalled Coyle. Burke and everyone worked seven days a week and often long after dark as the job demanded. "Many a night at midnight I was taking dictation," Coyle remembered, "as Father Burke made ready to board the midnight [train] for New York." While dictating, he paced, hands clasped behind his back. "He never ate properly or at regular hours," she said. Often, she brought him lunch from a local hotel, and he would snatch bites between appointments.[5]

Burke's first order of business was to apprise Muldoon about the budget necessary to sustain the work. He explained it would "be impossible to state a definite and detailed sum." For planning purposes, the old War Council had used the YMCA's rule of thumb, which was $25 per soldier. Estimating 700,000 Catholic servicemen, the amount needed by the Knights would come to $17.5 million, which was scaled back to $15 million ($300 million in 2024). The old council had planned a fund-raising drive, the money to be used first to support the Knights.[6]

Beyond their work, Burke estimated annual expenses of the CSWA would amount to about $27,000 ($540,000). It would take $50,000 ($1 million) more to make an accurate count of Catholic servicemen to secure a just proportion of Catholic chaplains. "Attempts are constantly being made to lower our portion," he told Muldoon. "They can be defeated only by accurate figures." It would take another $225,000 ($4.5 million) to equip chaplains and to print and distribute prayer books and New Testaments to Catholic servicemen free of charge. Moreover, Cardinal James Gibbons had insisted the council raise "a fund sufficiently large to meet all needs and the greater emergencies." For instance, the government already identified large hospitals from Boston down to Cape May, New Jersey, to receive the wounded. Such Catholic institutions would need more chaplains and supplemental funds. Money would also be needed to restore damaged churches in France. French Catholics were already asking for help. Burke estimated a fund of $5 million more ($100 million) for unforeseen needs.[7]

In April 1918, Muldoon went with the original figure and reported to the Board of Archbishops that it would cost $15 million ($300 million) for Catholic war work through June 1919, though that sum might have to increase as the war developed. The Knights had already collected over $5 million ($100 million), and Wall Street Catholics had amassed a sum just short of that.[8]

CHAPLAINS

Before leaving Washington after reorganization, the Administrative Committee saw Secretary of War Newton Baker and urged him to support the Chamberlain-Schallenberger bill for chaplains. Major General John Pershing, commander of the AEF, also advocated it. Baker agreed to cease obstruction and would try to have a Catholic chaplain on each transport to Europe. The bishops then saw Representative Hubert Dent, who said with Baker now behind the measure, the House committee would likely report it.[9]

The bishops also saw Senator George Chamberlain of Oregon about the proposed selective-service bill. They wanted to ensure it excluded not only clergymen but seminarians studying for the ministry. Chamberlain assured them there was no need of fear. Not trusting him, Muldoon told Burke to have Walter Hooke, his executive secretary, monitor matters.[10]

Burke did so. Baker told Hooke he now considered the chaplain bill "urgent" and planned to see Dent about it. When that meeting failed to occur, Burke had Fosdick pressure Baker into sending Dent a letter to have his committee pass the bill without delay, something that would solve a problem that just arose: "camp pastors." According to Burke's memorandum to Baker about that issue, the Committee of Six was to nominate volunteer chaplains and have the government appoint them for service in camps. Yet, some Protestant clergymen had already taken it upon themselves. Fosdick explained to Burke that Baker opposed not just the arbitrary action of those men, but the very idea of volunteer chaplains. He viewed the Chamberlain-Schallenberger bill as a way around them. Baker wanted the Committee of Six to convince those who had initiated this practice to see the reasonableness of his position.[11]

When Burke informed the committee, he and the members decided not only to continue the practice until passage of the chaplain bill, but to discuss with Fosdick and Baker its further use afterward. Baker was in no mood to bargain. In mid-February, he sent Burke word that once the Chamberlain-Schallenberger bill passed, he would issue an order forbidding volunteer chaplains. Thus the War Department and the Committee of Six were on a collision course. "I often wish you were here to advise," Burke wrote to Muldoon; "indeed I often wish I could talk matters over with you personally."[12]

Despite support from Baker, Fosdick, Pershing, and even President Woodrow Wilson, the chaplain bill stalled in the House committee through February and March 1918. Admitting in early April that he was a novice "in the ways of legislation," Burke appealed to Fosdick "to do all that you can do to secure the immediate passage of the bill." The next day, he learned it would finally come before the House. On behalf of the Committee of Six, Burke sent a circular to all congressmen explaining that the bill simply restored the traditional ratio of chaplains. "We voice not simply a small committee's opinion," he pleaded, "but the earnest demand, the urgent appeal of the millions of American fathers and mothers of Christian and Jewish belief."[13]

The House passed it, but with two troublesome amendments. The first opened the chaplain service to faiths which did not ordain ministers, like Christian Scientists, Mormons, and Jews. The second stipulated "the maximum age limit of chaplains in the Army shall be 45 years." This last caused Wilson to veto the bill because the wording could be interpreted to mean that a chaplain must be discharged when he turned forty-six, rather than the intended meaning that a man be appointed chaplain before that age.[14]

Meanwhile, in February the new selective service legislation was introduced in Congress, minus any exemption for seminarians. In the name of the Committee of Six, Burke urged Chamberlain to ensure that "the exemption of *bona fide* clerical students who have in good faith entered recognized theological schools since May 1917, be clear and fully stated." Chamberlain replied such an amendment was being embodied in a forthcoming joint resolution of Congress.[15]

A Southern Interlude

While Congress worked to meet the president's objection to the chaplain bill and to secure the joint resolution on clerical exemption, Burke took a long-deserved vacation to the South. Having burned the candle at both ends for a year, he needed rest. He told Colonel Harry Cutler that he was "quite tired at the present time" and did not believe Congress would act on the chaplain measure before his return.[16]

Mute testimony to Burke's heavy work schedule was the paucity of correspondence to loved ones during the intervening year. To be sure, he saw Grace Murray during his weekly days at *Catholic World* and may occasionally have visited Helen Lynch while in Manhattan. But in D.C., he practically never wrote to either. His only communication to Lynch was a brief note at Christmas 1917: "My absence from you would but lend emphasis to the heart in this message. I miss you and I miss the Cenacle which is ever like a restful benison to a soul distracted by many things. The call to war is a call to war in many senses."[17] No doubt this last sentence covered multiple issues: his struggles with the government, with Congress, with the Knights, and with his desire to be with loved ones rather than where he was.

His only letter to Murray was penned on a train back to Washington shortly after the New Year. That Burke wrote to her thus testified to his devotion because he hated writing on a moving railroad car. He did so this time because Murray was feeling overwhelmed by having to supervise the office in his absence. He tried to encourage her with the words of St. Paul: "Rejoice always in the Lord: again I say rejoice [Phil. 3:3]." Paul, he explained, had more to bear than either of them; he had care of all the churches. "We have the jealousy, incapacity, pig headedness of individuals: and bad luck." Burke said that by failing to be joyful, she "would lose so much." She should rejoice he was her spiritual father, "and I'm no angel," he added. Acknowledging her job had its difficulties, he urged her not to take it too seriously. She possessed love, devotion, and talent enough to do it well. "Learn to rule as a queen," he advised, "not in pride but in the confidence that Christ has given you as a gift. Be sure of self. Be patient with others.... Think and speak and act as Christ: be possessed by Him and possess Him." Burke closed, "Only love keeps me at this writing."[18]

Now, it was Murray who was there to see Burke off on his departure from New York for Charleston and points south. Yet, it was not with an "altogether light" heart that he left, and his first day at sea gave it no lift, "for there are certain things on which I must not let my mind dwell." Affairs at the CSWA weighed heavily on him, wrote Burke. He regretted deeply leaving Murray in charge at *Catholic World*. He sent fervent prayers that nothing would go wrong, yet from his experience as editor he warned, "You must be prepared to know that it will not go well." During the night, the ship hit a storm that lasted into the next day. So violent were waves that Burke was thrown from his berth, covers and all onto the deck. He made an attempt to set up an altar to say Mass in the morning, but it proved impossible and he gave up.[19]

On arrival in Charleston, Burke toured the old part of city near the battery where the blue bloods lived. He found them a depressing people, whose "principal occupation or interest in life ... is to worship their ancestors." They were "more mindful of past memories than of present opportunities," living life in isolation behind their wrought-iron gates. The war, however, was enlivening other parts of the city. The federal government was building shipyards, factories, and a naval training facility, which meant new people, new homes, and new activity. Burke found the condition of black people particularly distressing. On a drive into the countryside he saw "many colored families ... living in hovels that you would not think fit for a cow." Southerners claimed that blacks were happy. "They are essentially moody, changeable," he told Murray. "Quick to be cheerful, happy if they have enough to eat. But pigs may be happy." He considered white southerners' "lack of vision ... damnable." The South had a duty to uplift black people and it would pay the price for failing to do so.[20]

After several days in Charleston, he went down to Jacksonville, Florida, where he visited an army camp to see how the Knights were functioning. He was very disappointed. "The K. of C. building is not much either as a structure or in its equipment," he noted. Moreover, although the secretary was an amiable man, he was ill-suited to the work. "Opportunities pass him unnoticed," wrote Burke, and educational uplift was totally absent from the Knights' efforts. He feared this was "the case all over the country." "Catholics," he commented, "are rapidly getting the reputation of being the great champions of boxing." While that sport certainly had its place, the YMCA was offering classes in French which were attended by 3,000 soldiers, and the books checked out of its library were of "a serious high character." The Christian Scientists distributed tracts and pamphlets daily. The Knights, however, were doing nothing of the sort.[21]

In early May, Burke was ready to return to New York, waiting for a ship because he disliked traveling by train on vacation. He was worried about Murray. Her letters had not been upbeat about things at *Catholic World*, and he thought she might to be trying to shield him from problems lest she disturb him. "You have a big burden on your young heart," he told her, "and your heart loves ? me so much that it would bear any thing. Yet it must and can only bear in God and with God." The question mark was his. Burke advised that if she was doing her best, she should not think about whether he would be displeased with her performance or not, but "find the few moments of secret commune and thanksgiving with God that you have done all that you could for His dear sake."[22]

In fact, she was happy in her work. Murray wrote to friend Marie Murtaugh, whom Burke had brought from *Catholic World* to the CSWA, that she was aware of the spiritual benefit of being in the cloister. "I am only doing what I enjoy doing," wrote Murray, "and endeavoring to make some slight return for the wonderful opportunities and help that have been given to me since I came to the Paulist Press. Of course it all has such a wonderful appeal—that while doing God's own work and helping to work out our salvation we can at the same time earn our living. That is to me most consoling."[23] Here was testimony to the atmosphere Burke created in the editorial sanctum: he encouraged the spiritual growth of workers while they promoted the apostolate of Catholic literature and earned a livelihood to boot.

As for himself, Burke told Murray he was rested and had stored up strength. He had seen firsthand "the far reaching importance" of the work being done. "Here in the quiet and rest I make good resolutions of order, of patience, of deliberate mastery of the work," he wrote. "I wish some of it would remain with me in the midst of the actual conflict." He asked her to help him be more patient and more "the master … by leading me to speak oftener to you of spiritual truths and the betterment of your own self. You I feel can help me to use my days and my life to their best."[24] Again, Burke recognized that when he spoke to others of spirituality, he was also preaching to himself. Murray the pupil was to draw the master out.

Nor was Burke's burden to be eased by efforts to relieve him from work at *Catholic World*. Both Kerby and Monsignor Henry Drumgoole had urged Muldoon to ask the Paulists to assign Burke full-time to the CSWA because of increasing workload. Muldoon made the request to Father John Hughes, Paulist superior general. "I hope that Father Hughes will make the sacrifice as well as yourself," Muldoon told Burke. "The work is going to be more trying and absorbing as the weeks go on, and our case all along the line is a serious one." To improve chances, Muldoon had Cardinal Gibbons second the request. "I share heartily the high estimate that the Bishops place on Father Burke's character and work," he wrote by hand, no doubt to make the appeal more personal. The appointment would be "a signal service to the Church," and Gibbons was convinced "that this larger task calls in a voice that will not lack appeal to you."[25] Yet, lack appeal it did, and Burke continued to carry water on both shoulders.

Chaplains and Seminarians

By Burke's return to Washington, the chaplain bill—reworded as Wilson wished—had passed the Senate, but the House had yet to take it up. Because the measure had been delayed for seven months, Burke was ready to do battle. "If action is not taken … this week," he told Cutler, "we certainly ought to start something of a protest." In the end, the House endorsed the bill. Moreover, both houses passed the joint resolution granting an exemption to those who were enrolled in recognized seminaries as of 20 May 1918.[26]

Both pieces of legislation raised new concerns, one in the long term and the other in the short. Because the exclusion for seminarians applied only to those already studying for the ministry in May 1918, it left uncertain the situation of those who would come of age and enroll in the fall. More immediately, Burke confided to Muldoon his fear that because the chaplain bill opened that service to Jews, Christian Scientists, Mormons, and Universalists, the FCC would attempt to ensure that Catholics, rather than Protestants, suffered the reduction in chaplains to accommodate these other faiths. He had no objection to an equitable, across-the-board cut, but considered it "unreasonable" that his Church should bear it all. "It is to be regretted that we have not a definite census of Catholics in the service," he complained to Muldoon. "I have collected all the data I could, but it is by no means complete."[27]

Indeed, once the law was passed, Assistant Secretary of War Frederick Keppel sent to Burke a representative from the Christian Scientists, who was eager to have chaplains of that faith appointed. "So like St. Paul," Burke told Murray, "I have the solicitude of all the churches." The issue of appointing Christian Scientists would go unresolved until the war was practically over. The Committee of Six wanted that denomination to conduct a census of its military members so an apt proportion of chaplains could be allotted. Given the unlikelihood of that occurring, however, the committee recommended to the adjutant general that four or five chaplains be appointed for them.[28]

Of more immediate concern was the government's attempt to halt the practice of camp pastors. Some military men began to fear that such unauthorized ministers, especially those in traditionally Germanic faiths like Lutheranism and the Reformed Church, might foster antiwar sentiment or spread pro-German propaganda among the troops. With enactment of the chaplain bill, Keppel personally requested that the Committee of Six consider withdrawal of camp pastors because the number of military chaplains would be increasing. The committee, however, strongly advised otherwise until there was "a sufficient number of regular chaplains" to replace them. Nor was this advice to be interpreted as meaning "there will be no need for service of volunteer chaplains" once a full complement of military ones was secured. The committee thought if the War Department decided to end the practice, its directive should contain a provision for supplementary religious services in locations where needed.[29] A week later, Keppel showed Burke an order from Baker halting camp pastors altogether. "I don't like it," Burke told Murray, and he protested against it. Keppel agreed to delay its issuance until Burke could offer modifications. He suggested a clause which permitted volunteer chaplains to do some work in camps where necessary. Whether or not the final form of Baker's order would allow such, Burke could not say, but he hoped the final verdict "will not be as drastic as first framed."[30]

When Burke informed Bishop Hayes of the development, the latter grew concerned. He thought the order ought to apply only to camps and cantonments with a full quota of chaplains. He telegraphed Burke, "There must be a hundred places—small forts and barracks—which can hardly be cared for except by permitting local clergy to attend to them." Burke showed the telegram to Baker, who replied the order would contain an exemption for those situations. If Burke deemed the exemption insufficient, Baker "would issue one that would cover it." The matter went unresolved until late September 1918 when a compromise was reached. Accordingly, volunteers were permitted to continue on a limited basis, provided the commandant of the base invited the clergymen into the camp, the appropriate religious body and the War Department certified them, and the pastors worked under supervision of a military chaplain.[31]

On 23 June, Keppel informed Burke the War Department wanted to commission 237 Catholic chaplains. At that time, there were already 125 in service, but because of a clergy shortage, the church had few priests to nominate. "We have this day only 5 names to offer," Burke told Murray. "What a plight we are in!" Within days, however, he had been able to muster fifty-one more candidates, and in early July, Muldoon sent a letter to the hierarchy requesting priests for service. On the eleventh, Burke received word from the government it wanted 228 Catholic chaplains in twenty days or it would assign the billets to other denominations. That night Burke laid the situation before Archbishop Giovanni Bonzano, apostolic delegate, i.e., papal representative to the American hierarchy. Bonzano ordered him to telegram every bishop over his—the delegate's—signature, requesting nominations for chaplains. In essence, Burke went over the head of the Administrative Committee. "Some in authority may not like my action," he explained to Murray, "but I cannot help it. The need of souls, the vast interest of the Church demanded it." The nighttime telegrams had the desired effect. The quota was filled and there was never again a dearth of candidates.[32]

While Burke was trying to fill billets, the issue of a chief of chaplains reasserted itself, threatening to remove him from the CSWA. The FCC had been pushing for appointment of a Protestant to that post. Burke had consented to the idea, provided the government appoint a Catholic chaplain as deputy chief. At Baker's request, the judge advocate general of the army had drafted a bill for creation of such a position and introduced it into Congress. At the same time, however, the War Plans Division in the War Department resurrected the idea of a committee of three chaplains of different faiths to head the chaplain corps. In fact, Pershing had already established such a committee for the AEF. His General Headquarters for Chaplains consisted of three military ministers: Episcopal Bishop Charles Brent; Reverend Paul Moody, son of evangelist Dwight Moody; and Paulist Father Francis B. Doherty. This committee assigned all chaplains to their fieldwork in France and oversaw them. It is possible that the War Plans Division modeled its recommendation on Pershing's action. Doherty was then in Washington and informed Burke of the division's plan and that his name was apparently being considered as the Catholic representative on the proposed committee. "To serve would be to accept a commission and of course give up all other work," Burke confided to Murray. "There is grave danger that I will be asked and I hope I can avoid being asked—for if the government did ask direct it would be difficult to refuse." In fact, Baker had been persuaded to shift his support from appointment of a chief of chaplains to establishment of a committee, but then balked at both ideas. Nothing would come of either until 1920, when Congress authorized the Army Chaplain Corps.[33]

Meanwhile, a new multifaceted issue was unfolding around military insignia. From 1880 to 1899, in place of rank insignia, the symbol worn by chaplains was a shepherd's crook. After the latter date it became the Latin cross. In 1914, chaplains were also permitted to wear rank insignia to increase esprit de corps. With the opening of the chaplain service to Rabbis, the army chief of staff exempted Jewish chaplains from wearing the cross which they obviously found objectionable. Without some appropriate religious designator, however, Rabbinical chaplains were indistinguishable from line officers. The quarter master general asked Colonel Cutler to recommend an insignia which would be acceptable to both Orthodox and Reformed Jews. Cutler quickly replied that both would welcome the Star of David. The adjutant general, however, objected to use of that six-pointed star because the insignia of his staff was a five-pointed one, and staff members feared the two might become confused. So, he ordered that all chaplains revert to use of the shepherd's crook. Rumor soon spread that the change occurred because certain Jewish chaplains had objected to their Christian counterparts' use of the cross. Burke entered a protest. Then came word from France that Pershing's committee of chaplains had readopted the prior practice of military ministers' wearing no rank insignia and being addressed simply as "chaplain" in order to help them get closer to the troops. Pershing recommended the entire army resume the custom, and Baker approved. This brought objection from Major Alden Pruden, head of the chaplain-training school. Moreover, the War Department was considering moving that school from Camp Zachary Taylor near Louisville to a new location. So, the army asked the Committee of Six to investigate all these matters and make recommendations.[34]

In July 1918, the committee led by Burke accompanied Keppel on an inspection tour of the school. Deeming the location satisfactory, the committee recommended it remain there permanently. They further recommended that more time be allowed for spiritual exercises, prayer, and scripture reading, and also suggested that training conclude with a spiritual retreat. The War Department accepted the recommendations. Because the matter of rank insignia for chaplains affected the entire army, the committee believed "unity of action should prevail" between what Pershing's chaplains were doing and what the committee would recommend. It delegated Bishop Perry, who was about to visit the AEF, "to secure harmony of opinion on the question." With regard to the shepherd's crook, the committee protested against it. Cutler spoke emphatically for the Jewish Welfare Board declaring Jews not only had no objection to Christian chaplains wearing the cross, but would "consider it a distinct injury to the national welfare" to forbid them to do so. Jewish chaplains simply wished to wear the Star of David.[35]

Over the course of a month, the issue of the chaplains' insignia was resolved. In mid-July, the War Department rescinded the order about the shepherd's crook. Keppel informed Cutler that Baker still hesitated about the Star of David because of its "real or fancied resemblance" to the insignia of the adjutant general's staff and asked if there was some other appropriate design. Cutler looked to Burke, who recommended using the menorah. Cutler nixed the idea because that was the "emblem of a secret fraternal organization," B'nai B'rith. He thought the only alternative was an open scroll and urged Burke to secure it. He also asked him to put to rest the ugly rumor still circulating that Jews opposed use of the cross.[36]

Indeed, *America* magazine, the national Jesuit weekly, had recently run an editorial reiterating the rumor. Burke asked the editor, Father Richard Tierney, to publicize the revocation of the order about the shepherd's crook and explain that Jews "decidedly" favored Christians wearing the cross. Burke quoted the declaration Cutler made to the Committee of Six. Without making the retraction, Tierney skillfully turned Burke's request into a letter to the editor explaining the army's withdrawal of the order and the Jewish role therein. Burke continued to keep in touch with Keppel about the insignia device for Jewish chaplains. Meanwhile, the Jewish Welfare Board submitted two designs from which the War Department could choose. The insignia selected was the two Tables of the Law surmounted by a small Star of David.[37]

The decision about rank insignia caused a near mutiny. Perry and Pershing's chaplains agreed that the order against wearing any should stand. In late September after Pruden read the order to candidates at the chaplain school, he and the faculty expressed disapproval of it and encouraged the trainees to protest to their congressmen and ecclesiastical superiors. Six students, including Father John Holland, sent telegrams of protest directly to the adjutant general. The War Department considered this insubordination. Burke defended the men, arguing that responsibility lay with Pruden and the faculty who had put them up to it. He further contended that they could not be court-martialed because they were not yet members of the army, but simply candidates for commissions, despite the impression Pruden had given them that they were privates. The worst they could suffer was dismissal from the school.[38]

At Burke's urging, the War Department sent an inspector to conduct an investigation. Although Keppel had appealed to Adjutant General Peter Harris to stay the action against the six students until the investigation was completed, Harris ordered Pruden to dismiss them from the school. The situation seemed hopeless to Burke. "The military part of the War Department are very angry," he reported to Muldoon. Burke then begged Keppel to "so modify the order as not to exclude absolutely the appointment of these men as chaplains." Apparently, Keppel won a suspension of the dismissal until the office of the inspector general reported its findings. The results of the investigation were "drastic" regarding Pruden. While the six students were granted their commissions, the War Department relieved him and his faculty of their duties, considering this course of action the best way to avoid the negative publicity of a court martial in wartime. According to Burke, the faculty members were reassigned to a "strict disciplinarian" and none of them was to be permitted to serve in the AEF.[39]

While that was being resolved, the Committee of Six had reason to reverse its position on keeping the chaplain school at Camp Zachary Taylor. Burke noted that when the committee had visited the base, it had specifically asked that there be no impingement on the school's space. Ignoring this request, the army placed a construction battalion immediately next to it. "The juxtaposition of these … is altogether unnecessary and absolutely unwarranted," complained Burke. The school had a latrine with fifty toilets which 350 men were to use in space of a half an hour. Though soldiers of the construction battalion were forbidden to use the chaplains' latrine, they did so with impunity and most were "suffering from syphilis." This last comment bespoke the prevalent belief that venereal disease was transmitted in more innocent ways than sexual intercourse. Moreover, the army had provided no suitable place for Catholic priests to say Mass nor a conference room where Protestants could meet. Burke protested to Baker that the army had implemented none of the recommendations which the committee had made and the War Department had accepted.[40]

By late summer 1918, exemption of seminarians from the draft again became an issue. Army war plans called for deploying 4 million men to France by June 1919, with another 1.5 million at the ready in the U.S. This necessitated amending the draft law of 1917 to expand ages of eligibility. When the bill to amend had been introduced in Congress in February 1918, Burke requested, on behalf of the Committee of Six, that it explicitly exempt seminarians from the draft.[41] Instead, as seen above, Congress had handled the issue through a joint resolution excluding only those enrolled in a seminary as of 20 May 1918. Officials of the War Department now planned to act as if that exemption would automatically apply to the forthcoming legislation as well, despite the very specific date in the joint resolution.

In August 1918, shortly before the Senate took up the new draft bill, Burke pleaded with Baker to have it adjusted to exempt those who would enter seminaries in September. He explained that William Guthrie, a prominent New York attorney, advised that unless the bill explicitly extended the exemption, it could be construed as repealing the joint resolution. Baker replied that in the mind of the government, the bill did not revoke the existing exemption which would also cover those in seminaries at the time of the legislation's passage. He feared raising the issue because it "would provoke a serious debate in the House" and probably result in repeal of any exemption. Burke, however, insisted. So Baker dictated a memo to Judge Advocate General Enoch Crowder asking him to ensure the bill was explicit about the matter. Still unsatisfied, Burke demanded Baker speak personally with Crowder. That afternoon, he received word the two had spoken, and both agreed the present bill did not rescind the exemption. As judge advocate general, Crowder said he would interpret the new legislation accordingly.[42]

The assurance did nothing to settle Burke's mind. "It would be disastrous if new students for the ministry were to be cut off or greatly diminished," he wrote in a memorandum to himself. An army of the size contemplated by the War Department would demand 3,200 additional chaplains. In the Catholic church, it took six years of seminary education for ordination. "We feel our petition is just, when we asked that the incoming class be exempted."[43] Toward the end of August, Congress passed the bill with no explicit exemption, and Wilson signed it into law.[44]

Burke refused to let the matter go. Catholic students for the ministry, unlike their Protestant counterparts, were also in college seminaries as well as high-school seminaries and novitiates of religious communities—all of them preparatory institutions for entry into theological seminaries. So, Burke worked with Keppel and Colonel Charles Warren, Crowder's chief of staff, and secured a favorable ruling in mid-September 1918. Warren instructed that all students studying for the ministry in approved schools and novitiates, should answer affirmatively on the draft questionnaire that they were ministerial students in recognized seminaries. Burke sent a night telegram and a follow-up letter to all Catholic bishops and all rectors of seminaries and novitiates informing them of the decision, with the caution that the communication was "strictly confidential" and "should not under any circumstance receive publication" or be shared with anyone. A collective sigh of relief came from bishops and rectors around the country.[45]

Unfortunately, one of them made the telegram public and another filed it with a district draft board in Nebraska, bringing the matter to the attention of Crowder's staff, which demanded corrective action be taken immediately. Crowder referred the issue back to Warren and Keppel. Understandably upset, Warren told Burke it was "lamentable" his telegram had become public and "still worse" that it had been served on a draft board. Warren asked him to write a more carefully worded communication for approval by both himself and Crowder. Burke crafted new instructions which carefully stated the letter of the law, but worded in such way as to give wide berth to Catholics. In order to qualify for exemption, a man had to have been "a bona fide student for the priesthood" pursuing studies for that purpose prior to 20 May 1918 "in such an institution as directly and professedly fitted him for the priesthood and for the completion of his final courses in a major seminary [i.e., a theological seminary]." Burke stressed the government did not intend to determine which schools fell within the parameters of the exemption; such determination was to be according to the norms of each denomination, and local draft boards were to honor those norms. Making only minor adjustments, Warren and Crowder signed off on it.[46] Thus, Burke got his exemption for those entering major seminaries in September 1918. Virtually all enrollees had been students in college seminaries, which the Church considered institutions preparing bona fide candidates for priesthood.

Motion Pictures

Intimately connected with the spiritual care of soldiers was concern for their morality, and Burke sought to preserve servicemen from what he considered indecent motion pictures. Having served for years as head of New York's Catholic Theater Movement, Burke had reviewed many silent films and knew the medium well. No champion of censorship, he shared the Victorian, Christian moral standards of the Protestant and Catholic establishments.

Such matters as seduction, prostitution, white slavery, fornication, adultery, and unwed pregnancy were unsuitable topics for stage and screen, which should reinforce societal norms. Yet, these very subjects were becoming box-office draws, encouraging studios to push the envelope of moral standards.[47] Though an ardent advocate for and upholder of purity, Burke hated prudery. For him, sex was holy, part of God's creation. He could be scathing in his denunciation of religious who refused to allow themselves to think of it. It was an integral part of life.[48]

Burke and the CSWA worked closely with Fosdick to ensure wholesome conditions and entertainment for military personnel at home and abroad. The two worked well together. In April 1918, Fosdick reported the CTCA had eliminated prostitution and liquor traffic around military camps and was then trying to "to prevent prostitutes and other carriers of venereal disease from having access to troops." He requested help of Catholic organizations in that regard.[49]

At the same time, the CTCA launched an educational program through lectures to recruits, which promoted male continence as healthy and wholesome. As social historian Allan Brandt remarks, "The CTCA cast the war as a symbolic battle of virile manhood to protect 'pure' womanhood." The effort culminated in production of a feature film about continence entitled *Fit to Fight.* The first thousand feet showed pictures of and explanatory captions about lesions resulting from venereal disease. It then developed the story of five men from different backgrounds as recruits. The film introduced protagonist Billy Hale, a college quarterback, beating up a pacifist. The other four included boxer Kid McCarthy, a pursuer of wine and women; Chick Charlton, a wastrel, upper-crust, college student; Hank Simpson, a farm boy; and Jack Garvin, a jaded, traveling cigar salesman. Billy's girl back home wanted him to preserve his virtue for their marriage and wrote him about the danger of sexually transmitted diseases. On leave in town before deployment, prostitutes and bootleggers approached the five. Remembering his sweetheart's letter, Billy resisted temptation, while the others accompanied the women to a brothel. Afterward, Kid immediately sought medical attention and avoided disease. He called Billy a "mollycoddle" for his unmanly behavior. Billy decked him with one punch. With new-found respect for him, Kid reformed and the two became friends. The military qualified both for overseas duty, but rejected the other three as unfit. Chick contracted gonorrhea and was discharged. Hank and Jack were hospitalized with syphilis.[50]

The movie became part of military training and provoked intense protest from a number of Catholic soldiers and officers who considered it indecent and suggestive. In June 1918, the CSWA adopted a resolution that the film was inimical to the "high purpose" of the CTCA, which upheld continence as "the right and practical law of conduct for the soldiers." The CSWA advocated for "a constructive program showing the worth and value to the body and mind of sexual purity." Hooke sent the resolution to Fosdick. His Vice Chairman Malcolm McBride replied the film had been vetted by physicians, ministers, and women's groups before its release in camps and invited members of the CSWA to a screening.[51]

In July, Burke saw the film and sent a balanced review to Major William Snow. Considering the goal of the movie "in every way laudable," he objected to certain details that "mar … pervert an otherwise good piece of work." A major concern was the brothel scene, which lacked "verisimilitude." Burke noted the madam of such an establishment neither sat conspicuously observing the amorous behavior of clients and her girls awaiting a room—"the lifted dress, the abandon, the caresses"—nor did she take payment like a cashier in a restaurant. Moreover, prostitute and client did not exit such establishments a happy couple arm in arm. The scene could not be "justified," argued Burke, especially when the film "aimed at suppression and control of the sexual appetite." Rather, it would excite passion. "Suggestion is the most powerful weapon in the hands of an artist," he wrote. The film should simply show men being solicited, and those who succumbed entering the establishment. Thus the tale would be told "effectively and with that reticence which decency always demands." "It is well to leave something to the intelligence of the audience," argued Burke, "because the audience is then flattered."[52]

He also found unbelievable the scene of Hale's girl writing him about venereal disease. Such discussions occurred in "social hygiene circles," not with people one loved. "No pure-minded girl feeling the enthusiasm of love," wrote Burke, "touches upon such things with her beloved.… A message from the girl he loves, inspiring him to be a great, noble and pure man in every way would be far more effective, as it would be far more true to facts."[53]

Burke concluded that the strength of the film lay in its positive appeal, rather than fear of venereal disease. Sexual passion was powerful. To offset it, something more powerful was necessary. "In his ideals of self-respect and of reverence for women," said Burke, "man finds the sources of restraining and conquering power." He noted everyone attending the screening agreed there must be a stopping point for display of indecency. He asked for removal of the objectionable scenes. Fosdick had the scenes in the brothel shortened and the letter from Billy's girl excised. Moreover, the government promised to exhibit the film only to the military.[54]

The CTCA developed a companion piece depicting the female side of the issue. Professional prostitutes were not the only source of venereal disease. Teenage girls and young women found military camps exciting and attractive places. Some became "patriotic prostitutes," doing their part for the war effort. "One such girl," reported a CTCA social worker, "said that she had never sold herself to a civilian but felt she was doing her bit when she had been with eight soldiers in a night." Fosdick was concerned about such behavior and the alarming rate of pregnancy among young women near army camps. He established the Committee on Protective Work for Girls. Yet, his concern was less for feminine sexual purity than about keeping troops fit. So, the CTCA produced the movie *End of the Road*.[55]

The film was about two high-school graduates: Mary Lee and Vera Lynch. Mary, whose mother instructed her about love, marriage, and sex, left boyfriend Paul behind to become a nurse in New York City. Vera's mother encouraged her to marry rich. She too went to New York and became a shop girl. When a wealthy man promised to marry her, she became his live-in lover. Instead of getting a ring, she got syphilis. Mary and her employer Doctor Bell treated Vera. They took her to see the disease's ravages, shot live in the women's ward of the asylum on Blackwell's Island (present-day Roosevelt Island). The film continued with Mary encountering other women suffering from venereal disease, one an immigrant Irish lass working as a servant in a wealthy home. The chauffeur made love to her. Becoming pregnant, she begged him to wed her, but he refused and she shot him. In a fit of remorse, she held the crucifix on her rosary to his dying lips. Mary also met the invalid wife of a wealthy philanderer who had infected her with gonorrhea, resulting in blindness of their baby. The scoundrel husband then plied with liquor and seduced a young debutante who became pregnant. When he refused to marry her, she drowned herself. Disappointed with men, Mary also turned down the proposal of Doctor Bell. Later as a nurse in Europe, having witnessed the type of man Bell was, she married him.[56]

The army gave Burke a screening of the film, which was to go into general distribution. Its content haunted him "for many hours" that night because of its effect on the outlook, morals, and ideals of all who viewed it. He sent a lengthy letter unburdening his conscience to Fosdick. There was no question about "the ingenuity and cleverness" of the picture, which was of "a high order." "Indeed it may rightfully be asked," said Burke, "if the beauties of nature have not been artfully subsidized to give tribute to the allurement of sex." As he saw it, the entire film had that one dominant theme. Each female character had only sex on her mind. Burke argued that life was bigger and greater than sex. Civic, moral, and religious matters motivated people. "Therefore I must protest," he wrote, "against the radically false and perverted view of life and life's responsibilities which this picture will give to the young girl."[57]

Burke then addressed specifics. He asserted that the "moral virtue of the Irish girl is proverbial." Art should reflect life, not its exceptions. And artful the movie was. When the philandering father of the blind baby refused to marry the debutante, she walked out of his elegant estate in her lovely lace dress and down the road where windblown leaves beckoned her to a dock and the water that called to her. There she stood, eliciting pity from the audience, until "the kind waters give her peace." Burke considered it "a fitting moment for someone to rise and recite 'Once she was as pure as the beautiful snow.'" The unhealthy sentimentalism of the scene had nothing redeeming about it. "God knows and we know that weakness, failure are common enough," complained Burke. The message of this segment was that "suicide or prostitution" were the only alternatives. The ghastly footage from the syphilitic ward was worse than gratuitous. "Has our civilization become so beggared of worthy motive," he queried, "that we must ask the derelicts of humanity to parade themselves with timid, halting step, expose their rotting, diseased limbs that we may be inspired to virtue?" The only idea that this scare tactic inspired was that sexual intercourse was "not so bad if one knows how to avoid the consequences" or seeks timely treatment. The whole philosophy of the film was that knowledge of sexually transmitted diseases was "virtue and that ignorance is sin." "I must respectfully insist," concluded Burke, "that its exhibition be prohibited by official order."[58]

Fosdick referred Burke's letter to Snow. The major discussed Burke's complaint with various persons, including Catholic laymen and priests. "I think there will be plenty of dissenters from Father Burke's views," he reported. For the life of him, Snow could not understand how Burke could conclude the message of the movie was that knowledge was virtue and ignorance sin. The major said he intended to get a consensus opinion based on a wide sample, including audiences of women and girls.[59] The government made no adjustments to the film.

OFFICIAL RECOGNITION OF THE WAR COUNCIL

While Burke fought for decency in movies, events were afoot that would cause the government to transfer official recognition for Catholic war work from the Knights of Columbus to the War Council. In July 1918, Keppel met with Burke to inform him of unrest in the CTCA over the seemingly inflated budget submitted by the Knights for their war work. Keppel considered it "absurd" because it called for millions of dollars without itemization. A sizeable portion was to support the Knights' policy announced in the slogan "Everybody Welcome and Everything Free," meaning the Knights intended to give away candy, gum, cigars, cigarettes, pipes, playing cards, and more to soldiers. Keppel also thought the scope of Catholic endeavors went well beyond what the CTCA had authorized for the Knights. Burke explained to Baker that the CSWA, rather than the Knights, planned to engage in those broader activities, like the erection of hostess houses near training camps. Baker asked him to confer with both Keppel and Fosdick before any further action. They met on 24 July. "The important part of the interview," Burke told Murray, "was that Mr. Fosdick thought all the work ought to be under the name of the National Catholic War Council, not the K. of C." Fosdick said because the Knights were a fraternal organization, they were "causing the Government all kinds of trouble." He begged Burke to see if something could be done to make the War Council the official Catholic body for war work. "This would surely be a great turn-about in history," remarked Burke.[60]

The government's problem with the Knights became clear when Fosdick and Keppel met again with Burke. They told him other fraternal organizations, especially the Masons, were arguing they should be permitted to do war work in camps like the Knights. Burke explained the Knights were working not as a fraternal order, but as an agency of the Catholic Church. To Murray, he wrote: "The position of the K of C is weakened in the mind of Mr. Fosdick because he believes they have 'fallen down' in the work over seas and so expressed himself emphatically. He is even thinking of having the K of C go out of the camps." Adamantly opposing that, Burke urged Fosdick to make his concerns known to Muldoon. Indeed, Burke telegraphed the bishop that a "critical situation had arisen concerning our entire war activities and relations with government." It was imperative that he come to Washington. Burke confided to Murray his anxiety that some would blame him if the War Department recognized the War Council as the Catholic organization for war work. "Of course … I have labored diligently against just such an attitude," he wrote, "and the untruth should not disturb me. But to run against a falsehood is loathsome."[61]

On 30 July, Burke and Muldoon met with Fosdick, who explained his trouble with fraternal organizations. During his recent visit to France, Pershing had made it clear that he wanted no fraternal orders in the war zone. When Fosdick tried to convince such organizations that the Knights were an agency of the Catholic Church, none of them bought it. Muldoon and Burke asked what the government wanted done. Fosdick said both he and Baker would rather deal with the War Council than the Knights. The War Department classified war work as Protestant, Catholic, and Jewish. All Protestant work was under the YMCA, all Jewish work under the Jewish Welfare Board, and all Catholic work should be under the War Council. If this were done, it would remove "the present embarrassment" and effectively answer "the demands of the Masons and other fraternal organizations." The Masons were particularly insistent on being allowed into war work and backed their demand with the fact that 70 percent of congressmen were Masons. Fosdick said there was also tremendous opposition to the Knights in the South. In his view, the situation was such that it needed "but a match to start a conflagration." He meant no disparagement toward the Knights, but the government saw working with the War Council as the way around its problem. When Muldoon and Burke asked that he put the request in writing, Fosdick absolutely refused. He wanted no publicity. As Burke summarized it, the issue was "a family affair" among Catholics. Fosdick wanted their discussion kept "entirely private." If Burke and Muldoon could effect the change, "he would trust to us to do it quietly and privately, without any public announcement."[62]

Within a fortnight, the issue was resolved. On 1 August, the executive committee of the War Council met in New York to discuss the government's proposed national drive for war funds. The CTCA planned to let its subsidiary organizations, including the Knights, hold a nationwide campaign to raise money for their projects. After agreeing on a budget of $50 million ($1 billion in 2024) to support Catholic war work, the committee considered sponsorship of the campaign. All members were polled for their views. Every Knight believed "it should be a straight Knights of Columbus Drive." Every member of the CSWA thought it should be a War Council drive. The four bishops of the Administrative Committee considered these views and decided the drive would be under the auspices of the War Council, but promised the Knights their emblem would "be given every possible prominence and their achievements and their needs in this war brought strikingly before the public." The bishops further decided that the War Council should become the official Catholic agency recognized by the government for war work and that the council should be incorporated.[63]

A week later, the transfer of official recognition was finalized. Fosdick met in New York with Muldoon, Burke, and Knights Daniel Callahan, William Mulligan, and William McGinley. At this meeting, agreement was reached that the War Council would be responsible for all Catholic war work, and all government relations pertaining thereto would be conducted by the War Council. The council remained "free to choose such agents to carry on the work as it may deem wise," with the War Department's sole concern being "the work shall be well done." Moreover, any campaign for funds would be in the name of the War Council. For its part, the War Council chose the Knights as its agent for work with troops in camps at home and abroad.[64]

Burke's fear he would be blamed for this turn of events may have materialized in a form quite personal. His secretary Coyle remembered that in 1918, "something happened to mar the friendship" between Burke and O'Hern, though she could not recall what occasioned it. Although thinness of the historical record prevents exact dating of the harm, there are indications it occurred in August 1918, very likely over this transfer of power.[65]

Coyle averred Burke "had his troubles from 'within' his own organization and the rumblings backstage were loud and long." One of the grumblers was probably O'Hern, as Fosdick later explained to Burke in 1919. He said the Knights had repeatedly brought pressure "not to have him recognize in any way" the War Council or the work it was doing. They argued it was an age-old matter in Catholic America that the laity initiated a work and then the clergy tried to take it over to get hold of the funds. They had made this case forcefully to Fosdick before the New York fund-raising drive in March 1918. He said "that Father O'Hern came to see him with the Knights frequently and supported their appeal that he should not recognize the N.C.W.C." Fosdick said he at first believed the Knights, but because of his experiences with them and his later work with the War Council, his attitude had changed. He now regretted he had not gone straight to the hierarchy from the start to handle war work.[66]

Given O'Hern's support of the Knights, it is probable he considered the government's transfer of its recognition to the War Council as the final straw. O'Hern removed himself from War Council headquarters, though he continued as Bishop Hayes's executive secretary for military chaplains.[67] Neither Burke nor O'Hern is known to have written about the friction. Burke's account of Fosdick's conversation was objective, without judgment or self-justification. Such reporting befitted an editor familiar with the canons of journalism and a spiritual director who counseled that a Christian loved those with whom he disagreed, even if he felt betrayed by them. In fact, any damage to the relationship was temporary. The two remained lifelong friends, and Burke preached at O'Hern's funeral following his untimely death in December 1930.[68]

Death of a Poet

O'Hern's departure was not the only loss Burke suffered that summer. In mid-August, word arrived that poet Joyce Kilmer had been killed in France. "The news of his death was a great shock to me," Burke told Murray. "Pray for him." In 1912, a bewildered Kilmer had come to Burke in search of spiritual truth. When Burke spoke about the revealed word of God,

Kilmer's "soul was roused and attentive." He wanted to believe but could not. Never was it more apparent to Burke that faith was a gift. He and Kilmer met for months. "God's mercy was not slow," recalled Burke. "The gift came." No one proselytized or pushed Kilmer into the Church. "I had to jump," said the poet—the leap of faith. Burke counted him "a beloved, intimate friend."[69]

Shortly before deployment, the youthful thirty-year-old visited Burke at *Catholic World*, "so much like a boy, so much the man." He came to announce the birth of his youngest son and bid farewell. Now, news of his death stunned Burke, who telegraphed condolence to Kilmer's wife and then wrote an editorial eulogizing him.[70]

Burke pictured the convert Kilmer in Americanist terms: as the personification of Hecker's vision of a Catholicized America. The nation had a mission to the world. As Burke had declared at the War Council's founding, America's life was essentially spiritual, and only Catholicism unlocked the right principles of that life. Alluding to Wilson's war message, Burke recalled that at Kilmer's parting, "There was no anger nor excitement nor boastfulness in his voice nor in his heart.... As he talked he typified the great mystery of America's entry, America's determination, America's sacrifice in this War."

> Many could not or would not see ... the soul of America. They denied its existence or thought it ... incapable of a magnificent, spontaneous full response to the ideal of spiritual and political liberty for itself and for others.... The quiet, strong, sensitive soul of America was living and awake ... it was the soul of a people ... that did not forget its inheritance nor the traditions to which it must prove true if it were to be true to self.... It would sacrifice its best sons, millions of them, if necessary, and ... not ask nor accept indemnity. It did not seek one foot of territory. It would give itself that others might live. Greater love than this no man hath that a man should lay down his life for his friends.
>
> Joyce Kilmer ... typified all of this. He left high position, promising future ... young wife and four children, and quietly went

> forth to give his life—as he truly thought—for his country. He voiced America's soul.... His life is a wonderful evidence of how the Catholic faith begets the greatest patriots.... And it was that Faith that led him to make the supreme sacrifice ... that has crowned him before all his country and throughout history with the crown of a hero and a patriot.[71]

As overdrawn as the imagery was, penned in a moment of grief, Burke clearly viewed America as did Hecker: It was the redeemer nation, and Kilmer was an *alter Christus*, another Christ, a Protestant American who had perfectly conformed himself to the ideals of the country through conversion to Catholicism and had sacrificed all for their sake.

Endnotes to Chapter 5

1. Burke, *Christ in Us*, 67.
2. Burke to Muldoon, 6 March 1918, ACUA, NCWC 10:3:35 (second quote is here). The description of Muldoon is quoted in James P. Gaffey, *Francis Clement Kelley and the American Dream*, 2 vols (Bensenville, Ill.: The Heritage Foundation, Inc., 1980), 1:87. It was made by Father John T. Roche.
3. Williams, *Catholics in War*, 155; McKeown, *War and Welfare*, 88.
4. Kerby to Edward Garesché, S.J., 26 February 1918, copy, ACUA, NCWC 10:3:35 (first quote is here); Burke to Muldoon, 27 February 1918, ibid. (second quote is here); Coyle, Memories of War Council, ACUA, USCCB 10:72:24 (remaining quotes are here).
5. Coyle, Memories of War Council, ACUA, USCCB 10:72:24 (emphasis in original); Minutes of Adjourned Meeting of Supreme Board of Directors, 10 and 11 February 1918, AKC, SC–16–1–0041; McKeown, *War and Welfare*, 88.
6. Burke to Muldoon, 6 March 1918, ACUA, NCWC 10:3:35.
7. Ibid.
8. Minutes of the Board of Archbishops, 10 and 11 April 1918, AASL, RG 9 USA Hierarchy; Burke to Muldoon, 6 March 1918, ACUA, NCWC 10:3:35; Williams, *Catholics in War*, 178–80; McKeown, *War and Welfare*, 97–100.
9. Diary of Muldoon, 19 January 1918, ACUA, microfilm; Bishops of the Administrative Committee of the War Council to the Hierarchy, 22 January 1918, copy, AKC, SC–16–1–0045; Major General John Pershing to the Adjutant General, undated, printed in *Congressional Record*, 65th Congress, 2nd Sess., 56, pt. 5, 4807.

10. Diary of Muldoon, 19 January 1918, ACUA, microfilm; Muldoon to Burke, 22 January 1918, ACUA, NCWC 10:7:17.
11. Burke to Muldoon, 30 January 1918, copy, ACUA, NCWC 10:7:17; Fosdick to Burke, 1 February 1918, copy, ibid., 10:5:5; Burke to Fosdick, 5 February 1918, copy, ibid., 10:5:5; Minutes of the Executive Committee of the War Council, 13 November 1918, ibid., 10:6:7.
12. Minutes of the Committee of Six, 6 February 1918, ACUA, NCWC 10:5:10; Burke to Muldoon, 22 February 1918, copy, ACUA, War Council 10:7:17; Stover, *Up from Handyman*, 212–13.
13. Burke to Fosdick, 5 April 1918, copy, ACUA, NCWC 10:8:1; Burke, circular to Members of the House, 6 April 1918, copy, ibid., 10:5:5.
14. *Congressional Record*, 65th Congress, 2nd Sess., 56, pt. 5, 4807–10, 4879 (the quotation is on 4809–10); Woodrow Wilson to the Senate, 18 April 1918, printed in ibid., 5241.
15. Burke to George Chamberlain, 12 February 1918, copy, ACUA, NCWC 10:4:70; Chamberlain to Burke, 14 February 1918, ibid.
16. Burke to Cutler, 23 April 1918, ACUA, NCWC 10:5:9.
17. Burke to Lynch, 22 December 1917, AP, Burke Papers, box 5.
18. Burke to Murray, Somewhere in America, 15 January 1918, AP, Burke Papers, box 11. See also Burke to Murray, 15 February 1926, ibid., box 12.
19. Burke to Murray, 26 April 1918, AP, Burke Papers, box 11.
20. Burke to Murray, 28 April 1918, AP, Burke Papers, box 11.
21. Burke to Murray, 2 May 1918, AP, Burke Papers, box 11.
22. Burke to Murray, 6 May 1918, AP, Burke Papers, box 11.
23. Murray to Murtaugh, 18 April 1918, ACUA, NCWC 10:13:26.
24. Burke to Murray, 6 May 1918, AP, Burke Papers, box 11.
25. Muldoon to Burke, 2 June 1918, ACUA, NCWC 10:7:17; Burke to Murray, 5 June 1918, AP, Burke Papers, box 11; Gibbons to John J. Hughes, 9 June 1918, ibid., Official Papers of Superior General John J. Hughes, January 1916–May 1919; McKeown, *War and Welfare*, 92–93.
26. Burke to Cutler, 14 May 1918, ACUA, NCWC 10:5:9; *Congressional Record*, 65th Congress, 2nd Sess., 56, pt. 6, 5393, 6081–82 and pt. 7, 6621, 6741, 6818, 7233; Senate Joint Resolution 124, 20 May 1918, in *Selective Service Regulations: Prescribed by the President under the Authority Vested in Him by the Terms of the Selective Service Law*, 2nd ed. (Washington, D.C.: U.S. Government Printing Office, 1918), 356.
27. Burke to Muldoon, 24 May 1918, copy, ACUA, NCWC 10:7:17.
28. Burke to Murray, 23 June 1918, AP, Burke Papers, box 11; Burke to Brigadier General Peter Harris, 4 November 1918, copy, ACUA, NCWC 10:5:30.
29. Extract from Minutes of the Committee of Six, 17 June 1918, ACUA, NCWC 10:7:17.

30. Burke to Murray, 23 June 1918, AP, Burke Papers, box 11 (first quote is here); Burke to Muldoon, 24 June 1918, ACUA, NCWC 10:7:17 (second quote is here); McKeown, *War and Welfare*, 134–35.
31. Burke to Hayes, 23 June 1918, copy, ACUA, NCWC 10:5:23; Hayes to Burke, telegram, 3 July 1918, ibid. (the first quote is here); Burke to Hayes, 6 July 1918, copy ibid. (the second quote is here); Frederick Keppel to Fosdick, 21 September 1918, copy, ibid., 10:8:2; Stover, *Up from Handyman*, 212–13.
32. Burke to Murray, 23 June 1918, AP, Burke Papers, box 11 (first quote is here); Burke to Murray, 28 June 1918, ibid; Burke to Murray, 11 July 1918, AP, Burke Papers, box 11 (second quote is here); Burke to Muldoon, 24 June 1918, ACUA, NCWC 10:7:17; Minutes of the Executive Committee of the War Council, 27 February 1917, ibid., 10:6:7; Williams, *Catholics in War*, 243.
33. Burke to Murray, 30 June 1918, AP, Burke Papers, box 11; Stover, *Up from Handyman*, 220–22; *The Messenger* 37 (May 1902): 581.
34. Captain Simon Jacobsen to Cutler, 27 April 1918, copy, ACUA, NCWC 10:5:9; Cutler to Jacobsen, 30 April 1918, copy, ibid.; Burke, Memorandum on Meeting of the Committee of Six, 29 May 1918, enclosure with Burke to Muldoon, 31 May 1918, copy, ibid., 10:7:17; Muldoon to Newton D. Baker, 28 June 1918, copy, ibid., 10:5:3; Burke to Murray, 28 June 1918, AP, Burke Papers, box 11; Stover, *Up from Handyman*, 203–04, 215–16.
35. Minutes of the Committee of Six, 3 July 1918, afternoon, with memorandum of discussion, ACUA, NCWC 10:5:16; Minutes of Committee of Six, 3 July 1918, evening, ibid. (quote is here); Burke to Richard Tierney, S.J., 14 August 1918, copy, ibid., 10:5:5; Stover, *Up from Handyman*, 216–17; McKeown, *War and Welfare*, 136–37. With regard to the lack of implementation of the recommendations, see Burke to Baker, 15 October 1918, copy, ACUA, NCWC 10:5:3.
36. Burke to Cutler, 16 July 1918, copy; Keppel to Cutler, 19 July 1918, copy, (first quote is here); Burke to Cutler, telegram, 3 August 1918; Cutler to Burke, telegram, 3 August 1918 (second quote is here); Burke to Cutler, 3 August 1918, copy; Cutler to Burke, telegram, 5 August 1918; Cutler to Burke, 10 August 1918—all in ACUA, NCWC 10:5:10; Stover, *Up from Handyman*, 204.
37. Burke to Cutler, 13 August 1918, copy, ACUA, NCWC 10:5:10; Burke to Tierney, 14 August 1918, copy, ibid.; "The Chaplains' Cross," *America* 19 (27 July 1918): 382; Stover, *Up from Handyman*, 204. The edited version of the letter is in *America* 19 (24 August 1918): 477.
38. Burke to Hayes, 26 September 1918, copy, ACUA, NCWC 10:5:23; Burke to Muldoon, 26 September 1918, ibid., 10:3:36; Burke, Memorandum on

Training School for Chaplains, undated [October 1918], enclosure with Burke to Keppel, 6 October 1918, ibid., 10:5:26; Burke to Muldoon, 2 November 1918, copy, ibid., 10:7:19; Stover, *Up from Handyman*, 205–06.

39. Burke to Muldoon, 26 September 1918, ACUA, NCWC 10:3:36; Burke to Hayes, 26 September 1918, copy, ibid., 10:5:23 (second quote is here); Burke to Muldoon, 28 September 1918, ibid., 10:7:18 (first quote is here); Burke to Muldoon, 2 November 1918, copy, ibid., 10:7:19 (third and fourth quotes are here); Stover, *Up from Handyman*, 205–06.40. Burke, Training School for Chaplains, undated [October 1918], enclosure with Burke to Keppel, 6 October 1918, copy, ACUA, NCWC 10:5:26 (quotes are here); Burke to Baker, 15 October 1918, copy, ibid., 10:5:3; Brandt, *No Magic Bullet*, 21–22.
41. Burke to Chamberlain, 12 February 1918, copy, ACUA, NCWC 10:5:5; *Congressional Record*, 65th Congress, 2nd Sess., 56, pt. 9, 9200–01, 9230, 9506–07.
42. Burke, Memoranda, 13 August 1918, ACUA, NCWC 10:5:3; Burke to Baker, 13 August 1918, ibid.
43. Burke, Memoranda, 13 August 1918, ACUA, NCWC 10:5:3; Burke, handwritten thoughts, undated [August 1918], ibid.
44. *Congressional Record*, 65th Congress, 2nd Sess., 56, pt. 9, 9506–07 and pt. 10, 9573, 9676, 9704, 10129.
45. Burke to the hierarchy and heads of seminaries and novitiates, telegram, 13 September 1918, copy, ACUA, NCWC 10:4:71; Burke and Edward Kelly to the hierarchy, [17 September 1918] copy, ibid., 10:4:70 (quotations are here); Minutes of the CSWA, 13 September 1918, ibid., 10:1:6. For telegrams and letters thanking Burke for securing the exemption, see the correspondence in ibid., 10:4:70–71.
46. J. S. Easby-Smith to Enoch Crowder, 19 October 1918, copy; Crowder to Colonel Charles Warren, 24 October 1918, copy; Burke, Confidential Memorandum on Interview with Warren, 28 October 1918, (first and second quotes are here); Burke to the hierarchy, [28 October 1918], copy, (third and fourth quotes are here)—all in ACUA, NCWC 10:4:71.
47. Burke to Charles C. Pettijohn, 16 March 1921, copy, ACUA, USCCB 10:125:32; Gregory D. Black, *Hollywood Censored: Morality Codes, Catholics, and the Movies* (Cambridge: Cambridge University Press, 1994), 3–20; Tom Pollard, *Sex and Violence: The Hollywood Censorship Wars* (Boulder, Colo.: Paradigm Publishers, 2009), 11–20; Lary May, *Screening Out the Past: The Birth of Mass Culture and the Motion Picture Industry* (Chicago: University of Chicago Press, 1980), 3–95; Francis G. Couvares, "Hollywood, Main Street, and the Church: Trying to Censor the Movies Before the Production Code," *American Quarterly* 44 (December 1992): 584–87; Stephen Vaughn, "Morality and Entertainment: The Origins of the Motion Picture Production Code,"

Journal of American History 77 (June 1990): 39–42; Henry F. May, *The End of American Innocence: A Study of the First Years of Our Own Time, 1912–1917* (New York: Alfred A. Knopf, 1959), 3–51; Halsey, *Survival of American Innocence*, 26–28; Daniel Howe Walker, "American Victorianism as a Culture," *American Quarterly* 27 (December 1975):507–32; Arnold J. Sparr, *To Promote, Defend, and Redeem: The Catholic Literary Revival and the Cultural Transformation of American Catholicism, 1920–1960* (Westport, Conn.: Greenwood Press, 1990), 3–98; Joseph M. McShane, S.J., "Mirrors and Teachers: A Study of Catholic Periodical Fiction Between 1930 and 1950," *U.S. Catholic Historian* 6 (1987): 181–98.

48. Hawks, "Souvenir of Burke," AP, Burke Papers, box 10.
49. Fosdick to Muldoon, 25 April 1918, ACUA, NCWC 10:4:8; Brandt, *No Magic Bullet*, 70–77.
50. Brandt, *No Magic Bullet*, 61–70; Frank Walsh, *Sin and Censorship: The Catholic Church and the Motion Picture Industry* (New Haven: Yale University Press, 1996), 12–13; Kevin Brownlow, *Behind the Mask of Innocence* (Berkeley and Los Angeles: University of California Press, 1990), 61; Karl S. Lashley and John B. Watson, *A Psychological Study of Motion Pictures in Relation to Venereal Disease Campaigns* (Washington: United States Interdepartmental Social Hygiene Board, 1922), 7–8.
51. Minutes of the CSWA, 6 June 1918, ACUA, NCWC 10:12:1 Minute Book I; Hooke to Fosdick, 13 June 1918, ibid., 10:17:16; Malcolm McBride to Hooke, 18 June 1918, ibid; Walsh, *Sin and Censorship*, 13.
52. Burke to William Snow, 27 July 1918, copy, ACUA, NCWC 10:6:57; Walsh, *Sin and Censorship*, 13–14; Williams, *Catholics in War*, 332–33.
53. Burke to Snow, 27 July 1918, copy, ACUA, NCWC 10:6:57.
54. Ibid.; Burke to Muldoon, 7 June 1918, ACUA, NCWC 10:3:40; "Our Fight Against Unclean Films," *National Catholic War Council Bulletin* 1 (July 1919): 19–20; Walsh, *Sin and Censorship*, 13–14; Williams, *Catholics in War*, 332–33.
55. Quoted in Brandt, *No Magic Bullet*, 80–81; Brownlow, *Behind Mask of Innocence*, 66 and 517 n.157; Walsh, *Sin and Censorship*, 14.
56. Brownlow, *Behind Mask of Innocence*, 66–67; Walsh, *Sin and* Censorship, 14; *End of the Road* (1919) http://www.tcm.com/tcmdb/title/489623/The-End-of-the-Road/notes.html accessed 28 July 2012; *End of the Road* (1919) http://www.afi.com/members/catalog/DetailView.aspx?s=&Movie=15366 accessed 28 July 2012.
57. Burke to Fosdick, 12 October 1918, copy, ACUA, NCWC 10:6:57; Walsh, *Sin and Censorship*, 14–15.
58. Burke to Fosdick, 12 October 1918, copy, ACUA, NCWC 10:6:57.
59. Snow to Fosdick, 26 October 1918, ACUA, NCWC 10:6:57.
60. Burke, memorandum, [14 July 1918], ACUA, NCWC 10:13:27 (first quote is here); Burke to Muldoon, 19 July 1918, ibid. 10:3:35; Diary of Muldoon,

26 August 1918, ACUA, microfilm (second quote is here); Burke to Murray, 24 July 1918, AP, Burke Papers, box 11 (remaining quotes are here); *Boston Globe*, 13 October 1918; Kauffman, *Faith and Fraternalism*, 203–06.

61. Burke to Muldoon, telegram, 26 July 1918, ACUA, NCWC 10:3:35; Burke to Murray, 27 July 1918, AP, Burke Papers, box 11; McKeown, *War and Welfare*, 144; Kauffman, *Faith and Fraternalism*, 204–05; Lynn Dumenil, *Freemasonry and American Culture, 1880–1930* (Princeton, N.J.: Princeton University Press, 1984), 115–47.
62. Burke and Muldoon, Conference with Fosdick, 30 July 1918, ACUA, NCWC 10:8:1; another copy may be found in 10:4:80; Diary of Muldoon, 30 July 1918, ACUA, microfilm; McKeown, *War and Welfare*, 144–45.
63. Minutes of the Executive Committee of the War Council 1 August 1918, ACUA, NCWC 10:1:19; Report of the Administrative Committee to the National Catholic War Council, 4 August 1918, ibid. (quotations are here); Diary of Muldoon, 1 August 1918, ACUA, microfilm; Williams, *Catholics in War*, 183–85; Kauffman, *Faith and Fraternalism*, 219; McKeown, *War and Welfare*, 145–46.
64. Diary of Muldoon, 7 August 1918, ACUA, microfilm; Fosdick to Muldoon, 19 August 1918, ACUA, NCWC 10:4:8 (quotations are from here); Muldoon to Fosdick, 5 September 1918, copy, ACUA, War Council 10:7:18; *National Catholic War Council: Committee on Special War Activities Report to Commission on Training Camp Activities to January 1, 1919* (Washington, D.C.: NCWC, 1919), 6–8; Williams, *Catholic in the War*, 161–65.
65. Coyle, Memories of War Council, ACUA, NCWC 10:72:24; Burke, [Memorandum of Conversation with Fosdick], 29 May 1919, ACUA, USCCB 10:152:18.
66. Burke, [Memorandum of Conversation with Fosdick], 29 May 1919, ACUA, USCCB 10:152:18.
67. Kauffman, *Faith and Fraternalism*, 198.
68. "Father Lewis O'Hern Dies in Washington," *NCWC Review* 13 (January 1931): 6 and 29.
69. Burke to Murray, 19 August 1918, AP, Burke Papers, box 11 (the first two quotes are here); [Burke], "With Our Readers," *Catholic World* 107 (September 1918): 856–57 (the second, third, fourth, and final quotes are here); James J. Daly, S.J., *A Cheerful Ascetic and Other Essays* (New York, Milwaukee, Chicago: The Bruce Publishing Company, 1931), 76–80 (penultimate quote is here); Robert Cortes Holliday, ed., *Joyce Kilmer*, 2 vols (New York: George H. Doran Company, 1918), 1:51–56, 2:127–29.
70. Burke to Murray, 19 August 1918, AP, Burke Papers, box 11; [Burke], "With Our Readers," 107: 856–57 (the quote is here).
71. [Burke], "With Our Readers," 107:856–58.

Chapter 6

Postwar Reconstruction: Conflicts with the Knights of Columbus

> Charity seeks not her own. Charity as spoken of in his epistle to the Corinthians by St. Paul is primarily the supernatural life of God in us, the bond of life between God and us, by which He gives to us His life. Since it is God's life, it is God's love—not only the bond of love between us and God, but God's love given to us out of the inexplicable goodness of God, without merit or claim on our part. It is the love of God drawing us, inciting us, overflowing within us, asking, urging cooperation, eager to take us into itself that our life, our love, our self may be God's, more truly God's than it is our own. This is the charity of which St. Paul writes.[1]

Jesuitical Machinations on Behalf of the Knights

Though the Knights of Columbus acquiesced in the government's transfer of recognition for war work to the War Council, some still smarted over it. According to an adage, one never really knows another until the two divide an inheritance. The same can be said of organizations, though in this case it was not an inheritance but proceeds of the United War Work Campaign, a fund-raising drive in which all organizations working under the CTCA participated. Ironically, it began the day of the Armistice. Even before its launch, the proceeds became an issue. In September 1918, Joseph Pelletier, supreme advocate (attorney) of the Knights and unfriendly to the War Council, warned Bishop Peter Muldoon the transfer of recognition placed the order's war activities on shaky ground because the council was not incorporated. Thus, the Administrative Committee's agreement to give the

Knights their portion of the funds was simply a good-faith promise, not a legally binding one. So, the Knights lacked firm, financial footing for continuance of their war work and might have to withdraw to avoid possible embarrassment, leaving the War Council to take up the slack. Pelletier urged the necessity of immediate incorporation.[2]

To assuage the Knights, the council began that process and agreed to allocate them five-sixths of the Catholic share of proceeds. It decided, however, to hold and invest all funds, and have the Administrative Committee disburse them after approving expenditures by the Knights and CSWA. Supreme Knight James Flaherty himself seconded this motion. The sums in question would be considerable. The campaign netted pledges of $205 million (nearly $3.6 billion in 2024), well over the goal of $170 million. When the funds were divided proportionally among the participating organizations, the War Council would receive at least $30 million and perhaps as much as $36 million if the overage actually materialized, which meant the Knights would get $25 million ($440 million) or as much as $30 million ($529 million).[3]

When in October 1918, the CSWA approved Burke's plan to establish a service school for women to train them for war work (see next chapter), some Knights suspected the CSWA intended to duplicate, on expansive scale and at vast expense, the work they were already doing, using money from the order's share of the funds. In November, the Knights' Supreme Board directed its members on the War Council's executive committee to seek a reconsideration of the decision authorizing the Administrative Committee to hold and disburse funds. The issue was custody of the cash.[4]

At the same time, the Supreme Board prepared to enter into work assigned to the CSWA: vocational education for and re-employment of veterans. The board invited New York Jesuit Father John Wynne to address them on those issues at their meeting in Chicago. Wynne encouraged the Knights to take them up. The board authorized the immediate development of a program to do so, thereby muscling in on the CSWA.[5]

Meanwhile, Pelletier informed Muldoon that two men of the War Council claiming to be "agents of the Knights of Columbus," were investigating activities of the Knights at several military bases in Virginia. It was "rather disquieting," he said, to find the Knights were under investigation by the organization for which they worked. Given that the CSWA was establishing a hostess house in Norfolk where the Knights already had one, Pelletier suggested the CSWA might want to consult with them in the future before doing so.[6]

Muldoon asked Burke for explanation. Burke replied that one of the alleged "agents" was actually a field director of the CTCA and the other was a representative of the CSWA, who was seeking a location for its proposed service house. In fact, the Knights' Virginia State Deputy asked the CSWA agent to assist them in their work there. "We have never permitted … any investigation of the work of the Knights of Columbus," stated Burke. "We would dismiss at once any worker who sought for any reason to do it." He deeply regretted the disinformation.[7]

When the War Council's executive committee met in late November, it gave little satisfaction to the Knights. On the positive side, Muldoon announced the War Council had been incorporated. When, however, both Pelletier and Supreme Secretary William McGinley called for reconsideration about the Administrative Committee holding and disbursing funds, the motion failed with only four of the six Knights on the committee voting in favor.[8]

When the committee took up the matter of postwar reconstruction, Monsignor Michael Splaine reported initiatives being planned by his Committee on Reconstruction and hoped the service school for women might be funded from campaign funds. For his part, Pelletier announced the Knights would have their secretaries at home and abroad gather information about the help the soldiers wanted with vocational education and reemployment. He said Knight Peter Collins would develop a comprehensive plan for those efforts.[9]

Given the tension between the Knights and the CSWA, Muldoon asked for a frank discussion of their differences. According to Burke's account, Pelletier "unexpectedly" and "with great emphasis" accused him and the CSWA of sending out "detectives to spy on Knights of Columbus secretaries," of secretly opening a service club in Chicago (see below), and of surreptitiously establishing a service school to train female war workers. Caught by surprise, Burke, "with a good deal of heat and as emphatically as I could," countered that "the charges were absolutely false." He had investigated the allegations of spying; the CSWA had publicly announced its intention to establish the club in Chicago; he personally informed William

Mulligan, chairman of the Knights' War Activities Committee, about plans for the service school. According to Pelletier's version, Burke was calling him a liar. He approached Burke at meeting's end to shake hands and wish him a Happy Thanksgiving, "rather than let [him] depart in anger." His overture met with stony silence that left him unsettled. Burke's recollection was that Pelletier apologized, the matter was closed, and the two engaged in friendly conversation.[10]

The next day, with Pelletier on his way home, Burke and Mulligan teamed up to secure passage of a resolution stipulating neither the Knights nor CSWA would establish a hostess house where the other already had one without prior agreement between the two of them—Burke and Mulligan. The executive committee then instructed the CSWA's Committee on Reconstruction to develop a plan of action, complete with budget and timetable, and submit it within two weeks for approval by the Administrative Committee.[11]

Meanwhile, Pelletier stopped in New York to see Wynne and report his version of what transpired at the meeting. Wynne began to work with McGinley to discredit Burke and the CSWA, if not the War Council itself. Pelletier's account convinced Wynn the CSWA intended to compete in reconstruction work with the Knights, rather than the other way around. He believed Burke, the "Chief manipulator," was hoping to get half, or at least a third, of the War Council's campaign funds. "They want that money," Wynne told McGinley, "& if they can't get all they want, they'll take all they can." He considered the proposed service school a scheme by Burke's executive secretary, Walter Hooke, "for salary & influence in the 'reconstruction' movement." As will be seen, the idea for the school was Burke's and William Kerby's. Wynne urged the Knights to begin a publicity campaign "with a vengeance" about their reconstruction work. He doubted the CSWA had the first clue about how to educate veterans or help them find work. "The hardest part of every great enterprise," he told McGinley, "is to overcome the opposition of those who should be first *and strongest* to aid in it." For his part, Wynne said he would "try a few things … that will bring about a reconsideration on the part of these men."[12]

He got an unidentified New York Knight to write to Paulist Father Bertrand Conway. The writer averred that the Knights believed the Paulists favored and supported Catholic lay activity, so they found it hard to reconcile "why your most prominent member here, Father Burke, should be their downright enemy." Burke had antagonized them "bitterly" and turned others in the War Council against them. He treated Pelletier "shamefully and scandalously" at a meeting of the executive committee. He also sought to manipulate the Knights out of their war-work funds. "My God," the writer concluded, "is one man to undo all that Catholics have done in this work, and that man a member of the American Community which seemed born to promote lay activity?"[13]

Wynne also had an unidentified New York journalist write to Cardinal James Gibbons. Without mentioning Burke, the newsman said word leaked that the War Council wanted to divert campaign funds from the Knights "to other purposes for the Church or Churchmen." Local reporters were salivating over prospect of such a story and taunting the letter-writer "with this new proof as they regard it, that clericalism is as strong in the Roman Catholic Church in the U.S. as in France or Italy." The writer urged Gibbons to encourage the Knights and ensure that the funds were used for the purposes collected.[14]

Wynne himself spoke with Conway "about the feeling of the leaders of the Knights against Father Burke." Conway encouraged him to write Superior General John Hughes. Wynne explained to Hughes that he was not lodging a complaint against Burke; he was reporting "the sentiments" of the Knights so that Hughes might understand why their monetary generosity toward the Paulists might not be as much as in the past. Burke had made them feel they were no longer wanted in war work. As a postscript, Wynne said he wrote this letter "after a day of meetings with various groups of Knights, whom I have exhorted to hope for kindlier treatment and relations." Thus, he painted himself as peacemaker or impartial arbitrator, rather than the meddler, if not manipulator, he was.[15]

The next day Wynne wrote to Gibbons about strained relations between the Knights and the War Council for the past year and a half. The situation had become "serious." Without naming Burke, Wynne averred the War Council had given the Knights the impression their effort was "not fully appreciated" and now sought to limit their activity or "perhaps to do away with them entirely." Wynne believed a break between the two would be "deplorable" for the Church because it would justify the "reproach of clericalism." He offered to speak with Gibbons about this "menacing catastrophe."[16] Finding Wynne's news "painful" and earnestly desiring "harmony be restored as soon as possible," Gibbons invited Wynne to see him.[17]

Meanwhile, Hughes assured Wynne the Paulists always supported the Knights. Completely in the dark about matters, he could only pass Wynne's letter along to Burke, which was certainly not the outcome the Jesuit hoped for. Burke averred to Wynne that he had "never opposed the Knights of Columbus in any way." Indeed, he had supported, encouraged, and defended their work with servicemen. While promoting Catholic support of the war effort, he was careful that "no other organization has been allowed to interfere with the K. of C. nor to occupy the field which the K. of C. have put down as their own." So strongly did Burke feel about the accusation, he told Wynne: "I would offer my resignation in a minute if my presence were an obstacle or a hindrance in any way. And I think such resignation ought to be offered whether I thought myself innocent or blameworthy." He asked Wynne's permission to send the Administrative Committee copies of his letter so the bishops might judge for themselves whether he should resign. Burke thanked Wynne for his "good work in striving to promote Catholic unity in this work" and offered to meet with him.[18]

Wynne's letter gave Burke pause. Correctly identifying his outburst against Pelletier as source of the trouble, he sent Pelletier a friendly letter to say he felt no antipathy toward him. He said his emphatic response to accusations by the Knights was to show only they were false, "not to make any attack upon you personally." Burke thought their handshake and friendly words after the meeting had mended things. He asked pardon for any offense. The letter gladdened Pelletier, who assured Burke that though he had taken the remarks personally, he now understood Burke's irritation was at the charges, not at him.[19]

Even as Burke dealt with Wynne and Pelletier, a new issue arose. Rumor had it the CTCA's Committee of Eleven, which oversaw campaign funds, intended to withhold them until participating organizations submitted revised budgets in light of war's end. Muldoon told Burke to see John Agar about this since he belonged to that committee. Burke impressed on Agar "the urgent necessity" of taking some action to demonstrate the committee did not intend to impound the money. Before Agar could do anything, Knight James Phelan, also a member of the Committee of Eleven, made the matter public in Boston, causing great excitement. Splaine telephoned Burke from there to say "he was sitting on a lid which held down a good amount of explosive material." Phelan contended Agar was ineligible to serve on the committee and his failure to join the CTCA's trip to France left Catholic interests there unrepresented. In early December, Raymond Fosdick met with the Committee of Eleven's finance subcommittee whereat Agar introduced and secured passage of a resolution authorizing the treasurer of the War-Work Campaign to begin disbursing funds once 20 percent of pledges had been collected.[20]

Burked informed Muldoon of this successful outcome. "Not to let myself feel too comfortable," he added, "a well known Jesuit father wrote to my superior about my war work." He was awaiting permission to send the letter to the administrative bishops. Rather than meet with Burke or permit him to forward the complaint, Wynne asked return of the letter so that he could see what he had written because he had kept no copy. An untruth. After returning it, Wynne and Burke carried on a fruitless exchange over what had or had not been said to Pelletier at the November meeting.[21]

While this transpired, McGinley sent Wynne a "cheque, quite a generous one," to cover the expense of his trip to Chicago. Given the overpayment, Wynne replied, "I shall devote the additional to a little propaganda work, and hope to get some results in a week or so." He enclosed copies of his letters against Burke and the CSWA, along with those he had encouraged others to write to the Paulists and Gibbons. McGinley forwarded copies to the members of the Knights' Board of Directors.[22]

The next step in Wynne's propaganda campaign was to argue the case personally to Gibbons, whom he saw in mid-December. The cardinal was surprised there was friction between the Knights and War Council. He had nothing but praise for the order and its war work. He said there must be no thought of the Knights' withdrawal from it; such was unthinkable. Wynne explained the Knights believed the War Council wanted to withhold their share of funds and use the money to duplicate their initiatives on a large scale. Wynne stressed the Knights wanted their full share distributed to them as soon as the War Council got the money. Aware of rumors about the Committee of Eleven, Gibbons averred he could not see how it had authority to withhold money. Wynne told him Agar and Hooke had swayed the members. He claimed the Knights' "only fault" was that their total absorption in war work had prevented them from realizing the importance of frequent contact with the Administrative Committee. Wynne found Gibbons uninterested in such matters. Rather, he insisted on the main point: there must be harmony between the bishops and the Knights.[23]

Muldoon—still unaware of the specific accusations against Burke, Agar, and Hooke—informed McGinley of the Administrative Committee's approval of the plan submitted by the CSWA's Committee on Reconstruction including vocational education and re-employment. In a spirit of cooperation, he asked Burke and Splaine to consult with the Knights about it so "as far as possible to have it all a joint program." He hoped this could be accomplished "as we must work as one body in some of these activities."[24] Thus, he paved the way for the Knights' participation in reconstruction work as a cooperative effort. Following up on the matter, Burke wrote to McGinley to say that "it is more clear than ever that we ought to work together and know what each other is doing." Though he begged McGinley to appoint someone to interface with the CSWA about reconstruction, Burke would have to take that initiative.[25]

Just before Christmas, Wynne widened his attack, writing to Bishop Thomas Shahan, rector of Catholic University and close associate of Gibbons. He said he had "been working hard the past few weeks trying to prevent a break" between the Knights and War Council. He had held meeting after meeting "to get at the root of the trouble," but he doubted he would succeed. In these discussions, he had "learned that the Knights could not understand why so many of your men [faculty members] act as is [*sic* for if] opposed to them." He thought the Knights were justified, "at least by appearances," in this belief. It was "the devil's handiwork." The Knights had thought of approaching Shahan, but "had lost confidence." Wynne said he could not get them to approach the hierarchy at all.[26]

In fact, three of Shahan's faculty members belonged to the CSWA: Fathers Peter Guilday, William Kerby, and John O'Grady. The first two were members of committees not even remotely connected to the work of the Knights. O'Grady was secretary of the Committee on Reconstruction. Extant correspondence of the Knights mentions none of them.

Two days later, Wynne wrote to the Administrative Committee. He spoke of friction between the CSWA and the Knights and said members of the former "were determined, as far as possible, to eliminate the K of C from war activities." The Knights felt "their cooperation in war work was no longer wanted, and that they were disposed to retire." Wynne discouraged them from doing so. Unfortunately, actions of some at the November meeting did little to reassure them. The Knights believed neither the Board of Archbishops nor the Administrative Committee would approve of the actions of "those who appear to be running this affair," a thinly disguised reference to Burke, Agar, and Hooke. Wynne said the more he observed and spoke with those on both sides, the more he believed that even though those managing the council claimed "they do not wish to eliminate the K of C, they are, in effect, actually eliminating them." He thought a breach between the two organizations would scandalize Catholics. Action should be taken at once because the Supreme Board of the Knights was to meet in New York in January 1919 and would no doubt decide whether or not to continue their war work. "The Knights," said Wynne, "do not know I am writing."[27] The last statement was technically true. He did not forward a copy of this letter to the Knights, as previously.[28]

Scour the minutes of the War Council executive committee as one might, one is hard pressed to see how the Knights might feel unwanted or that they were being pushed out of war work, except for their pique at not being given custody of their portion of the United War Work funds. In fact, Pelletier continued to try to build a legal case that money to support work for servicemen had actually been contributed to the Knights rather than the War Council, although even Phelan considered his argument unconvincing.[29]

Muldoon told Wynne his letter was perplexing because he was unaware "of any severe antagonism between the Knights of Columbus and the other members of the National Catholic War Council." He said if Wynne's informant would read to him the minutes of the meeting in question, he could see for himself. Muldoon had always encouraged the Knights and CSWA to work harmoniously. He could not believe either McGinley or Flaherty would make such claims as Wynne expressed. "There is no friction, and there is no antagonism, as far as I, as chairman, am concerned," declared Muldoon, "and I know that I can speak for the rest of the Administrative Committee." He was "extremely sorry" Wynne had written to Gibbons, "as no doubt it will give him pain and he may get a wrong impression." He wished Wynne would have come to the Administrative

Committee first. Muldoon declared he would take no notice of the matter until he heard directly from the Knights themselves.[30]

Recounting to Burke what he told Wynne, Muldoon said he had written to Flaherty to express surprise that a complaint should have come in this manner. "Exactly what is in the wind I do not know," he wrote, "but I do think that gossip is partly accountable both for the condition of mind of some people and for [Wynne's] letter." Muldoon stated "very firmly" neither Wynne nor anyone else was "going to stampede me." "If there is any real reason for complaint," he told Burke, "we will take it up and settle it in a broad, honorable and businesslike way."[31]

Wynne could not understand why Muldoon was upset with him. He explained his information had come from the Knights themselves and also from members of the CSWA, though it remains a mystery who those might have been. He had written to Gibbons "not to give him pain, or a wrong impression, but to save him from both." Wynne even urged the Knights to make their case to the Board of Archbishops, but found them reluctant to do so. "I suppose I must bear with the proverbial fate of the peace-maker," he concluded, "but I shall accept it as a real beatitude if only proper relations be established between the parties now at variance."[32]

Meanwhile, Burke worked to smooth things over with the Knights. While in New York for the holidays, he met with McGinley on Christmas afternoon. He took with him, perhaps as a witness, Charles Denechaud, who was both a Knight and chairman of the CSWA's Committee on Men's Activities. Burke spoke of the necessity of cooperation between the two organizations and of his desire "not to do anything that would seem like interference or duplication." He explained the importance of having a Knight to collaborate with the Committee on Reconstruction. Such a Knight could join O'Grady in meetings with the Federal Board of Vocational Training and would be able to speak authoritatively about the Knights' role in the matter. Burke assured that the plans of the Knights would be given first consideration. Absent a Knight liaison, cooperation between the CSWA and Knights "would be impossible and steps would almost inevitably be taken that would beget misunderstanding." McGinley agreed and said until the Supreme Board made the appointment, Daniel Callahan, a member of the War Council's executive board, would serve as liaison.[33]

Two days later, Burke met with Callahan. He asked straightforwardly if the CSWA's reconstruction program interfered in any way with the work of the Knights. Callahan mistakenly thought that at the November meeting, the War Council executive committee had established a new Joint Committee on Reconstruction, consisting of Knights and members of the CSWA, to develop the plan recently submitted to the Administrative Committee. Burke showed him the minutes which clearly indicated that the CSWA's Committee on Reconstruction had been asked to develop the program. He explained its plan and urged the Knights to appoint a representative to collaborate with O'Grady. Callahan said that there was no need of that.[34]

At that point, O'Grady joined them. Burke explained that he told O'Grady that in the selection of leaders for the reemployment project, he give preference to Knights as a way of demonstrating cooperation with the order. This would come back to haunt Burke. O'Grady thought it would be good to have an official representative of the Knights to comment on the acceptability of those appointees. Callahan assured the two men the CSWA was not interfering with the work of the Knights. When Burke informed him of Wynne's letter to Muldoon about their dissatisfaction with the CSWA, Callahan was puzzled and told Burke to "send [Muldoon] word that there was really no cause for worry." He suggested Burke and William Mulligan serve as a coordinating committee of two. Until Mulligan returned from France, Callahan himself would act in that capacity. The Knight then urged Burke to attend the upcoming meeting of the Supreme Board of Directors in New York City, which the priest agreed to do.[35]

Burke reported to Muldoon: "One feels that there is something further back that has not been touched.... Mr. Callahan assures me everything is satisfactory—but I still doubt." He feared if Callahan's misconception about the appointment of "an entirely new sort of joint committee on Reconstruction" was widespread among Knights, "then they would think we weren't abiding by the decision of the Executive Board."[36] His misgivings were well founded, not because the Knights were confused about a joint committee, but because they planned to go ahead with their own separate reconstruction work. The rivalry begun in August 1917 continued to play itself out. Since the Knights considered themselves equal to and independent of the CSWA, they refused to collaborate with it. Coordination between the two organizations would happen, if at all, on the highest level—between their chosen leaders, Mulligan and Burke.

Muldoon replied that Burke had "done all possible and it is now up to the K. of C. to do their part." The bishop had gotten feedback indicating his letter to Flaherty would bring the issue to a head. "Time to stop gossip and deal as full gown men," he told Burke. "I will let you know what I hear. In the meantime plod on. Don't worry it is bad for the kidneys they say."[37]

On New Year's Day, Burke called on Bishop Patrick Hayes, a member of the Administrative Committee. Hayes said he too had received a letter from Wynne, but had not responded. Burke explained that Callahan had invited him to the meeting of the Supreme Board of Directors, and in light of Wynne's letters, he thought it wise to attend. Hayes concurred.[38]

When Burke returned to Washington, he learned Shahan was upset about relations between the Knights and the War Council and wanted an explanation. Burke gave him one, but complained to Muldoon that, "of course, it is a great loss of time to be 'explaining.'" He wished he could have seen Gibbons as well, but had to get back to New York for the meeting of the Knights. Instead, he wrote informing Gibbons of his meetings with McGinley and Callahan, and reporting both had assured him there was no dissatisfaction on the part of the Knights with the War Council. Burke promised to see him at once on his return from New York. "I trust Your Eminence will not be disturbed or worried about the matter."[39]

By the time Burke attended the meeting of the Supreme Board, he was well aware of Wynne's letter-writing campaign. On arrival at the Waldorf-Astoria Hotel, he ran into Wynne. In the exchange that followed, there was disingenuousness on Wynne's part. About his letter to Hughes, he asked, "You sent it to Bishop Muldoon, did you not?" His assumption that Burke had forwarded it brought the startled reply, "I did not." Burke reminded Wynne that he never received permission: "You asked its return saying you would like to formulate the definite charges of the Knights. This you did not do; and of course I never sent the letter." Wynne said the only reason he wrote to Muldoon was that he thought Burke had forwarded it. This remark was tantamount to saying Burke was not a man of his word, while covering the fact that Wynne's letters to the administrative bishops and to Shahan were part of his wider attack.[40]

Retiring to a room where they could talk privately, Burke found Wynne remarkably ill-informed about the constitution and make-up of the War Council. He explained that he and Mulligan were a committee of two to coordinate the efforts of the CSWA and the Knights. Rather pointedly, he remarked "how lamentable the gossip, falsehoods, [and] misunderstandings were; how we all owe a great duty to Catholic Unity and emphasized the necessity of having everything cleared up."[41] Burke intended to do just that: beard the lion in its den.

On joining the meeting of the Supreme Board, Burke was invited to speak. He declared straightway the reason that brought him there: "That it was stated that the National Catholic War Council was endeavoring to handicap the Knights of Columbus; to block their work; that I had shown myself antagonistic to the Knights of Columbus; that [the] Special Activities Committee [CSWA] had interfered with and was taking up the work of the Knights of Columbus; that Father Wynne had written letters to this effect to me and to the members of the Administrative Committee." Burke declared the accusations "were unfounded," that the Knights "were worried by groundless fears and unsupported rumor and gossip." He was present so they could confront him with their evidence; "that in a word all the cards should be placed face upward on the table: that for the welfare of the Church all should work in Catholic unity."[42]

Pointed questions followed. An excited Martin Carmody of Michigan wanted to know why Burke had voted against the resolution in November to give the Knights five-sixths of the campaign funds. The question convinced Burke that they had been misinformed. He replied he had not voted against the resolution because no such resolution had been proposed. A number of Knights asked why not. Others declared the War Council would give the Knights no money. Again, Burke averred their fears were groundless. He was certain the bishops of the Administrative Committee would support a motion to guarantee the Knights five-sixths of the funds and he himself would introduce it. Luke Hart of Missouri wanted to know why there had never been a clear division of work between the Knights and the CSWA. Burke told him that the Administrative Committee had indeed delineated the activities of each when the War Council was reorganized in January 1918. As recently as November, the committee had repeated the division of labor. Burke then explained which tasks were assigned to each.[43]

His reassurances had little immediate effect. Speeches that followed over the next four hours were impassioned, many of them long, and most of them calling for the War Council to pass a resolution guaranteeing the Knights five-sixths of the war funds. Burke restated his promise to introduce one. Fortunately, Hayes was in attendance and declared he would support the measure. He also praised the Knights for their war work. Burke begged for appointment of a committee of Knights to cooperate with the CSWA in order to avoid friction in reconstruction work. When Dr. Edward Buckley of Minnesota moved that the Knights' War Activities Committee cooperate with the CSWA, McGinley stated the resolution was unnecessary because the Knights' committee already had authorization to engage in reconstruction work independently of the CSWA.[44]

Then, Wynne made a plea for unity. Burke noted his remarks were not without a parting shot at the CSWA. Wynne claimed that two of its members—both unnamed—had shown animosity toward the Knights, and added that a professor at Catholic University—also unnamed—had told him that members of the CSWA believed O'Grady's appointment of Knights to its reemployment work was a way to absorb the order into the War Council. Thus did he picture Burke's attempt at cooperation with the Knights as evidence of sabotage. Still, Wynne averred that the day's session had produced much good. He now believed things would proceed smoothly.[45]

A frustrated Burke reported to Muldoon that the Administrative Committee must insist that some effective committee of Knights be appointed to interface with the CSWA because McGinley asserted the Knights and CSWA would each do their reconstruction work independently. "That is synonymous with friction," wrote Burke. Nor did he think the Knights on the War Council's executive committee were communicating clearly to their constituents the decisions it reached. He explained he had refuted many ungrounded statements, but had let many others pass, for "a man, corrected too often, gets angry." It was "unpleasant work and took hours of my time," he concluded, but thought it did good.[46]

Hayes filed his own report to Muldoon. He said some Knights wanted the order to quit war work. Their reasons were several: the absence of a guarantee of five-sixths of the funds; the executive committee's refusal to give them custody of the money; Burke's use of War Council stationery and his signing himself as chairman, giving the impression he and the CSWA were the War Council; O'Grady's appointment of Knights to do reemployment work for the CSWA, giving the impression it would rather collaborate with individual Knights than with the order itself. Hayes thought Burke's offer to introduce a resolution assuring the Knights of five-sixths of the campaign funds went a long way to defusing the situation.[47]

Muldoon thanked Burke for his efforts. "I hope now all will be quiet," he wrote. He believed all the excitement "was manufactured and absolutely unnecessary." The Administrative Committee had promised the Knights the money and told them they would get it. "Gossips and inter meddlers did it," concluded Muldoon. As Burke pondered over what had transpired, he became convinced the Knights' Board of Directors was "perfectly willing to do the right thing in the line of hearty cooperation." He thought rumors and misrepresentations were "due to one or two persons." He never named those he suspected. He had seen Cardinal Gibbons, who was now "entirely satisfied with the situation."[48]

The Knights did have a point about Burke's use of War Council stationery, though they were probably oversensitive about it. Convenience and frugality more likely explain the situation. No doubt, Muldoon intervened when Hayes brought the matter to his attention. For several months thereafter, Burke continued to use the letterhead, but was careful to sign himself as chairman of the CSWA. By May 1919, he was using specially printed CSWA stationery. Moreover, he kept his word to the Knights. When the executive committee met in January 1919, it put on record the order was to receive five-sixths of the Catholic portion of campaign funds. It also appointed Burke and Mulligan a committee of two to coordinate matters concerning joint work of the CSWA and the Knights.[49]

Inharmonious Cooperation

Despite hope for harmony, the relationship between the CSWA and the Knights continued its dissonant way. While driven by a vision of Catholic unity and cooperation, Burke was also a stickler for order. "Order is heaven's first law," he confided to his diary later in life, "and it is also the first law of a soul that honestly seeks God, for order is justice."[50] Order was part of his spirituality. Things must be done in orderly fashion. Each subsidiary of the

War Council—the Knights and CSWA—must stick to its assigned tasks. If the two were to enter the same field of endeavor, their efforts must be coordinated.

The troubles over funding, augmented by Wynne, left lingering tones of distrust, resulting in a contredanse rather than a pas de deux. The partnered agencies, one rivalrous and the other suspicious, began the dance to the tune of hostess houses. The CSWA had established one in Chicago named the Columbus Hotel. McGinley complained to Muldoon that it charged for beds, which the Knights' houses did not do, and its name caused confusion. Unconcerned about rental of beds, Muldoon advised Burke the name deserved "serious consideration." Upon investigation, Burke learned the Chicago chapter of the War Council had named it without thought of the Knights. Signage, however, made clear it was under the auspices of the War Council. Since McGinley's protest concerned only Chicago, the CSWA deferred to that chapter of the War Council for further action.[51]

Meanwhile, Burke learned from the CSWA's Pershing Club in Baltimore that the Knights proposed to establish a club there too. Burke sent McGinley a curt note reminding him that he and Mulligan were to agree on opening a second club in the same city. Before Burke got a response, Muldoon heard rumors the Knights intended to set up their own hostess house in Chicago. He urged Burke to meet with McGinley as soon as possible because this, "of course, will only cause friction and dissatisfaction."[52]

With Mulligan overseas, Burke saw Callahan about it. Burke said if there was a genuine need for a second house in Chicago, he would have no objection. If the Knights did go forward, he asked them to coordinate with the War Council's house to avoid "interference or public difference." Callahan agreed.[53] Burke, however, considered the proposed club in Baltimore a direct violation of their agreement. Callahan explained that without authorization, a Knight had approached Gibbons about opening one there. Yet, Burke had heard from McGinley the Knights officially obtained the cardinal's permission. "But one mustn't push things too closely towards the truth!" he told Muldoon.[54]

During the face-off over hostess houses, publicity became an issue. At the executive committee meeting in January, Pelletier suggested publication of an article about the war activities of both the Knights and the CSWA.

The committee thought it advisable to begin a monthly bulletin to advertise the work. Burke learned from Fosdick that United War Work funds could be used for publicity. The committee delegated Burke and Mulligan to develop a report on the cost of the project for approval by the Administrative Committee.[55]

Again, in the absence of Mulligan, Burke and Callahan agreed that Burke become editor of the *Bulletin of the National Catholic War Council.* The Knights would devise and carry out plans for its distribution. They would also write and submit their own material for inclusion. Burke told Muldoon he would submit a proposal for size and cost of the bulletin, including printing and distribution.[56]

Before he could develop a budget, the War Activities Committee of the Knights nixed the project. McGinley sent Burke and Muldoon a copy of its resolution that in light of important pressing reconstruction work, such a publication was "not desirable and would not accomplish sufficient to justify the expense."[57] Burke politely replied that the War Council had decided a bulletin should be published. He noted the Knights' own resolution admitted important work was ahead, rendering a bulletin valuable. As to its cost, he reminded McGinley "no amount . . . was decided upon, and it could be kept to whatever figure we might determine." "Might I ask if your cooperation in some way is not possible?" concluded Burke. To Muldoon, he said to call the Knights' resolution "outrageous would be . . . mild."[58]

The contredanse continued as McGinley responded that Callahan had given the War Activities Committee the impression the project was being proposed tentatively. The committee thought its opinion was being asked about the value of such publication. Thus did McGinley put a willful interpretation on the matter. As Burke had already correctly pointed out to him, the War Council had decided to publish a bulletin. "If you will let us have a definite statement as to expenses, etc.," concluded McGinley, "we will be very glad to reconsider the matter."[59]

Burke sent a "definite statement," not to McGinley, but to Muldoon as the council had ordered. He recommended publication of a small monthly bulletin with a print run of 50,000 copies to go gratis to priests, lay societies, convents, Catholic colleges, and Catholic institutions. Such would require $3,000 ($54,000 in 2024) in overhead and $2,000

($36,000) per month in printing and distribution. Muldoon forwarded the estimate to colleagues on the Administrative Committee. In his view, it was "important that the Bulletin be published as soon as possible if it is to accomplish any real good." The committee approved.[60]

Burke twice asked McGinley to have the Knights contribute an article to the first issue. Receiving no reply, he pleaded with Mulligan to give the matter "immediate attention" so the *Bulletin* could cover Catholic war activity "as a whole—of which the K. of C. forms such a notable part." Of course, McGinley had received both Burke's letters and forwarded them to Mulligan to ask if the War Council indeed decided on a bulletin. No doubt informed it had, McGinley chose not to respond to Burke. Mulligan, however, did. He explained the Knights' *Columbiad* went to its half million members and was read by more than 3 million people. Therefore, the Knights decided against "any further publication." Mulligan told Burke the Knights' News Service would provide him with information about their work "from time to time." He asked John Kennedy, director of that service, to send Burke an article.[61] It offered a brief, one-page summary of their war work, which concluded with a paragraph about the Knights' activity with re-employment of veterans—which would be the final step in the contredanse.[62]

In April 1919 the Knights assigned Collins to work full-time on re-employment. His plan called for each of the Knights' 1,750 councils to establish five committees covering agriculture, business, industry, professions, and vocations. The committees were to enlist members from those occupational groups to help find veterans jobs. This program paralleled that of the CSWA's Committee on Reconstruction which was establishing employment bureaus around the nation, many of them staffed by Knights.[63]

In May, Burke and Collins met to discuss overlap of effort. Burke said the Knights' program actually duplicated what the Administrative Committee had assigned to the CSWA. He had no desire to deprive them of entering that work; his sole concern was mutual coordination of effort "so that there might be concord and cooperation." Burke said Muldoon too "was very anxious" for harmonious action in it.[64] The two were then joined by Mulligan and O'Grady. The latter explained the Committee on Reconstruction had secured the services of P. J. Hanley, a prominent Knight in Oregon, to help coordinate the effort with Knights in the West. It had already established some twenty-eight offices around the nation and sixty more were being operated jointly with other organizations. Knights were running a number of the CSWA's independent offices.[65]

O'Grady presented a memorandum of agreement which he and Burke had worked out. It stipulated the CSWA should continue working in places it already was and the Knights in those offices would do so under supervision of the CSWA. All new work would be undertaken by special arrangement between the CSWA and the Knights. Finally, re-employment work in offices jointly operated was to be in the name of the "National Catholic War Council, Knights of Columbus."[66]

Burke reported to Muldoon he found Collins and Mulligan cooperative. The Knights accepted the memorandum as the best path forward, but said they must submit it to their War Activities Committee. "Father O'Grady was not hopeful of the outcome," commented Burke. "I cannot report to you that I am confident of a happy result. The organization [the Knights of Columbus], not the work, fills their vision." This last statement revealed that Burke understood the underlying conflict: his vision was of united, coordinated Catholic action (the Mystical Body); the Knights' vision was self-centered, on how the work would enhance their reputation. Muldoon replied he had seen Pelletier in Boston and told him "for the good of all concerned there must be cooperation." He hoped "there will be a fair understanding."[67]

Reporting to the Knights, Collins considered Burke's "rather far fetched" assertion that re-employment had been assigned to the CSWA as a preemptive strike to undercut their own claim to it. Betraying stunning ignorance, Collins said he had been and still was under the impression that the War Council "had either not been established or was not functioning as such" in early 1918. He could not understand why Burke, O'Grady, and Muldoon were so insistent on cooperation.[68] In other words, the CSWA was "butting in" on work begun by the Knights, one for which the order was eminently suited. In reality, the Knights were in fact entering a work given to the CSWA.

The War Activities Committee considered the memorandum in May, and both Collins and McGinley separately communicated its decision to Burke. They said Pelletier had begun plans for the Knights' re-employment work prior to the November meeting of the War Council executive committee, and they proceeded to carry them out. The War Activities Committee was unaware of any friction or duplication of work with the CSWA. The task was "approached from different points of view by different organizations and different civic bodies and there seems to be room enough for all."[69]

To Muldoon Burke wrote, "It is not a hopeful outlook but I do hope that by patience and careful handling we can avoid too great public friction." The Knights had completely disregarded that reemployment had been assigned to the CSWA. "But that," wrote Burke, "is an old story."[70]

In the practical order, there was more than enough work to go around, and the Knights' 1,750 councils provided a broader base of action than did the CSWA's nearly 100 employment bureaus. On the other hand, a matter of principle had been at stake. The Knights' independent course upset proper order of the War Council, which embodied Burke's vision of national Catholic unity. Their uncooperative attitude irritated him. Perhaps at the heart of it all were two diverse perceptions: what Burke viewed as right order, the Knights saw as domination. In existence since 1882, they were not about to bow before an upstart organization like the War Council, even if it did have episcopal blessing. Their continued unwillingness to bend or to play a subservient role portended future difficulties.

ENDNOTES TO CHAPTER 6

1. Burke, *Christ in Us*, 5.
2. Pelletier to Muldoon, 5 September 1918, ACUA, NCWC 10:4:29. For Pelletier's attitude, see Pelletier to Agar, 12 December 1917, copy, ACUA, NCWC 10:6:28.
3. Minutes of the Executive Committee of the National Catholic War Council, 18 October 1918, ACUA, NCWC 10:1:19; Williams, *Catholics in War*, 183–217; McKeown, *War and Welfare*, 149–54.
4. Minutes of Special Meeting of Supreme Board of Directors, 22–23 November 1918, AKC, SC–16–1–0103; Wynne to McGinley, ibid., SC–16–1–0103; Anonymous Knight to Bertrand Conway, C.S.P., 29 November 1918, copy, ibid.; A New York Journalist to Gibbons, 30 November 1918, copy, ibid; [Wynne, Memorandum of Interview with Cardinal Gibbons, undated (probably during the week of 9 December 1918)], ibid., SC–16–1–0114.
5. Minutes of Special Meeting of Supreme Board of Directors, 22–23 November 1918, AKC, SC–16–1–0103.

6. Pelletier to Muldoon, 29 October 1918, ACUA, NCWC 10:7:19; *National Catholic War Council: Committee on Special War Activities Report to Commission on Training Camp Activities*, 12.
7. Burke to Muldoon, 19 November 1918, copy, ACUA, NCWC 10:7:19.
8. Minutes of the Executive Committee of the National Catholic War Council, 26 November 1918, ACUA, NCWC 10:1:19.
9. Ibid.; Wynne to McGinley, Thanksgiving Day [28 November] 1918, AKC, SC–16–1–0104; Peter W. Collins to Burke, 28 May 1919, copy, ibid., SC–16–1–0148; Kauffman, *Faith and Fraternalism*, 224.
10. Minutes of the Executive Committee of the War Council, 27 November 1918, ACUA, NCWC 10:1:19; Burke to Wynne, 6 December 1918, copy, ibid., USCCB 10:153:14; Pelletier to Burke, 17 December 1918, ibid., copy in AKC, SC–16–1–0114.
11. Minutes of the Executive Committee of the War Council, 27 November 1918, ACUA, NCWC 10:1:19.
12. Wynne to McGinley, Thanksgiving Day [28 November] 1918, AKC, SC–16–1–0104; Pelletier to Burke, 17 December 1918, ACUA, USCCB 10:153:14.
13. Unidentified Knight to Bertrand Conway, [29 November 1918], copy, AKC, SC–16–1–0104.
14. A New York Journalist to Gibbons, 30 November 1918, copy, AKC, SC–16–1–0104.
15. Wynne to Hughes, 1 December 1918, ACUA, USCCB 10:153:14, a copy in AKC, SC–16–1–0109.
16. Wynne to Gibbons, 2 December 1918, AAB-AASMSU, Gibbons Papers 123T2; a copy in, AKC, SC–16–1–0109.
17. Gibbons to Wynne, 4 December 1918, copy, AKC, SC–16–1–0110.
18. Hughes to Wynne, 3 December 1918, copy, AKC, SC–16–1–0110; Burke to Wynne, 4 December 1918, AP, Official Papers of Superior General Hughes, January 1916 to May 1919. A copy of this letter is in AKC, SC–16–1–0110.
19. Burke to Pelletier, 6 December 1918, copy, ACUA, USCCB 10:153:14; Pelletier to Burke, 17 December 1918, ibid.
20. Burke to Muldoon, 4 December 1918, ACUA, NCWC 10:4:29.
21. Ibid.; Wynne to Burke, 5 December 1918, ACUA, USCCB 10:153:14; Burke to Wynne, 15 December 1918, copy, ibid.; Wynne to Burke, 16 December 1918, ibid.; Burke to Wynne, 17 December 1918, copy, ibid.; Wynne to Burke, 23 December 1918, ibid.; Burke to Wynne, 26 December 1918, copy, ibid.; Burke to Muldoon, 6 January 1919, ACUA, NCWC 10:4:29.
22. Wynne to McGinley, 4 December 1918, AKC, SC–16–1–0110.
23. [Wynne, Memorandum of Interview with Cardinal Gibbons, undated (probably 12 or 13 December 1918)], copy, AKC, SC–16–1–0114.
24. Muldoon to McGinley, 21 December 1918, AKC, SC–16–1–0126.
25. Burke to McGinley, 22 December 1918, SC–16–1–0115.

26. Wynne to Thomas Shahan, 21 December 1918, AAB-AASMSU, Gibbons Papers 124C13.
27. Wynne to Muldoon, 23 December 1918, ACUA, NCWC 10:4:29.
28. Wynne to McGinley, 4 December 1918, copy, AKC, SC–16–1–0110.
29. James J. Phelan to Pelletier, 7 December 1918, copy, ACUA, NCWC 10:4:29.
30. Muldoon to Wynne, 27 December 1918, copy, ACUA, NCWC 10:4:29.
31. Muldoon to Burke, 28 December 1918, ACUA, NCWC 10:7:20.
32. Wynne to Muldoon, 30 December 1918, ACUA, NCWC 10:4:29.
33. Burke, Memorandum of Conversation with William McGinley, 25 December 1918, enclosure with Burke to Muldoon, 28 December 1918, ACUA, NCWC 10:3:37.
34. Burke, Memorandum of Conversation with Daniel J. Callahan, 28 December 1918, enclosure with Burke to Muldoon, 28 December 1918, ACUA, NCWC 10:3:37.
35. Ibid.
36. Burke to Muldoon, 28 December 1918, ACUA, NCWC 10:3:37.
37. Muldoon to Burke, 29 December 1918, copy, ACUA, NCWC 10:7:20.
38. Burke to Muldoon, 3 January 1918, ACUA, NCWC 10:3:38.
39. Burke to Gibbons, 3 January 1919, AAB-AASMSU, Gibbons Papers 124F6; Burke to Muldoon, 3 January 1918, ACUA, NCWC 10:3:38.
40. Burke to Muldoon, 6 January 1919, ACUA, NCWC 10:4:29.
41. Ibid.
42. Ibid.; "Board of Directors: Minutes of Regular Quarterly Meeting at Hotel Waldorf-Astoria, New York, 4 January 1919," *Columbiad* 26 (February 1919): 11.
43. Burke to Muldoon, 6 January 1919, ACUA, NCWC 10:4:29.
44. Ibid.; "Board of Directors: Minutes," 11.
45. Burke to Muldoon, 6 January 1919, ACUA, NCWC 10:4:29; "Board of Directors: Minutes," 11
46. Burke to Muldoon, 6 January 1919, ACUA, NCWC 10:4:29.; Patrick Hayes to Muldoon, 6 January 1919, ibid., 10:4:11.
47. Hayes to Muldoon, 6 January 1919, ACUA, NCWC 10:4:11; "Board of Directors: Minutes," 11.
48. Muldoon to Burke, 9 January 1919, ACUA, NCWC 10:7:20; Burke to Muldoon, 12 January 1919, ibid., 10:3:38.
49. Minutes of the Executive Committee of the War Council, 22 January 1919, ACUA, NCWC 10:1:19.
50. Burke Diary, 2 August 1935, AP, Burke Papers, box 30.
51. McGinley to Muldoon, 17 January 1919, ACUA, NCWC 10:7:21; Muldoon to Burke, 28 January 1919, ibid.; Burke to Muldoon, 2 February 1919, copy, ibid.; Minutes of the Meeting of the CSWA, 13 February 1919, ibid., 10:1:6.

52. Burke to McGinley, 2 February 1919, copy, AKC, SC–16–1–0126; Muldoon to Burke, 26 February 1919, ACUA, NCWC 10:7:21.
53. Burke to Muldoon, 15 March 1919, copy, ACUA, NCWC 10:7:21.
54. Ibid.
55. Minutes of the Executive Committee of the War Council, 22 January 1919, ACUA, NCWC 10:1:19.
56. Burke to Muldoon, 15 March 1919, copy, ACUA, NCWC 10:7:21 (quote is here); Burke to Muldoon, 22 March 1919, ibid., 10:3:38.
57. McGinley to Burke, 20 March 1919, copy, AKC, SC–16–1–0135; McGinley to Muldoon, 20 March 1919, copy, ACUA, NCWC 10:7:21.
58. Burke to McGinley, 22 March 1919, AKC, SC–16–1–0135; Burke to Muldoon, 22 March 1919, ACUA, NCWC 10:3:38.
59. McGinley to Burke, 3 April 1919, copy, AKC, SC–16–1–0138.
60. Burke to Muldoon, 6 April 1919, ACUA, NCWC 10:3:39 (Muldoon's comment is written on the back of the letter with instructions to have it copied and sent to other committee members); Burke to Muldoon, 13 April 1919, ibid.
61. McGinley to Mulligan, 13 May 1919, copy; Burke to McGinley, 14 May 1919; Burke to Mulligan, 14 May 1919; Mulligan to Burke, 15 May 1919, copy—all in AKC, SC–16–1–0147.
62. John B. Kennedy, "Where the K. of C. War Work Stands," *NCWC Bulletin* 1 (June 1919): 4.
63. Leo Hillman, "Our National House Warming," *Columbiad* 26 (June 1919): 7–9; Peter W. Collins, "Stand Behind the Doughboy and God," ibid. (July 1919): 9–10; Kauffman, *Faith and Fraternalism*, 224–25; Aaron I. Abell, *American Catholicism and Social Action: A Search for Social Justice, 1865–1950* (Garden City, New York: Hanover House, 1960), 194.
64. Peter Collins to the War Activities Committee of the Knights of Columbus, 22 May 1919, AKC, SC–16–1–0148.
65. Ibid.
66. Ibid.
67. Burke to Muldoon, 21 May 1919, copy, ACUA, NCWC 10:7:22; Muldoon to Burke, 24 May [1919], ibid.
68. Peter Collins to the War Activities Committee of the Knights of Columbus, 22 May 1919, AKC, SC–16–1–0148.
69. Minutes of the Committee on War Activities of the Knights of Columbus, 24 May 1919, AKC, SC–16–1–0148; Collins to Burke, 28 May 1919, copy, ibid.; McGinley to Burke, 29 May 1919, copy, ACUA, War Council NCWC 10:3:40; Kauffman, *Faith and Fraternalism*, 460, n.149.
70. Burke to Muldoon, 31 May 1919, ACUA, NCWC10:3:40.

Chapter 7
From War Council to Welfare Council

> The love of our neighbor, since it comes from God, is a habit of the soul: a habit that must first be accepted, adhered to: that is obeyed only by constant effort. Love of our neighbor does not necessarily mean sensible affection. Because we cannot feel this, we feign would excuse ourselves from keeping the commandment consciously before us. Love of our neighbor is love of God—the love whereby we actively love all His creatures because they are His creatures and our brothers.[1]

National Service School for Women

While sparring with the Knights of Columbus, John Burke founded an institution he would remain connected with for the rest of his life: the National Service School for Women. In November 1917, William Kerby submitted a plan to the original War Council for training social workers at Catholic University to serve in military camps. The council authorized Burke to chair an ad hoc committee to confer with university officials about the matter.[2] Unfortunately, the reorganization of the War Council derailed the idea.

Meanwhile, the government approved the YWCA to work in hostess houses at home and abroad. Located on or near bases, such houses offered soldiers a place to experience a home-like atmosphere and to visit relatives or sweethearts who lodged there. During 1918, the War Council's Committee on Women's Activities united Catholic women behind the war effort, and Burke negotiated with the government to have them open and run Catholic hostess houses. The War Department finally acquiesced in September. Burke chaired a subcommittee, including Kerby and Father

John Montgomery Cooper, to draw up plans for a school to train women. The plan won immediate approval, and Burke was directed to implement it.[3]

He leased a mansion on forty acres of woods and meadows in Georgetown Heights. Known as Clifton, it had a commanding view of Washington, though a bit remote; the nearest streetcar line ended two miles away. Vacant for nearly twenty-five years, the house desperately needed cleaning and care. Burke served as president of the new institution. Bishop Peter Muldoon offered a member of his Rockford flock, Maud Cavanaugh, as dean. She arrived on Armistice Day 1918, and was joined by Helen Cronin of Springfield, Massachusetts. Burke approved their decision to have students handle cleanup and domestic chores to help train them for later fieldwork, while instilling in them a sense of community.[4]

The school opened in November with twenty-eight women and five resident teachers. Combining practice with theory, the curriculum prepared them for tasks they would face at home and in France. Adjunct instructors from Catholic University included Kerby, Father John A. Ryan, and Father John O'Grady. The first lectured on Catholic principles of social work, the second on relief of poverty, and the third on public health. Spirituality, the driving force of Burke's life, was the soul of Clifton. Each day began with Mass, and, in addition to classes, there were religious conferences, many delivered by Burke. The young women felt profoundly transformed by the experience. For instance, Margaret Hennessy wrote: "the course [of study] was particularly gratifying … [b]ecause of the spiritual and Catholic atmosphere … which surrounded the work…. Social Service has a new and fuller meaning. Looking at it from the Catholic viewpoint … it is a Holy Work that I am about to do." Marie McPoland told Burke his "inspiring and convincing" conferences had touched her so that it would take years for her to appreciate completely their "full meaning."[5]

The first cohort graduated in January 1919. Burke and Cavanaugh handpicked nine for service overseas and sent the other nineteen to posts at home. Before departure for France, Burke led the nine in a three-day retreat at the Cenacle of St. Regis, the convent of Sister Helen Lynch. The exercises concluded with the graduates' recital of an act of consecration, written by Burke, committing themselves to imitate the selfless service of Jesus on behalf of humankind.[6]

Overseas, "Father Burke's girls," as they became known, earned an enviable reputation. When Raymond Fosdick went to France to check on operations of various service organizations, he wired to Frederick Keppel: "The workers sent over by Father Burke's special committee [CSWA] ... are excellent and more could be effectively used. Suggest you take up with Burke advisability of sending in reasonably large numbers." The second cohort of students began in March 1919 with a program expanded to three months. Given the pressing need for workers, however, the course of study was reduced back to seven weeks for the third and fourth cohorts. Ultimately, Burke sent more than fifty graduates overseas.[7]

A matter destined to become linked with Clifton was the need for a national organization of Catholic women. In reply to Muldoon's question about works that should continue postwar, Burke wrote "the big field for Catholic women's activities in the future will demand the development and direction of latent forces in Catholic women's organizations." The CSWA's Committee on Women's Activities had erected hostess houses and instituted girls' clubs and community centers. Several houses must continue because they were on permanent military bases. Moreover, Catholic women were the only welfare workers at Walter Reed Hospital, the army's premier medical center. Burke argued that if that work was "to continue in Catholic hands, the organization that conducts it must necessarily be national, for it must be in touch with the government, capable of transferring its workers from one place to another." Otherwise, the work would pass to the YWCA, a "calamity" if that were to happen. "The time is ripe," urged Burke. "There never can be a Catholic Y.W.C.A. unless it be organized under and controlled by the hierarchy."[8]

The urgency increased when the War Department informed Burke of its plan for a large peacetime army, which would necessitate continuance of large training camps. The government intended to make welfare work for soldiers permanent. For that purpose, the War Department would draw women workers from both the YWCA and the War Council at government pay. Such workers needed training. Burke asked and received authorization to continue Clifton on an almost permanent basis. He and Cavanaugh expanded the curriculum to six months, adding courses in sociology, economics, ethics, community organization, Americanization, public speaking, and recreational activities. It went into effect in fall 1919. At Cavanaugh's suggestion, Clifton began charging tuition of $300 ($5,400 in 2024) a semester.[9]

Not all sailing was smooth. Muldoon forwarded Burke the complaint of a priest in Washington alleging extravagance at Clifton. He claimed it was paying "high priced professors" from Catholic University $3 an hour (equivalent to $54) to teach rudimentary subjects like penmanship, arithmetic, and grammar. Some ten of them were teaching two hours per day each. Muldoon said he had heard that members of the CSWA were "very lavish with money." He could not vouch for the truth of any of this, but he urged Burke to keep an eye open. "We cannot be too careful."[10]

After investigation, Burke reported that the federal government paid the instructors. The CSWA had spent only $600 ($10,800 in 2024) for recreational equipment at Clifton. "It is too bad that these rumors are sent abroad," lamented Burke. "These charges … are utterly unfounded." He said he had encountered the same sort of allegations when in New York. With regard to extravagance, Burke wrote, "I think in fact I know, there is truth in the charges." Some employees had gone to Atlantic City on business and stayed at its most expensive hotel. Burke ordered a halt to the practice. He thanked Muldoon for bringing it to his attention.[11]

Motion Pictures: From Protest to Americanization

Burke also sought to preserve the public from indecent motion pictures. At war's end, the CTCA added an epilogue to *Fit to Fight* and renamed it *Fit to Win*. Billy Hale returned from France, bringing Kid McCarthy's girlfriend the medal awarded him posthumously for bravery. Billy then visited Chick Charlton suffering at home from gonorrheal arthritis, his distraught mother ignorant of its cause. He sympathized with Hank Simon and Jack Garvin now recovered from syphilis, and counseled them to avoid prostitutes and keep clean as civilians. The film concluded with Billy and his sweetheart at the altar.[12]

Both *Fit to Win* and *End of the Road* passed into the hands of the American Social Hygiene Association, which worked with the U.S. Public Health Service to fight venereal disease. The war had revealed five of six soldiers suffering from it contracted it as civilians. So, the agencies distributed both films commercially. Public exhibition breached the government's promise that *Fit to Fight* would be used only for the military. Burke urged the 15,000 Catholic lay societies countrywide to oppose public screening of these "indecent and suggestive" pictures for alleged "educational purposes." "Let the Catholic laity speak," he wrote. "Although we are a patient people, we shall not tolerate any violation of the standards for which Catholic manhood and womanhood stand." As a result, the government withdrew its endorsement and the films eventually faded from view.[13]

Like other progressives, Burke considered movies a tool for education as well as entertainment. He intended to make innovative use of them to address Americanization of immigrants, the focus of national attention for several reasons. Foremost was the influx of twenty-one million people from Eastern and Southern Europe between 1890 and 1914. The nation's liberal residency laws enabled them to incorporate easily into economic life without incorporating politically through citizenship. These immigrants settled in urban ethnic enclaves where they maintained their language and culture and retained strong ties to their homelands.[14]

A related issue was German-Americans, who had entered in the decades before those just mentioned. Their intense ethnic pride manifested itself in German-language newspapers, societies, parishes, and parochial schools. During America's period of neutrality (1914–1917), German-American and Irish-American Catholics took the side of Germany rather than England and France, which won the sympathy of Anglo-Americans. The U.S.'s entry into the war unleashed a wave of 100-percent Americanism which equated patriotism with conformity.[15]

Public schools were increasingly viewed as the means for instilling that uniformity or Americanization. At the state level, a movement began for compulsory public schooling, which meant eradicating parochial and private education.[16] At the federal level, progressive schoolmen used the National Education Association (NEA) to secure introduction of the Smith-Towner bill, congressional legislation to create a department of education with a huge subsidy to redress a variety of problems, including illiteracy, unassimilated immigrants, and the need for standardization.[17] Catholic editors denounced the bill, believing it aimed directly or indirectly at eliminating parochial schools because they were "un-American, being under control of a foreign potentate, the pope of Rome."[18]

Burke's response was to mount a civic-education program through motion pictures, a project aimed at illiterates and unassimilated immigrants. The potency of movies derived in part from their lack of sound. Silent films conveyed their message through visual and emotional impact readily accessible to immigrants of any language. The War Council's Committee on Reconstruction produced a pamphlet outlining the initiative. Burke, an ex-officio member of its subcommittee on civic education, contributed ideas and probably wrote portions of it. The plan was to entertain and instruct through movies and lectures aimed at instilling patriotism and citizenship, while imparting advice about vocational opportunities and the means of learning English. The basic program consisted of six, weekly, ninety-minute sessions, with fifteen-minute films promoting health, sanitation, vocational opportunities, safety, recreation, current events, and "clean comics." Other reels taught citizenship, patriotism, and democracy. Interspersed among them were one or two fifteen-minute lectures, based on material in the book *Fundamentals of Citizenship*, issued by the War Council and translated into Italian and Polish. The continuation program ran for twenty-four weeks.[19]

Burke and the subcommittee strongly urged the basic program be offered free, with the cost of films, projector, screen, and textbooks defrayed by parish fund-raising. Where circumstances warranted, the CSWA would bear the total expense. The cost of the continuation course was conditioned upon whether a parish established a permanent movie venue on its premises. The CSWA would install the screen, projection booth, and projector at a 50 percent loss, selling the equipment to the parish at half-price: $200 (about $3,600 in 2024). The idea was that the local church would then use the equipment for similar programs and perhaps a weekly movie night for parishioners. If a parish did so, the CSWA would also split the cost of providing films for the continuation program, each party paying $10 per picture (about $180). The CSWA recommended opening the program to immigrants of all faiths, affording opportunity to promote citizenship according to "the Catholic ideal and the Catholic point of view."[20]

To implement it, Burke hired Charles A. McMahon, secretary of the Board of Education of Buffalo. Burke and O'Grady went there in mid-July to confer with him about specifics. Burke thought that the project would run about $500,000 ($9 million in 2024). He reported to Muldoon that launching it had been difficult, but he thought the CSWA was "on the way to doing a big piece of work." Muldoon advised "the most extraordinary care" be taken in approaching it, especially with regard to cost. The rumored the figures he had heard were $250,000 to $300,000 ($4.5 to $5.4 million).[21] Obviously, Burke and O'Grady were dreaming far larger than Muldoon was willing to spend, with consequences that would later be felt.

TRANSITION TO PERMANENCE

As Burke pursued effective use of movies, an event occurred that would eventually result in an institution that would occupy him until his death. In February 1919, seventy-five bishops met in Washington to celebrate Cardinal James Gibbons's fiftieth episcopal anniversary. Pope Benedict XV sent a Vatican official, Archbishop Bonaventura Cerretti, to speak about postwar work. He said Benedict recognized that only the U.S. possessed the resources necessary to assist war-torn peoples. The task facing the Church was "nothing less than the reconstruction of human society." He urged American Catholics to unite their efforts for the spread of justice and charity among all peoples of the world. "Rome," declared Cerretti, "now looks to America to be the leader in all things Catholic and to set the example to other nations"—a statement that would have made Isaac Hecker and the Americanists beam.[22]

The bishops discussed how to fulfill the pope's wishes. Bishop William Russell delivered a paper, written at Gibbons's request, about the need for a national Catholic agency in Washington to keep an eye on legislation so that the Church would never again be caught off guard as it had been with enactment of Prohibition, which necessitated negotiating with the government for use of sacramental wine. The bishops appointed a committee to propose a plan of action. The committee recommended the hierarchy meet annually and that a standing committee of five bishops be appointed to handle matters of general Catholic interest. Gibbons appointed the four bishops of the War Council's Administrative Committee to a new General Committee on Catholic Affairs and Interests with himself as chairman.[23]

Burke heartily supported this plan. He urged Kerby, who was traveling the Midwest and West to promote the idea of a permanent office in Washington. "In talking to … the Bishops," wrote Burke, "I think it well to lay stress on the advantages of a national committee actually at work here at the Capitol" to assist the General Committee on Catholic Affairs and Interests. Otherwise, the five bishops would have "no means of doing the work they would wish done."[24]

Burke soon got the opportunity to make the case himself. Russell devised a plan for that committee to supervise a bureau in Washington to safeguard Catholic interests on five matters. In order to shape Russell's plan into a proposal for consideration of the hierarchy when it met in September, Muldoon thought it best to seek help from people with practical experience in the areas to be covered. So in late July, the Committee on Catholic Affairs and Interests hosted thirty-six experts to a three-day gathering at University of Notre Dame.[25]

Muldoon divided attendees into three committees: press, missions, and social service. As editor of *Catholic World*, Burke belonged to the press committee. Burke and Charles Jaegle of the Holy Childhood Association wrote the committee's report. It recommended establishment of a National Catholic Publicity Bureau, complete with a news service to furnish Catholic and secular papers with information. Its reporters would keep abreast of secular papers, "a favorite medium for attack upon all things Catholic," so that items discrediting or misrepresenting the Church received corrective action. The bureau was to enlist "a corps of capable writers" known for their authority on a subject, their competence as interpreters of events, or their expertise in editorials, essays, short stories, and verse. Their writings too would go to both the Catholic and secular press. From such a nucleus would spring "groups of literary and professional men, reading circles, lecture clubs, forums and the like." The bureau should also ensure "an adequate supply" of youth literature and publish "a world library of Catholic classics" to form the core of a library in every Catholic home. "No more efficient method could be devised to recreate a love for Catholic writing and familiarity with Catholic thought." To foster these projects, the bureau was to have an organ of its own.[26]

Because the other two committees also recommended the establishment of national agencies—a National Bureau of Social Service and an American Board of Catholic Missions—a conference committee met to coordinate the three proposed entities. Of the five conferees, three belonged to the CSWA: Burke, O'Grady, and Edward Kelly. The conference committee recommended each agency be allowed to select its home city. Integration of the three would take place through a liaison committee, composed of the director and one representative from each. This committee would be responsible directly to the General Committee on Catholic Affairs and Interests and have its headquarters in Washington, D.C.[27]

This last recommendation certainly represented the thinking of Burke and his two colleagues on the CSWA. Their experience had convinced them of the need for official Catholic presence in Washington. Burke informed Kerby that the meeting had "prepared a big program," but he was unsure how much of it the hierarchy would accept, nor could he divine the future of the War Council. "Of one thing I feel certain," wrote Burke, "unless the Bishops continue some such National Committee we will go backward.... The Conference at Notre Dame agreed upon a national committee at Washington. In fact they were practically of one mind with regard to it. It remains for the Bishops to decide."[28]

Whatever the hierarchy might do, the CSWA needed a new headquarters. It would have to continue operating for some years to ensure it expended appropriately the War Work Campaign funds allotted it. The building where it rented space was up for sale, so it might need to leave on short notice. Burke wanted to purchase a large edifice at 1312 Massachusetts Avenue N.W. He told Muldoon that rental rates in Washington were prohibitive, and new zoning regulations made it "essential that we have a place wherein we can work for some time to come with security." The purchase price of $125,000 ($2.25 million in 2024) would come from money appropriated for that purpose, independent of campaign funds. The CSWA would sell the building on completion of war work. Muldoon approved the acquisition.[29]

Shortly thereafter, the Committee on Catholic Affairs and Interests hosted another meeting of eighteen men interested in Catholic education, including Burke and members of the executive board of the Catholic Educational Association. Their report declared that the preservation of the faith and its instilment in future generations depended on parochial schools. The difficulties facing Catholic education could be overcome "only through the united action of our Bishops." These problems included improvement and increase of parochial schools, recruitment and certification of teachers, establishment of tuition-free central Catholic high schools, encouragement of Catholic colleges, and strengthening of Catholic professional schools.

Moreover, something must be done to improve education of blacks and provide decent care for the deaf, dumb, blind, and feeble-minded. The conferees recommended establishment of a committee "to gather and disseminate information regarding our educational system and its interests and, in general, to act under the direction of the Standing Committee of the Bishops in such matters."[30]

Over the next day and half, the Committee on Catholic Affairs and Interests finalized plans. Its program called for organizing the Church nationally modeled on the reorganized War Council and Burke's CSWA. Accordingly, the hierarchy in its annual convention was to become the National Catholic Welfare Council (NCWC). Between conventions, an Administrative Committee, composed of seven bishops elected annually, was to handle business and have complete charge of all matters decided by the council. Five of those bishops would each head one of the five departments: Press, Lay Societies, Social Service, Education, and Laws and Legislation (three if not four of the same committees in the CSWA). To place the organization on firm financial footing, an endowment fund should be raised through a national collection. The goal of the drive was $25 million ($450 million in 2024) to be used for both the NCWC and other purposes. Missing from the proposal was any mention of a national headquarters in Washington, the very thing that Burke had insisted on. The committee sent the plan to the hierarchy for action at its convention in September.[31]

Casualties of War

Meanwhile, war work had taken its toll, real or feigned, on Burke and people close to him, particularly Grace Murray. With his shuttling weekly between Washington and New York, the daily running of *Catholic World* fell on her shoulders. Adding to her burden was her low level of confidence in her abilities, which in Burke's estimation were considerable. In the spring, she broke down physically while he was in New York. "Grace must go away at once," he wrote to Lynch. "She is worn out, and she must stay for at least six weeks." Murray's absence and pressing work at Clifton made him cancel leading the annual retreat for the sisters at the Cenacle. "I must go to Washington to night," he wrote. "It is now 10:30 [P.M.]"[32] Obviously, his schedule was exhausting.

For several months, Burke had been trying to get Murray to understand what "an awful fallacy and injustice" her self-doubt and low self-esteem were to both God and herself. He encouraged her to "rest" in all she had accomplished and God had permitted her to do. Burke's inability to help her break the cycle of thinking herself unworthy, fighting the thought, then listening to it, then repeating the process, and finally yielding to it "quite fully"—frustrated him. As she recuperated in Connecticut, he tried to turn the tables on her thought process by recommending a peculiar form of nightly examination of conscience. He wanted her to view self-doubt as sinful, as falsehood. She should ask herself: "Have I lied to myself to-day? Have I lied by doubting my ability to work? Have I really been a great help and comfort to my employers and yet given way to thoughts that I was quite a perfectly useless being?" The source of his peeve was positive. Writing from New York while attending the Paulist chapter, he told her: "Day by day here [at the office] shows what you did; and shows what a hole there is when you are not here. And these thoughts you've had that you weren't doing much are damned lies." To ease her mind, he assured her he was in "good humor" and that things were quite up to date at work. "You are improving," he told her. "I can tell that from your letters. Sleep as you wish to. It is nature restoring her strength in you."[33]

In reply, Murray chided herself for not having written more often. "It's a good test of friendship when we don't write—as you know from my *not* answering letters of friends oftentimes," Burke told her. "Don't bother about writing if for example you have a full day and just don't feel like it at night." He reiterated he could tell she was improving. He also sensed she blamed her predicament solely on her lack of self-confidence. If she did that, knew Burke, she would not improve as she ought. "Lack of self-confidence there was," he acknowledged: "it came on gradually: finally got a strong grip on you—and the cause all along was that you were doing too much. The physical structure broke down: couldn't stand the strain: the body refused to carry the mental load. The logical thing is to see this and admit it." He urged her not to worry about her return to the office. Just enjoy herself and the time away.[34]

As he had done with Lynch, he prayed God would grant her the "eyes of a saint," so that she may "see God's world as God's world." This gift resulted from a positive, loving, and energetic faith. Such faith was different from faith as an "abstraction." By the latter, Burke meant mere acceptance of religious truth "as an article of faith." Positive faith was real experience of the Holy Spirit, the very love of God Himself, dwelling within and energizing the Christian with love. With that came the ability "to see ourselves and ourselves as the creatures of God." To Lynch, Burke had expressed it thus: "In their [the saints'] own souls there is ever a joy of being with Him who loves to be with the children of men. That make merry with God. They shower Him with their cares: they burden Him with the questions that oppress their heart, they ask Him His secrets: they know the privileges of lovers: their delights are His: their love is its reward now and hereafter, for their love is the Divine Bridegroom Himself. With Him there is not time nor death. Neither are His lovers conquered by either of these. Youth knows its enthusiasm and age its unwithered freshness in consecration to and possession by Him." In short, it was to be in love with God and see the world with spiritual eyes.[35]

In Murray's next letter, she told Burke she "saw." "I'm glad you 'see,'" he replied. "Keep seeing and yet don't try to see. Just see even when depression comes." He told her to make "a positive rule" not to think of herself, about how she was doing or whether she was improving. If such thoughts came, "refuse to think of them. Do something."[36] She took this advice to heart. At end of July she wrote to say that by keeping herself occupied, her fearfulness had fled. "I am glad you have banished fear," Burke replied. "Keep to your rule of so interesting yourself in other things that you won't go back to fear. And then don't fear that if you don't fear what would happen if you did fear. That's rather ridiculous of course: but your thoughts here run in that direction a few times."[37] Rather than an end to her struggle, this surcease was but an interlude.

In June, the War Department awarded Burke the Distinguished Service Medal, a newly established decoration for exceptionally meritorious labor for the government in a duty of great responsibility. Muldoon congratulated him, "I am heartily glad that they recognized all your excellent work." Apparently mistaking the medal for the Distinguished Service Cross, the army's second highest decoration for valor in combat, he added, "You have a few wounds, and you have been in many engagements and how frequently under fire.—So it is entirely proper."[38] Kerby too sent Burke a warm note of congratulation. "No man will ever know what the work of the last two years has meant to me or cost me," replied Burke. "You know it more intimately than anyone else. And though you may protest against my saying it—your cooperation from the very beginning and your abiding sympathy at all times (and at all hours!) has been the greatest support and the most fruitful comfort."[39] Indeed, Burke had grown tired and weary. After the Notre Dame conference, he told Kerby: "Personally, I have no inclination to continue on the work. I have done my share and played my part. The motive of immediate service to country has gone. The motive of service to the Church would win my consent to further serve if I were asked. But it wouldn't be what I liked."[40]

When Murray returned to work, Burke gave her his Distinguished Service Medal for having given him the liberty to serve "God and Country." Of course, she returned it to him, "but his gesture of humility and gratitude," recalled Mary Hawks, "remained an ineffaceable memory."[41]

In late June, another associate was hors de combat. Walter Hooke apparently succumbed to fatigue and was "very near a break-down." His doctor ordered him to rest for at least a month, Burke explained to Muldoon. Two weeks later, physicians insisted Hooke take a sea voyage to recuperate, raising Burke's suspicions that something else was afoot. He released Hooke from duty, but "at his own expense and in no official capacity," so he could not interfere in the work of Clifton graduates in France.[42]

Burke suspected Hooke of embezzlement. Muldoon's earlier request for an inquiry into extravagant spending had likely alerted Hooke to the danger of disclosure. After Hooke's departure, Burke launched an investigation that revealed "grave irregularities in the way he kept accounts entrusted to him." Hooke had itemized no expenses and had received "monies from the comptroller for which he had no authorization." Burke laid the matter before the CSWA, which decided it best to ask for Hooke's resignation while maintaining the ruse that ill health was the reason. The incident was doubly distressing to Burke because Hooke was a convert who had entered the Church through instrumentality of the Paulists. He told Kerby he could hardly express the "the utter, utter disappointment" he felt. "It almost shakes one's faith in human nature," he wrote: "but no, it doesn't shake mine.... My heart feels weary at times and more and more must I be silent within myself."[43]

Of more immediate concern for Burke was the need to assure Kerby all was well with his assistant Father Cooper. Burke's secretary Mary Coyle commented years later: "Quite unassuming, dreadfully earnest ... was this John Montgomery Cooper." A priest of the archdiocese of Baltimore, he was six years younger than Burke and had earned doctorates in philosophy and theology in Rome. Burke thought him a real catch when he secured Cooper's release to work for the CSWA. For his part, Cooper respected Burke, Kerby, and Michael Slattery, but held other members of the CSWA in low regard.[44]

In August, Cooper sent Kerby a letter informing him of his intention to resign as executive secretary of the women's committee, a dispatch Kerby found waiting for him when he reached Sioux City a week later. Cooper complained the women's work lacked representation on the CSWA because Kerby never attended its meetings. Kerby's neglect of communicating and consulting with Cooper left him feeling like a "high class office boy." For him to continue, Kerby must at least attend meetings of the CSWA. Cooper complained to Burke that Kerby's usurpation of what little authority he had, resulted in diminished enthusiasm for and interest in the work. "I can not see just exactly what use I am to the cause," he wrote. He left his continuance with the CSWA to Burke and Kerby's judgment.[45]

When Burke received Cooper's letter, he sat him down for a serious talk, then wrote Kerby to say he hoped Cooper's letter had not worried or upset him and assured him the matter had been ironed out. "I'd love to be with you and free from all these troubles to talk and commune with you on those better things we both love," he told Kerby. "But the 'worse' part is mine just now"—a reference to the gospel story of Martha and Mary (who chose "the better part"), with Burke in the role of Martha (Luke 10:38–42).[46]

Denouement

In the fall, the foregoing strands came together in denouement. McMahon approached Burke with the idea of introducing the cinematic civic-education program with a feature-length movie about the War Council. The laity, he argued, knew very little about it. If they knew more, they would become more active in support of its program, especially the civic education one. He envisioned creating something along the lines "of a news feature [rather] than any attempt to tell the whole story of the Council."[47]

Burke launched the project in mid-August. He appointed a motion-picture committee under McMahon consisting of Frederick Sweet, an experienced film editor and caption writer; Robert Drady, former manager of a movie theater; and Michael Williams, a Catholic journalist. The committee took office space in New York. In little more than three weeks, it produced the first cut of *American Catholics in War and Reconstruction*, to be screened for the hierarchy when it met in late September. McMahon and his colleagues wanted to demonstrate to the bishops the value of motion pictures as a medium for both education and publicity.[48]

Burke sent him to Rockford for Muldoon's permission to screen the film for the bishops and arrange the time for it. Muldoon approved, provided the movie include a reel produced by the Knights about their war work. "Unbalanced program would be great mistake," cautioned the bishop. He also urged Burke to invite clergy and prominent Catholics of Washington.[49]

Unfortunately, there is no extant print of the film. All that remains is a programmatic flyer akin to a playbill which accompanied the revised final version. The picture consisted of five reels, the first an animated cartoon about how the grim shadow of world war descended on a peaceful globe in 1914, leaving in its wake desolation and lawlessness. The second recounted foundation of the War Council. The third depicted the Knights' pioneering work with soldiers on the Mexican border which prepared them to serve soldiers in camps at home and abroad.[50] Reels four and five focused on postwar reconstruction. The fourth identified the problems: binding up wounds, improving citizenship, promoting economic justice, abolition of child labor, and "bringing back the light of faith to the hearts of men." The fifth reel highlighted the "Bishops' Program of Social Reconstruction," which outlined the Catholic response to the problems identified in the fourth reel. It then spotlighted various works of the CSWA's Committee on Reconstruction: reemployment of servicemen, civic education through motion pictures, Clifton, hostess houses, service clubs overseas, and social service departments in hospitals.[51]

The convention of the hierarchy met at Catholic University in late September to consider the plan of the General Committee on Catholic Affairs and Interests. Almost all bishops favored making the hierarchy the NCWC, which would meet annually in convention and carry out its will between meetings through an Administrative Committee overseeing the five departments outlined above. A handful of conservatives, Cardinal William O'Connell of Boston chief among them, opposed the plan for two reasons. Jealous about the autonomy of each bishop, they worried about the binding force of decisions reached at the annual convention. To an even greater extent, they fretted over the Administrative Committee's authority and power for the same reason. By end of day, however, the hierarchy established itself as the NCWC. The bishops elected the following prelates to its Administrative Committee: Archbishops Austin Dowling of St. Paul, Dennis Dougherty of Philadelphia, and Edward Hanna of San Francisco, along with Bishops Peter Muldoon, Russell, Joseph Schrembs of Toledo, and J. F. Regis Canevin of Pittsburgh.[52]

That evening, an audience of about 150, mostly bishops and priests with a sprinkling of laywomen, gathered to view *American Catholics in War and Reconstruction*. McMahon introduced it, warning viewers used to the standard movie line of "dramatic high points, continuity of action and fascinating suspense," that they were in for a "quite formal recital" of American Catholic activities in the war its aftermath.[53] The warning was apt. According to newspaperman Edward Murtaugh, the picture was "sadly disappointing" as an exposition of Catholic war activities. It dragged on and "grew frightfully dull," causing many to leave. The film seemed a veritable "moving picture gallery" of prelates, priests, welfare workers, and buildings. Caption boards were heavily laden with text and statistics. There was "a decided lack of action." Worse was the absence of "good looking women," noted Murtaugh, "and that was commented upon greatly." Its producers should have hired "a few professional beauties" to relieve the monotony of all the plain girls (excepting his sister Marie). Search as one might, he would not find one memorable female face in the lot. "The whole picture in a word," concluded Murtaugh, "lacks a punch."[54]

Burke himself took a critical view. He found the first part too long. All the captions needed careful revision, especially the one describing the War Council and the Knights of Columbus as two separate organizations, when in fact the latter was an arm of the former. He asked McMahon to take better film of Clifton and "cut out the girls in bloomers." He also ordered him to delete the picture in front of the school wherein Burke himself appeared front and center in a group photo of faculty and students. Given the many other shots of him, he considered this depiction "infra dig[nitatem]"—beneath dignity. Scenes of the service clubs were too long and should be flashed quickly in succession, making for a better impression. Finally, he wanted community houses featured and their work with various ethnicities and social classes.[55]

The next day, the Administrative Committee met to arrange the NCWC's financial foundation. The hierarchy had nixed an endowment, authorizing instead an initial budget of $200,000 ($3.6 million in 2024) to come from proportional assessments against each diocese. Chairman Hanna then appointed the following members to head the five departments: Dougherty, Legislation; Dowling, Education; Muldoon, Social Action; Russell, Press; and Schrembs, Lay Activity. After adjournment, the bishops went to supper.[56]

During the meeting, Burke sent in word he wished to see Muldoon privately. Because the hierarchy had failed to establish a headquarters in Washington, he intended to unburden himself on that issue. Unable to break away until after supper, a tired Muldoon came out and greeted him with, "What is it you want, Father Burke?" "Bishop, I have something on my conscience to tell you," he replied. Burke then explained that war work revealed many grave needs facing the Church which could be met only by a national headquarters in Washington. After a recital of the exigencies, he concluded, "Bishop, this is no longer on my conscience—now it's on yours."[57]

Ten days later, an insistent Burke returned to the theme. He wrote Muldoon that since their meeting that night, he had "given constant and urgent thought to the future of Catholic needs and interests." Repeating the recommendation of the conference committee at Notre Dame, he urged the necessity of a national committee in Washington to interface with the government. Without such an agency, not only would work done by the War Council "fail," but any national Catholic "movements will be little short of hopeless." "I write strongly because I feel strongly—as you know," he told Muldoon, "and I believe you agree with me." He would send him a detailed memorandum on the subject. At the moment, however, doctors ordered Burke away for rest. Typical of him, any vacation was destined to be a working one. He was going to the Panama Canal Zone and told Muldoon he would write the memo while away. He urged the Administrative

Committee take no action until it had his document.[58] Muldoon replied he had spoken to the committee of the need to continue work begun by the War Council. He told Burke to make his memorandum "as clear and as urgent as possible."[59]

Burke left from New Orleans on the S.S. *Heredia* together with three companions, a Miss Callahan, Sadie Murphy, and Gertrude Delahunt; the last two worked at Chaplain's Aid and *Catholic World*, respectively. They sailed down the Mississippi and out into the Gulf of Mexico. Once at sea, they saw no land, save a glimpse of Cuba and couple of small islands. There were few other passengers aboard. "We have been by ourselves on the ship, a home complete," Burke wrote to Murray, "with the open spaces, the close horizon, the sun, the stars, and the moon each night." He and she were in an uneasy truce over her spiritual life. She may have been struggling again with self-doubt, and they were having a tussle over obedience. Burke had not heard from her in over a week. Apparently, they reached an agreement to leave the issue alone. He told her she was in his prayers constantly. "But I am not going to write in detail of yourself."[60]

In her last letter to him, Murray had Burke promise not to fret over her or work. "I have kept my promise to you and freed my mind from worry, and given myself to rest," he told her. "In fact the sea wins in the fight and makes one succumb. One has to desire to work." He admitted that thoughts of how things were going at *Catholic World* and the War Council passed through his head. "If I were to let my imagination run I would picture many things, but I won't," he wrote. "They in Washington will have to do the best they can." He said the *Heredia* had served as a troop transport during the war. "So I have a fellow feeling because of its patriotic service."[61]

Burke was also feeling separation from Lynch. Her religious community was sending her to Brussels to spend a year imbibing the European heritage and spirit of the Sisters of the Cenacle. He acknowledged the sadness and difficulty she must feel in leaving behind her home of the last seven years and sisters to whom she had grown close. He assured her she would find an equally warm community in Belgium where "loving and gracious hands" would help shape her into "the more perfect pattern that Our Lord wishes." Burke believed Lynch's religious order had an important role to play in the near future. The entry of women into politics (the Nineteenth

Amendment), industry, and social service demanded more than ever that Catholic women have an intelligent understanding of their faith and zeal for truth. Those of such substance "will refine and redeem the modern movements in which women will play so great a part," wrote Burke. The Sisters of the Cenacle were already engaged in the effort and God would prosper their work.[62]

As for their parting, Burke wrote: "You have gone from me but only physically. Distances don't exist in God. You will miss my frequent word, my help; but for what God takes away He gives a hundred-fold. And let us both make the sacrifice most joyfully; let not God be worried by the slightest whisper of murmuring, even in thought." Unknown to him at the time, although she was to have sailed while he was away, her departure had been postponed until January 1920.[63]

Sailing to and from Panama was the only respite Burke got. His trip was to investigate the situation of the military in the Canal Zone with a view to having the War Council lend such assistance as was warranted. On 13 October, he arrived at Cristobal, the city at the Caribbean end of the Zone. He immediately visited the YMCA facility, "a large but ill adapted recreation building intended primarily for soldiers and sailors." It lacked capability for housing men overnight, but construction was underway for quarters to sleep fifty. Burke then toured the Knight's facility in Colón just outside the Zone. It was located in an out-of-the-way place, accessible only through a seedy part of town. It did have "neat and orderly" rooms for lodging, but they were on the third floor of the building "necessitating quite a climb up stairs." The principal recreational equipment was a boxing ring. "The situation is not desirable" concluded Burke. "Even soldiers and sailors will go there only when there is some special attraction advertised, e.g., a prize fight." He then went about both cities in search of the best site for a community house.[64]

Burke crossed the isthmus by train to Balboa, the administrative seat of the Zone at the Pacific end of the canal. He stayed with Father Thomas McDonald, the Vincentian pastor of St. Mary's parish. The only recreational place available to the military was the "Club." Every town in the Zone had one, and all were government-supported and open to everyone, military or civilian. As far as Burke could tell, they had no definite purpose or aim and no program of entertainment. The YWCA was present, but as yet had developed no plans. In Burke's view, Balboa had great need of a Welfare Community House directed by women. He pictured it in "the nature of a 'home' house," providing "the home atmosphere: the quiet opportunity for reading: assembly: games: reading circle: classes in civic education, history, domestic science: lectures: educational movies etc." Dancing was the popular amusement in the Zone, but Balboa had no dance hall. He thought the proposed community house ought to have one open to all, of course "with proper supervision."[65]

The Zone's salient problem, in Burke's view, was the division between civilians and enlisted personnel. The American district was akin to a large military base, with civilian and military officials, male and female employees, families, and enlisted men. Work was being done for soldiers, but it pertained to them alone. Civilians had private clubs which excluded enlisted men. "Unless the problem is solved, the work of civil government and of military will grow more and more difficult," noted Burke. "The soldier will feel the stigma, will be convinced that he is not welcome to civilian entertainments and civilian society and will seek his recreation in circles far from desirable." He saw the proposed community house as a place which would "welcome with equal warmth" civilian, officer, and enlisted man—"a common meeting place for all classes." To be sure, there were other places the soldier and sailor could take recreation, "but nowhere can he experience that home welcome, that conviction that he is on equal footing with his fellow man in human society."[66]

Burke went forward with the idea. As for staffing, McDonald had a women's organization which was ready to lend a hand, but the CSWA would have to send trained representatives to supervise and manage work. Burke located three potential sites for the building, one particularly suitable. He stressed his desire for it to the civil governor, Chester Harding, and urged Lieutenant Colonel Jason Joy back in Washington to encourage Secretary of War Newton Baker to intercede in favor of the site. Eventually, military officials in Panama denied all three locations, offering three others as alternatives. Burke selected one for construction of a "splendid building." Completed a year later, the edifice was an elegant, two-story, colonnaded, stone structure whose exterior resembled a library or government building.[67]

While away, Burke wrote the memorandum arguing the necessity for a national committee with headquarters at Washington. The CSWA had learned by experience that interests of its various subcommittees could be represented and protected only by a committee headquartered in the nation's capital. So, he said no matter where the NCWC's departments decided to locate their centers, all had to be united in a practical, working manner. Because such coordination demanded daily attention, it was beyond the scope of the administrative bishops. Nor could it be accomplished by occasional meetings of representatives from the various departments. It warranted a standing committee in Washington. Unless this was established, warned Burke, the departments would "undoubtedly fail in the larger sense of their mission, and the condition of Catholic interests and Catholic progress will be little short of disastrous."[68]

Moreover, to protect Catholic welfare, the Church must have its finger on the pulse of power. Legislation began, not in Congress, but in executive meetings or in conferences called by national organizations. Departments of the NCWC had to be in touch with that process. They needed permanent representatives in Washington. The FCC had such deputies, and before the war they were a force to be reckoned with. During hostilities, the War Council had managed to hold them in check. Once the latter was out of the way, advised Burke, the FCC would again "be the sole voice of its kind at the national capitol." The Church needed an agency there. "I cannot stress this point too much," wrote Burke. "It is crucial. Our withdrawal now will practically leave the field clear to our opponents and the opponents of our Church." A national bureau should comprise a delegate from each department, a salaried chairman, an executive secretary, and four clerks. If each department bore the cost of its delegate, the rest of the bureau could be run at an annual expense of $26,300 ($468,000 in 2024).[69]

In effect, Burke was arguing that the NCWC participate in what contemporaries referred to as the "new lobbying." In the previous century, lobbying had been conducted secretly and in the interest of corporations. In the early twentieth century, given the Progressive Movement's reliance on governmental solutions to problems, the centralization brought about by the war, and the increasing organization of American life, lobbying underwent a transformation. Institutionalized, public, and conducted by voluntary organizations, it became an important means of wielding power. Lobbies, like the FCC and the NEA, wrote legislation, sought friendly congressmen to introduce it, exerted pressure on congressional committees by supplying facts and expert testimony to support the legislation, and attempted to secure public backing through publicity campaigns.[70]

Burke returned to Washington in early November. When the Administrative Committee of the NCWC met there in December, Muldoon read it his memorandum. The committee met with the CSWA to discuss its postwar works which the NCWC should assume. After discussion, the bishops agreed to take over works consonant with their portfolio. Burke presented a new, scaled-down version of his proposal for a central agency in Washington. The Administrative Committee then adopted a series of motions. The bishops decided to appoint an executive secretary—soon re-designated general secretary—to represent them at a Washington headquarters to be located in the CSWA building. The director of each NCWC department would reside in the capital, and they would collectively serve as an executive committee under the general secretary, who was to supervise their work. The bishops unanimously elected Burke general secretary.[71]

Endnotes to Chapter 7

1. Burke, *Christ in Us*, 62.
2. Minutes of the Executive Committee of the War Council, 13 November 1917, ACUA, NCWC 10:6:7.
3. Minutes of CSWA, 13 September and 19 October 1918, ACUA, NCWC 10:1:6; Williams, *Catholics in War*, 386–403; Lawler, *Full Circle*, 13–14, 17–18; Jeanne Petit, "'Up against a Stone Wall': Women, Power and the National Catholic Community Houses," *American Catholic Studies* 123 (Summer 2012): 31–37.
4. Sister M. Ignatia Fleming to Burke, 2 October 1918, ACUA, NCWC 10:5:18; William DeLacy to John M. Cooper, 26 October 1918, ibid., 10:15:10; Agreement of 18 November 1918 between Sallie D. Elverson and National Catholic War Council, ibid.; Coyle, Memories of War Council, ibid., 10:72:24; May M. Murphy, "The National Service School for Women," *NCWC Bulletin* 1 (June 1919): 12; Williams, *Catholics in War*, 410–11; Lawler, *Full Circle*, 18–22; L. E. Hartmann-Ting, "The National Catholic School of Social Service: Redefining Catholic Womanhood through the Professionalization of Social Work during the Interwar Years," *U.S. Catholic Historian* 26 (Winter 2008): 101–06.
5. Margaret Hennessy to Burke, 22 June 1919, ACUA, NCWC 10:5:18; A. Marie McPoland to Burke, 3 July 1919, ibid.; Williams, *Catholics in the War*, 411–15; Lawler, *Full Circle*, 22 and 28.

6. Suggestions to Overseas Workers, 11 January 1919, ACUA, NCWC 10:5:18; Williams, *Catholics in the War*, 415–20; Lawler, *Full Circle*, 22–24, 234.
7. Quoted in Lawler, *Full Circle*, 24–29, 33; "Clifton Graduates Another Class," NCWC Bulletin 2 (September 1920): 29–30.
8. Burke to Muldoon, 2 May 1919, with enclosed Memorandum, ACUA, NCWC 10:11:41 (the quotations are taken from both the letter and the memorandum); Lawler, *Full Circle*, 40–41.
9. Lawler, *Full Circle*, 29–30; "Clifton Graduates Another Class," 30.
10. Muldoon to Burke, 30 June 1919, ACUA, NCWC 10:7:23.
11. Burke to Muldoon, 5 July 1919, ACUA, NCWC 10:7:22.
12. Brownlow, *Behind Mask of Innocence*, 61; Lashley and Watson, *Psychological Study*, 7–8.
13. Quoted in Williams, *Catholics and War*, 331–34; *New York Times*, 18 May 1919; Burke to Muldoon, 7 June 1918, ACUA, NCWC 10:3:40; Matthias Nicoll Jr. to Muldoon, 21 July 1919, ibid., 10:7:23; Brandt, *No Magic Bullet*, 77–78, 123–24; Brownlow, *Behind Mask of Innocence*, 61–62.
14. *Historical Statistics*, 615–16; Richard M. Abrams, *Burdens of Progress, 1900–1929* (Glenview, Ill.: Scott Foresman, 1978), 53; Gary Gerstle, "Liberty, Coercion, and the Making of Americans," *Journal of American History* 84 (September 1997): 534–39; Ewa Morawska, "Immigrants, Transnationalism, and Ethnicization: A Comparison of This Great Wave and the Last," in Gary Gerstle and John Mollenkopf, eds., *E Pluribus Unum? Contemporary and Historical Perspectives on Immigrant Political Incorporation* (New York: Russell Sage Foundation, 2001), 179–87; Reed Ueda, "Historical Patterns of Immigrant Status and Incorporation in the United States," ibid., 295.
15. Coleman J. Barry, *The Catholic Church and German Americans* (Milwaukee: Bruce Publishing Company, 1953), 1–12; Philip Gleason, *The Conservative Reformers: German-American Catholics and the Social Order* (Notre Dame, Ind.: University of Notre Dame Press, 1968), 29–31, 159–171; Dolores Liptak, R.S.M., *Immigrants and Their Church* (New York: Macmillan, 1989), 92–101; E. Clifford Nelson, *The Lutherans in North America* (Philadelphia: Fortress Press, 1975), 295–98, 367, 398–99; John Higham, *Strangers in the Land: Patterns of American Nativism, 1860–1925* (New York: Atheneum, 1975), 194–212; Dean R. Esslinger, "American German and Irish Attitudes Toward Neutrality, 1914–1917: A Study of Catholic Minorities," *Catholic Historical Review* 53 (July 1967): 194–216; Edward Cuddy, "Pro-Germanism and American Catholicism, 1914–1917," *Catholic Historical Review* 54 (October 1968): 427–54.
16. "No God for the Child," *America* 18 (6 April 1918): 656; Higham, *Strangers in the Land*, 204–07; *Nebraska State Legislature*, 37th Sess., House Roll No. 4; Orville Zabel, *God and Caesar in Nebraska: A Study of the Legal Relationship of Church and State, 1854–1954* (Lincoln: University of Nebraska Press, 1955), 135.

17. Douglas J. Slawson, *The Department of Education Battle, 1918–1932: Public Schools, Catholic Schools, and the Social Order* (Notre Dame: University of Notre Dame Press, 2005), 1–34; David B. Tyack and Elisabeth Hansot, *Managers of Virtue: Public School Leadership in America, 1820–1980* (New York: Basic Books, 1982), 105–21; David B. Tyack, *The One Best System: A History of American Urban Education* (Cambridge: Harvard University Press, 1974), 126–76; Raymond E. Callahan, *Education and the Cult of Efficiency: A Study of the Social Forces That Have Shaped the Administration of the Public Schools* (Chicago: University of Chicago Press, 1962), 1–220; Morton Keller, *Regulating a New Society: Public Policy and Social Change in America, 1900–1933* (Cambridge, Mass.: Harvard University Press, 1994), 46–48.
18. "A Plot Against Our Schools," *Fortnightly Review* 25 (15 October 1918): 306; Slawson, *Department of Education Battle*, 22–23, 31–34, 41, 44.
19. Committee on Special War Activities, *A Plan for Civic Education through Motion Pictures*, July 1919, ACUA, NCWC 10:30:38; Charles McMahon et al. to Burke, 5 November 1919, ibid., 10:21:82; May, *Screening Out the Past*, 39, 52–59, 72.
20. CSWA, *Plan for Civic Education*, July 1919, ACUA, NCWC 10:30:38; Circular to the Clergy from John O'Grady, 24 July 1919, ibid., 10:21:80 (quote is here).
21. Charles McMahon to Larkin Mead, 23 July 1919, copy, ACUA, NCWC 10:21:80; McMahon to Burke, ibid., 10:7:10; Burke to Muldoon, 10 August 1919, copy, ibid., 10:7:23 (first quote is here); Muldoon to Burke, 7 September 1919, ibid., 10:7:24 (second quote is here); Williams, *Catholics in War*, 335–36.
22. Diary of Muldoon, 20 February 1919, ACUA, microfilm; *Baltimore Catholic Review*, 1 March 1919. The quotation about Rome looking to America is attested to by several sources: Diary of Muldoon, 20 February 1919, ACUA, microfilm; William Russell's draft of Gibbons's letter to the hierarchy, 1 May 1919, AASUS-AASMSU, RG 10, box 23; Louis Walsh to Russell, 7 February 1922, ADCh, 111–R6; *Report of the General Committee on Catholic Affairs and Interests Presented to the Catholic Hierarchy of America Assembled at the Catholic University, Washington, D.C., September 24, 1919, His Eminence, Cardinal Gibbons, Presiding*, (n.p.: [1919]) 1, ACUA, USCCB 10:227:1; Slawson, *Foundation of NCWC*, 48; Luca Castagna, *A Bridge Across the Ocean: The United States and the Holy See Between the Two World Wars* (Washington, D.C.: The Catholic University of America Press, 2014), 72–73.
23. Diary of Muldoon, 20 and 21 February 1919, ACUA, microfilm; Louis Walsh, Diary, 20 and 21 February 1919, ADP; Minutes of the Meeting of the Archbishops, 1919, AAB-AASMSU, 128 H7; John Glennon to Gibbons, 26 February 1919, ibid., 125 E12; Russell to Burke, 7 July 1921, ACUA, USCCB 10:98:26; Slawson, *Foundation of NCWC*, 47–54; Douglas J. Slaw-

son, "Wine for the Gods: Negotiations for the Sacramental Use of Alcohol during Prohibition," in Joseph C. Linck, C.O., and Raymond J. Kupke, eds., *Building the Church in America: Studies in Honor of Monsignor Robert F. Trisco on the Occasion of His Seventieth Birthday* (Washington, D.C.: The Catholic University of America Press, 1999), 161–73; Herbert Asbury, *The Great Illusion: An Informal History of Prohibition* (Garden City, N.Y.: Doubleday and Company, Inc., 1950), 121–34; Edward Behr, *Prohibition: Thirteen Years that Changed America* (New York: Arcade Publishing, 1996), 7–75; Sean Dennis Cashman, *Prohibition: The Lie of the Land* (New York: Free Press, 1981), 6–23; John Kobler, *Ardent Spirits: The Rise and Fall of Prohibition* (London: Michael Joseph, 1973), 198–212; Charles Merz, *The Dry Decade* (Garden City, N.Y.: Doubleday, Doran & Company, Inc., 1931), 1–42; Andrew Sinclair, *Era of Excess: A Social History of the Prohibition Movement* (New York: Harper Colophon Books, 1964), 63–82, 116–28, 152–66.

24. Burke to Kerby, 15 June 1919, ACUA, Kerby Papers 58:2:5.
25. Diary of Muldoon, 22 July 1919, ACUA, microfilm; Muldoon to Joseph Schrembs, 8 June 1919, copy, ACUA, NCWC 10:3:41; Muldoon to Burke, 30 June 1919, ibid., 10:7:23; Slawson, *Foundation of NCWC*, 49–57.
26. Burke and Charles Jaegle, "Report of the Committee on Catholic Press and Literature," in *Report of the General Committee*, 14–19, ACUA, USCCB 10:227:1; Minutes of the Meeting of the Committee on the Catholic Press, at Notre Dame, Indiana, ibid., USCCB 10:60:4.
27. Minutes of the Conference Committee, 24 July 1919, ACUA, USCCB 10:60:4.
28. Burke to Kerby, 15 August 1919, copy, ACUA, Kerby Papers 58:2:5.
29. Burke to Muldoon, 13 August 1919, copy; Muldoon to Burke, 16 August 1919; Muldoon to Arnold, 16 August 1919, copy—all in ACUA, NCWC 10:7:26.
30. Report of the Special Educational Committee to the Committee of the Hierarchy on Catholic Interests and Activities, [28 August 1919], copy, AASUS-AASMSU, RG 13, box 8; also in *Report of the General Committee*, 9–12, ACUA, USCCB 10:227:1; Minutes of the General Committee on Catholic Interests and Affairs, 28 August 1919, copy, AASUS-AASMSU, RG 13, box 9.
31. Minutes of the General Committee on Catholic Affairs and Interests, 29 and 30 August 1919, copy, AASUS-AASMSU, RG 13, box 9; *Report of the General Committee*, 37–41, ACUA, USCCB 10:227:1; Circular from the General Committee on Catholic Interests and Affairs, 30 August 1919, AAB-AASMSU, NCWC file. Because the details of how the organization took shape are not pertinent to this study, the material in this paragraph reflects the organization of the NCWC as approved by the hierarchy at the first annual convention. For an examination of the shaping of the NCWC, see Slawson, *Foundation of NCWC*, 60–69.

32. Burke to Lynch, undated [May or June 1919], AP, Burke Papers, box 5.
33. Burke to Murray, 27 June 1919, AP, Burke Papers, box 11.
34. Burke to Murray, 6 July 1919, AP, Burke Papers, box 11.
35. Burke to Lynch, undated fragment "From 'Away' (Quebec Vacation)," AP, Burke Papers, box 5; Burke to Lynch, undated fragment, ibid.; Burke to Lynch, 9 July 1915, ibid. (all quotations except "abstraction" are from here); Burke, Thoughts on the Holy Spirit for Lent, undated [1920?], ibid., Burke Papers, box 15 ("abstraction" is from here).
36. Burke to Murray, 10 July 1919, AP, Burke Papers, box 11.
37. Burke to Murray, [29 July 1919], AP, Burke Papers, box 11.
38. Muldoon to Burke, 6 June 1919, ACUA, USCCB 10:104:11.
39. Burke to Kerby, 15 June 1919, ACUA, Kerby Papers 58:2:5.
40. Burke to Kerby, 15 August 1919, ACUA, Kerby Papers 58:2:5.
41. Hawks, "Souvenir of Burke," AP, Burke Papers, box 10.
42. Burke to Muldoon, 29 June 1919, ACUA, NCWC 10:7:22 (first quote is here); Burke to Muldoon, 13 July 1919, ibid. (remaining quotes are here).
43. Burke to Kerby, 15 August 1919, ACUA, Kerby Papers 58:2:5.
44. John M. Cooper to Kerby, 7 August 1919, copy, ACUA, NCWC 10:38:66; Coyle, Memories of War Council, ibid., USCCB 10:72:24; Burke to Kerby, 15 August 1919, ibid., Kerby Papers 58:2:5; Gerard S. Sloyan, "John Montgomery Cooper: A Memoir," *American Catholic Studies* 120 (Fall 2009): 47–49.
45. Cooper to Kerby, 7 August 1919, copy, ACUA, NCWC 10:38:66; Cooper to Burke, 8 August 1919, ibid., USCCB 10:152:4; Petit, "'Up against a Stone Wall,'" 38–39.
46. Burke to Kerby, 15 August 1919, ACUA, Kerby Papers 58:2:5.
47. McMahon to Burke and O'Grady, undated [August 1919], copy, attachment to McMahon to Burke, 25 November 1919, ACUA, NCWC 10:7:10.
48. Burke to Frederick Sweet, 22 August 1919, copy, ACUA, NCWC 10:7:9; McMahon to Burke, 25 December 1919, ibid., 10:7:10; Memorandum Covering Introductory Remarks as Motion Picture Entertainment, ibid., 10:21:80 (quote is here); Williams, *Catholics in War*, 335–36; Black, *Hollywood Censored*, 23–24.
49. Burke to Muldoon, 8 September 1919, copy, ACUA, NCWC 10:7:24; McMahon to Burke, telegram, 11 September 1919, ibid., 10:7:9.
50. Program for *American Catholics in War and Reconstruction*, 6 December 1920, ACUA, NCWC 10:32:48.
51. Ibid.; John Tracy Ellis, ed., *Documents of American Catholic History* (Milwaukee: Bruce Publishing Company, 1962), 585–603; Curran, *American Catholic Social Ethics*, 30–44; Broderick, *Right Reverend New Dealer*, 27–47, 57–59, 104–05; Joseph McShane, S.J., *"Sufficiently Radical": Catholicism, Progressivism, and the Bishops' Program of 1919* (Washington, D.C.: Catholic University Press, 1986), 31–42, 175, 180, 187.

52. Slawson, *Foundation of NCWC*, 62–66.
53. Memorandum Covering Introductory Remarks as Motion Picture Entertainment, ACUA, NCWC10:21:80; Edward Murtaugh to Marie Murtaugh, 25 September 1919, ibid. 1:7:10.
54. E. Murtaugh to M. Murtaugh, 25 September 1919, ACUA, NCWC 10:7:10 (all quotes are here); McMahon to Burke, 25 November 1919, ibid.
55. Burke to McMahon, 27 September 1919, copy, ACUA, NCWC 10:7:9.
56. Minutes of the Administrative Committee, 26 September 1919, ACUA, USCCB.
57. Quoted in Iona McNulty to Paul Tanner, 6 May 1964, ACUA, USCCB 10:72:24; McNulty to Henry Lefebure, 5 June 1972, ibid.; Minutes of the General Committee on Catholic Affairs and Interests, 9 May 1919, AASUS-AASMSU, RG 13, box 9; Slawson, *Foundation of NCWC*, 54–55. Burke had recounted the incident with Muldoon to McNulty years after its occurrence. According to her recollection, it occurred at the meeting of the committee on 28 August 1919 shortly before the first convention of the hierarchy. Documentary evidence, however, argues for placing it immediately after that convention.
58. Burke to Muldoon, 5 October 1919, copy, ACUA, NCWC 10:7:24.
59. Muldoon to Burke, 8 October 1919, ACUA, NCWC 10:7:24.
60. Burke to Murray, 12 October [1919], AP, Burke Papers, box 11 (quotes are here); Burke to Murray, 4 October 1919, ibid.
61. Burke to Murray, 12 October [1919], AP, Burke Papers, box 11.
62. Burke to Lynch, 12 October 1919, AP, Burke Papers, box 5.
63. Ibid.
64. Burke, Report of the Chairman [CSWA] on Conditions and Needs in the Canal Zone, [October 1919], ACUA, NCWC 10:10:30; Lt. Col. Jason Joy to Commanding General, Panama Canal Zone, 4 October 1919, ibid.
65. Burke, Report of the Chairman [CSWA] on Conditions and Needs in the Canal Zone, [October 1919], ACUA, NCWC 10:10:30.
66. Ibid.
67. Ibid.; Burke to Joy, n.d. October 1919, copy, ACUA, NCWC 10:10:30; "Panama Community House Formally Opened in Balboa: President-Elect Harding, President of Panama, and bishop Rojas Assist," *NCWC Bulletin* 2 (December 1920): 1–3, and 27.
68. Burke to Muldoon, 9 November 1919, ACUA, NCWC 10:7:24; Burke, Memorandum on the Necessity of a Permanent National Committee with Headquarters at Washington for the Study: Advancement: Protection and Promotion of Catholic Needs and Catholic Interests, undated [November 1919], copy, ibid. Hereafter cited as Burke, Memorandum on National Committee.
69. Burke, Memorandum on National Committee, ACUA, NCWC 10:7:24.

70. Lynn Dumenil, *The Modern Temper: American Culture and Society in the 1920s* (New York: Hill and Wang, 1995), 40–2, 46–7; Lynn Dumenil, "'The Insatiable Maw of Bureaucracy,': Antistatism and Education Reform in the 1920s," *Journal of American History* 77 (September 1990): 508–09.
71. Burke to Muldoon, 30 November 1919, copy, ACUA, NCWC 10:7:25; Minutes of the Administrative Committee, 10 December 1919, with attachment: Burke, Memorandum to the Administrative Committee, 10 December 1919, appended to minutes, AASUS-AASMSU, RG 13, box 7.

Part II
“The Burden of the Day and the Scorching Heat” (Matt. 20:12)

Chapter 8
The Trials of a New Venture

> Nothing human comforts us so much in our sorrow as another who understands. The sorrow may not be lightened: but there seems more reason for bearing it when we are yoked with another. In like manner, nothing so eases suffering as the help and friendship of another. This is eminently true when suffering is so intense that we lose our courage: when pain routs us and the tears of utter weakness come and we are again but crying infants. For one who will not mock our weakness, for one who will still believe in our courage and tell us so, we are grateful, even though we cannot respond.[1]

Separations

New Year 1920 brought unwanted separations to John Burke, affording him ample opportunity to reflect on the spirituality of affection. The toll his appointment as general secretary would have on relations with family and friends was obvious. He loved family intensely. When Burke was in New York for business at *Catholic World*, he always went to his mother's flat where she lived with James, Will, and Lizzie. He and James were particularly close. Without fail, the two celebrated John's birthday and anniversary of his ordination together. The work of launching a new organization would curtail Burke's time with family.[2]

He was also close to women at *Catholic World*, especially Grace Murray, Gertrude Delahunt, and Mary Hawks. He celebrated their birthdays and anniversaries of hiring without fail. He loved rides with Murray up Riverside Drive along the Hudson as she took him to his mother's home. He especially liked their longer "more romantic" ones—in the nineteenth-century understanding of that term—down along the river to Battery Park. She had become his alter ego at *Catholic World* while he was in Washington.[3]

Of course, there was also Helen Lynch at the Cenacle of St. Regis in Hamilton Heights. In early January she finally left for Belgium. Burke wrote he had told her all he had to say about her going when he had written on his way to Panama. "You bear with you my heart's love," he now added, "and the deep earnest prayer that your going and your stay will be guided by the opportunity our Lord gives you for more intimate life with and knowledge of Him." The deepening of her spiritual life must "rise above all human considerations and feelings." Burke assured her his prayers would be with her daily. "This is a fare well, a God bless you," he concluded. "We are not parting. We are with and in Christ and may He ever find you His willing, listening child."[4]

Burke had to put his words into practice as he faced launching the work in Washington. News of his election as general secretary saddened the staff at *Catholic World*. Their reaction brought him face to face with his own feelings of separation. "You know what my going on the other work means to me," he confided to Murray. He told her he had never felt more "wretched" than when Archbishop Edward Hanna informed him of his election. Burke later admitted he cried at the news. It was not just because of longer absences from New York, but because "I am unfitted for the job that it is not to my taste."[5]

In early January, he went to deliver an address in Chicago. On the train, he pondered the pall of sadness his election cast over the staff at the magazine, dampening his own spirit. He "worried" throughout the speech, hoping he "would not break down or fizzle it." It was well received, but his ability to carry it off feeling as he did left him cheerless. "I succeed in a measure," he told Murray, "God knows why." One hearer told a colleague at the CSWA she had never seen "a speaker so self-possessed, so master of himself and his audience." She wondered what the secret was. The unspoken truth, Burke was equally surprised he could appear thus while feeling totally otherwise. Despite accolades, he missed "the comfort of connection."[6]

Burke feared he felt so because he was "too much attached to his loved ones." Yet he refused to view that attachment as a spiritual negative, as a sign of need for greater detachment. Echoing Isaac Hecker, he believed human sentiment was both a path to and gift from God. "Affection cannot be left behind like an old coat," he told Murray. "One must carry one's heart with him and it loves and beats and I would rather none than an inhuman one.... God's gifts ... are most worthiest when truest. And I never want my affections to be other than true and loyal and warm. I know that it means pain and suffering. So be it. So be it. The joy or rather the dignity of it is well worth the cost. For so we taste the love of God: so are we bound closer to Him in being bound one to another and the very affection whereby we love is a portion of that affection whereby we love God." Burke noted the First Epistle of John declared no person could truly love God while hating a neighbor. The Beloved Disciple called anyone who said otherwise "a liar" (1 John 4:20). To love God honestly, a person must sincerely love the neighbor.[7] Acknowledging this, however, did not make separation any easier; it simply confirmed human emotion was a gift from God to be cherished and lived to the fullest.

Little did Burke know the separation was to become deeper and more permanent than he imagined. The Administrative Committee considered it imperative he reside full-time in Washington. Splitting time between there and New York was out of the question. Hanna made the request to Thomas Burke, John's brother and the then-Paulist superior general. Cardinal James Gibbons also wrote, arguing no one was more conversant with issues or as agreeable to government officials as John Burke. "As a personal favor," he asked Thomas to make his brother's appointment permanent.[8]

Replying to Gibbons, Thomas reported he and his council agreed the assignment would be "temporary" lasting two years. No doubt, he consulted John on the matter. The Paulists wanted it understood the NCWC was to find and train another person to replace him "as soon as practicable."[9] In the short term, Thomas promised to appoint someone to help him with *Catholic World* so he could devote most of his time to the NCWC. That too failed to materialize, and John was to continue the editorship unaided until June 1922.[10]

Organization of NCWC Departments

As general secretary, Burke reported directly to Hanna. A native of Rochester, New York, Hanna had earned a doctorate in theology at the

Urban College in Rome. While on faculty at St. Bernard's Seminary in his home diocese, he authored two articles that brought him under suspicion as a Modernist. Perhaps because of that, Monsignor Filippo Bernardini, nephew of papal secretary of State Cardinal Pietro Gasparri and faculty member at Catholic University, made no secret of his opinion that Hanna was "a source of weakness to the [Welfare] Council." Burke's secretary, Iona McNulty, considered him "a Public Relations or Madison Ave. type—but … most likeable."[11] Throughout his tenure as general secretary, Burke kept Hanna well informed about operations at headquarters, though he tended to rely more on Bishop Peter Muldoon for advice.

Burke brought from the War Council the motion picture committee under Charles McMahon. McMahon hired the Famous Players–Lasky Corporation (later renamed Paramount Pictures) to provide material from its archive for the civic-education program. The company gave the committee space in its New York offices. The project did not go smoothly. By late winter, McMahon had Burke dissolve the committee, thereby leaving him sole project manager. Burke also brought the operation to Washington under his immediate supervision. It became the Motion Picture Bureau of the NCWC.[12]

Before its dissolution, the committee completely revised *American Catholics in War and Reconstruction* and released it in December 1919. Throughout the next year, it played mainly to Catholic audiences in parish halls and other venues in 663 locations from California to Maine. More than 900,000 viewed it, with those in the East and Midwest giving it a fine reception.[13]

The program for civic education through motion pictures launched in summer 1920. It enjoyed only modest success because under-funded; it received only one-fifth of the requested budget, rendering it impossible to assist parishes in the manner planned. Despite this setback, the program ran in eighteen cities around the nation using twenty-seven different five-reel films consisting of such things as travelogues, industrial movies, and patriotic pictures.[14] The Motion Picture Bureau then got out of the production business and turned to the matter of cleaning up the movie industry.

Burke also assisted with the organization of NCWC departments, though not every bishop who chaired one needed or sought his help. Muldoon, who led the Social Action Department, took the bull by the horns.

He first consulted with Burke, Father John Ryan, and Dr. Charles Neill about how to proceed. He then called a meeting of nationally known Catholic experts. They became the department's executive committee and decided it should have two co-directors: Ryan at Washington headquarters and John Lapp at an office in Chicago. Lapp had distinguished himself in the areas of civics, social insurance, and industrial and public health.[15]

In need of legislative advice, Burke had immediate, personal interest in the establishment of Archbishop Austin Dowling's Education Department. One of the most important issues Burke and the NCWC faced over the next twelve years was defense of parochial schools. As seen in the previous chapter, the Smith-Towner bill for a federal department with a massive subsidy would be used to induce states to accept minimum standards of schooling.[16]

At its 1919 convention, the hierarchy decided to support the Smith-Bankhead bill, which proposed to eradicate illiteracy among native-born people and teach English, citizenship, and homemaking skills to immigrants, two features of the Smith-Towner measure. The bishops believed enactment of this limited bill might defuse the drive for a department of education. When even the Smith-Bankhead seemed to go too far, Senator William Kenyon of Iowa introduced even more restricted legislation known as the Kenyon Americanization bill.[17]

In mid-January 1920, Burke informed Dowling of the Kenyon measure. Echoing Catholic editors, Burke cautioned "the danger to Catholic interests is that the Bill may furnish an opening wedge for State control of Catholic schools." On the other hand, he believed its appropriation should be shared with parochial schools so they too might participate in promoting Americanization. He considered it "at best … a debatable question" whether or not Congress would permit such sharing. "The vitally important thing," wrote Burke, was for Dowling to appoint an executive secretary to reside in Washington and authoritatively represent him. In Burke's view, the person "should not be a lobbyist: but one capable of presenting our side intelligently to those promoting the bill."[18]

Here, Burke was hinting at an important distinction, which several years later he would make explicit. A "lobbyist" was willing to trade money or votes to secure a political advantage. The Catholic Church could never do that because it would be entering directly into the political process. Such activity would either open the Church to manipulation by political parties or else compromise its ability to speak truth. Rather, the NCWC was to be a "voice" to present the Church's position "intelligently" to all parties, inviting them to see the reasonableness of its stand. No commitment would be made to anyone. The Church must remain free to be itself.

Dowling turned to Monsignor Edward A. Pace, vice rector of Catholic University. He held two doctorates, one in theology and a second in experimental psychology. Pace agreed to become executive secretary of Dowling's department on a temporary basis until other arrangements could be made. He was level-headed, eminently qualified, and already quite conversant with the federal education question. Burke thanked Dowling for assigning him and confirmed that he "will be an immense help." Indeed, during Burke's first year and more as general secretary, he would rely heavily Pace for advice and counsel.[19]

Burke assisted Bishop William Russell directly in forming the Press Department. He articulated its critical role in the NCWC in an address he prepared for delivery by Russell to the Catholic Press Association (CPA). It explained that while the NCWC was to unify all major Catholic activities—education, social action, and men's and women's organizations—the Press Department was to be the center of information and clearinghouse for the plans and activities of the others. It would be not only information-central, wrote Burke, "[it] will be the living voice of the whole body of the National Catholic Welfare Council, of which the other departments are the mind, the heart, and the hands. The Press Department is an organic part of the National Catholic Welfare Council. It cannot be separated from it without vitally injuring it."[20]

This allusion to the Mystical Body of Christ was classic Burke. No doubt he saw the heart of the NCWC as the education department which protected and promoted parochial schools, transmitters of Catholic life. The mind was the Social Action Department which applied Catholic principles to social problems. The hand was the Department of Lay Activities which mobilized Catholic men and women to implement the solutions. These agencies would use the Press Department as their means of publication. That department would have three subsidiary bureaus: one for news, another for information, and a third for publication. The news bureau would function much like the Associated Press, providing articles on foreign and domestic issues to Catholic and secular papers. The information bureau would answer inquiries about the Catholic position on public matters and about people in the public eye. The publication bureau would issue pamphlets and books of the departments.[21]

In late January 1920, Russell delivered the address at the national convention of the CPA, which he attended to solicit its cooperation with the Press Department. The association complied, passing several resolutions including one appointing eight members (its own officers among them) to the department's executive committee, and another turning over to the department the CPA's cable service with London and Rome. As part of the last arrangement, it stipulated membership in the CPA as a prerequisite for a subscription to that service.[22]

Burke and Russell wanted the Washington news bureau to be first-class and intended to secure a man of national repute as director. Doing so would cost a considerable sum in salary, $15,000 annually ($230,000 in 2024). That amount would put a huge dent in the department's $40,000 budget. While in New York, Burke sought to supplement funds by soliciting a sizable donation from wealthy Catholic Francis Patrick "Frank" Garvan, dean of Fordham University Law School. He explained the bureau in detail and pleaded with Garvan to "keep us from financial worry in order to do the work." "The fact that we planned a really high class efficient department appealed to him," Burke reported to Russell. Garvan pledged $60,000 ($925,000) to be given at the end of April.[23]

Back in Washington, Burke approached Justin McGrath, Washington bureau chief of the Hearst Press and Universal News Service. He had previously been editor of the *San Francisco Examiner.* After extensive interview, Burke considered him "an ideal man" for the post. He had a keen sense of news and understood distribution well. "Of his own accord he showed what he would do for the Catholic papers," Burke reported to Russell, "and how he could get Catholic news into the secular press." Burke found him "unassuming and quiet: yet he knows of what he is talking." McGrath agreed to the salary, but wanted two-years' work guaranteed.[24]

Since McGrath was one of William Randolph Hearst's "biggest men," Burke was unsure if the tycoon would let him go. Moreover, he wanted to make certain McGrath was "a practical Catholic." So, he telegraphed Hanna in San Francisco who knew McGrath well.[25] Hanna responded that

McGrath was "capable, honourable, and upright," though "not very ardent in the practice of his religion," which Hanna attributed to McGrath's need to be at the office until 2:00 or 3:00 on Sunday mornings to put the *Examiner* to bed. He favored the appointment.[26]

Burke went to New York to see Hearst about it. "Do you know you are asking for my best man?" was Hearst's comment. "Yes," replied Burke. He argued the case strongly before Hearst agreed to surrender his star. During their discussion, Hearst displayed great interest in the NCWC's news bureau and thought it would be of immense help to the secular press. Burke returned to D.C. to sign the deal with McGrath.[27]

Helping launch these departments added to Burke's burden of winding down the war work while continuing editorship of *Catholic World.* By mid-February, the toll became evident in the way he signed off on correspondence. To Muldoon, Burke commented, "I often wish you had to come on here to help me with this new work." A week later he concluded a letter to Dowling: "I would ask you to pray that I may be patient and very charitable in all of this work."[28] Never had he ended a letter in this fashion. He obviously felt overburdened and on edge. His already thin patience was about to be sorely tried.

Burke played an essential role in helping Bishop Joseph Schrembs establish the Lay Activities Department. The initial concern was what to do with the AFCS.[29] Schrembs asked several people, Burke among them, how to proceed. As Burke understood it, the hierarchy intended "to form a national men's council," not supplant any society or agency like the AFCS. Nor should it usurp the Knights of Columbus, which he thought would affiliate with the council if it did not try to supplant them. Burke believed local bishops would insist Catholic societies unite with it and operate under diocesan direction and supervision. "Our council can work only through the Bishops," advised Burke, "for they are not only the Ordinaries, they are also the members of the National Catholic Welfare Council." In his judgment, it would be "a wrong start" to make the AFCS the new national men's council. He thought it best to hold a national conference of existing societies about how a national council could help coordinate them and promote them.[30] Muldoon recommended the same course of action. Like Burke, he believed organizing diocesan councils was the ideal, but he considered it "a dream at present." Schrembs should start with existing societies and gradually work toward diocesan councils.[31]

Cardinal William O'Connell, who viewed the NCWC as a threat to his ambitions and had been unfriendly to its establishment, argued otherwise. He thought the proposed council should unite only "diocesan organizations properly constituted and under the *active* direction and *active* guidance" of their bishops. Unfortunately, only a few dioceses, like his own, had such organizations. As O'Connell saw it, Schrembs's first task was "to bring into existence the Diocesan forces, then to organize them as a Diocesan unit, and then to unify them in a national sense." Unless he took this approach, the men's council would meet the same fate as the AFCS, which O'Connell considered moribund. He asked Schrembs to let him know his plan because he had "no intention of giving either time or money to anything which does not promise some real and definite program." Schrembs decided to follow the recommendation of Burke and Muldoon.[32] While this course made the most sense, its noncompliance with O'Connell's suggestion did not augur well for either Schrembs's department or the NCWC as a whole.

Schrembs and Burke went forward with the creation of a national women's organization. Unfortunately Burke's role brought him head to head with the "dreadfully earnest" John Montgomery Cooper, a clash that did not end well. Schrembs placed Cooper, secretary of the War Council's Committee on Women's Activities, in charge of establishing the new entity. He called an organizational convention to meet in Washington in March and asked each bishop to send one to three delegates, and each society, one or two.[33]

Cooper then drafted a tentative constitution which established two organizations: a board of directors with national officers and a service bureau which functioned independently of the board. On seeing the plan, Burke objected that women were being summoned to meet under false pretenses, asking them to establish the board of directors, yet without giving it direct control over the service bureau. Cooper admitted that was his intention because he did not think women could manage their own affairs. Although agreeing they lacked experience in national organization, Burke argued the plan ought to establish a real association and then provide guidance in its management. Prior to the convention, Burked explained their differences to Schrembs, who sided with him. Cooper gamely admitted defeat and "gave full acceptance to the decision."[34]

The convention, chaired by Burke, had delegates from forty-four dioceses and fifty-seven women's societies. "For the most part," he noted, "they were a group of unusually intelligent keen experienced women and proof that, if we can create a national organization we can outstrip anything in existence."[35] His opening remarks appealed to the Mystical Body. "We ought to be united," he told the delegates: "we ought to stand as one body, magnificent in our corporate unity, splendid in our united will, giving and receiving help and inspiration from one another, all animated by the one purpose.... We should think of ourselves not as individuals, not as particular groups, not even as one large human group—but as members of that one Body of which Christ is the Head."[36]

Burke then appointed three committees, one to frame an order of procedure, another to develop a program, and the last to report a constitution. These labored through the rest of the day. Burke worked with the constitution committee, which produced a document establishing the National Council of Catholic Women (NCCW). It provided a board of directors comprised of twenty-one ladies to include a representative from each of the fourteen ecclesiastical provinces. The board was to choose national officers: a president, three vice-presidents, a treasurer, and a secretary. The next evening, the convention adopted the constitution.[37]

Meanwhile, a dangerous situation brewed around Lillian Slattery, personal representative of O'Connell. He had become persona non grata with the bishops of New England because of his elevation to the archbishopric of Boston through powerful Roman connections rather than the normal selection process. Thereafter, he used his office to amass vast sums of money and attempted to impose his will and Roman discipline on bishops of the province of New England. Most recently, it became known that two priests—David Toomey, O'Connell's personal chaplain, and James O'Connell, his nephew and chancellor—were both secretly married, leading double lives. The scandal was an open secret among New England Catholics and in clerical circles beyond. The bishops of the province were working diligently for O'Connell's removal.[38]

Sharing the New Englanders' distaste for O'Connell, Cooper had given Slattery a cool, if not unfriendly, welcome to the convention. He considered her O'Connell's puppet, there to impose his ideas on the nascent organization or "smash" it aborning. Adding insult to injury, he allegedly offended her in meetings of the program committee, wherein it was said, he called the Lenten resolutions of the Boston Archdiocesan League of Women cheap advertising.[39] Cooper's demeanor and actions were not without repercussion.

On the convention's third day, elections began and trouble erupted. "Politics had not only taken root," noted Burke, "but had flowered overnight."[40] At issue was the Boston problem, and the "casus belli [occasion of war]," as Burke put it, was Slattery. Delegates from New England, led by Father Daniel M. Tully, observer for Bishop Thomas Beaven of Springfield, Massachusetts, worked to block her advancement. Because the nominating committee had placed Cardinal Gibbons's personal representative on the ballot for board members as a courtesy, Burke advised it should do the same for O'Connell's. When the proposed slate of candidates included Slattery, Tully lobbied on the floor for her defeat. Still, she won a seat. "It isn't over important," acknowledged Cooper. "She is only one of 21 and if she doesn't get office it is all right." While the newly elected board conferred to select national officers, Tully, in Beaven's name, notified Schrembs that the diocese of Springfield would not join the new organization, and the rest of New England would probably follow suit. He even asked Schrembs to announce this publicly to the convention. Figuring the matter would work itself out, Schrembs refused to give it notice. Instead, with an eye to appeasing O'Connell, he paid tribute to Slattery's election to the board. News of New England's threat, however, spread and overshadowed the proceedings. As it turned out, Slattery was not elected a national officer. Even so, Cooper told Burke that the NCCW was finished because New England refused to join.[41]

The convention's adjournment failed to bring an end to the Slattery affair. Cooper was angry with Burke for his role in her election. After steaming for two days, he buttonholed Burke who was about to catch a train for New York. "Father Burke, I am resigning and I wish my resignation to take effect at once," said Cooper. When Burke asked why, Cooper replied: "Ecclesiastical politics have entered into the organization. Disingenuousness marks it and I can no longer retain my self respect [*sic*] and remain." He believed fear of O'Connell caused Burke to sacrifice the principles of the NCCW by advising Slattery's election to the board.[42]

Burke canceled his trip so they could speak that evening. Cooper told him he already had Gibbons's permission to resign. It surprised Burke he had approached the cardinal without consulting him. In addition to the Slattery matter, Cooper complained Burke had allowed the *NCWC Bulletin* to carry an article about women's work which he had nixed. Burke countered that in his review of page proofs, he "naturally thought" the article had Cooper's approval. "That is always the answer," said Cooper. "No one is responsible. I won't say it is dishonest: but it is disingenuous." Burke was crestfallen. To Muldoon, he lamented: "Father Cooper does not believe I am honest in the general acceptance of the word.... I might with both justification and indignation say much in rebuttal. In an ecclesiastical organization it is as impossible to keep out ecclesiastical politics as it is to keep all air out of a house and yet have the walls standing. No one wishes to sacrifice principle: but adjustment: judgment that may be faulty, are necessary." Burke let the matter go with the comment: "One [Cooper] cannot altogether protest against ecclesiastical politics when one's friends [the New Englanders] are also doing political work even if the latter be in the name of righteousness."[43]

Cooper defended his resignation to Bishop Russell. Slattery was an unworthy delegate. She had come to impose O'Connell's views on the organization. She forced her way onto the board of directors. Burke knew she was unworthy, but "coached" the convention into her election. Cooper considered it giving "preferential backing" to O'Connell, a prelate "who stands for what is least American and what is least Catholic in our life." Cooper lost confidence in Burke, a man whom he had respected. It was a matter of principle.[44]

Cooper's resignation left the women's council without an executive secretary and left Burke "in a big dark hole." "What I shall do I do not know," he told Muldoon. "Sometimes the clouds are so thick and so numerous that everything looks very black." He asked if Muldoon could lend him a priest for the job.[45] The bishop had no one to offer. Nor was he sorry to see Cooper go. "I think it a blessing in disguise," he wrote. "He will not work in harness, and dislikes a rein. Training will hardly change that." He suggested Burke replace Cooper with a lay person. Turning to events at the convention, Muldoon vented his own frustration: "Boston—Boston—Boston. Of course N[ew]. E[ngland]. should be big enough to follow the voice of the delegates and not stand on the personal. All were, no doubt, given a fair show and a good loser accepts the result." He believed that the affair was blown out of proportion. Still, it was the "vain and false rumors" now to be bandied about that might do the real harm.[46]

To Lynch in Belgium, Burke confessed being overwhelmed. The Paulists had yet to give him an assistant for *Catholic World*, something he could not understand and which made "the whole work doubly hard." He was laboring day and night and believed if he devoted his entire time solely to the NCWC, it would still be difficult to make it a success. "With me away over half the time, it is impossible," he told her. "Meanwhile I try to do the impossible; confounded in the process ... because of the work and the spiritual adjustment." His "best worker in the woman's field," Cooper, had resigned, leaving him "very sorry and very much depressed." "He leaves the work without a master and so far as he is concerned, ruined," wrote Burke. He took inspiration from reading the epistles of Paul who lived in dependence upon Christ. "I live and work for and in Him and Him alone," concluded Burke. "He lifts us above human personalities, human self-seeking and gives us the sole necessary confidence that the work is worth while and that He will see to its continuing: its success or failure, its ending and its consummation in heaven."[47]

The saga continued with the wholesale resignation of stenographers in Cooper's office who were very fond of him. Before leaving, he had summoned and urged them *not* to resign, which reminded Burke of the story about an avaricious priest who, in devout tone, informed a rich female parishioner, "Next Friday is my birthday. Kindly say a prayer for me." Still, Burke believed the work would continue. "I will probably put a woman in charge," he told Muldoon. "They will have to learn to manage on their own." In the end, Burke let the NCCW board of directors choose its own executive secretary. In May, it selected Agnes Regan who was to hold the post for many years. Within a month she began national organizing and eventually managed to enroll even anti-O'Connell New Englanders.[48]

There remained the pacification of O'Connell. Slattery had given him a negative report. Her reception had been unfriendly. While a rival delegate from Boston had received honors, she had been ignored. She told of Cooper's offensive, tactless attitude toward her and the program of the Archdiocesan League of Women. To Schrembs and Burke, O'Connell gave the NCCW a vote of no confidence. Trust in it, he declared, could be restored only by a thorough explanation of these matters.[49]

Burke sent a lengthy reply defending himself, Schrembs, and the NCCW. He thought Slattery mistaken because he and Schrembs had gone out of their way to welcome her cordially. He had no idea how Cooper had greeted her. Opposition to her there was, but it came from New Englanders and neither he nor Schrembs took it seriously or encouraged it. As to Cooper, he resigned from the War and Welfare Councils.[50] This deft reply apparently smoothed matters over with O'Connell for the time being—but only that. The New England matter would surface again, and the next time it nearly spelled the end of the NCWC.

COLLAPSE

The effort to launch departments brought Burke to near collapse. As the Cooper debacle played out, he took to bed in New York with a cold. Murray and others at *Catholic World* were concerned enough to summon his physician Dr. Mohan, who delivered Burke "rather severe warnings." Still, Burke continued doing correspondence from bed, explaining to Muldoon that he "had been knocked out a bit."[51] Over-anxious and irritable, Burke rose to return to Washington. He tried to write to Murray before his departure, but the effort proved too much, so he telephoned her in apparent anger. That evening, he wrote to her from Washington to say that his call that morning gave her an example "of just what you should not do and how you should not act." He explained he had lost his temper because he thought she was working too hard and he felt "deeply" that she must keep up her spirits and health. "God help me if you should get sick now," he told her. "I frequently wish I were more faithful to my own teaching," he confessed. "I know that you will be: and so I'll say no more.[52]

The following day, Burke told her he was feeling better, but actually he was back in bed. He was impatient because he found the office woefully defective in comparison to its counterpart at the magazine. "I should keep my patience, my good humor, and my appreciation of all the love and kindness," he explained, "—and I don't." He had to admit, however, the work was going well and was "blessed." Reading Murray's thoughts, he continued: "Then, you say, why aren't you happy? And I answer because seeing it go so well, and with such possibilities, I want to see it go best and fulfill all its possibilities. And you answer, why don't you take a dose of the medicine you so often gave me: and I answer I will—and then sometimes neglect it."[53] After several days in bed, Burke was still near exhaustion. "I walked yesterday (just think of it)," he wrote Murray. He apologized for not being present to celebrate her birthday and the anniversary of her coming to *Catholic World*. "My celebrations here are none at all and sometimes I feel like the Jews in Babylon."[54]

Murray was not alone in her concern. Other of Burke's lady friends shared it. Mary Hawks and the Merrick sisters, Mary and Mildred, were confidantes of each other and Burke. During war years, he had had no time to visit Mary and Mildred. The former complained: "We never see Fr. B. any more. Of course he is terribly busy." In summer 1919, Burke did see the sisters, but the occasion afforded little opportunity for conversation. Mary blamed the situation on Burke's two jobs: at the War Council and *Catholic World*. "It is too much for any one man," she told Hawks. Shortly after Cooper's resignation, Burke visited Mary Merrick and told her the story of his leaving. Hawks was glad Burke had unburdened himself. She told Mary he was walking "his own via dolorosa [way of the cross], and it brings acute suffering at times. His position is not an enviable one, but it can accomplish much for God and the Church, and he must suffer for it." Hawks was sorry about Cooper because she believed to two men could have done much good for each other. "But surely, if after all these months Dr. C. can so misunderstand, it must not be hopeful."[55]

Indeed the physical and emotional strain took its toll. Shortly before Holy Week, Burke's health began to cave. To Lynch, he admitted he suffered what he called "a sort of a breakdown." His physician was glad he "was at least sensible for giving heed to the warning" and sent him south to recuperate. Accompanied by fellow Paulist, Father John E. Burke, who recently arrived at the NCWC, Burke went to the Partridge Inn in Augusta, Georgia, "a very quiet place with really nothing to do but walk." There was a tennis court, but Burke did not feel up to playing. The weather and surroundings were pleasant, the accommodations comfortable. "What I lack is the old buoyancy," he explained to Murray, "the youthful spirit if I may so speak: there is a sort of tired feeling. But this is passing and I have felt excellent for the last few days." He asked her to keep his condition secret, chalking it up to too much work, something which must have been evident to her through his impatience and irritability. He was making good resolutions to take things easier and more quietly. He gave her permission to correct him without getting "irritable and excited" when she saw him resuming his old work ways, but to "calmly" keep after him to take care of himself. "The Lord does turn the tables and show us that we are all weaklings," he wrote. "You were away a year ago and had to take a rest. And now I am away and you must bear the work. It is a harder task for you than for me because I am more gifted." Yet, Burke assured her that she was "doing wonderfully well," indeed "valiant work."[56]

The remark about being more gifted may seem insensitive, perhaps to a degree it was. It was also humble. Humility is truth, and truth is objective. Hawks later recalled Burke "always stressed great objectivity." His own "objectiveness made him essentially just."[57] His comment to Murray was not a boast or comparison, but a statement of fact. It recognized that handling the work by oneself was more difficult for her than for him because of his native talent. At the same time, it was an admission that his talent was a gift, and nothing to be prideful about, especially in the context of their mutual weakness.

And weakness there was aplenty on Burke's side. On Good Friday, he went to the local church and spent from noon until 3:00 P.M. before the Blessed Sacrament in honor of Jesus' passion. When he returned to the inn, he found a letter from Murray awaiting him. It was apparently a letter of support, saying she was praying the Lord would bring Burke closer to himself. He considered it an appropriate day to receive it. He admitted he was "weak enough to say that I need a good deal of strength." While assuming she understood his meaning, he made it explicit: "I don't want the Welfare Council work," he told her. "I never went into the priesthood for it. I don't think I'm called in any way to direct the national work of the Catholic Church in the United States. It's a pain and just now little short of an agony to accept it." Burke acknowledged that although time spent that afternoon with the Lord was comforting, he needed someone with whom to share what he was going through. "There is extreme loneliness unless another soul knows," he wrote. "One wants some one else to understand him." He thought she would find it odd that as much as he welcomed news of the Paulists' intention to give him an assistant for the magazine, "yet it seemed to fix more surely what I dread—the other work." The high regard in which those at the NCWC held him left Burke comfortless and joyless. Power and authority held no allure. He pined to be with those he loved and who loved him: his family, Murray, the staff of the magazine, his brother Paulists.[58]

Burke explained he probably took the job of general secretary because of circumstances. Somebody had to do it, and the choice fell to him. While the "vision" of national Catholicism fascinated him, its realization lacked personal appeal; he had no inclination for it. "Whatever I do the vision is beyond the achievement," he told Murray. "Some one else ought to have been chosen and I would gladly have served in my own way." Having poured out his heart, he assured her he was going to soldier on. "I see the big things I ought to do and my soul is not going to quake nor go back," he told her. "It is going to push ahead with the same courage, the same determination, the same single, absorbing love of our Savior Jesus Christ. I want that love to consume me and burn me up on the altar of his sacrifice." Burke simply wished Murray to know what it was costing him. He bared his soul to her because he considered her brave enough to handle seeing "a supposedly big man unwilling to take a big job."[59]

When Hawks informed Mary Merrick of Burke's illness, she was "not surprised—only truly indignant" because he had to work two jobs. "It seems so unnecessary and so inevitable," she told Hawks. "I believe the moral or mental worry of Fr. C[ooper]'s leaving etc. was worse for him than work."[60]

After six more weeks of recuperation, Burke's darkest time was behind him enough that he dismissed his breakdown as nothing of the sort. He had "not really been ill at all," he wrote to Lynch who was back from Belgium. It had been "more the solicitation of friends than anything else." He did admit working very hard to get the NCWC off the ground at significant personal cost. Yet, the "consuming" part of the effort was finished, "the great lines have been laid," and work of the organization would keep him busy in the future. Burke averred he had learned "spiritual lessons" and gained "spiritual experience." "I have had much of sacrifice, of disappointment: of bewilderment and of bitterness," he told her. "And so the value of quiet out of all the noise: of integrity out of the confusion: of silence out of the discussion and debate has not altogether been lost to me." Burke welcomed Lynch home and greeted her "in the name of our dear Lord, in Whom our lives are one."[61]

COMPLETION OF THE ADMINISTRATIVE ARM

By mid-April 1920, Burke returned to Washington. Early the next month, he joined Schrembs in Chicago to establish the men's council. This time Schrembs took the lead and Burke served as vice chairman of the convention. About sixty representatives from nineteen national organizations of Catholic men attended. "The very atmosphere," recalled Michael Slattery, "was surcharged with doubt and uncertainty." Although the delegates feared a comprehensive plan of diocesan organization would be too difficult to accomplish, they were persuaded to undertake it, reluctantly. Remaining "frankly skeptical of results," they formulated only a provisional constitution that stipulated each society and diocese was authorized to send one delegate to the annual convention of the National Council of Catholic Men (NCCM).[62]

The council was to elect an executive board of twelve members as the governing body. The NCCM was not "to interfere with the field of activity or the autonomous direction and conduct of any existing society or organization," but to aid them in their particular endeavors, something Burke and Muldoon had earlier insisted. Its several purposes included animation of lay movements in every parish and diocese of the country; preparation of social workers; and management of international relations with other Catholic societies. The NCCM also adopted a resolution to raise a $25 million ($385 million in 2024) endowment to support the NCWC.[63]

The day after the convention, Burke and Schrembs met with the board of directors of the NCCW in Chicago. Burke wanted it to take charge of his beloved Clifton, the National Service School for Women, thus bringing it under the umbrella of the NCWC. The board unanimously resolved to maintain and support the institution. In September 1920, it placed the school under immediate care of the executive staff, that is, the six officers of the NCCW.[64]

Thus began a somewhat turbulent relationship between Burke and Gertrude Hill Gavin, president of the NCCW and daughter of railroad baron James J. Hill. Scarcely a month later, Burke confided to Murray: "As to Mrs. G[avin]'s attitude to the school, I think it a determination to give no help. She's against me, of course. I also think she's disgusted with Miss Regan." Regan had failed to draft a plan for a fund-raising campaign to support Clifton, so there was nothing to present to the upcoming convention of the NCCW. "So all in all the clouds look heavy," wrote Burke. Nor had he had time to cultivate the help of Frederick Keppel or Raymond Fosdick, who were both great admirers Clifton graduates. The overstretched Burke said of himself and Regan: "We have grave faults: I've neglected much: but I had hoped Mrs. G would be willing to bear with our shortcomings. We are understaffed and trying to save money."[65]

Burke's heart was "depressed" about Clifton. Apparently, he had hoped Gavin would personally contribute funds to its support, which she showed no sign of doing. As will be seen, he considered her a cosseted heiress, who was spiritually immature if not weak. Perhaps her sensing of his attitude accounted for her opposition to him. Still, there was no strategy for a fund-raising campaign, which made the school's future bleak. At this point, Burke considered it a "failure." In September 1920, it had graduated only fourteen students. He thought the six-month curriculum too short and incomplete. He hoped to get it extended and standardized so that Clifton would become a true, Catholic, training school for social workers taking its rightful place among the handful of other such institutions around the country. In the present situation, however, the vision dimmed. The incoming cohort, which just arrived, however, had twenty-seven students, almost twice the previous one. Their tuition amounted to a total of $8,100 ($125,000 in 2024), which helped defray expenses. A month and a half later, Burke reported Clifton was causing him only "some worry."[66]

The branch of the NCWC that remained something of a phantom throughout most of the council's first year of existence was the Legal Department. Archbishop Dennis Dougherty, who chaired it, tried immediately to resign. When the administrative bishops refused to accept his resignation, he simply hired a lawyer, James R. Ryan, and gave him a secretary. By November 1920, Burke concluded Ryan was "too small for the task." In early 1921, Burke hired William Cochran, a political commentator for the *Chicago Tribune*, to direct the department and appointed Ryan associate director under him, something which no doubt rankled the man and would come back to haunt Burke a few years hence.[67]

The last piece of the NCWC's administrative arm was of Burke's own making. With postwar resumption of immigration from Europe, he wanted to ensure that Catholic newcomers felt welcomed by their American coreligionists. When the NCWC had received incorrect information that the commissioner of immigration had entrusted all immigrants to care of the YMCA, Burke, Lapp, Regan, and Slattery decided it should establish an Immigration Bureau. Under Burke's immediate supervision, it was to open offices at Ellis Island and Boston first, while monitoring Baltimore, Philadelphia, and Providence to see to the need at those ports. Burke hired Bruce Mohler to direct the bureau. In fall 1920, Burke asked Assistant Secretary of Labor Louis Post, who oversaw immigration, to officially recognize the NCWC as an agent of the government in that regard.[68]

Governmental recognition was slow in coming. The delay resulted in part from the change in presidential administrations. Further delay occurred when the new incoming commissioner thought the Red Cross should care for all immigrants. Not until Burke insisted that Catholics be admitted to the work did the government act. In May, the commissioner authorized two NCWC workers at Ellis Island.[69]

As this final component of the Welfare Council took shape, Burke told Murray the work was growing so fast it was hard to keep pace with it. "And then with the imagination I have," he added, "it is harder still." He could envision what the council might become and do. Yet, that vision seemed unique to him. "Long ago I saw that I was the only one who saw what the Council ought to be," he explained. "You saw it with me. And as it grows I see in a measure where it must be a solitary work." It was too difficult to explain to others and convince them how the NCWC was to function. People easily understood departmental work, but "to get those who will see the whole coordinated is most difficult." Even harder was getting them to appreciate the spirit that should enliven it, the extent of its responsibilities, and "the care to be exercised with the thought that it is better to live and to act some, than to be too energetic and die soon."[70]

THE EDUCATION QUESTION

By 1920 a new nativism was abroad in the land and focused on education. In spring of that year, the Southern Jurisdiction of Scottish Rite Masons, an organization unfriendly to the Catholic Church and comprising the thirty-three states south of the Ohio River and west of the Mississippi, came out in favor of both compulsory public schooling and the establishment of a federal department of education. A second organization with an identical platform was the Ku Klux Klan. Resurrected in 1915 by Georgia fraternalist William Simmons, the Klan was committed to 100 percent Americanism and the supremacy of the Caucasian race. It swelled its ranks by pandering to racism, nativism, anti-Semitism, and anti-Catholicism. Klansmen saw themselves as the guardians of law and order (especially Prohibition), family life, Protestantism, and Victorian values, issues one historian has summed up under the rubric of "white, Protestant nationalism." The NEA quietly accepted support of both and prepared to pressure the national conventions of both political parties to endorse the bill in their platforms. The Republican advisory committee already recommended federal aid for education.[71] Catholics viewed this as a step toward endorsement of the Smith-Towner bill. An alarmed Dowling urged the NCWC to counteraction.[72]

Burke and Pace set to work. Pace drafted a protest to the Republican platform committee wherein he warned against "federal control of education." Admitting need of financial support for schools, he asserted funds should come from local governments. He also urged upholding rights of private educational institutions as "fundamental to American civic life." He and Burke had Cardinal Gibbons, who was to deliver an invocation at the convention, offer the protest as a personal letter to the committee. Burke wrote a cover letter for the protest explaining that the Welfare Council represented "officially the entire Catholic body of the United States." It said the Church opposed the bill "because we know that the forces back of its framing are seeking a federal subsidy for state education." He "earnestly" requested Ogden Mills, presumptive chairman of the Committee on Resolutions, ensure the platform contain no such endorsement.[73]

Burke sent Pace and Michael Slattery to the Republican convention in Chicago where they joined forces with Lapp. Fearful lest their efforts be discovered and exposed by use of Western Union for communication with Washington, Burke assigned code names to the principal politicians. For instance, Mills was "Henry" and National Committee Chairman Will Hays was "Brown." The day before the convention, Burke telegraphed Slattery that he had the cover letter and protest "personally handed to Henry" that morning and a special message given to Theodore Roosevelt Jr., code-name "Smith."[74]

The NCWC's agents found the NEA and its allies pressing hard for federalization of education. So, the three decided to concentrate on the two candidates for permanent chairmanship of the platform committee: Mills, who was Hays's choice for the post; and Indiana Senator James Watson, who was the Old Guard's pick. Lapp saw Watson, who opposed the Smith-Towner bill. Slattery, a Philadelphian, made contact with delegates from that city, who promised support, and then he hunted down Roosevelt, who was staying "under cover" with friends. Slattery urged him to put pressure on Mills. Unable to locate Mills himself, Slattery saw John King, national committeeman from Connecticut, who held the proxy of Old-Guard party-boss Boies Penrose, senator from Pennsylvania. Slattery told King he did not like the outlook and wanted action. King told him to be in Pennsylvania Governor William Sproul's room at 6:00 P.M. The governor promised to make the NCWC's fight his own. When Slattery found Mills at 7:00, the latter claimed he received no letter from Burke and "acted as if he was not with us." Slattery urged Burke to have all his New York friends wire protests to Mills.[75]

On opening day, things brightened. The Committee on Resolutions elected Watson permanent chairman, "showing," as Slattery informed Burke, "the Old Guard is in the saddle." Watson appointed a subcommittee of thirteen with himself in the chair to draft the platform. One of the thirteen was John Neylan, a California Catholic. Leaving nothing to chance, Slattery had Congressman Joseph McLaughlin of Pennsylvania, who had access to Penrose's private phone, tell him Catholics would fight the ticket in November if Republicans failed to protect parochial education. Still unsatisfied, Slattery wired his friends in Philadelphia to deliver the message personally to Penrose. Word came back Boss Penrose would act. That night, Sproul sent for Slattery to say Penrose had ordered nothing be done that might offend Catholics. "I see you are taking no chances with this thing," commented the governor.[76]

The next day, Burke telegraphed Slattery with orders to see Neylan. Having already done so, Slattery explained that Neylan was not only on the subcommittee, he was also floor leader for Senator Hiram Johnson of California, code-name "West," who was a presidential candidate. Slattery argued the case against federalization of education. He also spoke with Joseph Scott, a prominent Catholic attorney from Los Angeles. He told Burke Scott would reinforce to Neylan the arguments made earlier in the day.[77]

The next day, the Committee on Resolutions reported a platform that went out of its way to be inoffensive to Catholics. The education plank retreated from the advisory committee's blanket sanction of federal aid and endorsed it only for agricultural and vocational education, two areas in which the federal government was already involved. A plank escaping Catholic attention at the time, but that would soon greatly aid the cause, was a call for reorganization of federal departments "with a view to securing consolidation ... [and] the elimination of duplication." Yet another that would prove a boon called for reduction of public debt, a goal at odds with the large subsidy in the Smith-Towner bill.[78]

Burke considered accompanying Slattery to the Democratic convention in San Francisco, but had worn down again to the point of needing rest. He left William Kerby in charge of headquarters and departed for Lake George and his Paulist brothers. There, he remained in contact with only family, especially his sister Lizzie and brother Thomas. His brother James went with Slattery; their doings Burke followed from afar through the press, commenting to Thomas that "James must have had an interesting time ... judging from the newspaper accounts."[79]

Indeed, he did. A number of progressive Catholic Democrats, like Senator Thomas Walsh of Montana and Knight Patrick Callahan, were unsympathetic to the NCWC's position on the Smith-Towner bill. So, James and Slattery had to rely on non-Catholics, like Secretary of State Bainbridge Colby, to uphold the Catholic position in face of tremendous pressure by the NEA for a plank endorsing it. In this, they received assistance from Gavin, president of the NCCW, who supplied advice and applied her considerable political leverage. In the end, the platform committee rejected a full endorsement of the bill in favor of "cooperative federal assistance to the states" for the removal of illiteracy, the increase of teacher salaries, and the promotion of citizenship.[80]

Burke probably returned to work in August 1920, but he was still not rested enough to remain free from illness. He attended the annual convention of the NCCM and then set off on a lecture circuit, which took him city-hopping throughout the East. All the while he suffered a cold that waxed and waned. Between trips, he told Murray, he "had a little attack of the old fever," which was "to be kept quiet." This bout was probably similar to what sent him to the Partridge Inn earlier that year. Burke said he must give up "the lecture business" because there was so much work at the NCWC he was unable to keep up with it. "I would like to work nights," he explained, "but there would be a protest I suppose," no doubt from his physicians.[81]

Murray herself learned she was suffering from a thyroid condition. This news confirmed for Burke what he told her the previous summer: that aggravating her spiritual struggle was "a physical condition that is real: that needs care and that must at all costs be attended to." Knowing this, however, did not make her spiritual journey any easier. The two had apparently reached an agreement not to talk about her struggles further, though Burke remained with her in spirit. "I have not left you for a day," he assured her in mid-November: "and every morning at Mass I remember your name."[82] Clearly, he shared her pain.

Bethlehem and Nazareth

Christmas Day 1920 found Burke in Washington away from family and friends, and his thoughts turned to Lynch and Bethlehem and Nazareth. "It is farther away from you physically than usual, that I write this Christmas letter," he penned. "But 'tis no farther in the affections, rather close as the years go on." Jesus had gone forth from the cave in Bethlehem and his home in Nazareth to do the will of his Father, undeterred by affection for those left behind, but with love for them never less for having done so. The editorial sanctum at *Catholic World* was his and Lynch's Bethlehem and Nazareth. Memory carried him back to the 1910s before remodel of the building. "The blessings you brought to 60th Street long ago still endure with me and with you," he reminisced. "Often does the street itself speak of it—its flags may be unclean but your feet have sanctified them: the old stairs are gone but the door through which you entered is still there, and the stairs lead to the same room where the editor sat: and your room though enlarged has the same narrow closet for cloak and rubbers and old shoes." What Lynch had learned there, she carried forth into the wider world, said Burke, and resting over what she took was the peace of Nazareth.[83]

Amid the bustle of the apostolate, he cautioned, was temptation to consider action as the principal thing. "Doing is much: but the nature of the doing is still more," he reminded her. The Holy Spirit was "eternally within us urging us to peace," and peace consisted of sinking all things and oneself in Christ. "We must abide by His side morning, noon, and night." One must learn "to hide self until the hiding [became] habit," until one's life was hidden in Christ, and Christ lived in and through one. "'Tis vain for one to boast but our Lord has given me something of this in spite of all my sins," admitted Burke. "And it is the only thing that has helped me." Turning beyond himself, he told Lynch the work of the NCWC was growing beyond his dreams. "It is the Catholic Church in action," he declared. "It is Christ manifesting the unity of the Church and the power of His word before men. And He is its peace."[84]

Endnotes to Chapter 8

1. Burke, *Christ in Us*, 97–98.
2. Federal Manuscript Census, New York City, 1920; Coyle, Memories of War Council, ACUA, USCCB 10:72:24; Burke to Lynch, 11 June 1933, AP, Burke Papers, box 5.
3. Burke to Murray, 5 January 1920, AP, Burke Papers, box 11; Burke to Murray, 15 October 1929, ibid.
4. Burke to Lynch, 2 January 1920, AP, Burke Papers, box 5.
5. Burke to Murray, 5 January 1920, AP, Burke Papers, box 11 (quotes are here); Burke to Murray, 2 April 1920, ibid.
6. Burke to Murray, 5 January 1920, AP, Burke Papers, box 11.
7. Ibid.
8. Russell to Gibbons, 13 February 1920, AAB-AASMSU, 130U9; Gibbons to T. Burke, 18 February 1920, AP, Official Papers of Superior General Thomas F. Burke 1920; Slawson, *Foundation of NCWC*, 72.
9. Thomas Burke to Gibbons, 25 February 1920, ADCh, 717.50; Slawson, *Foundation of NCWC*, 72.
10. Burke to Murray, 2 April 1920, AP, Burke Papers, box 11; Burke to T. Burke, 30 September 1922, AP, Official Papers of Superior General Thomas F. Burke 1922; Slawson, *Foundation of NCWC*, 72.
11. James H. Ryan to Burke, 31 May 1924, ACUA, USCCB 10:153:4 (the first quote is here); McNulty to Henry Lefebure, 14 April 1972, ibid., USCCB 10:72:24 (the second quote is here); Richard Gribble, C.S.C., *An Archbishop for the People: The Life of Edward J. Hanna* (NewYork/Mahwah, N.J.: Paulist Press, 2006), 7–50.
12. McMahon to Burke, 26 September 1919, with enclosure A Program Submitted to the National Catholic War Council by the Famous Player's–Lasky Corporation to Demonstrate the Type of Material Available for Civic

Reconstruction, ACUA, NCWC 10:7:9; McMahon et al. to Burke, 5 November 1919, ibid., 10:21:82; Burke to McMahon, 22 November 1919, copy, ibid., 10:7:9; McMahon to Burke, 8 March 1920, ACUA, NCWC 10:7:12; Burke to McMahon, 8 March 1920, copy, ibid.; Sweet and Drady to Michael Slattery, 2 August 1920, ibid., 10:7:13; Williams, *American Catholics in War*, 337–40.

13. McMahon to Monsignor Thomas, editor of the *Baltimore Catholic Review*, 5 December 1919, ACUA, NCWC 10:7:9; National Catholic War Council Review, undated [probably January 1921], ibid., 10:32:48; Jason Joy to Burke, 29 January 1921, ibid., 10:7:13; Baker to Burke, 29 January 1921, ibid.; McMahon to Burke, 19 October 1922, ibid., USCCB 10:125:28.
14. McMahon to Burke, 25 November 1919, ACUA, NCWC 10:7:10; Burke to McMahon, 22 November 1919, copy, ACUA, NCWC 10:7:9; McMahon to Burke, 25 November 1919, ibid., 10:7:10; McMahon to Burke, 19 October 1922, ibid. 10:125:28.
15. Ellis, *Documents of American Catholic History*, 585–603; Curran, *American Catholic Social Ethics*, 30–44; Broderick, *Right Reverend New*, 27–47, 57–59, 104–05; McShane, *"Sufficiently Radical,"* 145–74; "N.C.W.C. Social Action Department," *NCWC Bulletin* 1 (March-April 1920): 27.
16. The literature on this point is vast. Perhaps the most helpful studies are Harold A. Buetow, *Of Singular Benefit: The Story of Catholic Education in the United States* (New York: Macmillan Company, 1970); Lloyd P. Jorgenson, *The State and the Non-Public School, 1825–1925* (Columbia: University of Missouri, 1987); Ray Allen Billington, *The Protestant Crusade, 1800–1860: A Study of the Origins of American Nativism* (New York: Rinehart and Co., 1952).
17. Slawson, *Department of Education Battle*, 49–51.
18. Burke to Dowling, 18 January 1920, copy, ACUA, USCCB 10:105:15.
19. Dowling to John Fenlon, S.S., 6 February 1920, AASUS-AASMSU, RG13, box 7 (first quote is here); Burke to Dowling, 21 February 1920, copy (second quote is here), ACUA, USCCB 10:105:15; McNulty to Lefebure, 14 April 1972, ibid., 10:72:24; Gribble, *Archbishop for the People*, 15 and 49; Patricia DeFerrari, "Edward Aloysius Pace (1861–1938," in, Michael Glazier and Thomas J. Shelley, eds., *The Encyclopedia of Catholic History* (Collegeville, Minn.: Liturgical Press, 1997), 1103–04; Slawson, *Department of Education Battle*, 66, 81–82.
20. "Address of Bishop Russell," enclosure with Circular of Russell, 13 February 1920, ADCh, 108–N5. This address lays out the plan of the department, which Burke told Murray he had worked out (Burke to Murray, 23 January 1920, AP, Burke Papers, box 11). The language of the address is clearly Burke's.
21. "Address of Bishop Russell," enclosure with Circular of Russell, 13 February 1920, ADCh, 108–N5. See also Burke to Muldoon, 30 November 1919, copy, ACUA, NCWC 10:7:25.

22. Russell, Report on the Press Convention, 13 February 1920, with enclosures, ADCh, 108–N5; Mary Lonan Reilly, O.S.F., *A History of the Catholic Press Association, 1911-1968* (Metuchen, New Jersey: Scarecrow Press, 1971), 34–53.
23. Burke to Russell, 1 February 1920, copy, ACUA, USCCB 10:98:26; McNulty to Tanner, 6 May 1964, ACUA, USCCB 10:72:24; John J. Delaney, *Dictionary of American Catholic Biography* (Garden City, N.Y.: Doubleday & Company Inc., 1984), 208. Burke never identified the donor, though his secretary Iona McNulty later did.
24. Burke to Russell, 1 February 1920, copy, ACUA, USCCB 10:98:26; *Lewiston Evening Journal* (New York), 18 May 1931 (McGrath obituary).
25. Burke to Russell, 1 February 1920, copy, ACUA, USCCB 10:98:26.
26. Hanna to Burke, 2 February 1920, ACUA, USCCB 10:99:15.
27. Burke to Russell, 18 February 1920, ADCh, 108–R3; Hawks, "Souvenir of Burke," AP, Burke Papers, box 10.
28. Burke to Muldoon, 15 February 1920, copy, ACUA, USCCB 10:152:28; Burke to Dowling, 21 February 1920, copy, ibid., 10:105:15.
29. Ede, *Lay Crusade*, 57–92, 355–57; Mary Adele Francis Gorman, O.S.F., "Federation of Catholic Societies in the United States, 1870–1920" (Unpublished doctoral dissertation, University of Notre Dame, 1962), 74–107, 254–74; Minutes of the Board of Archbishops, 18 April 1917, AASL, RG 9, U.S.A. hierarchy.
30. Burke to Schrembs, 10 January 1920, ADCl, Schrembs Papers. For the request for advice, see Schrembs to O'Connell, 3 January 1920, copy, ibid. Schrembs sent virtually identical letters to all recipients on this date.
31. Muldoon to Schrembs, 12 January 1920, ADCl, Schrembs Papers.
32. O'Connell to Schrembs, 8 January 1920, ADCl, Schrembs Papers; Schbrembs to O'Connell, undated [probably February 1920], ibid.
33. Burke to Muldoon, 9 March 1920, copy, ACUA, USCCB 10:152:28; Report of the Chairman, Department of Lay Activities, [September 1920], ADCl, Schrembs Papers.
34. Burke to Muldoon, 9 March 1920, copy, ACUA, USCCB 10:152:28; Petit, "'Up against a Stone Wall,'" 38–40.
35. Burke to Muldoon, 9 March 1920, copy, ACUA, USCCB 10:152:28.
36. Quoted in Michael Ready, "Father Burke: Apostle of Unity," *Catholic Action* 18 (December 1936): 18.
37. Ibid.; "National Catholic Women's Council," *NCWC Bulletin* 1 (March–April 1920): 8.
38. James M. O'Toole, *Militant and Triumphant: William Henry O'Connell and the Catholic Church in Boston, 1859–1944* (Notre Dame: University of Notre Dame Press, 1992), 23–190; Douglas J. Slawson, *Ambition and Arrogance: Cardinal William O'Connell of Boston and the American Catholic Church* (San Diego: Cobalt Productions, 2007), 16–87.

39. Michael Splaine, writing for O'Connell, to Schrembs, 15 March 1920, ACUA, USCCB 10:153:8; Splaine to Burke, 15 March 1920, ibid., 10:153:7; Cooper to Russell, 26 March 1920, copy, ibid., 49:39:2.
40. Burke to Muldoon, 9 March 1920, copy, ACUA, USCCB 10:152:28.
41. Ibid.; Schrembs to Burke, undated [after 15 March 1920], ACUA, USCCB 10:153:8; Splaine to Schrembs, 15 March 1920, ibid.; Burke to Splaine, 21 March 1920, draft, ibid.; Cooper to Russell, 26 March 1920, copy, ibid., NCWC 10:38:66.
42. Burke to Muldoon, 9 March 1920, copy, ACUA, USCCB 10:152:28 (all quotes are here); Cooper to Burke, 9 March 1920, with enclosure, Cooper to William Kerby, undated, ACUA, NCWC10:38:66; Cooper to Russell, 26 March 1920, copy, ibid.
43. Burke to Muldoon, 9 March 1920, copy, ACUA, USCCB 10:152:28; Schrembs to Burke, undated [after 7 March 1920], ibid.; Cooper to Daniel Tully, 10 March 1920, ACUA, NCWC10:38:66; Cooper to Russell, 26 March 1920, copy, ibid.
44. Cooper to Russell, 26 March 1920, copy, NCWC 10:38:66.
45. Burke to Muldoon, 9 March 1920, copy, ACUA, USCCB 10:152:28.
46. Muldoon to Burke, 12 March 1920, ACUA, USCCB 10:152:28 .
47. Burke to Lynch, 11 March 1920, AP, Burke Papers, box 5.
48. "The National Catholic Welfare Council: A Sketch of Its Organization," *NCWC Bulletin* 1 (September 1920): 7; Slawson, *Foundation of NCWC*, 79–80.
49. Splaine, writing for O'Connell, to Schrembs, 15 March 1920, ACUA, USCCB 10:153:8; Splaine to Burke, 15 March 1920, ibid., 10:153:7. Quotes are from both.
50. Burke to Splaine, 21 March 1920, draft, ACUA, USCCB 10:153:7.
51. Burke to Muldoon, 20 March 1920, copy, ACUA, USCCB 10:152:28; Burke to Splaine, 21 March 1920, draft, ACUA, USCCB 10:152:37; Burke to Mary Merrick, 1 April 1920, AP, Burke Papers, box 9.
52. Burke to Murray, Fourth Sunday of Lent, Laetare, [21 March] 1920, AP, Burke Papers, box 11; Burke to Muldoon, 20 March 1920, ACUA, USCCB 10:152:28.
53. Burke to Murray, 22 March 1920, AP, Burke Papers, box 11.
54. Ibid.
55. Mary Merrick to Hawks, 11 August 1918 and 14 August [1919], copy, AP, Burke Papers, box 10; Hawks to Mary Merrick, undated [March 1920], ibid.
56. Burke to Lynch, n.d. May 1920, AP, Burke Papers, box 5; Burke to Murray, Palm Sunday [28 March] 1920, AP, Burke Papers, box 11.
57. Hawks, "Souvenir of Burke," 7 and 8.
58. Burke to Murray, 2 April 1920, AP, Burke Papers, box 11.
59. Ibid.

60. Mary Merrick to Hawks, 11 April 1920, AP, Burke Papers, box 10.
61. Burke to Lynch, 18 June 1920, AP, Burke papers, box 5.
62. "National Catholic Laymen's Council," *NCWC Bulletin* 1 (May 1920): 27; Slattery, "Men's Council Stirs to Action Latent Forces of Catholic Laity," ibid. 2 (March 1921): 20 (quotes are here).
63. Richmond Dean to the hierarchy, 26 June 1920, with constitution enclosed, ACUA, Rector files; "National Catholic Laymen's Council," 27.
64. Lawler, *Full Circle*, 48–49.
65. Burke to Murray, 2 November 1920, AP, Burke Papers, box 11.
66. Ibid. (first and second quotes are here); Burke to Murray, Fourth Sunday of Advent [19 December] 1920, AP, Burke Papers, box 11 (last quote is here); "Clifton Graduates Another Class: Students of National Service School Present Splendid Record," *NCWC Bulletin* 2 (September 1920): 29–30; "Seventh Session at Clifton," ibid. (November 1920): 26.
67. Burke to Murray, Fourth Sunday of Advent [19 December] 1920, AP, Burke Papers, box 11; Slawson, *Foundation of NCWC*, 83.
68. Dudley Wooten to Burke, 29 October 1920, ACUA, USCCB 10:39:25; Résumé of Conference Called by Father Burke, 10 November [1920] to Consider the Immigration Problem, ibid.; A Meeting of Those Interested in the Immigration Department, 18 December 1920, with attachment: Immediate Steps to Be Taken, ibid.; Slawson, *Foundation of NCWC*, 74–75; Gribble, *Archbishop for the People*, 192–93.
69. Burke to William W. Husband, 29 March 1921, copy, ACUA, USCCB 10:39:25; Bruce Mohler, Memorandum: Interview with Husband, 4 April 1921, ibid; Husband to Burke, 30 April 1921, ibid.; Burke to Husband, 4 May 1921, copy, ibid.; Burke to Husband, 6 May 1921, copy, ibid.; Husband to Burke, 13 May 1921, ibid.
70. Burke to Murray, Fourth Sunday of Advent [19 December]1920, AP, Burke Papers, box 11.
71. "The Smith-Towner Bill and the Catholics," *New Age* 28 (February 1920): 69–70; Paul Blakely, "The Republican Party and the Smith Bill," *America* 23 (12 June 1920): 190; David Chalmers, *Hooded Americanism: The History of the Ku Klux Klan* (New York: Franklin Watts, 1976), 14–15, 28–38, 180, 284–85; Charles Alexander, *The Ku Klux Klan in the Southwest* (Lexington: University of Kentucky, 1966), 1–35; Kenneth T. Jackson, *The Ku Klux Klan in the Cities, 1915–1930* (New York and London: Oxford University Press, 1967), 3–255; Higham, *Strangers in the Land*, 86–99; Robert Moats Miller, "The Ku Klux Klan," in *Change and Continuity in Twentieth-Century America: The 1920s* (Columbus: Ohio State University Press, 1968): 215–56; Dewey Grantham, *The South in Modern America: A Region at Odds* (New York: Harper Perennial, 1995), 101–04; Otis Graham Jr, *Great Campaigns: Reform and War in America, 1900–1928* (Englewood Cliffs, N.J.: Prentiss Hall, Inc., 1971),

125; Robert Alan Goldberg, "Hooded Empire: The Ku Klux Klan in Colorado, 1921–1932" (Ph.D. dissertation, University of Wisconsin, 1977); Shawn Lay, ed., *The Invisible Empire in the West: Toward a New Historical Appraisal of the Ku Klux Klan in the 1920s* (Urbana and Chicago: University of Illinois Press, 1992); Leonard Moore, *Citizen Klansmen: The Ku Klux Klan in Indiana, 1921–1928* (Chapel Hill: University of North Carolina Press, 1991); Dumenil, *Modern Temper*, 235–44; Slawson, *Department of Education Battle*, 56–59; Francis Russell, *The Shadow of Blooming Grove: Warren G. Harding and His Times* (New York: McGraw-Hill, 1968), 367.

72. Dowling to Hanna, telegram, undated, AASF, NCWC files; Dowling to Burke, telegram, 4 June 1920, ACUA, USCCB 10:105:13; Slawson, *Department of Education Battle*, 59. Punctuation has been added and spelling corrected in the telegram to Burke.
73. Burke to Dowling, telegram, 4 June 1920, ACUA, USCCB 10:105:13; Slattery to Burke, 10 June 1920, ibid.; Burke to Ogden Mills, 6 June 1920, ibid.; Pace to Committee on Resolutions, undated draft in pencil, ACUA, Vice Rector files; *NCWC News Sheet*, 14 June 1920; Slawson, *Department of Education Battle*, 59–60.
74. Coyle, Memories of War Council, ACUA, USCCB 10:72:24 (the nickname "Slats" is here); Code Words, undated [June 1920], ibid., 10:105:13; Burke to Slattery, telegram, 7 June 1920, ibid., 10:105:13. The code names of others were as follows: Governor William Sproul was Jones; Senator Hiram Johnson was West; Senator Warren Harding was Ford; Governor Frank Lowden was Hudson; Senator Medill McCormick was Mack; Archbishop Dowling was Darlington; Cardinal Gibbons was Simmons; and Archbishop George Mundelein was Casey.
75. Slattery to Burke, 7 June 1920, ACUA, USCCB 10:105:13; Slattery to Burke, 9 June 1920, ibid.; James Watson to James Hugh Ryan, 5 November 1920, ACUA, Pace Papers; Russell, *Shadow of Blooming Grove*, 367–68; Wesley M. Bagby, *The Road to Normalcy: The Presidential Campaign and Election of 1920* (Baltimore: Johns Hopkins Press, 1962), 31–33, 87; Slawson, *Department of Education Battle*, 60–61.
76. Slattery to Burke, 4:00 A.M., 9 June 1920, ACUA, USCCB 10:105:13; Slawson, *Department of Education Battle*, 61–62.
77. Slattery to Burke, 9 June 1920, second of that date, ACUA, USCCB 10:105:13; Slawson, *Department of Education Battle*, 62.
78. George L. Hart, *Official Report of the Proceedings of the Seventeenth National Republican Convention Held in Chicago, Illinois, June 8–12, 1920, Resulting in the Nomination of Warren Gamaliel Harding of Ohio for President and in the Nomination of Calvin Coolidge of Massachusetts for Vice-President* (New York: The Tenny Press, 1920), 100–01, 108; Slawson, *Department of Education Battle*, 62.

79. Burke to Lynch, 18 June 1920, AP, Burke Papers, box 11; Burke to T. Burke, undated [5 July 1920], AP, Official Papers of Superior-General Thomas Burke, C.S.P., May 1920–July 1921; Burke to T. Burke, 10 July 1920, ibid. (John's quotations are from here); Elizabeth Burke to Burke, 12 July 1920, AP, Burke Papers, box 3; T. Burke to Burke, 17 July 1920, ibid.; Pace to Dowling, 16 June 1920, copy, ACUA, Vice Rector files. Rook is a trick-taking game played with a special deck of fifty-seven cards arranged in four differently colored suits numbered one through fourteen each, with the fifty-seventh card picturing a raven called the rook.
80. NCWC News Service, 12 July 1920; Slawson, *Department of Education Battle*, 63–66.
81. Burke to Murray, 2 November 1920, AP, Burke Papers, box 11.
82. Burke to Murray, 16 September 1920, AP, Burke Papers, box 11 (first quote is here); Burke to Murray, 14 November 1920, ibid. (second quote is here).
83. Burke to Lynch, Xmas [25 December] 1920, AP, Burke Papers, box 5.
84. Ibid.

Chapter 9
A Myriad of Troubles, Public and Personal

> The gospel of the daily Mass for the dead repeats the words of Christ, as reported by St. John, that he who will eat of His Flesh and drink of His Blood will never die. Holy Communion is Christ planting in us the seed of eternal glory. Every time we receive Holy Communion, we are not only strengthened in the belief that we will live forever—we are strengthened in and by the Life Itself. He Who lived and suffered, and did all things well, Who died and rose again from the dead, is day by day planting His seed in us. That we may not only be like Him but that we may be in Him, that we may live, and suffer, and do all things well, and die and rise with Him and in Him and through Him—unto Him in glory, Who is the glory of the Father.... Our Lord Jesus in Holy Communion is our pledge. Heaven and earth may pass away, but His word will not pass.[1]

Problems over Pronouncements and a Rivalry Revisited

In its second year, the NCWC began to function according to John Burke's vision that it serve as the voice of American Catholicism, but that voice sometimes spoke at cross-purposes, sometimes out of turn, and sometimes seemed less official than other contenders. Fortunately, its first pronouncement, about need for reform of motion pictures, was clarion-clear. As Progressivism waned in postwar years, there was weakening in the use of film to reinforce Victorian values. The Big Eight studios were emerging under almost exclusive control of Jewish moguls more attuned to popular preference and box-office receipts than Victorianism. These countervailing vectors permitted sexual exploitation of film. Cinematic historian Frank Miller notes, "Movies managed to promote morality while exploiting any possible violation of American standards." They framed stories so they came to a moral conclusion before which pretty much anything went.[2]

Cecil B. DeMille mastered the device. For instance, in *Male and Female* (1919), a film about gender and class, he lavished "his most insidious arts" on Gloria Swanson, playing Lady Mary. He shot a gratuitous scene in her boudoir, where she approached her bath in a gauzy dressing gown, which caressed her bottom suggesting she was nude. Her back to the camera and two maids holding her gown, Swanson stepped out of it baring her shoulders and backside. As she descended into the bath, the lighting through the sheer material revealed she was indeed naked, "the glorious Gloria … quite literally uncovered to view."[3]

This sort of film prompted John Quinn to launch the Motion Picture and Theatrical Association (MPTA) in 1920 for wholesome movies. Charles McMahon of the NCWC Motion Picture Bureau endorsed the organization.[4] Meanwhile, Rev. Dr. Wilbur Fiske Crafts, founder of the International Reform Bureau, launched a campaign for a "Puritan Sabbath." He condemned Jews for control of the film industry, which violated observance of Sunday as a day devoted to religious activities. He urged his organization to cooperate with representatives of the Catholic Church who were trying to clean up pictures, thus intimating that Catholics supported a Puritan Sabbath. When the Lord's Day Alliance leapt on the bandwagon to close New York theaters on Sunday, the MPTA initiated a counter campaign for display of decent pictures every day of the week. In December, Quinn called a protest meeting against the proposed blue law and asked the NCWC to send someone to state its position.[5]

Burke wrote a statement explaining Catholics held Sunday as a holy day, but not one of sadness "dedicated to the blues, wherein no wholesome recreation is allowed." The question was not one of "Blue Laws," but the "great White Law of public decency, which should first be championed." For years it had been "flagrantly outraged" on screen and stage, declared Burke, paving the way for an "intemperate reaction, which is likely to lead to laws as blue as the Volstead Act" that banned liquor. He said the NCWC would side with any agency or organization working "for public decency, for public morality, for the spiritual welfare of our children." The lure of sex plagued theater and movies. "Scarcely a play is presented in which adultery, unfaithfulness, moral laxity, indecent dressing or undressing are not features," wrote Burke. "This rottenness is eating into our body social." Given the choice between the abolition of movies on Sunday or continued presentation of the current fare, Catholics would opt for the former without question. "That is not judgment for or against Blue Laws," he concluded. "That is a judgment in favor of public decency, in which every self-respecting Catholic, Protestant, and Jew would heartily and cordially join."[6]

As Burke explained to Archbishop Edward Hanna, the statement avoided "the Scylla of the Blue Laws and the Charybdis of the open lawless Sunday. We know that back of the attack on the so-called Blue Laws is the materialistically minded Jew and the commercial powers without conscience, who would quickly quote us in their support. The game is skillfully played."[7] His carefully worded declaration clearly articulated that the Church favored wholesome movies and clean fun on Sundays. It opposed indecent entertainment and was willing to work with any and all for abolition of such. Finally, it distanced the Church from the antisemitism of Crafts by specifically including "self-respecting" Jews among supporters of public decency.

McMahon delivered the statement at the protest, and three days later the Knights of Columbus issued their own: a blanket condemnation of blue laws. They feared such legislation would have the opposite effect: people would either become indifferent to the law or contemptuously violate it. The Volstead Act was a perfect example. It had reared overnight the "sixth largest national industry—bootlegging." The Knights declared they would "oppose the movement for blue laws because the movement is an attack on the Constitution. It aims to pursue the pursuers of happiness."[8]

This declaration, rather than the NCWC's, was widely quoted as the Catholic position. In fairness, the Knights can hardly be blamed for the perception of others. They never claimed to speak for the Church. Still, the situation aggravated Burke. "Our work is hampered," he reported to Hanna, "and in part defeated." The council had to expend valuable time explaining the Knights' pronouncement was not the official mind of the Church. "Oftentimes, the explanation is unavailing," he lamented, "for the K. of C. is much better known than we are."[9]

McMahon and Michael Williams, editor of the *NCWC Bulletin*, recommended Burke mount a program for improving the motion picture industry. McMahon wanted to join forces officially with the MPTA and suggested the NCWC consider the question of national censorship through legislation.[10] Wary of censorship, Burke was "decidedly against any step at the present time" toward it. Moreover, he refused to approve formal membership in the MPTA. "I think it would be much better for us to work entirely independent," he told McMahon, "and not to lend ourselves to any other organization." He feared the MPTA might be a "commercial" venture, which, though not discreditable in itself, ought to keep the NCWC from joining it. Burke jealously guarded the council's position as a voice without commercial or political ties. He preferred the NCWC establish a program along "lines of moral influence," which would enlist support of other national religious bodies. Perhaps it should create a committee to view major movies "to get a line on them and be able to send out a favorable or disapproving word." It must definitely stir and lead organizations of Catholic men and women to form local committees for the improvement of films. "I think that we ought to push the matter at once," concluded Burke, "and push it with all the power at our command."[11]

Push it McMahon did. The NCWC mobilized the NCCM and NCCW against production and display of unclean movies. He urged parents to ensure they and their children saw only decent films. They should work for the elimination of objectionable ones through local authorities. He called for a boycott of theaters that persisted in showing obnoxious pictures. "The quickest and surest way to improve the motion picture," argued McMahon, "is to withhold patronage.... The exhibitor's conscience is often reached more quickly and effectively by the way of the 'box office' than in any other manner."[12] It would be another two years before the NCWC initiated movie reviews, as Burke had recommended.

At about the time Burke crafted the statement on motion pictures, he and John A. Ryan, issued an endorsement of the Sheppard-Towner Maternity bill, which seemingly undercut the Church's opposition to the Smith-Towner measure for a department of education. In 1919, about 9 percent of children under the age of one died, nearly half within a month of birth. Most deaths were preventable. That bill offered federal funds for care of indigent mothers and their new-born, provided states matched the money dollar for dollar and their use of it met approval of the Children's Bureau. The constitutional issues at stake in the measure (federal aid on a matching basis and federal involvement in a state matter) were identical to those in the Smith-Towner bill. Because American Catholics opposed contraception, Burke was inclined to favor the legislation because it counterbalanced the birth control movement of Mary Ware Dennett and Margaret Sanger. The bill also answered in part the call for social insurance in the Bishops' Program of Social Reconstruction.[13]

Officials in the NCWC's Department of Education had misgivings about the endorsement. Father Edward Pace regretted the pronouncement, commenting it might be possible to make distinctions between the amount and purpose of federal appropriations in the Sheppard-Towner and Smith-Towner bills, but they would not amount to much once "the general principle of ferderal [*sic*] aid has been admitted." Archbishop Austin Dowling agreed; it was a "grave error" to have endorsed the legislation. So did Father James H. Ryan, who would soon succeed Pace as executive secretary of Dowling's department. "It committs [*sic*] us," he told Dowling, "to the principle of federal aid and co-operation.... We will just have to squirm out of it some way or other."[14]

The squirming was not long in coming. The NEA established a legislative commission to pressure Congress to enact the Smith-Towner bill. The new drive spawned such interest that the NCWC received numerous inquiries about the Catholic position on it. In mid-December Burke and Pace decided to draft a statement.[15]

Carefully avoiding any suggestion that the Smith-Towner bill aimed at control or abolition of parochial schools, Burke and Pace praised its aims, but took issue with its method of achieving them. Because of the Sheppard-Towner endorsement, they had to waffle on federal aid. "We recognize the utility and even the necessity of extending Federal Aid to the States under certain conditions," wrote the pair. "It is not, therefore, a question of approving or condemning such aid as a matter of principle, but rather of discriminating between cases in which it would be wise to extend Federal aid and other cases in which it would be unwise and contrary to the best interests of the nation." So, they rested their argument on the revenue aspect of the bill. Burke and Pace averred it would increase taxation, falling disproportionately on prosperous states, with the result they would pay the educational costs of their weak counterparts. That was unjust. It was also prejudicial to states' rights. They considered federal grants to schools the surest "way of destroying State autonomy … [and] responsibility in … education." Such aid would reduce local spending for education. Federal money always came with strings attached, leading ultimately to federal control. The bill created a department of education whose secretary was to manage expenditure of the funds, the first step in centralization. Because the bill's purposes were laudable, they positively recommended establishment of a federal agency or commission—not a department—to investigate educational problems and disseminate findings to the states for their own action on them.[16]

The skillfully worded pronouncement was a gem. Not only did Burke and Pace skirt the Sheppard-Towner endorsement, they carefully avoided the religious issue of parochial schools. The NCWC sent nearly 17,000 copies to affiliates of the NCCM and NCCW with instructions to make no protest until Burke gave the order. The NCWC also sent copies to the nation's 21,000 parish priests asking them to get influential non-Catholic friends to protest when the order came. Catholics and non-Catholics alike were to avoid any mention of parochial schools and limit their objections to those outlined in the statement, especially the financial ones.[17]

The time for mounting a protest was not long in coming. Senator Hoke Smith of Georgia, one of the bill's sponsors, had lost his reelection bid in November 1920 and was eager to see the measure enacted in his final session of Congress. He made multiple interventions on the floor, each suggesting Catholics alone opposed the bill, thereby implying everyone else wanted it. Burke had enough and ordered Catholics to protest against it. When telegrams flooded Smith's office, he claimed Catholics misunderstood his bill and asked to address the Senate to demonstrate the irrelevance of their criticisms. He was granted time on 12 February.[18]

Burke had William Cochran of the Legal Department secure Democratic Senator William King of Utah to respond to Smith. Smith claimed Catholic opposition derived from a Jesuit priest's objection that the bill would subject all education to an autocrat in Washington, would negate parental rights, and would drive religion from schools. Smith explained the measure's provisions and showed its respect of local control. Nothing in it took away parental prerogative to send their child to their school of choice. Portraying the Church as a bastion of states' rights, King countered that Catholics opposed it because they "believe[d] in local self-government and the splendid individualism which Christianity inspires."[19]

The very day of the Smith-King exchange, the Knights undid Burke and Pace's careful work. Although the Supreme Council passed a resolution clearly in line with their statement, Supreme Knight James Flaherty gave an interview to the *New York Times* wherein he called the bill an attempt "to have all private and public education at the mercy of a Federal bureaucracy." Claiming the Knights opposed it "not so much on religious as on patriotic grounds," he declared "the Smith-Towner bill is ultimately aimed at the parochial schools."[20]

Flaherty's statement was disastrous. "Of course, this was just what the friends of the Smith-Towner Bill wanted," reported Burke to Hanna. They circulated Flaherty's words through Congress. When telegrams from Grand Knights around the country poured in, "the matter assumed very quickly the aspect of a religious issue." Joseph Ransdell, Catholic senator from Louisiana, went to Burke and, in the name of several Catholic colleagues, begged him to do something.[21] There was not much he could do, and matters soon became worse.

A week later, Supreme Secretary William McGinley issued a second statement proclaiming the Knights' opposition, but adding that behind them was "the entire ecclesiastical and lay organization of the Catholic Church in the United States." In other words, the hierarchy and NCWC were behind the Knights, not the other way around. McGinley argued ultimately, the measure would interfere with parental rights in education; it would also create a despotic authority in Washington. Nothing would prevent a secretary of education "from declaring against the Catholic parochial school system."[22]

Because of McGinley's statement, Congress now believed the Church opposed the bill solely on religious grounds. This had a deleterious effect. "Word is going round," Pace told Hanna, "that certain Catholics have done the best thing yet to secure the passing of the Bill." The Senate Committee on Education and Labor, which had been reluctant to report it, did so on 1 March. Fortunately, there were only three days left in the session, insufficient time to enact it.[23]

Both Burke and Pace suspected the Knights intentionally interfered with the NCWC. First was their statement about blue laws and now this one about Catholic schools. As Burke explained it: "This action of the K. of C. is not haphazard. It is too orderly: too consecutive: too studied for that." In order to confirm the basic correctness of their position, they waited for the NCWC to voice a statement. Then they released their own proclamation "to keep themselves before the American public ... [as] the leading exponents on Catholic public matters." Both men urged Hanna to do something about the situation. Informing Muldoon of the issue, Burke commented: "The situation is at times as critical and as unpleasant as in our own war days. It is too bad the K. of C. will seek to make organization capital out of a Catholic position." The Administrative Committee discussed the matter in April and asked Hanna to admonish by letter all national Catholic organizations. He promised to visit personally with the Supreme Council of the Knights when they met in San Francisco in the summer.[24]

Indeed, Hanna did so. Although there is no record of what he told them, his admonition had the desired effect; they issued no more statements in tandem with the NCWC. They even agreed to affiliate with the NCCM, but never did so.[25]

While dealing with the foregoing, Burke was caught in a tempest in a teapot over a statement John Ryan issued two months earlier. The sharp postwar depression (1920–1922) had caused many employers to make unrelenting war on labor unions by advocating the "open-shop," one hiring both union and non-union workers. Because such a workplace allegedly afforded the greatest freedom of contract to capital and labor, employers dubbed it the "American Plan."[26] In a statement issued by the "Social Action Department of the National Catholic Welfare Council," Ryan supported labor's right to organize. He argued the American Plan threatened "not only the welfare of the wage earners, but the whole structure of industrial peace and order." Given the economic climate, its real aim was destruction of unionization achieved through the "closed shop," one hiring only union men. Quoting both the Bishops' Program of Social Reconstruction and the Pastoral Letter of the Hierarchy (1919), Ryan averred the Catholic hierarchy backed labor's right to organize and bargain collectively.[27]

This statement portended trouble for the NCWC. Bishop William Russell of the Press Department sounded the alarm to Muldoon, warning that labor and capital understood Ryan's declaration as committing the NCWC to the closed shop. Indeed, Frank Garvan, who had given $60,000 to establish Russell's department, threatened to ask return of his donation.

Apostolic Delegate Giovanni Bonzano "was much provoked" by the pronouncement, not for what it said, but because it seemed to have the authority of the NCWC behind it. A number of bishops thought the Administrative Committee had pledged them to a course of action without their consent. Russell concluded, "The fact that this article appears to have the sanction or authorization of the N.C.W.C., will raise a perfect storm at our Sept. meeting [of the hierarchy]."[28] So it would.

Muldoon instructed Burke to see Ryan at once. Because Ryan was away, Burke replied that a careful reading convinced him the "unwisely worded and framed" statement had been "misunderstood and misinterpreted." It did not proclaim the closed shop as Catholic principle, nor did it object to an open shop. Rather, it protested against the open shop, "which under the cloak of being 'open' sought to kill the labor union by refusing to employ a union man." The declaration aimed at protecting the right to organize and bargain collectively. "No one may now deny," wrote Burke, "that these are two principles of Catholic economics." Admitting the situation was "serious," he added: "We must avoid if possible any public or external sign of internal difference. That one department acts without another and that we are a polyglot gathering not an organization—to have this appear would be bad."[29]

On his return, Ryan affirmed Burke's interpretation of the pronouncement. Burke believed the NCWC should issue a clarification. He drafted one and Ryan approved it. He asked Burke, however, to withhold publication until the executive committee of his department could review it. In the end, the committee decided against offering an explanation, no doubt because Muldoon considered the matter "exaggerated." Only Russell had complained to him, and several Catholic newspapers had covered the question well. Muldoon remarked to Burke with some irony that if every pronouncement of the hierarchy was called into question, "we will have a delightful time!"[30] Rather, the sort of time they were destined for would be quite otherwise.

The final flap over pronouncements came in spring 1921. The NCWC Department of Education opened a bureau at headquarters under the direction of Arthur Monahan, a Catholic with a distinguished career in public education.[31] One of the bureau's functions was "to outline a policy on the position of the Church in educational matters." So, Monahan drafted one and submitted it to Pace, his superior, for review. It declared the following as tenets of the Church: the right of parents to send children to their school of choice; the state's right to mandate a minimum school term and make English the language of instruction; the state's right to set standards and inspect all schools; the state's right to tax all citizens for the support of public schools; and the local control of education.[32]

In early June, in what Burke termed "another example of pronouncements made without proper order," Monahan used the statement as the core of his graduation address at St. Teresa's College in Winona, Minnesota, where he urged the hierarchy publically to endorse it. The NCWC news service publicized the speech, and Monahan included portions of it in an article he wrote for the *NCWC Bulletin*. More controversial was his endorsement, issued just prior to the Winona speech, of the Dacey Law in Michigan. It applied to both public and parochial institutions, and gave the state superintendent of schools power to withhold a school's operating license until he had approved its location, physical and sanitary conditions, course of study, and qualification of teachers. It also authorized him to revoke the license of a school that subsequently fell below standards. The bishops of Michigan supported it only because they hoped acquiescing to state supervision of Catholic schools would forestall reintroduction of the recently defeated amendment to the state's constitution for compulsory public education. What was for them a tactical maneuver was an ideal for Monahan. When the NCWC Legal Department asked his opinion of the Dacey Law, he declared proponents of Catholic education everywhere "should secure at as early a date as possible, legislative enactments similar to those provided in this bill." The Legal Department published his view as that of the Department of Education.[33]

These actions caused a storm of protest. Bishop Joseph Schrembs warned Burke: "Mr. Monahan is talking too freely. There is much bitter criticism on this score on the part of a number of bishops." Father James H. Ryan, who just replaced Pace as Monahan's superior, also reported many prelates objected to the statements. He had Burke draft a clarification regarding Monahan's utterances. Burke did so, but held the department accountable for Monahan's words. Monahan accepted responsibility for all he had said, and the department's executive committee recommended against issuing the clarification. "It is unfortunate that such things happen,"

Burke told Hanna. "We will and are seeing to it that they do not repeat themselves."[34] Yet, the damage had been done and with near disastrous results.

Succession Planning for the Death of Gibbons

At the 1920 convention of the hierarchy, it was clear Cardinal James Gibbons, chairman, might not survive until the 1921 meeting and the see of Baltimore might be vacant. Archbishop Edward Hanna had introduced a resolution proposing that in case of such vacancy, the chairman of the Administrative Committee would preside at the convention. Although it seemed the resolution carried, the convention's secretary, Bishop Denis O'Connell of Richmond, missed its inclusion in the minutes.[35] In March 1921, Gibbons died.[36]

In late April, Burke and Pace visited America's newest cardinal, Archbishop Dennis Dougherty, head of the council's Legal Department, for advice about new federal education legislation. Although danger to Catholic schools remained great, Dougherty displayed curious disinterest. Nor did he inquire about the NCWC. His sole concern was who was to call the next meeting of the hierarchy. Burke replied the bishops had elected Hanna vice-chairman, hence he would. "At once earnestness; nervousness; intense interest," noted Burke. "Indeed Catholic education … welfare of the Church; these were but corollaries to this question—Who should call and preside at the Bishops' meeting?" Dougherty denied any election had occurred. "A long and animated dispute" ensued wherein he asserted the NCWC was simply the Administrative Committee, not the hierarchy. When Burke and Pace "pertinaciously upheld" that it *was* the hierarchy, Dougherty categorically denied it. "Neither Dr. Pace nor I," wrote Burke, "could see what he meant. But we had aroused intense interest." Dougherty declared the new archbishop of Baltimore should preside. In that, he was correct; a Vatican decree of 1858 bestowed that right on the incumbent of Baltimore.[37]

Dougherty's peculiar attitude bespoke his estrangement from the NCWC. Although a member of the Administrative Committee, he almost never attended meetings. It disturbed him that the committee had recently incorporated itself as the NCWC, that is, the hierarchy of the United States.

He was also angry with statements issued by council agents, no doubt Monahan and John Ryan. They had, he later averred, "published utterances in the name of the hierarchy without consulting the bishops throughout the country" and had "sometimes uttered doctrines which I, for one, would not subscribe to."[38] The encounter augured ill for the NCWC.

Burke apprised both Hanna and Muldoon of Dougherty's view. Muldoon wondered how he could "so conceive of the N.C.W.C. and the Admin. Committee," and noted that it showed "how intense has been his study of the question." If Bishop O'Connell could not produce the minute about Hanna taking the chair, "What are we to do?" asked Muldoon.[39] Hanna himself agreed with Dougherty about Baltimore's right. He recommended if opportunity arose that Burke ask Dougherty's advice about what to do in case of a vacancy. "We ought before the meeting takes place to have a united agreement on the matter," he wrote, "and there must be no untoward incident to mar the harmony of our proceedings." In mid-July 1921, Burke consulted O'Connell and reported to Hanna, "He neither affirms nor denies."[40] Nor did Burke get a chance to solicit Dougherty's advice.

Meanwhile, Bishop Louis Walsh of Portland, Maine, and his fellow bishops in New England were planning to use the convention to repudiate Cardinal William O'Connell because of the secret marriages of Fathers James O'Connell and David Toomey. In April, the bishops confronted him about them. Walsh then went to Rome and spoke with Pope Benedict XV, who agreed that if fifteen or more bishops refused to attend a convention chaired by O'Connell and petitioned approval of their action, the pontiff would permanently withdraw him to Rome. Walsh returned to America and secured the necessary support.[41] A showdown was imminent.

A Mother's Death: A Son's Devotion

In spring 1921, Burke's seventy-six-year-old mother became terminally ill. As her end drew near, Burke went to her side. She was in considerable pain. Her suffering was particularly bad the night after his arrival, and all four sons remained with her. In the morning, she asked for Holy Communion, which Thomas administered. "A new light came into her eyes," noted Burke: "she was re-animated." He remembered his mother once told

Gertrude Gavin "it was by the Blessed Sacrament that she lived and that it sustained her during the day."[42]

Burke arranged Mass in her bedroom the Sunday before her death. His brother Thomas celebrated it with her children and three grandchildren present. When John and his mother spoke of it that evening, she told him, "Now I have had everything. I could ask for no more."[43]

Two days later she rallied and asked for communion, which John administered with all her children present. Unconscious all the next day, it was apparent she would not last the night. John, Grace Murray, and Gertrude Delahunt said the rosary at her bedside, and he stood watch from 2:30 to 3:30 A.M. She died at 5:22 in the morning with all her children but Annie at her side. It was the feast of Corpus Christi, the Blessed Sacrament by which she had lived.[44] The way she endured her suffering and death greatly touched Burke. He wrote his friend William Kerby, "Could I live and die what I have witnessed with my own eyes these last two weeks I would be more than content."[45]

On Burke's return to Washington, he wrote to Murray: "Life and work have changed. I hardly said a word on the trip down." It seems his mother was his true anchor to New York and her passing left him with a mysterious sense of being at one with her in God, which permitted him greater acceptance of his role as a national churchman. "This may be a 'public' life for me," he explained to Murray: "but it is a life wherein I am very much alone, not lonely, that is a different thing. And I am much alone with her who is no longer here in body, her whom my soul loves." Conversant with the fathers of the Church, Burke may have been borrowing from St. Ambrose, who had explained: "I am never less alone than when I seem to be so.... For then I summon at pleasure whom I will and associate to myself those whom I love most or find most congenial." Ambrose went on to reflect that in solitude one was open to the intrusion of God.[46]

In Burke's current rumination, he was clearly communing with both God and his mother. She loved her children; they "were her delight and her only delight." "I have thought and thought deeply," he told Murray. "Could I but know her as she is now, know how her soul felt, her mind thought, her heart endured. All that her kisses meant: all that her embraces expressed? The look of her eyes. I saw the look, and the soul therein, but I did not, I suppose I could not, see all the soul. The pressure of her hand.

Her silence. Her smile." He wished to know his mother the way God knew her, but such knowledge would happen only when Burke would see God, and he and his mother would each see the other in Him. Until then, such "privacies [were] reserved for God alone." Yet, he believed she had partaken on earth in the sincerity, integrity, and unselfishness of God and "possessed something in finite share, yet in reality of the Eternal Divine Life." Mary Burke was with God, glorifying and exalting his name, and wished her children to follow. "My heart pleads that I also may learn," he wrote: "and grow: and give up my faults and sins, and be permitted to share with her—to share her—to possess her for all eternity. Without that I can see nothing but night, night enduring. She is the light: Morning star: and mother may God see to it that I do follow."[47] God and mother were one. Jesus the light, his mother Mary the morning star, and Burke's own mother Mary became interchangeable—they were all one with and in God.

Clifton

During his mother's final illness, Burke and William Kerby were transforming Clifton into a professional school of social work. Burke viewed social welfare as "*the great need* of today." It would prove vain, however, unless founded on truth and justice. From the day the apostles appointed deacons to do welfare work for Christians in Jerusalem (Acts 6:1–6), declared Burke, the Catholic Church had become "the mother of civilized society," which alone taught "those definite truths that ensure the welfare of mankind." Thus, he argued female Catholic social workers must be trained in both knowledge of the faith and knowledge of the profession. Therefore, Clifton must be the equal of the best training school in the nation: a standard, two-year institution with a curriculum embracing all sciences and activities of social work, taught by instructors of recognized ability.[48]

Burke and Kerby secured a charter from D.C. for Clifton to award degrees as the National Catholic Service School for Women. To direct it, Burke hired Dr. Charles Neill, a cofounder of the original War Council and a man of considerable experience. After doctoral studies in economics at Johns Hopkins University, he served as United States Commissioner of Labor under two presidents. Muldoon congratulated Burke for landing such a strong candidate.[49]

At Neill's hire, the governance of the school was in flux. The self-constituted Board of Management consisted of Burke as chairman, Gavin, Agnes Regan, Florence Loeber, Mrs. Harry Benziger, and Father James H. Ryan. The official responsibilities of the board were yet to be worked out, so Neill's contract said he was to have control of the school under direction of Burke. Over the next year, the board's duties became formalized, altering the authority of the school's director. As will be seen in the next chapter, the change led to Neill's resignation.[50]

The faculty was quite strong. Neill himself taught economics and social legislation. Kerby covered sociology. John Ryan handled personal and social ethics. Paulist Father Thomas Verner Moore, a psychologist and physician, dealt with psychological, medical, and health issues. Rose J. McHugh, formerly of the Red Cross, supervised case work. Three original members of Clifton continued at their posts: Maud Cavanaugh as dean, Maria Ewing as director of studies, and Helen Cronin as teacher of household economics. The new two-year curriculum was quite thorough, consisting of eighteen courses including a research seminar. Tuition was $250 a year ($4,250 in 2024). In May, Burke announced a campaign to raise $500,000 ($8.5 million) to support the school.[51]

Throughout summer 1921, Burke grappled with the vexing problem of the school's location. The lease of Clifton would expire in October, and the price of renewal was substantially higher. The cost of purchase was exorbitant, nor was Clifton ideal. The house barely accommodated the current program, and its isolation rendered difficult both student field work and access by non-resident faculty. Burke and others went house hunting to no effect. The cost of new construction was prohibitive. So, the board decided to renew the lease.[52]

Then, the unexpected occurred. On feast of the Assumption, Burke went to Clifton to say Mass, accompanied by Regan. On the long walk back to the trolley, they branched off along a tree-lined road which edged Rock Creek Park and took them by the Fairmont School for Girls. It consisted of three buildings on two acres: a multi-story, nineteenth-century, red-brick residence known as Mintwood House, adjoining a modern four-story brick building designed as classrooms and student living quarters on 19th Street; the last, a four-story, frame home fronting on 20th Street. Combined, the three edifices had more than 100 rooms. Burke learned the school was willing to sell the fully furnished properties for a total of $354,000 ($6 million in 2024), with $104,000 of that as down payment. Over the next two months, funding for the deal came together, and the new National Catholic Service School for Women opened in November 1921.[53]

Prohibition and Sacramental Wine

With the advent of Prohibition, Gibbons had appointed Bishops Russell and Thomas Hickey of Rochester as an ad hoc committee to negotiate with the government for sacramental use of wine. In 1919, Commissioner Daniel Roper made a generously elastic interpretation to the Volstead Act. He gave bishops complete charge of the authentication process for its acquisition. He even approved issuance of permits to designated wholesalers around the country to sell wine to clergy, even though the law stipulated only manufacturers and importers could do so. His regulations went unchallenged until spring 1921.[54]

Just before the Wilson administration expired, Attorney General A. Mitchell Palmer ruled permits to wholesalers violated the Volstead Act, a position Harding's attorney general, Harry Daugherty, affirmed. Burke was alert to this ruling and in touch with the government about it though the NCWC could do nothing because Russell and Hickey had charge of the matter, and Hickey opposed seeking special concessions. Unfortunately, complaints inevitably went to the NCWC instead of the two bishops. Bishop Joseph Busch of St. Cloud, Minnesota, none-too-friendly to the organization, warned Burke unless the NCWC fixed the problem it may suffer a loss in confidence. Burke replied that the Legal Department was monitoring the situation, but the ad hoc committee had "entire power to act" in the matter.[55]

Fortunately Russell, a member of the Administrative Committee, brought the matter before it for discussion. The bishop then went to see Assistant Attorney General Guy Goff, who recommended that Russell propose a plan to outgoing Commissioner John F. Kramer. Russell delegated William Cochran of the Legal Department to draft the proposal. This action marked the beginning of gradual transfer of the issue to the NCWC.[56]

In mid-April, Burke met with three government officials: Goff, Kramer, and outgoing Assistant Attorney General Annette Abbott Adams, author of the Palmer ruling. Kramer and Adams steadfastly held that the Volstead Act permitted clergy to purchase wine only from manufacturers or importers, and the two latter could not appoint dealers as selling agents. The best Burke could secure was tentative agreement that a bishop could designate a priest as diocesan broker to negotiate with manufacturers for purchase of wine to be shipped directly to individual parishes. If that was unacceptable, the NCWC should either ask the secretary of the Treasury to seek a new ruling from Daugherty or press Congress to amend the law. "The matter as it stands is very difficult," Burke reported to Russell, "and to secure successfully what would be welcome to the Catholic priests would be difficult."[57]

Meanwhile, Russell had written to Goff urging wine be available through dealers. He also argued priests could obtain it from either wholesale or retail druggists because the Volstead Act permitted pharmacists to sell alcohol. Responding for Goff, Adams said she had given Cochran a copy of Palmer's ruling that clearly indicated druggists could dispense alcoholic beverages only for medicinal, not sacramental, purposes. The Church must obtain wine only from manufacturers or importers. Russell told Burke to see Goff about it.[58]

In late April, Burke, Cochran, Goff, Kramer, and Adams met and discussed the problem from every angle. Both Goff and Kramer appreciated the difficulties the ruling imposed and were willing to do everything to eliminate them. Burke urged the government to permit Catholic religious-goods houses to distribute wine. The three officials said their hands were tied. The best they could do was tentatively authorize each diocese to appoint an officer as broker for purchase of wine to be shipped directly to parishes. Goff said Daugherty would be willing to reconsider the Palmer ruling if requested by the Secretary of the Treasury, though he held little hope for a different outcome. Burke notified Hanna, adding there was "yet a chance" he might be able to get a ruling to permit agencies to sell wine. "Our interests have been complicated and handicapped," he explained, "by having a separate committee of two bishops who of course cannot be here to look after the matter."[59]

The "chance" Burke took was to ask Secretary of Treasury Andrew Mellon to request a new interpretation from Daugherty. He said the requirement of procuring wine directly from a manufacturer worked hardship on clergy far removed from wineries. For them, it made sense only to purchase a year's supply of wine and have it shipped. The cost of that amount and its delivery might work hardship on parish financial resources more amenable to periodic purchases of lesser amounts. Burke contended that even this solution was objectionable on two counts: "First, the quantity of wine would be greatly in excess of the immediate need, and secondly, the Prohibition Director of the respective States would naturally not understand why a priest should need wine in such large quantities." The former system had conveniently permitted a priest to purchase small quantities from a licensed local wholesaler at minimal expense.[60]

More cogent was Burke's legal argument regarding two stipulations in the Volstead Act. The first specifically stated "nothing" in the law should "be held to apply to manufacture, sale, transportation, importation, possession OR DISTRIBUTION of wine for sacramental purposes." That provision was "general and absolute," meaning that it must "not be interfered with or handicapped in any other way." In Burke's view, specific mention of distribution sanctioned permits for current wine merchants. The second stipulation stated a person who held a valid permit authorizing engagement in the foregoing activities was forbidden to sell wine to any but a person with a valid permit to purchase it, namely, a clergyman or a church officer duly designated for that purpose. Burke contended that this second stipulation was "intended to define *to whom*" sacramental wine may be sold, while the Palmer ruling understood it "to mean those who shall *sell* the wine." Burke argued the first stipulation defined "those who shall *sell* the wine and the second … those *to whom* the wine shall be sold." Given this reading, he respectfully requested Mellon ask for a new interpretation permitting a continuance of the former system.[61]

Mellon told Burke rules consistent with Palmer's decision would be prepared by David Blair, incoming commissioner, once he entered office. "It is believed," wrote Burke, "that such regulations can be so framed as to provide for the convenient distribution of sacramental wines without undue hardship to the clergy, importers, manufacturers or their agents." Mellon assured him the NCWC would be granted a hearing before new rules were finalized, and, in the event they proved unsatisfactory, he agreed "to take up further the matter of requesting reconsideration by the Attorney General."[62]

Mellon's mention of the word "agents" hinted at the direction the government was moving. Indeed, in mid-July Goff had asked Cochran to verify that an acceptable solution would be distribution of sacramental wine through dealers appointed as agents by manufacturers, provided the latter would be responsible for them. When the regulation was unveiled at a hearing in July 1921, Cochran, representing both Hickey and Russell, made no objection. The new stipulation was to take effect on 15 August. Because the intervening time would prove too short for current wine dealers to have themselves named agents of manufacturers, Burke secured an additional month's grace and informed the hierarchy of the new interpretation. Thus, the matter seemed to have been arranged, leaving the status quo virtually unchanged.[63]

This settlement immediately unraveled. Dealers protested the regulations because they now had to seek to become agents of wineries or importers; manufacturers protested because legal title to the wine remained with them, even though it might be in possession of dealers, thus placing wineries at risk for actions of remote agents. Faced with protests, Treasury referred the matter to Daugherty "for a specific ruling as to whether permits to sell and distribute wines for sacramental purposes may legally be issued to wholesale dealers such as are now in the business of supplying the clergy." Pending decision, Burke secured from Treasury indefinite suspension of the regulation. He also requested and was assured by the attorney general's office that the NCWC would receive a hearing before a final decision.[64]

A Dangerous Convention

When the hierarchy met in September, a dangerous situation brewed around Cardinal O'Connell. Bishop Walsh had arranged at papal approval a walkout of more than fifteen bishops if O'Connell attempted to preside. He had also petitioned the pope to sanction election of the chairman. On eve of the convention, Archbishop Bonzano informed Walsh the pontiff had upped the ante from fifteen to one-quarter of the bishops. Although Walsh believed more than that would bolt, Bonzano begged him to avoid the public scandal of a walkout or election. Next morning, he personally intervened to prevent untoward action, and O'Connell assumed the chair. Yet, he clearly understood the bullet he had just dodged.[65]

The second day brought discussion of the NCWC, actually a debate over its nature. Some, like Cardinals O'Connell and Dougherty, insisted it was only the Administrative Committee, whose agents had exceeded their portfolio by issuing statements in the name of the hierarchy. The majority, however, argued the NCWC was the hierarchy operating through that committee. Michael Curley, archbishop-elect of Baltimore, passionately defended the NCWC as "organized leadership," declaring the day of "*one man leadership* was gone," that is, the age of Gibbons was over. As Walsh saw it, the two cardinals intended either to "rule or ruin" the organization. It was either deference to the cardinalate or annihilation of the NCWC. In fact, O'Connell and Dougherty would make good their threat when opportunity presented itself. What prevented them imposing their will at the moment was the "humiliating condition" in which O'Connell found himself because of universal knowledge among bishops of the scandals in his archdiocese. That, Bonzano told Cardinal Pietro Gasparri, Vatican secretary of state, was the only thing that precluded O'Connell from assuming "the attitude of a ruler, to which, unfortunately, he seems to be prone by temperament."[66] Though Burke had nothing to do with what transpired, he would reap the repercussion of these events in both the short and long terms.

Illness and Recuperation

Indeed, when the convention met, Burke was not even in Washington. At the end of August, he had fallen ill and unable to say Mass from the 29th onward. Still, he continued to work on sacramental wine and other issues almost to mid-September. Word of his health reached Muldoon through Burke's brother Thomas. Muldoon encouraged John "to follow the physician[']s orders—I guess that will be a cross, but do not take any chances, even for the meeting [of the Administrative Committee]. Your services are too valuable and you must rest now to do more in the future." That meeting on 19 September occurred without him.[67]

Burke's condition had so worsened that shortly before the meeting he had someone at the NCWC drive him to St. Vincent's Hospital in New York. As he later described the incident to Lynch: "That wild night ride from Washington was miserable. The Lord directed me for I would not have been able to make it twenty four hours later." Although the nature of the illness is unknown, it was quite serious. "Every part of the body had been poisoned—and consequently weakened," he later told Lynch. "The poison has been got rid of or almost entirely. The ordeal sapped me of strength." Dr. Mohan ordered extensive bed rest.[68]

Burke went first to Tally-Ho-Rest, a convalescent facility in Tuckahoe, a suburb in Westchester. Nurses there made him eat and do nothing else. Murray, who had visited and assisted him at St. Vincent's, continued to see him. Lynch sent letters that were "a treasure" to him during this crisis, though he was unable to reply until 7 October. "If my body were as strong as the convictions of my heart I would write many pages of affectionate gratitude to you," Burke penned on that date. "I am not permitted to write much." He explained he had not contacted her before the frantic trip because he had no idea what was wrong. "Of course this thing will affect my coming years," he said. "But I have every reason to be most grateful to our Blessed Lord. It is a wonderful satisfaction to have been permitted to suffer with Him." Burke hoped to be allowed to say Mass for the first time since August on the coming Sunday, though the doctor had yet to authorize it and he considered the outlook "dark." "You who know me know the trial" was his comment about inability to offer Mass. Indeed, he had once told Mary Hawks without Mass "the day is inglorious." Moreover, he rightly feared Lynch would not see him for a long time.[69]

Toward the end of October, Mohan ordered Burke to go south out of the cold for recovery. The end of that month found him at the Bennett Hotel in Saint Augustine in the company of James H. Ryan along with a personal nurse, Barbara Sandmaier, whom Burke referred to as "Miss S." He told Murray the trip down had "cost [him] something" in the way of health. He had a slight fever during his brief layover in Washington, but it passed by the time he reached Florida. His days there were "full in a way." The morning consisted of "hours of personal attention," followed by an outing, lunch, sleep, another outing, and supper. Ryan was "excellent company." In the evening, they played rook. Several of their excursions had been to Castillo de San Marcos, the old Spanish colonial fort. The food at the hotel was average, although special dishes prepared for Burke were better fare than those of his companions. Ryan was happy when he got a meal out. "To ask [$]240 a week ($4,000 in 2024) for two was consummate nerve," commented Burke. Mohan wanted him to rebuild his strength through golf. On All Souls Day, Burke felt fit enough to manage seven holes. "Of course I'm tired but I didn't expect to be able to play at all," he told Murray. "Miss S. followed me over the links and 'restrained' me at various points." Because weather was "quite variable" rather than hot, the little party moved farther south for warmth.[70]

They lodged in the Ansonia Apartments at Miami Beach. Their quarters had an ocean view, though the sea was distant enough not to disturb them with sound of surf. "This is a very fashionable place," Burke told Lynch, "but there is no fashion here yet. The season is not open." The beach was deserted; the days were quiet. Unfortunately, the Catholic church was over four miles away, so Burke could say Mass only on Sundays. If he got money enough to rent a car, he thought he might try doing daily Mass, but nothing indicates he did. The circadian rhythm had altered little from the Bennett: breakfast, golf, lunch, sleep, a walk, and supper. He reported he had not been out in evening air since 28 August, the night before he fell ill, and it was now mid-November. He was doing practically no work, though he felt he could.[71]

His condition and his mother's death made him reflective and emotional. Murray wrote him a letter recalling the family gathering a year earlier on Armistice Day when his mother was still alive. "I can picture the seen [*sic*]," he replied. He feared his present condition worried his siblings and caused them pain. "I know they have thought of my mother as she sat there a year ago," he wrote. "Today I saw a woman coming towards me on the street in Miami, and I all but cried. My life will never be the same. Sometimes I think that she is there in 92nd St. reading the letters that I send, thinking of me, and that I will travel back to see her, and then I have to live again in the past." He knew, however, that there was no going back for the Christian: "I must travel forward to see her."[72]

Burke wrote Lynch in a similar vein. "This has been a long exile for me," he said. "I have passed somewhat through the valley of darkness and of death, for no one knows what I have suffered: nor can I tell of all the mystery and the perplexity with which my soul has been deluged." The way forward was the path. He mused on how the "unstable," broken self with its failures and vexations received so much attention. "Our risen self in Christ Jesus is almost too good to look at—too big to believe. As a consequence we cling to God in our weakness rather than in our strength."

Recent experience made him feel he could "speak with some warrant." The Christian's future was already present: the risen Christ living within (cf. Phil. 3:12–16). "No wonder the psalmist [*sic* for prophet and apostle] says that no man has conceived those things that God had prepared for those who love Him [Isa. 64:3 and 1 Cor. 2:9]."[73]

Murray had thought it might be good if she went down to be with him for Thanksgiving while Sandmaier would be away with her family. Burke discouraged her. "I desire to have you and I know you'd enjoy it," he explained. "But it shouldn't be just now." They had shared so much together that at times he longed to be with her "because without introduction you would understand my thoughts."[74]

On 19 November, a change of the guard occurred. William Slattery came down and Ryan returned to Washington. Burke and "Slats" played golf together and had a pleasant time. One day Burke even sat on the beach and read *Moby Dick*. He told Murray he knew he was getting stronger because he now understood that he had not been as well as he thought he was while in St. Augustine and appreciated just how weak he had been at Tuckahoe. Golfing took a little out him, but to no great harm. Burke doubted he could now work as of old, nor did he think he would ever be able to do so again. "My days were pretty full" at NCWC, he admitted. He at times felt impatient and rebellious against his enforced exile.[75]

On 22 November, he received word that Gavin's mother had died. He telegraphed condolences. She had visited him at Tuckahoe and offered him a gift of money. When he refused it, she complained he considered her gifts "poison." Burke wrote to Murray, "You know how I pray that Mrs. G may do the right thing." Gavin had written asking again he accept a monetary gift. Burke told Murray in light of Gavin's remark to him at Tally-Ho, he decided to accept half the amount offered. "Her letters are good, she has intelligent insight," he noted: "but she doesn't know how to spell obedience."[76]

At age thirty-nine, Gavin herself was ill. Burke considered her a woman much in need of reform. As president of the NCCW, she blamed everyone else for the condition it was in, while failing to recognize her own part through neglect of leadership. He told Murray he would give Gavin what help he could. It was likely this moment Burke sent her his spiritual reflection on his mother's suffering and death in order to steel Gavin's faith as she endured her condition. He explained it was easy to see Christ in the agreeable things of life. Much harder it was to see him in the unpleasant. "We actually shrink from the thought that the true God, the Perfect Man was ever like this suffering, repulsive, helpless one." People were tempted to be contemptuous of humanity, which so vaunted itself, and yet was so weak. "Strong faith is required to keep faith in our fellows and ourselves," he wrote. He had seen how his mother mastered pain until it mastered her. "And her mind died. Her face was worn with exhaustion. All comeliness had gone from it," he remarked. She lay a helpless victim until her spirit departed and her body was committed to the earth. The same had happened to Jesus on the cross. He was a reproach to men and helpless, pitiably weak. "And in my mother Christ suffered and she suffered with Him," he reflected. "He was there when she was unconscious and what He had done she was doing.... Christ in her so suffered that in Him her glory through him might be revealed." Jesus still loved her lifeless body, which would later know him as her spirit knew him now, on the final day when his voice would "call at the Last Judgment—'I know Mine and Mine know Me [cf., John 10:27].'"[77] These thoughts meant enough to Gavin that she treasured the document and returned it to the Paulists after Burke's death.

Early December found him feeling better. He was grateful to be well, able to care for himself, and feel his strength returning. "I have been through a long night," he wrote to Murray. "The dawn is good. What I have suffered I never told." He could not speak of it even to his brother, James, when he came to visit, nor could he do so now with her. His thoughts turned to Christmas. He had written Mohan to ask if he could go home, though he was not getting his hopes up. When word came a week later he must remain where he was and continue recovery, he found it hard to take. "There is no use kicking," he wrote. "If I put it [Mohan's letter] aside and went back and anything happened—well. I'd be pestered again with what I have heard a million times that I'm not obedient. I always have and will have my own way etc. etc." He resolved to bear with separation from loved ones. In breaking the news to Lynch, he remarked he "never thought it would take so long" to regain the strength he once had. He said the first Christmas, Jesus "came to receive us all; to include us all in His inheritance. Never does he deny it, never does He fail when we give Him the opportunity to deepen its sense." He wished he could give her this word in person.[78]

On New Year's Eve, Burke missed Murray and the others at *Catholic World* as well as their annual ritual of reviewing the year gone by and guessing at what the next would hold. So he did it by letter. "The year showed what you have always had, your fidelity, your love, your loyalty," he told Murray. "As I look back upon most anxious days, I see you ever true: ever one with me: often anticipating my requests and my needs: your heart feeling for me: you, devoted to those of my own family, most devoted to her who has gone but who is still ever near." Burke remarked on Murray's spiritual growth. She was obedient and understood the meaning of that virtue more than before. Through her sufferings, she had learned to live and think with Christ and take her heart to him. "For these things I have labored and to know that they are bearing fruition in you, makes you my joy in the Lord," he told her, "—as St. Paul would put it."[79]

Burke said he was much better. "I did 18 holes of golf," he wrote, "but I can't boast of how I felt at the 18th." If someone had sat him down afterward, he doubted he could have risen. His feet and ankles were still sore from the outing. "I walk lame at times," he admitted. "Of course I don't do anything like I used to." His recovery, he told Murray, was such that he felt "justified" in writing Mohan for permission to return to work. He wanted to participate in the meeting of the Administrative Committee in January 1922.[80] His physician approved.

ENDNOTES TO CHAPTER 9

1. Burke, *Christ in Us*, 52.
2. Frank Miller, *Censored Hollywood: Sex, Sin, & Violence on Screen* (Atlanta: Turner Publishing, Inc., 1994), 23; Adolph Zukor with Dale Kramer, *The Public Is Never Wrong: The Autobiography of Adolph Zukor* (New York: G. P. Putnam's Sons, 1953), 202–03; May, *Screening Out the Past*, 21–214; Black, *Hollywood Censored*, 3–28; Pollard, *Sex and Violence*, 11–24. The Big Eight were Paramount (Famous Players–Lasky Corporation), Twentieth Century-Fox, MGM, Universal, Warner Bros., Columbia, United Artists, and Radio-Keith-Orpheum.
3. Julian Johnson, "The Shadow Stage: A Review of the New Pictures," *Photoplay* 17 (December 1919): 73 (quotes are from here); *Male and Female*, directed by Cecil B. DeMille, produced by Famous Players–Lasky Corporation, 1919; Black, *Hollywood Censored*, 28–29; May, *Screening Out the Past*, 205–38; Pollard, *Sex and Violence*, 21–24.

4. "Producers Warned to Abolish Indecent Movies," *NCWC Bulletin* 2 (January 1921): 20 (quotation is here); McMahon to Burke, 13 December 1920, ACUA, USCCB 10:125:32; *New York Times*, 12 December 1920 and 28 December 1922; Black, *Hollywood Censored*, 29–30: Brownlow, *Behind Mask of Innocence*, 7–8; Garth Jowett, *Film: The Democratic Art* (Boston: Little, Brown and Company, 1976), 151–56; Samantha Barbas, "The Political Spectator: Censorship, Protest and the Moviegoing Experience, 1912–1922," *Film History* 11 (No. 2, 1999): 217–25.
5. McMahon to Burke, 13 December 1920, ACUA, USCCB 10:125:32; *New York Times*, 12 December 1920 and 28 December 1922; Neal Gabler, *An Empire of Their Own: How the Jews Invented Hollywood* (New York: Anchor Books, 1989), 460 n. 278; Merrill Edwards Gates, ed., *Men of Mark in America: Ideals of American Life Told in Biographies of Eminent Living Americans*, 2 vols (Washington, D.C.: Men of Mark Publishing Company, 1905), 1:245–46; Brownlow, *Behind Mask of Innocence*, 7.
6. "Producers Warned to Abolish Indecent Movies," 20. For Burke's authorship of the statement, see Burke to Murray, Fourth Sunday of Advent [19 December] 1920, AP, Burke Papers, box 11.
7. Burke to Hanna, 23 February 1921, copy, ACUA, USCCB 10:128:17.
8. *New York Times*, 19 December 1921.
9. Burke to Hanna, 23 February 1921, copy, ACUA, USCCB 10:128:17.
10. McMahon to Burke, 23 December 1920, copy, ACUA, USCCB 10:125:32; Williams to McMahon, 22 December 1920, ibid.; Black, *Hollywood Censored*, 13–15, 53.
11. Burke to McMahon, 28 December 1920, copy, ACUA, USCCB 10:125:32.
12. McMahon, "The Problem with the Movies," *NCWC Bulletin* 2 (January 1921): 16–17; "Producers Warned to Abolish Indecent Movies," ibid., 20; McMahon, "Cleansing the Movies: An Urgent and Important Task Awaits the Catholic Men and Women of America," ibid. (February 1921): 19 (quotes are here).
13. "Council Favors Sheppard-Towner Maternity Bill: Catholic Women urged to Combat Startling Mortality of Infants and Mothers," *NCWC Bulletin* 2 (January 1921):15, emphasis in original; *Historical Statistics*, 25; Pace to George Johnson, 9 December 1920, copy, ACUA, Pace papers; David M. Kennedy, *Birth Control In America: The Career of Margaret Sanger* (New Haven: Yale University Press, 1976), 72–94, 218–22; Constance M. Chen, *"The Sex Side of Life": Mary Ware Dennett's Pioneering Battle for Birth Control and Sex Education* (New York: New Press, 1996), 223–32; Jean H. Baker, *Margaret Sanger: a Life of Passion* (New York: Hill and Wang, 2011), 112–14, 131–36; Leslie Woodcock Tentler, *Catholics and Contraception: An American History* (Ithaca, N.Y.: Cornell Paperbacks, 2008), 15–57.
14. Pace to Dowling, 3 January 1920 [*sic* for 1921], copy, ACUA, Vice-Rector

files; Dowling to Pace, 20 January 1921, copy, ibid.; James H. Ryan to Pace, 6 January 1921, ACUA, Pace Papers.

15. Pace to Dowling, 12 December 1920, copy, ACUA, Vice Rector files; Slawson, *Department of Education Battle*, 68–69.
16. "Welfare Council Issues Statement on the Smith-Towner Bill," *NCWC Bulletin* 2 (February 1921): 24.
17. Minutes of the General National Committee, 13 January 1921, ACUA, USCCB 10:1 BV Interdepartmental Meetings, vol. 1; Minutes of the meeting of the Department of Education, 2 February 1921, ACUA, Pace Papers; Slattery to the clergy, 19 January 1921, ACUA, Pace Papers.
18. Pace to David I. Walsh, 28 January 1921, copy, ACUA, Vice Rector files; Slawson, *Department of Education Battle*, 71–73.
19. *Congressional Record*, 66th Cong., 3rd Sess., 1921, 60, pt. 3, 3044–49; Slawson, *Department of Education Battle*, 73.
20. Circular of McGinley to Grand Knights, 15 February 1921, AKC, Smith-Towner file; *New York Times*, 13 February 1921.
21. Burke to Hanna, 23 February 1921, copy, ACUA, USCCB 10:128:17.
22. *New York Times*, 20 February 1921.
23. Pace to Hanna, 26 February 1921, copy, ACUA, Pace Papers; Burke to Hanna, 23 February 1921, copy, ACUA, USCCB 10:128:17; Slawson, *Department of Education Battle*, 74–75.
24. Burke to Hanna, 23 February 1921, copy, ACUA, USCCB 10:128:17; Burke to Muldoon, 15 February 1921, ibid., 10:104:11; Pace to Hanna, 26 February 1921, copy, ACUA, Pace Papers. Minutes of the Administrative Committee, 6 April 1921, ACUA, USCCB.
25. Minutes of the Administrative Committee, 19 September 1921, ACUA, USCCB; Kauffman, *Faith and Fraternalism*, 356–57.
26. Hicks, *The Republican Ascendancy, 1921–1933* (New York: Harper and Brothers, 1960), 68; Abell, *Social Action*, 212; McShane, *"Sufficiently Radical,"* 252–53.
27. News Sheet of the Social Action Department, 22 November 1920, ACUA, USCCB Social Action Department files, box 175.
28. Russell to Muldoon, 20 January 1921, copy, enclosed with Muldoon to Burke, 24 January 1921, ACUA, USCCB 10:152:28; Russell to Edward Dyer, 20 September 1921 [*sic* for 20 January 1921], AASUS-AASMSU, RG 10, box 23 (the quotation is here); McNulty to Tanner, 6 May 1964, ACUA, USCCB 10:72:24.
29. Muldoon to Burke, 24 January 1921, ACUA, USCCB 10:152:28; Burke to Muldoon, 28 January 1921, copy, ibid.
30. Draft of a Statement of Explanation on the "Closed-Shop," enclosure with Burke to Muldoon, 3 February 1921, copy, ACUA, USCCB 10:104:11; Muldoon to Burke, 9 February 1921, ibid.; Muldoon to Burke, 17 February 1921, ibid.

31. Report of the Bureau of Education, NCWC Department of Education, 2 February 1921, copy, ACUA, Pace Papers.
32. Arthur Monahan to Pace, 15 March 1921, with enclosure: "Position of the Roman Catholic Church in Educational Matters," ACUA, Pace Papers; Slawson, *Department of Education Battle*, 86–87.
33. Burke to Hanna, 25 July 1921, AASF, NCWC files; *Buffalo Catholic Union and Times*, 26 May 1921; *NCWC News Sheet*, 13 June 1921; Arthur C. Monahan, "Work of the N.C.W.C. Bureau of Education," *NCWC Bulletin* 3 (June 1921): 18; Frank T. Martin, "The Michigan School Controversy" (Unpublished M.A. thesis, Catholic University of America, 1949), 1–13, 18–40; Timothy Mark Pies, "The Parochial School Campaigns in Michigan, 1920–1924: The Lutheran and Catholic Involvement," *Catholic Historical Review* 72 (April 1986): 221–24; Slawson, *Department of Education Battle*, 86–87.
34. Schrembs to Burke, 1 July 1921, ACUA, USCCB 10:99:30; Burke to Hanna, 25 July 1921, AASF, NCWC files; Minutes of the Department of Education, 25 June 1921, ACUA, USCCB Education Department 10:23:11.
35. *Minutes of the Second Annual Meeting of the Hierarchy, September 1920*, 10, ACUA, Bound Volumes; Slawson, *Foundation of NCWC*, 93, 123–25.
36. Ellis, *The Life and Times of Gibbons*, 2:622–27; Thomas W. Spalding, *Premier See: A History of the Archdiocese of Baltimore, 1789–1989* (Baltimore: Johns Hopkins University Press, 1989), 316–18.
37. Burke, Interview with Cardinal Dennis Dougherty, 23 April 1921, ACUA, USCCB 10:152:8; Dougherty to O'Connell, 15 December 1922, AABo, Annual Meeting of the Hierarchy file; Burke to Hanna, 3 May 1921, AASF, NCWC files; Slawson, *Department of Education Battle*, 82–83; Spalding, *Premier See*, 157–58. The quotes are from both the interview and Dougherty's letter.
38. Dougherty to O'Connell, 15 December 1922, AABo, Annual Meeting of the Hierarchy file. Incorporating the committee was a mistake that was corrected in September 1923 when the corporation was adjusted to include all members of the hierarchy (Slawson, *Foundation of NCWC*, 93–94, 206–07).
39. Muldoon to Burke, 6 May 1921, ACUA, USCCB 10:152.28.
40. Hanna to *Carissimo* ["dearest one": Burke], n.d. May 1921, ACUA, USCCB 10:99:15; Burke to Hanna, 25 July 1921, AASF, NCWC files.
41. Slawson, *Ambition and Arrogance*, 91–99; Slawson, *Foundation of NCWC*, 126–28; O'Toole, *Militant and Triumphant*, 194–97.
42. Burke, Memorandum on Mother's Final Illness [May 1921], AP, Burke Papers, Box 2.
43. Ibid.
44. Ibid.
45. Burke to Kerby, 31 May 1921, ACUA, Kerby Papers 58:4:4.
46. Burke to Murray, 15 April 1921, AP, Burke Papers, box 11; Burke to Murray,

Eve of SS Peter and Paul [29 June] 1921, ibid.; *The Letters of St. Ambrose, Bishop of Milan*, trans. by a member of the English Church, revised by H. Walford (Oxford: Devonport Society of the Holy Trinity, 1881), 317.

47. Burke to Murray, Eve of SS Peter and Paul [29 June] 1921, Paulist Archives, Burke Papers, box 11.
48. [Burke], "The Need of Social Welfare Work," *NCWC Bulletin* 2 (May 1921): 3; Lawler, *Full Circle*, 35–40; Hartmann-Ting, "Catholic Service School for Women," 105–09.
49. "Clifton to Be Permanent Social Service School." *NCWC Bulletin* 2 (May 1921): 2–4; Muldoon to Burke, 6 May 1921, ACUA, USCCB 10:152:28; Lawler, *Full Circle*, 40, 50–51; Hartmann-Ting, "Catholic Service School for Women," 109–10.
50. Burke to Muldoon, 4 March 1922, copy, ibid., 10:152:28; Burke to Charles P. Neill, 24 February 1922, copy, ibid., 10:152:35; "Clifton to Be Permanent School," 2; Lawler, *Full Circle*, 110.
51. [Burke], "Need of Social Welfare Work," 3; "'Clifton' Becomes Standard Service School: Opens in October with Dr. Charles P. Neill Director," *NCWC Bulletin* 3 (September 1921): 22–23; "National Catholic Service School: Splendid Faculty and Physical Plant Characterize New Institution," *NCWC Bulletin* 3 (November 1921): 8–9.
52. Lawler, *Full Circle*, 41–42, 51.
53. Ibid., 51–54, 57.
54. Slawson, "Wine for the Gods," 165–75; Asbury, *Great Illusion*, 121–34; Behr, *Prohibition*, 7–75; Cashman, *Prohibition*, 6–23; Kobler, *Ardent Spirits*, 198–212; Merz, *Dry Decade*, 1–42; Sinclair, *Era of Excess*, 63–82, 116–28, 152–66.
55. Joseph Busch to Burke, Thursday [31 March 1921], ACUA, USCCB 10:111:18; Walter Barron to Burke, memorandum, 4 April 1921, ibid.; Burke to Busch, 9 April 1921, copy, ibid.; Slawson, "Wine for the Gods," 175–76.
56. Minutes of the Administrative Committee, April 6, 1921, ACUA, USCCB 10:64:2.
57. [Burke], Conference with Colonel Goff, Assistant Attorney General, John F. Kramer, Commissioner of Prohibition, and Mrs. Adams, Assistant to the Attorney General, 22 April 1921; Burke to Russell, 22 April 1921, copy; Memorandum from William Cochran to Burke, regarding suggested letter to the NCWC Administrative Committee about sacramental wine, April 27, 1921—all in ACUA, USCCB 10:111:18.
58. Russell to Burke, 23 April 1921, copy, ACUA, USCCB 10:111:18; Annette Abbott Adams to Russell, 20 April 1921, copy, ibid.
59. Cochran to Burke, 27 April 1921, ACUA, USCCB 10:111:18; Burke to Hanna, 3 May 1921, AASF, NCWC files.
60. Burke to Andrew Mullen, 6 May 1921, copy, ACUA, USCCB 10:111:18.
61. Ibid. Emphasis in original.

62. Mellon to Burke, May 18, 1921, ACUA, USCCB 10:111:18; Slawson, "Wine for the Gods," 177–78.
63. Cochran to Russell, July 12, 1921, copy, ACUA, USCCB 10:111:18; James R. Ryan to Hickey, July 15, 1921, copy, ACUA, USCCB Legal Department 10:32:1; Hickey to J. R. Ryan, telegram, July 17, 1921, ACUA, ibid.; Boston *Pilot*, 23 and 27 July 1921; *New York Times*, 24 July 24 1921; Burke to Edmund Gibbons, August 29, 1921, ADA, NCWC files; "Report of the Chairman of the Department of Laws and Legislation," *The National Catholic Welfare Council: Reports of Administrative Committee and Departments Made at the Conference of the Hierarchy of the United States, Washington, D.C., September 21–22, 1921* (Washington, D.C.: NCWC, 1921), 23–24.
64. Burke to James Cantwell (chancellor of archdiocese of San Francisco), telegram, September 7, 1921, AASF, NCWC files; Burke to Harry Daugherty, 10 October 1921, copy, ACUA, USCCB 10:111:18; Mabel W. Willebrandt to Burke, ibid.; "Report of the Chairman of the Department of Laws and Legislation," 23–24; T.D. 3231 in Arthur W. Blakemore, *National Prohibition: The Volstead Act Annotated and Digest of National and State Prohibition Decisions* (Albany, N.Y.: Matthew Bender and Company, 1923), 588. The federal government considered the sale of sacramental wine to priests, ministers, and rabbis to be wholesale rather than retail—even though a retailer conducted the transaction—because the wine was to be used for professional purposes rather than for personal consumption (T.D. 3208 in Blakemore, *National Prohibition*, 583–84).
65. Slawson, *Ambition and Arrogance*, 95–100, 104–05; Slawson, *Foundation of NCWC*, 127–29.
66. Diary of Walsh, 22 September 1921, ADP (quotes of Curley are here); Bonzano to Pietro Gasparri, 25 September 1921, ASV, DAUS, IX, Boston 104; Bonzano to the Hierarchy, 22 March 1922, with enclosure the Vatican Decree Suppressing the NCWC, ADP, Walsh Papers; Slawson, *Ambition and Arrogance*, 100–01. Walsh had written over the head of the decree: "Threat of Boston & Philadelphia carried out—rule or ruin."
67. Muldoon to Burke, 9 September 1921, ACUA USCCB 10:152:28; Burke to Lynch, 7 October 1921, AP, Burke Papers, box 5; Minutes of the Administrative Committee, 19 September 1921, ACUA, USCCB 10:64:2.
68. Burke to Lynch, 7 October 1921, AP, Burke Papers, box 5 (first quote is here); Burke to Lynch, 24 October 1921, ibid. (second quote is here).
69. Burke to Lynch, 7 October 1921, AP, Burke Papers, box 5; Hawks, "Souvenir of Burke," ibid., box 10.
70. Burke to Murray, 2 November 1921, AP, Burke Papers, Box 11 (quotes are here); Burke to Lynch, 17 November 1921, ibid., box 5.
71. Burke to Lynch, 17 November 1921, AP, Burke Papers, box 5 (quotes are here); Burke to Murray, 17 November 1921, ibid., box 11.

72. Burke to Murray, 17 November 1921, AP, Burke Papers, box 11.
73. Burke to Lynch, 17 November 1921, AP, Burke Papers, box 5.
74. Burke to Murray, 17 November 1921, AP, Burke Papers, box 11.
75. Burke to Murray, 22 November 1921, AP, Burke Papers, box 11; Burke to Murray, 26 November 1921, ibid.
76. Burke to Murray, 22 November 1921, AP, Burke Papers, box 11.
77. [Burke, Reflection, undated], AP, Burke Papers, box 1; Burke to Murray, 29 January 1922, ibid., box 11; Burke to Murray, 12 February 1922, ibid.; Burke to Murray, 22 February 1922, ibid. Handwritten on the typescript of the reflection about his mother is that Gavin returned this to the Paulists, probably after Gavin's or Burke's death.
78. Burke to Murray, 1 and 8 December 1921, AP, Burke Papers, box 11 (quotations are from both); Burke to Lynch, 19 December 1921, ibid., box 5.
79. Burke to Murray, 1 January 1922, AP, Burke Papers, box 11.
80. Ibid. See also Burke to Mildred Merrick, 8 January 1922, AP, Burke Papers, box 9.

Chapter 10
Suppression and Restoration

> Sincerity is the honesty of the soul with itself. We cannot be insincere with men and sincere with God. The soul that gives itself to the habit of pretending one thing yet really seeking another: … or to take unfair opportunity: the soul that in its estimate of life accepts the standards of the world, which are of appearance, of outward show … of preferment, is offering serious obstacles to the strength which Christ would bestow.… Christ seeks to break down barriers: His love is true, therefore does it seek and ask full possession. Of us He asks sincerity.[1]

Back in Harness

Shortly before the Administrative Committee met in January 1922, John Burke was back in harness at headquarters. He had been sorely missed. Edward Pace reported to Archbishop Edward Hanna that Burke's absence had occurred at an "unfortunate" moment, as things at the agency were still fluid. Some departments felt they were making little progress. He hoped Burke's recovery would "enable him to take hold of the situation with renewed vigor."[2] Indeed, headquarters seems to have drifted. Burke met a pile of correspondence. "Letters I find were answered thus 'Father Burke is away. It will receive his attention when he returns etc.,[']" he told Grace Murray. "Of course anybody could answer letters in that fashion. So the problems facing me are many."[3] Three were especially urgent: education, the National Catholic Service School for Women, and sacramental wine.

Regarding federal education legislation, the NCWC received unexpected help from President Warren Harding, who wanted to reorganize the executive branch and create a department of public welfare which would house the Bureau of Education. The NEA resisted because it wanted a separate, subsidized department of education embodied in the Sterling-Towner bill, successor of the Smith-Towner. Supporting the NEA were the Ku Klux Klan and Southern Jurisdiction of Scottish Rite Masons. The NEA intended to force the bill out of committee. The Scottish Rite pledged $125,000 annually (almost $2.125 million in 2024) to publicize it.[4]

In late January, Burke, Pace, Father James H. Ryan, and William Burris, dean of education at the University of Cincinnati, met to discuss the situation. A friend of Ryan, Burris had seen Harding, who said he understood perfectly the motives of those supporting the Sterling-Towner bill and opposed them. He wanted no department of education. In an astute political move, Harding appointed Senator William Kenyon, a department advocate, to a federal judgeship, removing him from the chair of the Committee on Education and Labor. Next in line for the chairmanship was Senator William Borah of Idaho, who opposed the bill.[5]

In early February, Burke saw Harding about the Sterling-Towner and reorganization bills. Evidence suggests the two discussed having congressional Republicans toe the party line. Shortly after their meeting, Harding addressed the League of Republican State Clubs urging all Republicans to hew to the platform of 1920 which called for reorganization of the government, not a department of education. Burke informed Murray of the interview, commenting "I suppose you read [Harding's] statement in the paper."[6]

The rebuke had little immediate effect. Republican leaders of the House Committee on Education met informally with representatives of the NEA. Despite his desire to obey Harding, Chairman Simeon Fess felt compelled by colleagues and the NEA to report the bill.[7] On learning this, Burke urged Fess to hold a hearing before doing so; the chairman refused because there was no demand for one. If Fess needed such, Burke would provide it. He asked members of the Administrative Committee to have prominent men, preferably Protestants, telegraph Fess that public opinion demanded a hearing. A number of them did.[8]

Fortunately, the NEA Department of Superintendents was meeting then in Chicago. Burke had agents there work to steel the courage of previously silent opponents of the Sterling-Towner bill. A number found their voices, for there was significant opposition to the idea of either a department or federal aid or both. "I intend to keep working this way," Burke explained to Archbishop Michael Curley, "and look forward to even greater change with regard to N.E.A. sentiment at their annual convention in Boston next June." Burke said the telegraphic protest he organized and the meeting of superintendents demonstrated to Fess the educational community was disunited on the issue "and that public sentiment was by no means entirely behind the Bill." In early March, Fess sent his son to Burke with word it would remain in committee.[9]

When Burke informed Bishop Peter Muldoon of Fess's decision, he wisely added "this [word] may have been sent simply to lead me to let up our efforts." Explaining the Scottish Rite's drive to report the bill, Burke described the Masons as "the strongest lobby in the way of political influence that Washington knows," no doubt because so many representatives and senators were Masons themselves. It was also one of the most financially powerful.[10]

Three days later, Republican leaders of the House committee met again informally with agents of the NEA to digest Harding's definite message that no action occur on the bill until his own legislation on public welfare and reorganization came forward. Afterward, a chastened Judge Horace Mann Towner, cosponsor of the bill, announced, "We have decided not to do anything until we get the re-organization report." Republican majority leader Frank Mondell of Wyoming told the House he was determined no new subsidy bill, including the Sterling-Towner, would be enacted. Scarcely two weeks later, Senator Borah accepted chairmanship of the Senate Committee on Education and Labor.[11]

While Burke believed the subsidy in the Sterling-Towner bill would prevent its passage, he told Muldoon the Church would have to yield on creation of a department of education with the same functions as Bureau of Education. "The feeling for that is very strong throughout the country," he explained, "and I don't see on what ground we could effectively oppose it; nor do I see any harm that it would do to the cause of Catholic education."[12] To Bishop Edmund Gibbons, new chairman of the Legal Department, Burke made a similar point: "Our situation will be hopeless if we as Catholics oppose all federal remedial legislation simply because it is federal. We must show that in a particular instance federal aid will do more harm than good as for example in the control of general education by the Sterling-Towner Bill."[13]

While dealing with education, Burke faced a crisis in the Service School for Women. During his absence in Florida, its management was augmented and lines of authority were redrawn. Moreover, conflict had erupted between Director Charles Neill and the old Clifton faculty. Marie Ewing and Helen Cronin resented Burke's passing over Maud Cavanaugh for the directorship and balked at the new curriculum. They wanted the old military-style discipline. Burke told Muldoon that "in many ways they have made Dr. Neill's life miserable." As for Neill, he did not care for them either.[14]

By the time Burke returned to Washington, the three women had submitted their resignations, and Neill was apparently prepared to accept them. Burke explained that he himself no longer had oversight of school which was now under the authority of the NCCW, so Neill would have to consult the new board before doing so. This came as news to him.[15]

Several days later, the visibly agitated Neill saw Burke. He quoted the contract the latter signed at hiring him, stating he had charge of the school under the direction of Burke himself. Neill added his heart was with the school and he would continue to serve its academic side even without salary. He gave Burke a week to decide if he would honor their contract.[16]

Unfortunately, Burke came down with a cold. His Washington physician Dr. Marbury confined him to bed. So, Burke wrote to say if Neill was convinced he could not direct the school, he would be released. If that was not the case and "certain changes of the faculty" would suffice, Burke would gladly see to it. Neill asked for clarification about authority of the NCCW regarding the school's internal organization, its curriculum, its faculty, and its discipline. He wanted authority to dismiss teachers and administrators and hire new ones as he saw fit. In reply, Burke explained the NCCW now controlled the school in cooperation with the Social Action Department. The two entities had formed a joint committee of three consisting of John Ryan, William Kerby, and Agnes Regan who must agree on curriculum, faculty, and director of the school.[17] There the matter lay for nearly a month.

Burke informed Muldoon of all that transpired and explained Neill had cited his contract in support of his demand. "He seems to think," wrote Burke, "—in fact by speech intimated—that I was not entirely frank in drawing up the contract." Burke did not believe there had "been violation of the contract" because he could always act as go-between for the joint committee in its relations with Neill. It would be "preposterous," however, to grant him power of appointment and dismissal, which meant he must resign. Yet, his doing so "would be looked upon as a great victory for those who have so opposed at the School," which was equally unacceptable. "It is a most difficult situation," Burke told Muldoon.[18]

In mid-March, Neill told Burke if he had known the previous year that curricular and personnel issues were under the purview of the joint committee, he "would unhesitatingly have declined" the position. As painful as it was for him, he decided to withdraw as director at the end of term. At close of the year, Neill, Cavanaugh, Cronin, and Ewing all resigned.[19]

While handling mutiny in the Service School, Burke was again dealing with sacramental wine. During his long absence, sole care of it had transferred to the NCWC. The Attorney General's Office had taken under consideration Burke's argument about how the Volstead Act should be applied. Mabel Walker Willebrandt, assistant attorney general for prohibition, prepared a decision adverse to the NCWC, and James H. Ryan had appealed to Assistant Attorney General Guy Goff to review her decision. He agreed.[20]

When the Administrative Committee met on Burke's return, Goff summoned Hanna and Gibbons to say a new ruling would permit agents of manufacturers to distribute sacramental wine. The committee deemed it satisfactory if the government actually carried it out. Despite Goff's assurance, no decision was forthcoming until well into March. This delay caused Burke no little concern. "Nothing has been done by the department [of Justice] since you were here," he wrote Gibbons. "I am afraid that the present supply [of wine] may fail: and then with no ruling permitting a convenient distribution, we will face a terrible situation: and blame will fall upon the N.C.W.C." Burke assured Gibbons he was keeping after the matter.[21]

He just posted this letter when the Treasury tightened regulations on agents. The commissioner ruled no new permits for agencies would be granted except when clearly "necessary to accomplish adequate and economical distribution in the locality." Because some wineries established agencies without fully appreciating the liability, he spelled it out: business conduct of an agent "shall always be upon the manufacturer," and title to liquor in an agent's possession "shall remain with the manufacturer until title is transferred to a purchaser." The manufacturer must establish both sale price and the agent's compensation in a contract.[22]

William Cochran reported to Burke these new regulations were meant simply to forestall price gouging by dealers, a matter about which Burke himself was concerned. The government received complaints that although wineries made their product available to agents at reasonable rates, some hiked prices excessively. Cochran believed the Treasury would probably relax rules once the Justice Department had rendered a decision. He urged Burke to see Attorney General Harry Daugherty about it. The only good news was that the Prohibition Division permitted agents to replenish stocks for Passover, a ruling that also applied to Catholics.[23]

Hanna felt betrayed by the tightened regulations. Few wineries would want to risk appointment of an agent on "such [an] unreasonable and unbusinesslike basis"; the rules were tantamount to elimination of agencies altogether and served as a hindrance to legitimate distribution of sacramental wine. Hanna urged Gibbons to protest and have them amended.[24] Gibbons delegated the matter to Burke.

Burke saw Daugherty. He complained the new Treasury regulations were stricter than those issued the previous September, which Daugherty himself had suspended at request of the NCWC, pending his new ruling. Burke made the same argument he had made to Andrew Mellon: the Volstead Act specifically exempted *distribution* of sacramental wine. He wanted current distributors placed on the same footing as wineries to take delivery of bonded shipments in their own bonded storerooms for sale to properly approved applicants. This matter, said Burke, had been dragging on for over a year and he asked for its speedy resolution.[25]

Though sympathetic, Daugherty believed the law left no room: distribution must occur between individual priest and manufacturer directly. If the Church wished otherwise, it would have to ask Congress to amend. Given the Masons' pressure on Congress with regard to education, Burke considered that approach out of the question. He then convinced Daugherty that because the Volstead Act gave a bishop authority to supervise manufacture of sacramental wine, it implicitly granted him the lesser right to supervise distribution and even delegate it to a priest. Daugherty accepted this argument in principle. Burke wrote Hanna the issue was very involved, but he felt he "found a plan which will be accepted to meet our needs in distribution of wine." It would, however, take some weeks of further negotiation.[26]

A Bolt from the Blue

It was remarkable Burke was able to meet Daugherty with such composure because only days earlier a lightning bolt struck out of blue skies. Archbishop Curley had telephoned Burke that a letter just arrived from the apostolic delegate enclosing a Vatican decree dissolving the NCWC. It had gone to every bishop in the country. The news was quite literally stunning. As Archbishop Austin Dowling put it, "Everyone seems knocked on the head."[27]

Rumor of the decree spread through the NCWC staff. The day Burke saw Daugherty, headquarters was filled with uncertainty and consternation. Burke assembled employees and confirmed issuance of a document impacting the organization "fundamentally," but he had no idea how it might affect operations. All must await word from the Administrative Committee. Until it came, they should neither accept rumor as fact nor discuss it with outsiders. Burke said the committee would act rightly and justly. In any case, all should be prepared to give obedience and full acceptance to its decision. He encouraged them to pray. "This is a time that tries your soul and my soul," he said. He told them never had he worked with "a more devoted, loyal staff." "We have written a worthy record," he concluded. "Let not the pen falter now. We have our superiors—our leaders. Let us wait patiently and hopefully upon their word."[28]

Late that afternoon, Muldoon wired Burke that he had telegraphed Hanna to assemble the Administrative Committee. Burke replied an immediate meeting was necessary to see "what if anything can be carried on." He called Mary Hawks to express sorrow at the terrible news. As she later put it, "In his mind there was no question of anything but obedience." That evening, Burke informed Grace Murray. "My heart is ready to accept the Lord's will," he told her. "I cannot tell you what a burden it is here now." There was nothing to do but pray, and pray hard. "Talking … does no good nor discussion of why or how it happened. Silence, reticence will help our soul most. It is an hour to be with our Lord." To Helen Lynch, he wrote the NCWC had received "a severe blow." "What it means in detail I know not," he continued. "I think it means the end of the work." He begged her to pray: "It is a critical hour for the Church in America."[29] It was a critical hour too for his vision of that Church, a time that tried him dearly.

Next morning, Burked wired Hanna that the committee must meet immediately to decide if any work could continue, to do justice to employees, and perhaps to present the true situation to the Vatican. "Continue work," telegraphed Hanna. Unable to leave his archdiocese, he had wired Muldoon to call a meeting.[30]

News of the suppression leaked around the country. Two Catholic papers—the Buffalo *Echo* and *Denver Catholic Register*—telegraphed the Press Department for confirmation. Burke silenced both by replying he had received no official word and nothing should be published until the NCWC issued a statement. The secular press was also on the trail. The *New York Herald* reported rumor of the suppression and denial of it by an unnamed clergyman in that city, who said the NCWC was simply to be reorganized. Other papers reprinted the story, leading to further inquiries for confirmation by the News Service.[31]

Then came a cable from Monsignor Enrico Pucci, NCWC Roman correspondent: "News arrived these days from America papal condemnation NCWC. I interrogated immediately secretary of state [Cardinal Pietro Gasparri] who contradicted absolutely statement, confirming fully papal benevolence." Burke forwarded it to Muldoon, who ordered it wired to other members of the committee.[32] Bishop William Russell, head of the Press Department, advised Burke to publish the cable. Burke did so. When Bishop Joseph Schrembs saw the item, he urged Muldoon to have Burke stop Catholic papers from using it. "Denial of an official document of the Roman congregation, officially communicated, is a dangerous thing," warned Schrembs. "We are being placed in a wrong position." A chagrined Muldoon demanded Burke telegraph each Catholic paper not to publish the cable. "This is a terrible mistake and must be corrected at any cost," he admonished. "Cannot possible [*sic*] understand your action in this matter."[33]

The rebuff stung Burke. He complied then drafted a lengthy defense, explaining conflicting reports, demands for confirmation, and Russell's instruction to release the cable. In the end, however, he simply wired Muldoon: "Regret causing any embarrassment.... Situation here most difficult." He promised full explanation when the Administrative Committee met.[34]

It did so at Schrembs's residence in Cleveland. Just as the session began, a cable arrived from Michael Williams in Rome. He heard about the suppression and saw the undersecretary of State to inquire. The undersecretary denied Rome dissolved the NCWC, which he said had full papal approval. This was the third such indication the Vatican's right hand knew nothing of what its left was doing. Comparing impressions, the bishops arrived at the same conclusion. They believed the decree was the work of Cardinals William O'Connell and Dennis Dougherty, who were in Rome for election of a new pontiff to succeed Benedict XV. Although they arrived too late to cast a ballot, they engaged in mischievous business. At the instigation of either or both, the Consistorial Congregation hurriedly put together the decree and rushed it to the new pope, Pius XI, who had no idea of its nature and simply signed or orally approved it as routine business.[35] As it turned out, this conjecture proved remarkably accurate.

The story from headquarters was not encouraging. Burke said many local directors of the NCWC reported a membership dazed and bewildered. All wondered why Pius scrapped a work blessed by his predecessor. Field workers of the NCWC filed similar accounts. While the decree caused dismay among laity, it encouraged enemies of the Church to go on the offensive. After the news broke, reported Burke, Masonic organizations pressured their members in Congress to demand the Sterling-Towner bill be reported at once. If it came to the floor, said Burke, the House would certainly pass it.[36] He argued the NCWC was needed to champion the Catholic cause.

Besides defending Catholic rights, it must honor its obligations to the federal government. Burke noted that the NCWC's Immigration Bureau had a seat on the General Committee of Immigrant Aid at Ellis Island and belonged to the Organizing Committee of the National Conference on Immigration Policy.[37] Similarly, the NCWC was a federally authorized agent for Russian relief, an appointment with a curious Vatican twist. While the Holy See negotiated with Russia to allow Papal Relief into the famine-stricken country, Herbert Hoover's American Relief Administration (ARA) had secured the Riga Agreement with the Soviets. The accord recognized the NCWC as an authorized food distributor, so the easiest way for Vatican participation in relief was to have its agent, Jesuit Edmund Walsh, become the NCWC's agent. Burke had made the appointment, but unaware of Rome's overall intention, he had limited the commission to three months.[38]

Although this would result in future complications, the suppression presented a more immediate threat to American Catholic and thereby papal participation.

The Administrative Committee agreed quick action was necessary to prevent public injury to the Catholic cause. It decided to send a delegation to Rome to present its case. Schrembs would spearhead the effort, departing later in the month. Delegates who followed would carry two documents: a protest and petition against suppression to be written by Father John Fenlon; and a report written by Burke on the NCWC. First, however, the committee must win a stay of the decree. It sent a cablegram to Pius stating the NCWC was necessary to protect Catholic education and must fulfill its obligations to the government regarding immigration and Russian relief. It asked him to suspend the decree and prevent its publication in *Acta Apostolicae Sedis* [*Acts of the Holy See*] until it could fully report the importance of these works.[39]

At noon the following day, Burke and Muldoon received a telegram from James H. Ryan, saying Gasparri's nephew, Monsignor Filippo Bernardini, a professor at Catholic University, told Father Joseph Christopher, one of Muldoon's priests studying there, the decree was too severe and should be protested. He added that it blindsided the delegate, Archbishop Giovanni Bonzano. Next day brought a cablegram from Gasparri with word the Vatican would withhold publication and send further information through Bonzano, news that cheered both Muldoon and Burke.[40]

On return to Washington, Burke took to his bed. "Cleveland was a hard trip in the sense that it gave me no rest and much excitement," he told Murray. "I've been laid up since with a slight cold." From bed, he informed Muldoon of a conversation between Fenlon and Bernardini. The latter confirmed the decree was the work of O'Connell and Dougherty, who persuaded Cardinal Gaetano De Lai that the NCWC represented a grave danger of schism in America. Bernardini advised the NCWC to make a strong presentation of the case at Rome. He thought if sixty bishops protested, Rome would accede. Burke and Fenlon talked the matter over and believed the Administrative Committee should solicit written support from the hierarchy for its protest.[41]

Burke set to work on the report. The first two sections outlined the NCWC's history, composition, and purpose, which was to protect and promote the Catholic cause. The decree, wrote Burke, asserted it had been established only to facilitate postwar reconstruction. That was false. Catholics needed a permanent agency. Experience of the War Council held three lessons: (1) the Church's enemies were organized, so it behooved Catholics to be likewise; (2) if the hierarchy did not take the lead, the laity would; and (3) "the only effective Catholic organization is the divinely appointed Hierarchy, working in union with the Holy See, and organizing all the forces of the Church." The vastness of the nation, isolation of many dioceses, weakness of the Catholic body in many states, and increasing federal power combined to make united action imperative for protection of the Church's rights and interests.[42]

Burke then recounted the NCWC's various works, beginning with advancement and defense of Catholic schools, gemstones of the American Church. The council's Social Action Department popularized papal social teaching and helped keep workers within the fold and away from Socialism. The Immigration Bureau looked after hundreds of thousands of newcomers, most of them Catholics. The NCWC, moreover, fostered public morality by advocating decency in motion pictures, opposing birth control legislation, and inculcating civic decorum. The Press Department served eighty-nine Catholic papers, twelve of which it helped establish. It also supplied secular journals with Catholic news, doctrine, and opinion, thereby offsetting prejudice and spreading accurate knowledge of the faith. The Department of Lay Activities molded Catholics into a body under episcopal rule for promotion of piety, zeal, religion, and charity. Finally, the NCWC was recognized by the federal government as the Church's official representative in all legislative matters.[43]

When the Administrative Committee met again, it made minor adjustments to Fenlon's protest and Burke's report. Bernardini was to translate them into Italian, and Archbishop Henry Moeller of Cincinnati would carry them to Rome and join Schrembs. The committee accepted Burke and Fenlon's suggestion of soliciting support for the protest through a circularized signature form for endorsement. A final matter was the NCWC's desperate financial situation. Since the decree, few bishops contributed to its support. The committee ordered Burke to husband remaining funds and streamline business without public show so as to continue work as long as possible while concealing the NCWC's plight.[44]

At Burke's urging, Michael Slattery convinced the NCCM, whose budget was second in size only to the Press Department's, to raise its own funds after 1 June. Burke quietly ordered his own salary of $3,000 per year ($55,500 in 2024) stopped until further notice. Closing the purse strings on himself, he pulled political ones. Working with Senator Medill McCormick of Illinois, Burke had President Harding send word to the Vatican through the American ambassador in Rome that he would be greatly displeased and disappointed if the NCWC were suppressed.[45]

In early May, Moeller picked up the report in Washington, and Burke traveled with him to New York to get his reaction and offer advice. After poring over it, Moeller told Burke, "If the Holy Father reads that, the decree will be withdrawn." Burke then pressed him on a matter he had already insisted by letter to Schrembs in Rome: "No 'tolerari potest' from the Holy See will be sufficient." *Tolerari potest* is Latin for "it can be tolerated," meaning the NCWC could continue as an exception to the rule. Moeller agreed such a decision would be inadequate. The pope must not just tolerate the NCWC, he must order it continued. Burke likely insisted on other things he told Schrembs, namely, the hierarchy must be allowed to meet for purposes of common defense and promotion of common good, which could not be achieved by return to annual meetings of the Board of Archbishops. Nor would a national organization of men or women under a "bishop protector" suffice. It must be the hierarchy as a whole. In New York, they discovered the protest still needed to be printed. So, Moeller sailed for Rome without it. Burke and Fenlon decided to send it with James H. Ryan who was to follow Moeller to the Vatican.[46]

A WOUNDED ORGANIZATION

The Vatican decree left the NCWC wounded. It had previously enjoyed political clout as official voice of the Catholic Church. Now, with rumors of its imminent demise in the press, its influence began to erode. For instance, success in negotiations for sacramental wine had seemed certain. Now, Burke reported to Muldoon: "The solution … is mysteriously held up. We cannot get authorities to move. We are still respected: listened to: but we are no longer what we were."[47]

A pointed example occurred over the tariff. The Senate was considering the Fordney-McCumber bill, which already passed the House. The NCWC did effective work in protecting Catholic interests, keeping such items as altars, books, and ecclesiastical furnishings on the duty-free list. At the time of the decree, the last item to be negotiated was stained-glass windows. Over the NCWC's protest, the Senate Finance Committee recommended amending the House version to raise the duty on stained glass worth less than $15 per square foot from 30 to 60 percent. When the amendment came to the floor, Senator Reed Smoot of Utah said representatives of various churches had met with the committee and agreed to the hike. Burke wrote to ask Smoot the authority of his statement. When he made no reply, Burke sent a formal brief to Senator Porter McCumber, committee chairman, for him to read it to his colleagues.[48]

With that, Smoot summoned Burke, who demanded to know who spoke for the Catholic Church on the matter. Smoot explained a monsignor in New Jersey sent Senator Joseph Frelinghuysen a letter wherein the unnamed clergyman averred he had no objection to a 60 percent tariff on stained glass. Burke countered no cleric had the right to speak in the name of the Church unless authorized to do so. He had come to Smoot in just that capacity, official representative of the NCWC. At that, Smoot pulled from his pocket a press clipping from the *Brooklyn Daily Eagle* with boldface title "Catholic Welfare Council Dissolved by Action of Pope." Smoot asked if it was true. Burke replied it was inaccurate, the council still functioned authoritatively. Still, the message was clear, he wrote to Muldoon: "The N.C.W.C. … is today ineffective."[49]

The NCWC's influence among Catholics was also eroding. Its various departments had received notes from faithful around the country who declared the council was finished. For instance, the Department of Education had recently sent a questionnaire that fetched replies like "we obey the Holy Father," and "haven't you been ordered to close?" Burke himself had received letters asking, "Why do you still send me notices?" and "Did not a decree from Rome order you to quit?" Although he surely suffered at the disintegrating effectiveness of the organization embodying his vision of the American Church, his intention was not to complain. "I write these things," he explained to Muldoon, "to show the present situation: also to point out that I cannot tell when it will grow worse—when our authority will be directly and officially questioned and also to show how strong must be the approval of the authorities in Rome if we are to live and to work effectively."[50]

Indeed, Rome needed a functioning NCWC, as Russian relief reasserted itself. Father Walsh arrived in Washington with word the Vatican wanted the NCWC to extend his membership on the ARA. Burke had already written to Father Vlodomir Ledochowski, superior general of the Jesuits, explaining the uncertain status of the NCWC and asking if in light of that he wished Walsh reappointed. As the deadline approached, Burke was in a quandary. Walsh went to Bonzano, who said there was no reason not to reappoint him. So Burke cabled Colonel William Haskell in Russia that he renewed Walsh's membership on the ARA. Still, the situation was dicey. The government was having doubts about the NCWC's longevity and was considering removing it from the relief effort. Then Ryan cabled from Rome that Ledochowski wanted Walsh reappointed: "Delay very unfavorable." Indeed, the Vatican inquired of Bonzano how the Walsh mission was fairing. When Walsh received word Pius was sending the American bishops an appeal for monetary aid to Russia, he asked Burke if the NCWC would prepare the pope's circular and mail it. Burke hesitated, so Walsh again went to Bonzano, who told Burke to cooperate. To Muldoon, he complained: "Authorities in Rome seeing how useful N.C.W.C. is to their immediate purpose wish to use it. The lack of appreciation of the greater work the N.C. is doing here for the church is scandalous and deplorable."[51]

Soon thereafter, Burke heard from Ryan, who wrote that the suppression was the hottest topic of conversation at the Vatican. Schrembs had a brief meeting with Pius, who told him he knew nothing of the condemnation of the NCWC. "Do you think I am a man who can be believed?" asked the pope. "If so, I tell you as the Holy Father that I did not know what the decree meant." Ryan said everyone realized a mistake had been made, but the situation was very "muddled" with conflicting opinions about how to resolve it. Burke forwarded a copy of the letter to Muldoon.[52]

While Schrembs, Moeller, and Ryan were seeking to save the NCWC at the Vatican, Burke was dealing with a crisis at home with potential to sink the organization. In early June, Augustine McNally of the New York *World* was in Washington to cover what was happening to the NCWC. Burke put him off, then left for work at *Catholic World.* McNally then interviewed John Ryan who showed him a letter Burke received from Thomas Mason, a union man who bewailed Rome's dissolving the NCWC, a Catholic voice on behalf of labor. Its demise, wrote Mason, would be "a calamity! A tragedy!" because the Social Action Department had defended unionization. McNally insisted that capital's hostility toward the department had brought the decree. Sidestepping, Ryan mentioned that seventy-nine bishops had signed the protest to Rome. McNally, who knew of the protest, began taking notes. At that, Ryan emphasized, "Of course, this is not for publication: I am giving you this information in confidence." "I understand that," replied McNally, "and I will not publish this." He promised, moreover, to print nothing until he had spoken with Burke.[53]

The next day, McNally's article appeared. All of Catholic America, he wrote, was anxiously waiting to see if the NCWC's postwar policies would continue, given its suppression by the Vatican. Rome had issued a decree dissolving it without consulting the hierarchy. Since times had returned to normal, there was no need for its continuance. Because the decree followed on the heels of the papal election, most believed the American cardinals were responsible for it. When it reached the U.S., Hanna called a meeting that resulted in a letter asking the pope to suspend it. The dispatch was sent to every bishop with a request to endorse it. Seventy-nine did. Among those who refused were O'Connell and Dougherty as well as several others. Given the hierarchy's overwhelming response, the Administrative Committee felt justified in continuing its work until definite word came from Rome.[54]

The article continued that in trying to discover the reason for the condemnation, McNally questioned an anonymous bishop, who said: "Assign a reason if you can. I can't. Of course there are surmises." These McNally gladly took. The only one to make sense was that wealthy Catholics opposed Ryan's social theories. When news of the condemnation reached labor groups, letters of protest were sent to NCWC headquarters. One workingman, Thomas Mason, called the suppression "a calamity." When McNally "submitted these facts to officials of the Welfare Council, they were neither confirmed nor denied."[55] His article pieced the story together fairly well. With minor errors, it was accurate in the main. Such a correct account, with its comment that Rome had acted without consulting the hierarchy, could prove dangerous.

Burke was in New York when the story broke. The quotation from Mason pointed him in Ryan's direction. He asked the editor to publish that the NCWC had authorized no part of McNally's article and that it contained inaccuracies. Fearful of its effect if it reached Rome, Burke cabled

James Ryan: "Newspapers here publishing much. Nothing given out or sent by our office. Contradict any statement to contrary."[56]

When Burke returned to Washington, Ryan confessed his part in the leak, but pleaded McNally promised the information would be off record. To Muldoon, Burke explained Ryan had not "intentionally" leaked information, "but nevertheless he is old enough not to confide in a newspaper man." Burke said he did not see Bonzano about the article because he would have asked its source. "I would have had to speak of Dr. John Ryan," wrote Burke, "and my explanations would not have been sufficient." Muldoon found the column disturbing, especially because a principal informant was a bishop.[57]

Cardinal O'Connell sent a copy of it to Bonzano and held the NCWC responsible. He wanted the council put out of business. Agreeing it was deplorable, Bonzano advised nothing could be done about the NCWC. The Administrative Committee had appealed to Rome, as O'Connell well knew. The issue now rested with the Consistorial Congregation, which would soon act definitively.[58]

The article brought a deluge of inquiries to the NCWC. To keep publicity from getting out of hand, Burke drafted a statement discreetly setting the record straight. It acknowledged issuance of a decree affecting the NCWC, the Administrative Committee's request for a hearing, the support of bishops, and the presence of Moeller and Schrembs in Rome for that purpose. Meanwhile, work of the NCWC was to continue. "Speculations made in the press as to reasons which led to … the decree are not based upon accurate information," concluded the statement. "Most of them we believe to be highly unjustified and therefore most deplorable since they are calculated to arouse conclusions which have little or no warrant in fact." Burke telegraphed the draft to both Hanna and Muldoon with a request to publish it over the former's name.[59]

While he awaited reply, McNally ran another article insisting opposition to the Social Action Department was at least partially responsible for the decree. The *World's* persistence was the last straw. Hanna gave Burke approval to release the statement. On 21 June 1922, Burke gave it to the Associated Press's Universal Service and sent it to all Catholic papers. It appeared in the *World* together with a self-justification by McNally. Within days a host of Catholic journals carried the item.[60] Finally, there was official word about the NCWC. Ironically, it was issued on the eve of success. The next day James Ryan cabled Burke from Rome: "Victory won. Details tomorrow. Keep secret." Four days later, Schrembs cabled that Burke should prepare the program for the annual meeting of the hierarchy, adding that official notice of the Vatican's decision would be sent the following week: "Hard struggle. Complete victory."[61]

Simultaneous with Rome's vindication of the NCWC was Attorney General Daugherty's decision regarding distribution of sacramental wine. He officially accepted Burke's argument that because the Volstead Act gave bishops the right to produce wine, it implicitly conferred the lesser right of distribution. That meant a bishop could appoint a priest to stockpile wine and dispense it throughout his diocese. The Church would have complete control over distribution. New regulations would be forthcoming about implementation of this decision.[62]

When Muldoon received word of the victory at the Vatican, he wired his abstemious friend Burke: "If I were near by I would try to induce you to violate the 18th Amendment." Although reputed a teetotaler, Burke was not. He refused to drink in clerical circles because he believed it led to discussion of ecclesiastical politics, a subject he loathed. Iona McNulty recalled that when the Administrative Committee turned to such talk, Burke excused himself and went to his office explaining: "I can't stay in there when they get started on ecclesiastical politics. They're playing ducks and drakes with the Catholic Church, the Body of Christ." O'Connell and Dougherty had certainly been playing such a game during the suppression crisis, and the former would continue to do so for some time to come.[63]

Anxious Waiting and Collapse

Burke and the Administrative Committee anxiously awaited the new decree. Until it arrived, they could publish nothing about victory. Yet Catholic and secular papers continued to puzzle over reasons for the suppression in ignorance of Rome's reversal. Worse, the rest of the bishops knew nothing of the Vatican's decision. Many refused to contribute money to the NCWC, and none planned on an annual convention of the hierarchy in September.[64]

At the end of June, Burke went to New York for the Paulists' general chapter. Just prior to its opening, he suffered an attack of the old fever and was hospitalized at St. Vincent's. After several days, his temperature subsided, but Dr. Mohan kept him for observation for over a week. Burke told Lynch this trouble "saps one's strength." "And even when one feels well," he continued, "he knows by experience that any exertion will lead to tire and tire is ominous. This is a hard situation for an apparently able bodied healthy man. Bodily and mentally one has to refrain. May the virtue of temperance be mine and the gift of knowledge so that I may know what to do."[65]

By mid-July, Burke was out of the hospital, but under doctor's orders to rest. So, he retired to the Paulist house. That, however, did not prevent him from worrying. "I have been most anxious … for the arrival of official word," Burke told Muldoon. He had received James Ryan's final letter from Rome recounting Schrembs's farewell papal audience, wherein he asked and received permission to make public the withdrawal of the decree. Burke argued that Schrembs's cable about complete victory, coming as it did after the final audience, was intended to be published so as to reassure American Catholics. Burke begged Muldoon to ask Bonzano for word of the new decree as soon as it arrived.[66]

Next day, Burke heard from Justin McGrath of the Press Department that Bernardini told officials of Catholic University news of the revocation. He feared the embarrassment that would come to his department if it leaked to Catholic papers. When the News Service sent no word out about the original decree, many commented "we did not know we were dead," he wrote Burke. He feared if the service got scooped on the reversal, they might "declare that we did not know we were alive, which would be worse than their first accusation." Burke sent Muldoon another letter explaining the situation and reiterating his plea of the day before.[67]

He was obviously pressing Muldoon to ask Bonzano for permission to publish official word. Muldoon doubted the prudence of trying to get the delegate to commit himself. In any case, the Administrative Committee would be meeting in three weeks. Having waited so long already for the document, it might just as well wait longer.[68]

Then came bad news on the educational front. Burke received an urgent letter from Archbishop Alexander Christie of Oregon City with word the Ku Klux Klan and Southern Jurisdiction of Scottish Rite Masons had sponsored a state referendum for compulsory public education of all children ages eight to sixteen. If it passed in the November election, it would end parochial schools in Oregon, and similar legislation would be attempted in other states. Christie organized a campaign against it, but needed financial resources. He asked Burke to place the matter before the NCWC.[69]

Alerting the Administrative Committee, Burke opined to Christie that the Klan and Masons had chosen Oregon because its population closely resembled the old-stock, Anglo-Saxon, Protestant American ideal. He agreed if it succeeded there, a similar attempt would be made in other states, leading to federal legislation for compulsory public schooling or even an amendment to the Constitution. Burke explained the NCWC was hampered in its ability to offer monetary aid because of the decree of suppression. He did not tell Christie it had only $23,000 left in the bank. Yet, he promised the Administrative Committee would do all in its power.[70]

Indeed, taking shape was a battle pitting advocates of 100 percent Americanism against Catholics, with the most treasured possession of each at the struggle's center, each side viewing its school system as prototypically American. For old-stock Protestants—so-called Nordic types—public schools were mainstays of democracy because they were the instruments for instilling patriotism and traditional social values in segments of the population viewed as alien. For Catholics, parochial schools were descendants of the traditional religious schools of the nation's colonial and early republican heritage, established by the founding fathers. They were places where the next generation could safely be schooled for citizenship while preserving religious and cultural values. With both sides championing their institutions as truly American while suspecting those of the other, the situation was explosive. Historian Lynn Dumenil remarks, "They were in effect at war over the right to define what it meant to be American."[71]

On the heels of the news from Oregon came word from Slattery that the Treasury had totally bollixed the new instructions on sacramental wine. When Burke read them, he declared them "wholly inadequate"; they changed nothing, "and there we are—just where we started." They were not at all what Daugherty had approved. "They cannot be accepted," wrote Burke. He would risk a trip to Washington to get them altered, but hoped Slattery could get them postponed until the meeting of the Administrative Committee.[72]

While underlings in the Treasury bungled regulations, Rome finally issued its new decree and instructions, sending their own mixed signals. At the Vatican, the NCWC had been caught in a power struggle between conservatives and progressives. The progressives, led by Gasparri, won and if he had written the instructions, they would have been a forthright endorsement of the status quo ante for the NCWC. Unfortunately, De Lai, who headed the conservatives, got to write the instructions because he issued the original decree. He made them as restrictive as he could get away with. When they arrived at the end of July, Bonzano summoned Muldoon and Dowling to Chicago to discuss them. Muldoon told Burke the delegate wanted to know if anything should be changed in them, though Bonzano did not know if he had power to do so. Muldoon considered the instructions fine and urged the delegate to send them to the bishops at once. Ever the optimist, he thought they made no major changes in affairs, though they might have been clearer in parts. Dowling was not so sanguine. What Muldoon saw as lack of clarity, he viewed as obstacles, if not threats. He told Burke, "The ironed-out instructions are full of broken glass."[73]

Before going to Chicago for the meeting of the Administrative Committee, Burke spent more than a week recuperating on Fishers Island on Long Island Sound. He stayed with the local pastor and played golf, enjoying it very much. He felt well, but his legs continued to tire and become painful. He hoped the condition would "wear away" with time.[74]

To Murray, he confessed feeling out of place in NCWC work. The past year and a half held many trials for him. He was still "bitter" at losing the life he had at *Catholic World*. As much as he loved and was zealous for the NCWC, he told her "it is not my home." Perhaps the gospel promise applied to his case: those who left home for the Lord would receive a hundredfold. The work needed to be done, even against fear it would fail—indeed, even "against evidence that humanly speaking only prophesies its failure." This last was certainly a reference to the suppression crisis. Yet, the seed had been planted, even though it might disappear and the place of its planting be forgotten. In God's own time, he would give it increase, for that was the way the Church progressed. Burke admitted he was not always confident. Human failure and his sinfulness made the glory of Christ disappear. Nevertheless, his honest self knew the truth of divine ways. His mother, the "saint," protected him and he desired to be with her. "So often here I longed for peace," he wrote, "that it would not be hard to die." Burke assured Murray this admission was not meant to depress her. These thoughts were "sober" but "uplifting." "I miss you," he told her, "because once I talked to you my daily heart and soul and that was a help and joy." Assuring her of his prayers, he traveled to Chicago for the meeting.[75]

At that gathering, Burke delivered Christie's letter. Although sympathetic, the bishops could offer no financial aid. They directed Burke to offer the staff's assistance in every way possible. In particular the NCCM should furnish suitable defensive literature. Burke and Slattery explained negotiations for distribution of sacramental wine, which Daugherty had approved but Treasury had misunderstood. The bishops directed Burke to convey their dissatisfaction to the government and to secure just regulations.[76]

The committee turned to the Vatican instructions. According to De Lai's version, the NCWC was not to be identified with the hierarchy and should be renamed something like the National Catholic Welfare Committee, which represented the O'Connell-Dougherty claim that it was the Administrative Committee. Because the instructions also said the annual meetings of the hierarchy were for friendly conference, the Administrative Committee took the position the NCWC was indeed the hierarchy, not as a canonical body, but as a voluntary conference with the committee its administrative arm. It decided to recommend the organization be renamed the National Catholic Welfare Conference, in keeping with Gasparri's understanding of the institution. Burke told his sister Lizzie, that "while the situation with regard to the NCWC looks favorable, there are still many complications and some dark clouds." He explained to his brother, Thomas, the instructions left it to the hierarchy to decide if it wished to continue the NCWC, so the upcoming convention would be "a crucial one."[77]

Burke weathered the Chicago meeting health-wise, but remained under doctor's orders to rest. So, he returned to New York and directed Slattery and Cochran to reenter negotiations about sacramental wine. He greeted the two heroes returning from Rome, Schrembs and Ryan, who regaled him with the stories of what happened. At the Vatican, they had discovered that O'Connell, aided by Dougherty, engineered the suppression, and Pius signed the decree as routine business without knowing what he was endorsing. As the bishop and priest visited each cardinal of the Consistorial Congregation, they learned only De Lai and Rafael Merry del Val knew anything about the decree. The rest were surprised the NCWC had been dissolved. So, there never had been a plenary session of the congregation that allegedly voted to do away with it. Pius reopened the case and ordered a true plenary session to hear it. He armed Gasparri with a papal veto in case the vote went against the NCWC. As Burke told his brother, Schrembs had done "a magnificent piece of work" and Ryan was "full of the story of Roman procedure."[78] In wake of the crisis, he confided to Mary Hawks, "Never, did I think I would ever question a decision of the Holy See."[79]

Meanwhile, Slattery and Cochran reached an agreement that accorded with Daugherty's ruling, namely, a bishop could appoint a priest or layman to distribute sacramental wine within his jurisdiction.[80] The Treasury formulated the new regulations, omitting mention of laymen. The rules reiterated manufacturers might sell their wares directly to clergymen. Or, the bishop might appoint a priest to supervise distribution of sacramental wine in the diocese. In this instance, the clergyman would have to post bond to possess wine, while title remained with the manufacturer until it reached the pastor who needed it. In either case, all applications for wine had to be authenticated by the bishop or his appointee before wine could be distributed. Bishop Gibbons drafted a circular to the hierarchy stating the new rules were "extremely liberal" and showed the government was "well disposed and eager to provide as convenient a distribution of sacramental wine as possible under the law." On 18 August, Burke returned to Washington to oversee personally adjustments to the announcement and its dissemination.[81]

Meeting there in late September, the Administrative Committee agreed to fight for the name National Catholic Welfare Conference at the annual convention. The following day sixty-four bishops met. Burke commented they "showed united support" for the NCWC. They cheered reports about its departments. When "a warm discussion" occurred about its nature, most insisted it was the hierarchy gathered in voluntary annual assembly. O'Connell insisted it was simply the Administrative Committee. The bishops agreed it should be called the Welfare Conference and directed the Administrative Committee to consider the matter and report back at the next annual convention. In the meantime, the name Council was to stand.[82]

Burke saw the divine hand at work in the convention. "The result has been a miracle," he told Murray, "for no human agency could have brought about such a united action." He wrote his brother Thomas, "It is simply that God wished it as it was done against every sign to the contrary." Burke believed the NCWC was now a permanent fixture of the American Church. He reminisced that when he created the War Council, he never dreamed it would grow into the NCWC, which he worked so hard to promote. It was time for him to stop.[83]

Indeed it was. When Thomas had released him for service as general secretary, he stipulated the appointment be for two years. Those were now up. Then, too, John's efforts at the War and Welfare Councils had taken a toll on his health. The only relief he received had come just three months earlier with his removal from editorship of *Catholic World*, freeing him to devote his full time to the NCWC. "I have labored in this," he told Thomas, "and I feel that my labor is done." When the Administrative Committee met after the convention, it elected him for another term as general secretary. Burke accepted on condition he serve only one more year to provide time to find and prepare his replacement. The bishops said, "They would cross that bridge when they came to it." Some averred they would be unable to find a candidate the equal of Burke. He said if the work was to continue, they must prepare men to handle it. He told Thomas that he was confident of the correctness of his decision.[84]

Obviously, the committee had great confidence in Burke's leadership and abilities. Shortly after the meeting, he wrote to Murray he was still of the mind in which he wrote her from Fishers Island: that he felt out of place in the work and bitter at being away from the magazine. Yet, a month later, his thoughts grew questioning. Two years earlier, he had urged Lynch, and by extension himself, to hide "self" in Christ so that Christ could live in them. Now, his spirituality had matured to the point of understanding that self itself could be self-deceptive and was in need of purification. Self comprised much that was "unconsciously selfish": habit, traditional views, obstinacy in one's own judgment and experience, personal wishes and desires mistaken for truth, and blind adherence to self. If Christ was to live in him, these must be stripped away. Burke begged the Holy Spirit to do so even if he "be flayed in the process."[85] This was his prayer as he set out on what was hopefully his final year as general secretary.

ENDNOTES TO CHAPTER 10

1. Burke, *Christ in Us*, 164.
2. Pace to Hanna, 10 January 1922, AASF, CUA file.
3. Burke to Murray, 29 January 1922, AP, Burke Papers, box 11.
4. Slawson, *Department of Education Battle*, 79–95.
5. J. H. Ryan to Dowling, 1 February 1922, copy, ACUA, USCCB 10:105:16; Slawson, *Department of Education Battle*, 96.
6. Burke to Murray, 12 February 1922, AP, Burke Papers, box 11; *New York Times*, 12 February 1922.
7. Burke to Archbishop Michael Curley, 13 March 1922, AAB-AASMS, B2048; NEA Bulletin on the Sterling-Towner Bill, 15 March 1922, copy, ACUA, Vice Rector files. The NEA Bulletin indicated that at the February meeting with the House committee, Fess and his colleagues argued persuasively that the bill could not be reported until the Reorganization committee issued its findings, but Burke's contention that Fess intended to report the measure is more compelling, also borne out by evidence external to his correspondence.
8. Burke to Hanna, telegram, 1 March 1922, AASF, NCWC files; Muldoon to Burke, 10 March 1922, ACUA, USCCB 10:152:28; Burke to Michael Curley, 13 March 1922, AAB-AASMSU, B2048; NEA Bulletin on the Sterling-Towner Bill, 15 March 1922, copy, ACUA, Vice Rector files.
9. "Department of Superintendents," NEA *Addresses and Proceedings, 1922* 60 (1922): 1322–46; Burke to Curley, 13 March 1922, AAB-AASMSU, B2048 (quote is here); Burke to Muldoon, 4 March 1922, copy, ACUA, USCCB 10:152:28; J. H. Ryan to Muldoon, 13 March 1922, copy, ACUA, USCCB 10:144:46; NEA Bulletin on the Towner-Sterling Bill, 15 March 1922, copy, ACUA, Vice Rector files; *Congressional Record*, 67th Cong., 2d sess., 1922, 62, pt. 4, 3627; Slawson, *Department of Education Battle*, 90–99.
10. Burke to Muldoon, 4 March 1922, copy, ACUA, USCCB 10:152:28; Robert K. Murray, *The Harding Era: Warren G. Harding and His Administration* (Minneapolis: University of Minnesota Press, 1969), 128, 190, 314–16; Robert K. Murray, *The Politics of Normalcy: Governmental Theory and Practice in the Harding-Coolidge Era* (New York: Norton, 1973), 43–47. Burke believed Fess did not wish the Sterling-Towner bill reported because he opposed the measure, but evidence argues that Fess did support it but wanted to await the report of the Reorganization Committee before pressing for it (*Congressional Record*, 67th Cong., 2nd sess., vol. 62, pt. 8, 8072–73).
11. Burke to Curley, 13 March 1922, AAB-AASMSU, B2048 (quote is here); Burke to Muldoon, 4 March 1922, copy, ACUA, USCCB 10:152:28; J. H. Ryan to Muldoon, 13 March 1922, copy, ACUA, USCCB 10:144:46; *Con-*

gressional Record, 67th Cong., 2d sess., 1922, 62, pt. 4, 3627; Slawson, *Department of Education Battle*, 90–99.
12. Burke to Muldoon, 4 March 1922, copy, ACUA, USCCB 10:152:28.
13. Burke to Edmund Gibbons, 21 March 1922, ADA, NCWC files.
14. Burke to Muldoon, 4 March 1922, copy, ACUA, USCCB 10:152:28; Burke to Muldoon, 8 June 1922, copy, ibid.; Burke to Murray, 22 February 1922, AP, Burke Papers, box 22; Lawler, *Full Circle*, 60–64, 110; Hartmann-Ting, "Catholic Service School for Women," 110.
15. Burke to Muldoon, 4 March 1922, copy, ibid., 10:152:28; Burke to Neill, 24 February 1922, copy, ibid., 10:152:35.
16. Burke to Muldoon, 4 March 1922, copy, ACUA, USCCB 10:152:28; Hartmann-Ting, "Catholic Service School for Women," 110.
17. Burke to Neill, 5 February 1922, copy, ACUA, USCCB 10:152:35; Neill to Burke, 7 February 1922, ibid.; Burke to Neill, 24 February 1922, copy, ibid.
18. Burke to Muldoon, 4 March 1922, copy, ACUA, USCCB 10:152:28.
19. Neill to Burke, 18 February [*sic* for March] 1922, ACUA, USCCB 10:152:35; Burke to Muldoon, 8 June 1922, copy, ibid., USCCB 10:152:28; Lawler, *Full Circle*, 63–64.
20. J. H. Ryan to Goff, 8 December 1921, copy, ACUA, USCCB 10:111:18; Slawson, "Wine for the Gods," 179–82.
21. Burke to Gibbons, 21 March 1922, ADA, NCWC files; Minutes of the Administrative Committee, 26 January 1922, ACUA, USCCB 10:64:2; Slawson, "Wine for the Gods," 182.
22. U.S. Treasury Department, Bureau of Internal Revenue, T.D. 3300, March 10, 1922, ACUA, USCCB 10:111:19; Slawson, "Wine for the Gods," 183.
23. Cochran to Burke, 24 March 1922, ACUA, USCCB 10:111:19; [Burke], memorandum, undated [December 1921], ibid., 10:111:18; Slawson, "Wine for the Gods," 183.
24. Hanna to E. Gibbons, telegram, March 22, 1922, copy, ADA, NCWC file (punctuation added); Slawson, "Wine for the Gods," 183–84.
25. Burke to Daugherty, In the Matter of the Sale and Distribution of Sacramental Wine: Supplemental Statement of the National Catholic Welfare Council Representing the Hierarchy of the Catholic Church in the United States, 27 March 1922, copy, ACUA, USCCB 10:111:19 (emphasis in original).
26. Burke to Slattery, 28 July 1922, copy, ACUA, USCCB 10:111:19; Burke, "Report on Sacramental Wine," addendum to Minutes of the Administrative Committee, 11 August 1922, ACUA, USCCB 10:64:2.
27. Dowling to J. H. Ryan, 27 March 1922, ACUA, USCCB 10:60:11; Slawson, *Foundation of NCWC*, 137–38.
28. Address of the Reverend John J. Burke, C.S.P. to N.C.W.C. Employees, 27 March 1922, ACUA, USCCB 10:60:2.

29. Hawks, "Souvenir of Burke," 13; Burke to Murray, 27 March 1922, AP, Burke Papers, box 11; Burke to Lynch, undated [late March 1922], ibid., box 5; Muldoon to Burke, telegram, 27 March 1922, ACUA, USCCB 10:60:20; Burke to Muldoon, telegram, 27 March 1922, ibid.
30. Burke to Hanna, telegram, 28 March 1922, ACUA, USCCB 10:60:14; Hanna to Burke, telegram, 29 March 1922, ibid.
31. Slawson, *Foundation of NCWC*, 139–41.
32. Burke to Muldoon, telegram, 2 April 1922 (the Pucci cable is quoted here); Muldoon to Burke, 2 April 1922—both in ACUA, USCCB 10:60:20.
33. Schrembs to Muldoon, telegram, 4 April 1922, copy; Muldoon to Burke, telegram, 4 April 1922—both in ACUA, USCCB 10:60:20.
34. Burke, draft of telegram never sent, 4 April 1922, ACUA, USCCB 10:60:20; Burke to Muldoon, 4 April 1922, ibid.; *New York Times*, 2 April 1922.
35. Minutes of the Administrative Committee, 6 April 1922, ACUA, USCCB; J. H. Ryan to Burke, two telegrams, 7 April 1922, ibid., 10:60:24; Burke to Hayes, 9 April 1922, copy, ibid., 10:60:14; Louis Walsh, Diary, 6 April 1922, ADP; Walsh to Curley, 9 April 1922, AAB-AASMSU, W271.1.
36. Burke for Muldoon to O'Connell, undated [May 1922], draft, ACUA, USCCB 10:60:22.
37. "Bishops Authorize N.C.W.C. to Expand and Intensify Activities: Annual Conference of Hierarchy Lauds Splendid Work of Welfare Council," *NCWC Bulletin* 4 (October 1922):7.
38. Edmund Walsh to Burke, cable, 13 February 1922, ACUA, USCCB 10:26:10; Burke to Walsh, cable, 17 February 1922, copy, ibid.; Walsh to Burke, radiogram, 28 February 1922, ibid.; Burke to Walsh, cablegram, 1 March 1922, copy, ibid.; Burke to Colonel William Haskell, cablegram, 1 March 1922, copy, ibid.; Burke to Herbert Hoover, 4 March 1922, copy, ibid.; Walsh to Burke, 24 April 1922, copy, ibid.; Louis Gallagher, S.J., *Edmund Walsh, S.J.: A Biography* (New York: Benzinger Brothers, Inc., 1962), 14–15; Patrick McNamara, *A Catholic Cold War: Edmund A. Walsh and the Politics of American Anticommunism* (New York: Fordham University Press, 2005), 23–33; Castagna, *Bridge Across the Ocean*, 92–93.
39. Minutes of the Administrative Committee, 6 April 1922, ACUA, USCCB 10:64:2. The entire cablegram is quoted herein.
40. J. H. Ryan to Muldoon, telegram, 7 April 1922, ACUA, USCCB 10:60:20; Ryan to Burke, telegram, 7 April 1922, ibid.; Burke to Hayes, 9 April 1922, copy, ibid., 10:60:14; Muldoon to Hanna, 7 April 1922, AASF, NCWC files.
41. Burke to Murray, 10 April 1922, AP, Burke Papers, box 11; Burke to Muldoon, undated [probably 11 April 1922] ACUA, USCCB 10:60:18.
42. *Report to His Holiness, Pope Pius XI, on the Work of the Administrative Committee of the National Catholic Welfare Council, 25 April 1922*, pp. 1–12, ACUA, USCCB 10:60:29.

43. Ibid., 13–39.
44. Minutes of the Administrative Committee, 26 and 27 April 1922, ACUA, USCCB.
45. Minutes of the Executive Board of the NCCM, 1 and 2 May 1922, ACUA, NCCM 10:2:4; Edward Arnold (comptroller of the NCWC) to J. H. Ryan, 24 April 1922, ACUA, USCCB 10:144:1; [Burke] to the NCWC Financial Department, memorandum, 4 May 1922, ibid.; Burke to Muldoon, 10 May 1922, ibid., 10:60:18.
46. Burke to Schrembs, 7 May 1922, copy, ACUA, USCCB 10:60:25; Burke to Muldoon, 10 May 1922, ibid., 10:60:18.
47. Burke to Muldoon, 9 June 1922, copy, ACUA, USCCB 10:152:28.; Slawson, *Foundation of NCWC*, 152–53.
48. Burke to Porter McCumber, 2 June 1922, copy, ACUA, USCCB 10:128:3; Burke to Chairman and Members of Senate Committee on Finance, 2 June 1922, copy, ibid.; Burke to Curley, 10 April 1922, ibid., 10:60:10; Burke to Muldoon, 9 June 1922, copy, ibid., 10:152:28; *Congressional Record*, 67 Cong., 2nd Sess., 1922, 62, part 7, 7477–7479.
49. Burke to Curley, 10 April 1922, ACUA, USCCB 10:60:10; Burke to Muldoon, 9 June 1922, copy, ibid., 10:152:28; *Brooklyn Daily Eagle*, 28 May 1922.
50. Burke to Muldoon, 9 June 1922, copy, ibid., 10:152:28.
51. Burke to Muldoon, 8 June 1922, copy, ACUA, USCCB 10:152:28; Walsh to Burke, 8 June 1922, ibid., 10:26:10; J. H. Ryan to Burke, cablegram, 5 June 1922, ibid., 10:60:24; Burke to J. H. Ryan, cablegram, 5 June 1922, ibid.; Burke to Hanna, 22 June 1922, AASF, NCWC files.
52. J. H. Ryan to Burke, 25 May 1922, ACUA, USCCB 10:60:24; Burke to Muldoon, 8 June 1922, copy, ibid., 10:152:28.
53. Burke to Muldoon, 19 June 1922, ACUA, USCCB 10:60:18 (Ryan and McNally quotes are here); Thomas Mason to Burke, 16 May 1922, ibid., 10:60:9.
54. New York *World*, 14 June 1922.
55. Ibid.
56. Burke to J. H. Ryan, cablegram, 15 June 1922, copy, ACUA, USCCB 10:60:24; Burke to the editor of the *World*, 14 June 1922, copy, ibid.,10:60:27; Burke to Muldoon, 19 June 1922, ibid., 10:60:18. The inaccuracy was that two more bishops had endorsed the petition, so the actual number was eight-one, not seventy-nine.
57. Burke to Muldoon, 19 June 1922, ACUA, USCCB 10:60:18; Muldoon to Fenlon, 17 June 1922, AASUS-AASMSU, RG 13, box 7.
58. Bonzano to O'Connell, 19 June 1922, AABo, O'Connell correspondence.
59. Burke to Hanna, 16 June 1922, copy, ACUA, USCCB 10:60:14.
60. New York *World*, 19 and 21 June 1922; Burke to Hanna, 22 June 1922, AASF, NCWC file. For example, see San Antonio *Southern Messenger*, 22 June 1922;

Buffalo *Echo*, 22 June 1922; Omaha *True Voice*, 23 June 1922; Los Angeles *Tidings*, 23 June 1922; Belleville *Messenger*, 23 June 1922; Saint Louis *Catholic Herald*, 23 June 1922; Providence *Visitor*, 23 June 1922; Sacramento *Catholic Herald*, 1 July 1922.

61. Burke to Hanna, telegram, 22 June 1922, AASF, NCWC files (first quote is here); Burke to Dowling, 26 June 1922, ACUA, USCCB 10:60:11 (second quote is here).
62. Burke to J. H. Ryan, cablegram, 18 June 1922, ACUA, USCCB 10:60:24; Boston *Pilot*, June 24, 1922; *New York Times*, July 17, 1922; Burke to Hanna, 22 June 1922, AASF, NCWC files; Burke to Slattery, 28 July 1922, copy, ACUA, USCCB 10:111:19; [Burke], Report on Sacramental Wine, addendum to Minutes of the Administrative Committee, 11 August 1922, ibid.
63. Muldoon to Burke, telegram, 23 June 1922, ACUA, USCCB 10:60:20; McNulty to Tanner, 6 May 1964, ibid. 10:72:24; Sheerin, *Never Look Back*, 236.
64. Slawson, *Foundation of the NCWC*, 180–81.
65. Burke to Lynch, 9 July 1922, AP, Burke Papers, box 5; Burke to Muldoon, 12 July 1922, ACUA, USCCB 10:60:18.
66. Burke to Muldoon, 12 July 1922, ACUA, USCCB 10:60:18; J. H. Ryan to Burke, 23 and 25 June 1922, ibid., 10:60:24.
67. McGrath to Burke, 13 July 1922, ACUA, USCCB 10:60:17; Burke to Muldoon, 13 July 1922, ibid., 10:60:18.
68. Muldoon to Burke, undated [probably 15 or 16 July 1922], ACUA, USCCB 10:60:18.
69. Alexander Christie to Burke, undated [13 July 1922], copy, ACUA, USCCB 10:14:7; David B. Tyack, "The Perils of Pluralism: The Background of the Pierce Case," *American Historical Review* 74 (October 1968): 75–76; Paul M. Holsinger, "The Oregon School Bill Controversy, 1922–1925," *Pacific Historical Review* 37 (August 1968): 330; Lloyd P. Jorgenson, "The Oregon School Law of 1922: Passage and Sequel," *Catholic Historical Review* 54 (October 1968): 456–58; Lloyd P. Jorgenson, *The State and the Non-Public School, 1825–1925*, (Columbia: University of Missouri Press, 1987), 205–09; Thomas J. Shelley, "The Oregon School Case and the National Catholic Welfare Conference," *Catholic Historical Review* 75 (July 1989): 440–42; Dumenil, *Freemasonry*, 143–45; Slawson, *Department of Education Battle*, 107–08.
70. Burke to Christie, 30 July 1922, copy, ACUA, USCCB 10:14:7; Dowling to the Administrative Committee, 14 July 1922, ibid., 10:60:11.
71. Dumenil, "Tribal Twenties," 30; Slawson, *Department of Education Battle*, 107–10; Slawson, *Foundation of NCWC*, 191–92.
72. Treasury Department regulations 60, Amended, Effective 1 August 1922, undated, enclosure with Slattery to Burke, 26 July 1922, ACUA, USCCB 10:111:19; Burke to Slattery, 28 July 1922, copy, ibid.

73. Muldoon to Burke, [1 August 1922], ACUA, USCCB 10:60:18; Dowling to Burke, 21 August 1922, ibid., 10:60:11. In fact, there were two versions of the instructions. Gasparri dictated to Schrembs his version of what they were to be; De Lai's interpretation became the published version. For a comparison see Slawson, *Foundation of the NCWC*, 175–77.
74. Burke to T. Burke, 2 August and 4 September 1922, AP, Official Papers of Superior General Thomas F. Burke 1922.
75. Burke to Murray, undated [from Fisher's Island, August 1922], AP, Burke Papers, box 11.
76. Minutes of the Administrative Committee, 11 August 1922, ACUA, USCCB 10:4:2.
77. Ibid.; Burke to E. Burke, 17 August 1922, AP, Burke Papers, box 3; Burke to T. Burke, 4 September 1922, ibid., Official Papers of Superior General Thomas F. Burke 1922; Walsh, Notes for the Meeting of the Administrative Committee, 11 and 12 August 1922, ADP, NCWC files.
78. Burke to T. Burke, 4 September 1922, AP, Official Papers of Superior General Thomas F. Burke 1922; Slawson, *Foundation of the NCWC*, 137–78 (a complete account of the Roman fight); Slawson, *Ambition and Arrogance*, 112–19. A less helpful account is in Sheerin, *Never Look Back*, 68–84.
79. Hawks, "Souvenir of Burke," AP, Burke Papers, box 10.
80. Untitled Report on Conference of Slattery and Cochran with C. P. Smith, E. L. Lloyd, and James J. Britt, 17 August 1922, ACUA, USCCB 10:111:19.
81. U.S. Treasury Department, Bureau of Internal Revenue, T.D. 3391, 25 August 1922, ACUA, USCCB Legal Department 10:32:1; Gibbons to the hierarchy, 11 October 1922, ADR, NCWC files. A summary of these is presented in "Synopsis of New Government Regulations Covering Distribution of Sacramental Wine," *NCWC Bulletin* 4 (September 1922): 8.
82. Minutes of the Administrative Committee, 25 September 1922, ACUA, USCCB 10:64:2; Burke to T. Burke, 4 September 1922, AP, Official Papers of Superior General Thomas F. Burke 1922; *Minutes of the Fourth Annual Meeting of the Hierarchy, 1922*, 3–4, 6–7, ACUA, Bound Volumes; Slawson, *Foundation of NCWC*, 184–87.
83. Burke to T. Burke, 30 September 1922, AP, Official Papers of Superior General Thomas F. Burke 1922; Burke to Murray, 4 October 1922, ibid., Burke Papers, box 11.
84. Burke to T. Burke, 30 September 1922, AP, Official Papers of Superior General Thomas F. Burke 1922; Burke to Murray, 4 October 1922, ibid., Burke Papers, box 11; Minutes of the Administrative Committee, 29 September 1922, ACUA, USCCB 10:64:2.
85. [Burke, Meditation], 13 November 1922, AP, Burke Papers, box 5. See also Burke to Lynch, Xmas 1920, ibid.

Chapter 11
Between Illnesses

> We who preach Christ must, even as Christ, know the needs of those to whom we preach. We must be able to have them recognize their needs: confess their needs to themselves: desire to have their needs redeemed unto positive life. This includes not alone needs that are sinful: but those also that are not—temporal, physical, economic needs. Our voice must have the accents of human, personal understanding. We must know the needs of our generation. We must feel for them, even if they are sinful needs. We must know their temporal necessities: their outlook upon life: the measure of their own spiritual outlook or lack of it. Then, perhaps, we, like Christ, may become the effective servant of many more.[1]

The Film Industry and the NCWC

The NCWC's increasing association with the film industry coincided with the suppression crisis. In March 1922, movie mogul Adolph Zukor took a step that would bring them together. Public dissatisfaction with moviemakers increased as off-screen activity of some actors mirrored the worst of film fare. With acquittal of comedian Roscoe "Fatty" Arbuckle for manslaughter of a starlet at an alcohol-fueled party, Zukor organized the Motion Picture Producers and Distributors of America (MPPDA) "to establish and maintain" the highest possible moral and artistic standards in films. To lead it, the MPPDA hired Postmaster General Will Hays. Hays convinced Zukor to cancel all contracts for exhibition of Arbuckle's pictures, an action widely interpreted as banning him from the industry.[2]

In June, Hays held a national meeting of social-improvement organizations "to discuss frankly and advise fully" how best to achieve the

MPPDA's goal. He was "particularly anxious" to have Father John Burke and Charles McMahon attend. Burke hoped to be present, but was prevented by the suppression crisis. He sent McMahon and others. More than 100 participants organized themselves as the Committee on Public Relations of the MPPDA, with McMahon a member of its executive board. He secured a resolution for establishment of a committee to preview pictures of questionable character.[3]

In mid-October, the board asked constituents to appoint competent critics to review films and suggest changes and "things to be avoided" in future. If a picture deserved support, the critic would recommend his organization have members urge theaters to screen it and encourage attendance thereat. The idea was to build demand for wholesome pictures, thereby prodding producers into making better movies.[4]

McMahon argued the importance of this action. He told Burke this system offered "a splendid opportunity to correct many film evils before the pictures [were] presented to the public." It also enabled the NCWC News Service and *NCWC Bulletin* to carry condensed criticisms of forthcoming films. As the "mouthpiece of enlightened Catholic opinion," the NCWC was duty-bound to address morality in movies and promote decent pictures.[5]

Burke appointed him NCWC film critic. The Committee on Public Relations began reviewing in October. Almost immediately, it wrestled with the use made of critics' comments. Jason Joy, executive secretary, submitted them to Hays who communicated them to producers. This raised the question of whether producers should be permitted to publicize favorable mention of their films. McMahon opposed such exploitation. He favored, however, commending worthwhile movies through the NCWC News Service.[6]

Burke was adamant the committee should not permit itself to be used for commercial purposes. Going further, he insisted it reach "a corporate view as to whether the particular picture should receive the Committee's approval or should be changed." Expression and collection of individual opinions "mortally imperiled" its efficacy and purpose. Such practice permitted producers to pick and choose among them. McMahon must "take care not to make any commitment as to giving publicity to any picture, even one that is in every way to be commended."[7] In Burke's view, endorsing a film was not the committee's job.

In mid-November, the board decided all communications between members and Joy were to be considered "privileged correspondence" and "not be made use of by the producers either with or without the consent" of the reviewer. Members remained free, however, to communicate to their parent organizations any comments they wished.[8]

Shortly thereafter, Joy asked if member organizations would recommend a movie their critic found unobjectionable. McMahon thought the NCWC could not officially approve any picture because however wholesome, someone would disagree with the judgment. He suggested the Motion Picture Bureau begin distribution of critiques to Catholic papers so the faithful could "select the good and avoid the bad in motion picture productions" for themselves. McMahon asked Burke's advice.[9]

Burke averred the NCWC must "be prepared to answer definitely" queries from Catholics about films suitable for viewing and "a review of a motion picture would necessarily entail approval or disapproval." To undertake the responsibility of reviewer, McMahon must see every movie and in rendering an opinion must "play absolutely safe, that is to say, any picture recommended should be above criticism."[10] For reasons explained below, it would be some time before McMahon could implement this directive in even modified form.

In December, Hays ignited a firestorm of criticism and created a crisis for the Public Relations Committee. In the spirit of Christmas, he pardoned Arbuckle for good behavior. McMahon issued a press release, declaring Hays had completely "misjudged the temper of the American people." He further argued Arbuckle's restoration grossly traduced the high purpose of the MPPDA. His acquittal aside, McMahon contended "sufficient evidence was brought out at his three trials clearly to establish his unfitness to appear on the screen." Although Hays's charitableness was "commendable," it was "insufficient justification for the flaunting of this discredited actor before the American people."[11]

The *New York Times* printed the statement along with other protests. Joy called a meeting of the committee so that Hays could explain his action. Burke told McMahon the NCWC's position "must be made very clear" and gave specific instructions. If Hays indicated he would continue to act independently, McMahon must withdraw from the committee. With regard to Arbuckle, Burke said McMahon must stand by his press release. If the committee supported Hays's action, he must resign; likewise, if the committee failed to protest both the reinstatement and Hays's action. "There can be no half measures nor any compromise on our part," declared Burke, "for we as Catholics must stand as high as, and indeed higher than, any other body."[12]

In January 1923, Hays explained people had misunderstood his persuading Zukor against release of Arbuckle's films. He never intended the actor's permanent banishment from movies. The public now misconstrued his current position as reinstatement of Arbuckle. Hays said it was not in his power to reinstate him; all he could do was refuse to stand in the way of Arbuckle's finding work in the industry.[13]

The committee opposed display of Arbuckle movies and his return to the screen. Allowing either to happen would demoralize youth and run counter to principles of the MPPDA. On the other hand, no one objected to Arbuckle's finding work off screen. McMahon formulated a resolution encapsulating this thinking. While reaffirming the committee's dedication to improvement of movies under Hays's leadership, it recommended he advise producers against exhibiting Arbuckle's films or letting him act on screen. The committee adopted the resolution. Zukor agreed to release no Arbuckle movies and the man himself foreswore acting in favor of becoming a director for the Reel Comedies Company.[14]

Settlement of the Arbuckle problem permitted McMahon to focus on finances. Many NCWC staffers were paid with War Council funds because they worked for both entities. That money was fast depleting. Moreover, the suppression crisis caused some bishops to cease contributions altogether. McMahon was concerned about ability to fund his plans for the Motion Picture Bureau. He wanted to install projectors on trans-Atlantic liners to show films promoting civic education to immigrants en route to America, and also to inaugurate movie reviews in the *NCWC Bulletin* and issued through the News Service. Estimating cost at $17,500 per year ($315,000 in 2024), he needed to make it self-supporting.[15]

In February 1923, McMahon began a six-month dance with Burke about ways to finance the bureau. He recommended establishing a Cooperating Committee for Better Motion Pictures whose membership would be by subscription among movie producers. Because the bureau would endorse quality films through reviews, he thought producers would gladly subscribe.[16] Appreciating his initiative, Burke nixed the idea because it would create mutual indebtedness between producers and the NCWC, compromising its independent voice.[17]

McMahon tried again. He recommended a direct appeal, with no strings attached, for donations of $100 from Catholics employed as producers, directors, actors, financial backers, and the like. Moreover, like Catholic newspapers, the *Bulletin* might accept paid advertisements for fine films. Absent funding, argued McMahon, the bureau would exist only on paper. Again, Burke refused. He could never approve soliciting contributions from those in the industry. "That would create at once an indebtedness on our part to them," he said, "—even if it be but an indebtedness of courtesy." Ardently committed to maintaining the NCWC as an independent Catholic voice, he saw an unsolicited donation for support of the bureau from a wealthy Catholic as the only solution. He gently reminded McMahon of the resources at his disposal—the *Bulletin*, the News Service, the NCCM, and NCCW—Burke encouraged him to undertake what initiatives he could. He especially liked the idea of movie reviews.[18]

McMahon forged ahead with them. In October 1923, he began issuing endorsements of wholesome films through the News Service, thus giving his views a wide readership. The first films he recommended were Samuel Goldwyn's *Potash and Perlmutter* and Metro Pictures' *Scaramouche*. Six months later, the *NCWC Bulletin* began publishing a list of decent movies, asterisking those especially suitable for young viewers.[19]

Defense of Catholic Schools

In November 1922, voters in Oregon passed the compulsory public-education law, confronting the Church with abolition of its schools in that state, effective September 1926. Indeed, there was a rising tide of anti-Catholicism throughout the nation, much of its animus focused against parochial education. Successful passage of the Oregon law touched off similar endeavors in other states.[20]

In December, Archbishop Austin Dowling; Edward Pace; Admiral William Benson, president of the NCCM; and Burke met in Washington to discuss the situation with influential Catholic Democrats. Senators Joseph Ransdell and David Walsh believed the Church had brought the present disaster on itself. Catholics, especially priests, were too critical of public education and opposed legislation like the Sterling-Towner bill. Worse, they publicly boasted about defeating such measures. Protestants, said Ransdell, held misconceptions about the Knights of Columbus, which contributed to the situation. Many thought the Knights were engaged in a religious joust with knights of the Ku Klux Klan. Senator Thomas Walsh said Senator Joseph Robinson had recently been invited to join the Klan because it was just a Protestant version of the Knights. Burke wondered if Masonic ill will resulted from Masonry's having been excluded from war work while the Knights and Catholic Church were allowed to engage in it. Constantine Smyth, chief justice of the U.S. Court of Appeals in D.C., believed the separate-but-equal style of Catholicism whereby the Church established organizations paralleling those in the larger society, created a great deal of opposition among Protestants. Burke thought a reasonable statement of facts would influence most Americans, so the Church should issue a statement of its position on education. He remarked a number of "very high class educators" advocated a national school system because they considered private schools, Catholic or non-Catholic, antithetical to development of American democracy. All agreed the Church should make a forthright declaration in favor of both public and private education. In fact, the hierarchy at its last convention authorized a pastoral letter setting forth the Church's position on that matter. The method of crafting one, however, proved unworkable, so the NCWC Department of Education would eventually produce a statement it released through the Catholic Educational Association.[21]

Convinced the Oregon Law was not a local issue, Archbishop Edward Hanna invited Archbishop Alexander Christie to meet with the Administrative Committee in January 1923. In preparation, Burke turned for legal advice to William Guthrie, professor of constitutional law at Columbia University. Guthrie replied the issue was "novel and difficult" because no court had yet ruled on a state's power to compel children to attend a particular type of school. In his view, such compulsion violated the spirit of the Fourteenth Amendment. He added the law also involved interference with property rights, though he advised a decision based solely on that ground might not adequately protect Church schools in the future. Burke thanked him for his "excellent summary" and promised to keep him abreast.[22]

The Administrative Committee met days later with other legal counsel present. Judge John Kavanaugh, a Knight and Christie's personal attorney, said Christie wanted the matter resolved by the U.S. Supreme Court. The law was unconstitutional and should be tested on the basis of property rights. Judges Patrick Hally of Detroit and Thomas O'Brien of St. Paul advised otherwise. Given the present Court's strong advocacy of religious and parental rights, they thought the attack should be made on those grounds rather than property. Burke read Guthrie's letter, which supported them.[23]

Excusing the jurists, the committee considered the case. Hanna said Christie had met earlier with the Supreme Board of the Knights, which agreed to fund litigation and authorized an immediate grant of $10,000 ($180,000 in 2024) to cover initial expenses. Christie, however, wanted to depend on the hierarchy rather than laymen. Given the national Catholic interest at stake, the committee agreed to lead the fight, with Hanna, Dowling, and Bishop Edmund Gibbons managing and coordinating the case in cooperation with Christie. The committee would ask the hierarchy for $100,000 ($1.8 million) to fund it.[24] This action set the stage for a revival of rivalry with the Knights.

Cooperation seemed in doubt from the start. Without consulting the other members, Christie sent Kavanaugh to New York to retain Guthrie. Kavanaugh seemed to be playing a double game. He reported to Burke and Dowling that he discussed the case with Guthrie, especially how to introduce it in the courts. Guthrie said he would leave that to Kavanaugh. So, Kavanaugh offered to retain him, but left the arrangement tentative because Guthrie was ill and on verge of a nervous breakdown, necessitating a three- to four-month rest in the Mediterranean. Uncertain what to do, Kavanaugh went to see Burke in Washington. Burke read to Kavanaugh the minutes of the Administrative Committee that Christie was to coordinate with Hanna, Dowling, and Gibbons. Burke told him to maintain constant contact with Dowling and obtain his prior approval regarding counsel. He should also send copies of correspondence and agreements to NCWC headquarters.[25]

Burke informed Hanna what had transpired and urged a swift decision about chief counsel. Hanna had his attorney Garret McEnerney telegraph Guthrie to confirm his inability to take the case and recommend alternative lawyers. Guthrie wired back he was "greatly surprised" by Kavanaugh's version of their meeting. He admitted he was going abroad for two or three months for health, but had "distinctly agreed" he would "act in the Oregon matter ultimately," that is, before the Supreme Court. This led Hanna to think Burke must have misunderstood what Kavanaugh told him about the conversation with Guthrie.[26]

Meanwhile, Kavanaugh and Christie asked Dowling if they should secure Guthrie's services or those of someone else as "associate counsel."[27] Use of that term was ominous. In mid-February, Burke again insisted the matter of chief counsel be resolved, noting Guthrie seemed the candidate all had agreed upon. Hanna went to Portland to speak with Christie and Kavanaugh. Kavanaugh then visited San Francisco to confer with Hanna and McEnerney. It was agreed Kavanaugh would handle the case in Oregon, while Guthrie and McEnerney would argue it before the Supreme Court.[28] Sadly, the arrangement would not last.

In late February, the Supreme Court heard *Meyer* v. *Nebraska*, litigation bearing on the Oregon law; Nebraska had mandated that all instruction in both public and private schools be given in English.[29] Guthrie filed an amicus curiae brief pointing out the constitutional principles of the case. In fact, the brief offered opportunity to apprise the Court of the Oregon Law and the assumption on which it rested: "that the police power of a state over the education of minors is virtually unlimited." While upholding a state's right to set "minimum standards" and "prohibit certain species of additional instruction duly found to be inimical to the public welfare," it denied a state had the authority to arrogate to itself the education of all children or to forbid any and all instruction in addition to the prescribed course of study. To allow a state such power would be to ape Soviet Communism.[30]

Burke attended oral arguments and reported the justices were unusually interested. Chief Justice William Taft inquired about the history of education and rights of the state therein. An associate justice pointedly asked if a state could compel children to attend public schools. "It is evident," Burke confided to Muldoon, "that they are expecting the Oregon case. If the Nebraska case is decided in favor of Nebraska, we will have a difficult time, indeed."[31]

Fortunately, it was not. In June 1923, the Court ruled the Nebraska law violated Fourteenth Amendment liberties. Writing the majority opinion, Justice James McReynolds argued parents had the duty to provide for education of their children while the state had the right "to compel attendance at some school and to make reasonable regulations for all schools." He conceded the state might go far to improve the quality of its citizens, but must respect the rights of individuals, especially parents. "It is the natural duty of the parent to give his children education suitable to their station in life," noted McReynolds. Though it might be advantageous for everyone to be competent in English, a state could not accomplish that by unconstitutional means, which the Nebraska law did. The decision almost ensured the Court would overturn the Oregon law. Burke felt greatly heartened.[32]

The decision in the *Meyer* case caused Kavanaugh to rethink his deal. Guthrie told Burke Kavanaugh wanted to argue before the Supreme Court. Burke notified Muldoon "some little trouble has arisen." Indeed, Kavanaugh was urging Christie to let him and his associates handle the case alone. If the NCWC refused to pay him, the Knights pledged $50,000 for the litigation. Kavanaugh filed suit on behalf of the Society of the Sisters of the Holy Names of Jesus and Mary. The vexing matter of legal counsel dragged on through summer before agreement that Kavaugh would sit second chair to Guthrie when the case reached the Supreme Court.[33]

Thereafter, the case proceeded smoothly. Shortly before Christmas 1923, Kavanaugh filed for an interlocutory injunction against enforcement of the law and asked that the request be heard by a panel of three federal judges, two from the district and one from the circuit court of appeals sitting en banc. Appeal from such tribunal was immediate to the Supreme Court, which could not refuse to hear the case. Arguments were scheduled for mid-January 1924.[34]

NATIONAL CATHOLIC SERVICE SCHOOL

A bright spot in Catholic education was the Service School for Women. It started the 1923–1924 academic year with sixteen students, "a hopeful number" in Burke's terms. Gertrude Gavin took deeper interest it. Given her poor health, Grace Murray now lived with and helped her. Any part Burke may have played in the arrangement remains unknown. Gavin told him, however, "You know I couldn't live without Grace now." He thought this truer than she knew. He saw vast improvement in the woman, which he attributed to Murray.[35]

Moreover, the school's new director, Dr. Anne Nicholson, had undergone a change of heart about the role of spirituality in it. When she took the job, she told Burke religion was something between the individual and God. She could not understand students' need for spiritual conferences and daily Mass. For Burke, religion had everything to do with life and society. In April 1923, he gave a retreat to students and staff who engaged in it completely, unlike during the mutiny the year before. It was "little short of wonderful," wrote Burke. After his concluding Mass and sermon, which focused on the social dimension of religion, Nicholson was so enthusiastic about his remarks that she sought him out to express her appreciation. For his part, he found it difficult to understand the effect his words had on people. "What I say in sermons is so clear to me that I'm afraid I am dry and common place," he told Murray. His hearers, however, were deeply affected, so much so that he found it "both terrifying and encouraging."[36]

Burke, Gavin, and Murray collaborated on decorating the chapel. At first, Gavin wanted nothing to do with the project. "Of course, I would not hear of this," Burke told Murray. "I gave little thought to the matter and I think her taste better than mine: But I think your taste and selection of color and blend of color is far better than either Mrs. G or myself." He relied on Murray's eye for this. She chose green brocade drapery to serve as backdrop of the sanctuary. The altar was a simple dark wood table with a small tabernacle mounted on it. The table was unusually tall, built to accommodate his six-foot-three stature. Burke insisted on a traditional sanctuary lamp hung from the ceiling. Because the ceiling was low and he was tall, congregants always expected a collision with his head that never occurred.[37]

Meanwhile, Burke had the school's third building, the multistory frame house fronting 20th Street, repaired and refurbished as residence for himself and other NCWC clerical officials. A series of passageways connected the three edifices, which shared an expansive, park-like lawn with trees and shrubs on the half block across their southern facades. Of course, domestic arrangements of the school and NCWC residence were completely separate.[38]

BIRTH CONTROL

In January 1923, Burke and the NCWC confronted the first legislative attempt to promote birth control. Back in 1919, the movement's two principal proponents, Mary Ware Dennett, executive secretary of the National Birth Control League (NBLC), and Margaret Sanger, editor of *Birth Control Review*, had parted company over tactics. Dennett wanted to remove every mention of contraception from the Comstock Obscenity Act of 1873. Sanger believed the public needed to be educated and won over on the subject before approaching Congress. After leaving the NBLC, Dennett formed the Voluntary Parenthood League (VPL). Burke had been monitoring her efforts through Sara Laughlin, a Catholic social worker in Philadelphia. To gain inside information, she became a member of the VPL in 1920. She twice visited Dennett, concluding each meeting with "you have no idea what this has meant to me." Her visits convinced her Dennett sincerely believed she was "doing a service to woman kind." Besides keeping Burke informed, Laughlin fed confidential reports to *Woman Patriot*, a national paper for defense of home and nation against woman suffrage, feminism, and socialism, leaving Dennett puzzled as to the source of the leak in her organization. In January 1923, the VPL introduced an amendment to the Comstock law through the auspices of Senator Albert B. Cummins of Iowa and Representative John Kissel of Brooklyn. This marked the first legislative effort of the birth control movement.[39]

The Catholic position on birth control was absolute. The biblical injunction to increase and multiply meant the purpose of sexual intercourse was procreation, and every act must be open to that. Hence, the Church opposed contraception. The only acceptable method of limiting family size was abstinence. Most Protestant denominations opposed birth control for the same reason, though most maintained a decorous silence about it, leaving the impression only Catholics oppose it. In the VPL mouthpiece *Birth Control Herald*, Dennett insinuated there was division of opinion developing among Catholic clergy. She noted Archbishop Patrick Hayes held any avoidance of conception was criminal, while Father John Ryan said restricting conception through abstinence was unquestionably lawful. Laughlin sent a copy to Burke, who wrote Dennett there was no difference in their teaching: Hayes referred to use of contraceptive devices, not abstinence from marital relations. He asked her to publish his letter, but Dennett never did.[40]

Burke organized a small protest against the Cummins-Kissel bill through the NCCM and NCCW. He also sent Laughlin contact information for senators and representatives on the judiciary committees and urged her to have twenty non-Catholic friends send letters of protest. In his view, the matter "did not demand anything like a show of strength." Burke believed once committeemen realized there was public opinion against it, they would take no action. He himself wrote to Dr. George Stewart of the New York Academy of Medicine to complain the medical profession was "unbecomingly silent" on the bill and called for his organization to reassert leadership over an issue which was obviously a matter of medical science.[41]

As NCCW president, Gavin protested to both committees. Knute Nelson, chair of the Senate panel and old friend of her father, replied he was surprised Cummins had introduced the bill. He called Dennett "the most persistent woman" he ever saw. She and a coterie of followers were "pestering senators" to hold a hearing. Nelson had appointed a subcommittee for that purpose, but members were "very loath to take any action." Dennett herself admitted they considered the "subject distasteful." She considered Nelson "an utter ignoramus."[42]

Kissel, too, responded to Gavin. He claimed every other "civilized country" disseminated information about birth control and asserted "the greater number of intelligent American parents" already practiced it. Lack of such knowledge among millions of poor families caused economic hardship and unnecessary suffering. It also contributed to the high rate of infant mortality and to "immense cost to the public for the care of orphans and for imbecile or criminal offspring." He contended countries, like Holland, distributed contraceptive information and had a much lower infant-death rate. Gavin's secretary Murray asked Burke for assistance in replying. Burke thought Gavin should point out Kissel's stunning ignorance. Dutch law was second only to German law in being "the most severe on this matter of all Europe." Indeed, there were no public clinics in Holland. He recommended commending Kissel for interest in the poor, while pointing out that instead of advocating "a living wage" to enable a man to maintain wife and children in comfort, Kissel would have him tailor family size to his income. Burke called that "base materialism." Moreover, Kissel would save society from care of orphans and the feeble-minded "by prematurely killing them, which is the last word in paganism." Like other Catholic progressives, Burke believed economics was at the root of the birth control movement: the unwillingness of capital to pay workers an ample wage. Moreover, contraception was "a menace" to national welfare because it already lowered the birth rate below the level necessary to maintain current population, let alone increase it.[43]

With Congress about to expire, Dennett redoubled her efforts for action on the bill. As Burke told Laughlin, the woman was "certainly going at it very madly," but the prospects of success were slight. Catholic letters and telegrams to committeemen bore fruit. Burke informed Hanna the NCWC had kept the measure "from coming to a vote even in committee."[44]

He then faced birth control in Puerto Rico, an American possession. Nearly a year earlier, Luis Muñoz Marín, scion of a prominent political family, published an article asserting overpopulation was the root of the island's economic woes. Its inability to sustain the vast number of people resulted in widespread poverty. He advocated adoption of Sanger's ideas and called for distribution of contraceptives at cost. In late April 1923, Burke received a letter from Father Mariano Vassallo, secretary of Bishop George Caruana of San Juan, with word that a legislator would soon introduce a bill permitting physicians and others to disseminate information about birth control. The legislator implied such laws already existed in the most progressive states of the U.S. Vassallo asked Burke to send any literature he might think useful.[45]

Burke sent a summary of criminal statutes demonstrating only four of forty-eight states failed to prohibit distribution of contraceptive information: Georgia, New Hampshire, New Mexico, and North Carolina. He included a synopsis explaining those states were not only unprogressive, but also three of them were among the most backward in the nation. Burke said the legislator promoting the idea was "either very ignorant or very dishonest, or both." He gave Vassallo permission to quote him or the NCWC about the untruth of the man's statement.[46]

Burke complained to Major General Frank McIntyre, chief of the Bureau of Insular Affairs, and to Horace Mann Towner, governor general of Puerto Rico. He explained to McIntyre the legislator in question was placing the U.S. in a false light. To Towner, he said representing birth control as a progressive view in the U.S., would rouse Puerto Ricans against the American government. He urged Towner and McIntyre to take whatever steps proper to halt the effort. Towner assured Burke there was "not the slightest danger of such legislation being put through or even proposed." He had heard nothing about it, nor did he believe the Chamber of Representatives would countenance it. "I think perhaps it is unnecessary to add," he wrote, "that no proposition of that sort would meet with my approval."[47] There, the matter ended for ten years before reappearing with a vengeance.

Haiti

As with birth control, Burke's concern for the Church in Haiti extended back to 1921 when he sent Michael Williams there to investigate the situation. In 1915, the U.S. had invoked the Roosevelt Corollary to the Monroe Doctrine to invade Haiti, ostensibly to restore civil and political order, but in reality as part of a plan to control the Caribbean. With construction of the Panama Canal (1904–1914), American hegemony over that sea assumed new importance. The violent overthrow of President Vilbrun Guillaume Sam and the need to restore order served as the pretext for the invasion.[48]

The suppression crisis and aftermath had prevented Burke from doing anything about Haiti until September 1922. In that month, Senator Medill McCormick, who led a Senate investigating committee there a year earlier, advised Archbishop Giovanni Bonzano, apostolic delegate, that unless Catholic authorities opened more schools in Haiti, Protestant denominations would. Burke, who wrote Hanna's annual report to the hierarchy, used it to apprise the bishops. He wrote that whatever the U.S. government did in Haiti would either promote or injure the Catholic Church there. He pleaded for American Catholics to do "something" for the Church in Haiti. "This is the more important and urgent," stressed Burke, "because the Protestant churches are already planning to introduce technical schools—the evil effect of which is much feared by the Archbishop of Port-au-Prince."[49] The bishops listened politely but took no action.

Although the hierarchy was indifferent, the American government was not. Its attitude toward Haiti was one of racist, paternalist Progressivism.

Administrators at home and onsite viewed Haitian blacks as childlike, happy, harmless, generous, and uncivilized peasants incapable of self-governance. Those same innocents, however, under influence of alcohol or vodou, were capable of savage barbarism, even cannibalism. American occupiers tried to suppress vodou and introduced modern technology and administrative principles to create the infrastructure to uplift the people. In belief that blacks were fit only for manual pursuits, they intended to use vocational education to turn Haitians into docile drudges.[50]

Education became the battleground between Haiti and the U.S. By Concordat with the Vatican, the Church held a privileged role in public education; schools, both private and public, were to teach Catholicism. Moreover, the Haitian system offered classical education of the French model. The treaty between Haiti and the U.S. was silent about education, so Haitians used it as basis for resisting American interference in the matter. Because the treaty conceded control of Haitian finances to the United States, the occupier used funding to assert control over the national school system. When Haitian officials parried the effort, the occupiers decided in 1922 to establish their own system of industrial and agricultural vocational education, known as Service Technique de l'Agriculture et de l'Enseignement Professionnel, or Service Technique for short. Haitians resisted the schools as purveyors of Yankee materialism and utilitarianism. The occupiers then used power of the purse to starve the Haitian system.[51]

Unsuccessful in rousing the hierarchy, Burke went over the bishops' heads. He and McCormick went to Bonzano to beg him to do something for Haiti and suggested that since the U.S. occupied it, it should be placed under Bonzano in his capacity as apostolic delegate to the U.S. As a matter of fact, Archbishop Pietro Benedetti, apostolic delegate to Cuba, was already interim regent of the apostolic internunciature of Haiti.[52]

In fall 1923, Benedetti went to Washington, where Burke arranged for him to meet with McCormick. Burke and James H. Ryan accompanied him. Sympathetic to the Haitian people and their plight, McCormick told Benedetti there was "no question" that the U.S. would withdraw from Haiti, but he was silent about when. Meanwhile, that country needed technical education, instructors for Catholic schools, and priests who could speak French. In McCormick's view, the American Catholic Church should take charge of the problem, because if it failed to act, Protestant or secular forces in America would. McCormick said he would write to John Russell, commissioner general of Haiti, to extend every courtesy to Benedetti during his visit there. Once outside, Benedetti told Burke "this Calvinist (McCormick) was more interested in the Catholics of Haiti than the Catholic bishops of America."[53]

Because Burke insisted Benedetti see Undersecretary of State William Phillips and Secretary of State Charles Evans Hughes, he had to rearrange the archbishop's schedule. Benedetti had previously committed himself to a luncheon and booked a 3:00 P.M. train to Philadelphia. Running late, the group reached the hotel at 1:30. "Why people will allow these social or quasi social functions to interfere with the work of God, I don't understand," wondered Burke. "Of course it is very kind: but there is a kindness higher." In his mind, spiritual welfare of the Haitian people took precedence. He arranged for Benedetti to catch the 4:30 train, and, after "a hearty lunch," he and Benedetti made "an uncivil get-away" to see Phillips.[54]

At first, Phillips was unwilling to say when the U.S. would evacuate Haiti. Finally, he told Benedetti and Burke the occupation would definitely last until 1936—the date stipulated in the treaty—and perhaps longer. Burke had him invite Hughes to join them. Asked if he thought it advisable to send French-speaking American priests to Haiti, Hughes said he could give no definite answer. He was predisposed to the idea, but it needed careful examination. If sending priests would cause ill will, none should go. Burke remarked that Hughes "was clear cut in his talk, deliberate and ... covered his tracks well." Still, he found the man sympathetic and cordial to American Catholic action in Haiti.[55]

Returning to the NCWC, Benedetti again "deplored the indifference of the U.S. bishops" to the needs of Caribbean and South American countries. He wanted Burke to draw up a report on Haiti for the Vatican. Burke was disinclined because Rome would not want to hear what he had to say, especially since the Church was unprepared to implement his recommendation.[56]

Burke committed his thoughts to paper. The best approach to Haiti was through lay missionaries. Family life, proper housing, public health, education, just industrial conditions, decent standards of living, political liberty, participation in government—"all these are duties, obligations that belong to the laity," believed Burke. Where Catholic lay people took no interest in them and left them to the clergy, they inevitably became the "plaything of shrewd, unscrupulous politicians." Benedetti had admitted clericalism was the problem in Haiti. The Breton clergy there were extremely clannish. They would not welcome non-Breton priests, even French ones. Burke believed lay missionaries stood a better chance of acceptance by the Haitian people. Laymen and laywomen could meet them as equals and through humble service help them improve their homes, childcare, nutrition, and medical attention. Through such, they would lead Haitians to knowledge of redemption while teaching them dignity, self-protection, and self-assertion. The Haitians would be won over because "the tongue that spoke in the same name as the hand that helped[,] would not be denied."[57]

Yet, Burke thought his idea chimerical. American Catholics prided themselves as "strong and even progressive," but "those who so boast do not see deeply or think seriously." Science was lost to the Church as was literature. The American Church was a clerical institution run by priests and religious. Exposition and defense of the faith was in the hands of clergy. Religious almost exclusively conducted Catholic education. Priests edited practically every Catholic magazine and newspaper. They also ran Catholic charities in nearly every diocese. Burke pondered why this was so. "I think the fundamental answer is that we have forgotten the call of perfection was issued by Christ not alone to priests and religious, but to all without exception," he wrote. "We practically preach the contrary.... We have assumed that decision and direction of all matters Catholic belong to the clergy. And the people have allowed the assumption to rest with us." He thought if the laity were entrusted with the responsibility for Catholic truth regarding familial, social, political, industrial, and literary life, the Church and America would be a different reality. "All this may seem far away from Haiti," he wrote, "but I do not think it is." The laity in America and Haiti alike needed to be empowered. To put these thoughts in a report to the Vatican "would be quite useless unless one could also explain how de facto it could be done." The obstacle to effective assistance for Haiti was quite simple: "We have not the vision, we have not the machinery or organization to carry out this work. Last September it was put before the bishops: but the answer was silence." Burke concluded perhaps French-speaking, American priests should, after all, be sent to Haiti. Perhaps such men would see the need for lay action "and make their appeal heard. But we ask, how long, how long."[58]

Burke kept these dispirited thoughts to himself. At Christmas he wrote to Benedetti in Haiti with word that after further enquiries, he was able to confirm Phillips's opinion that the U.S. would likely remain there indefinitely. He expressed forlorn hope of sending a few lay missionaries, who might later be followed by French-speaking American priests.[59]

Reminiscing into Continuance

The September 1923 convention of the hierarchy was to have been Burke's last, but it seems he had reminisced himself into continuing at the helm of the NCWC. In April of that year, Murray had asked how it was doing, which launched Burke into recollections about its origin. He told her there were indications of its widespread acceptance, that it was "beginning to be understood and to be needed." No doubt its efforts regarding the Oregon School Law, birth control, and motion-pictures contributed to this altered atmosphere. As one who knew his "heart and soul in this matter," Murray understood this recognition of the NCWC owed much to his "obstinate fidelity to one idea and the belief that it would be accepted because so plainly Catholic and so plainly necessary." Burke told her since those days long ago when he had first discussed with her his vision, he had suffered many "disappointments and sad hours." "You saw I think more clearly than I the sacrifices and the hardships," he wrote. "I was too thoughtless and too reckless to count them." If he knew then what he knew now, he would have lacked the courage to take the first step. It was simply the work of God and succeeded only because it was His work. Burke had no idea why he was chosen for it: "There it was and I lived it and I am more than grateful if God has given me share in it to His glory." Burke considered it "good" and "profitable" to dwell on such things.[60]

He told Murray he often thought of those old days when they were together at *Catholic World* morning, noon, and night; how he had poured out his heart and soul to her, seeking to give her all he had and to shape her as best he could into a child of the Lord. The work of the NCWC had taken its physical toll. "I'm not what I was when you first knew me," he wrote. It was time to let her fly on her own. "I must leave you to our Lord's care, to the guidance of the Holy Spirit," he said. "And this for me is an act of faith in you. I can't keep you with spoken word and personal contact every day: but with the bonds of holy hope I keep you near."[61] Their friendship would continue through life, but Burke would no longer be her spiritual director.

And so it was that seven months after he had told the Administrative Committee it had a year to find his replacement, he recalled the NCWC was the product of his obstinate vision, given him by God to live. He had already been replaced as editor of *Catholic World*, and his release of Murray to the hands of the Holy Spirit was tacit acknowledgment he would be remaining in Washington where he was already refurbishing a lodging next to his beloved Catholic Service School. In the months that followed, he never broached the idea of his departure from the NCWC with any member of the Administrative Committee. When it met in September after the hierarchy's convention, neither the bishops nor he brought the matter up. The prelates simply reelected him general secretary without comment or protest and business continued as usual. The only change to occur was the name of the NCWC: the hierarchy agreed it should be called the National Catholic Welfare Conference.[62]

Federal Education Question

When the new Congress opened in December 1923, the NCWC again faced the federal education question. The NEA had its legislation for a funded department reintroduced as the Sterling-Reed bill, still backed by Masonry and the Ku Klux Klan. The political situation had, however, altered since the previous Congress. President Harding died unexpectedly, and Calvin Coolidge succeeded him. A governmental minimalist, Coolidge considered education a "peculiarly local problem," an endeavor that must "always be pursued with the largest freedom of choice by students and parents." He opposed federal aid to education. Since he was fulfilling Harding's unfinished term, He felt morally bound to support his predecessor's Reorganization bill that called for a department of education and welfare.[63]

In mid-January 1924, while Burke was away in New York City and Cleveland, the NEA maneuvered the Senate Committee on Education and Labor into holding a hearing on its bill. Burke thought the tactic "rather underhand work," causing him to coordinate a counter effort by long-distance telephone. He and James H. Ryan discussed the situation by wire.

They considered support of the reorganization bill as means to derail the Sterling-Reed, but Burke had grown wary of attempts to solve problems with federal legislation. Fortunately, the NCWC Department of Education was meeting at the time and able to provide collective wisdom. Ryan drew up a brief rejecting the Sterling-Reed bill and delivered it himself before the Senate committee. He called for appointment of a national commission to study the needs of schools and make recommendations. He proposed a federal board of education to integrate and direct various educational agencies scattered throughout the government. Intelligence Burke gleaned from Congress indicated most senators on the committee opposed sending the NEA bill to the floor.[64]

Later in January, it held a hearing on the Reorganization bill. Burke and Ryan considered whether to tackle such complex legislation. Because the Administrative Committee had given Burke no instruction on it, the two thought it best to limit objection to the educational aspect in the measure. So, Ryan submitted the same brief he sent to the Senate. Burke believed there was no likelihood Congress would do anything about reorganization in the current session.[65]

In late February, he reported to Muldoon there was "a marked change of sentiment" in Washington regarding federalization and establishment of new departments. In the wake of Harding's death came revelations of scandals in his administration. The most prominent was the Teapot Dome Oil affair, wherein the secretary of Interior coaxed the secretary of the Navy to transfer naval oil reserves to his department and then took bribes to lease them to petroleum magnates. As Burke saw it, revelation of the crime had "played its part" in keeping the Sterling-Reed bill in committee. "To relief work in Russia and to the Teapot dome [*sic*] the N.C.W.C. may yet be historically both grateful and indebted," he told Muldoon. Russian relief had proven how valuable it was in furthering Vatican purposes; Teapot Dome helped stall the movement for a department of education which, like the Oregon Law, threatened parochial schools.[66]

Immigration Restriction

A key feature of the Sterling-Reed bill was its mandate for Americanization of immigrants, one tine of a two-pronged movement; the second was restriction of immigration. The Klan backed both. So did many old-stock Americans who sought to preserve dominance in the country of the Anglo-Saxon, Nordic race. They wanted to stem the influx of eastern and southern European Catholics and Jews, people deemed racially inferior and resistant to the "melting pot." In 1921 Congress had passed the Emergency Quota Act aimed at temporarily curbing immigration for one year. It limited the annual influx from each country to 3 percent of the number of its nationals in the U.S. according to the 1910 census.[67]

While it was under consideration, the NCWC had registered no opposition. Those at its helm were Catholic progressives deeply committed to the Church's social teaching, especially promotion of a living wage. The nation was then in a sharp postwar depression with widespread unemployment. Advocates of labor argued immigrants willing to toil for lower pay would jeopardize the welfare of American workers by deflating wages and weakening the power of unions.[68] Catholic bishops came alive to the act's negative aspects only after passage, when the quota feature caused hardship to married immigrant men whose wives and families wanted to join them in America. Many were prevented because of exhausted quotas, a situation severely affecting Puerto Ricans, Italians, and Poles. The hierarchy referred the matter to the NCWC's Immigration Bureau. Meanwhile, the life of the Emergency Quota Act was extended for two years.[69]

Between 1921 and 1924, racialization of southern and eastern Europeans hardened as old-stock Americans came to view the melting pot as a false, dangerous idea. In December 1923, Representative Albert Johnson of Washington, chairman of the House Committee on Immigration and Naturalization, introduced patently discriminatory legislation that excluded all Asians and Africans and continued the quota system until 1927, though reducing each country's allowance from 3 to 2 percent of the number of its people resident according to the 1890 rather than the 1910 census. Because the 1890 census antedated the massive influx of eastern and southern European immigrants, the bill virtually eliminated future migrations from those areas. After 1927, total European immigration was not to exceed 150,000 annually and quotas were to be assigned on a proportional basis according to national origin of residents in the 1920 census. This feature essentially slammed the door on eastern and southern Europeans. Many Catholics correctly viewed the legislation as aimed at them.[70]

Setting aside the implied anti-Catholicism of the Johnson bill, Burke drafted a protest attacking it on patriotic grounds. He considered it contrary to traditions, principles, and ideals of America. From its foundation, the country had opened its doors "to the world"; it had shown itself to be "mother and refuge of the people of all lands." Every American was a beneficiary of that generosity. America owed a debt to every other nation for its growth and strength. This legislation was "a studied attempt to exclude immigrants from certain countries: to favor immigrants from other countries." Burke did not oppose restriction of immigration as such. He opposed the present bill for its betrayal of the country's "mission," something that would "excite the anger of other nations against us, because of its very plain insult," and render Americans "a pharisaical class." He believed the country was strong enough to assimilate all who would come, just as it had assimilated those who had earlier arrived.[71]

Burke declared it would be hard to think of a more efficient way to prevent Americanization of immigrants already in the country than by this bill. The principal obstacle to assimilation was breaking down nationalism of ethnic groups. The "patent discrimination" in the bill, branding people of the targeted lands as "undesirable aliens," would anger rather than assuage their countrymen in America, thereby making them defensive of their national heritage. Its message was not one of good will and equal justice to all, but one of discrimination and dislike. Burke suggested a more just basis of judging suitability for admission to America would be literacy, skill, and general fitness for citizenship.[72]

He and Bruce Mohler of the Immigration Bureau discussed changes desired in the bill. Burke wanted the quotas based on the 1910 or, even better, 1920 census. Both thought the minimum quota of 200 for targeted nations was too small and should be raised to at least 500. Applauding the bill's inclusion of a non-quota class for wives and unmarried children of citizens of the U.S., they urged, for "moral and humane" reasons, extension of that privilege to spouses and children of permanent resident aliens and those who intended eventual naturalization. Unlike the Emergency Quota Act, which permitted priests and ministers to enter without restriction, the bill required foreign clergymen to have four years of ministerial experience at home prior to entry as non-quota immigrants. This stipulation was meant to prevent fraud by demonstrating a clergyman's permanent, fixed profession. Burke thought the bill should retain the clerical exemption of the Emergency Act. He asked Mohler to draft a brief for submission to Congress embodying Burke's protest and the NCWC's desired changes.[73]

Mohler incorporated almost all of Burke's protest into the text of the brief, though he toned down or eliminated one or two of the more accusatory remarks. Still, it made a powerful statement. Burke had him send it to both the House and Senate Committees on Immigration. The reception it received was anything but welcome; Burke told Hanna, "I need not review … the experiences and opinions with which we met." Doubting the bill would pass, he said indications suggested quotas would be based on either the 1900 or 1910 census.[74]

To Muldoon, Burke explained the "strange" feeling of anti-Catholicism in Congress "—the extent of it, the ground of it—and the colorings, light or heavy, it displays." The respect congressmen had for the Church was, he wrote, "significant and universal." Yet at the same time there was feeling, even "a deep settled conviction," the Church did not work with the country or was working against it. At other times, opposition to the Church resulted, not from conviction, but from political expediency, the need to take into account sentiment of constituents. Burke believed anti-Catholicism had never been so widespread as it then was, yet he thought earlier bouts of it had "been far more deep and more dangerous." "In other words," he told Muldoon, "if circumstances and events serve us, it will contract."[75] That was not to happen for several years.

THE KU KLUX KLAN

The Ku Klux Klan was virulently anti-Catholic. By early February 1924, a presidential election year, Burke sensed growing pressure among Catholics to have the two parties adopt an anti-Klan plank. In fact, in January, the NCCM's Indianapolis branch held its first diocesan convention, which passed a resolution demanding both parties adopt one. The man who seconded the motion was on the payroll of the Republican state committee. Burke had no doubt the resolution was being used by political agents to secure support for one candidate or another.[76]

As general secretary, he considered it his duty to formulate "some definite policy" for the NCWC to follow and committed his thoughts to paper.

"My own judgment," he wrote, "is that it would be a very serious and perhaps a fatal error to work for the insertion of such a plank, to demand it, or to lay public stress and approval upon the statement and position of those who do favor it." He feared if the Church sought or supported such a plank, either or both parties would demand Catholic support in return. In his view, the Klan was not a Catholic issue, but an American one. Thousands also saw it that way and thought the best way to solve it "as an American issue is to leave it alone." If Catholics began playing politics, they would become tools of particular interests and become mired in "political hypocrisy and political chicanery." "The day that it [the NCWC] is termed a political body," concluded Burke, "that same day its usefulness will cease." The best thing Catholics could do to defeat the Klan and the intolerance and prejudice it expressed was to work constructively for the country through civic education, immigrant aid, decent motion pictures, etc., rather than political protest.[77]

This memorandum reiterated Burke's position that the NCWC was a Catholic voice. The agency articulated Catholic positions on issues and attempted to sway Congress and the government to its point of view. What kept it from being a political machine was its unwillingness to trade Catholic support for party favor. When occasion finally demanded Burke's articulation of this policy, he would do so from the sidelines.

Endnotes to Chapter 11

1. Burke, *Christ in Us*, 170–71.
2. Motion Picture Producers and Distributors of America, Inc., Certificate of Incorporation Filed in the Office of the Secretary of State of New York, 11 March 1922, and in the Office of the County Clerk of New York County, 13 March 1922, and By-Laws Adopted at the Meeting of Incorporation on 7 April 1922, 1 (the quotation is here), FULSC, MPPDA Record 2030, 2–0011 to 2–0040 accessed 16 February 2013 http://mppda.flinders.edu.au/records/2030; Stenographic Report of the 4 January 1922 Meeting of the Committee on Public Relations, ibid., MPPDA Record 77, 1–0086 to 1–0129 accessed 16 February 2013 http://mppda.flinders.edu.au/records/77; *New York Times*, 19 April 1922; Zukor and Kramer, *Public Is Never Wrong*, 203–04; Barbas, "Political Spectator," 218, 225–26; Black, *Hollywood Censored*, 30–32; Brownlow, *Behind Mask of Innocence*, 13–15; Pollard, *Sex and Violence*, 27–29; Miller, *Censored Hollywood*, 28–29; Thomas Doherty, *Hollywood's Cen-*

sor: Joseph I. Breen & the Production Code Administration (New York: Columbia University Press, 2007), 33–36; Tropiano, *Obscene, Indecent, Immoral*, 29–30; Raymond Moley, *The Hays Office*, (New York: The Bobbs-Merrill Company, 1945), 32–35; Jowett, *Film*, 159–66; Couvares, "Main Street and the Church," 589; Stephen Vaughn, "Morality and Entertainment: The Origins of the Motion Picture Code," *Journal of American History* 77 (June 1990): 41.

3. Burke to Ralph Hayes, 15 June 1922, ACUA, USCCB 10:125:32; Addresses Delivered at the Get-Together Meeting of the MPPDA at the Waldorf Astoria, 22 Jun 1922, FULSC, MPPDA Record #5, 1–0333 to 1–0454 accessed 16 February 2013 http://mppda.flinders.edu.au/records/5; Resolutions Adopted at the Meeting Held at the Waldorf Astoria, 22 June 1922, ibid., Record #4, 1–0014 to 1–0016, accessed 8 February 2013 http://mppda.flinders.edu.au/records/4; Jason Joy, Brief Résumé of the Facts Pertaining to Affairs of the Committee to Date, 22 March 1923, ibid., Record #81, 1–0167 accessed 17 February 2013 http://mppda.flinders.edu.au/records/81 accessed 23 February 2013; Minutes of the Meeting of the Committee of Twenty, 7 July 1922, ibid., Record #7, 1–0032 to 1–0034, accessed 8 February 2013 http://mppda.flinders.edu.au/records/7; NCWC New Service, 26 June 1922; Ruth Vasey, *The World According to Hollywood, 1918–1939* (Madison: University of Wisconsin Press, 1997), 31–32; Moley, *Hays Office*, 134–35.
4. Minutes of the Committee of Twenty, 18 October 1922, FULSC, MPPDA Record #14, 1–0041 to 1–0043 accessed 9 February 2013 http://mppda.flinders.edu.au/records/14 (copy in ACUA, USCCB 10:125:28); Moley, *Hays Office*, 132–34, 136.
5. McMahon to Burke, 19 October 1922, ACUA, USCCB 10:125:28.
6. McMahon to Burke, 11 November 1922, ACUA, USCCB 10:125:33; Joy, Memorandum to the Chairman of the Committee on Public Relations, 10 November 1922, FULSC, MPPDA Record #33, 1–0028 accessed 23 February 2013 http://mppda.flinders.edu.au/records/33; Moley, *Hays Office*, 136.
7. Burke to McMahon, 11 November 1922, AUCA, USCCB 10:125:33.
8. Minutes of the Informal Meeting of the Executive Committee, 13 November 1922, FULSC, MPPDA Record #17, 1–0055 accessed 16 February 2013 http://mppda.flinders.edu.au/records/17; Moley, *Hays Office*, 136.
9. McMahon to Burke, 16 November 1922, ACUA, USCCB 10:125:28.
10. Burke to McMahon, 20 November 1922, copy, ACUA, USCCB 10:125:28.
11. *Oakland Tribune*, 20 December 1922; McMahon Press Release, 21 December 1922, ACUA, USCCB 10:125:33; *New York Times*, 22 December 1922; Stenographic Report of the Meeting of the Committee on Public Relations, 4 January 1923, FULSC, MPPDA Record 77, 1–0086 to 1–0129 accessed 16 February 2013 http://mppda.flinders.edu.au/records/77; Jowett, *Film* 174–75; Moley, *Hays Office*, 136–37. Arbuckle had two mistrials before finally being acquitted.

12. Burke to McMahon, 2 January 1923, copy, ACUA, USCCB 10:125:33.
13. Stenographic Report of the Meeting of the Committee on Public Relations, 4 January 1923, FULSC, MPPDA Record 77, 1–0086 to 1–0129 accessed 16 February 2013 http://mppda.flinders.edu.au/records/77.
14. Minutes of the Meeting of the Committee on Public Relations, 4 January 1923, FULSC, MPPDA Record #78, 1–0130 to 1–0142 accessed 9 March 2013 http//mppda.flinders.edu.au/records/78; Hays to Hanmer, 31 January 1923, ibid., MPPDA Record #23, 1–0143 to 1–0144 accessed 17 February 2013 http://mppda.flinders.edu.au/records/23.
15. McMahon to Burke, 19 October 1922, ACUA, USCCB 10:125:33; Burke to Muldoon, 19 August 1923, copy, ibid., 10:104:12; McMahon to Burke, 19 April 1923, ACUA, USCCB 10:125:28; Minutes of the Luncheon Meeting of the Executive Committee, 20 March 1923, FULSC, MPPDA Record #27, 1–0156 to 1–0161 accessed 16 March 2013 http://mppda.flinders.edu.au/records/27; Slawson, *Foundation of NCWC*, 187.
16. McMahon to Burke, 15 February 1923, ACUA, USCCB 10:125:28.
17. Burke to McMahon, 17 February 1923, copy, ACUA, USCCB 10:125:28.
18. McMahon to Burke, 19 April 1923, ACUA, USCCB 10:125:28; Burke to McMahon, 28 April 1923, copy, ibid.
19. NCWC News Service, 22 October 1923; Edith H. Jarboe, "When the Movies are Worth While," *NCWC Bulletin* 5 (April 1924): 10.
20. Slawson, *Department of Education Battle*, 111–15. See also, McGrath to Burke, 20 April 1922, ACUA, USCCB 10:60:17.
21. Notes on meeting held Monday, 11 December 1922, ACUA, Vice Rector files; Slawson, *Department of Education Battle*, 111, 115–16. On a Catholic "separate but equal" subculture, see Halsey, *Survival of American Innocence*, 37–60; Paula M. Kane, *Separatism and Subculture: Boston Catholicism, 1900–1920* (Chapel Hill: University of North Carolina Press, 1994), 1–48; Slawson, *Foundation of NCWC*, 10–15.
22. John Carroll to Burke, [ca. 15] December 1922, handwritten on J. A. Walsh to Carroll, 7 December 1922, ACUA, USCCB 10:14:7; Burke to Carroll, 20 December 1922, copy, ibid.; William Guthrie to Burke, 20 December 1922, ibid.; Guthrie to Burke, 5 January 1923, ibid.; Burke to Guthrie, 6 January 1923, copy, ibid.; Shelley, "Oregon School Case," 443.
23. Minutes of the Administrative Committee, 11 and 12 January 1923, ACUA, USCCB 10:64:3.
24. Ibid.; Slawson, *Department of Education Battle*, 111; Kauffman, *Faith and Fraternalism*, 282–83.
25. Dowling to Burke, 18 January 1923, ACUA, USCCB 10:14:7; Burke to Dowling, 22 January 1923, copy, ibid.; Burke to Hanna, 24 January 1923, AASF, NCWC files; Kavanaugh to Dowling, 31 January 1923, copy, enclosure with Kavanaugh to Hanna, 31 January 1923, ibid.

26. Burke to Hanna, 24 January 1923, AASF, NCWC files; Garret McEnerney to Guthrie, telegram, 2 February 1922, ibid.; Guthrie to McEnerney, telegram, 3 February 1923, ibid.; Hanna to Dowling, telegram, 5 February 1923, ibid.
27. Kavanaugh to Dowling, 31 January 1923, copy, enclosure with Kavanaugh to Hanna, 31 January 1923, AASF, NCWC files.
28. Burke to Dowling, 14 February 1923, copy, ACUA, USCCB 10:14:7; Hanna to Burke, 26 February 1923, ibid.; Minutes of the Meeting of the Administrative Committee, 12 April 1923, ACUA, USCCB 10:64:3.
29. Orville B. Zabel, *God and Caesar in Nebraska: A Study of the Legal Relationship of Church and State, 1854–1954* (Lincoln: University of Nebraska Press, 1955), 140–47.
30. William D. Guthrie and Bernard Hershkopf, *Brief of Amici Curiae: Supreme Court of the United States, October Term 1922, Robert T. Meyer v. State of Nebraska,* printed copy in AASF, NCWC files; Slawson, *Foundation of the NCWC,* 195. The brief was actually written by Garret McEnerney, perhaps with the help of Hershkopf, Guthrie's partner.
31. Burke to Muldoon, 2 March 1923, copy, ACUA, USCCB 10:152:29; Burke to John Kavanaugh, 1 March 1923, ibid., 10:14:7; Burke to Hanna, 27 February 1923, AASF, NCWC files.
32. *Meyer* v. *Nebraska*, 262 U.S. 390 (1923); Burke to Muldoon, 21 June 1923, copy, ACUA, USCCB 10:14:7; Zabel, *God and Caesar*, 147–48.
33. Burke to Muldoon, 21 June 1923, copy, ACUA, USCCB 10:14:7; Kavanaugh to Christie, 21 June 1923, AASF, NCWC files; Carroll to Dowling, 9 July 1923, with enclosures, ibid.; Dowling to Muldoon, 4 July 1923, ACUA, USCCB 10:14:7; Hanna to Dowling, undated [mid July 1923], copy, enclosure with Dowling to Muldoon, 20 July 1923, ibid.; Dowling to Hanna, telegram, undated [19 July 1923], AASF, NCWC files; Minutes of the Administrative Committee, 25 September 1923, ACUA, USCCB 10:64:3; Slawson, *Foundation of the NCWC*, 197–99.
34. Guthrie to Kavanaugh, 5 October 1923, copy, ACUA, USCCB 10:14:7; Burke to Guthrie, 3 January 1924, copy, ibid., 10:14:8; Guthrie to Burke, 3 January 1923, with enclosure Guthrie to Kavanaugh, 3 January 1924, copy, ibid.; *Berea College* v. *Kentucky*, 211 U.S. 45 (1908); *Oregon School Cases: Complete Record* (Baltimore: Belvedere, 1925), 36–58; "The Three-Judge Court Act of 1910: Purpose, Procedure, and Alternatives," *Journal of Criminal Law, Criminology, and Police Procedure* 62 (June 1971): 205–19.
35. Burke to T. Burke, 30 September 1922, AP, Official Papers of Superior General Thomas F. Burke 1922; Burke to Murray, 26 October 1922, ibid., Burke Papers, box 11.
36. Burke to Murray, 21 April 1923, AP, Burke Papers, box 11.
37. Ibid.; Lawler, *Full Circle*, 70–71.
38. Lawler, *Full Circle*, 57–58.

39. Chen, *"Sex Side of Life,"* 181, 205–35 (first quote is here); Sara Laughlin to Burke, 24 February 1921, ACUA, USCCB 10:116:34 (second quote is here); Minutes of the NCWC Interdepartmental Meeting, 18 January 1923, ibid., USCCB 10:1: Minute Book I; Kennedy, *Birth Control,* 94, 220–21; *Margaret Sanger: An Autobiography* (New York: W. W. Norton & Company, Inc., 1938), 180–81, 414–15; Tentler, *Catholics and Contraception,* 45–46, 53–55; Baker, *Sanger: Life of Passion,* 132–37, 170–72, 204–06; Ellen Chesler, *Woman of Valor: Margaret Sanger and the Birth Control Movement in America* (New York: Simon & Shuster, 1992), 231–33; Hartmann-Ting, "Catholic Service School for Women," 101–02 and 109.
40. Burke to Mary Ware Dennett, 5 January 1923, copy, ACUA, USCCB 10:117:2; Tentler, *Catholics and Contraception,* 5–54.
41. Burke to Laughlin, 29 January 1923, copy, ACUA, USCCB 10:117:2; Burke to George Stewart, 14 February 1923, copy, ibid.
42. Knute Nelson to Gavin, 10 February 1923, ACUA, USCCB 10:117:2; Dennett, handbill 19 February [1923], enclosure with Laughlin to Burke, 23 February 1923, ibid. (her comment about the committees is here); Chen, *"Sex Side of Life,"* 224 (the comment about Nelson is quoted here).
43. John Kissel to Gavin, 3 March 1923, copy, ACUA, USCCB 10:117:2; Burke to Murray, 6 March 1923, copy, ibid.; Tentler, *Catholics and Contraception,* 48–49; Kennedy, *Birth Control,* 236–38.
44. Burke to Hanna, 27 February 1923, AASF, NCWC files; Burke to Laughlin, 21 February 1923, copy, ACUA, USCCB 10:117:2 (quote is here); Dennett, handbill 19 February 1923, enclosure with Laughlin to Burke, 23 February [1923], ibid.; Burke to Laughlin, 24 February 1923, copy, ibid.
45. Mariano Vassallo to Burke, 29 April 1923, ACUA, USCCB 10:117:2; Annette B. Ramírez de Arellano and Conrad Seipp, *Colonialism, Catholicism, and Contraception: A History of Birth Control in Puerto Rico* (Chapel Hill: University of North Carolina Press, 1983), 16–19; Elisa Julian de Nieves, *The Catholic Church in Colonial Puerto Rico (1898–19164)* (Río Piedras: Editorial Edil, Inc., 1982), 133–34.
46. Burke to Vassallo, 9 May 1923, copy, ACUA, USCCB 10:117:2.
47. Burke to Frank McIntyre, 9 May 1923, copy; Burke to Horace Towner, 9 May 1923, copy; Towner to Burke, 21 May 1923—all in ACUA, USCCB 10:117:2.
48. Michael Williams to Burke, 23 December 1921, ACUA, USCCB 10:98:19; Douglas J. Slawson, "Rev. John J. Burke, the National Catholic Welfare Conference, and the American Occupation of Haiti, 1915–34," *Catholic Historical Review* 100 (Summer 2014): 514–19; Hans Schmidt, *The United States Occupation of Haiti, 1915–1934* (New Brunswick, N.J.: Rutgers University Press, 1971), 1–100; David Nicholls, *From Dessalines to Duvalier: Race, Colour and National Independence in Haiti* (New Brunswick, N.J.: Rutgers University

Press, 1996), 126–37, 142–47; Kate Ramsey, *The Spirits and the Law: Vodou and Power in Haiti* (Chicago and London: University of Chicago Press, 2011), 1–10, 54–134, 139–47; Brenda Gayle Plummer, *Haiti and the United States: The Psychological Moment* (Athens and London: The University of Georgia Press, 1992), 81–91; Mary Renda, *Taking Haiti: Military Occupation and the Culture of U.S. Imperialism, 1915–1934* (Chapel Hill & London: University of North Carolina Press, 2001), 10–181; Anne Greene, *The Catholic Church in Haiti: Political and Social Change* (East Lansing: Michigan State University Press, 1993), 82–84; Michel-Rolph Trouillot, *Haiti: State against Nation, the Origins of and Legacy of Duvalierism* (New York: Monthly Review Press, 1990), 50–51, 65–82, 99–102; Leon Denius Pamphile, *La Croix et le Glaive: L'Église Catholique et l'Occupation Américaine d'Haïti, 1915–1934* (Port-au-Prince: Éditions des Antilles, S.A., 1991), 21–50, 135–53; Leon D. Pamphile, *Clash of Cultures: America's Educational Strategies in Occupied Haiti, 1915–1934* (Lanham, Md.: University Press of America, Inc., 2008), 1–37.

49. "Report of the Chairman of the Administrative Committee, NCWC," pp. 5–6; Williams to Burke, memorandum, September 22, 1922, ACUA, USCCB, 10:98:12; Slawson, "Burke and Occupation of Haiti," 524–25.
50. Schmidt, *Occupation of Haiti*, 135–50; Ramsay, *Spirits and the Law*, 121–58; Renda, *Taking Haiti*, 89–130; Plummer, *Haiti and the United States*, 74–80, 106–09; Slawson, "Burke and Occupation of Haiti," 525–26.
51. "Report of the Chairman of the Administrative Committee, NCWC," 5–6; Greene, *Catholic Church in Haiti*, 98; Pamphile, *Clash of Cultures*, 26, 31–32, 40–58, 67–114; Pamphile, *La Croix et l'Glaive*, 53–89.
52. Burke, Memorandum, 31 October [1923], ACUA, USCCB 10:39:11; Giuseppe De Marchi, *Le Nunziature Apostoliche dal 1800 al 1956* (Roma: Edizioni di Storia e letteratura, 1957), 141. Burke wrote that this visit to Bozano occurred about a year earlier.
53. Burke, Memorandum, 31 October [1923], ACUA, USCCB 10:39:11.
54. Ibid.
55. Ibid.
56. Ibid.
57. Ibid.
58. Ibid.
59. Burke to Pietro Benedetti, 22 December 1923, copy, ACUA, USCCB 10:39:11.
60. Burke to Murray, 21 April 1923, AP, Burke Papers, box 11.
61. Ibid.
62. Minutes of the Administrative Committee, 27 September 1923, ACUA, USCCB 10:64:3.
63. Calvin Coolidge, "First Annual Message Delivered at a Joint Session, 6 December 1923," in Fred Israel, ed., *The State of the Union Messages of the*

Presidents (New York: Chelsea House—Robert Hector Publishers, 1966), 3:2650–51, 2652; Slawson, *Department of Education Battle*, 122–27; Paul Johnson, "Calvin Coolidge and the Last Arcadia," in John Earl Haynes, ed., *Calvin Coolidge and the Coolidge Era: Essays on the History of the 1920s* (Washington, D.C.: Library of Congress, 1998), 4–7; Claude M. Fuess, *Calvin Coolidge: The Man From Vermont* (Hamden, Conn.: Archon Books, 1965), 381–82; Robert H. Ferrell, *The Presidency of Calvin Coolidge* (Lawrence: University Press of Kansas, 1998), 167–75; Robert Sobel, *Coolidge: An American Enigma* (Washington, D.C.: Regnery Publishing, Inc., 1998), 310–13; George B. Nash, "The "Great Enigma' and the 'Great Engineer,'" in *Coolidge and the Coolidge Era*, 149; William Allen White, *A Puritan in Babylon: The Story of Calvin Coolidge* (New York: Macmillan Company, 1938), 267–68.

64. Burke to Muldoon, 27 January 1924, copy, ACUA, USCCB 10:104:13 (quotes are here); Burke to Hanna, 9 February 1924, AASF, NCWC files; Minutes of the Department of Education, 22 January 1924, ACUA, USCCB Education Department 10:23:12; Report of the Chairman of the Department of Education for the Year Ending 30 June 1924, attached to the Minutes of the Department of Education, 28 January 1925, ACUA, Vice Rector files.
65. Burke to Hanna, 9 February 1924, AASF, NCWC files.
66. Burke to Muldoon, 24 February 1924, copy, ACUA, USCCB 10:152:29; Russell, *Shadow of Blooming Grove*, 488–507, 609–37; Hicks, *Republican Ascendancy*, 76–77.
67. Robert A. Divine, *American Immigration Policy, 1924–1952* (New Haven: Yale University Press, 1957), 6–10; [Finley Peter Dunne], *Observations by Mr. Dooley* (New York: R. H. Russell, 1902), 49–54; Edward P. Hutchinson, *Legislative History of American Immigration Policy, 1798–1965* (Philadelphia: University of Pennsylvania Press, 1981), 178–81; Roger Daniels, *Guarding the Golden Door: American Immigration Policy and Immigrants since 1882* (New York: Hill and Wang, 2004), 47–49; Jonathan Peter Spiro, *Defending the Master Race: Conservation, Eugenics, and the Legacy of Madison Grant* (Lebanon, N.H.: University Press of New England, 2009), 143–67, 202–10; Gary Gerstle, "Liberty, Coercion, and the Making of Americans," *Journal of American History* 84 (September 1997): 534–39; Ewa Morawska, "Immigrants, Transnationalism, and Ethnicization," in Gerstle and Mollenkopf, *E Pluribus Unum? Contemporary and Historical Perspectives on Immigrant Political Incorporation* (New York: Russell Sage Foundation, 2001), 179–87; Reed Ueda, "Historical Patterns of Immigrant Status and Incorporation in the United States," in *E Pluribus Unum?*, 295; Evelyn Savidge Sterne, "Beyond the Boss: Immigration and American Political Culture from 1880 to 1940," in *E Pluribus Unum?*, 37–57; Desmond King, "Making Americans: Immigration Meets Race," in ibid., 143–51, 158–66; Abrams, *Burdens of Progress*, 45, 51–53; Kirschner,

City and Country, 14–16, 27–38, 117; Dumenil, *Modern Temper*, 204–7, 260–63; Higham, *Strangers in the Land*, 150–63, 312–24; William Leuchtenburg, *Perils of Prosperity, 1914–1929* (Chicago: University of Chicago Press, 1965), 66–83; Frederick Lewis Allen, *Only Yesterday: An Informal History of the 1920s* (New York: Harper & Row, Publishers, 1964), 38–62; Harvey Green, *The Uncertainty of Everyday Life:, 1915–1945* (New York: Harper Perennial, 1993), 33–36.

68. Gribble, *Archbishop for the People*, 193; Higham, *Strangers in the Land*, 234–63, 303–12; Richard M. Linkh, *American Catholicism and European Immigrants, 1900–1924* (Staten Island, N.Y.: Center for Migration Studies, 1975), 148–51, 177–78; Divine, *American Immigration Policy*, 7–11.
69. *Minutes of the Fourth Annual Meeting of the Hierarchy, September 1922*, p. 8, ACUA, USCCB 10:70:7; Higham, *Strangers in the Land*, 312.
70. Burke to Muldoon, 23 December 1923, ACUA, USCCB 10:152:29; Dumenil, *Modern Temper*, 204–7, 260–63; Linkh, *Catholicism and European Immigrants*, 178–79; Hutchinson, *History of Immigration Policy*, 187–95; Daniels, *Guarding the Golden Door*, 49–55; Spiro, *Defending Master Race*, 220–33; Mae M. Ngai, *Impossible Subjects: Illegal Aliens and the Making of Modern America* (Princeton: Princeton University Press, 2004), 21–27; Higham, *Strangers in the Land*, 150–63, 264–99, 312–24; Divine, *American Immigration Policy*, 11–18; Jeanne Petit, "Our Immigrant Coreligionists: The National Catholic Welfare Conference as an Advocate for Immigrants in the 1920s," in Rachel Ida Buff, ed., *Immigrant Rights in the Shadows of Citizenship* (New York and London: New York University Press, 2008), 316–18; Gribble, *Archbishop for the People*, 194.
71. [Burke, undated (December 1923), untitled protest], ACUA, USCCB 10:42:1. The language and idiosyncratic punctuation clearly indicate that Burke wrote this protest. Burke was not alone in viewing the bill as a reversal of America's traditional policy of immigration. His contemporary William Van Vleck, dean of the Law School of George Washington University, also saw it as "a complete about face" from the "policy of the open door, of encouragement of immigration" (*The Administrative Control of Aliens* [New York: The Commonwealth Fund, 1932], 21).
72. [Burke, undated (December 1923), untitled protest], ACUA, USCCB 10:42:1.
73. Mohler to Muldoon, 7 January 1924, with enclosure Mohler to the House Committee on Immigration and Naturalization, 7 January 1924, copies, ACUA, USCCB 10:104:13.
74. Mohler to House and Senate Committees on Immigration and Naturalization, 7 January 1924, copies, CMS, 023/28 and 023A/7/80; Burke to Hanna, 9 February 1924, AASF, NCWC files; Burke to Muldoon, 24 February 1924, copy, ACUA, USCCB 10:152:29.

75. Burke to Muldoon, 24 February 1924, copy, ACUA, USCCB 10:152:29.
76. [Burke], Memorandum, 2 February 1924, ACUA, USCCB 10:78:24 and also 10:5:28.
77. Ibid.

Chapter 12
Sidelined

> That He, the Life, might give life to all men, Christ suffered. His work was not simply passive: not simply an endurance. His work was supremely positive: active for all time and in all men.... He loved the world and loving it He loved it unto the end. If we view only the suffering of our Lord we will miss the life and the love that accepted the suffering, offered it and brought us to power, to triumph and to glory. The work of Jesus is not primarily to aid us to suffer, but to give us life—His life—and give it more abundantly. By making of our Christian faith simply an acceptance and a resignation we are in danger of losing the whole content of that faith. For primarily the Christian faith is the positive power of Jesus Christ, the power of God in the individual soul giving that soul a life more exacting in its activity, in its achievement, in its creativeness than any merely natural life.[1]

"In Weary Ways, Where Heavy Shadows Be"

Mid-February 1924 found John Burke once again under the shadow of ill health. The previous year, he was relatively free of ailment except for a spell prior to and during the convention of the hierarchy in fall 1923. In winter, he felt something was wrong with his heart. His Washington physician Dr. Marbury told him although it was fine, it was not beating normally. So, he had him see a cardiologist: Dr. Lee. Lee agreed Burke's heart was healthy, but racing too fast. He ordered absolute rest. Burke confined himself to quarters in the refurbished residence adjacent to the Catholic Service School. He continued to do some work at home until end of February.[2]

The situation of the school weighed heavily on him. First there was its director, Dr. Anne Nicholson, whose "devotion and unselfishness" were praiseworthy. Difficulties, however, arose between her and faculty that became so aggravated she and Burke agreed it best for her to take a "leave of absence"—in fact retirement—which the Board of Management granted. Burke wanted the board to consider Mary Hawks for the post, but it requested he persuade a reluctant Father William Kerby to become the acting director, a position he would hold for six years.[3]

Of greater concern were the school's finances. It lived a precarious existence and survived thanks to refinance of its mortgage and two generous $50,000 donations ($900,000 in 2023) by an anonymous benefactor. Rather astonishingly, before leaving office, Nicholson and school officers agreed to establish a social service department at Georgetown University Hospital to serve as fieldwork center for the new medical social-service courses, which would strain already straitened circumstances. Burke pursued the Laura Spellman Rockefeller Memorial Foundation for three annual grants of $15,000 ($270,000 in 2024) to support the school.[4]

Because illness kept him from the office, Burke decided it best to relinquish reins of the NCWC and appointed Father James H. Ryan acting general secretary. After turning over command, Burke was in bed twenty-two hours a day and up in a chair for the remainder. No visitors were permitted, though Kerby and Agnes Regan did drop by for short periods. Dr. Lee forbade Burke to engage in correspondence or say Mass. "The N.C. work is out of my hands, except for a more important matter now and then," Burke wrote Helen Lynch. He felt very tired and unwilling to take up problems. To Murray, he confessed he was living "a lazy, indifferent life.... I have lost, or given up, my zeal." Yet, hours went by quickly because he read much, but nothing "of a consecutive or studious kind."[5]

News of his condition gave his friend, Mary Merrick, a heavy heart. She reminded him he was not idle in sickness, just as Jesus was not idle on the cross, when "those hands and feet ... for me were nailed unto a tree." Unaware of the interdiction on correspondence and after some time, she wrote she was "getting quite hungry for a little personal word" of his condition. Cobbling together excerpts from two poems—"He Leadeth Me" and "The Hound of Heaven"—she consoled: "I fear the way seems long to you just now, but it's still *the Way* [John 14:6], not always do we go the sunny way, 'sometimes He in kindness leadeth me in weary ways where dreary shadows be,' but I know you know that after all[,] the dark is but the shadow of His hand 'outstretched carressingly [*sic*].'"[6]

After six weeks in bed, Burke reached the conclusion Dr. Lee was "a very severe man." He avoided visiting Burke the previous week, causing him to believe the absence was purposeful so as not to have to deny his return to work. By mid-March, Lee permitted Burke to write a few letters and resume saying Mass, though not daily. At month's end, Burke reported to Hanna he should be back at his desk in two or three more weeks.[7]

In early April, Ryan sought Burke's help on birth control. When the new Congress had opened in December, Mary Dennett and the VPL had their bill reintroduced. Dennett then had league members in Philadelphia pressure George Graham of that city, chairman of the House Judiciary Committee, to hold a hearing on it. A joint committee of the House and Senate scheduled one. Still abed, Burke sent telegrams to Dr. George Stewart, president of New York Academy of Medicine, and Dr. Edward Keyes, president of American Social Hygiene Association, to have them protest against the bill. Keyes was in Europe, and before Stewart responded, Burke took a turn for the worse.[8]

He informed Lynch he "had a rather bad set back," necessitating return to St. Vincent's Hospital for surgery. "What exactly it is to be," he told her, "I do not know." The record is silent about the type of operation, which occurred near Easter (20 April). It is unlikely it was heart surgery, something scarcely in its infancy at the time, yet it was far more serious than Burke had anticipated. The medical staff dressed his wound for the first time exactly a week after Easter.[9]

Nor was there rest for the weary. Within days of the operation, Ryan approached Burke about the immigration restriction bill. In late February, David Reed of Pennsylvania introduced its companion in the Senate. His version lacked the non-quota feature for clergy contained in Johnson's, and both excluded aliens ineligible for citizenship. Two years earlier, the Supreme Court had ruled that since Japanese were not Caucasian, they could not become citizens. In his protest to Johnson's bill, Burke had argued that this feature constituted an insult to races against which it was prejudiced. That was exactly how the Japanese took it. Their reaction was universally hostile, prompting rallies in Tokyo and elsewhere. Their government objected to

Secretary of State Charles Evans Hughes, who complained to Congress it was an affront to a friendly nation. Rear Admiral Shinjiro Yamamoto, the most prominent Catholic in Japan, twice cabled Archbishop Pietro Fumasoni-Biondi, apostolic delegate to the United States and former delegate to Japan, urging him to do whatever he could to halt the bill's passage.[10]

Fumasoni-Biondi summoned Ryan. The delegate felt he himself could do nothing. Yet, he was concerned because the FCC and Methodists had protested the exclusion of Japanese, while the Catholic Church remained silent. Moreover, he feared angry mobs in Japan might attack Catholic and Protestant churches. Although the Administrative Committee should take no stand on exclusion, he believed a statement of international friendship, world peace, and common humanity might create a favorable atmosphere. Fumasoni-Biondi wanted his intervention kept completely out of the affair.[11]

Ryan sought Burke's advice about suggesting such a statement to the committee. His concern was that Hanna had often spoken against the FCC's propaganda on behalf of Japan. Burke replied, "Strange, I was just about to write on the matter," indicating even in the aftermath of surgery his mind was on NCWC business. With the self-deprecating comment his "head may not be working so well—if it did ever work well," he drafted a statement and also a cover letter to make it seem the idea was his, rather than the delegate's.[12]

The essential portion declared there were heartening signs of enduring peace among nations previously at enmity with each other. Its preservation should govern America's thoughts, aims, and dealings. While the nation must look to its own welfare, it should refuse "to give offense" and "need not unfairly discriminate against particular peoples." Under divine providence, the country must take the lead in many fields of world activity. "Charity as well as justice to all, ill-feeling and discourtesy to none," concluded Burke in Lincolnesque terms, "will keep us as a nation in the way of righteousness." The Administrative Committee adopted and issued the statement.[13]

In the end, the NCWC was unable to secure the changes it wished in the Reed-Johnson bill. When the Senate and House appointed a conference committee to resolve differences in their versions, Bruce Mohler conferred with congressmen who assured him the Senate would accept the non-quota feature for clergy in the House version favored by the NCWC, but in return the House would have to accept the restriction clauses. In fact, Congress met the Church only half-way about clergy, reducing from four to two the number of years a priest must serve in ministry before being permitted to migrate to America. It turned a deaf ear to the NCWC's plea that the non-quota class include wives and children of permanent resident aliens intending citizenship. From bed, Burke did his best to explain in a circular to the hierarchy the NCWC's efforts and what prevented a satisfactory outcome. Even so, Ryan reported the matter greatly "aroused" the bishops. A large number were "quite upset" because they recruited students in foreign seminaries to serve in their dioceses, and now recruits would have to wait two years after ordination before entry into the country.[14]

By end of the first week in May, Burke was permitted out of bed and out of doors. He walked for two blocks near the hospital and hoped Dr. Mohan would allow him to say Mass Sunday, but that was not to be. Shortly thereafter, Mohan released him, and Burke returned to Washington for a day or two. "The trip … did not go so well," he told Lynch. He suffered a physical setback in D.C., and left for more rest at the Homestead, a resort hotel in Hot Springs in the Alleghenies of Virginia. Burke took up residence in one of the resort's outlying cottages. Given the elevation, nights and mornings were cool. "It is set in the bowl of the mountains: ringed about by them," he wrote to his niece, Elizabeth Salmon. "They make an attractive setting." It was quiet and his existence retreat-like. He was physically unable to play golf, the only amusement there. He hoped to regain strength by taking walks, but weather did not permit. It was rainy and cool, and what he needed was warmth. Having to give so much attention to himself tried him and took away from work for the NCWC. He kept up on its correspondence, though not without a great deal of rest. When James R. Ryan of the Legal Department visited him, he reported Burke had not risen until afternoon. He said Mass on 26 May for the first time since Passion Sunday (13 April), "and the ordeal seemed too much for him."[15]

At the end of the month, James H. Ryan, who had negotiated on Burke's behalf with the Rockefeller Foundation, told him it granted the Service School only $15,000 (270,000 in 2024). The news was disappointing. "Anyway one third of a loaf is better than none," wrote Burke. Ryan explained the foundation could not have acted otherwise. It never made annual grants to an unincorporated institution, and the Service School belonged to the NCCW.[16] This information charted the course Burke and the school would follow on his return to work. He negotiated to have it incorporated as the National Catholic School of Social Service (the NCSSS), placed jointly under the Administrative Committee and the NCCW. With that, the foundation awarded the next two annual payments of $15,000.[17]

Of more immediate concern was the Ku Klux Klan. As seen in the previous chapter, the Indianapolis branch of the NCCM demanded an anti-Klan plank of both parties. It had done so without required permission of the local bishop or NCWC. Now, a representative of the NCCM called for the Indiana State Democratic Convention to endorse an anti-Klan plank. James H. Ryan telegraphed news to Burke. He wired back that if the NCCM's national board authorized the action, Ryan must veto it at once. After pondering overnight, Burke telegraphed the next morning it would be a mistake to force a retraction by the chapter. Ryan agreed. Burke was adamant, however, the national NCCM must remain neutral.[18]

This incident caused Ryan grave concern. The political situation was "full of dynamite," he told Burke. It called for subtlety rather than "strong-arm methods." Thus far, no one at headquarters had injected religion into the mix, but Ryan feared the upcoming Democratic national convention might be the catalyst for it. The Klan was strong enough to hope it might nominate the presidential candidate. Anti-Klan Senator Oscar Underwood of Alabama, a front-running nominee, intended to place Ku-Kluxism squarely before the convention. Another front-runner was Al Smith, Catholic governor of New York, so the religious issue would be a highlight. Ryan particularly worried about press director Justin McGrath, who was almost manic about the Klan. Ryan suggested Burke send him a letter cautioning against imprudence.[19]

Instead of singling out McGrath, Burke sent Ryan a lengthy instruction for all at headquarters. He said the mind of the Administrative Committee was definite: the NCWC would never trade political support for concessions. This was an absolute and cardinal principle. It was also "a primary truth" that the NCWC was "absolutely opposed to Ku Klux Klanism," as should be every American. Admitting all Catholics instinctively hoped both parties would adopt an anti-Klan plank, Burke declared the NCWC could never come out for one party or another simply because it stood for or against the Klan. "It would be a sad and wretched mistake," he said, "for the Church … to barter for political advantage her spiritual independence." He considered the action of the Indianapolis chapter "unfortunate" and "lawless." As individuals, Catholics were free to support or oppose whatever they chose and to vote for whomever they pleased. The NCWC stood "for political liberty." In his absence, Burke wanted Ryan to reinforce this policy among department heads. Although he thought coreligionists might criticize the NCWC for being insufficiently Catholic on a supposedly "critical Catholic question," it must remain free from partisan politics. "As the charge against the Church is that she is a political power or aims to be such," concluded Burke, "We to whom has been entrusted her public national position must sacredly strive to keep her position intact, above suspicion."[20]

Regarding the party conventions, the NCWC had two objectives: prevent endorsement of the Sterling-Reed bill and avoid official involvement on the Klan issue. Burke told Ryan to attend those of both parties. "But I strongly believe that you should have a layman as the one who would appear generally at committees and at meetings," he advised. "Indeed unless it would come to a very critical point, I don't think you, a priest, should be known as 'appearing' or advocating." Burke suggested he take Frank Crowley, new director of the Bureau of Education. When Underwood declared he would attack the Klan for anti-Catholicism and anti-Semitism, Burke advised Ryan against approaching any Democratic leaders directly for the time being.[21]

In fact, Ryan was to take William Cochran of the Legal Department to both conventions, probably because of his political connections as well as personal tie with Homer Cummings, who was the apparent choice for chairmanship of the Democratic platform committee. Before departing for the Republican convention in Cleveland, Ryan informed Muldoon that at Burke's instruction he would make no appearance nor have any direct contact with party members unless pressure for endorsement of the Sterling-Reed bill became too strong.[22]

The Republican convention coincided with the twenty-fifth anniversary of Burke's ordination to the priesthood. Typically, this occasion was celebrated as a jubilee event, much like a silver wedding anniversary. Given his circumstances, however, the forty-nine-year-old Burke expected to celebrate it alone. He was surprised when his sister Lizzie, brother James, Grace Murray, and Gertrude Delahunt showed up at Hot Springs. He said Mass for them. Helen Lynch and the sisters of the Cenacle sent him a model of a cathedral they made by hand. Inside its several doors were well wishes from various nuns. Burke gave it place of honor on the cottage mantelpiece. His secretary Iona McNulty, who considered him a mystic, though of a practical sort, sent greetings wherein she congratulated him on dreaming up the NCWC.[23]

The next day, Burke responded to her with a letter wherein he intended simply to describe the celebration. McNulty's mention of his part in creation of the NCWC, however, sent him into a spiritual reflection on his life in Christ. He explained he had not "thought out" the NCWC; it had been "given" to him. He considered it a "self evident proposition." "Granting Christ and the Church" he wrote, "it is nothing else but Himself living in the Church and we living in Him and her." McNulty was correct that he spent himself in realizing the vision. Doing so had probably cost him his health "and some years of life," but it also had saved him. "What I have done, I would for Christ's sake do again —if He again gave me the power," he explained.

> For apart from all work and all men I do love Him with a passionate love. I think He is everything. He gave Himself for me. He is not only all Truth: He is ever truth. He is not only all Love He is ever love. He to me is my mother, my father, my brothers and sisters.... He is not only all Beauty, He is every beauty. And what I try to express in truth or love or beauty is but part of Christ.
>
> Yet, what wins me is His love for me. He would love me with the same infinite love were I the only creature. He spends Himself for me: He watches He follows: He draws me from the pit of my own shame. He seeks not Himself—He is the daily Mass, offering Himself for me, giving Himself to me. His love is so great that it actually craves me, and with infinite, ceaseless native honesty it is seeking me.... And yet I may say I love Him not for myself, not for what He can bring to me, I love Him for

> Himself. In one sense I care not what may happen to me for I know I love Him and in that love is all my joy. I love Him for Himself, conquering, consuming, glorious. I long to give. It is not sacrifice nor do I wish Him to think it so: it is joy, it is delight, it is life.... He won't withdraw himself. He comes with His wisdom when I am confounded: and I have found Him joyfully in suffering and known His presence in the bleak long hours of night. A terrible, long re-birth this being born of Him yet His patience is inexhaustible. His Hands skillful, and we know His will, is being done.

When Burke finished this stream-of-conscious reflection, he reread it and told McNulty he had written "what I did not intend to write." Like Pontius Pilate, he let it stand; he had written what he had written. "Tell the words to no man," he ordered her: "and let not the letter ever be seen whether I am in the flesh or out of it. It is but aspirations and I am poor in the accomplishment—a spiritual Lord Jim."[24]

This was the sort of letter Burke would have written to Lynch. To her, however, he simply described events of the anniversary and told her it would take too long to recount his inner feelings about it. He said his time at Hot Springs was like being on retreat, yet he was in almost daily contact with headquarters and was still directing much of the work, especially about the education question.[25]

Indeed, the day after the celebration, Ryan telegraphed that the platform committee would likely recommend the position Coolidge had taken in his first state-of-the-union message. It would go no further than "recommendation of [the] Reorganization Committee." The wire puzzled Burke because of his tentative recollection of what Coolidge said. Yet, his return telegram showed he correctly remembered. Burke told Ryan if the resolution upheld the president's declaration that education was primarily a local matter and federal assistance should be limited to advice, he could accept the plank. If the party simply recommended the Reorganization bill without committing to it, he could accept that too. "No indirect or equivocal support [of] centralization to be permitted," ordered Burke.[26]

Usually, the words "recommendation" and "commitment" are roughly equivalent terms implying endorsement. Yet, in this case, Burke clearly intended a distinction between them, with "recommendation" signifying a preference for one among several options versus a definite endorsement of (commitment to) a particular option. In other words, if the convention simply "recommended" the Reorganization bill with its proposed department of education and welfare, that would be acceptable. If it committed itself to (endorsed) the measure, that was not. Clearly, Burke now definitely considered the Reorganization bill a step—"indirect or equivocal"—toward further centralization. In fact, however, that was not how Coolidge or the party understood it. For them, it aimed simply at more efficient coordination of existing federal functions.

Two days later, the convention adopted a platform declaring the government's educational aid to states should be limited to the "benefit of its counsel." To coordinate the government's "numerous and important" activities, the party endorsed "the suggestion" for a department of education and relief. Ryan telegraphed news to Burke, with the comment the plank was "very innocuous" and "satisfactory." At the convention's end, he explained to Burke: "Party loyalty practically compelled them to do this much. There is not the slightest chance of this measure passing the short session of Congress." Ryan made the same point to Muldoon, adding some type of reorganization of the government's educational functions was necessary.[27]

On 30 June, Ryan and Cochran went to New York for what turned out to be "a very exciting week" at the Democratic convention. The political atmosphere was explosive. With the Klan in control of several state delegations, Underwood allied himself with Smith's supporters to ask for condemnation of the Hooded Empire by name, resulting in an acrimonious fight that split the convention in two. The Klan had no choice but to back the third front runner, William Gibbs McAdoo, a Georgia-born Californian. Despite the volatility, Ryan took a high profile because the NEA, rebuffed by the Republicans, came to New York in force to press endorsement of the Sterling-Reed bill. He saw Cummings, chair of the platform committee, and other members to explain the Catholic position. They were receptive and, as he later expressed it, "stood behind us loyally."[28] That was an understatement. The party adopted an education plank coauthored by Ryan and Edward Pace. Upholding the "sovereign right" of states in education, each was responsible for the instruction of its citizens and "for the expenditure of the moneys collected by taxation for the support of its schools." The plank added the federal government should offer "such counsel, advice and aid as may be made available through the Federal agencies."[29]

The real excitement, however, occurred around the Klan. Calls for its condemnation by name, touched off raucous demonstrations and fist fights on the floor. Meanwhile, the platform committee engaged in contentious debate for two days. Cummings tried to draw from Ryan the NCWC's stand on the Klan, "but of course, I had nothing to say about it," he told Burke. Not so, prominent Knight of Columbus Patrick Callahan, who testified before the committee that he spoke for the American Catholic hierarchy. Ryan told Burke he had previously advised Cummings no one had the right to speak for the bishops on this matter. After much wrangling, the committee endorsed a plank proposed by William Jennings Bryan: a reaffirmation of constitutionally protected liberties without mention of the Klan. When the platform came before the convention, the minority report called for condemnation of the Klan. After two hours' debate, the convention adopted Bryan's plank by one vote.[30]

Throughout this time, Burke's health remained tenuous. After his anniversary, he told Murray while he felt better, he at times suffered a weakness he could not explain nor did he know if it was imaginary or real, whether it was caused by mental work or not. When it overtook him, all he could do was "lie down and be quiet." It did not happen often, so he urged her not to worry and tell no one. Two weeks later, Burke was well enough to tell Ryan he would return to Washington on 7 July to spend a couple of days arranging the program for the hierarchy's annual convention. On the Fourth, however, he had an attack of the old fever. That morning he went up to the hotel to hear distinguished orator Chauncey Depew speak. Afterward he took a walk and had lunch. At 3:30 the fever struck and lasted until about 8:00 P.M. the next evening. Nurse Barbara Sandmaier came down to assist him, and Dr. Pohle, a local physician, attended him daily for five days without charge. Both Pohle and Burke wrote to Dr. Mohan in New York, who wanted Burke to come up for examination, something Burke considered "almost laughable." A week later he felt well enough to return to Washington to draft the program, after which he planned to join his sister, Lizzie, in the White Mountains of New Hampshire.[31]

Once the program was out, however, Burke went instead to the Buena Vista Springs Hotel in the Alleghenies at the southern border of Pennsylvania. He found it difficult to settle in, thinking of the missed trip to New Hampshire and harking back to the "secluded, private cottage" in Hot Springs, a place far more beautiful. He told Lynch the only thing that made the place bearable was a chapel on its grounds. His room was "fairly good," but he knew a great many lodgers from whom he found it hard to get away. He played golf for the first time in a year. Burke confided to McNulty his experience of the previous months had been "unsatisfactory": awareness of the NCWC's work, but not being part of it; subjection to medical directions with which he often disagreed; being mastered by circumstance rather than mastering it. "Yet all I can see is an acceptance," he told her: "a waiting upon a sphinx like future." Evidence suggests he informed his superior general about resigning and had left a letter of resignation with McNulty as he pondered whether to send it. "After all in one way my going (if such is to be) can in one way be looked upon as if it were not. What is, endures," he explained to her. "Of course it may not be: it may be my superiors will wish me to keep on with the work."[32]

Burke was pleasantly surprised when Lizzie came down with Delahunt to stay with him rather than go to New Hampshire. The two women liked Buena Vista Springs and its peace and quiet.[33] Burke repaid his sister's kindness by writing a novena to the Holy Spirit for her. Each of the nine days of the devotion opened with the prayer "Come, Holy Spirit, fill the hearts of your faithful ..." to be followed by the Sequence—a hymn in irregular meter—from the Mass of Pentecost. He wrote conferences for each day, an introductory one for the opening day and a concluding one for the ninth, while the intervening seven treated consecutively each gift of the Holy Spirit. The initial conference stressed devotion to the Spirit as of "the supremest [sic] importance" because He was "the source of all love: the soul of our prayers." Burke rightly noted the gift of fear of the lord was neither servile nor motivated by punishment. Rather, it was born of overwhelming love of God making one fear "to fail in duty: to miss opportunity, to give offense to God," to disappoint a loving Father. That gift was closely related to piety, which consisted in living in the house of one's soul always in the presence of "Our Father," knowing and trusting in his tenderness and care, eagerly cooperating with him. "By the gift of piety the Holy Spirit enables us to realize this."[34]

About the gift of knowledge, Burke held even the simplest truths concerning created things were insufficient unless related to their origin: God. The acquisition of true knowledge consisted in breaking the bars of desire and letting go of one's "lesser self" to place oneself in "right relation to true knowledge." That knowledge came only from God the creator. "Through the Holy Spirit He created," wrote Burke. "The same Holy Spirit dwells in us, to give us that knowledge of created things and of God which is also the highest knowledge of self."[35]

The gift of counsel was related to piety, which led to abandonment of self to God: the willingness to make oneself his instrument. Amid daily anxiety and strife, the soul yearned to know what God would have it do or decide. Burke noted the Holy Spirit was always within, awaiting the soul's attention. "Thoughtful consultation with Him will bring the true answer," he said. "By habit we can become His faithful disciples and always know what it is the Lord would have us do."[36]

A self-described spiritual Lord Jim, Burke understood the need for the gift of fortitude. He realized "the vast difference between resolution and accomplishment." As alluring as was intention to follow Christ, execution was "distasteful, difficult, uninviting." Courage to brave it came only from God through the Holy Spirit. By the gift of fortitude the Spirit supplemented the weak will, moving it to sacrifice to become one with Christ.[37]

The gift of understanding was deep appreciation of what God had done for humans. "The most efficient incentive to love is the esteem in which one is held by the beloved," wrote Burke. When a person began to understand even slightly the partnership to which God invited the soul, it compelled love. The mystery of the Trinity; a person's creation and redemption in Christ; oneness with him in the Holy Spirit; the Eucharistic bread which eternally quenched hunger [John 6: 32–35]; the universal motherhood of Mary—Burke considered these the "solid meat which nourish the virile Christian life." Through understanding, the Holy Spirit made all "these intelligible practical truths to us, that we, by some means, may apprehend wherein we also are apprehended by Christ Jesus."[38] This gift enabled the Christian to participate in the inner life of the Trinity, including the mission of Jesus.

The gift of wisdom was "to see as God sees," which gave insight to the meaning of the Christian life. "The nearer one draws to Him, the harder life becomes," wrote Burke. "The old peace passes: suffering, misfortune seem to mark those who love God." As the letter to the Hebrews said, God tried those whom he loved and scourged those he received (Hebrews 12: 5–6). Burke may also have been thinking of St. Teresa of Avila, patroness of Paulists, who was reputed to have told God that if this was the way he treated his friends, it was no wonder he had so few. "To be a faithful lover it is necessary not only to know: not only to understand but to taste how sweet is the love of God," advised Burke. "To love the word of God, and to trust it, to find therein our delight is wisdom.... Only the Light of God Himself can show us that sense and desire and human sight will of themselves lead to darkness." To see oneself, creatures, and created things with the eyes of God was wisdom.[39]

The final conference returned to the Holy Spirit. Burke would not have Lizzie "forget the Giver, in thinking of the gifts." The Spirit brought forth all of creation and overshadowed Mary, who conceived the redeemer. The Spirit descended as fire on the apostles bringing forth the Church. The Spirit dwelt in the soul of every faithful believer. Therein the Spirit initiated and completed the work of sanctification. "Love labors for that which it loves," wrote Burke. "To Thee I owe every inspiration, every good deed accomplished & every help I have been to others, every ray that I will add to the glory of God. To ears that are open Thou speakest: to eyes watchful Thou revealest: to hand ready Thou givest power: possess me. Every day will I be attentive to Thy voice.... I will love Thee as my wisdom, knowing that Thou wilt build me up, incorporate me into Him, the Perfect Man, my God and my Saviour, Jesus Christ."[40]

While Burke was at Buena Vista Springs, the Administrative Committee voted him an extended vacation. For his part, Burke decided to resign. In late August, he asked advice of his brother, Thomas, who himself was recuperating from a serious illness. Thomas told John not to submit his resignation at this time. Both Hanna and Muldoon had told Thomas, unsolicited, that apart from John's illness, the bishops would have given him the vacation just for the change and rest it would afford him. To tender his resignation at this moment, explained Thomas, would only embarrass them by calling into question their motive for awarding him time away. In any case, they certainly would not accept it. He was also convinced Superior General Joseph McSorley shared this view. John's accomplishments for the

Church and country deeply gratified the Paulist community upon which those achievements reflected. The fact that McSorley had not reassigned John meant he wanted him to continue where he was. Thomas told his brother to take the vacation and make it a real one, completely away from NCWC work. If afterward, he felt he could not continue, then he could tender his resignation.[41]

A TURBULENT FORCED REST

By September, Burke's thoughts were neither about vacation nor rest nor resignation. He felt well and suffered no setbacks. "My hope is that I will be allowed to go back definitely to the work," he told Lynch. "With care and restraint I think I could handle it." To Murray, who knew his concerns at the NCWC and how seriously he took them, he explained he could not just cast them on God; he had to play his part, but without going beyond his strength, so he must "leave much to God." He promised to exercise temperance with regard to work.[42]

McSorley was glad he was feeling better. His concern was about Burke's living situation when he returned to the NCWC. The recent general chapter called for reuniting Paulists in community life, and he inquired if Burke would be willing to live at either of the two Paulist houses in Washington instead of the NCWC residence. Burke explained that as general secretary, he represented the Administrative Committee, which in turn represented the hierarchy. He feared by living in a Paulist house, people might think his work was for the community rather than the Church. Priests on staff lived together in the home next to the Service School, and, when the bishops of the committee were in Washington, they visited there. Moreover, the house was just blocks from the apostolic delegation. The delegate often visited to discuss issues concerning the NCWC, and frequently summoned Burke to see him about important matters. Living elsewhere would seriously hamper these relationships. Finally, Burke was chaplain at the Service School, which work would be seriously affected. As a loyal Paulist, however, he placed himself "unreservedly and without reluctance" at the will of the General Council and would abide by its decision.[43] McSorley and the council permitted him to live apart.

This letter illustrates Burke's understanding of Paulist obedience, which differed from military obedience. As a Paulist, one first expressed his best mind about a matter to his superior, then followed whatever the superior ordered. It was the sort of obedience he inculcated in and sought from others.[44]

McSorley was not about to let Burke get away with going directly back to work. He spoke with Dr. Mohan, who insisted that rest was "imperative" at least through January 1925. If Burke was "reasonably careful" after that, he would probably be able "to get into the harness again and work for an indefinitely long period." Mohan wanted him to see Dr. Lee and get his advice. McSorley expected him to carry out Mohan's instruction. Within a week, Drs. Marbury and Lee weighed in on the situation. Both wanted Burke to continue resting, and the heart specialist advised he play no more than nine holes of golf at any one time. Burke's brother, Thomas, agreed that as soon as the hierarchy's convention was over, his sibling should leave Washington. McSorley was of like mind. "Away down deep in your heart *you know* that you will work if you are there; it would be almost superhuman to do otherwise," he wrote. "Then, after Christmas, we can find out if you are fit to buckle on the harness again,—and in the meantime we can let all other questions rest."[45]

Already, however, a matter was brewing that would soon intrude on Burke's time away. Shortly after the political conventions, the Conference for Progressive Political Action nominated Senator Robert LaFollette of Wisconsin as independent candidate for president, with the intention of forming a third party after the election. John Lapp, co-director of the Social Action Department, informed Muldoon of his intention, as private citizen, to speak on LaFollette's behalf. Muldoon warned him it would be practically "impossible" not to be identified with the NCWC. Still, Lapp publicly announced he would stump for LaFollette. An Associated Press release in the *Washington Star* identified him with the NCWC. When Burke read the item, he immediately telegraphed Muldoon "this must be a mistake" because agents were not to get involved in politics. Muldoon replied there was no mistake. When he recently stopped in Chicago on his way to Providence, Rhode Island, he saw Lapp, who said he expressly told the AP not to report his position in the NCWC. He was surprised it made the identification against his wishes. Still, he defended his right to speak as citizen.[46] His attitude did not bode well for Burke's rest.

When the Administrative Committee met in September, Burke said his doctors and superior general had ordered him to travel for extended rest. The bishops expressed sympathy and regret that "his hard work for the NCWC should have entailed such sacrifice on his part." They reappointed James H. Ryan interim general secretary. Indeed, Burke had much need of vacation. The strenuous work for the convention of the hierarchy left him "fatigued, and 'knocked out' afterwards," delaying his departure. He reported to Lynch the bishops of the committee had been "very kind" to him. "It is embarrasing [*sic*] to see the trust they place in me," he told her. "Their appreciation is unmerited."[47]

In early October, Burke finally left Washington, destined for St. Paul. Archbishop Austin Dowling had invited him to rest there until he was ready to travel. Burke told Murray he felt "almost criminal" leaving, driven out like Hagar and her unborn son Ishmael (Gen. 16:6). He said neither Mohan nor McSorley trusted him not to work if he remained at home. He made a brief stop in Chicago where he dined with Lapp, who wore a large LaFollette button on his jacket. Burke was not pleased, but kept his thoughts to himself. He considered it best to stay for a week of rest with Muldoon in Rockford before continuing to the Twin Cities. He felt well, no attack of fever or tiredness. "Am leading a lazy life and don't particularly care for it," he told McNulty. Rockford was beautiful at that time of year. "The leaves are falling: the cold of fall announces its coming. I think it particularly attractive to see at night from the street the homes and the lights therein, they speak of comforting love and security … against an 'outside' world," he wrote. "It is the 'reminder' of what once was mine, and the hope of what will be mine forever. The autumn always reminds me of the warm fire and the cracking and eating of nuts and a sort of harvest mood."[48]

When Burke reached St. Paul, he came down with a terrible cold, landing him in bed. He occupied the time by writing several short verses:

"No thorn a grape can ever yield"
    All nature says "amen"
But Thou hast made the wood to bleed
    And pour forth wine to men.

*****

O Christ is my weak prayer
    Part of Thy strong grace?

And is the world made bare
That we may see Thy face?
*****

Christ to Thee upon the Tree
I shall dedicated be.
This my whole philosophy
Not to please myself but Thee.

Burke asked Murray to give them titles, for he could think of none. He told Lynch she might think he had time on his hands, but the kindness of his hosts left him no time alone. Although there was no golf to be played in St. Paul, he and Dowling's secretary, Father Rudie Nolan, played cribbage voraciously. And Burke was a skilled cribbage player, winning most of the games. Still, he missed his spiritual daughters. "I'm hungry for some news from you," he told Murray. His word to Lynch: "Please drop all work and write me."[49]

At this point, work intruded on his forced rest. At issue was the Child Labor Amendment and the LaFollette campaign's use of the NCWC. Congress had before it eighteen different amendments to end child labor, one of them coauthored by John Ryan. Burke had asked the Administrative Committee if it wished to endorse one. The bishops refused, considering the matter best left to the states. Ryan, however, had gotten the annual convention of the NCCW to pass a non-binding resolution in favor of such an amendment. When Congress held a hearing on the issue, Regan appeared to support such a measure. In June 1924, Congress passed the Child Labor Amendment, and three months later the Social Action Department released two newsletters which, without endorsing it, defended it and explained why advocates cited the Bishops' Program of Reconstruction in its favor.[50]

While Burke was in St. Paul, Cardinal William O'Connell renewed his attack on the NCWC using that amendment as his weapon. He ordered Boston Catholics to vote no on the state's advisory referendum on it.[51] To Bishop Edmund Gibbons of the Legal Department, O'Connell accused Burke, Regan, and John Ryan of being "tied up with some of the dangerous influences at the Capital" in favor of "that nefarious and bolshevik" amendment and of crediting their views to the hierarchy. Unless corrected very soon, warned O'Connell, they were "driving fast toward a public condemnation."[52] He told Bishop Joseph Schrembs of the Lay Activities Department the three were "lacking in certain fundamentals and had better be watched." "Bureaucracy knows how to get a hold of some of our agents—who want a job," continued O'Connell, "and unless their loyalty is beyond question, before we know it we shall be compromised and involved." He wanted Schrembs to investigate "whether our agents are on the right side."[53] Schrembs informed Burke of O'Connell's accusations and urgently requested information. Unaware that Burke was in Minnesota, he sent the letter to D.C., so it took several days to make its way to St. Paul.[54]

Meanwhile, O'Connell sent Monsignor Michael Splaine, to Washington to have Regan call a meeting of the Executive Committee of the NCCW to repeal the organization's non-binding support of an amendment. She refused. Splaine then tried to get John Ryan to change his position. He too refused. Two days later, O'Connell's Boston *Pilot* ran an editorial quoting the Vatican instructions on reinstatement of the NCWC that it was not to be identified with the hierarchy. So, declarations of its departments were not "authoritative." Both the Press and Social Action Departments recently released articles commending the Child Labor Amendment. In this case, NCWC agents aired views "wholly unrepresentative of the true position of the Hierarchy."[55]

James H. Ryan considered the editorial "very unfair." He reported to Schrembs neither Press Department nor Social Action Department took a position on the amendment. Ryan ordered Regan to stand her ground and sent a letter to Father George Leech, secretary of the apostolic delegate, to explain the situation. He thought Burke ought to write O'Connell denying the charges and stating his opposition to the amendment. In fact, both Burke and James Ryan objected to it as the wrong approach to the problem. Burke refused to "plead [his] personal views to escape a corporate responsibility and a corporate loyalty." Instead, he explained to Schrembs: "The hidden and chief falsity of the editorial is the supposition made therein that the Hierarchy has taken a positive position on the Child Labor Amendment and that that position is against. Having ingeniously [disingenuously?] supposed this, given that impression to readers (but giving absolutely no proof) the editorial charges that the agents of the Bishops … are … misrepresenting the Hierarchy." Burke reminded Schrembs the Administrative Committee had taken no position on the amendment. Nor had either the Press or Social Action Departments endorsed it. He hoped authorities in Rome would not be misinformed about the matter.[56]

In the midst of this flap came word the LaFollette campaign used the Social Action Department in support of a plank in its platform. Because the Supreme Court had struck down laws curbing child labor, the platform called for a constitutional amendment for direct election of all federal justices for fixed terms and authorizing Congress to override a judicial veto of legislation. The LaFollette headquarters quoted a statement by the department countering arguments against this amendment. Scarcely had Burke sent the above letter to Schrembs when the rector of the St. Paul seminary, the rector of the pro-cathedral, and the head of the archdiocesan social study club arrived at Dowling's door to show Burke the circular and demand to know what was going on. When they left, Burke telegraphed John Ryan to ask the source of the extract. Ryan replied it came from a news sheet the department issued, but was used without permission.[57]

The next day brought a letter from James H. Ryan who also received a copy of the circular. "It seems to me that the Social Action Department has, in spite of all warnings, come over bag and baggage to the Third Party," he told Burke. Recounting the visit by the three clergymen, Burke replied Dowling was very upset by the situation and insisted something be done "to clean it up." "The Social Action [Department] lacks dignity and reticence," wrote Burke. "Innocently enough perhaps they talk to these outsiders—and the outsiders do the rest." So, he drafted a release acknowledging newspapers had recently carried various declarations claiming to have approval of the NCWC or phrased in such way as to give that impression. "We wish to state that no authorized pronouncement on any political question has been made or will be made, by the N.C.W.C. or any of its departments," read the release. "The N.C.W.C. does not consider it within the scope of its activities to enter into political campaigns. It has made no statement in favor of or against any political party or candidate." When Dowling approved it, Burke sent a copy to Muldoon for his blessing. He then telegraphed it to Justin McGrath with orders to issue it over Hanna's signature as chairman of the Administrative Committee to the Associated Press and the United Press services and every Catholic newspaper.[58]

Bringing McNulty up to date on events, Burke gave her a blow by blow of what had transpired. He said O'Connell had no more interest in child welfare than he had "in polar expeditions." Burke noted the cardinal supported reelection of President Calvin Coolidge, whose platform endorsed the Child Labor Amendment, but "consistency must not be looked for." He said O'Connell had also sent Muldoon a letter about the situation, "and mirabile dictu he [the cardinal] writes he must protect the good name of the NCWC. (This is the place to laugh.)"[59]

Burke lamented he lacked command to help in the matter as he wished. Nor had he, sidelined as he was, the resources necessary to do it. "All this demands a momentary touch with the work," he told Murray, "actual reading of all correspondence, free use of telephone and telegraph, and a secretary, a typist, one who can tell you whether you've answered a letter or not, one who can take dictation intelligently, keep copies of letters, get things for you, keep your table in order, bear the expression of anger at your own mistakes as if she were to blame, meet every exaction, bear unjust blame and smile complacently, you know the type of saint required."[60] Indeed she did. This was Burke's admission to her of the sort of exacting perfectionist he was.

In early November, O'Connell demanded Archbishop Michael Curley, chancellor of Catholic University, require John Ryan, James Ryan, and William Kerby, alleged supporters of the amendment, "either cease their crooked and false activities or leave the University and the offices of the N.C.W.C." Instead, Curley explained their positions and defended the three faculty members. James Ryan informed Burke of this attack, reporting people at the university and headquarters were disturbed and agitated by it. "It seems I have been honored," remarked Ryan, "by being put in the radical camp."[61]

Shortly after the election, Burke was in Cleveland to meet with Schrembs and James Ryan. He said he and Dowling believed the situation was serious enough to warrant a written report to the apostolic delegate and the Vatican about the Administrative Committee's position on the amendment. Dowling already expressed his opinion on the affair to Hanna: "Boston is doing his *damndest* to bust the N.C.W.C. once more." When Burke spoke with Muldoon by phone about a written report, the bishop thought only a verbal update should be given the delegate. Ryan and

Schrembs, on the other hand, agreed with Burke and Dowling. They wanted Burke to draft for Hanna's signature a letter explaining the mind and actions of the committee. Hanna should send it to Cardinal Pietro Gasparri, Vatican secretary of State, and also to Cardinal Gaetano de Lai, secretary of the Consistorial Congregation. Burke wrote the letter, but, admitting his "need [of] a 'keeper,'" mixed it with correspondence he was taking to Washington for filing. It was two weeks before the error was caught and McNulty could forward the letter to Hanna. Nothing indicates that he took the desired action.[62]

Meanwhile, James Ryan wrote and submitted to the apostolic delegate a memorandum explaining the amendment, the NCWC's position, and O'Connell's accusations. Early in December, he reported to Burke, who was then away in the Caribbean, that "Boston is still making noise but I think that everybody is on to him." The delegate, Fumasoni-Biondi, certainly was. He reported to Gasparri that O'Connell was again seeking to assert dominance over the hierarchy, but the "dislike of the episcopate for him remains unchanged and total."[63]

Endnotes to Chapter 12

1. Burke, *Christ in Us*, 159.
2. Muldoon to Burke, 14 November 1923, ACUA, USCCB 10:152:29; Burke to Murray, 26 February 1924, AP, Burke Papers, box 11; Burke to Lynch, 23 March 1924, ibid., box 5.
3. Burke to Hanna, 9 February 1924, AASF, NCWC files; Burke to J. H. Ryan, 27 May 1924, ibid., 10:153:4; Burke to Hawks, 27 March 1927, AP, Burke Papers, box 10; Lawler, *Full Circle*, 113–14.
4. Burke to Hanna, 9 February 1924, AASF, NCWC files; Burke to J. H. Ryan, 28 February 1924, ACUA, USCCB 10:153:4; Lawler, *Full Circle*, 93–98.
5. Burke to Murray, 26 February 1924, AP, Burke Papers, box 11; Burke to Lynch, 23 March 1924, ibid., box 5.
6. Mary Merrick to Burke, undated [probably late February or early March 1924], first quote is here; [11 March 1924]; [14 or 21 March 1924] second quote is here; undated [probably late March 1924] third quote is here—all in AP, Burke Papers, box 7. Merrick substitutes "deary" for the correct "heavy" in the subheading of this chapter. See, J. Wilbur Chapman, (Boston: United Society of Christian Endeavor, 1899); D. H. S. Nicholson and A. H. E. Lee, eds. *The Oxford Book of English Mystical Verse* (Oxford: The Clarendon Press, 1917).

7. Burke to Murray, 20 March 1924, AP, Burke Papers, box 11(quotes are here); Burke to Lynch, 23 March 1924, ibid., box 5; Burke to Hanna, 29 March 1924, copy, ACUA, USCCB 10:152:13.
8. Dennett to Philadelphia Members of the Voluntary Parenthood League, 19 March 1924, copy, ACUA, USCCB 10:117:3; Burke to Stewart, telegram, 2 April 1924, ibid.; Howard Jeck (for Edward Keyes) to Burke, 3 April 1924, ibid.; William Snow to Burke, 9 June 1924, ibid.; Chen, *"Sex Side of Life,"* 233–34.
9. Burke to Lynch, 12 April 1924, AP, Burke Papers, box 5; Burke to J. H. Ryan, 27 April 1924, ACUA, USCCB 10:153:4.
10. J. H. Ryan to Burke, 25 April 1924, ACUA, USCCB 10:153:4; *Ozawa* v. *United States*, 260 U.S. 178 (1922); *Congressional Record*, 68th Cong., 1st sess., 1924, 65, pt. 3, 2829, pt. 5, 4395, pt. 7, 6644–49, pt. 8, 8218–24; Izumi Hirobe, *Japanese Pride, American Prejudice: Modifying the Exclusion Clause of the 1924 Immigration Act* (Stanford: Stanford U. Press, 2001), 21–45; Divine, *American Immigration Policy*, 22–23; Castagna, *Bridge across the Ocean*, 95.
11. J. H. Ryan to Burke, 25 April 1924, ACUA, USCCB 10:153:4.
12. Ibid.; Burke to J. H. Ryan, 27 April 1924, ACUA, USCCB 10:153:4.
13. [Burke], "Plea for World Peace Issued by N.C.W.C. Administrative Committee," *NCWC Bulletin* 5 (June 1924): 3; Minutes of the Administrative Committee, 1 May 1924, ACUA, USCCB 10:64:3.
14. J. H. Ryan to Burke, 25 April 1924, ACUA, USCCB 10:153:4; J. H. Ryan to Muldoon, 7 May 1924, copy, ibid., 10:104:13; Burke to the hierarchy, 2 June 1924, copy, ibid., 10:42:1; J. H. Ryan to Burke, 18 June 1924, ibid.; J. H. Ryan to Burke, 3 July 1924, ibid., 10:153:4; *Congressional Record*, 68th Cong., 1st sess., 1924, 65, pt. 7, 6644–49, and pt. 8, 8218–24; "In the Field of Immigration," *NCWC Bulletin* 5 (June 1924): 8.
15. Burke to Lynch, 8 May and 4 June 1924, AP, Burke Papers, box 5 (quotes are from the second); Burke to Elizabeth Salmon, 31 May 1924, ibid., box 4; J. H. Ryan to Muldoon, 7 May 1924, copy, ACUA, USCCB 10:104:13; Burke to Kerby, 23 and 28 May 1924, ACUA, Kerby Papers 58:4:5; Burke to J. H. Ryan, 23 May 1924, ibid., 10:153:4; James R. Ryan to J. H. Ryan, 28 May 1924, ibid.
16. Burke to J. H. Ryan, 29 May 1924, ACUA, USCCB 10:153:4; J. H. Ryan to Burke, 31 May 1924, ibid.
17. Burke to Hanna, 10 February 1925, copy, ACUA, USCCB 10:99:16; Hanna to Burke, telegram, 16 February 1928, ibid.; Minutes of the Administrative Committee, 23 April 1925, ibid., 10:64:4; Malloy, "John Joseph Burke," 723; "National Catholic School of Social Service," *NCWC Bulletin* 8 (September 1925): 21–22; Lawler, *Full Circle*, 97, 100, 110–12.
18. Minutes of the Administrative Committee, 1 May 1924, ACUA, USCCB 10:64:3; J. H. Ryan to Burke, telegram, 25 May 1924, ibid., 10:153:4; Burke

to J. H. Ryan, telegram 25 May 1924, ibid.; Burke to J. H. Ryan, telegram, 26 May 1924, ibid.; J. H. Ryan to Burke, 26 May 1924, ibid.

19. J. H. Ryan to Burke, 2 June 1924, copy, ACUA, USCCB 10:153:4; J. H. Ryan to Muldoon, 20 May 1924, copy, ibid., 10:144:46; Robert K. Murray, *The 103rd Ballot: Democrats and the Disaster in Madison Square Garden* (New York: Harper & Row, 1976), 52–53; David M. Chalmers, *Hooded Americanism: The History of the Ku Klux Klan* (New York: New Viewpoints, 1976), 79–80, 204–05. See also J. H. Ryan to Burke, 23 May 1924, ACUA, USCCB 10:153:4.
20. Burke to J. H. Ryan, 3 June 1924, ACUA, USCCB 10:153:4.
21. J. H. Ryan to Muldoon, 20 May 1924, ACUA, USCCB 10:144:46; J. H. Ryan to Muldoon, 8 July 1924, copy, ibid.; J. H. Ryan to Burke, [23 May 1924], ibid., 10:153:4; Burke to J. H. Ryan, 2 June 1924, ibid.
22. J. H. Ryan to Muldoon, 6 June 1924, copy, ACUA, USCCB 10:144:46.
23. McNulty to Tanner, 6 May 1964, ACUA, USCCB 10:72:24; Burke to McNulty, 10 June 1924, AP, Burke Papers, box 14; Burke to Lynch, 11 June 1924, ibid., box 5.
24. Burke to McNulty, 10 June 1924, AP, Burke Papers, box 14.
25. Burke to Lynch, 11 June 1924, AP, Burke Papers, box 5.
26. J. H. Ryan to Muldoon, 8 July 1924, copy, ACUA, USCCB 10:144:46; J. H. Ryan to Burke, telegram, 9 June 1924, ibid., 10:5:28; J. H. Ryan to Burke, telegram, 11 June 1924, ibid.
27. *New York Times*, 12 June 1924; J. H. Ryan to Burke, telegram, 11 June 1924, ACUA, USCCB 10:5:28; J. H. Ryan to Burke, 18 June 1924, ibid., 10:153:4; J. H. Ryan to Muldoon, 18 June 1924, copy, ibid., 10:144:46.
28. J. H. Ryan to Burke, 24 June 1924, ACUA, USCCB 10:153:4; J. H. Ryan to Gibbons, 8 July 1924, copy, ibid., 10:144:10; J. H. Ryan to Muldoon, 8 July 1924, copy, ibid., 10:144:46; J. H. Ryan to Burke, 30 June 1924, ibid., 10:153:4; Chalmers, *Hooded Americanism*, 204–12; Murray, *103rd Ballot*, 90, 104, 108–09.
29. *New York Times*, 29 June 1924.
30. J. H. Ryan to Burke, 30 June 1924, copy, ACUA, USCCB 10:153:4; Chalmers, *Hooded Americanism*, 203–12 (the quotations of the delegates are on 206); Murray, *103rd Ballot*, 164–218; Burner, *Politics of Provincialism*, 107–35; Hicks, *Republican Ascendancy*, 94–97.
31. Burke to J. H. Ryan, 1 July 1924, ACUA, USCCB 10:153:4; Burke to Murray, 13 June and 13 July 1924, AP, Burke Papers, box 11.
32. Burke to McNulty, Saturday [20 or 27 July 1924], AP, Burke Papers, box 14 (first quote is here); Burke to McNulty, 30 July 1924, ibid. (last quote is here); Burke to Lynch, 14 August 1924, ibid., box 5.
33. Burke to Lynch, 14 August 1924, AP, Burke Papers, box 5
34. Burke, Novena to the Holy Spirit with Prayers from the Missal and Short

Conferences, Done at Buena Vista Springs, Pa., and Transcribed There for Elizabeth by My Own Hand in August 1924, AP, Burke Papers, box 52.

35. Ibid.
36. Ibid.
37. Ibid.
38. Ibid.
39. Ibid.
40. Ibid.
41. T. Burke to Burke, 5 September 1924, AP, Burke Papers, box 3.
42. Burke to Lynch, 5 September 1924, AP, Burke Papers, box 5; Burke to Murray, 6 September 924, ibid., box 11.
43. Burke to McSorley, 15 September 1924, copy, AP, Burke Papers, box 21.
44. Hawks, "Souvenir of Burke," AP, Burke Papers, box 10.
45. McSorley to Burke, 9 September 1924, AP, Burke Papers, box 21; McSorley to Burke, 18 September 1924, ibid.; Burke to Murray, [16 October 1924], ibid., box 11.
46. Burke to Muldoon, telegram, 9 September 1924, ACUA, USCCB 10:104:13; Muldoon to Burke, 15 September 1924, ibid.; John A. Lapp to Muldoon, 16 September 1924, copy, ibid.; John D. Hicks, *The Republican Ascendancy, 1921–1933* (New York: Harper and Row, 1960), 97–101; George H. Mayer, *The Republican Party, 1854–1966* (New York: Oxford University Press, 1967), 397–99; David Burner, *The Politics of Provincialism: The Democratic Party in Transition, 1918–1932* (New York: Alfred A. Knopf, 1968), 128–30; Karl Schriftgiesser, *This Was Normalcy: An Account of Party Politics During the Twelve Republican Years, 1920–1932* (Boston: Little, Brown and Company, 1948), 189–97.
47. Minutes of the Administrative Committee, 23 September 1924 (first quote is here) ACUA, USCCB 10:64:3; McSorley to Burke, 3 October 1924, AP, Burke Papers, box 21; Burke to Lynch, 18 October 1924 (second quote is here), ibid., box 5.
48. Burke to Murray, [16 October 1924], AP, Burke Papers, box 11 (first quote is here); Burke to McNulty, [11 October 1924], ibid, box 14 (remaining quotes are here).
49. Burke to Murray, [16 October 1924], AP, Burke Papers, box 11; Burke to Lynch, 18 October 1924, ibid., box 5; Rudie Nolan to Burke, 9 May 1925, ACUA, USCCB 10:105:17; Burke to Nolan, 13 May 1925, copy, ibid.
50. Slawson, *Foundation of NCWC*, 219–20; Slawson, *Ambition and Arrogance*, 154–56; Broderick, *Reverend New Dealer*, 97–98, 126–27; Vincent McQuade, O.S.A., *The American Catholic Attitude on Child Labor Since 1891: A Study of the Formation and Development of a Catholic Attitude on a Specific Social Question* (Washington, D.C.: Catholic University of America Press, 1938), 72–73, 79.
51. Thomas R. Greene, "The Catholic Committee for the Ratification of the Child Labor Amendment, 1935–1937: Origin and Limits," *Catholic Historical*

Review 74 (April 1988):248–49; O'Toole, *Militant and Triumphant* 132–33; James M. O'Toole, "Prelates and Politicos: Catholics and Politics in Massachusetts, 1900–1970," in Robert E. Sullivan and James M. O'Toole, eds., *Catholic Boston: Studies in Religion and Community, 1870–1970* (Boston: Roman Catholic Archdiocese of Boston, 1985), 29; McQuade, *Child Labor*, 74–78, 82– 89.

52. Quoted in Gibbons to J. H. Ryan, 23 October 1924, copy, ACUA, J. A. Ryan Papers 11:39:24.
53. O'Connell to Schrembs, 14 October 1924, ADCl, Schrembs papers.
54. Quoted in Gibbons to J. H. Ryan, 23 October 1924, copy, ACUA, J. A. Ryan Papers 11:39:24; O'Connell to Schrembs, 14 October 1924, ADCl, Schrembs Papers; Schrembs to Burke, 17 October 1924, copy, ACUA, USCCB 10:135:1.
55. Boston *Pilot*, 18 October 1924; J. A. Ryan to Muldoon, 23 October 1924, ACUA, J. A. Ryan Papers 11:39:24.
56. J. H. Ryan to Schrembs, 21 October 1924, copy, ACUA, USCCB 10:144:77; Burke to Schrembs, 22 October 1924, copy, ibid., 10:135:1.
57. Burke to J. H. Ryan, 25 October 1924, ACUA, USCCB 10:153:4; Burke to Muldoon, 26 October 1914, copy, with enclosure "Supreme Court Reform," ibid., 10:104:13; "The La Follette Platform of 1924," in Henry Steele Commager, ed., *Documents of American History*, 9th ed., 2 Vols (Englewood Cliffs, N.J.: Prentice Hall, 1973), 2:194–97.
58. Burke to McGrath, telegram, 26 October 1924, ACUA, USCCB 10:135:1; Burke to J. H. Ryan, 25 October 1924, ibid., 10:153:4; Burke to Muldoon, 26 October 1924, copy, ibid., 10:104:13; Burke to Murray, 29 October 1924, AP, Burke Papers, box 11.
59. Burke to McNulty, 28 October 1924, AP, Burke Papers, box 14; O'Toole, *Militant and Triumphant*, 123–29, 132–33.
60. Burke to Murray, 29 October 1924, AP, Burke Papers, box 11.
61. O'Connell to Curley, 2 November 1924, AAB-AASMSU, 0278 (copy in AABo, Catholic University file); J. H. Ryan to Burke, 2 November 1924, copy, ACUA, USCCB 10:153:4; Slawson, *Foundation of NCWC*, 224–25; Slawson, *Ambition and Arrogance*, 161–62.
62. Dowling to Hanna, 31 October 1924, AASF, NCWC files; Burke to Hanna, 8 November 1924, with enclosed statement, ibid.; Burke to Muldoon, 8 November 1924, copy (the comment about a "keeper" is here), ACUA, USCCB 10:135:1; McNulty to Hanna, 21 November 1924, copy, ibid.
63. J. H. Ryan, Memorandum on the Child Labor Amendment, 21 November 1924, copy, ACUA, USCCB 10:135:1; J. H. Ryan to Burke, 9 December 1924, copy, ibid., 10:153:4; Pietro Fumasoni-Biondi to Pietro Gasparri, 26 March 1925, copy, ASV, DAUS, IV, Liste Episcopali, 93.

Chapter 13
A Caribbean "Vacation"

> To every one of us according to the will of Christ there is the obligation, because we have received His life, to work, to labor—in prayer, in mental and manual labor, in personal and social influence and interest—to extend the kingdom and the reign of Jesus Christ throughout the world.[1]

Puerto Rico

In mid-October 1924, John Burke planned a vacation to the Greater Antilles. He asked Father Raymond McGowan, a housemate at the NCWC residence, to accompany him. Burke felt that McGowan had more of the spirit of St. Francis of Assisi than any priest he knew. For his part, McGowan considered Burke "the greatest and kindest man" he ever met. The two would travel to Puerto Rico, an American possession, with Bishop George Caruana of San Juan. Maltese born, Caruana was a priest of the Brooklyn diocese who had served as a military chaplain in Puerto Rico and the Panama Canal Zone. Burke spent the night before departure in the garden guesthouse of the Cenacle, home of Helen Lynch, and said Mass for the sisters in the morning. Gertrude Gavin picked him up and headed for Brooklyn and the S.S. *San Lorenzo*. Losing their way and misdirected by policemen, they reached the dock to find McGowan awaiting them and the ship underway in the harbor. A tug ferried the two priests out and they climbed aboard through a porthole.[2]

Once at sea, Burke wrote to Grace Murray that he felt he was going away for a long time, leaving everything and everyone he loved behind. He tried to banish the thought because he did not want to lose the spiritual benefit he hoped to gain from the vacation. The transit to Puerto Rico was pleasant and took almost four days on calm seas under clear skies. The three clergymen said Mass every morning and on Sunday had quite a crowd in attendance. Burke and McGowan played cribbage to while away hours, the latter a more formidable opponent than Rudie Nolan.[3]

They reached San Juan on 17 November and lodged with the American Redemptorist Fathers, "a proper thing for a Paulist to do," noted Burke, since Isaac Hecker had belonged to that community. Their hosts made the two comfortable and entertained them. San Juan itself was quite picturesque: the sea to the north, the low green hills close across the bay to the south, and the mountains in the distance. The food, however, left much to be desired. There was very little for breakfast and wherever they went, the other two meals consisted of a steady diet of eggs, rice, black beans, and a bit of fish or meat. As Burke wrote, it was always "*huevos y piscado y arroz y habichuelas*"—the relentless fare of the Puerto Rican working class.[4]

On their third day, Burke and McGowan called on Governor General Horace Mann Towner, former cosponsor of the NEA's bills for a department of education. Looking "old and quite worn out," Towner received them coldly at first, but then became friendly enough. The three conversed about religious matters there. "With some heat," Towner asked, "have the Catholics in the U.S. lost their missionary spirit?" He explained the extreme need for priests in Puerto Rico. There were not quite 100 for a population of 1.3 million, while there were 400 Protestant ministers laboring there. Towner noted that American Catholics sent millions of dollars to China, yet for a much smaller amount, they could accomplish a proportionally greater good on the island. "We are aiming at the same end the mental and spiritual betterment of these people, people fundamentally good and really Catholic," Towner told the pair. "But you leave them without priests. There are districts in the Island wherein thousands are getting no word of religious training." Having spent only two days in San Juan, Burke and McGowan felt unqualified to discuss the matter because of their unfamiliarity with conditions. They agreed to call again when more acquainted with the situation, but the opportunity never presented itself.[5]

The next day, the two traveled to the place where worked Consuelo Delgado, a graduate of the National Catholic Service School. She was delighted to see Burke. Everyone admired and respected her accomplishments, which made him proud of the school. The people, as elsewhere on the island, were desperately poor. Large agricultural industries, producing tobacco, coffee, and especially sugar, dominated the economy and landownership, siphoning off the wealth. The country was overpopulated and the inhabitants impoverished by corporate capitalism, American and domestic, which turned them into meagerly paid wage-workers no longer able to grow their own food. Four out of five families were landless. Their staple diet of rice, beans, and codfish had to be imported from the United States. "The housing and living conditions are indescribable," wrote Burke in his diary. "The streets are unpaved.... Houses have no water nor toilet ... and [were] divided by thin boards into small rooms. These rooms rent for from 5 to 8 dollars a month ($90 and $144, respectively, in 2024)—far more than would be asked in N.Y. City. No windows. Most scanty furniture. No sewerage. One would not believe that human beings could live under such conditions. Disease and immorality rampant." He and McGowan visited a family of five. The physician in attendance said the youngest child was dying. The second youngest would not survive because of tuberculosis. Three had measles. One of the Redemptorists told Burke that 45 percent of children died before age five.[6]

Over the next several days, he and McGowan traveled through central and southwest Puerto Rico. They learned that many in high civil positions were former Catholics or non-practicing ones, and a number were Masons. There were one Catholic senator, two Catholic assemblymen, no Catholic Supreme Court justice, and only two Catholic district judges. "The Chief Justice of Supreme Court once a Catholic now says Porto Rico must change its language and its religion if it is to progress," noted Burke. The commissioner of education was an Evangelical Protestant who was a preacher in his church. Textbooks used in the schools were anti-Catholic. In sum, a Protestant minority ruled the island. Catholics were losing prestige, and Catholic men believed they must dissociate themselves from the Church to secure advancement. A Dominican priest at Yauco stressed "that if help were not given—more priests and some financial aid—Porto Rico in a generation would be non-Catholic."[7]

In his first week, Burke had several conversations with priests and nuns about the NCWC. It was disappointing how little they grasped its spirit, which made him reflect on the Mystical Body. He thought the fundamental cause of their inability to comprehend the nature of the NCWC was "their failure to keep before the mind that the Church is not so much an organization as an organism." They saw it as an institution, battling for the Catholic cause. For Burke, it arose from "the very nature of the Church's economy." "The Church as an organism presupposes the orderly, united action of priests and people," he wrote: "it presupposes the injection of that action into every sphere of human activity.... Not to grasp that is [to] understand Christ only in part. That the Church as an organism, as the living Body of Christ, into which we are all incorporated with every human interest we have, presupposes such comprehensible thought and all inclusive action.... If we do not shape our special work with this as the background it is not shaped well: it is not Catholic nor will it endure as Catholic."[8]

Burke had a deep sense of the incarnation as redemptive of all creation. People were not simply spiritual or religious beings. "Man has a body as well as a soul," he wrote. "That body and all that relates to the welfare of that body was touched by the hand of Christ and redeemed under God." He believed no one could serve God unless physically healthy. Spiritual welfare presupposed bodily welfare, basic human dignity. Burke considered the absence of order or well-being in any part of creation as unacceptable because all creation was "of God." It bothered him deeply when he heard priests express fear for the Church if its people were better educated. He found the social condition of the islanders "lamentable." "Foreign capital waxes fat on cheap labor," he complained: "on the underfed, poorly housed mothers and fathers and children."[9]

Burke and McGowan continued their touring while awaiting return of Bishop Caruana from Havana where he had gone to see the apostolic delegate, Archbishop Pietro Benedetti. The Redemptorists told Burke that Caruana was quite discouraged, and they hoped he might be able to hearten him. On 3 December, he and McGowan visited him. Caruana described the situation that had confronted him. The former rector of the seminary, Father Pérez, had reported to the Vatican that all the native priests were bad and that those from the United States were trying to Americanize the island. He also accused the venerable vicar general, Monsignor José Torres Díaz, of repeated attempts to murder the previous apostolic delegate, Archbishop Tito Trocchi. Trocchi believed the accusation true because on visits to San Juan he had heard noises at night in his room in the episcopal residence. The frightened delegate had the door lock changed numerous times.

At Rome, Pérez's word was accepted as gospel. When Caruana's predecessor Bishop William Jones died, Caruana had refused to become bishop unless the Vatican corrected the situation. Promises were made, but went unkept.[10]

Once in office, Caruana had solved the mystery of the nightly noises in the guestroom. His young nephew had come to visit and slept there. In the middle of the night, the pale, trembling lad awakened his uncle. He said he had heard noises, ghosts, and refused to return to the chamber. Caruana learned that the vicar general had told the boy the portraits in the guestroom were of dead clergymen—the alleged ghosts. The bishop found that the bottom of the door was cut so cats could pass through. When they did, the door shook and rattled. He had solved the mystery. The break with Pérez came when the priest absconded with a woman and $18,000 ($324,000 in 2024). Caruana obtained a copy of the marriage license and sent it to Benedetti along with a report, concluding with the words of Pontius Pilate: "Ecce, homo [Behold! The man (John 19:5)]." On reading the report, Benedetti's terse reply was, "O, felix culpa [O, happy fault]." Benedetti sent report and license to Rome. Burke remarked, "If it wasn't a bishop who told the story, one would say it was comic opera."[11]

Burke believed that the root of such troubles was Spanish influence in both Puerto Rico and the Vatican. Rome refused to make the island part of the American Catholic Church as a suffragan diocese. He asked Caruana if it would be better if he were under the apostolic delegate to the U.S. The reply was yes and that Benedetti thought so too.[12]

Two days later, Caruana showed Burke around San Juan and used the occasion to unburden himself. On the way to St. Augustine College, the bishop explained he could get no religious community to run that institution. He had to pay laymen $14,000 a year (over $252,000 in 2024) to teach there and the school was running an annual deficit of $4,000 to $5,000 ($762,000 to $90,000 respectively). The president was a former Jesuit priest of Cuba. He had been a rising star in that order and was about to become president of the Jesuit Colegio de Belén in Havana when it came to light that he had embezzled funds from that institution and "was inveigled with a woman." He went to New York and worked in a hotel, until the provincial of the Vincentian Fathers, Frederick Maune, brought him to Caruana's attention. The bishop lived in daily dread that news of the scandal would reach Puerto Rico. Burke considered Caruana's charitable disposition toward the fallen clergyman risky. "Mercy, yes," he commented in his diary: "but here the stakes are too high." When Burke met the erstwhile priest, he felt "the greatest sympathy for the man." "I will pray that silence on the part of those who know will graciously give him his full opportunity," he wrote. "And may he answer to the merciful providence of God."[13]

On their way to Immaculate Conception school, Caruana confided that the diocese was on the brink of bankruptcy. Nor did he have the heart to ask Rome for permission to sell more property. He said that the older generation of Puerto Ricans had at least the tradition of love for the Catholic faith; the younger generation lacked even that. Burke asked if Caruana could get together a small group of Catholic men to support him. He answered with an emphatic no. He felt he could trust no one. For Puerto Rican Catholics, religion was a matter of processions and erecting altars. They had neither knowledge of nor taste for the real meat of Christianity. Burke wrote to his friend William Kerby that the situation of the Church there was "deplorable and full of problems: but not so deplorable that it may not be mended." He had no doubt that if Puerto Rico became part of the American Church, matters would quickly improve.[14]

As Elisa Julian de Nievas, historian of Catholicism in American-held Puerto Rico, notes, the people of the island and the American bishops and clergy were of two different types. The latter were "an exotic breed … not only aggressively Catholic but also compellingly American." From their perspective, Puerto Rican Catholicism sorely lacked "enterprise and drive."[15]

Hispañola

On 8 December, Burke and McGowan departed for Hispañola on the *S.S. Catherine*, a vessel described by the former as "a small boat … not very comfortable" and one whose name he would forever remember "not in joyfulness." They were headed to Santo Domingo, and fortunately the sea was smooth and the voyage short, only twenty-four hours in unpleasant accommodations. They arrived early next evening. After a quick visit to the National Palace, the pair booked into a "miserable" hotel, the Français, an old building with rooms off a second story balcony overlooking a yard "filled with many things, particularly wash." There was a common bath at the far end of the balcony. Burke noted that the "first meal was promising: Soup: then green beans: then a stuffed tomato: then broiled chicken with no vegetables: bananas 'dolci'—cheese, coffee."[16]

The next morning he and McGowan visited Archbishop Adolfo Alejandro Nouel y Bobadilla, who was courteous without being welcoming. He spoke with them about the archdiocese. Burke got the impression that "he evidently wished to conceal things from me—and there are very many to conceal." Indeed three years earlier, Michael Williams had visited Santo Domingo and reported to Burke about "certain scandals affecting the morality and probity of too large a number of the clergy." After leaving the archbishop, the pair saw the Cathedral of Santa María la Menor, the oldest one in the Americas. Then, an acquaintance of Burke's brother James toured them around the countryside.[17]

Although the two were to have traveled overland the next day to Haiti, morning found Burke ill with one of his "old time attacks" of fever. His surroundings were hardly comforting in sickness: the room had no windows, the bathroom was about a half block away, and there was no hot water except the meager amount a serving girl brought. McGowan found an American doctor who wanted to get Burke out of the hotel. At the time, the United States controlled the customs house in Santo Domingo, and the American deputy collector had offered to let the two priests stay with him. McGowan took him up on the offer. The collector and an American Red Cross worker helped McGowan get Burke to the home. The next day, McGowan came down with dengue fever. The doctor and Red Cross worker nursed the two clergymen for several days. It was almost a week and a half before the physician cleared Burke for travel.[18]

On Sunday, 21 December, he said Mass in the old cathedral, a dispiriting experience. "No one received communion," wrote Burke. "No one followed along. Some stood throughout, even during consecration. Many did not kneel even for the blessing." Early that afternoon he and McGowan headed northwest across the island in a chauffeured car. They made it as far as Santiago, a city of mud. "Everywhere mud," wrote Burke: "wet, thick mud." Spending the night there, they continued on "through a barren almost desert country of cactus: burros: goats … and poor-looking long-horned cattle. Mile after mile of monotonous barrenness." They stopped briefly at Monte Christi, a small coastal town in the northwest corner of the Dominican Republic, before driving south to Dajabón on the Massacre River, which formed the border. They forded the river and drove up the hill to the town of Ounaminthe in American-occupied Haiti where Captain Frank Verdier, the marine in charge of the Gendarmerie there, awaited them. Burke and McGowan stayed with the Breton Père Tilly at the local parish.[19]

That evening Verdier and Lieutenant Wilkins joined the three clergymen for dinner. During the meal, conversation turned to Vodou or voodoo, a term used for traditional Afro-Haitian religious beliefs and practices. As historian Kate Ramsey and others have pointed out, white Westerners and Haitian elites viewed African traditions and customs as indicators of primitivism and savagery, a perspective reinforced by tales of cannibalism and child sacrifice. This outlook engendered in the American occupiers a sense of superiority and paternalism. In reality, Haitian popular religion was deeply spiritual. The people believed in a remote, transcendent God who created the universe as well as spirits (*lwa*) who functioned as intermediaries with humans. Yet, nothing happened apart from the will of the "Good God." Devotees referred to their religious practice as serving the spirits, who included deceased ancestors. The common folk of Haiti had syncretized vodou with Roman Catholicism.[20]

Verdier explained that there was a Haitian law against sorcery, and his police were always on the lookout for vodou meetings. In fact, prior to the occupation, that law had gone largely unenforced. Its function seems to have been symbolic, a way for elites to prove to themselves and Western nations that Haiti was not primitive: it had outlawed "superstition." With little understanding of the language, people, or customs, the marines now strictly enforced the law. Verdier told Burke and McGowan that there was to be a vodou ceremony the next evening to cure a local school teacher. She would set out in the morning for the distant, hidden place of the meeting, which the captain had come to know. She would pay the religious healer $40 (about $720 in 2024) and provide food for all participants. "They will kill a chicken: pour its blood into a cup and pass the cup that all may drink," Burke wrote in his diary. "To the sick woman will be given some extract of herbs. All will partake of the food: make their incantations, etc. It is a superstition that seeks to placate by sacrifice of blood and apparently of an innocent victim the mysterious threatening powers of nature." Verdier hoped to capture the lot of them.[21]

After hearing the captain's account, Burke stepped out onto the back porch and into the night. The absence of electricity served only to enhance the inky blackness. The stars above were radiant, but "on the earth was darkness and the imaginative mystery that darkness inevitably brings." Burke could hear voices in the night around him and the sound of people moving about. "It was not strange that the dark—which deprived them of sight and of power—should demand a certain mastery as well as mystery and that the same should be accorded," he thought. "What faint glimmer of light there was only gave emphasis to the dark." The folk of Haiti were simple, uneducated, natural. "Before voodooism is lifted," he wrote in his diary, "they must be taught that they are the masters of nature. The thick forest … the fantastic dark—must for them be robbed of its apparent power." Like the American occupiers, Burke believed that the means for doing so were "vocational schools, home economics, primary education, better roads, easier communications, community centers with moving pictures, general entertainments, etc." His solution was to uplift of the country through modernization, opening it to "every kind of light."[22] Unlike the occupiers, Burke believed that the process of modernization should be respectful of Haitian culture and life.

When the two marines departed, the three clergymen conversed in Latin because Tilly spoke no English. He told them that there were 22,000 people in his parish. All were baptized and nearly all had been confirmed. But there had been only thirty-five church weddings in the current year. Civil ones were more common, but concubinage was the norm. The people were simple, ignorant, and superstitious. The pastor spoke admiringly of some whose devotion and unfaltering faith were heartening. It was a mission country, and missionary work must be done.[23]

The next morning Burke and McGowan continued on to Cape Haïtien on the north coast and arrived just in time for lunch with Bishop Jean-Marie Jan, coadjutor of the diocese, described by Burke as "an admirable: zealous: progressive bishop." Jan affirmed that concubinage was commonplace in Haiti. The country had a population of 2.3 million, but only 150 priests. After lunch they climbed up the mountain for a visit with seventy-seven-year-old Bishop François-Marie Kersuzan, a tall man with a full white beard and saintly countenance. He had had charge of the diocese for thirty-eight years. He told them the Haitian Church needed priests, money, sisters, and lay workers. Kersuzan insisted that Haiti was "absolutely" a problem and an obligation for the Catholics of the United States.[24]

Burke and McGowan spent Christmas in Cap Haïtien. After supper, Burke had a long conversation with Jan, who explained that the Church and clergy in Haiti enjoyed the full confidence of the people. There were indications, however, of some lessening of that spirit because of the clergy's sympathy with the American occupation. Love of liberty was inborn in the Haitian people. They were growing angry with the American interpretation and use of the treaty which governed the occupation. It seemed the Americans were seeking greater dominion over Haiti in order to make it a possession of the United States. The occupiers controlled every department of government except the judiciary, which Brigadier General John Russell, high commissioner, seemed intent on taking over. The bishop advised that the American government should send military officers to Haiti who spoke French and were free of racial prejudice. He told of rumors that the United States intended to send American priests to Haiti because the Breton clergymen were obstacles to Americanization and their Latin culture must give way to the Anglo-Saxon. Burke commented in his diary: "Interesting, important conversation."[25]

The next morning Burke and McGowan began the long auto journey down to Port-au-Prince. At 9:30 A.M., they stopped at Plaisance where the local pastor offered breakfast. When they declined, he insisted that they have some claret wine which was followed by chartreuse. "We were beginning early," commented Burke. The pastor had the church bells rung. Burke thought it must be for a religious service, but when they went into the church, no one was there. Still the bells rang. Burke asked, "*Pourquoi les cloches* [Why the bells]?" The pastor replied, "*Pour vous* [For you]." They reached the capital at about 7:00 P.M., and Archbishop Julien Conan welcomed them to his residence. Burke was happy the long trip from Santo Domingo to Port-au-Prince was behind them. "It is one of those journeys one is glad to have taken—after it is over," he wrote, "—but which one would not, without cause, take again."[26]

Next morning, the pair of travelers visited Russell, who spoke at length of the plans to create agricultural schools under Dr. George Freeman. Russell considered the American system of public education the best. Burke asked if the agricultural schools would interfere with the Haitian public schools wherein religion was taught. No, answered Russell. Burke reminded him that Haitians were almost all Catholics and that "the American administration's work was not to graft American methods on to Haiti but to build up Haiti according to its own beliefs and traditions: that religion … the Catholic religion, was the only possible foundation for civic responsibility: moral and personal dignity, etc." Burke said that many "forward-looking men" in the United States deplored the absence of religion in their public schools. The conversation was not adversarial, and Russell praised the work of the Breton priests, brothers, and nuns as having saved Haiti from chaos. Yet, as Haitian historian Leon Pamphile has pointed out, the Americans intended to establish their own separate system of Service Technique schools and financially starve the Haitian system.[27]

Later in the day, Conan took Burke and McGowan to meet Haitian President Louis Borno, a distinguished-looking mulatto with a "studied manner of courtesy, giving at times an impression of insincerity." He spoke English quite well and emphasized that Haiti was a Catholic country and that the government had a duty to support the Church, Catholic schools, and Catholic worship. He noted, however, that William Cumberland, the American financial adviser who controlled Haitian funds, oftentimes opposed such support. Burke told Borno the same thing he had told Russell: the job of the American occupiers was to keep Haiti Haitian, not make it American. "You have spoken goldenly," replied the president, "and I hope you will succeed in changing the mind and attitude of Mr. Cumberland."[28]

That evening Conan showed Burke the memorandum Benedetti had written, requesting the Haitian government increase the salaries of priests from $18.75 a month to $40 ($337 and $720 respectively in 2024). Borno and his council had approved the raise, but Cumberland vetoed it. The wages of others were also quite low: hospital sisters received $10 ($180) a month and rural school teachers $6 ($108). By comparison, a laborer earned $6 a month, and a skilled one $20. The archbishop pointed out that Cumberland approved salaries as high as $20,000 ($360,000) a year —an exaggeration— for experts from America, money that came from the Haitian treasury, not the United States. He added that marine officers who commanded the Haitian gendarmerie drew two salaries: one from the Haitian government and their regular one from the Marine Corps.[29]

The following day Burke and McGowan met with a delegation of

Christian Brothers. Their superior, Brother Hyppolyte, expressed fear that the American agricultural schools would prove inimical to Catholic ones and introduce education without religion. The Brothers believed that was Freeman's intention. Burke commented in his diary: "It grows more and more evident that [the] occupation is not at all acceptable to the Haitian people. And if the American administration continues encroaching, as it has, on Haitian governmental departments, there will be serious trouble.... The American administration needs larger brains and bigger hearts than it gives evidence of at present."[30]

The next evening, Conan, Burke, and McGowan dined with Russell, his wife Mabel, and William and Edith Cumberland at the high commissioner's home. Burke found Mabel an entertaining hostess "according to the standard of the Federation of Women's Clubs." The Russells served no wine or liquor, but Mabel and Burke chain-smoked throughout the evening and she won the contest. "Otherwise we were orthodoxically Puritan," he noted. Although the gathering was pleasant, he thought that some of the stories the Americans told about Haitians did no credit to their own intelligence. For instance, both Russells claimed that children dashed across the road in front of an oncoming car so that it would run over their shadow and kill it. Then it would never follow or bother them again. "Now, Fr. McG. and I have travelled [*sic*] hundreds of miles in Haiti," recorded Burke. "We never saw one child do anything that resembled this." When he later asked Conan about it, the archbishop said it was untrue. Perhaps it was the condescending view of the colonizer for the indigenous folk.[31]

On the afternoon of New Year's Eve, a great number of clergy and religious gathered at the archbishop's residence. Conan expressed gratitude to those present for their work. He thanked Burke for coming to see conditions and carry word back to the American hierarchy. Then, Burke had to go around and give the kiss of peace to all the priests and brothers assembled, white and black alike. "Physically it was a task," was his comment, and he was not talking about exhaustion. Afterward, they all drank Coca Cola. "Why it was not wine I cannot understand," complained Burke.[32]

Burke, McGowan, and Conan then left for a reception thrown by President Borno. It was the first "popular" New Year's reception he had given. Previous ones were just for high officials and their families. Russell later told Burke that even members of the political opposition were present, something new for Haiti. This gathering boasted a number of Haitian elites, most of them mulattoes derisively dubbed "the shoe class" by Marine Major Smedley Butler, who considered them little better than the peasants who went barefoot. "As I looked on these Haitians, men and women, I thought of the other Haitians, the thousands, men and women whom we had seen trudging the roads mile after mile in Haiti: without stockings or shoes and wearing probably a single garment," wrote Burke. "Here at the reception they were clothed, men and women, à la mode: whether they were of any more right mind is a question. After all *l'habit ne fait pas le moine* [the habit does not make the monk]. But as far as it went it was a good sign." They had punch, sandwiches, and cakes.[33]

Over the next few days Burke learned more of Haitian life. The pastor of the parish in Pétionville explained why concubinage was so prevalent. Before a couple could be married in the Church, they must first have a civil marriage, which cost more than most could afford. A conversation with Conan, moreover, revealed that the archbishop had as clear an idea of vodou as any white man was likely to get. He told Burke that it was difficult to know the truth about it. Even those convicted of practicing it said nothing: "You the white man have your ways: we the black men have our habits our customs and we must keep them as our own." There was an element of family indebtedness about vodou. The Haitians believed in many spirits between the individual and God. For example, a man might become sick because he had not done right by his parents, and their spirits were angry. Conan averred that the Americans' enforcement of the law against sorcery had certainly curbed the practice in Port-au-Prince by arresting most of the male religious leaders, men called *papaloi* or *oungan*.[34]

On 4 January 1925, Burke and McGowan left Port-au-Prince for Aux Cayes out west on the southern peninsula. Bishop Jules Pichon, who had heard of their coming, went east to meet them in Aquin. The three then traveled together to Aux Cayes. After supper, they talked of the country's situation. According to Pichon, "America saved Haiti but America has not and is not living up to its obligations." American authorities had promised that when a loan of $40 million ($720 million in 2024) had been floated, salaries of the clergy would be increased. After the loan, no raise came. The two travelers then retired to Spartan and soiled accommodations. "With all charity," Burke commented in his diary, "more consideration might be given to cleanliness here. It would cost no more. No clean soap: only one towel. And I see there are no electric lights. As it happens I write this with the poor light of an oil lamp. I don't know yet—at 9 o'clock—where the toilet is. The toilets we had to use en route—well, were as poor as those of the pioneers in the U.S."[35]

The next day, the three toured religious institutions in the city. Burke wrote of the Breton clergy and religious: "Truly these men really love the blacks as their fellow men and with a burning zeal for Christ." He had witnessed similar devotion everywhere in Haiti. Pichon was not in favor of having American priests work there. The Breton priests were strongly bound together in a credo to save Haiti and keep it safe. No American priests would do what they did. Two Americans had come to Haiti. One by the name of Halpin, said the bishop, "would have nothing to do with the 'nigger.'" He gave communion only to white nuns. "Do you think I would put my fingers into the mouth of a black man?" Halpin had asked Pichon. "Well he should have had to kiss them as I did," wrote Burke. The real problem was the cultural conflict between the Haitians and American occupiers. The latter were "not against but certainly not with" the former, and, "in tendency," they were "ultimately antagonistic."[36]

On Little Christmas (6 January), Burke and McGowan headed back to the capital. While awaiting the car, Burke and Pichon conversed. The bishop said that vodou, in its extreme practices, was dying out, but it was still strong in other ways. The American campaign to halt secret meetings and dances had done effective work. He told Burke that human sacrifice, adult or infant, happened "*rarissime* [most rarely]." His priests had informed him of only three instances. The sacrifice of animals was far more common. It seems that Burke took such talk with a grain of salt. Two years hence, he would comment that the Haitians were "capable of a high degree of development" and their superstitions were "exaggerated." The car arrived and the pair of travelers departed.[37]

Toward the end of his stay, Burke came to question what he was even doing there: "Sometimes I ask myself why I ever came to Haiti—why I chose this as a recreation and vacation. I spend all my days in the consideration of problems that affect the Church here: from morning until after sun down I am hurried for time. I take long arduous trips and I am disgusted at the accommodations furnished for our physical comfort. Yet I am here." Indeed, Burke wrote to Kerby that the visit to Haiti was being interpreted as "official." The Americans thought he and McGowan were there on behalf of the U.S. State Department, while the clergy and religious, "well, you'd think we were of high and important standing." With all the meetings, conferences, and travel, Burke said he was as busy as he would have been if he stayed at NCWC headquarters. "It is one of the mysteries of God's Providence," he wrote in his diary. "In some way and in spite of my sins God is using me and He has used me for His purposes *hic et nunc* [here and now]. May His mercy continue and may he not cast me off at the end." Burke felt that if his visit there resulted in aiding the Catholics of Haiti, that would be repayment enough.[38]

The bishops asked him to see Russell on their behalf about matters pertaining to the concordat. On 8 January Burke did so. He reminded Russell that a concordat—a treaty—existed between the Vatican and the Haitian government. Whether or not an American thought this appropriate was of no consequence. The United States had pledged to observe it. In Burke's view, the occupier was not keeping faith. Foremost was the issue of pay for the clergy. "I said the present salary was an insult," Burke recounted. Russell explained that A. J. Maumus, a former American financial adviser who was Catholic, had disallowed any increase because priests had other sources of income from stipends for sacraments. Burke countered that for the majority of the clergy those were negligible. Russell seemed unconvinced.[39]

Burke then spoke of Cumberland, who controlled Haitian treasury funds. The man refused to abide by the letter or spirit of the concordat. He was unsympathetic to religious education and refused to permit religious goods or educational equipment for Church schools to enter the country duty-free. Burke protested against Cumberland's attitude and said he would have to do so back in Washington as well. Russell responded that making distinctions among imported goods was difficult and that "if the privilege was granted to one it would have to be granted to all." Burke countered that it was easy to distinguish between goods of an educational or religious nature.[40]

He asked the commissioner if religion was being taught in the Service Technique schools as required by Haitian law. Russell answered no, but he would see that it was. When Burke spoke about the construction of Church buildings, the commissioner denied that the concordat contained any obligation to build churches. Burke contended any plain reading of that document and the organic conventions pursuant thereto proved otherwise. He suggested "the need and advisability" of Russell's consulting with the Haitian bishops as a group regarding appropriations for the salaries of priests and the building of churches and presbyteries as well as other matters pertaining to the concordat. Russell replied that he would do so in future.[41]

Burke considered Russell a cordial and sincere man, who was trying to do his best for the Haitians, although he was handicapped by political considerations and political appointments. After the interview, Burke gave an account of it to Archbishop Conan, whose only comment was that the assertion about priests not having other sources of income was perhaps too strong. Clergy in long-established parishes did receive stipends.[42]

Cuba

The next morning, Burke and McGowan departed Haiti for Cuba. Russell had arranged for them to sail on the U.S.S. *Woodcock*, a former mine sweeper converted into a gunboat. The only other passenger aboard was a navy dentist. They arrived at Guantanamo Bay Naval Station at 5:00 A.M. the following morning and at 11:00 sailed on along the coast to Santiago, which they reached in early evening. The next day they toured nearby battle fields of the Spanish-American War. At El Caney, Burke saw a memorial tablet listing those killed, and among the names was that of Captain John Drum, who was his training master at St. Francis Xavier High School. "I never thought I would see his name in bronze at the battle site on which he died," commented Burke. The following day they boarded a train for the long overnight trip to Havana. "Such was the swerving," wrote Burke, "... that one went to sleep with the conviction that he would awake on the floor."[43]

In Havana, Burke and McGowan lodged with the Augustinians at St. Augustine's College. They called on the American ambassador to Cuba, retired Major General Enoch Crowder, with whom Burke had dealt as judge advocate general. Crowder told them of all the corruption in the government of Cuba, to which the Catholic Church turned a blind eye. He said that he would be willing to explain his conviction about the failure of the Church in this regard to the newly appointed apostolic administrator of the archdiocese: Bishop José Rúiz y Rodríguez. The Augustinian superior agreed to arrange an interview for him with the bishop.[44]

After lunch, Burke and McGowan aimlessly strolled the boulevards and avenues of Havana. Everywhere they turned, sexual images assaulted and insulted them: "picture, book, magazine of crude suggestiveness, of bald nakedness" were commonplace on newsstands, in book stalls, and in windows. "The streets literally drip with this filth," wrote Burke. "It is tolerated. It is supported. No voice against it is heard in the wilderness [cf., Isa. 40:3]." Seeing this and recalling what Crowder had told them, Burke reflected in his diary on his firm conviction that purity was the basis of a peoples' life, of a nation's life, just as it was the basis of the dignity and uprightness of an individual. "And dishonesty and betrayal of a people will not be lifted from public life until this blinding rottenness and selfishness are lifted from the hearts of men and women," he concluded.[45]

Several days later, Bishop Rúiz told Burke the archdiocese had only twenty-five secular priests to cover 7,000 square miles. The Augustinian superior later explained to him that the majority of children received no religious instruction. Only the wealthy had ability to educate their children in private schools where religion was taught. For the rest there was only Sunday school, but middle-class children would not mix with their poor counterparts. So, the former took religious instruction on Sunday, and the latter on Saturday. Even so, a great many never attended. Moreover, the poor children did not attend Sunday Mass because their poverty embarrassed them.[46]

Yet the greatest religious need in Havana was the rehabilitation of the secular clergy. People who went to confession did so to priests belonging to religious orders, not to a secular priest. "They do not respect or trust him." The Augustinian superior averred that not one church in the hands of a secular had been repaired, enlarged, or built since the Spanish American War (1898). Some seculars did not live in their parishes, but dwelt far removed from them. They were in boarding houses, whose matrons were often procurers bringing in prostitutes. "How can a priest live pure under such circumstances?" wondered Burke. He thought that the seculars ought to be compelled to live in their parishes. The danger, as he saw it, was that the archdiocese would end up in the hands of religious clergy rather than secular priests.[47]

On 22 January 1925, McGowan left to return home. Burke was sorry to see him go. They had been together for over two months, and he could not have asked "for a more agreeable, willing and zealous companion." His departure put Burke in a reflective mood about his own return. He had earlier told both Murray and Kerby that he missed the NCWC, "the work I love," as he phrased it to the former. That expression spoke volumes about the great change in his attitude since 1920. He complained that he had heard nothing about what was going on in Washington, and felt "in exile." He had written to Kerby of his eagerness to return to the NCWC, but confided, "Sometimes the fear haunts me that I will not go back."[48]

Now, with McGowan's departure, he confessed in his diary: "I feel strange about going back at all. There has been something of a burial and there is something of a feeling akin to that of Lazarus," that is, being called forth from the tomb. The NCWC had been with him throughout the trip, and Burke felt that the welcomes tendered to him were really meant for it. He was returning to something he loved dearly, had given his all, had been plucked away from, and now would return to. He did not know what he felt. "Is it because the joy is incredible?" he wrote. "Is it the fear that has in a measure ever possessed me that another could do it better and that my service is ended." Burke admitted that in times past he had been so tired he had "to whip" himself to the work. He had lost his old vigor. At other times he felt renewed and able to do much. Of late, his love for things spiritual had grown as had his desire and willingness to be alone. He thought this might be "a giving way to a desire for physical and mental rest." In any case, he hoped he would always do what was for the glory of God. "I go into the future knowing He is here and He is there," he concluded and wished himself and his diary "good night."[49]

On 27 January 1925, Burke sailed from Havana for Florida and home. His comment to Murray: "It seems strange to be going back as it was strange to go away."[50]

Endnotes to Chapter 13

1. Burke, *Christ in Us*, 160.
2. Burke to E. Burke, 15 November 1924, AP, Burke Papers, box 3; Burke to Lynch, 16 November 1924, ibid., box 5; Burke to Murray, 16 November

1924, ibid., box 11; McNulty to Lefebure, 14 April 1972, ACUA, USCCB 10:72:24; McGowan, "Tribute of a Co-Worker," 23; Elisa Julian de Nieves, *The Catholic Church in Colonial Puerto Rico, 1898–1964* (Río Piedras, Puerto Rico: Editorial Edil, Inc., 1982), 99.

3. Burke to Murray, 16 November 1924, AP, Burke Papers, box 11; Burke to E. Burke, 15 November 1924, ibid., box 3; Burke to Lynch, 16 November 1924, ibid., box 5.
4. Burke to Murray, 16 and 29 November 1924, AP, Burke Papers, box 11; Burke, Puerto Rico Diary, 30 November 1924, ibid., box 70; Burke to J. H. Ryan, 4 December 1924, ACUA, USCCB 10:153:4; Nieves, *Catholic Church in Puerto Rico*, 141; Ramírez de Arellano and Seipp, *Colonialism, Catholicism, and Contraception*, 5; César J. Ayala and Rafael Bernabé, *Puerto Rico in the American Century: A History Since 1898* (Chapel Hill: University of North Carolina Press, 2007), 39; Eric Williams, *From Columbus to Castro: The History of the Caribbean, 1492–1969* (New York: Vintage Books, 1984), 450–51.
5. Burke to Lynch, 6 December 1924, AP, Burke Papers, box 5; Burke to J. H. Ryan, 4 December 1924, ACUA, USCCB 10:153:4 (first quote is here); Burke, Puerto Rico Diary, 19 November 1924, AP, Burke Papers, box 70 (remaining quotes are here); Truman R. Clark, *Puerto Rico and the United States, 1917–1933* (Pittsburgh: University of Pittsburgh Press, 1975), 48–75; Arturo Morales Carrión, *Puerto Rico: A Political and Cultural History* (New York: W.W. Norton & Company, Inc., 1983), 204–10.
6. Burke, Puerto Rico Diary, 20 November 1924, AP, Burke Papers, box 70; Burke to Murray, 29 November 1924, ibid., box 11; Burke to J. H. Ryan, 4 December 1924, ACUA, USCCB 10:153:4; Nieves, *Catholic Church in Puerto Rico*, 141; Ramírez de Arellano and Seipp, *Colonialism, Catholicism, and Contraception*, 5–8, 23–26; Ayala and Bernabé, *Puerto Rico in the American Century*, 19–20, 25, 33–50; Williams, *Columbus to Castro*, 428–33, 435–38, 444–48; 451–454.
7. Burke, Puerto Rico Diary, 20–24 November 1924, AP, Burke Papers, box 70; Slawson, *Department of Education Battle*, 58.
8. Burke, Puerto Rico Diary, 23 November 1924, AP, Burke Papers, box 70.
9. Ibid.
10. Burke, Puerto Rico Diary, 3 December 1924, AP, Burke Papers, box 70; Burke to Murray, 29 November 1924, ibid., box 11.
11. Burke, Puerto Rico Diary, 3 December 1924, AP, Burke Papers, box 70. "O felix culpa" is taken from the *Exultet*—Easter Proclamation—in the Roman Missal.
12. Burke, Puerto Rico Diary, 3 December 1924, AP, Burke Papers, box 70; Burke to J. H. Ryan, 4 December 1924, ACUA, USCCB 10:153:4.
13. Burke, Puerto Rico Diary, 5 December 1924, AP, Burke Papers, box 70.

14. Ibid.; Burke to Kerby, 6 December 1924, ACUA, Kerby Papers 58:4:4; Burke to J. H. Ryan, 4 December 1924, ACUA, USCCB 10:153:4.
15. De Nieves, *Catholic Church in Colonial Puerto Rico*, 126.
16. Burke to Kerby, 7 January 1925, ACUA, Kerby Papers 58:4:4 (first three quotes are here); Burke, Puerto Rico Diary, 8 and 9 December 1924, AP, Burke Papers, box 70 (remaining quotes are here).
17. Burke to Kerby, 7 January 1925, ACUA, Kerby Papers 58:4:4 (first quote is here); Williams to Burke, 23 December 1921, ACUA, USCCB 10:98:19 (second quote is here); Burke, Puerto Rico Diary, 10 December 1924, AP, Burke Papers, box 70 (remaining quotes are here).
18. Burke, Puerto Rico Diary, 11–20 December 1924, AP, Burke Papers, box 70 (quote is here); Burke to Kerby, 7 January 1925, ACUA, Kerby Papers 58:4:4; Herring, *Colony to Superpower*, 272–73.
19. Burke, Puerto Rico Diary, 21–22 December 1924, AP, Burke Papers, box 70.
20. Ramsey, *Spirits and the Law*, 1–176; Greene, *Catholic Church in Haiti*, 82–84; Renda, *Taking Haiti*, 10–181.
21. Burke, Puerto Rico Diary, 22 December 1924, AP, Burke Papers, box 70; Ramsey, *Spirits and the Law*, 1–10, 54–134, 139–47.
22. Burke, Puerto Rico Diary, 22 December 1924, AP, Burke Papers, box 70
23. Ibid.
24. Burke, Puerto Rico Diary, 23 December 1924, AP, Burke Papers, box 70.
25. Burke, Puerto Rico Diary, 25 December 1924, AP, Burke Papers, box 70; Renda, *Taking Haiti*, 127–28.
26. Burke, Puerto Rico Diary, 26 December 1924, AP, Burke Papers, box 70: Burke to Lynch, 10 January 1925, AP, Burke Papers, box 5.
27. Burke, Puerto Rico Diary, 27 December 1924, AP, Burke Papers, box 70; Greene, *Catholic Church in Haiti*, 98; Pamphile, *Clash of Cultures*, 26, 31–32, 40–58, 67–114; Pamphile, *La Croix et l'Glaive*, 53–89.
28. Burke, Puerto Rico Diary, 27 December 1924, AP, Burke Papers, box 70
29. Ibid.; Burke to Kerby, 7 January 1925, ACUA, Kerby Papers 58:4:4; Burke to Lynch, 10 January 1925, AP, Burke Papers, box 5.
30. Burke, Puerto Rico Diary, 28 December 1924, AP, Burke Papers, box 70.
31. Burke, Puerto Rico Diary, 30 and 31 December 1924, AP, Burke Papers, box 70.
32. Burke, Puerto Rico Diary, 31 December 1924, AP, Burke Papers, box 70.
33. Ibid.; Butler's comment is in *Hearings before a Select Committee on Haiti and Santo Domingo, United States Senate, 67th Cong., 1st and 2nd sess. Pursuant to S. Res. 112*, 2 vols (Washington, D.C., U.S. Government Printing Office, 1922), 1:517.
34. Burke, Puerto Rico Diary, 2 January 1925, AP, Burke Papers, box 70.
35. Burke, Puerto Rico Diary, 4 January 1925, AP, Burke Papers, box 70.

36. Burke, Puerto Rico Diary, 5 January 1925, AP, Burke Papers, box 70 (quotes are here); Burke to Murray, 31 December 1924, ibid., box 11.
37. Burke, Puerto Rico Diary, 6 January 1925, AP, Burke Papers, box 70; Burke to George Caruana, 20 April 1927, copy, ACUA, USCCB 10:39:12.
38. Burke, Puerto Rico Diary, 4 January 1925, AP, Burke Papers, box 70; Burke to Kerby, 7 January 1925, ACUA, Kerby Papers 58:4:4.
39. Burke, Puerto Rico Diary, 8 January 1925, AP, Burke Papers, box 70; Burke to Benedetti, 16 February 1925, copy, ACUA, USCCB 10:39:12.
40. Burke, Puerto Rico Diary, 8 January 1925, AP, Burke Papers, box 70.
41. Ibid.
42. Ibid.; Burke to Caruana, 20 April 1927, copy, ACUA, USCCB 10:39:12.
43. Burke, Puerto Rico Diary, 9–12 January 1925, AP, Burke Papers, box 70.
44. Burke, Puerto Rico Diary, 13–14 January 1925, AP, Burke Papers, box 70.
45. Burke, Puerto Rico Diary, 14 January 1925, AP, Burke Papers, box 70.
46. Burke, Puerto Rico Diary, 18–19 January 1925, AP, Burke Papers, box 70.
47. Burke, Puerto Rico Diary, 19 January 1925, AP, Burke Papers, box 70.
48. Burke to Murray, 29 November 1924, AP, Burke Papers, box 11; Burke to Kerby, 7 January 1925, ACUA, USCCB 58:4:4.
49. Burke, Puerto Rico Diary, 21 January 1925, AP, Burke Papers, box 70.
50. Burke to Murray, 21 January 1925, AP, Burke Papers, box 11.

Chapter 14
"So Many and Grave Problems," 1925 and 1926: Part I

> Our own life is not without its many problems. We have problems from within and from without. We have great problems.... We have problems of our own causing: and problems caused by others or by circumstances over which we have no control.... We have to face the uncertainty of time, and creature, and circumstance.... To abide in the trust of our Father will give that strength in self, that patience, that spiritual leisure and composure absolutely necessary for hearing the quiet voice of the Holy Spirit.[1]

Haiti

Back in Washington, John Burke faced "so many and grave problems," not the least of which was Haiti. Awaiting him was a letter from Archbishop Julien Conan, with a list of requests from the Haitian hierarchy to the U.S. government. In mid-February 1925, Burke presented the requests to Francis White, who had the Haitian desk at the State Department, and Dana Munro, State's Caribbean economist. The three discussed matters, particularly education. White and Munro were surprised to learn the Service Technique schools offered no religious instruction as required. The department had summoned Commissioner John Russell and asked Burke to draft a plan for education to be taken up with him. Later, Burke had second thoughts. Given the concordat and Haitian law, he believed the Haitian bishops and Vatican must be involved in planning. Indeed, the secretary of State should preside at a meeting with him, Russell, and a bishop empowered to act for both the Haitian hierarchy and the Vatican.[2]

Burke made this recommendation to Archbishop Pietro Benedetti, internuncio to Haiti, who took the matter up with Cardinal Pietro Gasparri and Pius XI. Both Gasparri and the pope appreciated Burke's work and wanted him to proceed along the lines he suggested. The Haitian bishops also approved. Benedetti went to Washington in May to confer with Burke. Together, the two met with Democratic Senator Peter Gerry of Rhode Island and several senatorial colleagues. The senators agreed to gather information about the Haitian situation and present it to the Senate, the Departments of State and Navy, and officials of the occupation. Sadly, Gerry would be the only senator to take action. Convinced that an American churchman must represent the situation before the federal government, Benedetti commissioned Burke to act on his behalf: "Haitian matters are now in your hands." Specifically, Burke was to secure Catholic instruction in every grade at every school in Haiti, an increase of salaries for priests and religious, and establishment of the final two dioceses specified in the Concordat.[3]

The plight of Haitian Catholicism turned Burke's thoughts to the laity and the immature status of the NCCM and NCCW. If these two were better organized and more experienced, "if their interest and support could be aroused and expressed," wrote Burke, "easier would be made the way of salvation, temporal and eternal, to hundreds of thousands of Haitians"—indeed to people of all nations. He believed the American Church had a spiritual mission to the world, and the apostles of that mission were the laity. "Yet many Bishops ask why an N.C.C.M or an N.C.C.W.," lamented Burke. "There must be some sad days in heaven."[4]

Meanwhile, he told the Administrative Committee about conditions in the Antilles. In Puerto Rico, wealthy Americans and Spaniards owned most of the land. The country had desperate need of priests, Catholic hospitals, and Catholic education. Only about 7 percent of the population was Protestant, but those enjoyed "great prestige on account of the American Government and the idea that America is Protestant." As for Haiti, Burke said the occupiers failed to abide by the concordat. They established the Service Technique, which had every appearance of developing into a "national system of secular schools." American administrators received huge salaries, while priests and Catholic teachers were "miserably paid." The people were largely ignorant with "a tendency to revert to Voodooism."[5]

The committee called for a study of problems in those countries in preparation for the hierarchy's annual meeting. It intended to recommend redefinition of the American Home Missions to include U.S. possessions and dependencies. Unfortunately, when the hierarchy met, it simply noted the Vatican no longer treated Puerto Rico and Haiti as its wards, nor did the American Home Missions consider them under its purview.[6]

Just before Christmas, Burke saw President Calvin Coolidge. "Tell it not in Gath [2 Sam. 1:20]," he wrote to Bishop Peter Muldoon, "but Mr. Coolidge thought we had withdrawn from Haiti." So, Burke updated him on the situation. In the New Year, he reminded White of the concordat and hoped to speak to him soon about issues hinging on it. Unfortunately, critical matters recounted in the next chapter diverted Burke's attention. Still, his current effort bore fruit. The State Department apparently ordered that students in Service Technique schools receive religious instruction which was now being taught.[7]

In June 1926, Archbishop Conan and Bishop Jean-Marie Jan were in Washington and met with Burke. He wanted them to see Coolidge, but they declined because President Louis Borno was also there, and they feared a meeting with Coolidge might be misinterpreted back home as a political act. So, Burke, Conan, and Jan conferred with Gerry and other senators about education. The three clerics said William Cumberland opposed Catholic education. He claimed Haiti had three different systems: state schools, religious schools under Catholic brothers and sisters, and presbytery schools under bishops. Cumberland used this claim as "a sort of smokescreen" for introducing a fourth "secular and sort of federal system." Consensus emerged that the Haitian government and Church could set aside differences in order to incorporate agricultural education in all schools. Burke discussed the idea with Archbishop George Caruana, new apostolic delegate to the Antilles and Mexico, who was then in D.C. Caruana believed he could arrange such agreement between Church and government.[8]

Gerry proposed the plan to Secretary of State Frank Kellogg arguing the Service Technique was impractical and wrongheaded. The majority of Haitians were illiterate and needed introduction to new ways by those they trusted: French religious brothers and sisters already conducting schools. Agricultural training could be incorporated into them if the occupier released sufficient funds.[9] To give it careful consideration, Kellogg delayed responding until November. His reply correctly surmised Gerry's real concern was the Service Technique. Kellogg nixed the plan because it represented a "fundamental change of policy," necessitating reconsideration of the problem, requiring new legislation from the Haitian government, and perhaps causing loss of progress already made.[10]

Reporting the decision to Conan, Burke said he would continue to appeal to officials for "justice to the church in Haiti." Making it a political issue in Congress, he said, "would avail nothing at the present time."[11]

EDUCATION

In April, Burke and James H. Ryan informed the Administrative Committee the NEA abandoned hope of securing a department of education with financial aid, the controversial feature in previous ones. Instead, it would propose creation of a department of education for scientific investigation and research, something virtually all schoolmen supported. Burke and Ryan asked for guidance. The bishops thought the NCWC should participate in the NEA meeting to draft the bill and advocate something positive without committing the hierarchy to anything. It authorized Edward Pace, president of the American Council on Education, who would attend the meeting in that capacity, to represent the NCWC as well.[12]

Meanwhile, the Oregon School Law was argued before the Supreme Court. Burke attended the oral arguments. Oregon's lawyers claimed parents had no more control over their offspring than over themselves. Since the state could reasonably limit rights of adults for the common good, it could do the same with children. One attorney even claimed the state stood as *parens patriae* [national parent] to minors and therefore had unlimited control over them. The Fourteenth Amendment did not abridge a state's right to legislate for the common good, which demanded all children be educated in public schools, the only safeguards against foreignism, religious distrust, and disloyal teaching. Both William Guthrie and John Kavanaugh argued the law aimed at destruction of private education. To accomplish this, it negated liberties of private schools, of teachers who taught in them, of parents who sent their offspring to them, and of children who attended them. It was a gross assault on Fourteenth Amendment rights.[13]

Burke told the Administrative Committee the justices displayed "the utmost respect for Guthrie, in marked contrast to treatment of opposing counsel." He was convinced the Court would uphold the lower tribunal either unanimously or with one dissenting vote. In fact, when the chief justice happened on NCWC counsel before the session, Burke overheard him say, "In principle, this case is simply the *Meyer* case over again." Two months later, the Court handed down a unanimous opinion upholding the lower bench. While admitting a state could reasonably regulate and supervise all schools, wrote Justice James McReynolds, the practical effect of the Oregon law was destruction of private and parochial education without sufficient warrant for such drastic use of state police power. He continued "the child is not the mere creature of the state." Parents had the right and duty to prepare their offspring for obligations beyond citizenship. This decision gave unprecedented security to parochial schools. It stunned both the Ku Klux Klan and Southern Jurisdiction of Scottish Rite Masons, but left both undeterred in their belief that all children belonged in public schools.[14]

Shortly thereafter, the NEA unveiled its new bill, calling for establishment of a department of education to house both the Bureau of Education and Board of Vocational Education. Through research and dissemination of information, the secretariat would help states establish and maintain better school systems, devise improved financing, design modern classroom buildings, and develop state-of-the-art teaching methods and curricula. It was the first half of the former bill.[15]

The NEA's strategy was not lost on the NCWC. Ryan reported it deleted the aid package, but really yielded nothing. It aimed at federalization of education. What it previously attempted in one step, it now sought in two.[16] Burke told the hierarchy that once a department was established, the NEA would ask for aid. Given strong sentiment among educators for a department, and since aid was no longer in the bill, he proposed the bishops reopen the question at their annual convention and weigh the wisdom of intransigent opposition.[17]

The day before the convention, the Administrative Committee discussed the matter. On one hand, the Oregon ruling secured parochial schools. On the other, Catholics suspected the new bill foreshadowed federal control of education. Indeed it had the support of the same anti-Catholic groups backing its predecessors, especially Masonry and the Klan.

The committee decided to recommend taking a neutral position regarding the NEA bill.[18]

When the hierarchy considered the question, several bishops wanted to endorse the bill. Others argued the NEA was the Church's principal opponent on schooling. Moreover, public sentiment opposed every form of centralization. Sensing the drift, Archbishop Austin Dowling asked if the bishops wanted to oppose the bill openly or informally. He warned that open opposition would ensure its passage. The hierarchy adopted a resolution declaring their unwillingness to take a formal stand against it, but that "informally" they opposed any legislation tending toward further federalization of education. Cardinal William O'Connell, chairman, emphasized Dowling's Department of Education was to be unhampered in its activity and at liberty to use its discretion in directing its informal course of action.[19]

So, the Administrative Committee directed Burke to make no open opposition to the bill, but to counter informally—quietly—federal control. If public action became necessary, he was to consult with the committee.[20] This directive was problematic: neither Congress nor the Catholic press knew the hierarchy had muted, not abandoned, its opposition to federalization. This situation would bring Burke into disrepute among some Catholics and cause them to question the nature and authority of the NCWC itself.

Motion Pictures

In March 1925, the Public Relations Committee of the MPPDA decided the latter needed a more definite and effective structure than the committee itself to accomplish the important work of improving motion pictures. It called for establishment of a Public Relations Department inside the MPPDA with an "Open Door" policy to the public. With that, the committee dissolved, and the MPPDA launched the new department under Jason Joy.[21]

Since October 1923, the NCWC's Charles McMahon, a member of the committee, had been screening films and issuing reviews of wholesome ones. With its demise, he announced a three-year program of expansion of Motion Picture Bureau. Approved by Burke, it called for hiring a full-time, experienced critic. It also proposed a campaign through lectures, radio, and special articles for three ends: to inform about motion-picture production; to develop a sympathetic and constructive point of view toward the screen; and to encourage patronage at local theaters to make "exhibition of worth-while pictures financially profitable." When Joy and Will Hays saw the plan, they agreed to contribute $10,000 annually (equivalent to $190,000 in 2024) for its support. McMahon informed Burke, and the two agreed it would be improper to accept it, no doubt because it would compromise the NCWC's independence.[22]

McMahon launched the program in early 1926 with an address on "Motion Pictures and the New Year" over radio station WJZ, flagship of NBC Blue. He said the industry's outstanding achievement was having studio heads recognize "moral responsibility toward the public." Acknowledging not all "movies were 100 per cent perfect," their level was now comparable to legitimate theater and current literature. None of them would be perfect until public taste became perfect. Rather than fault-finding, the Motion Picture Bureau followed the slogan "Boost the Best." Opposed to censorship, it promoted decent films and roused people to responsibility for welfare of their communities and the nation.[23]

Alfred Young, Burke's former associate in the Catholic Theater Movement, heard the address and wrote a letter to the editor of the Brooklyn *Tablet*. McMahon so impressed him that, though not a moviegoer, he saw two films, the first about an attractive "gold digger," who flirted with men to secure favors, but rebuffed them when they sought favors in return. The second, *A Woman of the World*, starred Pola Negri who, Young was told, reveled "in the vampire role." It took every opportunity for suggestiveness. His negative reaction surprised a movie-going friend who considered both films standard fare, as apparently did McMahon who said the NCWC opposed "legalized censorship." Noting the *Tablet* had recently called for such, Young suggested the matter be presented to the "tribunal" of the NCWC "with all the reverend judges [bishops] in session."[24]

To Burke, Young complained the influence of film was so "potent and insidious" it could seduce "well-meaning Catholics," even those in positions able to do "infinite harm." He hoped Burke could see his "way clear" to lay the case before the NCWC. He offered to come discuss it.[25] Nothing indicates Burke replied. In defense, McMahon sent the *Tablet* a screed to which

Young responded. He then sent Burke a formal request to "appeal" to the NCWC—the "Higher Court"—against McMahon's position, which opposed "the distinctively Catholic side."[26]

In mid-April, Burke laid the matter before the "tribunal": the Administrative Committee. He noted Young objected to the NCWC's policy against legal censorship, something Burke himself opposed. He explained it was difficult to secure voluntary censorship because of lack of "good faith" on the part of theater managers. The committee thought any attempt to enforce censorship was unlikely to be successful. It directed McMahon continue to work with producers for elimination of indecent films.[27]

At the same time, Burke put the NCWC on record as opposed to federal regulation of the movie industry. Democrat William Upshaw of Georgia introduced a bill in Congress for establishment of a six-person, federal commission empowered to prohibit films containing sexual matters such as illicit affairs, white slavery, passionate lovemaking, nudity, and scantily clad persons. It required everyone engaged in film-making to register with the commission.[28]

When a House committee held a hearing on it, Burke protested, arguing every state and municipality possessed the power to protect public morals through censorship. To authorize the federal government to override that power was "inimical to the American sense of liberty and local self-government." It would abridge peoples' right to choose the films they wished to see. Enactment would serve as precedent for federal censorship of press and stage. Burke objected to investing arbitrary power in six individuals to decide what movies the nation would see. He trembled at thought of the "blunders of private judgment" and "personal prejudice" they might perpetrate. Such "unlimited" authority had never been granted any federal agency. Although the NCWC desired and worked for clean films, Burke declared it was "unalterably opposed to the un-American procedure" proposed in the bill. The measure died in committee.[29]

In early July 1926, Will Hays informed Burke that Cecil B. DeMille was shooting *King of Kings* about the life of Jesus and wanted advice from Catholics, Protestants, and Jews. Hays thought the movie might be "the greatest picture ever made" as well as "the greatest sermon of our time." While interested in what religious consultants might say, DeMille sought their cooperation more as a ploy to preempt criticism. Hays asked Burke to be Catholic adviser. Unable to devote the time, he promised to appoint a qualified person. After negotiations "that would try a man's soul" to find someone, Burke secured Jesuit Priest Daniel Lord, a drama professor at St. Louis University.[30]

Burke was concerned because he learned from a "rather reliable authority" the film was based on Bruce Barton's best seller *The Man Nobody Knows* (1925), which portrayed Jesus as a man's man and described him as a world-class salesman. In Burke's view, Barton practically denied the divinity of Jesus. He feared the NCWC might not be able to approve the film. Sources indicated the FCC and Jews had already reviewed and blessed the screenplay, which led him to be "very sceptical [*sic*]." Still, he thought it incumbent upon Catholics to be "even more than fair" and judge the picture on study of the script and its film depiction. He instructed Lord to render no judgment on it to DeMille or Hays, but tell them his report would go to Burke. If Lord determined only drastic changes would make it acceptable, he could inform DeMille his report would be negative. Such might prompt him to make "sweeping changes," in which case Lord could say he would await "hopefully on the ultimate result." Lord replied that if based on the book, he too foresaw problems; he considered it "flippant and ignorant." In fact, DeMille used Barton as a consultant and the book served as his commercial inspiration.[31]

After meeting with Hays and Burke, Lord went to Los Angeles and spent ten days with cast and crew, five in a studio and five on Catalina Island where DeMille shot outdoor scenes. While on location, Lord spent nights either on DeMille's yacht or in camp with cast and crew. He found DeMille "more than cordial," and the two conferred for hours. Lord reported to Burke that DeMille was risking his personal fortune and expected to lose money. He considered the director deeply sincere in his desire "to make Christ known and loved." Some crew members said at the project's start, DeMille called them together and urged them to work in a spirit of reverence and devotion: "No scandals of any sort; no profane talk; no quarrelling [*sic*] or ill feeling." Many were Catholics, and Lord said Mass for them daily on Catalina.[32]

He reviewed the script and saw all footage shot thus far. Lord found everyone open to suggestions and eager to adapt the film to Catholic tastes.

Jeanie MacPherson, screenwriter, was a Christian. She built the first half to climax at intermission with the "Our Father," using the Protestant ending "For thine is the power and the glory, etc." Lord counseled her to delete it because there was question whether Jesus spoke those words and Catholics did not use them. Even though the conclusion of the first half depended on them, MacPherson agreed to drop them from prints for Catholic countries and probably those in the United States.[33]

Lord told Burke that to condense the film, MacPherson depicted only the last part of Jesus' ministry, taking considerable liberty with chronology for dramatic interest and effect. For instance, the cleansing of the temple occurred at conclusion of the first half, rather than on Palm Sunday. The scene began with the Widow's Mite, which Mark and Luke placed later in Holy Week. When Jesus saw a buyer and seller trying to cheat the poor woman, he drove all such from the temple, to cheers of a crowd waving palms and proclaiming him king, a clear allusion to Palm Sunday. As Jesus looked over the rejoicing throng, Satan showed him all the world's kingdoms and promised them in return for his homage—the temptation on the Temple parapet, which happened at the beginning of Jesus' ministry (Matt. 4:5–10). This scene ended the first half of the film, concluding with Jesus uttering the "Our Father."[34]

Something sure to cause controversy was the manner in which DeMille opened the movie: an elaborate Romanesque, banquet-scene filmed in Technicolor. Mary Magdalen, "nude from the waist except for large jeweled plates at her breasts and a loose robe over her shoulders," hosted the opulent feast, a foil to the humble poverty of Jesus. The sequence featured carousing drinkers, dancing girls, and zebras harnessed to a chariot. One chair at the table was empty: the seat of Judas, implying she was his mistress. Magdalen asked where he was, only to be told he went to follow a carpenter. "I will bring him back," she replied. DeMille explained the scene established opposition: Christ and goodness versus Magdalen and evil. Lord told Burke he had DeMille cut from it "a sensual kiss; the leering of an old roué at her leg; a procession of dancing girls; a long scene of her making up for her [lost] conquest [Judas]." DeMille admitted the opening was classic "C. B. DeMille, the rest is the Evangelists."[35]

Lord told Burke he could render no final judgment because the film was not finished. His verdict based on what he had seen, was "entirely in favor" and would be "absolutely" so if he could review the finished product. DeMille wanted him to return after Christmas for the final cut and to edit caption boards. In the report's cover letter, Lord admitted DeMille's "very cordial" reception of and friendship for him had made the priest "an enthusiast about him and his work." Lord believed, however, that he had maintained objectivity.[36]

Burke read the report carefully, noting his concerns which were several. Use of the Protestant version of the "Our Father" bothered him. He remarked on the absence of any mention of Jesus' divinity. The looseness with chronology deeply troubled him, especially placing the temptation of Jesus on Palm Sunday. Troublesome too was the suggested relationship between Judas and Magdalen. Related to it was DeMille's opinion that Jesus' ability to win Judas from her and then convert her was what made him a "real" hero.[37] That was not the element that made him a hero to Christians. Burke gave Lord a guarded response. Since Lord withheld final determination pending completion of the film, so would he.[38] Yet Burke had serious reservations.

He asked McMahon's thoughts on the report. McMahon said Lord had done all he could to secure changes at present. It would be difficult to get more at the final cut, but he should be there to do what he could. Despite Lord's favorable attitude toward the film, McMahon doubted "the wisdom of giving it an 'official N.C.W.C. endorsement,'" which would set a "dangerous precedent." He predicted Catholic critics would take a wide variety of positions on it.[39]

Toward mid-November, the MPPDA Public Relations Department sent the NCWC photos of Lord saying Mass for the company of *King of Kings*, noting they memorialized the first religious ceremony on a movie set. Given Lord's role as Catholic consultant, McMahon asked if there was objection to using the pictures in the NCWC News Service. Burke did object. "It seems to me a sort of method to force a quasi-commitment from us," he told McMahon. "If the Moving Picture People are going to push us this way, it may be necessary for us to dissociate ourselves by positive statement, and that would be unpleasant and certainly a thing I do not wish to do."[40] There the matter lay until the final cut.

A DEATH, VACATION, AND RESENTMENT

In summer 1925, Burke coped with an unexpected death. William Cochran, director of the Legal Department, had been unwell for some time. Physicians discovered he had cancer and in July performed surgery that seemingly went well. Five days later, Cochran's condition worsened and soon thereafter became hopeless. Burke hurried home from vacation in Canada, but arrived too late. He sang the high requiem Mass in St. Paul's church and performed Cochran's interment at Mount Olivet Cemetery.[41]

Burke reported to Bishop Edmund Gibbons, chairman of the Legal Department, his eagerness to secure a replacement quickly because of pressing matters. He discounted promoting James R. Ryan, department attorney, because "his usefulness is in another line." Burke was considering Grattan Kerans, an "excellent Catholic" possessed of wide acquaintance with public men. He worked in the Press Department. Gibbons counseled Burke to proceed slowly. The two had often discussed the Legal Department's future, and both hoped to hire a high-class Catholic lawyer to head it. Gibbons urged checking with Justin McGrath, head of press, before talking to Kerans to ensure he had no objection. Burke feared McGrath would indeed want to keep him.[42]

About a week after the funeral, Burke resumed vacation on Shelter Island at Gardiner's Bay, Long Island. He hoped "for many hours" to himself and time to write to Helen Lynch and Grace Murray. On the anniversary of Lynch's taking the veil, he told her: "We will not know until eternity comes, what the consecration of oneself to Christ means.... He is the beginning and the end; the All in All; He is finality and He gives to us the sense of finality that with Him in us all will be well."[43]

Reminiscing on his years at *Catholic World* and their shared spiritual endeavors, Burke told Murray he often thought "upon the past" because "fidelity and gratitude demanded it." He recalled that while she, Gertrude Delahunt, Mary Hawks, and he worked together on the magazine, they also worked on themselves. He pictured them as a foursome in golf. Rather than opponents, they "played on the greens of God" and "gave one another points on the game: without rivalry and with much love." They all "looked to the same course: all played to read the same final green, which is death—which is heaven." They thought they would remain close, within earshot of each other, until the last fairways. But, no. They were still on the course, each hitting from the same tee to reach the same green, yet "out of sight of one another, nor can we always know how the others are doing." They were still a foursome on the same "earthly green of God" and knew they were "not playing a lone game: that the others are behind or ahead, hoping to catch up, or hoping that we will advance." God had separated them only that they "may play the better, without ever forgetting our first lessons and the companionship together: nor the aims and standards that I think were the best we ever had." He doubted not that God would give them "a good approach at the last—and time to put [*sic* for putt] carefully and thoughtfully on that last green from which He will take us to Paradise." Burke told Murray to share the letter at some point with Delahunt and Hawks, "for after all, all of the foursome should know about it." The letter was an artful, wistful way of putting the best face on the separation of spiritual friends. He signed it off with blessings "from one who just now is in the fairway."[44]

On return to Washington, Burke began the hunt for Cochran's successor, a matter complicated by the ambition of James R. Ryan, who coveted the position. He and his friends lobbied Gibbons hard. As for Kerans, McGrath refused to let him go. Burke knew the Legal Department must function at a higher level within its current resources. Neither the late Cochran nor Ryan were "equipped to do more work if asked." Burke told Gibbons the financial straits of the NCWC prevented him from securing "a capable lawyer." William Kerby highly recommended William F. Montavon. Though not an attorney, he had wide contacts in the State Department, extensive foreign service in the Philippines and South America, and fluency in Spanish and French. Described by Burke as "an elderly, presentable man"—he was only a year older than Burke—he was willing to work for an annual salary of $6,000 (equivalent to $105,600 in 2024), half his previous pay because he wanted "to get into Catholic work." Moreover, he had plans to "build the dept in a way that entails no expense." Gibbons approved the appointment.[45]

Then the trouble began. Resentful at being passed over, Ryan considered Montavon totally unfit for the directorship because he lacked legal training and had little familiarity with domestic policy. He asked Burke for independent control of all legal matters. Burke and Gibbons refused because the department must function as a unit. Gibbons also considered

Ryan "very light weight legally" and questioned his ability to function independently. When Ryan refused to accord Montavon "the simplest courtesies," Burke pleaded with him. As he told Murray, "I have been kindness itself to Mr. Ryan." Finally, in January 1926, after more than a month of such behavior, Ryan resigned.[46] He departed a bitter man: one determined to destroy Burke.

IMMIGRATION

After passage of the Reed-Johnson Immigration Restriction Act of 1924, Burke and Bruce Mohler spent much time, often unsuccessfully, assisting various bishops and religious orders in overcoming hurdles to get individual priests, sisters, and brothers into the U.S.[47] At the same time, Burke worked at securing relaxation of the law to hasten entry of foreign-born clergy and religious. At its passage, the NCWC had convinced Congress to cut the required experience in ministry from four years to two prior to immigration. Even so, this stipulation caused uproar in the American hierarchy. So, Burke sought to further shorten the wait.[48]

In April 1925, he came up with an idea to halve that time again. He and Mohler met with Secretary of Labor James Davis and Assistant Secretary Edward J. Henning to apply that non-quota exemption to deacons. Burke argued that ordination to the diaconate fulfilled the Labor Department's definition of a "minister" under the law. Davis was hesitant because in his Baptist church, deacons were simply lay people appointed to that office. Burke argued the Catholic Church ordained deacons after five years of study. They were bound by vows and could administer the sacraments of baptism and matrimony as well as perform other duties in common with the priesthood. Davis asked Henning to take it up with the department's solicitor general.[49]

In fact, Burke was not trying to get deacons admitted into the United States. His idea was to start the waiting period for priests at the date of their ordination to the diaconate, which occurred a year before priesthood, thus reducing the wait-time from two years to one. Although his argument was technically true, it was a bit misleading. While deacons had power to baptize and marry, in the early twentieth century there was little opportunity for that in a seminary.

Burke reported to the Administrative Committee he was hopeful the government would recognize deacons as ministers. Within days, Mohler announced the solicitor general agreed with Burke's argument. The government would so instruct all U.S. consuls. A foreign priest recruited for work in America would have to provide evidence of the date of his diaconate. He would also need an attestation of acceptance for ministry from the bishop in whose diocese he would work.[50]

Having succeeded in shortening the wait-time for priests, Burke turned to the matter of religious sisters. In December 1925, he and Mohler spoke with Representative Albert Johnson and Senator James Wadsworth of New York about having the law amended to place foreign nuns in a non-quota class. Failing to gain support, they asked to place such sisters in a new quota class specifically for admission to American territories and insular possessions. The two congressmen offered to support such a measure, "provided a suitable phraseology could be agreed upon" between the NCWC and Commissioner of Immigration William W. Husband.[51]

Burke and Mohler had a long meeting with Husband in January 1926 and reached an understanding on wording, which the NCWC put into a bill to amend. The measure created a separate quota class for sisters and brothers seeking to immigrate to U.S. possessions with a limit of 100 per calendar year for each territory.[52] Burke was not sanguine about its chances. When Archbishop George Caruana came through Washington in April, Burke took him to see Johnson. The two made a special plea, particularly with regard to Puerto Rico. Johnson, however, now refused to introduce the bill. He explained the House Committee on Immigration would not accept it and therefore it would be unwise to propose it. Burke believed him sincere "because there is a strong feeling here that if any exception at all is made in the immigration restriction, the door will be opened wide to many others."[53]

In mid-April, Bishop Edwin Byrne of Ponce, Puerto Rico, informed Burke he had been able to secure some Spanish sisters through the regular quota for Spain, which was now exhausted and there was need of more nuns. He asked if anything was being done about it. Burke reported his efforts thus far were "unsuccessful and there is no light upon the horizon." He suggested that since the Reed-Johnson Act permitted open migration from Central and South American countries, Byrne seek help from communities of sisters in those regions.[54]

On the domestic scene, the NCWC was concerned about the nation's hostile mood toward immigrants within. Many Americans viewed the Mass of resident aliens as "a national menace." Burke, Mohler, and Montavon found this attitude disconcerting. NCWC agents who traveled the country reported such hostility was causing resident aliens to feel "less and less certain" about their status and to sense that "their security is menaced." In some cases, this feeling was about to or had reached "a condition of panic."[55]

In December 1926, Congress sought to tighten even more the grip on immigrants already within. It entertained various bills for registration of aliens. The several versions of these measures called for issuing an identification card to each immigrant upon entry into the U.S. They also required aliens, legal or illegal, to obtain a card that would identify personal characteristics and perhaps require a photograph and fingerprint. It would also list any court actions regarding the person. These bills required aliens to renew registration at least once a year and with each change of address.[56]

Burke wired Hanna and Muldoon for explicit direction to oppose the bills. Advocates, he said, claimed their purpose was threefold: to hasten acquisition of citizenship; to enforce more effectively the 1924 law; and to curb smuggling of illegal aliens. Burke believed the measures constituted an "unnecessary and unwarranted surveillance" of those aliens already legally in the nation prior to the Reed-Johnson Act. He said "goading" aliens into citizenship ran counter to American tradition. Signing of an oath of allegiance did not make a citizen. The mind and heart of a person must be prepared for that goal. "To subject the alien to multitudinous unnecessary annoyances will never accomplish this," argued Burke. Moreover, enforcement of such laws would require a vast army of agents who would be used "to harass the alien into either acquiring citizenship or abandoning the country." The proposed legislation affected not only immigrants, but also international observers studying American institutions, tourists, foreign students in American schools, and businessmen acting as agents for foreign financial, commercial, industrial, and scientific institutions.[57]

Of equal concern was the bill to be known as the Deportation Act of 1926. It authorized expulsion of any alien who entered the country illegally or under false pretenses; who belonged to a forbidden group like anarchists; who remained in the country longer than authorized; who became a public charge; who was an idiot, imbecile, feeble minded, epileptic, insane, psychopathic, or chronic alcoholic; who committed a crime warranting a sentence of one or more years; who committed more than one minor offense with aggregate sentences amounting to eighteen months; who was involved in any manner at all with prostitution. The legislation authorized immigration administrators to implement deportation through summary procedures. The measure prompted one legal scholar to conclude the government had "devised a system of administrative procedure, of executive justice, with a maximum of powers in the administrative officers, a minimum of checks and safeguards against error and prejudice, and with certainty, care and due deliberation sacrificed to the desire for speed."[58]

Burke sent Montavon to the House hearing. His statement walked the fine line between recognizing the nation's right to regulate immigration and the proper method of doing so. No doubt coached by Burke, he said the goal was eventual citizenship of newcomers. After recounting the feeling of uncertainty among resident aliens, Montavon argued the correct approach to them was "a missionary one … which required humanity and sympathy and charity." He argued the government would never turn "these millions of aliens into satisfactory citizens" if it attempted to accomplish it by the methods proposed. He believed sympathy for immigrants existed, but the present focus on the "undesirable alien" eroded the faith of resident aliens in that sympathy. The NCWC believed the present measure would accelerate erosion. "The tendency which is manifested in this Bill to subject the alien to a summary procedure … under administrative officers who are apt to be inefficient and even hostile to the alien," said Montavon, "is foreign to our institutions." The House passed the bill, but it died in the Senate.[59]

Birth Control

In summer 1925, Burke geared up for the expected renewal of Mary Dennett's campaign for birth control. He had eleven leaflets printed, objecting to contraception from various angles, Catholic, Protestant, and secular. For instance, one reprinted the *New York Times* challenging Malthusianism. Another reprinted an article from *Collier's Weekly* by an actuarial statistician demonstrating a declining birth rate and a rising death rate in America. Yet another contained Anglican Bishop Charles Gore's testimony, pronouncing "unnatural" the separation of sexual intercourse from procreation.[60]

In August, Burke sent a circular to Catholic newspapers and magazines with the leaflets enclosed. He urged they bring them to the attention of readers and asked for names of ten people in their locales who would be interested in receiving the leaflets and in actively working against birth control. Similarly, he circularized heads of various organizations, like the New York Society for the Suppression of Vice.[61] Bishop Gibbons suggested encouraging eminent physicians, Catholic and non-Catholic, to protest against change in the law. He thought the Catholic Hospital Association might also be of assistance. "Better that Bishops should not figure [in]," he advised, "—or the charge that *Rome* was interfering might be raised."[62]

In October, Sara Laughlin sent Burke the newsletter of Margaret Sanger's ABCL. Like Burke, Sanger was of Irish descent. Unlike his devout Catholic parents, her father was a freethinking apostate who refused to have his children baptized as infants or to permit his pious wife to attend Mass. He encouraged his children to think for themselves, and Sanger eventually became a free-love radical. Laughlin described her as "a very good looking scoundrel." In the newsletter, Sanger announced her intention to amend the Comstock law. As Burke saw it, incorrectly, Dennett and Sanger had joined hands. In fact, the physically and financially exhausted Dennett had abandoned the birth control movement.[63]

In late November, Burke cast a wider net for opponents to the proposed amendment. He argued it represented "a challenge to the patriotism of every true American" and confronted the nation "with a moral crisis of great magnitude." This plea went to a wide array of organizations, secular and religious. When Burke saw Coolidge in December 1925, he spoke about birth control. The president opposed the movement: "Of course, Father Burke, every Church organization will join you in protest." "When I returned to my office," wrote Burke to Muldoon, "I found a letter from the United Congregationalists who said they would not."[64]

In January 1926, Sanger sent Anne Kennedy, legislative secretary of the ABCL, to establish an office in Washington and sound out congressmen on their willingness to support a birth control amendment. Senator Albert Cummins and Representative William Vaile, who sponsored Dennett's, refused to sponsor Sanger's. Burke claimed they declined because of NCWC activities, especially its successful effort to line up at least twenty prominent non-Catholic organizations to oppose it.[65]

Kennedy called at the NCWC to see Burke. To say she was not altogether forthright in her motive would be polite. From the following, it is clear she and Sanger were trying to elicit, and perhaps color, information to use against the Church in what Kennedy already knew was an uphill and probably fruitless struggle to secure congressional sponsors.

Burke's office referred her to Patrick Ward, who handled birth control. Kennedy presented herself as just another "walk-in" interested in learning the Catholic position. According to Ward, they engaged in friendly, rambling conversation about the value of sexual intercourse in a marriage, the Church's efforts against birth control, and the alleged benefit of contraception in helping mothers raise children they already had. Most memorable to Ward was Kennedy's remark that aside from procreation, sexual intercourse possessed "of itself a spiritual and uplifting (!) value which it was intended have by the Creator" to express the "supreme attachment and the unity of two beings." He responded the value she placed on the act was "purely emotional and sensual." The real spirituality in intercourse came at conception when "a human being was being brought into existence endowed with a soul in God's image" destined for eternal bliss. Only toward the end of their conversation did it occur to Ward to ask if Kennedy represented any organization. She then admitted she was from the ABCL.[66]

As Ward showed her out, Father John Ryan entered. Ward introduced Kennedy and averred she had come to discuss birth control. Ryan told her, "Well, I suppose Mr. Ward is well up in the subject." With that, she departed.[67]

Two weeks later, Kennedy returned with a written report of her version of the visit and asked Ward to correct inaccuracies. He found it "a garbled distorted version of our more or less disjointed conversation." He later explained to Burke his attempt to correct "some of the more absurd statements," while others were so preposterous no one who understood Catholic theology would think a Catholic had made them. Those he let pass, seeing "it was hopeless to make the document a truthful record." He specifically told Kennedy even the amended version could not be viewed as an official statement of the NCWC.[68]

Her report said that as Roman Catholicism was the true faith, the Church was "responsible for the morals of the entire human race." So, it had the duty to block legislation affecting morals of non-Catholics. The purpose of marriage was procreation, and continence by a married couple was "practicable and healthful," the form of birth control endorsed by hundreds of leading psychologists, psychiatrists, and gynecologists. Aware of the difficulties parents had in rearing a large family, the NCWC held most were of human origin and could be eliminated by "less capitalistic control of the labor market, higher wages, better housing, etc." Catholics believed the ABCL was attempting "to correct those great social error[s] by advocating another error."[69]

Burke learned of the situation only gradually. His first inkling came in reading the March edition of Sanger's newsletter, which reported widespread acceptance of birth control except in religious circles, especially among Catholics, who "seemingly … closed their minds to reason." The ABCL's work in Washington was going so well "the opposition has had to come out in the open to fight us." The NCWC organized a committee against it and gathered support of non-Catholic organizations behind it. "They frankly state," said Sanger, "that they intend to legislate for non-Catholics according to the dictates of the church."[70]

Burke wrote to her that statements in the newsletter were "untrue." The NCWC had not just "come in the open"; it had been there since Dennett launched her campaign. It organized no committee, but operated through its various branches. Finally, it never said it intended to legislate Catholic morality for all. He asked correction of these falsehoods in the next edition.[71]

Sanger sent Burke a copy of Kennedy's report as adjusted by Ward and asked if he objected to it. He did, categorically. It was the first he saw of it, "and it has in no way the approval of the National Catholic Welfare Conference; nor is there warrant for publishing it as the mind or position of the Conference." This came as a "great surprise" to Sanger because she understood the interview was "official" and the statement had "the approval of the other members of the Conference." Ward had told Kennedy he spoke authoritatively. After checking with him, Burke denied Ward ever said he spoke for the NCWC. Sanger claimed Kennedy had spoken with "Mr. Ward as the person in authority of the matter," adding Ryan "informed her that Mr. Ward was qualified and authorized to speak on the subject." She met Ward a second time so he could ensure the report's accuracy. "I trust that this clearly establishes the fact that the interview was an authorized one," insisted Sanger.[72]

Burke spoke with Ward, who wrote a three-page memorandum about what occurred.[73] Based on it, Burke assured Sanger that Ward had never claimed to speak for the NCWC. He had no such authority. Conceding for argument's sake that she published the statements in belief they were correct, she now knew they were not. "Common justice" demanded she make the corrections. "I again ask you," wrote Burke, "to repair the error and to see that justice is done." Sanger agreed, but urged him in future to make clear to subordinates their power to speak for the organization. "If they are not authorized," she chided, "—they should not be permitted to talk to anyone." Insinuating Ward kept the "truth concerning this interview" from Burke, she considered his "repudiation" of the report's authoritative nature "an amazing procedure on the part of an organization that speaks of common justice." Burke fired back that Kennedy never volunteered she was an agent of the ABCL gathering information for a report to its board. Ward had to extract it from her at the end of the interview.[74] The preponderance of evidence indicates Sanger and Kennedy had attempted to ambush the NCWC.

In her autobiography, Sanger wrote she did not let the matter rest there. Insisting Kennedy had interviewed both Burke and Ryan, she gave the report to H. L. Mencken, acerbic editor of *American Mercury* magazine in Baltimore, who "had knocked down a great many gods, chiefly along political and religious lines." She hoped he would take the Catholic Church down a peg or two for the alleged remark about ensuring non-Catholics lived by Church doctrine. Mencken explained he had too many Catholic friends in Baltimore for him to attack the Church. "I gained the impression he was out to slash and hit where the cause was obviously popular," wrote Sanger, "but had no intention of leading a forlorn hope or playing the role of a pioneer for freedom." In the short term, it was her hope that was forlorn. Kennedy failed to secure congressional sponsors and closed down the Washington office five months after her arrival, ending any prospect of federal action for several years.[75]

Sacramental Wine

In late 1925, sacramental wine again became an issue because of the amount going astray through fake rabbis. The regulations of 1922 limited

Jews to two gallons of wine per family member a year. Contrary to expectation, the volume of wine distributed for religious purposes increased from a total of 2.13 million gallons in 1922 to 2.94 million in 1924. In April 1925, Coolidge appointed retired General Lincoln Andrews assistant secretary of the Treasury with full authority over Prohibition. In fall, Andrews sought to curtail abuses by issuing new regulations. He sought Burke's advice to ensure they contained nothing "inconsistent with existing practices, so far as your church is concerned, or anything which you think would be a mistake for the Government to put out."[76]

The draft version of the new regulations would have upset wine distribution for Catholics, so Burke saw Andrews and straightened out the matter. "Changes I made were O.K.," he reported to Muldoon. "So the waters are smooth again and sky is fair. (But don't tell the Methodists or the Fellowship Forum about this)." The *Forum* was the Klan newspaper. The new regulations cut the amount of wine allotted to Jews to one gallon per adult a year, not to exceed an annual total of five gallons for any family. The directives had the desired effect, decreasing total amount of sacramental wine from 2.25 million gallons in 1926 to 648,871 in 1927.[77]

Yet, the sky was less clear than Burke thought. In early 1926, information reached the NCWC that James Jones, national director of Prohibition, ruled that in the future priests could no longer procure application forms for wine from chancery offices or wineries, but only from the district director of Prohibition. This unofficial regulation apparently aimed at halting wineries from issuing pirated copies of the form with their names and addresses preprinted as vintner of sale. Such forms were distributed to clergy almost as advertising. Burke saw Andrews, who assured him the regulation was warranted, but that the clergy could continue to secure blank applications from chancery offices and wineries.[78]

Nothing more came of it until the summer 1926. While Andrews vacationed, Jones informed Burke of his intention to mandate that clergy procure application forms from either the district director or the chancery office; wineries would no longer be permitted to issue them. As Charles Fay, vice president of Beaulieu winery told Burke, "It would appear … the mice begin to play as soon as the cat is away."[79] Burke went at once to complain to Jones that the new order violated the understanding reached with Andrews. He said that Keith Weeks, federal supervisor in control of wine, had assured him that, although abuses needed correction, there would be no change in regulations until Andrews returned. Wineries could continue to dispense applications. Jones, however, contended Weeks informed him just before Andrews's departure that wineries could no longer issue forms. At length, both Burke and Jones agreed nothing would be changed for the moment and another conference would be held at a later date to reach a final agreement.[80]

Meanwhile, Burke checked with the Administrative Committee to determine what regulations would be satisfactory. No member objected to the government's refusing wineries permission to issue applications, and all expressed willingness to use chancery offices for distribution of such forms to "help the government in the administration of the law." In mid-October, the NCWC informed Andrews of its endorsement of the proposed regulations.[81]

While these negotiations occurred, the NCWC worked on delivery of sacramental wine. Regulations stipulated only a bonded carrier could transport it, and each carrier was to receive an authenticated copy of the application for purchase. Thus, a rural priest would have to know route of delivery and number of carriers in order to fill out the requisite number of applications. Bonds ranged from $1,000 to $5,000 ($17,000 and $85,000 respectively in 2024). Prior to Andrews, these regulations were widely ignored and unenforced. It was not uncommon for an unbonded parishioner to pick up a shipment of wine at the train station without ever receiving a copy of the application. Andrews, however, cracked the whip. He raised the bond to between $5,000 and $25,000 ($425,000) and required an authenticated copy of the application for each carrier on every leg of the journey.[82] Since no parishioner could post such a sizable bond, the priest himself would, as purchaser, have to pick up the wine.

The NCWC negotiated with the Treasury for more than a year before the matter was resolved to Catholic satisfaction. In October 1926, while Burke was again ill and absent, Father James H. Ryan suggested a possible solution: attachment of a special label to the container (bottle, jug, or case) of wine. The chancellor of a diocese would have sole charge of labels, sign them, and send them to the winery for attachment when he sent the application for purchase. At the end of the year, he would report to the government how many labels he issued.[83] The label served as an authenticated application form attached to the container, thereby obviating necessity of multiple forms. Montavon reported that Andrews was "sympathetic" to the Catholic position, but held the regulations were "indispensable because of abuses which have been committed, in no case by Catholic Priests, but by clergymen of other denominations, especially Jewish."[84]

Apparently, persistence paid off. Unfortunately, no record exists of Burke's negotiations with the Treasury after his return to work, only the resolution reached, which was a modification of Ryan's suggestion. The government approved a new label for wine. In essence, it was a blank form with gum adhesive on the back. Before distributing the labels to diocesan chancellors, the district prohibition administrator had to sign them. When the chancellor received an application for wine, he had to sign, number, and fill out the label, specifying the name and address of the priest to receive shipment as well as the quantity, kind, and brand of wine being sent. When such labels were used, common carriers sufficed.[85] A pleased Burke reported the new label would "decrease the number of certificates to be signed and do away with the necessity in rural places of a bonded carrier."[86] There would be no further complications about procurement of wine for sacramental purposes before repeal of Prohibition.

ENDNOTES TO CHAPTER 14

1. Burke, *Christ in Us*, 12–13.
2. Conan, Requests of the Bishops of Haiti, 20 January 1925, ACUA, USCCB, 10:39:12; Burke, Interview with Francis White and Dana Munro, 11 February 1925, ibid.; Burke, Memorandum—Conference on Haiti, 13 February 1925, ibid.; Burke to Benedetti, 16 February 1925, copy, ibid.; Burke to Conan, 12 December 1925, copy, ibid., 10:98:14; Burke to Murray, 9 February 1925, AP, Burke Papers, box 12; Pamphile, *La Croix et Le Glaive*, 99–100.
3. Burke, Interview with Benedetti, 18 May 1925, ACUA, USCCB, 10:153: Interview Book (quote is here); Benedetti to Burke, 6 June 1925, ibid., 10:39:12; Burke, Report to the Administrative Committee, September 1925, ibid. An internuncio was the Vatican diplomatic grade just below nuncio. A nuncio was equivalent to an ambassador and an internuncio was equivalent to a special envoy and minister plenipotentiary.
4. Burke, Interview with White and Munro, 11 February 1925, ACUA, USCCB, 10:39:12 (quotes are here); [Burke], "Hecker and Present Problems," 564–72.

5. Minutes of the Administrative Committee, 23 April 1925, ACUA, USCCB 10:64:4.
6. Ibid.; *Minutes of the Seventh Annual Meeting of the Hierarchy*, September 1925, p. 10, ACUA, USCCB Bound Volumes.
7. Conan to Burke, 22 October 1925, ACUA, USCCB 10:98:14; Burke to Peter Muldoon, 23 December 1925, ibid., 10:152:30; Burke, Interview with White, 11 January 1926, ibid., 10:153: Interview Book; Burke to Caruana, 20 April 1927, copy, ibid., 10:39:12. David's lament over the death of King Saul: "Alas! The glory of Israel, Saul, slain upon your heights; how can the warriors have fallen! Tell it not in Gath, herald it not in the streets of Ashkelon, lest the Philistine maidens rejoice, lest the daughters of the strangers exult!" (2 Sam. 1:20).
8. Burke to Muldoon, n.d. July 1926, ACUA, USCCB, 10:104:13.
9. Peter Gerry to Frank B. Kellogg, 11 August 1926, NA, RG59, 838.42/35; Pamphile, *Clash of Cultures*, 76–77, 87–90.
10. Kellogg to Gerry, 17 September 1926, NA, RG59, 838.42/35; Kellogg to Gerry, 18 November 1926, ibid. (quotes are here).
11. Burke to Conan, 20 April 1927, copy, ACUA, USCCB 10:98:14.
12. Minutes of the Administrative Committee, 23 April 1925, ACUA, USCCB10:64:4; Slawson, *Department of Education Battle*, 143–45.
13. *Oregon School Cases*, 626–96.
14. Quoted in Burke to Thomas O'Mara, 23 March 1925, copy, ACUA, USCCB 10:14:10; *Pierce* v. *Society of Sisters*, 268 U.S. 510 (1925). Minutes of the Administrative Committee, 22 April 1925, ACUA, USCCB 10:64:4; Slawson, *Department of Education Battle*, 151–52.
15. Slawson, *Department of Education Battle*, 145–46.
16. Minutes of the Departmental Meeting, 3 July 1925, ACUA, USCCB 10:1:BV Volume 2.
17. Program for the Meeting of the Bishops at the Catholic University of America, 16–17 September 1925, ACUA, Annual Meeting of Hierarchy file.
18. Minutes of the Administrative Committee, 14 September 1925, ACUA, USCCB 10:64:4, Chalmers, *Hooded Americanism*, 284–85.
19. *Minutes of the Seventh Annual Meeting of the Hierarchy, September 1925*, 5–8; Slawson, *Department of Education Battle*, 147–48.
20. Minutes of the Administrative Committee, 17 September 1925, ACUA, USCCB10:64:4.
21. Final Report of the Committee on Organization of the Committee on Public Relations, 21 March 1925, FULSC, MPPDA Record #3264, 2–0790 to 2–0804 accessed 17 March 2013 http://mppda.flinders.edu.au/records/3264; Vasey, *World According to Hollywood*, 34–37; Moley, *Hays Office*, 138–39; Jowett, *Film*, 176.
22. NCWC News Service, 22 October 1923; Edith Jarboe, "When the Movies are Worth While," *NCWC Bulletin* 5 (May 1924): 11; McMahon to Michael

Ready, 9 April 1940, with enclosure A Statement of the Work of the Motion Picture Bureau of the National Catholic Welfare Conference, 1925, ACUA, USCCB 10:125:31.

23. Brooklyn *Tablet*, 9 January 1926.
24. Brooklyn *Tablet*, 17 January 1926.
25. Alfred Young to Burke, 26 January 1926, ACUA, USCCB 10:125:32.
26. Brooklyn *Tablet*, 30 January and 6 February 1926; Young, An Appeal to the Higher Court of the National Catholic Welfare Conference, [16 February 1926], ACUA, USCCB 10:125:22.
27. Minutes of the Administrative Committee, 15 April 1926, ACUA, USCCB 10:64:4.
28. Burke to the House Committee on Education, 14 April 1926, ACUA, USCCB 10:125:32; Tropiano, *Obscene, Indecent, Immoral*, 26–27.
29. Burke to the House Committee on Education, 14 April 1926, ACUA, USCCB 10:125:32.
30. Hays to Burke, telegram, 3 July 1926, ACUA, USCCB 10:125:33 (first quote is here); Hays to Burke, 7 September 1926, ibid.; Burke to Robert Lucey, 11 September 1926, copy, ibid.; Burke to Daniel Lord, 11 September 1926, copy, ibid. (second quote is here); Walsh, *Sin and Censorship*, 52.
31. Burke to Lord, 11 September 1926, copy, ACUA, USCCB 10:125:33; Lord to Burke, 13 September 1926, ibid.; Richard Maltby, "*The King of Kings* and the Czar of All the Rushes: The Propriety of the Christ Story," *Screen* 31 (Summer 1990): 192–203.
32. Lord to Burke, 13 September 1926, ACUA, USCCB 10:125:33; Daniel A. Lord, S.J., Report on Cecil B. DeMille's New Film "*The King of Kings*" Submitted to the National Catholic Welfare Council, [October 1926], 3–4, ibid.; Walsh, *Sin and Censorship*, 52; *Played by Ear: The Autobiography of Daniel A. Lord, S.J.* (Chicago: Loyola University Press, 1956), 276–84. The account in Lord's report and subsequent supplemental report (see Chapter 16) are to be preferred over the account in his autobiography.
33. Lord, Report on "*The King of Kings*," [October 1926], pp. 1–2, ACUA, USCCB 10:125:33. The Protestant ending of the Our Father is not in the gospels, but only in the version of the prayer found in the Didache.
34. Ibid., 4–5.
35. Ibid., 6–7; Walsh, *Sin and Censorship*, 52–53; *Played by Ear*, 281–82.
36. Lord, Report on "*The King of Kings*,"[October 1926], ACUA, USCCB 10:125:33, 7; Lord to Burke, undated [9 October 1926], ibid.
37. [Burke, Notes on Lord's Report, undated (October 1926)], ACUA, USCCB 10:125:33.
38. Burke to Lord, 1 November 1926, copy, ACUA, USCCB 10:125:33.
39. McMahon to Burke, 2 November 1926, ACUA, USCCB 10:125:33.

40. McMahon to Burke, 10 November 1926, ACUA, USCCB 10:125:33; Burke to McMahon, 11 November 1926, copy, ibid.
41. J. H. Ryan to Burke, telegrams, 23, 28, 30 July and 1 August 1925, ACUA, USCCB 10:153:5; Burke to Hanna, 7 August 1925, copy, ibid., 10:99:16; Burke to E. Gibbons, 7 August 1925, copy, ibid., 10:103:26; Burke, note, 6 August 1934, ibid., 10:153: Interview Book.
42. Burke to E. Gibbons, 7 August 1925, copy, ACUA, USCCB 10:103:26; E. Gibbons to Burke, 14 August 1925, ibid.; E. Gibbons to Burke, 12 December 1925, ibid.
43. Burke to Lynch, 13 August 1925, AP, Burke Papers, box 5.
44. Burke to Murray, 16 August 1925, AP, Burke Papers, box 12.
45. Burke to E. Gibbons, 14 October 1925, copy, ACUA, USCCB 10:103:26; Burke to E. Gibbons, 21 November 1925, copy, ibid. (quotes are here); E. Gibbons to Burke, 23 November 1925, ibid.
46. Burke to Murray, 15 February 1926, AP, Burke Papers, box 12 (quotes are here); E. Gibbons to Burke, 12 December 1925, ACUA, USCCB 10:103:26.
47. Cf., ACUA, USCCB 10:39:28–36.
48. Burke, Interview with James Davis and Edward Henning, 6 April 1925, ACUA, USCCB 10:42:1.
49. Ibid.
50. Minutes of the Meeting of the Administrative Committee, 23 April 1925, ACUA, USCCB 10:64:4; Mohler to Muldoon, 28 April 1925, ACUA, USCCB 10:39:28; Richard Gribble, C.S.C, "Church, State, and the American Immigrant: The Multiple Contributions of Archbishop Edward Hanna," *U.S. Catholic Historian* 16 (Fall 1998), 13–14.
51. Burke to E. Gibbons, 29 January 1926, copy, ACUA, USCCB 10:103:27; Burke to Hanna, 13 February 1926, copy, ibid.,10:99:16.
52. Burke to E. Gibbons, 29 January 1926, copy, ACUA, USCCB 10:103:27; Draft of H.R. __, In the House of Representatives, April __, 1926, ACUA, USCCB 10:42:1.
53. Burke to Hanna, 13 February 1926, copy, ACUA 10:99:16; Burke to Edwin Byrne, 3 May 1926, copy, ACUA, USCCB 10:41:1.
54. Byrne to Burke, 15 April 1926, ACUA, USCCB 10:41:1; Burke to Byrne, 3 May 1926, copy, ibid.
55. [Burke], Registration of Aliens, undated [1926], ACUA, USCCB 10:42:1 (first quote is here); [Montavon, Statement before House Committee on Immigration, 26 March 1926], ibid. (remaining quotes are here); Higham, *Strangers in the Land*, 264–99.
56. [Burke], Registration of Aliens, undated [1926], ACUA, USCCB 10:42:1; Burke to Hanna, telegram, 29 December 1926, copy, ibid.; Burke to Muldoon, telegram, 29 December 1926, copy, ibid.

57. [Burke], Registration of Aliens, undated [1926], ACUA, USCCB 10:42:1.
58. [Montavon, Statement before House Committee on Immigration, 26 March 1926], ACUA, USCCB 10:42:1; *Jewish Daily Bulletin*, 13 June 1926; Van Vleck, *Administrative Control of Aliens*, 224 (quote is here); Hutchinson, *History of Immigration Policy*, 198–200.
59. [Montavon, Statement before House Committee on Immigration, 26 March 1926], ACUA, USCCB 10:42:1; Van Vleck, *Administrative Control of Aliens*, 20–21.
60. *The Question of Birth Control: Malthus Cross-Examined* (1925); *The Question of Birth Control: A Competent Authority Analyzes Our Birth Rate* (1925); *The Question of Birth Control: Bishop Gore's Views* (1925)—all in ACUA, USCCB 10:117:3; Tentler, *Catholics and Contraception*, 54.
61. Burke, circular to editors, 10 August 1925, ACUA, USCCB 10:117:3; Burke, circular to organizations, 29 August 1925, ibid.
62. Notes of Edmund Gibbons, September 1925, ACUA, USCCB 10:117:3.
63. Laughlin to Burke, 23 October 1925, with enclosure Sanger, Newsletter of American Birth Control League, October 1925, ACUA, USCCB 10:117:3; Laughlin to Burke, 13 February 1921, ibid., 10:116:34 (first quote is here); Burke to Laughlin, 3 November 1925, copy, ibid. (second quote is here); Laughlin to Burke, 26 February 1926, ibid., 10:117:4; *Autobiography of Sanger*, 11–23; Chesler, *Woman of Valor*, 21–43, 89–127; Chen, *Sex Side of Life*, 236–38; Baker, *Sanger: Life of Passion*, 15–19, 63, 71, 167, 212. Baker notes that Sanger was baptized without her father's knowledge at age fourteen and was confirmed a year later, but obviously without much effect because she followed her father's way of thinking.
64. Burke, circular to organizations, 18 November 1925, ACUA, USCCB 10:117:3; Burke to Muldoon, 23 December 1925, ibid., 10:152:30; Report on the Inquiry from American Religious and Social Bodies As to Whether They Were Prepared to Protest against Birth Control Legislation, 13 April 1926, ibid., 10:117:4; John A. McGlinn to Burke, 25 May 1926, ibid.
65. Burke to Thomas G. Carroll, 1 February 1926, copy, ACUA, USCCB 10:117:4; E. J. Kelly to Burke, 23 February 1926, ibid.; Burke to Laughlin, 2 March 1926, copy, ibid.; Report on the Inquiry from American Religious and Social Bodies As to Whether They Were Prepared to Protest against Birth Control Legislation, 13 April 1926, ibid.; Sanger, Newsletter, March 1926, ibid., 10:117:5; *Autobiography of Sanger*, 415; Kennedy, *Birth Control*, 223–24.
66. Patrick Ward, Memorandum to Father Burke, 20 February 1926, ACUA, USCCB 10:117:4; Ward to Clarence Little, 18 March 1926, copy, ibid., 10:117:5; Ward to Burke, Memorandum, 26 June 1926, ibid.; Chesler, *Woman of Valor*, 233.
67. Ward to Burke, Memorandum, 26 June 1926, ACUA, USCCB 10:117:5.
68. Ibid.

69. Marked-up draft of Report of an Interview with Mr. P. J. Ward of the National Catholic Welfare Conference, Washington, D.C., undated [2 March 1926], ACUA, USCCB 10:117:5; Anne Kennedy, Report of an Interview with Mr. P. J. Ward of the National Catholic Welfare Conference, Washington, D.C., (Mr. Ward is the Executive Directing the Organized Work Against Birth Control and Has the Authority to Speak on This Matter for the Entire Council), 2 March 1926, ibid.; Ward to Burke, Memorandum, 26 June 1926, ibid.; *Autobiography of Sanger*, 415–16. In fact, Burke and Ward understood quite well the difference between the amendment proposed by Dennett and Sanger (Burke to Laughlin, 2 March 1926), copy, ACUA, USCCB 10:117:4.
70. Sanger, Newsletter, March 1926, ACUA, USCCB 10:117:5; Chesler, *Woman of Valor*, 233.
71. Burke to Sanger, 21 April 1926, copy, ACUA, USCCB 10:117:5; Chesler, *Woman of Valor*, 233–34.
72. Sanger to Burke, 26 April 1926; Burke to Sanger 5 May 1926, copy; Sanger to Burke, 13 May 1926; Burke to Sanger 12 June 1926, copy; Sanger to Burke, 24 June 1926—all in ACUA, USCCB 10:117:5.
73. Little to Ward, 13 March 1926, ACUA, USCCB 10:117:5; Ward to Little, 18 March 1926, copy, ibid.
74. Burke to Sanger 3 July 1926, copy, ACUA, USCCB 10:117:5; Sanger to Burke, 17 July 1926, ibid.; Burke to Sanger, 28 July 1926, copy, ibid.; Chesler, *Woman of Valor*, 234.
75. *Autobiography of Sanger*, 416 (quotes are here); Kennedy, *Birth Control*, 223–24.
76. Lincoln C. Andrews to Burke, 31 October 1925, ACUA, USCCB 10:111:20; Laurence Schmeckebier, *The Bureau of Prohibition: Its History, Activities and Organization* (Washington, D.C.: Brookings Institution, 1929), 9–10, and 98; Behr, *Prohibition* 223. Thomas M. Coffey, *The Long Thirst: Prohibition in America, 1920–1933* (New York: W. W. Norton and Company, Inc., 1975), 169; Sinclair, *Era of Excess,* 185.
77. Burke to Muldoon, 9 November 1925, copy, ACUA, USCCB 10:152:30; U.S. Treasury Department, Bureau of Internal Revenue, T.D. 3779, 30 November 1925, copy, ibid., 10:111:20; Schmeckebier, *Bureau of Prohibition*, 98.
78. Burke circular to the hierarchy, 26 March 1926, copy, ACUA, USCCB 10:111:22.
79. Burke to M. J. Hoferer, 10 July 1926, copy, ACUA, USCCB 10:111:22; Charles Fay to Burke, 15 July 1926, ibid.
80. Burke interview with James Jones, 10 July 1926, ACUA, USCCB 10:153:21.
81. Minutes of the Administrative Committee, 13 September 1926, ACUA, USCCB 10:64:4; J. H. Ryan to Burke, memorandum, October 12, 1926, ibid., 10:111:22.

82. William Montavon to E. Gibbons, 5 February 1926, ADA, NCWC files.
83. J. H. Ryan to Burke, memorandum, 12 October 1926, ACUA, USCCB 10:111:22.
84. Ibid.
85. J. M. Doran to Burke, 4 February 1927, with enclosures (blank label and copy of Andrews to Prohibition Administrators, 1 February 1927), ACUA, USCCB 10:111:23.
86. Burke to Muldoon, 9 November 1925, copy, ACUA, USCCB 10:152:30; Burke to E. Gibbons, 18 November 1926, ADA, NCWC files; Burke to E. Gibbons, 10 February 1927, ADA, NCWC files.

John J. Burke, editor of *Catholic World*, circa 1910. Courtesy of Special Collections, The Catholic University of America, Washington, D.C.

Ordination photograph of John J. Burke in Paulist cassock, June 1899. Courtesy of the Archives of the Missionary Society of St. Paul the Apostle.

Group of boys of St. Paul the Apostle Church, circa 1884. John J. Burke (seated farthest right) probably age eight; his older brother Thomas F. Burke (standing second from right) probably age twelve.

Investiture of John J. Burke (kneeling) as a monsignor, 21 September 1936.
Courtesy of the Archives of the Missionary Society of St. Paul the Apostle.

Portrait of Monsignor John J. Burke, September 1936. Courtesy of the Archives of the Missionary Society of St. Paul the Apostle.

John J. Burke and classmates at College of St. Francis Xavier pulling poses, circa 1896. Burke is standing second from right in a hat. Courtesy of the Archives of the Missionary Society of St. Paul the Apostle.

Group of boys, probably altar servers of St. Paul the Apostle Church, circa 1889. John J. Burke, age twelve or thirteen, is on the left end of the far back row. Courtesy of the Archives of the Missionary Society of St. Paul the Apostle.

John J. Burke, General Secretary of the National Catholic Welfare Conference, circa 1920. Courtesy of the Archives of the Missionary Society of St. Paul the Apostle.

Chapter 15
"So Many and Grave Problems," 1925 and 1926: Part II

What matters to one who loves is not how he fares, but how his beloved fares. What matters to the lover of God is not how the lover fares, but how God, the Beloved fares. Or, since we cannot affect God Himself, how His glory fares among men. When this thought comes to the soul, it begins to realize that its primary duty is not the thought or care of self, but rather how self can promote the glory of God: Can keep God before itself as God is, love Him and devote itself to His love.[1]

Crisis over the NEA Bill

When Congress opened in December 1925, Senator Charles Curtis of Kansas and Representative Daniel Reed of New York introduced the new NEA bill for a department of education without federal aid. Despite the Oregon decision, both the Southern Jurisdiction of Scottish Rite Masons and Ku Klux Klan remained committed to compulsory public education and supported the bill as a step toward that. James H. Ryan wrote an article arguing that, given public opinion against further federalization as an encroachment on states' rights, it had little chance of passage in the first session.[2]

Under orders not to oppose it openly, John Burke shared Ryan's assessment. In mid-December he told Fathers Wilfrid Parsons and Paul Blakely of *America* magazine, ardent opponents of the NEA's bills, that they credited too highly the NEA's influence. The trend toward federalization was weakening, so there was no need for aggressive opposition at the moment.

Such action, said Burke, would have greater impact if delayed until warranted. Several days later, he saw Coolidge who agreed Congress would pass no education bill.[3]

Two bishops, Francis Howard of Covington, Kentucky, and Michael Curley, were concerned the NCWC was softening its opposition to the bill. Though the hierarchy had decided against open attack, it "emphatically opposed" it. Curley, who had missed the convention, criticized the bishops' lack of spine. In his view, they should have simply ordered the NCWC to fight the bill.[4]

While seeing Burke about a different matter, Curley mentioned his intention to argue publicly against the bill and asked Burke's opinion. Burke said the Administrative Committee directed him not to oppose it openly, but to watch and wait. Curley answered the hierarchy said the NCWC should be positively opposed to the bill; there was no doubt about that. Burke held Congress would pass no education bill, and Coolidge said the same. Relenting, Curley said he would make no public pronouncement.[5]

The NCWC's silence raised suspicions about its intention toward the bill. Parsons informed Curley a "very trustworthy" source warned "some sort of a deal is on foot at Washington by which the N.C.W.C. is favoring, or to favor, the Federal Department of Education." Parsons noted that Burke had urged *America* to abate its opposition. Curley replied the hierarchy refused to formally counter the bill, but "individually" (rather than "informally" as the minutes state) the bishops opposed it. "There is no question about the minds of the Hierarchy on the matter," he told Parsons, "consequently I cannot understand Father Burke's attitude."[6]

As Burke understood his instructions, he was to work against the bill informally, which meant checking on its prospects with the president and Congress, actions he had taken. Everything indicated the issue was quiescent. He could hardly have guessed proponents would take Catholic silence as consent. Indeed, word seems to have been circulating in political circles to that effect, no doubt giving rise to Parsons's suspicions.[7]

Parsons took his concern to Cardinal William O'Connell. Burke got a letter from the chancellor of Boston that O'Connell heard the NCWC was about to announce "in favor of the Federal Department of Education or, at least, has given assurances … that the [NCWC's] Department of Education favors the Curtis-Reed Bill." O'Connell wanted the truth. Burke replied neither the NCWC nor its departments planned any such action. Headquarters was abiding strictly by instructions of the Administrative Committee.[8] Burke's suspicions about the source of O'Connell's information were soon confirmed.

On New Year's Day, *America* carried the brief editorial "An Alarm and A Warning," which stated: "As this edition goes to press an ugly rumor is circulated referring to 'a political deal to put the Curtis-Reed Federal education bill across.' The details, which would tell a curious story, need not now be stated. Are the guardians of our interests betraying them?" Monsignor Filippo Bernardini at the apostolic delegation told Burke he feared it was aimed at the NCWC. Burke considered the piece "outrageous."[9]

He fired a letter to Parsons explaining "one of the highest ecclesiastical dignitaries in the country" had recently been informed the NCWC favored the Curtis-Reed bill. Now came *America*'s editorial with a similar rumor. Burke wondered if the two were connected and asked if "the guardians of our interests" referred to the NCWC. When Parsons replied his information was confidential, there followed a fruitless exchange of letters.[10]

To Bishop Peter Muldoon, Burke bitterly lamented Parsons's willingness to believe such a thing of the NCWC, especially in view of the money and energy it had expended in defeating the various NEA bills and Oregon Law. To Dowling, Burke questioned the wisdom of continued silence. The problem was not with Congress, because the bill lay dormant in committee. The issue was with Catholics, who were "beginning to think we really favor the bill, because we are doing nothing." He affirmed that NCWC silence gave them some justification. Presciently, he concluded: "It may be that through silence we would be jockeyed into a false position. That would be grossly unfair and unjust to the work of the N.C.W.C." He suggested the Administrative Committee meet soon to develop a plan of action. Dowling encouraged him to worry less and keep a sense of humor.[11] In this instance, Burke, an inveterate fretter, was more accurate than Dowling, who grossly underestimated the situation of both the education question and the NCWC itself.

Indeed, Burke felt beset and alarmed. He had New Year's supper with the Merrick sisters before departing for St. Louis and then to Rockford for a visit with Muldoon. Afterward, Mary Merrick wrote to Mary Hawks: "I hope that Bishop XXXX [Muldoon] will be able to help him. He feels all this criticism."[12]

Several days later, an agitated Curley told Edward Pace that the hierarchy definitely wanted a public protest against the bill, but Burke had told *America* to soft-pedal opposition. Curley agreed with *America*: passage of the bill would be the first step to federal aid and then complete federal control of education. Pace tried to calm him. In his view, opposition at this time would be interpreted as opposition to public education in general.[13]

Knowing Burke would attend a celebration that evening with Curley present, Pace telephoned to warn him of the archbishop's anger. He added that he would stop by after the function to "view the dead on the battlefield." At the event, however, Curley was the soul of cordiality with Burke. Still, the latter confided to Muldoon the temper of those insisting on active opposition was "angry: unwilling to be deliberate: or calculating: or thoughtful." Again, he urged the committee to meet with the NCWC Department of Education in Chicago to discuss the situation.[14] Again, his advice was not taken, which, in view of subsequent events, was a mistake.

In mid-January, Burke had the Legal Department check the pulse of Congress, while he made his own inquiries. He reported to Dowling the legislative mood on education "just now is 'nothing doing.'" Congress was preoccupied with other matters. At least, that was the word. Four days later, Burke learned of the House and Senate's intention to hold a joint hearing on the NEA bill, concurrent with the meeting of NEA Department of Superintendents in Washington. He telegraphed Ryan in Chicago where the NCWC Department of Education was to meet next day. "All our opposition said to be removed because absence of appropriation," read the message.[15]

The department discussed the situation. Pace argued against considering the bill on its merits because the hierarchy opposed federalization. Rather than take a purely negative stand, he thought the NCWC should show support for public schools by advocating something positive like the old Dallinger bill to expand the Bureau of Education which the NCWC endorsed in 1924. Department members agreed, and Dowling wired the decision to Burke, who just received a telegram from Muldoon arguing headquarters should abide by the hierarchy's guideline not to oppose openly. Burke summarized the contents of both wires in a third to Archbishop Edward Hanna, cautioning that following Muldoon's advice would be construed by Congress as consent to the bill. Hanna telegraphed he favored a "definite protest," but asked Burke to see if Curley agreed.[16] There is no doubt about the latter's position.

Burke complained to Senator Lawrence Phipps of Colorado, chairman of the hearing, that because it coincided with the NEA meeting, "it looks very much to me as if the 'game' were not being played fair." He demanded a fair and just amount of time for the NCWC to present its case. Phipps, who opposed the Curtis-Reed bill, gave him half the hearing.[17]

Burke and headquarters went into crisis mode. Agnes Regan sent a circular urging local units of the NCCW to protest against the bill to Phipps and their own congressmen, and Ryan did the same with 133 presidents of Catholic colleges. Through the good offices of a Knight of Columbus in Dunkirk, New York, co-sponsor Reed's hometown, the Legal Department mounted a campaign of criticism in the congressman's district. Burke lined up forty-three witnesses, both Catholic and non-Catholic, to appear before the Joint Committee. O'Connell sent a representative and Cardinal Dennis Dougherty sent a written protest.[18]

After making these preparations, Burke went to visit the Merrick sisters to get a few days rest before the hearing. From there, he sent Grace Murray a letter explaining that pressing business had kept him from going to New York for many weeks and any time to write had been "suddenly whipped away." He was feeling "cut off: and alone: and deprived of much." He told her, "This work here is endless, and mixed up with such human problems that one is often bewildered and lost." There had been one bright spot. A few weeks back Burke traveled to Rockford to see his friend Muldoon. The two reminisced about the "old days" of the War Council. Muldoon said it was "his conviction that no human hands shaped the forming of the N.C. War C. But that it was manifestly the inscrutable hand of God." This word heartened Burke. He told Murray he realized he had been but an instrument of the divine will. Yet, he felt uplifted that God deigned to use him for His own purpose and in His own way.[19]

Burke purposely secured more people to speak at the hearing than its schedule permitted because he wanted "to show the Committee that others were left who wished to protest but that the time was not sufficient." He told Dowling all senators on the panel opposed the bill, but such was no guarantee they would not favor it, as had happened with the Prohibition Amendment. Conduct of the NEA, whose members would run the proposed department, indicated "they would not be friends to liberty in education." Its witnesses occupied the first day, and then NEA officers also demanded the second to force the NCWC's out-of-town witnesses to return home. Burke was able to forestall the maneuver. Parsons came from New York and was as "conspicuous as is a nervous hen at all the sessions," Burke told Muldoon. "He is making a mistake. But of course it is useless to speak to him. Probably 'America' will have led the fight single-handed.... So it will be a great historical question as to who saved the day—if the day is saved. There won't be any question as to who lost it, if it is lost."[20]

Afterward, Burke reported to the hierarchy that NCWC witnesses made an "effective impression" on the joint committee. Evidence suggested it would not act on the measure, but that remained to be seen. So, the NCWC must prepare to counter the bill on the Senate and House floors. Burke cautioned against over-confidence.[21] Although Catholic Representative Loring Black of New York, a member of the House committee, soon communicated that it would not report the bill, the NEA and affiliated organizations exerted tremendous pressure on it to do so, as did the Klan and the Masons.[22]

Given the pressure, Burke followed the recommendation of Dowling's department: the way to ensure the bill's demise was to offer a viable alternative like the old Dallinger bill. He had the Legal Department draft one expanding the duties of the Bureau of Education to include those in the Curtis-Reed bill. Burke asked Phipps to introduce it, which he agreed to do if the NCWC promised to endorse it. So, Dowling issued a statement in its favor. Within two months, the House committee deferred action on the NEA bill until the second session of Congress; the Senate counterpart reported the Phipps bill as the only viable education legislation.[23]

MEXICO

While Burke handled the NEA bill, the Church-state conflict in Mexico preoccupied him and would require much of his attention for the remainder of his life. In the half year following the Curtis-Reed hearing, the conflict monopolized his time. In spring, he told Helen Lynch, "The Mexican situation ... excludes practically all other work." At the end of July, the message was the same, "The Mexican situation meets us every day." He begged her for prayers.[24]

In February 1917, Mexico's revolutionary government promulgated the Querétaro Constitution extending state sovereignty over natural resources and religion. Article 27 nationalized all land, including Church property, thereby divesting foreign businesses while placing religious temporalities in the hands of the government. Article 3 forbade parochial education, and article 130 made the priesthood a profession requiring civil registration, allowed states to regulate the number of priests, and confined the ministry to native-born Mexicans.[25] A combination of pressure from the U.S. to protect American oil interests and the need to consolidate the revolution had prevented implementation of these articles.[26]

Matters changed dramatically under the Presidency of Plutarco Elías Calles (1924–1928), who went by his middle name. Actively anti-Catholic, he won election with support of two revolutionary factions: peasants and industrial laborers—the former wanted land reform and the latter control of oil.[27] A key element of Calles's program was agrarian reform. To alleviate the plight of peasants, he intended to build up a yeomanry through a system of state-sponsored agricultural schools, irrigation projects, and land banks.[28] His efforts pitted government against Church, which had its own system of schools to impart an opposing philosophy and encouraged the formation of the National Catholic Labor Federation (NCLF, 1922). In 1925 the NCLF laid plans for a National League of the Middle Class and, even more disturbing to the state, for a National Catholic Peasant League.[29]

Calles's crusade against the Church unfolded gradually. In February 1925, he reminded states of their duty to keep a close eye on the clergy. There followed an attempt to establish a schismatic Mexican national church, which prompted the formation of the National League for Religious Defense under the guidance of Miguel Palomar y Vizcarra, Luis Bustos, and René Capistrán Garza. Two months later Archbishop Serafino Cimino, new apostolic delegate, arrived in Mexico City determined to bring peace. His stay was brief. In May illness forced him to seek health in Denver. When he tried to return, the Mexican government refused him reentry.[30]

In spring 1925, Burke informed the Administrative Committee about Mexico. It directed him to ascertain facts and inquire if Mexican bishops wanted American Catholics to act. Archbishop Pietro Fumasoni-Biondi, apostolic delegate to the U.S., sent Burke and James H. Ryan sub-rosa to

New York City to get Cimino's confidential report about conditions in Mexico. Explaining to Burke and Ryan that he never wrote one, Cimino discussed the situation with them. He recounted the circumstances of his expulsion and emphatically opposed protest meetings by American Catholics, averring Mexican bishops felt the same. If such meetings occurred and failed to alter matters, the Church's predicament "would be even worse than it is now." Cimino recommended informing American Catholics and the American public of "the real conditions prevailing at present in Mexico." On learning this, Fumasoni-Biondi instructed Burke to confine activities to fact-finding and their publication.[31]

In early June, Burke saw Franklin Gunther, head of the Mexican Division at State, to hear what he knew about conditions. Gunther told him there had been a change for the better and Calles would cease anti-Catholic tactics. In fact, both Gunther and James Sheffield, American ambassador to Mexico, believed that to be true. Burke said American Catholics were deeply interested in freedom of the Mexican church and asked the U.S. government to exercise its good offices to end such tyranny. Gunther reassured him things would be getting better. Spain's ambassador to the U.S. used his office to good effect with the Mexican government. Gunther promised to keep Burke abreast of information received. When Burke explained his intention to send Charles Phillips, a former editor and current professor of literature at the University of Notre Dame, to investigate the situation of the Mexican church, Gunther said that was no problem.[32]

When Burke next saw Gunther, Sheffield was there with him. Sheffield thought things were improving until the government entrusted the parish of La Soledad in Mexico City to schismatic priests. Calles intended to create a national Catholic church to divide the people and destroy Roman influence. Though Sheffield deplored Calles's treatment of the Church, he could do nothing about it. His role was limited to protection of American citizens and property. Burke warned that American Catholics would not accept that situation complacently; once they learned the facts, they would protest.[33]

From mid-summer through October, Phillips's articles appeared in the NCWC News Service. On return to the U.S., he told Burke he had spoken with nine Mexican bishops, who like Cimino wanted facts publicized but warned that demonstrations by American Catholics would do more harm than good. During the fall, the position of the Mexican church deteriorated.

The state of Tabasco effectively ended worship by decreeing only married priests could function and exiling those who were celibate. Condemning the action, Archbishop José Mora y del Río of Mexico City telegraphed the news to Burke. Burke gave Gunther copies of all of Phillips's articles, surprising him with how well informed the NCWC was about Mexican matters. Burke described affairs in Tabasco and said the U.S. government should inform Mexico the NCWC had protested against it. Gunther promised to do so. He added that State intended to insert in the forthcoming Treaty of Amity and Commerce with Mexico, a clause exacting a promise to halt religious persecution. Three days later, Washington papers reported the Mexican government had ordered Tabasco to reinstate the exiled priests. Mora telegraphed the news to Burke.[34]

In the winter of 1926, the situation of the Mexican church became enmeshed with that of American oilmen, at least in the mind of Calles. The Mexican Congress passed a law giving foreign petroleum companies until the end of that year to surrender their deeds to Mexican land in return for fifty-year leases backdated to the moment they had begun extracting hydrocarbons. The American petroleum cartel filed suit and clamored for protection by the U.S. government. At the same time, the Church's position deteriorated as more than fifteen states enacted repressive legislation, limiting the number of priests who could function and closing Catholic schools. When Mora issued a statement renewing the Church's objection to the anticlerical articles of the constitution, Calles considered the action collusion with American oil interests. He retaliated by expelling foreign clergy.[35]

As the situation worsened, the Mexican church found an advocate in Archbishop Curley, an ardent Catholic partisan. Despite advice against public demonstrations, and without consulting the NCWC, he launched a crusade against the Calles administration. In an address to Washington Knights of Columbus, Curley denounced the American government's unwillingness to protest the persecution in Mexico, all but accusing it of being in collusion with that country. Hinting the Coolidge administration's inactivity sprang from anti-Catholic bigotry, Curley urged his twenty million coreligionists in the U.S. to rise in protest. In reporting the speech, the *Baltimore Catholic Review* took a thinly veiled swipe at Burke and the NCWC: "Some there are in this capital city who are supine and who believe in reticence."[36]

Indeed, the NCWC's seeming passivity disturbed Curley. Already irritated at what he erroneously considered Burke's independent action handling the NEA bill, he wrote to Fumasoni-Biondi, it might be good to get the Welfare Conference into action. "At times like this, one does not know just who or what the N.C.W.C. is," sniped Curley. "In its ultimate analysis, it seems to be Father John Burke and nobody else."[37]

Curly's blast at the government took Burke by surprise. The next day, he lunched with Monsignor Paolo Marella, auditor of the apostolic delegation, who said Curley had dined with him the previous day and spoke of his intention to make the address. In the absence of Fumasoni-Biondi, Marella had given approval, despite knowing Cimino and the Mexican hierarchy had warned against such action. He even asked, "Father Burke, why do you not hold meetings of Catholics that will protest?" Burke explained he was acting under guidance of the Mexican bishops. Marella said no more.[38]

Then, Archbishop George Caruana arrived in Washington with word he was new apostolic delegate to Mexico. He worked with Burke and the American apostolic delegation for entry into that country. Caruana and Burke devised a code for their communications. The archbishop asked that Father Ray McGowan accompany him into Mexico and remain with him for a week or so. Although Caruana's U.S. passport indicated he was a clergyman, he intended to wear lay attire and declare he was entering as a professor to observe, study, and gather information. Burke agreed to let McGowan go with him, but disliked the ruse. He worried about the Mexican government's reaction once it wakened to the scheme. He thought Caruana should seek to enter that country openly as apostolic delegate, and if the Mexican government refused him entry, so be it. Burke sent Sheffield a letter of introduction, and the ambassador promised to offer Caruana assistance. Burke's first hint he was odd man out in the affair occurred as Caruana and McGowan departed. Burke said to Caruana, "You will communicate with me as arranged." "Oh," he replied, "I've arranged another code with the [American Apostolic] Delegation. I made three copies and one of them is for you. They will give it to you." They never did.[39]

Meanwhile, Curley published articles in the *Baltimore Catholic* exhorting coreligionists to follow his lead. In this, he enjoyed support of Fumasoni-Biondi, who said Sheffield, too, expressed hope to Caruana that Curley would continue his protests. The ambassador considered Curley "expert at swinging the shilleily [*sic*]." In early March, the Knights held a Mass rally in Washington to excoriate Mexico. Addressing the assembly, Representative John Boylan, a New York Catholic Democrat, declared the Calles government would collapse if the U.S. withdrew diplomatic recognition. He urged the Knights to lobby for that.[40] Curley summoned Boylan and virtually dictated a resolution demanding the government sever relations with Mexico until Calles amended his religious ways. The House scheduled a hearing for 30 March 1926.[41]

On the 24th, Boylan told Burke that Curley wanted him to appear on behalf of the NCWC in support of the resolution. Burke said he had no authority to do so, but would write to the Administrative Committee for direction. That evening, in a state of "great anxiety," Burke saw Fumasoni-Biondi to warn him that severing relations might injure Caruana's work in Mexico. "Had I told him it might rain tomorrow he might have been more excited or moved than he showed himself," commented Burke. The delegate simply shrugged his shoulders and said, "Well, the worst is that B[isho]p. Caruana will be driven out." Sheffield would be expelled, continued Burke, and Americans in Mexico attacked. Without Sheffield's protection, Caruana might be killed. None of this produced an increase of interest. "Well, the worst could be that he (Bp. C.) would be driven out," repeated the delegate, adding, "Arch[bishop] Curley is very zealous about this isn't he?" He then asked if Burke thought the Volstead Act would be modified.[42]

Reflecting on events, Burke confided his thoughts to paper. He realized he was out of the loop. No one had consulted him prior to taking action, not Curley, not Boylan, not Fumasoni-Biondi, who seemed detached. The game had changed and he was not a player. Something is "afoot of which we know not," wrote Burke, "—but which we can surmize [*sic*]." He believed the Vatican had given Curley marching orders to rouse American Catholics "to angered protest"; to discomfort the American government and threaten it with Catholic opposition until it broke relations with Mexico; and to discredit Calles, thereby provoking revolution below the border. If Curley succeeded, believed Burke, he would be summoned "to Rome to receive the Red Hat."[43] While such a scenario seemed plausible enough, evidence does not support it. The record does, however, show both Fumasoni-Biondi and Caruana favored Curley's course of action.

When Burke heard back from the bishops of the Administrative Committee, three favored support of Boylan's resolution, two of them without enthusiasm. Four opposed. So, Burke concluded he lacked authorization to endorse it. One of the opponents, Bishop Thomas McDevitt of Harrisburg, did, however, urge him to appear at the hearing, not in support, but to put the NCWC on record as objecting to the persecution. Burke telephoned Boylan to say although the committee nixed endorsement, it wanted him to present evidence of and object to the persecution. Boylan told him unless he was prepared to demand immediate severance of relations, he should stay home.[44]

Meanwhile, heartened by Curley's speeches, the Mexican National League for Religious Defense sent two representatives to Baltimore with a letter from Archbishop Mora. Curley referred them to Burke. Mora now wanted American Catholics to hold protest demonstrations. Burke informed the Administrative Committee. The bishops ordered him to prepare on their behalf a press release and a letter of protest to Coolidge. Burke should establish a national committee to publicize the persecution and have the NCCM and NCCW initiate protests.[45]

Burke and James H. Ryan collaborated on the two documents. The letter argued that when the U.S. granted diplomatic recognition to the government of Venustiano Carranza in 1915, it did so on his promise "of conceding religious and educational freedom to all" in accord with Mexico's 1857 constitution then in force. Both the 1917 constitution and the Calles government breached that commitment. While applauding the Coolidge administration's efforts to protect American property rights in Mexico, it was equally important to protect religious ones. Making the same argument in the press release, the two went a step further. "We [the bishops] are … not only amply justified, but … obligated, to call upon our Government … that its original request upon which recognition to Mexico was granted, be lived up to by the Government of Mexico." The statement stopped short of the Boylan resolution by not demanding severance of diplomatic relations.[46] The claim that the 1917 constitution and Calles's persecution violated Carranza's promise according to the 1857 constitution would cause problems.

Accompanied by Burke, the bishops met with Coolidge in April to present the letter. After reading it, Coolidge asked what the prelates wanted the government to do. Hanna said they made no specific request; they simply called attention to the persecution of religion by the Mexican government. The bishops felt it their "solemn duty to present their views." Coolidge agreed to let the committee publish the letter, provided Secretary of State Frank Kellogg concurred. The following day, the bishops issued their press release.[47]

Unfortunately, their letter did not please Kellogg. Coolidge asked that his friend Father Charles Lyons, president of Georgetown University, and Burke see Kellogg.[48] The latter took exception to the portion of the letter stating the American government was interested only in property rights. It had done everything it could "legitimately" do to protect human rights, he told Burke. He also called "unwarranted" the claim that diplomatic recognition had been conditioned on religious freedom. He argued the American government had sought from Carranza assurance he would uphold it under the then existing 1857 Constitution. It could not bind future actions of the sovereign state in "purely private [internal] matters." Kellogg wanted to know what the bishops' letter was "really" demanding of the government. Burke repeated what Hanna told Coolidge: it asked nothing specific. It was an expression of deep concern. If Kellogg felt the government had done all it could, he should state that clearly in a reply. The secretary said his reply would have to point out inaccuracies in the letter, which would be to the discredit of the bishops. He asked Burke to arrange a meeting with them. Lyons asked if Kellogg thought publication of the letter would work to the benefit of the Calles government. "I believe it certainly would," he replied.[49]

Burke asked the committee to return at once, but only Muldoon and McDevitt were able. Burke accompanied them to see Kellogg. Muldoon asked why he did not want the letter published. Kellogg replied, "Because I do not wish to be compelled to say that Mexico in doing what she has done is within her rights." He repeated this over and over in the interview. He told the three, "I wish you had addressed this to the public at large." Muldoon asked if State would forward without comment a protest from the NCWC to Mexico and whether he and/or Coolidge would find an opportunity to declare publicly their desire that all nations uphold religious freedom. Kellogg responded such might be done in a general way. He did promise to inform the Mexican ambassador of the embarrassment the persecution caused the American government.[50]

Back at headquarters, Muldoon and McDevitt agreed to change the letter and, together with Burke, rewrote it entirely. Less a protest, the second iteration recounted in mild fashion the religious persecution in Mexico and acknowledged "limitations of the influence of one government upon another and the courtesies of diplomatic relations." Too, it recognized the administration's present interest and effort in the matter. "We petition," concluded the letter, "a continuation of those good offices and of your watchful interest." Burke submitted it to Kellogg, who "found it perfectly satisfactory" and wrote a reply, saying he would informally bring the bishops' protest and those of other Catholics to the attention of Mexican Ambassador Manuel Téllez. He asked Burke not to publish the letter until he (Kellogg) spoke with Téllez and promised to notify him immediately afterward.[51]

Burke waited for two weeks without hearing from him. Meanwhile, Kellogg had sent Gunther to Téllez with a stack of Catholic protests, the bishops' letter among them. Finally, Burke went to Gunther and impressed on him the importance of the letter's publication. He said American Catholics "expected" the Administrative Committee "to take some definite action in presenting the matter to our own government." The bishops had done so a month earlier, but because of Kellogg's request, no word of its action had gone out to the Catholic people, leading them to believe the bishops had done nothing. Burke averred the government failed to treat the bishops "with the consideration and courtesy which their position demanded." Visibly agitated, Gunther replied, "If you are going to talk this way I wish you would talk directly to the Secretary of State." Turning to the revised letter, Gunther took exception to several parts and told Burke he should decide for himself whether to publish it. He said State still opposed publication because it had done all it could. He reported to Kellogg that Burke seemed to believe that Catholics were so politically important that the government should be taking more action. For his part, Burke deleted the objectionable passages and released to the press the now twice revised letter along with Kellogg's reply on behalf of Coolidge.[52]

At the same time, Burke received news that Calles gave Caruana six days to leave Mexico on grounds he allegedly entered the country under fraudulent papers and functioned as a clergyman. In fact, the Mexican government itself had doctored the documents. Certain the charges were untrue, Sheffield objected to deportation of an American citizen. When Burke learned of the expulsion order, he urged Kellogg to prevent violation of Caruana's rights. "Speaking for the Catholic citizens of the United States," he wrote, "I wish to state that their indignation at such an unwarranted action on the part of the Mexican Government would be limitless." He tried to increase pressure by having the hierarchy telegraph Kellogg protests against the expulsion, but the effort came too late. It would have made no difference. Kellogg and Sheffield fought hard against the deportation but lost. Caruana left Mexico on 16 May.[53]

Back in the U.S., Caruana addressed an open letter to Kellogg clarifying the facts of his entry and brief stay in Mexico. His purpose was to counter the Mexican government's publicity in the U.S. alleging his expulsion was for noncompliance with Mexican law. American papers denounced the deportation, prompting the Mexican government to further self-justification. Arturo Elías, Consul General in New York, published a photostat of Caruana's doctored entry papers, and consular offices around the U.S. released a rabidly anti-Catholic pamphlet, *The Church Problem in Mexico*, which included an article about the "truth" of the expulsion.[54]

Kellogg summoned Burke to discuss the affair. He said he was determined not to respond publicly to Caruana's letter because a reply would have to admit the Mexican government had the right to expel foreigners, and he did not want "to give any encouragement to such a position." He thought Elías's release of the doctored papers "showed to what extreme the Mexican Government was driven to defend itself." He thought the overwhelming newspaper support for Caruana was ample vindication of him. Kellogg asked Burke if he thought the expulsion meant Calles wanted no apostolic delegate whatsoever or just wanted Caruana gone. Burke replied the expulsion of Caruana's predecessors indicated Calles wanted no delegate. Kellogg seemed anxious there be one in Mexico and inquired if one of the Mexican bishops might be suitable for the post. Burke could recommend none, but thought an impartial and independent outsider would be a better fit. Kellogg said he was going to have Sheffield make confidential inquiries about Mexico's willingness to accept a delegate. Yet, he seriously doubted any good intention of the Calles government. He hoped it would see the light, but now felt "there was no profit in dealing with them considerately and kindly, nor in trusting them in anything." Disgusted with the regime, Kellogg angrily allowed he was "seriously contemplating lifting the [arms] embargo," thereby "setting Mexico adrift."[55] Of course, none of that happened.

In mid-July Burke told Dowling as long as the Mexican situation was considered "a Catholic question our State Dep't. will do nothing positive, irrespective of the merits of the case." Protestant, Masonic, and Ku Klux Klan influences were too strong. "The Mexican Government," he said, "knows the game and plays it shrewdly." To Lynch, Burke wrote he daily faced the Mexican issue. "I never dreamt I would have such problems to meet, and I feel altogether unfitted," he told her.[56]

Burke succeeded, however, in getting State to take one positive action. The Mexican government's misuse of diplomatic courtesy by its consulates prompted him to urge Hanna to protest to Kellogg. The objection spurred State to begin an investigation. Kellogg confronted Téllez about issuing through the Mexican consular service anti-Catholic propaganda that served no useful purpose, but tended to stir up public sentiment in the U.S. Téllez promised to discontinue the practice.[57]

To offset Mexican propaganda, Burke established the publicity committee the bishops mandated: the National Committee for the Protection of Religious Rights in Mexico, chaired by Judge Morgan O'Brien of New York. Launched in late summer 1926, it was composed of regional representatives of both the NCCM and the NCCW. Its purpose was twofold: first, to disseminate facts about the persecution and convince Americans the true intention of the Mexican government was to destroy the Catholic Church in that country; second, to undertake relief measures. The latter program never got off the ground because the Knights of Columbus were already involved in that work, thus rendering a second organization superfluous. Operating solely on donations, the committee published two pamphlets by September and issued numerous fliers by the end of the year.[58]

Meanwhile, Calles declared war on the Church with the so-called Calles Law issued on 2 July, implementing the anticlerical articles of the constitution. "The hour is coming when the definitive battle will be joined," he told *El Universal* at the end of the month; "we are going to see if the revolution has conquered reaction or if the triumph of the revolution has been temporary."[59] According to a British diplomat in Mexico City, Calles intended to provoke the cessation of religious worship, "calculating, as he told his friends, that if once the habit of church-going could be broken, the Indians would forget it." The ploy worked. In response to the Calles Law, the National League called for a nationwide economic boycott, and the episcopal committee ordered a halt to public worship, effective 1 August.[60]

In late July 1926, James H. Ryan went to Rome where he had an audience with Pius XI. The pope spoke of many things, Ryan wrote to Burke, including the NCWC, "with which he is au courant —very pleased." The pontiff talked about the Oregon Law and the NEA bill. With regard to Mexico, Ryan remarked there was "not a word here about Curley or his speeches." The pontiff confided: "Between us ... Calles is a *brigand.* He has the mania of a persecutor." Pius understood the position of the U.S.: that economic interests prevented intervention. "He is very calm about the outcome," concluded Ryan. Indeed, at the very time of his writing, the Vatican announced it would not negotiate with the Calles government until the persecution stopped. It would place all its force and hope "in the invincible arm of prayer."[61]

In the U.S., admirers of Calles supported him with their feet. The Ku Klux Klan had, in the words of historian David Chalmers, "a feeling of protective warmth" for his regime, which pursued the kind of religious liberty the Invisible Empire appreciated. In August 1926, thousands of hooded Americans paraded in the national capital and passed a resolution, directing Kellogg to maintain a hands-off policy south of the border.[62]

Despite pressure to the contrary, State became more sympathetic to the Catholic cause, largely at the insistence of Sheffield. Disgusted by the Calles Law and the man himself, he asked Kellogg to rethink policy toward Mexico. How, after all, could the U.S. claim world leadership in religious liberty if it "refused to take notice of so drastic and abhorrent a decree aimed at all religion." He held his own country responsible, at least in part, for the evils of Calles. The memorandum struck a responsive chord. If the domestic nature of the Church-state conflict prevented intervention, Kellogg could still register official displeasure. In a note to the Mexican Foreign Ministry, he declared the American government "regrets to observe that the [Calles] Law as a whole appears to contravene the principle of freedom of religious worship which prevails in the United States, has been productive of the most satisfactory results in this country, and is in accord with the liberal spirit of the age."[63]

PILLORIED

Burke's hard work on behalf of Mexico and in defense of Catholic education got him pilloried both privately and publicly. Regarding both matters, he simply followed orders: in the case of Mexico acting in accordance with the wishes of the bishops of that country, and regarding education by carrying out the instructions of the Administrative Committee to avoid public opposition to the NEA bill. As seen above, *America* insinuated Burke and the NCWC betrayed Catholic interests.[64] Feeling Burke had muzzled him on education, Curley complained to Fumasoni-Biondi that Burke seemed to be independently setting NCWC policy.[65] In February 1926, Burke learned James R. Ryan, disgruntled former attorney of the Legal Department, was maligning him around the country. One priest-editor informed Burke that Ryan said he would expose him before the country. "This is one instance of the perfidy one must endure," Burke lamented to Murray.[66]

In the face of these attacks, Burke wrote a memorandum and, with a good deal of "hesitation" because of personal involvement, gave it to Muldoon for presentation to the Administrative Committee. The committee considered it in executive session. The memo explained there was "a tendency and a habit" on the part of some to minimize the committee's direction of headquarters. "Rumors, charges are made," wrote Burke, "that the policy and activity of the Conference are practically shaped and carried out by the staff ... and particularly by the General Secretary." For example, in executing instructions regarding the NEA bill, headquarters had been subjected to public or private questioning by *America* magazine, Cardinal O'Connell, and Archbishop Curley. *America*'s criticism "had a very appreciable effect ... throughout the country in weakening, for the time at least, the position and the leadership of the N.C.W.C." Likewise, headquarters, in accord with instructions, had not agitated the Mexican question, only to have its "active interest" about the persecution questioned. Curley thought the NCWC was too passive regarding Mexico and complained to Fumasoni-Biondi about him. Burke asked the bishops to make known operations were under their "immediate care, attention and direction."[67] Whatever their deliberations, they took no action at the time, leaving Burke and other officers at headquarters to suffer in silence the avalanche of criticism released in *Fortnightly Review*.

Owned and edited by Arthur Preuss, *Fortnightly* was a German-American, Catholic magazine that had never been friendly to the NCWC. In May 1926, it launched a year-and-a-half-long attack on Burke and other agents. It enjoyed a wide, powerful readership. At the expense of Patrick H. Callahan, it went to every bishop and Catholic newspaper in the country. Preuss attacked Charles Dolle, executive secretary of the NCCM, who had appeared at the hearing on the NEA bill for claiming to represent all Catholic men in America. Similarly, he blasted William Montavon of the Legal Department for daring to claim to represent the entire American Catholic population.[68]

James R. Ryan, who was then practicing law in D.C., distributed copies to congressmen and government officials. In late June, the secretary of a New York congressman informed him that a perturbed Burke had made the rounds on Capitol Hill trying to eradicate the bad impression made by Preuss's attack, which had caused something of a sensation and stimulated considerable demand for copies of the hearing.[69]

Ryan then used *Fortnightly* to make good his threat to expose Burke. "His vanity, his greed for power, and his resentment of counsel," Ryan told Preuss, "coupled with his complete lack of discretion make him a dangerous occupant of his place of power." He congratulated Preuss on his article. Quite possibly the source behind *America's* New Year's editorial about the guardians of Catholic interests, Ryan alleged it was Burke's decision to remain neutral on the NEA bill. "I strongly suspect, but cannot prove," he wrote, "there was a 'deal' between certain officials of the N.C.W.C. and some of the proponents of this character of legislation." When *America* drove Burke to "a perfunctory opposition" of it, he and his supporters endorsed the Phipps bill, which represented the first step toward a federal department of education. Ryan urged Preuss to attack that legislation. Furthermore, he argued Burke's "meddling" in the Mexican Church-state conflict was responsible for the failure of Archbishop Caruana's mission and his expulsion. "The full facts of Father Burke's pernicious interference in this instance," wrote Ryan, "would be a startling revelation for many of the Hierarchy." He said the Vatican was "displeased" with Burke's "unofficial part" in the affair.[70]

Ryan remained friends with Grattan Kerans in the Press Department. In late June 1926, the pair began feeding Preuss articles. They proposed to attack Burke and other officers until the convention of the hierarchy in September in hope the bishops would sack them. The most telling of the articles appeared in August. It was unsigned, giving the impression Preuss himself had written it, thus protecting the ghostwriters. Entitled "The N.C.W.C. and Diocesan Autonomy," it quoted the Vatican instructions reinstating the organization as forbidding its agents to trespass on authority of a local bishop. The piece said over the course of six years, Burke and others had violated that injunction by advocating the Sheppard-Towner Maternity Act, the Child Labor Amendment, and now the Phipps bill. Because federal legislation operated throughout the country, it affected every diocese. Although some bishops opposed those measures, their antagonism was "nullified by the action of the N.C.W.C." If it was to avoid becoming a divisive or destructive influence in the Church, its agents must be chosen with utmost care. "Their record thus far," concluded the piece, "is one of arrogance and incompetence. Further intervention by the Holy See to correct these abuses need surprise no one."[71]

Two weeks before the annual convention, *Fortnightly* published a letter signed "*Ignotus* [Unknown]," written by Ryan in a tone suggesting he was a prominent clergyman. It stated executives at the NCWC were endangering Catholic interests regarding federalization of education. They were either "unconsciously misrepresenting or boldly misrepresenting the Catholic mind" in the matter of parochial schools. Echoing *America*, Ignotus/Ryan said the executives, posing "as the guardians of Catholic principles and rights," had no room for complaint when Catholics mistrusted their judgment. He applauded Preuss for articles demonstrating the need to correct the executives and believed the proper ecclesiastical authorities would take appropriate action. Ryan even appended an editorial note allegedly by Preuss, indicating the letter was but one of many similar the magazine had received, concluding: "We share the writer's view that the abuses chargeable to the N.C.W.C. will in due time be corrected—EDITOR."[72] The purpose of the letter and note was to encourage bishops at the convention to take action. "As we lawyers would say," Ryan explained to Preuss, "the indictment has been presented, the evidence is all in and now comes the motion for a directed verdict, putting the matter squarely up to the court (Hierarchy)."[73]

Fortnightly was not the only critic of Burke and the NCWC. Three days before the convention, Cardinal O'Connell summoned Burke to

Oblate College in Washington. Concerned about the Phipps bill, O'Connell wanted to know what the NCWC had done about it. He heard Burke had "sold out" on education by yielding to the federalizers. Moreover, he asserted Phipps was anti-Catholic. Not a Klansman himself, Phipps was friendly to the Invisible Empire and had received its backing in his 1924 election.[74]

Without mentioning that the NCWC drafted the Phipps bill, Burke explained events leading to its endorsement as an alternative to the NEA bill. Again, O'Connell asked what headquarters had done about it. Burke carefully sidestepped any admission of authorship. "If your Em[inence]., means what have we done … in pushing the Phipps Bill, beyond what I have told you," he said, "I would answer 'nothing.'" The Administrative Committee would press for it only if the NEA bill seemed likely to pass.[75]

O'Connell reminded Burke the hierarchy instructed headquarters to make no public opposition against the NEA bill, but counter further federalization. In his view, the secretariat violated this directive completely. It actively opposed the NEA bill and supported the Phipps bill, which he considered yielding to federal control. Burke explained the hierarchy's orders put headquarters in an untenable position. Congress interpreted its silence as consent to the NEA bill. The Administrative Committee had no choice but to oppose it. The endorsement of the Phipps bill was a tactical maneuver to ensure defeat of the NEA measure. This set O'Connell off on a rambling, three-hour discourse against Americanism wherein he made clear he considered Burke and the administrative bishops guilty of that heresy.[76]

The next day, Burke met with the Administrative Committee to discuss the Phipps bill. Reexamining the text, the board concluded it contained nothing unreasonable or objectionable.[77] The real hurdle, however, would be getting the hierarchy to approve Dowling's endorsement of it. At the convention, Hanna reported the actions of headquarters regarding the NEA bill. Curley said angrily Burke had tried to silence him on it and refused to support the Boylan resolution. He suggested Burke dictated Church policy because in emergencies he acted without seeking the Administrative Committee's advice. Bishop Edmund Gibbons said on both issues Burke consulted the board and had carried out its instructions. When Dowling reported endorsement of the Phipps bill, one bishop took exception to it, but the hierarchy approved and accepted the report.[78]

Burke's efforts at the many problems since his return to work in January 1925 caught up with him. After the convention, he was to give a series of talks in the Midwest. On his way to the first in Milwaukee, he fell ill in Chicago and checked himself into a hospital. The doctor told him his system was overtaxed and ordered rest. He urged Burke to halt his trip and limit work to mornings.[79]

When Congress reopened in December 1926, the Catholic press lined up against the Phipps bill, and leading the charge was *Fortnightly Review.* An article ghostwritten by J. R. Ryan and Kerans hinted at Burke and Montavon's authorship of the bill "which bears the Senator's name but was drafted by men who should have known better." Readers were erroneously told Phipps headed the Klan wing of the Republican Party in Colorado and therefore was not "the kind of official to whom the safety and interests of Catholic education could be entrusted." Yet Burke, Dolle, and Montavon had urged his bill on the Catholic people.[80] Thus, the magazine suggested they were at best stupid or at worst conscious traitors to the Catholic cause.

In the face of criticism, Burke and those at headquarters maintained silence. Clearly, they felt they were being misrepresented and Catholic readers were being misled. Yet, Burke directed those under him to answer no charges nor engage accusers in controversy. Still, he "regretted" these public misrepresentations went unchallenged by his superiors. For the time being, however, he refused to bring the matter to their attention.[81]

When the Senate placed the Phipps bill on the calendar for action, Burke sought Hanna's advice. Counseling against further endorsement, he warned that if the NCWC Administrative Committee ordered positive action, it better "be prepared to meet the criticisms that are sure to come, not from the non-Catholic but from the Catholic press." On the day scheduled for the bill's consideration, the Senate passed it over, dealing it a quiet death.[82]

ENDNOTES TO CHAPTER 15

1. Burke, *Christ in Us*, 27.
2. J. H. Ryan, "Educational Legislation Affecting Private Schools," *Catholic Educational Review* 20 (January 1926): 5–6; William J. Cochran, "The Beginning of the End of Paternalism," *NCWC Bulletin* 7 (July 1925): 6–7, and 31; Fuess, *Calvin Coolidge*, 370–71; Nash, "'Great Enigma,'" 149.

3. Burke to Lynch, 20 December 1925, AP, Burke Papers, box 5; Burke to Muldoon, 2 January 1926, copy, ACUA, USCCB 10:152:30.
4. Curley to Howard, 14 and 19 December 1925, copy, AAB-AASMSU, H1415 and H1417.
5. Burke to Muldoon, 2 January 1926, copy, ACUA, USCCB 10:152:30.
6. Parsons to Curley, 24 December 1925, AAB-AASMSU, P235; Curley to Parsons, 26 December 1925, copy, ibid., P236.
7. The evidence here is cryptic but clear. John Cochran, secretary of Representative Hawes, made it plain to Frederick Kenkel that an organization had apparently changed its view toward federal education legislation. Kenkel's later correspondence makes it evident that the organization at issue was the NCWC. See J. J. Cochran to Kenkel, 15 and 23 January 1926, AUND, Kenkel Papers II, box 8; Kenkel, circular to Central Verein, 3 February 1926, copy, AUND, Kenkel Papers II, box 8.
8. Richard Haberlin to Burke, 28 December 1925, copy, AASF, NCWC files; Burke to W. H. O'Connell, 30 December 1925, copy, ibid.
9. "An Alarm and a Warning," *America* 34 (2 January 1926): 271; Burke to Muldoon, 2 January 1926, copy, ACUA, USCCB 10:152:30; Burke to Murray, 15 February 1926, AP, Burke Papers, box 12 (quote is here).
10. Burke to Wilfrid Parsons, 1 January 1926, copy, ACUA, USCCB 10:152:30; Parsons to Burke, 4 January 1926; Burke to Parsons, 5 January 1926, copy; Parsons to Burke, 7 January 1926; Burke to Lawrence Kelly, 18 January 1926, copy; Parsons to Burke, 8 February 1926—all in ibid. 10:152:40.
11. Burke to Muldoon, 2 January 1926, copy, ACUA, USCCB 10:152:30; Burke to Dowling, 2 January 1926, copy, ibid.,10:105:17; Dowling to Burke, 6 January 1926, ibid.
12. Mary Merrick to Hawks, 2 January 1926, copy, AP, Burke Papers, box 10. Merrick left blank the bishop's name.
13. Burke to Muldoon, 7 January 1926, copy, ACUA, USCCB 10:152:30; Curley to Howard, 8 January 1926, copy, AAB-AASMSU, H1420.
14. Burke to Muldoon, 7 January 1926, copy, ACUA, USCCB 10:152:30.
15. Burke to Dowling, 22 January 1926, copy, ACUA, USCCB 10:152:30 (first quote is here); Burke to J. H. Ryan, telegram, 26 January 1926, ibid., 10:122:25 (second quote is here); Burke, Interview with Peter Gerry, 22 January 1926, ibid., 10:153:21; Slawson, *Department of Education Battle*, 159–60.
16. Minutes of the Department of Education, 27 January 1926, ACUA, USCCB Education Department 10:23:12; Burke to Hanna, Telegram, 28 January 1926, AASF, Diocesan Files (Hanna's reply is handwritten on back); Slawson, *Department of Education Battle*, 125–26.
17. Burke to Lawrence Phipps, 12 February 1926, copy, ACUA, USCCB Legal Department 10:58:23; Burke, Confidential Letter to the Hierarchy, 27 February 1926, ibid., USCCB Education Department 10:15:14.

18. Circular from Agnes Regan, 15 February 1926, copy, ACUA, Vice Rector files; Circular from J. H. Ryan, 12 February 1926, ibid., USCCB Education Department 10:15:14; Burke to Muldoon, 26 February 1926, copy, ibid., USCCB 10:152:30; Burke to hierarchy, 27 February 1926, AASF, NCWC files.
19. Burke to Murray, 15 February 1926, AP, Burke Papers, box 12.
20. Burke to Hanna, 2 March 1926, AASF, NCWC files (first quote is here); Burke to Dowling, 14 February 1926, copy, ACUA, USCCB 10:105:17 (second quote is here); Burke to Muldoon, 26 February 1926, copy, ibid., 10:152:30 (remaining quotes are here).
21. Burke, Confidential Circular to the Hierarchy, 27 February 1926, ACUA, USCCB Education Department 10:15:14.
22. Slawson, *Department of Education Battle*, 166–68.
23. Burke, Memorandum, 6 March 1926, ACUA, USCCB 10:153:21; Slawson, *Department of Education Battle*, 168–69.
24. Burke to Lynch, 31 May and 31 July 1926, AP. Burke Papers, box 5.
25. For a close study of the formulation and significance of the anticlerical articles of the constitution, see E. V. Niemeyer Jr., *Revolution at Queretaro: The Mexican Constitutional Convention of 1916–1917* (Austin: University of Texas Press, 1974), chapter 3. See also Charles C. Cumberland, *Mexican Revolution: The Constitutionalist Years* (Austin: University of Texas Press, 1972), chapter 9; Jean Meyer, *The Cristero Rebellion: The Mexican People Between Church and State, 1926–1929*, trans. Richard Southern (Cambridge: Cambridge University Press, 1976), 13–21; Christopher J. McMullen, "Calles and the Diplomacy of Revolution: Mexican-American Relations, 1924–1928" (Unpublished doctoral dissertation, Georgetown University, 1980), 1–29.
26. For Carranza's attitude toward the Church, see Douglas W. Richmond, *Venustiano Carranza's Nationalist Struggle, 1893–1920* (Lincoln: University of Nebraska Press, 1983), 182–88; Cumberland, *Mexican Revolution*, 379–81. On Obregón, see D. C. Bailey, "Obregón: Mexico's Accommodating President," in George Wolfskill and Douglas W. Richmond, eds., *Essays on the Mexican Revolution: Revisionist Views of the Leaders* (Austin: University of Texas Press, 1979), especially 89–90; D. C. Bailey, "Álvaro Obregón and Anticlericalism in the 1910 Revolution," *The Americas* 26 (October 1969): 183–98. For diplomatic pressure, see Lorenzo Meyer, *Mexico and the United States in the Oil Controversy, 1917–1942*, trans. Muriel Vasconcellos (Austin: University of Texas Press, 1972), 42–106; McMullen, "Diplomacy of Revolution," 1–16.
27. McMullen, "Diplomacy of Revolution," 12–29; Luis Gonzalez, ed., *Historia de la Revolución Mexicana*, 23 vols. (Mexico City, Colegio de Mexico, 1977) vol. 11: *Estado y Sociedad con Calles*, by J. Meyer, Enrique Krauze, and Cayetano Reyes, 279.

28. Arnaldo Córdova, *La ideologia de la Revolucion Mexicana: la formacion del nuevo regimen* (Mexico City: Ediciones Era, 1974), 307–34; J. Meyer, *Cristero Rebellion*, 17–21; J. Meyer, Krauze, and Reyes, *Estado y sociedad*, 54–56; McMullen, "Diplomacy of Revolution," 12–29.
29. J. Meyer, *Cristero Rebellion*, 17–24 (quote is on 23). See also Quirk, *Mexican Revolution*, 115–31; J. Meyer, Krauze, and Reyes, *Estado y sociedad*, 54–56, 79, 217, 279–80; McMullen, "Diplomacy of Revolution," 12–21; Córdova, *La Ideologia de la Revolución*, 307–34.
30. David C. Bailey, *¡Viva Cristo Rey!: The Cristero Rebellion and the church-State Conflict in Mexico* (Austin: University of Texas Press, 1974), 23–58; J. Meyer, *Cristero Rebellion*, 34–35; J. Meyer, Krauze, and Reyes, *Estado y sociedad*, 11 and 220; Matthew A. Redinger, *American Catholics and the Mexican Revolution, 1924–1936* (Notre Dame: University of Notre Dame Press, 2005), 7–8; Peter Lester Reich, *Mexico's Hidden Revolution: The Catholic Church in Law and Politics since 1929* (Notre Dame: University of Notre Dame Press, 1995), 12–13.
31. [Burke], Interview with his Excellency, Most Reverend Serafino Cimino, O.F.M., Apostolic Delegate to Mexico, held in New York City, at 15 Thompson Street, 26 May 1925, ACUA, USCCB 10:145: Interview Book I; Burke, A Page from Contemporary History [25 March 1926], ibid., 10:150:16.
32. Burke, Interview with Franklin Mott Gunther, 8 June 1925, ACUA, USCCB 10:145: Interview Book I.
33. Burke, Interview with James Sheffield, 12 July 1925, ACUA, USCCB 10:145: Interview Book I.
34. Burke, Page from Contemporary History [25 March 1926], ACUA, USCCB 10:150:16; Burke, Interview with Gunther, 4 November 1925, ibid., 10:145: Interview Book I; Burke to Muldoon, 9 November 1925, copy, ibid., 10:152:30; Burke to Muldoon [26 February1926], copy, ibid.; Burke to Hanna, 2 March 1926, AASF, NCWC files; Redinger, *American Catholics and the Mexican Revolution*, 68; Bailey, *¡Viva Cristo Rey!*, 56–67; Robert E. Quirk, *The Mexican Revolution and the Catholic Church, 1910–1929* (Bloomington: Ind.: University of Indiana Press, 1973), 151–54.
35. *NCWC News Sheet*, 8 March 1926; L. Meyer, *Oil Controversy*, 53–129; McMullen, "Diplomacy of Revolution," 49–97; James Morton Callahan, *American Foreign Policy in Mexican Relations* (New York, 1932), 596–606; Samuel Flagg Bemis and Robert H. Ferrell, eds., *The American Secretaries of State and Their Diplomacy*, 18 vols. (New York, 1963) vol. 11: *Frank B. Kellogg–Henry L. Stimson*, by Ferrell, 27–28, 36–37; J. Meyer, *Cristero Rebellion*, 41–45; Bailey, *¡Viva Cristo Rey!*, 59–67; Quirk, *Mexican Revolution*, 151–54.
36. *Baltimore Catholic Review*, 19 and 26 February 1926; Douglas J. Slawson, "The National Catholic Welfare Conference and the Church State Conflict in Mexico, 1925–1929," *The Americas* 47 (July 1990): 60; Redinger, *American*

Catholics and the Mexican Revolution, 39–41; Sheerin, *Never Look Back*, 110; Spalding, *Premier*, 349–50.

37. Curley to Fumasoni-Biondi, 19 March 1926, copy, AAB-AASMSU, Roman Letters.
38. Burke, Page of Contemporary History [25 March1926], ACUA, USCCB 10:150:16; Burke to Muldoon [26 February 1926], copy, ibid., 10:152:30.
39. Burke, Page of Contemporary History [25 March1926], ACUA, USCCB 10:150:16; Burke to Muldoon [26 February 1926], copy, ibid., 10:152:30; Burke to Muldoon, 25 March 1926, copy, ibid.; Caruana to Curley, 14 April 1926, AAB-AASMSU, Roman Letters; Caruana to Kellogg, 14 May 1926, copy, AASF, NCWC files.
40. *Baltimore Catholic Review*, 12 March 1926; Fumansoni-Biondi to Curley, 17 March 1926, AAB-AASMSU, Roman Letters; Caruana to Curley, 14 April 1926, ibid. (quote is here); Quirk, *Mexican Revolution*, 168; Slawson, "NCWC and Mexico," 60; Reddinger, *Catholics and Mexican Revolution*, 39–41; Spalding, *Premier See*, 349–50.
41. *Congressional Record*, 69th Cong., 1st Sess., 1926, 67, pt. 5, 5443; Burke, Page of Contemporary History, [25 March 1926], ACUA, USCCB 10:150:16; Burke to Joseph Schrembs, 24 March 1926, ADC, Schrembs papers; Slawson, "NCWC and Mexico," 60; Spalding, *Premier See*, 350; Redinger, *American Catholics and the Mexican Revolution*, 152–53.
42. Burke, Page of Contemporary History [25 March1926], ACUA, USCCB 10:150:16; Burke to Muldoon, 25 March 1926, copy, ibid., 10:152:30; Burke to Joseph Schrembs, 24 March 1926, ADC, Schrembs papers; Reddinger, *American Catholics and Mexican Revolution*, 152–53; Slawson, "NCWC and Mexico," 60–61; Spalding, *Premier See*, 350.
43. Burke, Page of Contemporary History [25 March1926], ACUA, USCCB 10:150:16; Spalding, *Premier See*, 350; Sheerin, *Never Look Back*, 111–12.
44. Answers from Members of the Administrative Committee to Father Burke's letter re: Hearing on Boylan Resolution, undated [30 March 1926], copy, ADC, Schrembs papers; Burke to Schrembs, 30 March 1926, ibid.; Burke, Telephone Interview with Boylan, 29 March 1926, ACUA-USCCB, 10:145: Interview Book I; Slawson, "NCWC and Mexico," 61.
45. Minutes of the Administrative Committee, 15 April 1926, ACUA, USCCB 10:64:4; Bailey, *¡Viva Cristo Rey!*, 71–72; Redinger, *American Catholics and the Mexican Revolution*, 23–25.
46. Hanna et al. to Coolidge, 15 April 1926, copy, ACUA, USCCB 10:144:43 (first quote is here); *NCWC News Sheet*, 19 April 1926 (second quote is here).
47. Burke, Interview with Gunther, 21 April 1926, ACUA, USCCB 10:145: Interview Book I; *NCWC News Sheet*, 19 April 1926; Reddinger, *American Catholics and Mexican Revolution*, 5–6, 25, 70.

48. Burke to Muldoon, 19 April 1926, copy, ACUA, USCCB 10:152:30; Burke to Hanna, 20 April 1926, ibid., 10:99:16.
49. Burke, Interview with Kellogg and Gunther, 21 April 1926, ACUA, USCCB 10:145: Interview Book I.
50. Burke to Hanna, 20 April 1926, copy, ACUA, USCCB 10:99:16.
51. Administrative Committee to Coolidge, 23 April 1926, copy, AASF, NCWC papers; Minutes of the Administrative Committee, 13 September 1926, ACUA, USCCB 10:64:4; *New York Times*, 19 May 1926; Reddinger, *American Catholics and Mexican Revolution*, 25; M. Elizabeth Ann Rice, O.P., *The Diplomatic Relations between the United States and Mexico, As Affected by the Struggle for Religious Liberty in Mexico, 1925–29* (Washington, D.C.: The Catholic University of America Press, 1959), 83.
52. Burke, Interview with Gunther, 14 May 1926, ACUA, USCCB 10:145: Interview Book I; *New York Times*, 19 May 1926; Quirk, *American Mexican Revolution*, 164; Reddinger, *Catholics and Mexican Revolution*, 25 and 69; Rice, *Diplomatic Relations*, 84–86.
53. Burke, Report on Phone Conversation with Gunther, 14 May 1926, ACUA, USCCB 10:145: Interview Book I; Burke to Frank B. Kellogg, 14 May 1926, copy, ACUA, USCCB 10:144:43 (quote is here); Kellogg to Burke, 18 May 1926, published in *NCWC News Sheet*, 24 May 1926; Burke to Thomas O'Leary, 16 May 1926, copy, ACUA, USCCB 10:144:43 (a penciled note on the top margin states that this letter was sent to all bishops); Burke to Hanna, 7 July 1926, AASF, NCWC files, with enclosure of handwriting experts testifying that Caruana's papers had been altered; Bailey, *¡Viva Cristo Rey!*, 68 n. 84; Rice, *Diplomatic Relations*, 74–77; Reddinger, *American Catholics and Mexican Revolution*, 70–71.
54. Caruana to Kellogg, 4 June 1926, copy, ACUA, USCCB 10:144:43; Burke, Interview with Kellogg, 3 July 1926, ibid., 10:145: Interview Book I; *NCWC News Sheet*, 12 July 1926.
55. Burke, Interview with Kellogg, 3 July 1926, ACUA, USCCB, 10:145: Interview Book I.
56. Burke to Dowling, 23 July 1926, copy, ACUA, USCCB 10:105:17; Burke to Lynch, 31 July 1926, AP, Burke Papers, box 5.
57. Burke to Hanna, 7 July 1926, AASF, NCWC files; Hanna to Kellogg, undated [July 1926], copy, ibid.; Rice, *Diplomatic Relations*, 103–04, especially n. 106.
58. *NCWC News Sheet*, 9 August 1926; Minutes of the Administrative Committee, 13 September 1926, ACUA, USCCB 10:64:4; Burke to Hanna, 13 December 1926, draft (never sent), ibid., 10:152:13; Kauffman, *Faith and Fraternalism*, 295; Redinger, *American Catholics and the Mexican Revolution*,119–21.
59. Quoted in J. Meyer, Krauze, and Reyes, *Estado y sociedad*, 223; Bailey, *¡Viva Cristo Rey!*, 76; Quirk, *Mexican Revolution*, 167; Redinger, *American Catholics and the Mexican Revolution*, 8–9; Reich, *Mexico's Hidden Revolution*, 13.

60. Quoted in J. Meyer, *Cristero Rebellion*, 44; Quirk, *Mexican Revolution*, 168–78, 192–93; Bailey, *¡Viva Cristo Rey!*, 76–95, 101–02, 128.
61. J. H. Ryan to Burke, 12 August 1926, ACUA, USCCB, 10:153:5; *New York Times*, 11 August 1926 (quote from the Vatican is here).
62. Chalmers, *Hooded Americanism*, 284–90.
63. Quoted in Bailey, *¡Viva Cristo Rey!*, 101-02; Quirk, *Mexican Revolution*, 172.
64. Parsons to Curley, 24 December 1925, AAB-AASMSU, P235.
65. Curley to Fumasoni-Biondi, 19 March 1926, AAB-AASMSU, Roman Letters.
66. Burke to Murray, 15 February 1926, AP, Burke Papers, box 12 (all quotes are here); J. R. Ryan to Arthur Preuss, 30 August 1926, ACBCCU, Preuss Papers, reel 6.
67. [Burke to the Administrative Committee], undated [April 1926], copy, ACUA, USCCB 10:152:1; Minutes of the Administrative Committee, 13 April 1926, ibid., 10:64:4.
68. "By What Authority?" *Fortnightly Review* 33 (15 May 1926): 215–16 (quote is here); "More Light on the Activities of the N.C.W.C.," ibid. (15 June 1926): 259–60; Slawson, *Department of Education Battle*, 164 and 170.
69. J. R. Ryan to Preuss, 21 June 1926, ACBCCU, Preuss papers, reel 6; Ryan to Preuss, 25 June 1926, ibid.; Slawson, *Department of Education Battle*, 171.
70. J. R. Ryan to Preuss, 21 May 1926, ACBCCU, Preuss Papers, reel 6; J. R. Ryan to Preuss, 30 July 1926, ibid. (quotes are from both).
71. "The N.C.W.C. and Diocesan Autonomy," *Fortnightly Review* 33 (15 August 1926): 355–56; Slawson, *Department of Education Battle*, 171–72.
72. *Ignotus* to the Editor, *Fortnightly Review* 33 (1 September 1926): 393–94; J. R. Ryan to Preuss, 23 August 1926, ACBCCU, Preuss Papers, reel 6.
73. J. R. Ryan to Preuss, 23 August 1926, ACBCCU, Preuss Papers, reel 6.
74. Burke interview with O'Connell, 12 September 1926, ACUA, USCCB 10:153: Interview Book 1925–1931; Kenneth T. Jackson, *Ku Klux Klan in the City, 1915–1930* (New York: Oxford University Press, 1967), 226–28; Robert Alan Goldberg, "Hooded Empire: The Ku Klux Klan in Colorado, 1921–1932," (University of Wisconsin: unpublished doctoral dissertation, 1977), 118 and 131; Chalmers, *Hooded Americanism*, 127–29.
75. Burke interview with O'Connell, 12 September 1926, ACUA, USCCB 10:153: Interview Book 1925–1931.
76. Ibid.
77. Minutes of the Administrative Committee, 13 September 1926, ACUA, USCCB 10:64:4.
78. *Minutes of the Eighth Annual Meeting of Hierarchy, September 1926*, 6, ACUA, USCCB 10: Bound Volumes; Schrembs to Sincero, 25 March 1927, copy, ibid., 10:153:8; J. R. Ryan to Preuss, 21 June 1926, ACBCCU, Preuss papers, reel 6; Slawson, *Department of Education Battle*, 174–75.

79. Muldoon to Burke, 23 and [24] October 1926, ACUA, USCCB 10:152:30; Burke to Lynch, 26 October 1926, AP, Burke Papers, box 5.
80. "Senator Phipps and the Phipps Bill," *Fortnightly Review* 33 (1 October 1926): 433; J. R. Ryan to Preuss, 23 September 1926, ACBCCU, Preuss Papers, reel 6; Slawson, *Department of Education Battle*, 175.
81. Burke to Hanna, 13 December 1926, never sent, ACUA, USCCB 10:152:13.
82. Burke to Hanna, 13 December 1926, copy, ACUA, USCCB 10:99:16; Montavon to J. H. Ryan, 8 February 1927, copy, ACUA, USCCB Legal Department 10:58:23 and 24.

Chapter 16
"The Situation Is Too Much for Me," 1927 and 1928

> "Greater love than this no man hath, that a man lay down his life for his friends" (John 15:13).... To keep within us abiding faith in our fellows is a most difficult task. The cynics of this world apparently have the stronger argument. The distrustful, the suspicious, the calculating attitude is as easy and inviting as the Christian standard is difficult. Yet whatever other fidelities we possess, we may well ask ourselves if we do not lack the supreme one unless we are willing to love our fellows and love them to the end. Love means kindness: unselfishness: consideration: the more favorable interpretation, the happier outlook. Love means the giving of self even after such giving has been rejected.[1]

Under Attack

Despite failure to have the hierarchy sack John Burke in September 1926, J. R. Ryan and Grattan Kerans continued to attack him and the NCWC anonymously in *Fortnightly Review*. They considered the agents he sent to the hearing on the NEA bill stupid and incompetent. Regarding the Phipps bill, they thought Burke and the NCWC needed sound legal advice, noting Montavon was "not a lawyer and has no lawyer associated with him." Echoing an earlier theme, they argued Burke and the NCWC violated canonical autonomy of local bishops by supporting the Phipps bill, which some opposed.[2]

Giving the argument a new twist, Ryan and Kerans declared the pope would eventually condemn the NCWC as he had *Action Française*, a French movement that identified nationalism with Catholicism in a way making the latter servant of the former. The Church's principal safeguard against nationalism was autonomy of the local bishop. Yet, NCWC advocates wanted it "recognized and operated as a 'great central agency' which should 'represent and protect' Catholic 'causes, rights and interests' in a 'national way,'" thereby invading diocesan autonomy in violation of "the [1922] decree of the Holy See."[3] Equating *Action Française* with Americanism, *Fortnightly* warned: "Leo XIII checked a similar movement here with his famous brief 'Testem Benevolentiae,' but 'narrow earth-bound nationalism' is not by any means dead yet in America."[4] In short, Burke and the NCWC were exponents and promoters of Americanism.

Then came an assault from Archbishop Michael Curley. Bristling at the Administrative Committee's defense of Burke at the hierarchy's convention, Curly lashed out against the NCCM and NCCW, considering them "a failure." He proclaimed their attempt to create a national organization of laity had failed. The way to unite Catholic laity, declared Curley, was to return to the plan of the AFCS.[5] Calling Curley's "appraisement of the Men's and Women's Councils ... a Big Bertha," J. R. Ryan fed *Fortnightly* an article quoting liberally from Curley's remarks.[6]

Walter Johnson, president of the NCCM, complained to Burke about this "vicious attack," blaming Curley's own "indifference and lack of recognition and support" for failure of the two councils in Baltimore.[7] Burke sent copies of *Fortnightly* to the Administrative Committee, reporting to Bishop Joseph Schrembs, chairman of Lay Activities, that Curley's words had demoralized their organizers, but they had learned "not to talk of or to answer criticism." Burke feared other papers might reprint the article.[8] Little did he know it would make its way to Rome.

Unable to understand how the NCCW had upset Curley, Schrembs believed it resulted from "his peeve [at the NCWC], and to be consistent therein, he strikes at that which is within his reach." Schrembs considered it imperative to conciliate him and urged Burke to see Curley with a firm resolution "not to lose patience or your temper no matter what he says. The cause is bigger than we are."[9] Burke wisely demurred. Persona non grata, he replied, "I do not think a visit from me to Archbishop Curley would be in order."[10]

The attacks of Curley and *Fortnightly* discouraged him. The "unjust criticisms" of both pushed him several times to the verge of writing Archbishop

Edward Hanna about defending headquarters. Finally, Burke did. "I feel very deeply that an answer should have been made by the Bishops of the Administrative Committee," he told Hanna, "... yet no word is said in rebuttal." In the archdiocese of Baltimore, where headquarters lay, he averred "here we have no standing."[11] To Grace Murray, he lamented Curley's opposition to the NCWC or at least "the present Administrative Committee." If Hanna were nearer and in direct charge of things, perhaps Curley might be better disposed. "But personally to continue working in a diocese wherein one knows the Ordinary is against the work, is not pleasant," he told her.[12] He confided to Muldoon he felt physically ill-equipped to deal with the many sides of the affair. Admitting he was "not without fault" in its management, he wrote to Hanna, "The situation is too much for me."[13]

The situation only worsened as Curley found a new target: Father John O'Brien, a member of Dowling's department and promoter of the Catholic Foundation. The foundation was forerunner of present-day Newman Clubs on campuses of secular universities. In 1925, O'Brien declared: take religion out of a Catholic college and all that remained was secular education; inject religion into a secular college through the Catholic Foundation, and the essence of Catholic education was preserved. This view ran counter to the prevailing Catholic understanding that religion was not just a branch of learning; it was the basis of all education and ideally should color every other subject. Curley accused O'Brien of denigrating Catholic schools and colleges.[14]

The Administrative Committee supported Catholic Foundations, but not as a substitute for Catholic colleges. In January 1927, Dowling warned O'Brien to be prudent because his actions would redound on the department. Within months Dowling would ask for his resignation. At issue was his open stance toward non-Catholics in an age of increasing ecumenism.[15]

Bigotry fomented by Helen Jackson, a professional ex-nun employed by the Ku Klux Klan, ravaged the town of Champaign, home of the University of Illinois where O'Brien was chaplain of the foundation. The Klan held several parades and five cross-burnings, three at Catholic churches, one of them O'Brien's, and two at boarding houses of Catholic students. To allay religious hatred, Reverend James Baker wrote a non-denominational prayer for tolerance for use in all Protestant churches. Addressed solely to God the Father, it read in part: "Almighty God: We who are members of different races and faiths desire together to acknowledge Thy

Fatherhood and our kinship with each other.... Open our eyes to see that as nature abounds in variation so differences in human beings make for richness in the common life ... regardless of race, color or circumstances. Deepen our respect for unlikeness and our eagerness to understand one another." Baker secured its endorsement by O'Brien and Rabbi Benjamin Frankel. The NCWC News Service published the prayer, reporting their collaboration in "sweeping aside old racial and religious animosities and acknowledging kinship in the Fatherhood of God."[16]

Apostolic Delegate Pietro Fumasoni-Biondi summoned Burke and read him the item. Asked for his view, Burke answered he had seen the prayer in the Washington *Star*, but names were omitted. He could not believe a priest would have collaborated on it or approved it. Monsignor Paolo Marella, the delegate's auditor, said the News Service should never have issued it. Burke defended press director Justin McGrath, who obviously considered the prayer a news item. The conversation then turned to a general discussion of Catholic attendance in secular universities, O'Brien's unfitness to be a chaplain, and steps to be taken for his removal.[17]

Three days later, Curley's alter ego Vincent de Paul Fitzpatrick, editor of the *Baltimore Catholic Review*, telephoned McGrath objecting that the prayer was heterodox and warning that the NCWC was conniving at unorthodoxy. Days later, the paper protested against the release of a prayer dangerously close to heresy. Fitzpatrick claimed he asked the NCWC to stop the item. The director of its Press Department refused, declaring he had no intention of suppressing news. When McGrath saw the piece, he told Burke Fitzpatrick never asked him to kill the story.[18]

Marella visited Burke to see if O'Brien belonged to the NCWC's staff. When Burke said no, Marella urged him to check. James H. Ryan told Burke O'Brien was a member of his department. Burke informed Marella, who replied O'Brien should retract the prayer. To keep him in the department was to cast suspicion on his colleagues. Membership in it gave him undeserved prestige and backing. Marella urged Burke to do what had to be done. Immediately, Burke informed Dowling of Marella's advice.[19] More than a week would pass before Dowling acted.

Meanwhile, Cardinal Dennis Dougherty of Philadelphia, never friendly to the NCWC and furious because it closed its immigration office there, picked up the theme. His archdiocesan newspaper, *Catholic Standard and*

Times, published an editorial on religious indifferentism, "one of the most insidious evils against which the Church has to contend in these days." It was surprising, therefore, that the NCWC released a prayer co-authored by a priest that swept "aside the fundamental principles of Christianity" by failing to mention Jesus or the Holy Spirit. The paper refused to print it and thought the NCWC lacked judgment in releasing it. Calling for "rigorous supervision" of the News Service, it denied the agency represented the hierarchy.[20]

Marella urged Burke to defend himself and the NCWC because both Curley and Dougherty intended to press the issue. Out of corporate loyalty, Burke refused because it might give the impression of excusing himself at the expense of the Administrative Committee. This confused Marella who thought the general secretary had complete charge of headquarters. Burke explained that although he could advise directors, their immediate superiors were the bishops who chaired their departments. He had no right to censor McGrath's news; that belonged to Bishop Philip McDevitt. This surprised Marella, who urged that Burke explain it to Fumasoni-Biondi who was similarly uninformed of the NCWC's inner workings. Still, Marella thought something must be done. A layman should not decide what news was released by the NCWC, an organization of the bishops whose approval attached itself to all that went out.[21]

Burke sent the Administrative Committee copies of editorials from Curley's and Dougherty's papers and summaries of his talks with Fumasoni-Biondi and Marella. Dowling replied that he demanded O'Brien resign from his department. "It is open season for heresy hunting," he commented, "& I feel that O'B. is not the one the Inquisitors are after. All I can see in O'Brien is a fool." Clearly, Dowling knew critics were after the NCWC. He asked Burke if he was going to do anything about McGrath. "The notice he sent out was more than news," remarked Dowling: "'sweeping aside old racial and religious animosities' is propaganda."[22]

Schrembs, too, was concerned about being labeled heterodox. "The very fact that the prayer was published in the Catholic News Service," he told Burke, "would readily lend itself to the interpretation that those responsible for the News Service considered the prayer a wonderful advance in the matter of broadmindedness." Like Marella, he thought the incident proved need of censorship over the press bureau. He forwarded a letter just received from Giuseppe Pizzardo, undersecretary of state at the Vatican, who sent two recent issues of the journal *Fede e Ragione* [*Faith and Reason*], published in Florence, Italy, attacking the NCWC with information from *Baltimore Catholic Review* and *Fortnightly Review*. "It shows," said Schrembs, "that the storm is raging even in Rome."[23]

Assuming the mantle of Charles Maignen, who in 1898 exposed an alleged Americanist plot to subvert European Catholicism, *Fede e Ragione* issued a similar warning against the NCWC. "Since the exploits of this famous organization become more noisy," declared the paper, "so that the fame thereof flies across the ocean, and tries to stir up the emulation and the ambition of similar European associations, we think it necessary, for the cause of justice and virtue, to put on their guard the ingenuous ones and the admirers of American novelty, against this nest of false prophets and hirelings." The article praised Curley for revealing "to the American Catholics what an imposture the 'National Catholic Welfare Conference' is." Following *Fortnightly*, it hammered at Burke, Montavon, and Dolle for having betrayed Catholic educational interest by supporting the Phipps bill. It further alleged the NCWC had succumbed to the "Satanic spirit of the modern State" by yielding on the matter of birth control, a charge patently false. In short, the NCWC was a traitor to Catholicism.[24]

In its defense, Schrembs sent Vatican Cardinal Luigi Sincero, a supporter of the NCWC, an explanation of Curley's and Preuss's attacks. Burke prepared a formal point-by-point rejoinder to the article. After revising the document, the Administrative Committee signed it and sent copies to Cardinals Gaetano de Lai, Donato Sbarretti, and Alfonso Maria Mistrangelo, archbishop of Florence.[25]

Meanwhile, Burke drafted for McDevitt's signature a letter to Dougherty in defense of the Press Department. Surprised his paper accused it of heresy, Burke reminded Dougherty that at the celebration of his reception of the red hat, a rabbi offered latitudinarian remarks that "shocked and scandalized" Catholics present. They recognized, however, Dougherty was in no position to repudiate them. They understood his silence was not endorsement, explained Burke. Yet, his newspaper printed the rabbi's remarks in full, apparently with Dougherty's approval, implying his indifference to the evil consequences. Burke's draft included a direct comparison of the rabbi's remarks to those in the prayer O'Brien endorsed. Although politely worded, the substance of the letter was inflammatory. McDevitt discussed it with Schrembs, Archbishop John Glennon of St. Louis, and Bishop Hugh Boyle of Pittsburgh. All agreed no good would result from sending it; rather, the letter would only further antagonize Dougherty. "Hence the letter dies," McDevitt told Burke.[26]

One wonders at Burke's failure to see how incendiary it was. Perhaps the pressure of being under constant attack without defense clouded his judgment. Indeed, he told his friend Muldoon: "I wish you were here to direct me. Amid it all I know not sometimes where I am or what I ought to do or what will happen next." To Murray, Burke wrote, "The problems are manifold and I know not at times how to walk."[27]

Given Dowling and Schrembs's criticism of McGrath with which McDevitt agreed, Burke felt compelled to discuss it with the editor. He told McGrath his responsibility was not to subscribers of the News Service, but to the Administrative Committee. Three of its bishops considered his action a mistake. Burke asked if there was anything to be done. McGrath said no. He believed as director of the department, it was his responsibility to decide what news went out. The department was providing a service to Catholic newspapers. If their editors thought it was under censorship, they would distrust it, and that would be the end of it. He told Burke he would not refuse advice; indeed he would seek it. But he felt any change of policy would be harmful to the Church's interest. Burke told McGrath he communicated the opinions of the bishops to him in fairness, and it "had cost" him something to do it. He asked him to think over the import of the matter. The editor thanked him, but said he could in conscience take no other position.[28]

In late March1927, Curley, unaware Dowling had already acted, urged him to dismiss O'Brien. He denounced the priest to Fumasoni-Biondi on grounds he was doctrinally unsafe and then took the affair directly to Cardinal Raphael Merry del Val, secretary of the Holy Office. Curley sent him copies of the NCWC news releases and his letter to Fumasoni-Biondi. Moreover, he publicly questioned O'Brien's orthodoxy in an address to the Washington chapter of the International Federation of Catholic Alumnae. He recounted the charges against O'Brien while thrice mentioning the NCWC, thus implicating it by association in his guilt.[29]

Burke saw Fumasoni-Biondi, who seemed unworried by Curley's and Dougherty's attacks. He told Burke the NCWC was experiencing "something of a storm, as any organization might." Burke said at times "it was deeply discouraging: misrepresentation: inability or uselessness of answering: disedification and even scandal to the workers ... at these attacks from Church dignitaries." To his surprise, Fumasoni-Biondi told him not to be disturbed. "I have reported well on it [NCWC] and will so report," he declared. "It is doing a very good and a very necessary work. No hierarchy in the world is so united as the American hierarchy." The words heartened Burke.[30]

In mid-April, the delegate asked Curley to refrain from further utterance because the matter was under investigation. The archbishop replied: "I am through with the affair. What I did I did as a matter of duty to the people over whom I have been placed."[31]

If Curley was through, Ryan and Kerans were not. They continued their assault with three articles ghostwritten for Preuss. The first was the most significant, praising Fitzpatrick for his exposé of and stand against O'Brien's prayer. They argued "it would be a mistake to suppose that the sending out of this semi-heretical stuff was an inadvertent blunder." Behind it was "a definite and deliberate tendency." If allowed to continue unchecked, the movement would poison Catholic public opinion and evoke from the Vatican a new condemnation of "Americanism."[32]

A month before the convention of the hierarchy, Ryan and Kerans attacked Burke and the NCWC again. They pointed out both Curley's and Dougherty's newspapers had denied the NCWC was the hierarchy and quoted the 1922 Vatican instructions in support of that position. Since their issuance, Burke endorsed the Phipps bill and made pronouncements on the Mexican situation. "It may be that Father Burke is responsible for these and other dangerous adventures," they declared; "but if so, who is responsible for Father Burke?!?" The two denied the NCWC was agent of the hierarchy. If the bishops themselves would not definitively settle the matter, Ryan and Kerans were "confident the Holy See will."[33]

Apprehensions within the NCWC soon calmed as allies in Rome and America reported back. From the Vatican, Sincero wrote he was unsurprised by the assault of *Fede e Ragione*: "In times past, this same journal attacked the Holy Father and Cardinal Gasparri. This periodical has absolutely no importance."[34] Later, Burke learned from Filippo Bernardini at the apostolic delegation that the author in *Fede e Ragione* was an excommunicated priest.

Even more encouraging, at the request of the Administrative Committee, Fumasoni-Biondi and Bernardini drafted a letter to be issued by Pius XI, praising the work of the NCWC, especially its efforts for the Church in Mexico (see next chapter). In summer Bernardini carried it to Rome, and the pope signed it on 10 August 1927.[35]

Ryan and Kerans made a final plea in *Fortnightly* for the convention of the hierarchy to distinguish between itself and the NCWC. The article proved to be their swan song. Ryan took a job in New York City, and serious illness forced Kerans to take an extended leave of absence from the NCWC. Although they remained in contact, their collaboration on articles against Burke and the organization ceased.[36]

HAITI

While under attack, Burke dealt with Haiti. In January 1927, the Vatican appointed Archbishop George Caruana internuncio to that country. He asked Burke for "his frank opinion" about American administrators there as background for his upcoming visit.[37] Burke advised him to choose his words carefully because they would be publicized in the U.S. "and of course will be used as either for or against the American Occupation." Every Haitian government since the concordat had supported the Church. The same could not be said of American administrators. Occupation officials would blame the Haitian government for the current refusal to support the Church adequately, but there was "no truth in the statement." The Haitian people were thoroughly Catholic and "capable of a high degree of development." American officials will tell "of their superstitions, their filthy habits, etc., etc., but these are exaggerated and the work which the Church is doing, long and tiresome as it is, is showing good results." Caruana would find Haitians passionate, boisterous lovers of liberty, who despised the occupation. Although they appreciated medical work being done for them, they felt exploited by William Cumberland, financial adviser who controlled the treasury and used Haitian money to pay bloated salaries to American officials while offering miserable recompense to local teachers, judges, priests, and religious.[38]

Even before Caruana reached Haiti, three newspapers there belonging to Protestants or radicals attacked him as "a 'jingoist and imperialist American,'" whose coming was to further the ambitions of the U.S. He told Burke the papers linked their names: "We are birds in the same nest!!! Cave canes [beware of the dogs]!!!" Caruana found things in Haiti exactly as Burke described. Though a frank and honest man, Cumberland was an unbeliever who viewed the concordat "as a commercial treaty rather than an agreement among two friends seeking each other's mutual benefit." Caruana explained his purpose was to depart Haiti on friendly terms with all parties. He kept his speeches to pious platitudes and "'the usual sweet nothings.' The situation is such that I deemed it best to hold all my sentiments *locked* up." He urged Burke to do his best to persuade Cumberland to justice toward the claims of the church.[39]

Though Burke thought there was little chance of that, Cumberland, shortly before resigning, engaged in perhaps a parting act of kindness. Burke told the Administrative Committee Cumberland approved raises for religious brothers and sisters teaching there, "but nothing like justice had been done in the matter as yet." In December 1927, Arthur Millspaugh, "a different and better type of man" in Burke's judgment, took Cumberland's position. Before Millspaugh left for Haiti, Burke met with him and had a long talk about the situation there. In 1928, Burke pressured the U.S. government into having Haitian funds approved for the erection of the final two dioceses stipulated in the concordat: Gonaïves and Port-de-Paix.[40]

Meanwhile, Caruana had become persona non grata to the Haitian people and established residence in Cuba. Believing the Haitian government would not permit him to reenter, he appointed his chargé d'affaires, Monsignor Pietro Cogliolo, apostolic administrator to work in Port-au-Prince under his supervision. Burke still remained in direct contact with Caruana,[41] but his active involvement ceased until the denouement of the American occupation, which he would help bring about.

The King of Kings and The Callahans and The Murphys

When Father Daniel Lord returned to Hollywood in February 1927 for the final cut of *King of Kings*, Burke was more forthcoming than in his guarded reply to Lord's preliminary report. He told him in light of that report, the NCWC could not approve the film without "extensive and radical changes." Lord was free to suggest the alterations and say that without them the NCWC would not recommend it. Burke added he was "surprised—

and not a little bit concerned—" by public announcements indicating a Protestant minister, a Catholic priest, and Jewish rabbi had already approved the film. He hoped DeMille and Will Hays would live up to their understanding that the NCWC would have final say about Catholic approval.[42]

Lord assured Burke the MPPDA had issued no religious approvals of it and neither he nor Rev. George Reid Andrews, Protestant consultant, had expressed any opinions about it. Catholic endorsement must come from Burke. Lord explained that many priests and even some bishops attended shootings and were uniformly positive about the picture. He was disturbed to learn Burke thought it required major changes. The only part he thought might be offensive was the opening scene with Mary Magdalen. He assured DeMille had made all recommended adjustments to it. As for the rest, Lord judged it "a magnificent and very reverent treatment." He urged Burke to wire about the scenes of concern so he could inform DeMille.[43]

Burke telegraphed that the opening contained some of the questionable footage. The preliminary report described "such scenes of luxury and undress as [the] Conference would not approve." He said NCWC approbation was "vastly different from general toleration and acceptance." From data at hand, Burke wrote it was impossible to give specific instructions and urged Lord to do his best.[44]

In late February, Lord filed a gushing supplemental report. Several viewings of the final print convinced him Burke would be "deeply impressed" with it. Lord's only qualm remained the banquet sequence. He and DeMille had gone over it multiple times, cutting and cutting, until Lord thought it "well within the range of approval." The director trimmed it from 2,000 to 500 feet. The only possible objection might be to Magdalen's costume, but Lord convinced DeMille to eliminate all close-ups of her. Similarly, he cut all shots of dancing girls except one where they clustered about Magdalen.[45]

Lord found actor Henry Warner's portrayal of Jesus "more impressive with every reel." He thought viewers would be so drawn into the character of Christ, every thought about the actor would vanish. Caption boards contained only words spoken by Jesus in the gospels, using the Catholic Douay translation except in instances where the Revised Standard Version was better known. The film still took "considerable liberty" with chronology, "but not in a way to jar." The entire second half depicted the passion from betrayal of Jesus in the Garden of Gethsemane to the Resurrection and Ascension, "a magnificent, reverent, astonishing presentation." It would leave Burke "speechless," just as it had Lord. The portrayal of Jesus's mother Mary was "wonderfully beautiful." After her son, she was the most conspicuous figure in the passion. Like the opening, the Resurrection was in Technicolor and "marvelously beautiful." The Risen Christ's first appearance was to his mother.[46]

Lord said DeMille and Hays would give Burke a preview in New York City. DeMille was eager for NCWC approval and seemed willing to do almost anything to get it. Lord urged Burke to put together a representative committee to review the film with him. He considered it a "great, impressive, lavish, wonderfully acted" story that would do "untold good."[47]

Burke recommended to Hays ten New York Catholics, including Father Wilfrid Parsons of *America*, Father James Gillis of *Catholic World*, Michael Williams of *Commonweal*, and Rita McGoldrick of the International Federation of Catholic Alumnae. Hays assured Burke the MPPDA would ask no opinion of attendees; those would be addressed to him. As it turned out, Burke would hear from only one. He himself planned to attend, but work prevented him.[48]

He had no need to preview the picture when it came to a decision about NCWC endorsement. Burke put his thoughts on paper. Certain that DeMille and the MPPDA wanted official approval of the NCWC, FCC, and Jewish Board to ensure the film's success, he considered it shortsighted on the industry's part and actually inimical to its interest. By seeking it, the MPPDA would acknowledge, if not constitute, religious censorship. If it submitted *King of Kings* for approval, why not all films? And why thereafter should not churches demand such? The principle at stake was "acknowledgment of direct, positive church censorship in matters of public recreation and entertainment," which violated the principles and traditions of the country. Choice of entertainment should be left to the "informed conscience" of individual and parent. Burke felt the Church had a duty to instruct and inform, but she "also must depend on her children. Her coercive office must be as limited as possible." Religious bodies had the right to protest, warn, and admonish. They might even have the right to command their adherents regarding moral conduct. That, however, was an "interior right, of conscience, of obedience." Churches had no right in the "open domain of general public activity," except regarding moral principles enshrined in civil law as foundations of decency and social stability. What DeMille and the MPPDA sought for *King of Kings* would best be done indirectly, through laudatory reviews in the press of various denominations. Burke believed in this instance, the producers had done "a conscientious, worthy piece of work." They should put it before the public and let the public decide.[49]

This memorandum indicates Burke had come around to Lord's view of the film as an honest and worthy production. It also suggested just how far he was willing to go in meeting the wishes of DeMille and Hays. The NCWC would neither endorse nor condemn the picture. It would, however, give it a review.

Shortly thereafter, Burke heard from Father Joseph Husslein, associate editor of *America*, who attended the screening. He considered the film artistically successful. Everything about Jesus, his mother, Last Supper, and crucifixion was reverent. Religiously, much was "edifying and charming." There was also ground for severe criticism. Everything from the opening banquet to the conversion of Magdalen was "entirely out of place … and very offensive." Husslein credited Lord for toning down "these sensuous scenes." A non-Catholic with wide film experience told him "the first part was De Mille, the rest was the religious picture." Husslein shared Burke's problem with chronology: "It is the movie that must yield to the Scripture and not the Scripture to the movie." Moreover, DeMille embellished on the gospel. For instance, scripture said the earth quaked and rocks were rent at the Resurrection. Yet the film depicted fearful chasms opened into which fell masses of people. "The exaggerations created an air of unreality that almost destroyed … the entire effect the picture is intended to produce," concluded Husslein. "It destroyed its sincerity."[50]

When the Administrative Committee met, Burke explained the NCWC's part in consulting on the film. He set forth his own views about an official endorsement and summarized Husslein's critique. The committee decided to make no statement about the picture.[51]

In June 1927, more than a month after the film's release, Burke saw *King of Kings* during a visit to New York City. He told Mary Hawks he did not like Technicolor, "but that's a detail." He found the entire picture "reverent, and to me deeply impressive." He said he had gone with expectation of objecting to any representation of Jesus, but the film made him feel "how practical, and real, and human" was the example and love of the Lord. "I was much affected by the presentation," wrote Burke. "I think it will do much good."[52]

Though he and the NCWC were pleased with *King of Kings*, they would soon break with the movie industry. The parting came with Metro-Goldwyn-Mayer's (MGM's) release of *The Callahans and the Murphys*. Based loosely on the novel by Kathleen Norris, a Catholic, it was low comedy about a pair of now-feuding-now-friendly Irish tenement housewives and their families. Mrs. Murphy's son, Dan, a bootlegger, was romantically involved with Mrs. Callahan's daughter, Ellen, who became pregnant, leaving viewers to believe the child was illegitimate; Ellen gave birth in the countryside and left the baby at her mother's door. Mrs. Callahan adopted the child and later learned Ellen and Dan had been secretly married, but were living apart until Dan gave up bootlegging. The film clearly indicated the two families were Catholic. Crucifixes hung on walls, and Mrs. Callahan routinely crossed herself at appropriate moments in conversations. She did so correctly when sober, but incorrectly in her cups. Comedic highlights featured the drunken antics of the two stars, Marie Dressler as Callahan and Polly Moran as Murphy. At a St. Patrick's Day picnic, the pair quaffed beer after beer ("This stuff makes me see double and feel single!") and then began pouring it down each other's blouse. The scene concluded with an Irish donnybrook.[53]

When the film premiered in Los Angeles, it seemed MGM had a hit. Adverse criticism came only from local Irish-American organizations which asked its withdrawal. As it played around the country, especially in regions with large Irish-American populations, objections began to pour in. The MPPDA and MGM grew alarmed and began working with Irish-American groups to cut offensive scenes. As historians Francis Couvares and Frank Walsh have pointed out, the NCWC was among the MPPDA's best supporters in promoting self-regulation of the industry. Probably for that reason, Carl Milliken, head of the Public Relations Department, turned to McMahon. He telephoned to ask that he and Burke see the picture.[54]

If he was looking for help in the situation, he was in for a rude awakening. Burke and McMahon went to a nearby theater. They found the film deeply offensive, and both wrote to Milliken immediately. "I never witnessed a more vulgar travesty on the Catholic Irish and the Catholic Irish Americans," complained Burke. "No editing or correction will eliminate the offence of the picture which is carried throughout." The movie should be pulled, and he "anxiously" awaited word of what the MPPDA intended to do.[55]

McMahon was similarly harsh. "I am frank to say that never before have I been so disgusted with a picture and so incensed at a company that could be so lacking in good sense," he told Milliken. He enclosed a statement and an editorial which he had just written for release through the News Service. He agreed with Burke that nothing could be done to make the movie satisfactory; it must be withdrawn. McMahon hoped MGM would have the intelligence and decency to do that.[56]

His release called the film "a gross insult, deliberate or otherwise, to the ancient faith and culture of the Irish people." It reeked "from start to finish with vulgarity and indecency," and was offensive to the Catholic religion. McMahon was at a loss to understand how MGM could produce such a thing. The "Donnybrook Irishman" had disappeared from the "legitimate stage," he wrote, and it was time from him to do so from the silver screen. He concluded such an outrageous movie would "make the usually tolerant and liberty-loving Irish-Americans" clamor for legal censorship as loudly as the most ardent reformer.[57]

The editorial was equally harsh, declaring the picture "a particularly vicious contribution to the bigotry and hatred from which the Irish … have suffered at the hands of the Ku Klux Klan and its abettors." Situating this "crass caricature" of the Irish within a Catholic atmosphere—"the name of St. Patrick, the Crucifix, the Sign of the Cross"—was "hideous defamation" of the church's beliefs and practices.[58]

McMahon's mention of the Ku Klux Klan probably explains the vehemence of his and Burke's reaction. It was anti-immigrant, anti-Catholic, and pro-Prohibition. The movie's lampooning of Irish Catholic immigrants and their descendants and associating them with booze and bootlegging played into old-stock, Protestant, fundamentalist stereotypes just at the time when these prejudices were about to become very political in the presidential campaign.

The Irish and Catholics were not the only ones upset by the film. *Life* magazine carried a review by distinguished critic R. Emmet Sherwood, who called the picture "loathsome" and extremely vulgar. Without wishing to be "unfair to other terrible movies," he wrote, "at the moment I seriously believe that this is the most terrible picture I have ever seen." Fitzpatrick of *Baltimore Catholic Review* contacted Norris to ask her opinion. Her agent replied she "regrets the film ... as much as you do."[59]

Milliken delayed responding to Burke until MGM had a chance to revise it. He enclosed a letter that studio executive William Orr sent Hays explaining the steps the company had taken. In defense, Orr said MGM had carefully selected Irish people for key parts: Edgar Mannix supervised production, Moran played Murphy; Dressler, Callahan; and Sally O'Neil, Ellen. The studio had cut all "minor shots in which one of the characters used a symbol of worship" and reported the Ancient Order of Hibernians now approved the film. Admitting the revisions would probably not satisfy Burke, Milliken hoped he would at least see MGM made an honest effort. Burke was unmoved. He told Milliken the adjustments failed to meet the protest he sent, which demanded withdrawal. He added not only were Irish-Americans justified in protesting, but so were "all who had a reverent sense of religion and a love for the common decencies of life."[60]

The NCWC publicly declared the revisions inadequate and again demanded MGM withdraw the film. *Harrison's Reports*, an important reviewing service without ties to the industry, agreed. Notwithstanding adjustments, it encouraged subscribers to continue to protest and theater managers not to show the film. Protests continued into the fall with Cardinal Dougherty demanding it be pulled, and New York City threatening legal censorship. MGM finally surrendered. The incident helped turn McMahon against the MPPDA. He now believed Hays used the former Committee on Public Relations and the current Public Relations Department as a means "to hoodwink the public." He dubbed the MPPDA's boasting of its accomplishments in cleaning up movies "a lot of 'bunk.'"[61]

A Signal Honor

On 14 October 1927, the staff of the NCWC and members of the faculty of Catholic University gathered with Archbishop Fumasoni-Biondi in the meeting room of the Administrative Committee to witness the bestowal of a signal honor. When Burke was ushered in, the delegate, in the name of the pope, awarded him an honorary doctorate in sacred theology, a degree rarely granted for exceptional literary excellence or exceptional service to the Church, and only after the most exhaustive examination of the writings and work of the recipient. In this case, the award came to Burke "because of the integrity of his life, his zeal for religion and devotion to the Holy See, as well as his knowledge of theology." Expressing deep and humble appreciation, he averred, "I can but say that by the grace of God and as far as in me lies, I will endeavor to be … somewhat worthy of the honor that has been conferred upon me, and of working for the glory of Christ's Church, for the good name of the Holy See throughout the world, and for the cause and interests of our beloved country."[62]

IMMIGRATION

When President Calvin Coolidge delivered his state-of-the-union address in December 1927, he called for legislation to reunify immigrant families, a matter for which Burke had "deep concern." Senator Royal Copeland of New York introduced a joint resolution to permit wives and minor children of so-called declarants—resident aliens who filed initial citizenship papers stating their intent to become naturalized—to enter the country in a non-quota class. Unwilling to grant non-quota status, the Senate Committee on Immigration amended it to give them preference within the quota of their country. The Senate passed it. The House version required 50 percent of all national quotas for the next two years to be placed in a special pool: the Relief for Separated Families Quota Fund to be administered without regard to nationality. The news excited Burke, who asked Hanna's permission to send a copy of the resolutions to every bishop with a cover letter declaring the Administrative Committee supported them and urging the prelates to do the same. Hanna agreed.[63]

Before Burke could circularize the hierarchy, the House held hearings on its version. He wrote Chairman Albert Johnson a letter, reminding him that in 1924 the NCWC had begged for an adjustment in the Reed-Johnson bill to prevent the very thing the present joint resolution now tried to fix. Everyone recognized "the inhumanity of keeping apart husband and wife, parent and child," declared Burke. Yet, the 1924 law produced thousands of such cases. The NCWC "earnestly" asked legislative relief of "this situation, so intimately connected with the social, moral, and religious life of our country." Burke signed Hanna's name to the letter and informed him of what he had done.[64]

Burke sent Mohler, Dolle, and Agnes Regan to the hearing. Mohler presented the Burke-Hanna letter and entered into the record pertinent passages from the NCWC's 1924 brief, especially the part which predicted the shattering of families. "Gentlemen, that very thing has happened," testified Mohler who cited examples. Regan urged humanitarian reasons. "All civilized countries recognize that the family is the unit of society," she pointed out, "yet we are presenting to the world an attitude which definitely separates families." She begged the committee to allow those who had immigrated before 1924 to bring their wives and children into the country now. Similarly, Dolle stated the reunification of families was "a very serious matter" which the resolution would remedy without weakening the present immigration law. Burke reported to Hanna that from what he had heard, the three "made an effective presentation of the case." With regard to the circular to the hierarchy, he now advised it was "too early" to send it because Congress was moving on the matter much slower than anticipated.[65]

In May, the House Committee replaced the content of the Senate resolution with a new measure drafted by Representative Thomas Jenkins. It did away with the quota relief fund of the original House resolution. Instead, he divided the annual quota of each country into two equal parts. The first half was devoted to two groups: (1) foreign parents of adult U.S. citizens; (2) skilled farmers, their wives, and their children under age eighteen. The second half of the quota, and any residue of the first, gave preference to wives or husbands and unmarried children under age 21 of aliens lawfully admitted for permanent residence. The House passed the measure in mid-May, and the resolution went to conference committee. While pleased something was being done to reunify families, the NCWC pointed out, "The measure of course will do little to solve the question of separated families of those [countries] possessing small quotas."[66]

The conference committee made minor adjustments. It removed foreign husbands of American wives from the non-quota class and placed them in the first 50 percent of the national quota along with farmers and foreign parents of adult American citizens. Congress passed the joint resolution at end of May.[67] The law thus began reunification of families within the current quota system but only over time. By giving preferential treatment to family members within the current system, it would also significantly reduce the number of new immigrants without familial connections in the United States.

In early January 1928, Senator David Reed of Pennsylvania introduced a bill to amend the act of 1924 to eliminate the requirement of two years' teaching experience before permitting immigration of foreign educators for employment in a college, university, academy, or seminary. Burke had the NCWC support this measure because it would facilitate the entry of religious brothers and sisters who taught at the post-secondary level. The Senate passed the measure, but the House failed to act on it.[68]

Education

While Congress considered immigration reform, the NCWC again faced the Curtis-Reed bill for a department of education. In March 1928, cosponsor Daniel Reed delivered an impassioned plea for its passage on the House floor. Although the NEA decided against pushing for consideration until after the presidential election, the Klan and Scottish Rite continued to support the bill as a step toward ending parochial schools. Burke informed Bishop John Murray that the Klan even moved its national headquarters from Atlanta to Washington, almost directly across Massachusetts Avenue from NCWC headquarters. "So we must be even more circumspect," he commented. With Catholic Alfred Smith of New York almost certain to become Democratic nominee for president, the religious issue would figure in the next round in the battle for a department of education.[69]

Until February 1928, Burke felt certain Congress would take no action on the bill. Then Reed had his speech printed and distributed to every member of the House, causing rumors in Congress he intended to hold hearings on it. Indeed in early April, Reed informed the NCWC the House committee would conduct one. The NCWC's effort of lining up witnesses lacked the urgency of two years earlier, probably because the Senate refused to participate, signaling there would be no action on the bill. Burke played a reduced role in organizing the opposition because of his deep involvement in the Mexican Church-state conflict (see next chapter).[70]

The religious issue was in evidence at the hearing. Two Catholic Democratic committeemen, Loring Black of New York and John Douglass of Massachusetts, tried to corner proponents into admission that the bill aimed at standardizing education. Testimony of Dolle and Regan led Republican committeeman John Robsion of Kentucky, egged on by his adviser Elmer Rogers, a Southern Scottish Rite Mason, to accuse the Catholic Church of opposing public schools, a charge that led to angry exchanges.[71]

Because the NEA was sure to seek endorsement of its bill in party platforms, Montavon began preparations. He considered the wording of the 1924 Democratic education plank, written by James H. Ryan and Edward Pace, too elastic. He warned Burke that its encouragement of the federal government to offer "counsel, advice or aid" for schooling, left "open the door for practically everything that the advocates of a Federal Department of Education have been demanding." The certainty of Smith's nomination made the task of eliminating those words and blocking the NEA delicate. Montavon recommended Burke send politically adroit individuals to work both conventions.[72]

Burke sent him to the Republican convention and asked the NCCW to assign him a companion. It appointed Mrs. August Kech. Burke instructed them to ensure the party adopted no plank for a department. They were to give no impression the NCWC or hierarchy urged this. Arguments were to be based solely on the best interests of the country. If the two were questioned about the Catholic position, their response should be, personally speaking, they thought most Catholics opposed the NEA bill as did the majority of "informed" educators who understood "the genius of our country." Burke suggested to Montavon it might be opportune for Republicans to adopt a plank against increased bureaucracy along the lines of Coolidge's recent address to the Daughters of the American Revolution (DAR). Warning that tyrants had always held people in bondage with the plea it was for their own good, and noting the populace usually submitted because it was easier than self-rule, Coolidge urged a return to local self-government. So much did Burke like the idea of an anti-bureaucracy plank, he drafted a model and sent it to Colonel William Joseph Donovan, assistant U.S. attorney general and Catholic winner of the Medal of Honor, to transmit it to the convention.[73]

En route to Kansas City, Montavon and Kech strategized how to accomplish their mission without implicating the NCWC or the Church.

She would identify herself with the Pennsylvania delegation and work with its representative on the Resolutions Committee. Donning the mantle of a foe of increased bureaucracy, including a department of education, Montavon would make representations to party leadership, which was trying to calm a restive Farm Bloc seeking a bureaucratic solution to its economic woes.[74]

On the convention's opening day, more than three hundred banner-waving farmers marched into the Platform Committee's first session demanding relief. During the disruption, Montavon saw Vice-chairman Hiram Bingham of Connecticut to gauge reaction to the NEA's request for support of its bill. Bingham said the committee was so preoccupied with other matters it might simply re-adopt the 1924 plank recommending a department of education and relief. Montavon reminded him that he (Bingham) opposed increased bureaucracy. He agreed to do his best to keep the 1924 plank out. Montavon telegraphed the news to Burke.[75]

Through the night the drafting committee met in executive session. Maintaining contact with it, Montavon suggested the best way to derail the Farm Bloc would be to stand firmly against further bureaucracy by deleting the 1924 plank and adopting a home-rule plank along the lines of Coolidge's address to the DAR. By sunrise the committee scrapped the education endorsement, but made no move toward home rule, though Bingham and others were working to that end.[76]

That morning Montavon met Kech. He urged her to contact Pennsylvania party boss William Vare, a member of the Resolutions Committee, to encourage him to vote for a home-rule plank. Together with colleagues in the delegation, Kech made the representation, and Vare promised to do his best. Apparently he and Bingham did quite a bit. In its final form the platform not only scrapped the 1924 plank, but concluded with a home-rule plank deploring further federal encroachment on regional affairs and encouraging local communities to become self-reliant and solve their own problems. Montavon wired the good news to Burke.[77] While it would be too much to claim Montavon and Kech were responsible for inclusion of a home-rule plank, they certainly played a key role in its adoption.

Even while the Republican convention was in session, Burke looked ahead to its Democratic counterpart, which presented a far more risky situation with much less at stake. Burke's sole objective was deletion of the word "aid" from the 1924 education plank. At Montavon's suggestion, he contacted Edward Dore, who was in touch with Judge George W. Olvany, boss of the Democrats' Tammany Hall machine. Burke asked Dore to do what he could to get the word "aid" out of the 1924 plank and have Democrats adopt one for home-rule. Olvany was sympathetic to both ideas. Burke also contacted Senator Peter Gerry to secure his help to ensure the Democrats removed the word "aid" and refused to endorse the NEA bill.[78]

As circumspect as removal of that word might be, political realities made it impossible. By 1928, Democrats were sharply divided, pitting rural, Protestant, conservative "drys" against a coalition of urban, immigrant, Catholic "wets" and urban, middle-class, liberal "wets." Indeed, Prohibition emerged as an issue symbolic of the hegemony of old-stock Americans.[79] As the convention approached, tension mounted because Smith was the front runner for the nomination on an anti-Prohibition ticket.

Burke sent Montavon to Houston to protect Catholic interests. On arrival, he realized there would be a fight to the finish between liberals led by Smith and those who opposed him because of his religion. A "dry" head quarters had been established in the Rice Hotel, and local Baptist and Methodist churches held revival meetings and sent word to coreligionists around the country to pray against the anti-Prohibition movement which would overturn "Protestant Civilization." Montavon said their intention was to secure a bone-dry plank in the platform so that if nominated, Smith would have to repudiate it, either ensuring his defeat or giving Democrats who opposed him because of religion a safe pretext for rejecting him. Members of the Resolution Committee were split on the issue.[80]

Regarding the education plank, Montavon learned it would be impossible to remove the word "aid" from it. Smith's attitude toward public schools had been questioned and some charged he would destroy them if elected. Any tampering with the education plank would involve the committee in an uncontrollable fight. So, Montavon sought to forestall endorsement of the NEA bill by stressing how contradictory it would be for Democrats promoting states' rights to endorse the creation of such a secretariat.[81]

When the Resolutions Committee held hearings, no one appeared on behalf of the NEA, and talk of a department of education generated little interest. So, the committee ignored it and readopted the 1924 plank, including the word "aid." Montavon informed Burke that given the situation, this "was the best that it was possible to obtain."[82]

Indeed the religious question was volatile, as events surrounding the Prohibition plank showed. Some 2,000 bone-dry advocates. roused to fever pitch at a Baptist rally, marched on the convention and threatened to bolt the party unless it adopted an appropriate plank. While protesters disrupted the general session, the Resolutions Committee held a public hearing that almost degenerated into a fistfight. Bone-dry members and wet members engaged in heated debate. In the end, the committee accepted an innocuous plank condemning Republican law-breaking while pledging Democrats to make "an honest effort to enforce the Eighteenth Amendment and all other provisions of the Federal Constitution." The next evening, the convention adopted it. Montavon reported to Burke, "In this way ended what, by a great majority of observers in Houston, was declared to be the fiercest fight for religious liberty ever waged in the United States."[83]

If that was true, it went for naught. Smith accepted the party's nomination with a telegram declaring the solution to bootlegging and lawlessness was "real temperance" rather than Prohibition. Repudiation of the mild compromise plank opened the way for insurgency. To be sure, Smith's Catholicism and anti-Prohibitionism (the two were historically interchangeable: Rum and Romanism) played a part in his loss of the election, as recent historical studies have shown.[84] Yet even if dry Democrats had not bolted the party, it is unlikely Smith could have won, for the nation was riding a tide of prosperity associated with the Republicans.

ENDNOTES TO CHAPTER 16

1. Burke, *Christ in Us*, 59–60.
2. "Unsafe Representatives of the Catholic Cause in the N.C.W.C.," *Fortnightly Review* 33 (1 December 1926): 527–28; "The General Secretary's Mistake," ibid. (15 December 1926): 555; "The N.C.W.C. and Legal Advice," ibid. 34 (1 January 1927): 12; "Canonical Status of the N.C.W.C.," ibid. (15 January 1927): 31–32; "Mysterious Maneuvers of the N.C.W.C., ibid. (15 March 1927): 130–31; Davenport *Catholic Messenger*, 11 November 1926.
3. "'Nationalism' in Catholic America," *Fortnightly Review* 34 (15 February 1927):79. On *Action Française*, see Adrien Dansette, *Religious History of*

Modern France, 2 vols., trans. John Dingle (New York: Herder and Herder, 1961), 2:280–84; Aubert, *Church in Secularized Society*, 549–51.

4. "The Action Française and Nationalism," *Fortnightly Review* 34 (1 March 1927): 95.
5. *Baltimore Catholic Review*, 5 November 1926; Curley to Leonard McGreevy, 9 November 1926, copy, AAB-AASMSU, Mc631; Spalding, *Premier See*, 346.
6. J. R. Ryan to Preuss, 6 November 1926, ACBCCU, Preuss papers, reel 6; Ryan to Preuss, 13 November 1926, ibid. (quote is here); "Archbishop Curley on the National Councils of Catholic Men and Women," *Fortnightly Review* 33 (1 December 1926): 523–24.
7. Walter Johnson to Burke, 7 November 1926, ACUA, USCCB 10:152:15.
8. Burke to Schrembs, 15 November 1926, ADCl, Schrembs papers.
9. Schrembs to Burke, 19 November 1926, ACUA, USCCB 10:153:8.
10. Burke to Schrembs, 2 December 1926, copy, ACUA, USCCB 10:153:8.
11. Burke to Hanna, 19 March 1927, copy, ACUA, USCCB 10:152:13.
12. Burke to Murray, 22 March 1927, AP, Burke Papers, box 12. Regarding Curley's attitude toward the committee, see Curley to Fumasoni-Biondi, 19 March 1926, AAB-AASMSU, Roman Letters.
13. Burke to Muldoon, 9 March 1927, copy, ACUA, USCCB 10:152:30; Burke to Hanna, 19 March 1927, copy, ibid., 10:152:13.
14. Slawson, *Foundation of the NCWC*, 266–67.
15. *Minutes of the Eighth Annual Meeting of the Hierarchy, September 1926*, 14–17, ACUA, USCCB 10: Bound Volumes; Dowling to Burke, 22 March 1927, ACUA, USCCB 10:152:38; Dowling to Curley, 29 March 1927, AAB-AASMSU, D1287; Slawson, *Foundation of the NCWC*, 268; H. O. Evennett, "Catholics and the Universities, 1850–1950," in George Andrew Beck, ed., *The English Catholics: Essays to Commemorate the Restoration of the Hierarchy of England and Wales* (London: Burns Oates, 1950), 303–13; Pius XI, "The Promotion of True Unity," *Sixteen Encyclicals of His Holiness Pius XI, 1926–1928* (Washington, D.C.: NCWC, 1937); Barry Till, *The Churches Search for Unity* (Harmondsworth, England: Penguin Books, 1972), 193–208; Ruth Rouse and Stephen Charles, eds., *A History of the Ecumenical Movement, 1517–1948*, 2nd ed. (London: S.P.C.K., 1967), 355–455.
16. NCWC News Service, 7 March 1927; O'Brien to Edmund Dunne, 23 March 1927, copy, ACUA, USCCB 10:152:38; Chalmers, *Hooded Americanism*, 159, 179.
17. Burke, Memorandum to Administrative Committee—First Interviews, undated [14 March 1927], copy, ACUA, USCCB 10:152:38; Burke to Muldoon, 9 March 1927, copy, ibid., 10:152:30.
18. Burke, Memorandum to Administrative Committee—First Interviews, undated [14 March 1927], copy, ACUA, USCCB 10:152:38; *Baltimore Catholic Review*, 11 March 1927.

19. Burke, Memorandum to Administrative Committee—First Interviews, undated [14 March 1927], copy, ACUA, USCCB 10:152:38; Burke to Dowling, 14 March 1927, copy, ACUA, USCCB 10:152:9.
20. Philadelphia *Catholic Standard and Times*, 19 March 1927; Burke to Muldoon, 9 March 1927, copy, ACUA, USCCB 10:152:9.
21. Burke, Memorandum to the Administrative Committee—Second Interview, 18 March 1927, copy, ACUA, USCCB 10:152:38.
22. Dowling to Burke, 22 March 1927, copy, ACUA, USCCB 10:152:38; Dowling to O'Brien, 22 March 1927, copy, ibid.
23. Schrembs to Burke, 21 March 1927, ACUA, USCCB 10:153:8; Giuseppe Pizzardo to Schrembs, 28 February 1927, copy, ibid.
24. Quoted in Memorandum to Rome from the Administrative Committee, undated [April 1927], copy, ADC, Schrembs Papers.
25. Schrembs to Luigi Sincero, 25 March 1927, copy, ACUA, USCCB 10:153:8; Memorandum to Rome from the Administrative Committee, undated [April 1927], copy, ADC, Schrembs Papers; Minutes of the Administrative Committee, 26 April 1927, ACUA, USCCB 10:64:4.
26. [Philip R. McDevitt to Dougherty], undated draft by Burke [March 1927], ACUA, USCCB 10:152:38; McDevitt to Burke, 26 March 1927, ibid., 10:152:33.
27. Burke to Muldoon, 19 March 1927, ACUA, USCCB 10:152:30; Burke to Murray, 5 April 1927, AP, Burke Papers, box 12.
28. Burke to McDevitt, 26 March 1927, copy, ACUA, USCCB 10:152:33.
29. Curley to Dowling, 25 March 1927, copy, AAB-AASMSU, D1284; Curley to Fumasoni-Biondi, undated [29 March 1927], copy, ibid., Roman documents; Curley to Merry del Val, 13 April 1927, copy, ibid., M1219; *Baltimore Catholic Review*, 1 April 1927.
30. Burke to Muldoon, 7 April 1927, copy, ACUA, USCCB 10:152:30.
31. Dowling to Curley, 29 March 1927, AAB-AASMSU, D1287; Curley to Fumasoni-Biondi, 23 April 1927, copy, ibid., Roman documents; Spalding, *Premier See*, 349.
32. "The N.C.W.C. News Service as Promoter of Dangerous Tendencies," *Fortnightly Review* 34 (1 April 1927): 149–51.
33. "On the Necessity of Settling the Official Status of the N.C.W.C.," *Fortnightly Review* 34 (15 August 1927): 214.
34. Quoted in Schrembs to Burke, 23 May 1927, ACUA, USCCB 10:153:8.
35. Burke to Schrembs, 4 June 1927, copy, ibid., 10:153:8; Burke to Schrembs, 13 July 1927, copy, ibid.; Minutes of the Administrative Committee, 16 April 1927, ACUA, USCCB 10:64:4; Pius XI to the American hierarchy, 10 August 1927, printed in *Minutes of the Ninth Annual Meeting of the Hierarchy, September 1927*, 5–6, ibid., 10: Bound Volumes, and also in the *NCWC Bulletin* 9 (October 1927): 4.

36. "The Hierarchy and the N.C.W.C.," *Fortnightly Review* 34 (15 August 1927): 336–37; J. R. Ryan to Pruess, 12 November 1927, 6 December 1927 (two letters under the same date), and 17 January 1928, ACBCCU, Pruess Papers, reel 8.
37. Burke to Caruana, 4 March 1927, copy, ACUA, USCCB 10:39:12; Caruana to Burke, 9 March 1927, ibid.
38. Burke to Caruana, 20 April 1927, copy, ACUA, USCCB 10:39:12; Pamphile, *Clash of Cultures*, 106–15. See also Minutes of the Administrative Committee, 23 April 1925, ACUA, USCCB 10:64:4.
39. Caruana to Burke, 4 May 1927 (first and second quotes are here); Caruana to Burke, 17 May 1927 (fourth quote is here); Caruana to Burke, 29 May 1927 (third quote is here)—all in ACUA, USCCB 10:39:12.
40. Minutes of the Administrative Committee, 12 September 1927, ACUA, USCCB 10:64:4; Joseph-Marie LeGouaze to Burke, 16 November 1927, ibid., 10:98:14; Burke to LeGouaze, 7 December 1927, copy, ibid.; Burke to Pietro Cogliolo, 15 June 1928, copy, ibid., 10:39:12; Burke, Interview with Francis White, 12 July 1928, ibid.; Pamphile, *La Croix et Le Glaive*, 123–25.
41. Burke, Report of the General Secretary, April 1930, ACUA, USCCB 10:62:10.
42. Lord to Burke, 5 February 1926 [*sic* for 1927], ACUA, USCCB 10:125:33; Burke to Lord, 10 February 1927, copy, ibid.
43. Lord to Burke, undated [16 February 1927], ACUA, USCCB 10:125:33; Lord to Burke, telegram, 16 February 1927, ibid.
44. Burke to Lord, telegram, 17 February 1927, copy, ACUA, USCCB 10:125:33.
45. Lord to Burke, undated [late February 1927], ACUA, USCCB 10:125:33.
46. Ibid.
47. Ibid.
48. Burke to Hays, 15 March 1927, copy, with list of recommended previewers; Hays to Burke, 16 March 1927; Frederick Munroe to Burke, 9 April 1927; Burke to Munroe, 12 April 1927, copy; Burke to Lord, 21 April 1927, copy—all in ACUA, USCCB 10:125:34.
49. Burke, Memorandum Re Official Church Approval of "The King of Kings," March 1927, ACUA, USCCB 10:125:34.
50. Joseph Husslein, S.J., to Burke, 26 April 1927, ACUA, USCCB 10:125:34.
51. Minutes of the Administrative Committee, 27 April 1927, ACUA, USCCB 10:64:4; Burke to Husslein, 10 May 1927, copy, ibid., 10:125:34.
52. Burke to Hawks, 1 June 1927, AP, Burke Papers, box 10; Burke to Hawks, undated [June 1927], ibid. (the quotations are from here).
53. Walsh, *Sin and Censorship*, 36–37; Couvares, "Hollywood, Main Street, and Church," 605; *The Callahans and the Murphys* (1927): Review Summary (quote is here), http://www.nytimes.com/movies/movie/86485/The-Callahans-and-the-Murphys/overview (accessed 10 January 2015).

54. McMahon to Milliken, 23 July 1927, copy, ACUA, USCCB 10:30:20; Couvares, "Hollywood, Main Street, and Church," 599–605; Walsh, *Sin and Censorship*, 32–35, 38–39; Jowett, *Film*, 176.
55. Burke to Carl Milliken, 23 July 1927, copy, ACUA, USCCB 10:30:20.
56. McMahon to Milliken, 23 July, 1927, copy, ACUA, USCCB 10:30:20.
57. McMahon, Statement for the NCWC News Service on *The Callahans and the Murphys*, 23 July 1927, released in the NCWC News Service, 25 July 1927. The statement also appeared in the *NCWC Bulletin* 9 (August 1297): 2.
58. [McMahon, editorial,], NCWC News Service, 25 July 1927.
59. McGrath to Burke, 4 August 1927, with clipping from *Life* of the same date, ACUA, USCCB 10:30:20; *Baltimore Catholic Review*, 2 September 1927.
60. Milliken to Burke, 26 August 1927, with enclosure William Orr to Hays, 23 August 1927, copy, ACUA, USCCB 10:30:20; Burke to Milliken, 7 September 1927, copy, ibid.
61. McMahon to Burke, interoffice memo, 10 November 1928 (first quote is here), ACUA, USCCB 10:125:29; McMahon to McNulty, 18 May [1929] (second quote is here), ibid.; Dolle, "Revised 'Callahans and the Murphys' Still Obnoxious," *NCWC Bulletin* 9 (September 1927): 21; Walsh, *Sin and Censorship*, 39–45; Couvares, "Hollywood, Main Street, and Church," 605–06.
62. "Holy See Signally Honors Father Burke," *NCWC Bulletin* 9 (November 1927): 4.
63. Burke to Hanna, 13 March 1928, copy, ACUA, USCCB 10:99:17; Hanna to Burke, 19 March 1928, ibid.; Mohler to McMahon, 14 November 1936, copy, ACUA, Mohler Papers 141:30:7 (the quotation is here); Coolidge, "Fifth Annual Message," 6 December 1927; *Congressional Record,* 70th Cong, 1st Sess., Vol 69, Part 1, 351, and Part 3, 2684–87; Hutchinson, *History of Immigration Policy*, 203.
64. Hanna to Johnson, 26 March 1928, in *Hearings before the Committee on Immigration and Naturalization, House of Representatives, Seventieth Congress, First Session on H.J. 234, H.R. 8540, and H.R. 159, March 27 and 28, April 10 1928* (Washington: U.S. Government Printing Office, 1928), 10–11, hereafter *Hearings on Immigration*; Burke to Hanna, 27 March 1928, copy, ACUA, USCCB 10:99:17.
65. *Hearings on Immigration*, 10–16, 22–26; Burke to Hanna, 27 March 1928, copy, ACUA, USCCB 10:99:17.
66. *Congressional Record,* 70th Cong, 1st Sess., Vol 69, Part 9, 9389–95; "N.C.W.C. Activities in the Field of Immigration," *NCWC Bulletin* 9 (May 1928): 11; Hutchinson, *History of Immigration Policy*, 203.
67. *Congressional Record,* 70th Cong, 1st Sess., Vol 69, Part 10, 10302 and 10451.
68. Burke to Mohler, 14 February 1928, ACUA, USCCB 10:42:2; Burke to Hanna, 2 March 1928, ibid., 10:99:17; *Congressional Record,* 70th Cong, 1st

Sess., Vol 69, Part 2, 1222, and Part 3, 3428; Hutchinson, *History of Immigration Policy*, 205–06.

69. Burke to John Murray, 14 March 1928, ACUA, USCCB 10:152:31; Slawson, *Department of Education Battle*, 181 and 183–86.
70. Montavon, interoffice memo to Burke et al., 23 February 1928, ACUA, USCCB Legal Department 10:58:24; Montavon to J. H. Ryan, 2 March 1928, ibid.; Burke to J. Murray, 2 March 1928, copy, ACUA, USCCB 10:152:31; J. H. Ryan to Presidents of Catholic Colleges and Universities, 14 April 1928, ACUA, USCCB Department of Education 10:15:16.
71. Slawson, *Department of Education Battle*, 187–93.
72. Montavon to Burke, 9 June 1928, ACUA, USCCB 10:103:11.
73. Burke to Montavon, 9 June 1928, copy, ACUA, USCCB 10:103:11; Burke to Lillis, 9 June 1928, copy, ibid.; Burke to Colonel Donavon, 11 June 1928, copy, ibid.; Minutes of the Executive Committee of the NCCW, 7–10 June 1928, ACUA, USCCB NCCW 10:13:2.
74. Montavon, Memorandum Report on the Republican National Convention Held at Kansas City, 12–15 June 1928, ACUA, USCCB 10:103:11 (hereafter cited as Memorandum Report); Gilbert Fite, *George N. Peek and the Fight for Farm Parity* (Norman: University of Oklahoma Press, 1954), 3–202; Farrell, *Presidency of Coolidge*, 88–94; Sobel, *Coolidge*, 274–76, 326–27, 330–34.
75. Montavon, Memorandum Report, ACUA, USCCB 10:103:11; Montavon to Burke, Telegram, 12 June 1928, ibid.; *NCWC News Sheet*, 18 June 1928.
76. Montavon, Memorandum Report, ACUA, USCCB 10:103:11.
77. Ibid.; Montavon to Burke, telegrams, 13 and 14 June 1928, ACUA, USCCB 10:103:11; *New York Times*, 15 June 1928.
78. Burke to Edward Dore, 9 June 1928, copy, ACUA, USCCB 10:136:22; Dore to Burke, 12 June 1928, ibid.; Dore to George Olvany, 12 June 1928, copy, ibid.; Burke to Dore, 13 June 1928 copy, ibid.; Burke to Peter Gerry, 13 June 1928, copy, ibid., 10:152:11; Louis Eisenstein and Elliot M. Rosenberg, *A Stripe of Tammany's Tiger* (New York: Robert Speller and Sons, 1966), 43–44.
79. Dumenil, *Modern Temper*, 226–35; Hicks, *Republican Ascendancy*, 203.
80. Montavon to Burke, Memorandum (Confidential) on the Democratic National Convention Held at Houston, Texas, 26–30 June 1928, ACUA, USCCB 10:102:11 (hereafter cited as Memorandum [Confidential]). The most recent study of the 1928 campaign corroborates Montavon's assessment of evangelical strategy (Allan J. Lichtman, *Prejudice and the Old Politics: The Presidential Election of 1928* [Chapel Hill: University of North Carolina Press, 1979]).
81. Montavon, Memorandum (Confidential). For questions about Smith's position on public education, see Charles C. Marshall, "An Open Letter to the Honorable Alfred E. Smith," *Atlantic Monthly* 139 (April 1927): 543-46; Edmund A. Moore, *A Catholic Runs for President: The Campaign of 1928* (New York: Ronald Press Company, 1956), 25, 61, 69.

82. Montavon, Memorandum (Confidential); Democratic Party, *The Official Report of the Proceedings of the Democratic National Convention Held at Houston, Texas, 26–29 June 1928* (Indianapolis: Bookwalter-Ball-Greathouse, 1928), 198–99.
83. Democratic Party, *Official Report*, 197; Montavon, Memorandum (Confidential). First quote is from the former; the second from the latter.
84. Moore, *Catholic Runs for President*; Lichtman, *Prejudice and Old Politics*; Leuchtenburg, *Perils of Prosperity*, 229–40; Hicks, *Republican Ascendancy*, 201–14; Paul F. Boller, Jr., *Presidential Campaigns* (Oxford and New York: Oxford University Press, 1985), 223–27; Kirschner, *City and Country*, 41–53.

Chapter 17
Mexican Church-State Conflict, 1927 and 1928

> The will of God is the perfect unchanging will of justice, of love, of mercy.... God's will is that all men should do good and serve justice. God has left to the free choice of men whether they will do good or evil: serve justice or injustice.... What is to be deplored is the unwillingness of men ... to do the good and to serve justice. What is to be remembered is that we must accept—not as God's directly, but as man's—a world that has been estranged from God by man's sin: a world of which we are a part: a world wherein we will inevitably ... have to suffer pain: endure injustice: see our beloved suffer: witness to far-reaching calamities, to wars wherein millions are slain and hatred planted more deeply in the hearts of the living: ... to debased public morals: ... to recognized social systems that make way for what the world calls progress, inconsiderate of the physical and spiritual welfare of the multitude.[1]

From Bewilderment to Diplomacy

"I am bewildered in soul and hardly know what to say or do," wrote John Burke on a January night in 1927. On New Year's Day, Mexican Catholics launched the Cristero Rebellion against President Elías Calles. The source of Burke's confusion was the gap between principle and practice. The previous summer the Vatican announced it would trust the power of prayer to end persecution of the Church in Mexico. In November, Pius XI issued *Iniquis Afflictisque* (*From Unjust and Shattered Conditions*), urging Catholics worldwide to ask the Virgin of Guadalupe to beg forgiveness for injuries inflicted on Mexican Catholics and pray God for peace in Mexico. In

December, the American hierarchy issued a pastoral letter urging trust in prayer and opposing resort to violence. Yet in spring 1926, Archbishop Michael Curley had fostered nationwide protests and virtually wrote the Boylan resolution for immediate severance of diplomatic relations with Mexico, the first step to war. In August, the Knights of Columbus endorsed it and demanded end of the arms embargo. When they denied their intent was intervention, the *New York Times* argued the wording of the endorsement belied their denial. Anti-Catholic Senator Thomas Heflin accused them of trying to start war with Mexico. In response, Burke had Senator Thomas Walsh get the pastoral of bishops printed in the *Congressional Record.* For their part, the Knights called for a mass meeting at the end of January in Washington to denounce Calles.[2]

It seemed "cruelly evident" to Burke some Church authorities were "of a double mind," or worse, were single-minded, "believing one thing in their hearts and saying a different thing with their lips." Their sympathies lay with those who wanted war or would not mind if it came. He obviously had Curley in mind and believed the same of Apostolic Delegate Pietro Fumasoni-Biondi and others at the delegation. When Curley launched his attack on Calles in spring 1926, they wondered why Burke and the NCWC had not followed suit. The delegate seemed unconcerned about success or failure of Archbishop George Caruana's mission to Mexico. Leaders of the Knights, too, seemed to talk with forked tongue. Now, on the very evening of their mass meeting in Washington, Fumasoni-Biondi was hosting a dinner in honor of Joseph Scott, the keynote speaker.[3]

Burke's thoughts grew darker. If Fumasoni-Biondi, now in charge of Mexican affairs, supported the Knights, it was "not unreasonable to conclude that the Holy See knows and approves what [he] is doing." Burke had declined the delegate's invitation to dine with the Knights that evening. "I cannot join in with it all," he wrote. "I don't see how we can serve two masters—prayer and the sword: the spiritual and the temporal: I don't see how we can refuse to work persistently for what we profess. I'm probably 'mixed-up'—or a tyro. But … I'm bewildered."[4] With good reason. The delegate kept Burke out of the loop from the start of Caruana's failed mission. He had only the words and deeds of those around him to judge by, and they left him confused. Yet, his bewilderment did not last long.

The rebellion made Calles expel Bishop Pascual Díaz y Barreto, secretary of the episcopal committee and alleged director of the revolt. Díaz entered the U.S., and Fumasoni-Biondi asked Burke if he should remain there or go to Rome. Given the critical nature and uncertainty of Mexican affairs, Burke wanted Díaz nearby for advice. Fumasoni-Biondi agreed.[5]

Initially pro-resistance, Díaz turned irenic in exile. He undermined the attempt of rebel leader René Capistrán Garza to raise money in the U.S. and told Burke the Mexican hierarchy wanted the NCWC to discountenance advocates of armed rebellion. Burke complied. He found Díaz an "intelligent, gifted, balanced: up to date, full blooded Indian." Burke thought publicizing his photograph in the U.S. would be the most effective answer to the question: "What has the Catholic Church done for the Indian in Mexico"?[6]

By May, Calles exiled more than half the Mexican hierarchy. Most entered the U.S. where Díaz became their unofficial leader. "I do not think the revolution against Calles is making great headway," Burke wrote matter-of-factly to Helen Lynch, adding, "I wish that he were deposed for he is fanatical in his hatred of the Church."[7]

Having abandoned the State Department "to its own plans" in January, Burke was drawn back into American diplomacy. In July, Secretary of State Frank Kellogg asked Ambassador James Sheffield to resign for his seeming insistence only war with Mexico would end troubles there, something he denied. President Calvin Coolidge replaced him with Dwight Morrow, a classmate from Amherst College. Coolidge and Kellogg believed Morrow could manage diplomacy and hoped he might possibly win Calles to easement of the persecution. Cardinal Patrick Hayes and Judge Morgan O'Brien urged him to see Burke.[8]

Morrow and Undersecretary of State Robert Olds met with Burke in mid-October. He found both with a "meagre" understanding of the Catholic Church, the Mexican constitution, and Calles's decrees regarding religion. After filling them in, he said Calles's goal was "to destroy organized religion." Both Morrow and Olds wished Calles and his predecessor Álvaro Obregón gone, but could think of no one to fill the void and create a stable government. Burke had no one to suggest. Morrow asked what would happen if the U.S. withdrew diplomatic recognition. Burke replied they both knew Calles would fall. Morrow wondered how he could help the Church;

his position precluded religious matters. Burke said if some opportunity arose "to have justice restored and I could be of any service, I gladly offer it." Morrow urged he keep in touch with Olds and said this conversation disabused him of any thought his mission would be easy.[9]

As Morrow assumed his post, the situation in Mexico darkened. Calles summarily executed two rivals in the upcoming presidential election. Burke warned Archbishop Edward Hanna the murders might aggravate the rebellion, which meant the U.S. must remain completely neutral. Burke asked if he should insist on that course to Coolidge and Kellogg or trust they would take it. Before Hanna replied, a new outrage occurred. Catholic radicals attempted to assassinate Obregón, who was also running for president. Police arrested the ringleader, an accomplice, and two brothers, Humberto and Miguel Pro, the latter a priest, both innocent. Calles had the four shot without trial.[10] Their executions, especially Father Pro's, greatly disturbed Catholics on both sides of the border. Morrow reported the deed was dreadful enough to shock many Mexicans "hardened by revolutionary events."[11]

Notifying Hanna of his intention, Burke saw Coolidge whom he urged to notify Calles that the U.S. opposed such methods. Deploring them, Coolidge said there was little he could do. "If I were to send such protest," he told Burke, "a tart note would come in answer from Mexico." Other nations would support its sending such reply. The U.S. would be forced to retreat or answer with an equally tart note, escalating the situation. "I do not want war with Mexico," said Coolidge. He wanted to win Calles's confidence and lead him to a more just position. That was the reason he sent Morrow there. "He has instructions to win the good will of the present administration," explained Coolidge. "He has further instructions to see what he can do to bring order and justice to the country." Burke asked if Coolidge would forward without comment a protest from American Catholics. He replied it would depend on wording and told Burke to see Kellogg about it. He averred he would give the matter careful thought.[12]

Burke saw Kellogg and asked if the government could do something to improve conditions in Mexico. Irritated, Kellogg insisted the government had done all it could. Under no circumstance would he protest to Calles, which might lead to Morrow's withdrawal and war with Mexico. Burke asked if Kellogg would transmit without comment a Catholic protest. He emphatically refused; such would carry with it "tacit approval" of the government, leading to the same complications as a government protest. Kellogg reiterated what Coolidge had said about Morrow's instructions. Burke said the Administrative Committee had no intention of thwarting American diplomacy, but had a right to protest to its own government against the murder of Mexican Catholics. He told Hanna the two interviews "were both long, and, I must say, not easy."[13]

There followed another outrage. Considering Archbishop Francisco Orozco y Jiménez of Guadalajara a rebel leader responsible for the activity of "religious fanatics" in Jalisco, Calles sent a detachment of cavalry to hunt him down and bring him back "dead or alive." Burke sent Coolidge a letter explaining Orozco was one of the few bishops who remained in Mexico to tend his flock. "To kill this Archbishop in cold blood and without due trial," he declared, "… would be a crime against civilization." He begged Coolidge to use his good offices to have Orozco's life spared, "by exile if necessary." Burke sent a copy to Kellogg.[14]

Burke saw Olds to protest a summary execution of Orozco. He spoke of the archbishop's faithful service to his people and explained he was "a Cardinal Mercier" to the Mexican people. The world would be "indignant" if he were summarily shot, "a crowning example of inhumanity." Burke asked if word could be gotten to Orozco encouraging him into voluntary exile. Olds immediately instructed Morrow "earnestly" to request Calles to spare Orozco's life if captured. Morrow would do so and thought having him escorted to the border a good idea.[15]

Indeed, Morrow already believed "some better modus vivendi" must be found if Mexico was to have peace and reform. A week earlier, he sent Olds a confidential letter admitting the U.S. could do little about "this domestic controversy" except "strictly keep … hands off," yet he felt it needed resolution. The approach to Calles must come from the Church itself. Although he did not think Calles would surrender principle, "it would seem to me … not impossible," he wrote, "that a modus vivendi could be worked out without loss of dignity to either side if … a liberal Catholic of the type of Father Burke … were dealing directly with President Calles." Morrow had gained Calles's confidence and if he could retain it, he might later be of "some small assistance" in composing this "trouble." Kellogg encouraged him to look for an opportunity to broach the religious issue informally with Calles.[16]

Olds summoned Burke to say Morrow would speak with Calles about Orozco, adding he was going to "entrust" Burke with "a confidence rarely given." Morrow had sent a "confidential" letter that would not be logged into department files. Olds let him read it. When finished, Burke said it contained nothing of news to him. "You read the last part?" asked Olds. "Yes," replied Burke. "But the idea of my going to Mexico on such a mission is out of the question." The Administrative Committee had no authority to send him. Olds said he agreed with Morrow. "Well," concluded Burke, "I guess that is about all we have to talk of this morning."[17]

Nine days later Burke saw Olds about Orozco. Olds said Morrow was confident Calles would spare his life. He asked what it would take for Church-state reconciliation. Burke said Calles would have to make the first move. Public exercise of Catholicism was forbidden. Calles opposed "all religion," so it was "impossible" for the Church to exist. Constitutional clauses denying it the right to hold property or conduct schools must be changed. Calles would claim he upheld religious liberty because Mexicans could believe privately whatever they wanted. If he was sincere about negotiations, he would accept an apostolic delegate and begin them. Olds returned to Morrow's letter, but Burke refused to discuss it. Ignoring him, Olds rambled on, giving the impression Morrow had already approached Calles about meeting with Burke, which he had not. "Like a bolt from the blue," said Olds, "it may be that some day Morrow will send word that we should ask you to go down and see Calles." Burke ended the meeting.[18]

Panicky, he sent transcripts of the interviews to Hanna and asked for a meeting of the Administrative Committee. "Convinced to the point of anxiety and distress" that he was out of his depth, Burke wanted it to scotch the idea. "Personally, I need not say I think my going on such a mission is little short of the ridiculous," he wrote. "I do not know Spanish. I haven't the slightest reason to believe that my going would do the slightest good. I think it would do harm."[19]

Two observations should be made. First, Burke was acting on the assumption Olds and Morrow had concocted a plan for him to see Calles. This was certainly untrue of Morrow and probably untrue of Olds, who was apparently playing matchmaker to bring Burke and Morrow together when both were reluctant to involve themselves in the Church-state conflict. Second and ironically, Burke's panicky response accelerated his involvement.

Hanna called the committee to meet in Washington in January 1928, but only Bishops Edmund Gibbons and John Murray were able to go. Because the Vatican had authority regarding Mexico, they saw Fumasoni-Biondi.[20] Admitting lack of jurisdiction, they explained the committee might lose face if after all its agitation, the government offered it the opportunity to negotiate and it refused. Fumasoni-Biondi took a jaded view of Yankee diplomacy: the government was indifferent to religion; Morrow was in Mexico only to protect business interests. The delegate wanted to bide time. Supporters of Obregón recently assured an American bishop that if elected president, he would grant religious freedom. Gibbons and Murray reminded the delegate that 1928 was an election year, so Republicans wanted to resolve the Mexican problem to gain Catholic support, especially as Catholic Al Smith seemed destined to receive the Democratic nomination. Fumasoni-Biondi summoned Monsignor Filippo Bernardini, who recommended cooperation with the State Department. The delegate agreed, insisting the only one qualified for the mission was Burke.[21]

Burke informed Olds that the Administrative Committee stood ready to help if circumstances warranted. Olds denied there were plans for him to meet with Calles, only a suggestion such might be worthwhile. Olds wanted Burke to talk with Morrow, who would be in Havana for the Conference of American States. Burke wanted to think it over. Olds argued the importance of his seeing Morrow. If he decided to go, the meeting must be private. Reporters should not see them together nor should Burke's departure be publicized.[22]

Burke saw Fumasoni-Biondi and found him "very much changed," now taking it for granted Burke would meet with Morrow. Burke was surprised at "the seriousness and dignity" Fumasoni-Biondi gave the mission, which Burke considered informal, simply to learn why Morrow thought it worthwhile for them to meet. Fumasoni-Biondi and Bernardini stressed the importance of the mission and opportunity it presented. The delegate told Burke Rome's position was that Calles must allow exiled bishops to return and public worship to resume. That was the pope's ardent wish. "Father Burke," said Fumasoni-Biondi, "you have a big mission." "You have got me into a very unpleasant task," he replied, "one that is entirely against the tenor of my life.... It has upset me a great deal." The delegate told Burke that he was "deliberate and just ... the best person fitted to undertake the task."[23]

RELUCTANT DIPLOMAT

Burke and Morrow met the evening of 17 January 1928. The two dined privately in Morrow's room in Havana. Morrow said Calles was an obstinate, self-confident fanatic without education or historical sense to understand or appreciate principles; only the concrete appealed to him. He was the sole, absolute power in Mexico; the constitution was a farce. Calles was Mexico, and the Church his enemy. Morrow confessed he became ambassador only out of friendship for Coolidge. "Do all you can to keep war with Mexico out of my administration," said Coolidge. "I don't want war: the people don't want war." The religious problem vexed Morrow. Mexico was a Catholic country and would remain so. "The solution," he said, "lies in the winning over of Calles," But how? Failing to see a way, he thought it best to await the coming election, which he believed Obregón would win. Yet, Morrow did not consider him "dependable." If Calles could be won over and gave his word, the matter "would be settled for a generation at least." His obstinacy was the problem. Morrow asked Burke what he thought and what might be done.[24]

Burke explained he was there to learn just that: what might be done. He thought Calles and Foreign Minister Aarón Sáenz had misinformed Morrow about the Church. Sáenz had filled his head with nonsense concerning the indifference, immorality, and rottenness of the clergy. After countering these charges, Burke explained in detail how civil registration of priests threatened the very life and authority of the Church. The anticlerical articles as a whole denied Catholicism its identity. Despite this, the pope counseled peace. Although the Mexican bishops were eager to return and shepherd their flocks, the "Church could return only as a Church."[25]

Over and over, Morrow brought up Calles's obstinacy. His hopelessness about it evoked a strong rejoinder. Burke objected it was ridiculous to allow one man's stubbornness to block religious welfare of an entire people. Mexico would have no peace until it resolved the Church-state conflict; the U.S. would have none until Coolidge discountenanced Calles's tyranny. If he withdrew moral and financial support, the Mexican government would collapse. America held the key to religious peace; Burke held his country responsible for Calles.[26]

Morrow suggested a committee of Mexican bishops meet with Calles to try to change his attitude. Burke countered Bishop Díaz and Archbishop

Leopoldo Ruiz y Flores of Morelia had tried that in August 1926. Calles refused to settle the conflict. Morrow thought maybe a committee of Mexican laymen should approach him. In Burke's view, "the shortest, most effective and the practical way" to solve the problem was for Calles to accept an apostolic delegate, to let the Mexican bishops return to their sees, and to negotiate outstanding issues later. Unsure Rome would agree, Burke thought Morrow should propose this to Calles. The meeting ended for the night. The ambassador felt hopeless; the priest, "disappointed and depressed."[27]

The next afternoon the two picked up where they left off: who would make the approach to Calles? Reminding Burke the religious problem was a domestic affair, Morrow could broach it only unofficially, personally. Calles might turn it into a crisis, demand his recall, and put both nations on the brink of war. Morrow still thought a committee of Mexican bishops should ask to negotiate a settlement. Burke said the bishops had by letter recently asked Calles to open the matter for discussion.[28] Calles could take them up on the offer. If Morrow thought that was the path to follow, well and good. Burke considered it a bad idea because bargaining would be protracted, the bishops might differ among themselves, and the agreement would still need Vatican approval. Better to let the bishops return to Mexico, allow entry of an apostolic delegate, and then negotiate. Religious services would resume; a delegate would mediate authoritatively.[29]

Suddenly Morrow declared: "It is outside my office, but I will do it. I want to have this religious persecution settled. If I make the attempt and fail, it will be Morrow's failure." He then asked Burke if he would meet with Calles. Replying he "hadn't the slightest taste for such a job," he agreed only out of appreciation for what Morrow was doing. Given his own inexperience and the obstinacy of Calles, Burke held "no great hope." Morrow thought the two of them should enter the conflict unofficially. "I would want you to come with a like authorization that you had in coming to me," he said, "—not official, nor authoritative, but so that I might say to Calles that the Church knew of your coming." At this point, Morrow turned the tables on Burke by asking him to send Calles a letter expressing willingness to meet with him. Burke was tempted to say no; Calles must write him. "But I felt," he noted, "I was not the one to say how far I should humiliate myself. I answered … that I thought the first step should be made in writing by Calles:

but … I would personally be willing to go." Neither man felt hopeful a conference with him would be successful. Still, they planned to try.[30]

When Burke returned home, he wrote Mary Hawks: "I find now that I am 'loaned' to the Holy See: and the fear of having to go away again keeps me from making engagements. Keeps me from initiating what I may not be able to carry out." His sole focus had been work of the NCWC, which his involvement with Mexico "upset." "There is no one at the office to take my place," lamented Burke. "You will see that I have need of all the prayers you can offer."[31]

Back in Mexico, Morrow had a frank talk with Calles. As a friend, he said Mexico's economic recovery depended on domestic tranquility and good relations with the U.S. No matter the diplomatic path one took, it led to the Church-state quagmire. Its resolution was essential. Morrow told of Burke's willingness to confer about it, and Calles agreed. He had reason to be receptive: the rebellion was gaining momentum and his religious policy split the Revolutionary Party in two. Moderates, led by Obregón, favored negotiation and peace with the Church; radicals, led by Luis Morones, opposed compromise. With Obregón running for president, an election he would surely win, the alternative was civil war, which Calles eschewed. Obregón wanted resolution of the religious issue to coincide with his return to office, so Calles had little choice but to cooperate. He needed a face-saving solution that enabled him to uphold the anticlerical articles of the constitution yet allowed the Church to function.[32]

Morrow arranged for Burke to meet privately with Calles in Mexico City in mid-February 1928. Just before departure, Luis Bustos, Alberto María Carreño, and José Ortiz Monasterio met with Burke and William Montavon to say they established the National Union Party to supplant the National League. They opposed settlement of the religious question by Church authorities without the party's prior consultation. They warned any settlement must include restoration of civil rights to Mexican Catholics. In effect, they demanded inclusion in negotiations. Burke said the Church had the right to act on its own. Their demand for civil rights prior to restoration of public worship was "un-Catholic," a total misunderstanding of the Church's mission. He forced them to admit the absence of clergy in Mexico was hurting the faithful. A settlement permitting return of the bishops and resumption of the sacraments was necessary. All else could be negotiated once that occurred. They relented and promised to support that plan.[33]

Burke also met with Morrow's friend Walter Lippmann, editor-in-chief of the New York *World*. Until recently, the paper had been pro-Calles, but just reversed itself. Unknown to Burke, Lippmann was on his way to Mexico where he and Morrow would work on a settlement of the problem. Burke shared many facts about the present situation. He suggested the best way to solve the religious issue was for Calles to accept an apostolic delegate who could negotiate definitively for the Vatican. He spoke too about the registration law and the government's power to establish a quota of clergymen.[34]

The day before Burke's departure, the *New York Herald-Tribune* published a story out of Mexico City reporting his coming as papal emissary to negotiate an end of the religious persecution. Burke contacted Olds to see if the trip was still on. Next day, Olds phoned to say with all the publicity and excitement in Mexico City, Calles would have to receive him publicly with no opportunity for private discussions. So, it was best to cancel.[35]

Burke wrote to Lynch that his mission was off and the hunt was on for the "nigger in the wood pile, or perhaps the traitor in the camp." He wondered if Bustos, Carreño, and Monasterio had broken their promise and leaked the story to friends in Mexico. If so, the National Union Party opposed the Vatican's course of action and wanted no settlement until it achieved its political ends. "Such Catholics," wrote Burke, "are trying to have the Church depend upon military and political victory. To my mind, in that way lies disaster." He told Lynch he found it "hard, interiorly to bear the disappointment; in a way the defeat." It was equally difficult to be patient "with the confusion; the double-dealing; the lack of candor." All of this weighed on his soul and tired him more than physical exertion. "I am sure that all through it the wisdom and love of Our Lord rules and reigns," he wrote. "I try not to depart from Him." Burke later came to believe one or more of the exiled Mexican bishops derailed the mission.[36]

Despite the setback, Morrow and Lippmann continued unperturbed, looking for another opening. Breakfasting at his ranch with Morrow, Calles expressed desire for a fair religious settlement, even saying had Burke been able to come down, the first step toward one would have probably occurred. Morrow said he hoped the two could still meet. Olds let Burke read Morrow's letter reporting this conversation. He still wanted Burke to meet with Calles. When Kellogg stepped in to Olds's office, he said that was his wish too.[37]

Lippmann sent Burke a letter describing his conversation with Calles. Avoiding any mention of Burke, he asked Calles the purpose of the registration law. Calles explained that because churches were Mexican property, the government needed a record of the priest entrusted with them. Lippmann asked if the government had authority to refuse to register a priest appointed by a bishop. Calles answered absolutely not. The law was "unequivocally statistical," without intent to interfere in internal Church affairs. In the event of a settlement, Lippman wondered if the Mexican federal government could prevent a state from setting an unreasonable quota on the number of clergy. Calles assured him he had ways to persuade local authorities. Lippmann told Burke his belief Calles was "reliable" in the sense that he would abide by the terms of an agreement.[38]

Meanwhile, Ernest Legarde, chargé d'affaires at the French embassy in Mexico, went to Washington at Morrow's request to convince Olds and Burke the time was ripe for a meeting with Calles. Legarde told Burke that Morrow was "morally certain" Calles was willing to settle the religious question and ready to make definite statements on the independent personality of the Church, the statistical nature of the registration law, and a liberal interpretation of the quota feature in the constitution. Burke deeply impressed Legarde, and both saw eye-to-eye on the path forward. Neither believed the religious issue could be settled at the level of principle, but a practical adjustment was possible. Legarde told Fumasoni-Biondi, Bernardini, and Paolo Marella what he told Burke and Olds. He insisted a settlement be reached with Calles because of his reliability whereas Obregón, who seemed certain to succeed him, was untrustworthy.[39]

Morrow sent Olds a telegram suggesting a way to resolve the matter. If some authorized person, perhaps one or more of the Mexican bishops, would address a letter to Calles indicating the hierarchy's willingness to return, provided the government recognized the identity of the Church and interpreted the laws of registration and quotas as simply statistical, Morrow believed he could get an interview with Calles, who would then respond with declarations to that effect. Morrow hesitated to ask Burke to write the letter in the mistaken belief he would refuse unless assured Calles would respond positively.[40]

Olds had no such hesitation because Burke saw him daily, eager to do anything to resolve the affair. Explaining to Burke Morrow's telegram proposing an exchange of letters, Olds wanted him to write one to Calles indicating willingness of the Mexican bishops to return under appropriate conditions. Calles would reply affirmatively. With such assurance, one or more Mexican bishops would send Calles a letter similar to Burke's. Olds would extend to him "the courtesy of the United States mail pouch."[41]

When Morrow learned how eager Burke was to hazard any chance to settle the religious question, he proposed a text for the letter, which Olds relayed. "But here comes something that has surprised and worried Mr. Morrow very much, as it worries me," Olds told Burke. Morrow had a handwritten letter by "one of the highest ecclesiastical dignitaries" in Mexico who claimed to speak for the bishops, stating the Cristeros were doing the right thing. It went on to say if the U.S. lifted the arms embargo, the triumph of Catholicism would be certain. Olds said this showed the Church supported the rebellion. Burke explained the Church's attitude and denied that the statement of one bishop, if it was a bishop, spoke for the Church as a whole. Despite Burke's rejoinder, Olds now saw no way to a solution.[42]

Next evening, Lippmann, back from Mexico, visited Burke and James H. Ryan. He said the Mexican minister of finance, Luis Montes de Oca, a close friend of Calles, assured him the attitude of those in Calles's administration was different from those who wrote the 1917 constitution. Those wanted to crush the Church; present ministers did not. Lippmann spoke with all but one, and each shared the view of Montes de Oca. They wished "to see the Church live so long as it does not interfere in politics." Lippmann discussed the matter twice with Calles, who assured him he had no intention of destroying the Church nor denying its personality. He wanted priests to stay out of politics. The registration law and quota article were merely statistical. Lippmann considered the president "an intelligent man, but a slow thinker." In speaking to him about an apostolic delegate, Lippmann explained Calles was just beginning to understand the function of such a diplomat, and, given time, he might see the value of receiving one. Burke and Ryan stressed "the advisability, and even the necessity," that Calles ask for a delegate.[43]

Two days later, Burke made the same point to Olds, who turned the conversation to Orozco who, he claimed, was certainly a revolutionist and probable author of the letter in Morrow's possession. Convinced of this, Olds told Burke his plea for the man's safe conduct out of Mexico had been unwarranted. Burke would later learn the real author of the letter was Archbishop Miguel María de la Mora y Mora of San Luis Potosí.[44]

Then plans changed again. Morrow sent Olds a lengthy telegram with the proposed text of a new letter he wanted Burke to send Calles. Morrow believed it had a good chance of winning a meeting between the two. Olds gave Burke the news and said he wanted the letter the next morning. He told Burke to be ready to depart at once by rail for Mexico City. Olds urged him to take a companion, and Burke tapped Montavon.[45]

That evening, Burke wrote the letter based on Morrow's text, with only slight changes. It said he learned reliably of Calles's declaration that he never sought "to destroy the identity of the Church nor to interfere with its spiritual functions." Although the Mexican bishops wanted to restore public worship, they believed the laws, if enforced antagonistically, would mar the Church's identity. If Calles would issue a statement denying his intention of doing so and committing the government to periodic discussions of mutual concerns, the clergy would resume spiritual duties. If, moreover, Calles would entertain such an approach, the bishops or their representative would communicate with him.[46]

MEETING WITH CALLES

At the end of March, Burke and Montavon boarded a train for St. Louis where they changed lines for Laredo. They were met at the border by American Albert Smithers, a Catholic, married to a Mexican woman, and half-brother of James Smithers, Calles's personal interpreter. They boarded a train for the two-day journey to Tacuba outside Mexico City, whence they took an automobile to the station in the capital and a private rail car in the train for Veracruz. The Mexican president was vacationing there in the island fortress of San Juan de Ulúa.[47]

On the morning of 4 April, Morrow and the Smithers brothers saw Calles. Within an hour, Bert Smithers returned for Burke alone. The five met in the reception area of Calles's bedroom. Seated next to Calles, Burke explained the nature of the NCWC and the Administrative Committee, which lent him to Archbishop Fumasoni-Biondi who doubled as apostolic delegate to Mexico. He said the pope was eager for peace and desired return of the Mexican bishops and restoration of public worship. Burke came as personal representative of the delegate "with no power to promise, with no final authority and with no power to accept anything." He came to make clear the mind of the pontiff and to ask if Calles would be willing to recognize the Church and "its own organized life" and interpret laws regarding registration and limitation of clergy in such way as to permit resumption of worship. Burke's presentation was long and the tension in the room was palpable, visible. Calles uttered not a word.[48]

When Burke finished, Calles said: "Father Burke, you are all wrong with regard to the facts. I will tell you the facts." Without anger, but in slow, measured, emphatic terms, which Burke needed no translator to understand, Calles said he had never intended to implement the anticlerical articles of the constitution, but Archbishop Mora's proclamation against the constitution in February 1926 had compelled him to do so. It aimed at destroying the government and was an act characteristic of the Mexican hierarchy. The bishops called for a boycott aimed at crippling the economy and closed all churches. They went to the U.S. and sought to have it sever diplomatic relations. Calles tried to uplift the poor of Mexico, but priests told them poverty was their lot. By keeping peons ignorant, bishops sought to rule politically. Calles averred he had no idea of the Vatican's attitude, but he had "been given to understand" it supported the bishops "in their political and revolutionary efforts" against him. He was not opposed to the Church, but he insisted on "fidelity to the institutions and laws of Mexico." Calles concluded with the statement, "Father Burke, what have you to say to this?"[49]

Burke replied, "I will give you the same answer you gave me, Mr. President, you are all wrong." After assuring that the Vatican was not backing any political movement for his overthrow, Burke refused to argue over facts. That would lead nowhere. His frank reply eased tension in the room. Burke said the pope was asking if the president would permit the Church to return to Mexico and freely exercise its spiritual functions with the understanding the laws of registration and limitation of the clergy would leave it unhindered internally. Pleased to be assured of the Vatican's position, Calles answered he never intended to destroy the Church nor did he intend to interpret laws so as to interfere in its internal life. He launched into a long discourse about how good it would be if bishops and priests returned and truly sought to help people. Afterward, the group adjourned for lunch.[50]

On resuming, they conferred about Burke's letter and the one Calles would write in response. Burke posed the matter of an apostolic delegate. Calles said the Church could appoint any official or dignitary it chose. A delegate could live and work in Mexico, but would not receive diplomatic recognition. "I must not be asked whether I approve or disapprove," said Calles. If the delegate was a foreigner, however, he would not be permitted to officiate at any public function. His influence in Mexico "would depend upon his capability and his personal contact with the officials." The letter Calles gave Burke declared it was "not the purpose of the Constitution nor of the laws, nor my own purpose, to destroy the identity of any church, nor to interfere, in any form, in its spiritual functions." It said the president was always disposed to "to hear from any person, be he a dignitary of some church or merely a private individual." This last expressed Calles's willingness to meet with an apostolic delegate.[51]

Calles asked the next step. Burke said he had to report to Fumasoni-Biondi, who would refer the matter to Rome. Calles advised that if the Mexican bishops were coming back, they do so while he was in office. Unless a settlement occurred under his tenure, a successor might not agree to one for fear of appearing less revolutionary than Calles. As the more than five-hour interview came to a close, Calles handed his letter to Burke, thanked him for making known the mind of the Vatican, and, to Burke's "utter amazement," added, "I hope your visit means a new era for the life and people of Mexico."[52]

Burke discussed the interview with Montavon on their return to Mexico City. They concluded "Calles was rather of the [Francisco] Madero type of revolutionist than of the radical and 'red flagger' type." The next day, they boarded a train for the U.S. The two parted at San Antonio, as Burke was to meet Fumasoni-Biondi in Albuquerque. The letters and Burke's report pleased the delegate, who ordered him directly to Washington whence the report would be sent to Rome. Burke arrived home on 12 April, and, after several days of follow-up work, fell ill and was confined to bed until the twenty-fourth.[53]

Burke found waiting for him an Easter message from Lynch, complete with "beautiful blue birds." From his sickbed, he wrote secrecy prevented him from explaining why he had not been at the Cenacle as planned for Easter nor had the chance to write letters. "So I will have to endure and even be silent with regard to all I have done and which brought on this attack of weakness and fatigue," wrote Burke. He wished he could see Lynch "and talk over some spiritual things." Yet, he had no idea when the Lord would afford him that opportunity.[54]

Meanwhile, Fumasoni-Biondi changed his mind about sending the report and letters to Rome. He wanted first to hear from exiled Mexican bishops about their desire for a settlement. He sent Archbishop Ruiz to San Antonio to confer with the eleven there, but keep secret the agreement. He had three questions: (1) were bishops willing to return home and resume public worship? (2) were they willing to accept a Vatican decision in that regard? (3) would they stipulate any conditions for such decision? Unanimously, they voted yes on the first two and no on the third, though they did offer suggestions: they would like a clearer statement from Calles about laws restricting the clergy, religious instruction in primary grades, and return, if possible, of alienated Church property.[55]

Burke put their suggestions in a carefully worded letter. Rather than ask, he *assumed* Calles would agree to the recommendations. Olds sent the dispatch to Morrow urging him to have Calles affirm the assumptions correctly interpreted his thinking. Morrow telephoned Olds it was hopeless to win such concessions, especially by mail. He recommended Burke and Ruiz come to Mexico immediately and present them to Calles and Obregón, who knew and approved of the Burke-Calles exchange. Olds told Burke he and Ruiz should go, and Ruiz should have authority to act definitively. Burke could not believe Calles would meet with Ruiz and said he doubted Ruiz would get authorization to close a deal; Fumasoni-Biondi would want to see any agreement. Olds suggested Burke and Ruiz stay in Mexico City until Fumsoni-Biondi rendered a decision. Burke said that would be up to Fumasoni-Biondi. He told Olds he did not want to go, but would do what the delegate ordered. That night, Fumasoni-Biondi directed Burke and Ruiz to make the trip.[56]

On 12 May, Burke, Montavon, and Ruiz departed Washington. When the three reached Laredo, Bert Smithers took them across the border where they embarked for Mexico City. After Ruiz retired, Smithers told Burke Calles's reaction to the bishops' suggestions. Regarding registration, those in charge of government buildings had to be enrolled. There was no problem with religious instruction to children, but it must be in church, not in a school building. There were mixed messages about return of Church property. Smithers said Calles thought it unnecessary that Burke come, but Morrow insisted. On learning Ruiz would come too, Calles balked, considering it a mistake; Ruiz would stir up his friends and make public pronouncements to agitate the people. Calles relented because Morrow and Burke wanted him there. Burke was flabbergasted. "I thought … that Calles knew and approved it all," he said. That was a deciding factor in the decision to come. Another was the presence of Obregón because "it was very necessary … to know that whatever was done would endure." Smithers made no reply. Burke absolutely refused to see Calles unless he would "receive Ruiz." Smithers thought that could be arranged.[57]

Back in Washington, Olds saw James H. Ryan to say the party would reach Mexico City the following morning. Burke and Ruiz would meet with Calles, and Olds expected news of the interview shortly thereafter. If acceptable terms were reached, they should "be cabled immediately to Rome for quick action." Ryan relayed this information to Fumasoni-Biondi. Agitated, the delegate blurted: "These Americans are crazy. They want to rush things. It can't be done. Rome does not act in that way. She is eternal." Ryan acknowledged the truth of that, but said if Rome received positive news in the cable, it might act. Fumasoni-Biondi doubted it, but agreed to send one.[58]

Upon their arrival, Morrow came to see Burke and the two spoke privately. Morrow said Calles had been "very opposed" to Ruiz's coming, but finally yielded. Morrow thought it quite an accomplishment for Ruiz to be allowed to accompany Burke. Yet, Calles had no intention of letting him attend the interview. Burke considered that "very insufficient and unsatisfactory." Calles must receive Ruiz too. Morrow replied it was both "impossible" and "entirely inadvisable." Burke insisted: Ruiz would be present or he would not see Calles at all. He averred neither would have come except assurance was given Calles would receive them both. For Burke to see him without Ruiz would be "an insult to the Mexican Hierarchy" on whose behalf he worked. Among the most bitter things Calles told Burke at Veracruz was "no member of the Mexican Hierarchy ever visited him." "Here I was, bringing the senior [bishop] of the Mexican Hierarchy," noted Burke. "It would be well for Calles to prove his word." Morrow understood his point and agreed. He went to see Calles. A short while later, he sent word Calles would receive them both.[59]

Absent Obregón, Calles met with Morrow, Burke, Montavon, Ruiz, and the two Smithers. Shaking hands with Burke and Ruiz, Calles welcomed them, but without smile. Burke realized he was expected to begin because Calles sat in utter silence. Thanking him for receiving them, he explained Fumasoni-Biondi had wanted to sound out the exiled Mexican bishops about a settlement, so Ruiz conferred with them. He inquired about their desire to return. Burke said they came not to alter or revoke the conversations at Veracruz, but to continue them. He presented the bishops' suggestions and asked what Calles thought of them.[60]

Turning to Ruiz, Calles said, "Archbishop Ruiz and all the other bishops know the law very well." The registration act did not interfere in the internal life of the Church. Only priests authorized by a bishop would be registered. Registration was necessary because the government owned church buildings. Neither Calles nor the constitution had the right to deny the right of religious instruction. Yet, such instruction could not occur in school buildings; it must be in church. With regard to church buildings, the government had sold some to individuals and had converted others to public use. It would be difficult to get them back. Moreover, an avalanche of requests beset him to dedicate more to municipal use. He felt compelled to acquiesce unless the bishops came back to use them for religious purposes.[61]

Ruiz told of the San Antonio meeting. The bishops were not intransigent; they were eager to return. They placed no conditions on that, but left it to the Vatican. In fact, they preferred the pope make the decision. "You know and I know," Ruiz told Calles, "it would be better for the Holy See to order the bishops back." Burke asked that Ruiz and Calles exchange the same letters he and Calles exchanged at Veracruz—with one addition. Burke urged Calles to endorse the recent words of José Manuel Puig y Casauranc, minister of education, who declared the Catholic faith had made Mexico great and was the faith of the Mexican people. The president agreed to do so if Ruiz could get Roman approval for the exchange of letters.[62]

Afterward, Morrow and Burke telegraphed Fumasoni-Biondi that the interview was satisfactory. Arrangements were made regarding registration of priests by having bishops send names to Ruiz, who would submit them to the government. The plan was for Ruiz to celebrate a pontifical Mass on Pentecost Sunday, 27 May, in the cathedral at Mexico City, thus resuming public worship. The message pled the necessity of Fumasoni-Biondi's communicating this to Rome with an urgent request to approve resumption of worship. The telegram included the text of both letters exchanged between Ruiz and Calles. It concluded by stating Burke and Ruiz would remain in Mexico to await word from the Vatican.[63]

The message clearly cast the situation in the best light. It mentioned nothing about religious education or Church property because the chief obstacle to return of the clergy was the registration law. Burke, Morrow, and Ruiz never intended their effort as a permanent settlement. So, the question put to Rome was to approve resumption of public cult ten days hence. While the message was being coded, Burke phoned Ryan to let him know he would be receiving a telegram that night. Action must be taken. He would await telegraphic word back from the delegate.[64]

The telegram reached Ryan the next morning. He hand-delivered it to Fumasoni-Biondi., who summoned him back an hour later. With Fumasoni-Biondi were Bernardini, Marella, and Monsignor George Leech, secretary of the delegation. They asked Ryan's thoughts about the message. He said they should cable it in full to Rome. They countered the Vatican would never make a decision based on a cablegram; someone would have to go there to speak personally with the pope. Moreover, Fumasoni-Biondi was concerned because the message said nothing about religious education or return of Church property, two matters Ruiz was to have raised with Calles. So, Ryan crafted a memorandum stating the delegate would inform Rome of the interview. While pleased with the good will displayed by Calles, Fumasoni-Biondi was certain the Vatican would not act "on mere telegraphic advices." He desired the immediate recall of Ruiz who would be sent to Rome on the first ship.[65]

Ryan gave the memorandum to Olds, who was taken aback. Nevertheless, he promised to communicate it to Morrow. Its effect, he said, would be to disappoint Burke and Ruiz about a settlement. Olds urged Ryan to impress on the delegate the need for quick action, as the political situation might change any moment. He believed if worship resumed, it would be a positive gain for the Church in Mexico. Ryan relayed this information to the delegate. That night, a worried Burke telephoned Ryan because he had not received telegraphic reply from Fumasoni-Biondi. So, Ryan sent an uncoded wire to the embassy in Mexico in language cryptic enough to be intelligible only to recipients: "Chief wishes party to return immediately. Both of you to go across as soon as possible. This is the quickest and only sure way to achieve purpose."[66] Ryan's use of the phrase "both of you" instead of simply "Ruiz" would further confuse matters.

Burke got the telegram next morning. It "bewildered and puzzled" Morrow, who told Burke that Olds had just phoned to say the delegate wanted them to stay put until word came from Rome. Evidence indicates it was Olds himself who wanted that; he had not communicated Ryan's memorandum to the party in Mexico. The telegram left Morrow deeply disturbed and depressed. He had no idea which message—the one from Olds or the one from Ryan—contained the latest word or how to reconcile them. As Burke put it, "Morrow was losing faith and hope and interest." He even convinced himself the delegate sent nothing to the Vatican. Sometime after 4:00 that afternoon, Burke and Morrow reached Ryan by phone. Burke asked if their message had been sent to Rome with the delegate's approval. Ryan said yes. Burke inquired if the whole report went. No. Had the Vatican cabled any word back? No. Ryan asked if Burke and Ruiz were coming home. Burke said they were leaving that night. When he hung up, Morrow was "visibly improved." Burke told him what he had learned. "That's better," said Morrow.[67]

Burke wrote Calles a letter explaining and apologizing for his abrupt departure. Though the two had hoped to talk again, that was now out of the question. He showed the text to Morrow, who approved. Then the two said their goodbyes. "God bless you, Father Burke," said Morrow. "I hope we can get the Church back to these people."[68]

Roman Complications

When Burke and Ruiz reached Washington, Fumasoni-Biondi sent Ruiz alone to Rome. Anticipating his mission there would fail, the delegate did not want Burke involved so as to keep the door open with Calles. In Paris, Ruiz gave an interview to the press. Thus, the story of secret negotiations and Morrow's part became public. Obstinate Mexican Catholics pressed the Vatican to demand repeal of the obnoxious legislation as condition for restoration of worship. Cardinal Pietro Gasparri, however, agreed with Burke's report. He prepared a summary and he and Ruiz met with Pius XI to plea for a return of the bishops. The pope read the report and said it was good as far as it went. He asked Ruiz, "But do you not think it would be a scandal to the Catholics for the Mexican Bishops to return on these assurances?" When Ruiz replied it would, Pius took a harder stance. The incident convinced Gasparri that Ruiz suffered from "one great fault": "He agreed with the man he talked with last," in this instance the pope. Gasparri cabled to Fumasoni-Biondi: "The Holy Father wishes Your Excellency to thank Ambassador Morrow for his good offices and to ask him to insist with Calles that he (the latter) make some acceptable proposition." The delegate showed Burke the cable. In Burke's view, Rome seemed to consider his and Morrow's effort an attempt at full settlement of the Church-state issue, when in fact all they sought was a modus vivendi to restore public worship.[69]

The delegate ordered Burke to have Olds give the cable to Morrow, who was then in Washington, without comment. Burke objected that it was "unhappily" worded and expected Morrow to do the impossible. Fumasoni-Biondi insisted. So Burke had Olds relay it without explanation. The next evening, Burke met with Olds and Morrow. Morrow told Olds to pretend he never relayed the cable, and Olds asked Burke to do the same. Morrow said he would never accept such a communication from his own government. While he appreciated the Pope's thanks, the remainder of the message "would mean the killing of all his good offices." He would have to present the cable to Calles, which would destroy respect for the Vatican that Burke instilled in him at Veracruz. Olds was equally emphatic. The cable "formalized" a relationship between Morrow and the Church that never existed. "It was full of T.N.T.," he said. Morrow explained he would receive a cable worded differently: perhaps thanking him for his efforts and encouraging him to "continue them to the end that acceptable propositions be secured from President Calles." Like Burke, he felt Rome misunderstood what they all had attempted to do. Both Morrow and Olds repeatedly insisted Burke should go to the Vatican to explain matters. They wondered why Fumasoni-Biondi had not sent him with Ruiz. For his part, Burke withdrew the cable.[70]

The following day he read to Fumasoni-Biondi and Marella his memorandum of the previous evening's interview. It shocked them and caused the delegate's temper to flare. Totally ignoring that he ordered Burke to deliver the cable without comment, the delegate scolded Burke for not verbally communicating the gist of it: the pope wanted Morrow to continue his effort to secure more acceptable terms. Marella explained that in many cases it was necessary to "lie" in conveying Vatican messages. That afternoon, Burke told Morrow and Olds that Fumasoni-Biondi wanted Morrow to act as if he had never received the cable. He wished him to continue his good offices toward a more acceptable proposition. Burke said the delegate intended to cable the Vatican for details about "acceptable proposals."[71]

Several days later, Rome sent further word. Pius reserved the right to discuss terms of any proposals. Acceptable propositions would be "(a) such as will not permit the slightest impression to be made that the Holy See or the Bishops had abandoned or discounted in any way the faithful of Mexico who had undergone such sacrifices for the faith of their fathers; (b) some expression or form of satisfaction to the Bishops and clergy, (c) explicit and sufficient guarantees for the future of the church in Mexico." Fumasoni-Biondi was certain the pope wrote or dictated the message. Marella told Burke "to put a suit and overcoat over the wording of the cable and make of it a letter to Calles." Fumasoni-Biondi said to express it as kindly as possible. In giving the letter to Morrow for transmittal to Calles, Burke could inform him of its contents, but without any reference to the sufferings Mexican Catholics had endured.[72]

Burke met with Morrow and Olds. Rather than mince words, he told them exactly what the Vatican wanted: no odium should be visited on Mexican Catholics who suffered so much nor should the impression be given the Vatican abandoned them; satisfaction must be made to the bishops; more definite guarantees for the future of the Church. Morrow asked if the Vatican suggested anything to meet these concerns. Burke said no. Both Morrow and Olds recommended Burke leave out everything from the letter except the actual message of the Vatican. Morrow explained his job would be easier if knew what it considered "sufficient guarantees." He believed Rome was shifting their process to a permanent settlement. He and Burke aimed at only restoration of public cult. He thought amending the constitution was impossible until after the bishops returned. Morrow was not at all sanguine.[73]

When Burke reported on the interview, Fumasoni-Biondi explained his aim too was simply restoration of worship, regardless of limitations still imposed on the Church. He agreed Burke's letter should contain only the Vatican's message and now wanted it addressed to Morrow, not Calles. After making the changes, Burke met with Morrow, Olds, and Fumasoni-Biondi who approved it. Morrow assured the delegate he would do all he could. Once back in Mexico, he saw Calles, who made it clear he awaited a simple yes or no answer from the Vatican. Given that, Morrow informed Burke "no good purpose would be served" by giving Calles a copy of the letter. "I feared that he might possibly construe [it] … as a definite disavowal by the Vatican authorities," explained Morrow.[74]

The day after Morrow wrote, José de León Toral, a fanatical Catholic, assassinated President-Elect Obregón. Burke received authorization from Hanna to issue a statement in his name, calling the deed "an outrage against every law of God and man" and declaring his "utter condemnation of it and all connected with it cannot be made too emphatic." Diaz also issued a long statement condemning the murder. Burke had Montavon cable Ruiz in Rome to inform him of Diaz's action and for him to take a similar step if questioned. Burke saw Arthur Bliss Lane, chief of the Mexican desk at State, who said Morrow telephoned and he "he had never heard [his] voice so hopeless." Burke informed Lane of the telegrams and asked him to convey word of them to Morrow so that Calles would know the Church's attitude. Lane did so.[75]

Two days later Calles issued a statement blaming the Church for the assassination. Burke immediately wrote a message to Morrow explaining that at news of the assassination, he (Burke) had Catholic authorities condemn the deed. Still, without any evidence, Calles asserted "clerical action was directly connected to the crime." "Calles knows," wrote Burke, "this is the end of anything like fair or promising negotiations." He urged Morrow to have him qualify his statement in some way. If he refused, wrote Burke, "I will report my own mind to my ecclesiastical superiors … that further negotiations with President Calles are impossible. I think the situation very serious and critical."[76] Burke showed the message to Fumasoni-Biondi, who approved presenting it to officials at State. Burke gave it to Lane who passed it to Kellogg. The latter told Burke to do nothing until hearing from him. For his part, Lane read the message over the phone to Morrow. Both Kellogg and Lane thought Burke was acting in "a very rash manner."[77]

Two days later, Burke and Montavon met with Lane and Bert Smithers. Lane had just gotten off the phone with Morrow who advised that Burke "sit tight" for a couple of weeks. Everyone expected Calles to make a strong statement. At the moment, feeling against the Church was intense in Mexico City. Morrow believed it would dissipate in a fortnight making it again possible to discuss matters reasonably. The night of the assassination, Morrow spoke with Foreign Minister Genaro Estrada to advise against drastic punishment of Toral without proof that would satisfy the civilized world. He further urged if any statement were made about Catholic involvement, it distinguish between individuals and the Church. Three days later, Morrow gave Estrada a copy of Hanna's statement. Estrada said he had given Calles Morrow's advice about distinguishing between individual Catholics and the Church. Calles explained he meant only militant Catholics in his statement; he agreed with Morrow. The latter asked Estrada to encourage Calles to make that distinction clear publicly.[78]

On learning Morrow's assessment, Burke, Montavon, Lane, and Smithers drafted a telegram. The message said that allowing Calles's statement to stand was "dangerous because of its implication and incompleteness." Burke suggested that Calles himself or someone like Estrada find opportunity to qualify it. Kellogg sent the telegram.[79] Several days later, Morrow reported that Calles would probably issue a statement, but because of conditions, it must be a guarded one. Morrow believed given more time, Calles would be willing to issue a forthright clarification. He advised waiting. Burke agreed, but did not want to wait too long. In early August, Calles issued a statement that in his accusation of clerical involvement in Obregón's death, he did not mean the Church or Church authorities, but some individual Catholics.[80]

Matters became complicated by untoward words from Rome. In mid-July, *L'Osservatore Romano* (*The Roman Observer*), a semi-official Vatican paper, suggested Calles was another Nero involved in Obregón's assassination and scapegoated the Church for it. Shortly thereafter, it flat out accused him of ordering the murder. Moreover, the New York *World* reported Ruiz as saying Obregón's murder did not surprise him; Calles would continue as president, and he wanted a religious settlement only because he needed money. When Morrow went to discuss the religious question, Calles said it was altogether inopportune. Referring to *L'Osservatore Romano* and the

World, he told Morrow if the bishops and priests were unwilling to return in a spirit of good will, he did not want them back. Toward the end of the interview, Calles declared, "The religious situation is a closed incident." Morrow's words for Burke were: "Sit tight on this. Don't get discouraged. In another week or two we may be able to go on. It is essential to make settlement with Calles as it will be harder for his successor to make it." Burke confided to Lynch, "The Mexican situation … is about as dark as it can be.… I'm told to keep on and do my best. I will obey; but at times the invisible Lord is my only refuge."[81] Soon thereafter, *L'Osservatore Romano* widened its attack in a scurrilous article on Morrow. So indignant was Burke, he briefly thought of resigning from the NCWC.[82]

Well into fall 1928, efforts at a settlement stalled. In early November, Fumasoni-Biondi told Burke the pope gave new instructions. In essence, if incoming provisional President Emilio Portes Gil would put in writing the same guarantees about the registration law that Calles had given Burke, the bishops could return to Mexico and resume public worship. Ruiz was on his way to the U.S. to meet with the exiled bishops to secure their backing.[83]

When Ruiz arrived, he informed Kellogg that Pius XI was ready to negotiate with the Mexican government, preferably at Rome, for changes to the constitution. Meanwhile, bishops and clergy could return to their dioceses and resume worship, provided the government conceded sufficient securities. He neglected to mention that this offer applied to incoming Provisional President Portes Gil. Kellogg sent word to Morrow, who met with Calles. He agreed if the bishops returned in a spirit of conciliation and good will, he would admit them at once—on condition they immediately enter amicable discussion with him on a satisfactory interpretation or amendment of the laws, decrees, and articles of constitution. Burke communicated this information to Fumasoni-Biondi. The delegate, however, had received instructions from the Vatican that he was to deal with Portes Gil, not Calles.[84]

On 30 November, Portes Gil became provisional president. He informed Morrow of his willingness to pursue Calles's negotiations with Burke, but not with a Mexican bishop. Returning to the U.S., Morrow told Burke, who reminded him Rome wanted more guarantees, and that a representative of the Mexican government would probably have to negotiate with the Vatican in Rome. Morrow thought Portes Gil would never go that far, but might perhaps negotiate with Fumasoni-Biondi.[85]

Burke hosted a meeting with Fumasoni-Biondi, Morrow, and J. Reuben Clark, undersecretary of state. Morrow said vast numbers of Mexicans were indifferent to religion, and the number of Catholic rebels was few. With apologies to Fumasoni-Biondi, he thought the Mexican Church kept putting its trust in the wrong man. He urged moving forward with a settlement. Fumasoni-Biondi replied the Vatican wanted further guarantees, and Mexico should send an official representative to Rome to negotiate. Morrow said the government was unprepared to do that and asked Fumasoni-Biondi if he would to go to Mexico. He would not think of it except at Rome's express command and with plenary power to conclude an agreement. The conversation turned to Burke's going. He said he would do whatever the delegate wished. Fumasoni-Biondi explained that whatever might eventuate would need Vatican approval. The Church thought "in terms of centuries," he told Morrow. With a pleasant laugh, Morrow replied "the [Mexican] Church was thinking in terms of weeks or months."[86]

Afterward, Fumasoni-Biondi told Burke he should have his bags packed in case an invitation came for him to come to Mexico. He understood this as permission, even encouragement, to pursue this avenue with Morrow, who suggested they draft a letter which Portes Gil might sign giving stronger guarantees than Calles.[87]

The two worked on one for Portes Gil's signature. Quoting the letter Calles had exchanged with Burke in April and the speech delivered by Puig weeks later, Portes Gil would affirm both. The draft, however, contained an unfortunate disclaimer about the registration and quota laws for priests. When Burke showed it to Fumasoni-Biondi, he replied: "It is not nearly as strong as the letter Calles signed for you. Tell Morrow not to do anything on the matter until he hears expressly from you." When Morrow learned this, he asked Burke to have the draft destroyed. Morrow was at a complete loss about what he could possibly do. He told Burke that once back in Mexico, he would watch, hold himself in readiness, but take no positive steps.[88] There the matter lay until the definitive breakthrough occurred.

Endnotes to Chapter 17

1. Burke, *Christ in Us*, 193 and 195.
2. [Burke, memorandum], 27 January 1927, AP, Burke Papers, box 70; Burke

to Lynch, 24 January 1927, ibid., box 5; Burke to Muldoon, 9 March 1927, ACUA, USCCB 10:152:30; Pius XI, *Iniquis afflictisque* (18 November 1926), http://w2.vatican.va/content/pius-xi/en/encyclicals/documents/hf_p-xi_enc_18111926_iniquis-afflictisque.html (accessed 18 December 2014); "Bishops of the United States Issue Pastoral Letter On Mexico," *NCWC Bulletin* 31 (January 1927): 30–39; *New York Times*, 6 August and 2 September 1926 and 28 August 1927; Redinger, *American Catholics and the Mexican Revolution*, 117–20; Kauffman, *Faith and Fraternalism*, 292–93.

3. [Burke, memorandum], 27 January 1927, AP, Burke Papers, box 70.
4. Ibid.
5. Burke to Muldoon, 9 March 1927, copy, ACUA, USCCB 10:152:30; Bailey, *¡Viva Cristo Rey!*, 121–30, 142–43; Quirk, *Mexican Revolution*, 200–02.
6. Burke to Hawks, 11 February 1927, AP, Burke Papers, box 10; Minutes of the Administrative Committee, 26 April 1927, ACUA, USCCB 10:64:4.
7. Burke to Lynch, 17 May 1927, AP, Burke Papers, box 5; Bailey, *¡Viva Cristo Rey!*, 121–30, 142–43; Quirk, *Mexican Revolution*, 200–02.
8. Burke to J. H. Ryan, [2 January 1927], ACUA, USCCB 10:153:5; Burke Interview with Kellogg, 28 November 1927, copy, ibid., 10:145: Interview Book I; Bailey, *¡Viva Cristo Rey!*, 176–78; Sheerin, *Never Look Back*, 117–18; Rice, *Diplomatic Relations*, 109–11; Harold Nicolson, *Dwight Morrow* (New York: Harcourt, Brace, and Company, 1935), 338–42; Ferrell, *Frank B. Kellogg-Henry L. Stimson*, 41.
9. [Burke], Memorandum of Interview with Ambassador Morrow, 13 October 1927, ACUA, USCCB 10:145: Interview Book I; Sheerin, *Never Look Back*, 117–18.
10. Burke to Hanna, 7 November 1927, ACUA, USCCB 10:99:17; *Chicago Tribune*, 6 November 1927; Bailey, *¡Viva Cristo Rey!*, 164–68; Quirk, *Mexican Revolution*, 212–13; Jürgen Buchenau, *Plutarco Elías Calles and the Mexican Revolution* (Lanham, Md.: Rowman & Littlefield Publishers, Inc., 2007), 135–40; Héctor Aguilar Camín and Lorenzo Meyer, *In the Shadow of the Mexican Revolution: Contemporary Mexican History, 1910–1989*, trans. Luis Alberto Fierro (Austin: University of Texas Press, 1993), 92.
11. Dwight Morrow to Robert Olds, 9 December 1927, copy, ASCACL, Dwight Morrow Papers 10:5:114. This and subsequent passages are quoted by permission of the Trustees of Amherst College.
12. Burke to Hanna, telegram, 25 November 1927, copy, AASF, NCWC files; Burke to Hanna, 3 December 1927, ibid.; [Burke, Interview with Coolidge], 26 November 1927, ACUA, USCCB 10:145: Interview Book I; Sheerin, *Never Look Back*, 118.
13. [Burke, Interview with Kellogg], 28 November 1927, ACUA, USCCB 10:145: Interview Book I; Burke to Hanna, 3 December 1927, AASF, NCWC files; Sheerin, *Never Look Back*, 118–19.

14. *New York Times*, 6 December 1927; *Chicago Tribune*, 6 December 1927; Burke to Coolidge, 10 December 1927, copy; Sanders to Burke, 12 December 1927; Kellogg to Burke, 13 December 1927; Kellogg to Burke, 17 December 1927—all in ACUA, USCCB 10:149:17.
15. [Burke, Interview with Olds], 20 December 1927, ACUA, USCCB 10:145: Interview Book I; Morrow to Olds, 21 February 1928, ASCACL, Morrow Papers 10:5:114. Cardinal Désiré-Joseph Mercier, archbishop of Malines, Belgium, was a patriot and outspoken defender of the Belgian people during the German occupation of his country during World War I.
16. Morrow to Olds, 30 November 1928 (first quote is here); Morrow to Olds, 9 December 1928 (remaining quotes are here); Kellogg to Morrow, 17 December 1928—all in ASCACL, Morrow Papers 10:5:114.
17. [Burke, Interview with Olds], 20 December 1927, ACUA, USCCB 10:145: Interview Book I.
18. [Burke, Interview with Olds], 29 December 1927, ACUA, USCCB 10:145: Interview Book I. In fact, Morrow had told Calles that in World War I, the Germans had every right to execute Edith Cavell, but they were fools for doing so. "Even if you think you have the right to shoot this Archbishop," Morrow advised Calles, "you would be a d__ fool to do it." With that, the president agreed to exile Orozco if apprehended (First interview between Mr. Morrow and Father Burke, Havana, Cuba, 17 January 1928, copy, AASF, NCWC files).
19. Burke to Hanna, 30 December 1927, AASF, NCWC files.
20. Memorandum of meeting of Administrative Committee members, 3 January 1928, copy, AASF, NCWC files.
21. [Burke], NCWC Interview with Delegate, 3 January 1928, AASF, NCWC files; Sheerin, *Never Look Back*, 119–20.
22. [Burke, Interview with Olds], 4 January 1928, AASF, NCWC files.
23. [Burke, Interview with Fumasoni Biondi and Bernardini], 5 January 1928, ACUA, USCCB 10:145: Interview Book I; Burke to Hanna, 7 January 1928, AASF, NCWC files; Redinger, *American Catholics and the Mexican Revolution*, 77–78; Bailey, *¡Viva Cristo Rey!*, 181.
24. First interview between Mr. Morrow and Father Burke, Havana, 17 January 1928, copy, AASF, NCWC files; Sheerin, *Never Look Back*, 120.
25. First interview between Mr. Morrow and Father Burke, Havana, 17 January 1928, copy, AASF, NCWC files; Sheerin, *Never Look Back*, 120.
26. First interview between Mr. Morrow and Father Burke, Havana, 17 January 1928, copy, AASF, NCWC files; Sheerin, *Never Look Back*, 122.
27. First interview between Mr. Morrow and Father Burke, Havana, 17 January 1928, copy, AASF, NCWC files.
28. Ibid. In a speech on 1 January 1928, Calles blamed the Cristero rebellion in part on "the resistance of the higher clergy, who refuse to obey the laws." The

Mexican episcopal committee responded with an open letter explaining its position and asking the president to reconsider the bishops' 1926 petition to amend the constitution (Pascual Diaz, for the committee of bishops, to Plutarco Elias Calles, 8 January 1928, copy, ACUA, USCCB J. H. Ryan papers).

29. Second interview between Mr. Morrow and Father Burke, Havana, 18 January 1928, copy, AASF, NCWC files.
30. Ibid.
31. Burke to Hawks, undated [February 1928], AP, Burke Papers, box 10.
32. Bailey, *¡Viva Cristo Rey!*, 157–61, 191; Quirk, *Mexican Revolution*, 205–06, 221; J. Meyer, *Cristero Rebellion*, 48–63; J. Meyer, Krauze, and Reyes, *Estado y sociedad*, 21, 25, 234, 262; McMullen, "Diplomacy of Revolution," 179–83, 213–14.
33. [Burke, Interview with Luis Bustos, Alberto María Carreño, and José Ortiz Monasterio], 6 February 1928, AASF, NCWC files.
34. Burke to Hanna, 8 February 1928, AASF, NCWC files; Walter Lippmann to Burke, 7 March [1928], copy, ACUA, USCCB 10:145: Interview Book I; Ronald Steel, *Walter Lippmann and the American Century* (Boston: Little, Brown and Company, 1980), 241; Redinger, *American Catholics and the Mexican Revolution*, 79.
35. *New York Herald-Tribune*, 10 February 1928; Burke to Hanna, 13 February 1928, AASF, NCWC files; Sheerin *Never Look Back*, 122.
36. Burke to Lynch, 16 February 1928, AP, Burke Papers, box 5; Burke to Hanna, 13 February 1928, AASF, NCWC files; Alan F. Winslow, Memorandum, 13 February 1928, ASCACL, Morrow Papers 10:5:114; Burke, Memorandum, [16 March 1928], ACUA, USCCB 10:150:35.
37. Burke, [Interview with Olds], 3 March 1928, ACUA, USCCB 10:145: Interview Book I; Morrow to Olds, 21 February 1928, ASCACL, Morrow Papers 10:5:114; Steel, *Lippmann*, 241–42; Redinger, *American Catholics and the Mexican Revolution*, 79.
38. Lippmann to Burke, 7 March [1928], copy, ACUA, USCCB 10:145: Interview Book I.
39. Burke, Memorandum, [21 March 1928], ACUA, USCCB 10:150:35; Olds to Morrow, 9 March 1928, ASCACL, Morrow Papers 10:5:114.
40. Morrow to Olds, 13 and 16 March 1928, ASCACL, Morrow Papers 10:5:114.
41. Burke, Interview with Olds, 15 March 1928, ACUA, USCCB 10:145: Interview Book I; Burke, Memorandum, [16 March 1928], ibid., 10:150:35; Olds to Morrow, 9 March 1928, ASCACL, Morrow Papers 10:5:114; Morrow to Olds, telegram, 13 March 1928, ibid.; Redinger, *American Catholics and the Mexican Revolution*, 80.
42. [Burke, Interview with Olds], 23 March 1928, ACUA, USCCB 10:145: Interview Book I; Morrow to Olds, 16 March 1928, ASCACL, Morrow Papers 10:5:114.

43. [Burke, Interview with Lippman], 24 March 1928, ACUA, USCCB 10:145: Interview Book I; Sheerin, *Never Look Back*, 122–23.
44. [Burke, Interviews with Olds], 26 March 1928, ACUA, USCCB 10:145: Interview Book I; [Burke, Memorandum,] 19 May 1928, ibid., 10:145: Interview Book II.
45. [Burke, Interviews with Olds], 27 and 28 March 1928, ACUA, USCCB 10:145: Interview Book I; Morrow to Olds, telegram, 27 March 1928, ASCACL, Morrow Papers 10:5:114.
46. Burke to P. Elías Calles, 29 March 1928, addendum to [Burke], First Interview with President Calles, April 1928, ACUA, USCCB 10:145: Interview Book II; Rice, *Diplomatic Relations*, 202–03. See also Bailey, *¡Viva Cristo Rey!*, 192–94; Quirk, *Mexican Revolution*, 222; Ellis, "Dwight Morrow," 487; Sheerin, *Never Look Back*, 125–26.
47. [Burke], First Interview with President Calles, April 1928, ACUA, USCCB 10:145: Interview Book II; Burke to T. Burke, 30 May 1928, AP, Burke Papers, box 3; Sheerin, *Never Look Back*, 126.
48. [Burke], First Interview with President Calles, April 1928, ACUA, USCCB 10:145: Interview Book II; Redinger, *American Catholics and the Mexican Revolution*, 81–82 (containing his account of the interview); Sheerin, *Never Look Back*, 126–27 (containing his account of the interview).
49. [Burke], First Interview with President Calles, April 1928, ACUA, USCCB 10:145: Interview Book II; Conference among Burke, Montavon, Clark, and Lane, 12 October 1928, ASCACL, Morrow Papers 10:5:117 (last quote is from here).
50. [Burke], First Interview with President Calles, April 1928, ACUA, USCCB 10:145: Interview Book II; Conference among Burke, Montavon, Clark, and Lane, 12 October 1928, ASCACL, Morrow Papers 10:5:117 (opening quote is here).
51. [Burke], First Interview with President Calles, April 1928, ACUA, USCCB 10:145: Interview Book II; P. Elías Calles to Burke, 4 April 1928, addendum to the interview.
52. [Burke], First Interview with President Calles, April 1928, ACUA, USCCB 10:145: Interview Book II.53. Ibid.; Burke to T. Burke, 30 May 1928, AP, Burke Papers, box 3; Burke to Lynch, 19 April 1928, ibid., box 5; Olds to Morrow, 25 April 1928, ASCACL, Morrow Papers 10:3:119.
54. Burke to Lynch, 19 April 1928, AP, Burke Papers, box 5; Burke to T. Burke, 30 May 1928, ibid., box 3.
55. Burke to T. Burke, 30 May 1928, AP, Burke Papers, box 3; Burke to Hanna, 30 May 1928, AASF, NCWC files; Bailey, *¡Viva Cristo Rey!*, 199–200; Redinger, *American Catholics and the Mexican Revolution*, 83; Rice, *Diplomatic Relations*, 129.
56. Burke to Calles, 8 May 1928, ASCACL, Morrow Papers 10:3:96; Olds to

Morrow, 9 May 1928, ibid., 10:5:16; Burke, Interview with Olds, 10 May 1928, ACUA, USCCB 10:145: Interview Book II; Burke to T. Burke, 30 May 1928, AP, Burke Papers, box 3; Bailey, *¡Viva Cristo Rey!*, 200–01; Quirk, *Mexican Revolution*, 228; Ellis, "Dwight Morrow," 490-91; Rice, *Diplomatic Relations*, 129–30.

57. [Burke, Memorandum on Trip to Mexico], 12 May 1928, ACUA, USCCB 10:145: Interview Book II; Sheerin, *Never Look Back*, 128.
58. J. H. Ryan, Interview with Olds, 16 May 1928, USCCB 10:145: Interview Book II.
59. [Burke], Second Interview with President Calles at Chapultapec Palace, 17 May 1928, ACUA, USCCB 10:145: Interview Book II.
60. Ibid.; Redinger, *American Catholics and the Mexican Revolution*, 83–84 (containing his account of the interview); Sheerin, *Never Look Back*, 129 (containing his account of the interview).
61. [Burke], Second Interview with President Calles at Chapultapec Palace, 17 May 1928, ACUA, USCCB 10:145: Interview Book II.
62. Ibid. (quote is here); Summarized Report from Archbishop Leopoldo Ruiz and Rev. John J. Burke, C.S.P., 22 May 1928, copy, ACUA, USCCB 10:145: Interview Book II; Burke to T. Burke, 30 May 1928, AP, Burke Papers, box 3.
63. Morrow to Olds, telegram, 17 May 1928, ASCACL, Morrow Papers 10:5:116; [Burke], Memorandum, 17 May 1928, ACUA, USCCB 10:145: Interview Book II; J. H. Ryan, Memorandum, 17 May 1928, ibid.; Burke to Hanna, 26 June 1928, AASF, NCWC files; Sheerin, *Never Look Back*, 129–30.
64. J. H. Ryan, Memorandum, 17 May 1928, ACUA, USCCB 10:145: Interview Book II.
65. J. H. Ryan, Memoranda, 18 May 1928, two of same date, ACUA, USCCB 10:145: Interview Book II; J. H. Ryan, Memorandum, 20 May 1928, ibid.; Sheerin, *Never Look Back*, 130.
66. J. H. Ryan, Memoranda, 18 May 1928, two of same date, ACUA, USCCB 10:145: Interview Book II.
67. [Burke, Memorandum], 19 May 1928, ACUA, USCCB 10:145: Interview Book II.
68. Ibid.; Burke to Calles, 19 May 1928, ASCACL, Morrow Papers 10:5:116.
69. [Burke, Interview with Fumasoni-Biondi and Marella], 13 June 1928, ACUA, USCCB 10:145: Interview Book II; [Burke, Interview with Morrow and Olds], 13 June 1928, ibid.; [Burke, Interview with Fumasoni-Biondi], 3 August 1928, ibid. (quotes are here); Burke to Hanna, 26 June 1928, AASF, NCWC files; New York *World*, 7 June 1928; Quirk, *Mexican Revolution*, 230–32; Ellis, "Dwight Morrow," 492; Rice, *Diplomatic Relations*, 133–35; Redinger, *American Catholics and the Mexican Revolution*, 84–85.

70. [Burke, Interview with Fumasoni-Biondi and Marella], 13 June 1928, ACUA, USCCB 10:145: Interview Book II; Burke, [Interview with Morrow and Olds], 13 June 1928, ibid.; Sheerin, *Never Look Back*, 131.
71. [Burke, Interview with Fumasoni-Biondi and Marella], 13 June 1928, ACUA, USCCB 10:145: Interview Book II; [Burke, Interview with Morrow and Olds], 13 June 1928 (second of this date), ibid.
72. [Burke, Interview with Fumasoni-Biondi and Marella], 18 June 1928, ACUA, USCCB 10:145: Interview Book II.
73. Burke, [Interview with Morrow and Olds], 27 June 1928, ACUA, USCCB 10:145: Interview Book II; Burke, Memorandum, 27 June 1928, ibid.
74. [Burke, Interview with Fumasoni-Biondi and Marella], 28 June 1928, ACUA, USCCB 10:145: Interview Book II; Burke, [Interview with Fumasoni-Biondi, Morrow, and Olds], 29 June 1928, ibid.; Morrow to Burke, 16 July 1928, copy, ibid.; Burke to Morrow, 29 June 1929, copy, ibid., 10:150:35.
75. Burke, Journal for 17–19 July 1928, ACUA, USCCB 10:145: Interview Book II; Bailey, *¡Viva Cristo Rey*, 216–18; Quirk, *Mexican Revolution*, 232–34.
76. Burke, Memorandum, with attachment, 19 July 1928, ACUA, USCCB 10:145: Interview Book II.
77. Burke, [Interview with Lane], 19 July 1928, ACUA, USCCB 10:145: Interview Book II (all but last quote are here); Lane to Morrow, 25 July 1928, ASCACL, Morrow Papers 10:5:116 (last quote is here).
78. Burke, [Interview with Lane, Montavon, and B. Smithers], 21 July 1928, ACUA, USCCB 10:145: Interview Book II; William R. Castle Jr., 19 July 1928, Diaries, HLHU; Morrow to Kellogg, telegram, 20 July 1928, ASCACL, Morrow Papers 10:5:124.
79. Kellogg to Morrow, telegram, 21 July 1928, ASCACL, Morrow Papers 10:5:124; Burke, [Interview with Lane, Montavon, and B. Smithers], 21 July 1928, ACUA, USCCB 10:145: Interview Book II
80. Montavon to Burke, telegram, 27 July 1928, ACUA, USCCB 10:145: Interview Book II; Burke to Montavon, telegram, 27 July 1928, ibid.; Montavon, Memorandum, 27 July 1928, ibid.; [Burke, Interview with Lane], 3 August 1928, ibid.; *New York Herald-Tribune*, 3 August 1928.
81. [Burke, Memorandum], 17 August 1928, ACUA, USCCB 10:145 Interview Book II; Minutes of the Administrative Committee, 12 November 1928, ibid., 10:64:5; [Burke, Interview with Lane], 9 August 1928, ACUA, USCCB 10:145: Interview Book II; Minutes of the Administrative Committee, 12 November 1928, ibid., 10:64:5; Burke to Lynch, 13 August 1928, AP, Burke Papers, box 5.
82. [Burke, Memoranda], 17 August 1928 (two of same date), ACUA, USCCB 10:145: Interview Book II; Minutes of the Administrative Committee, 12 November 1928, ibid., 10:64:5; Rice, *Diplomatic Relations*, 147–50, 154; Bailey, *¡Viva Cristo Rey!*, 223; Quirk, *Mexican Revolution*, 236; Sheerin, *Never Look Back*, 136–37.

83. [Burke, Interview with Fumasoni-Biondi], 3 November 1928, ACUA, USCCB 10:145: Interview Book III; Bailey, *¡Viva Cristo Rey!*, 226–27, 229–30.
84. Montavon to Burke, 20 November 1928, copy, ACUA, USCCB 10:145: Interview Book III; Leopoldo Ruiz et al. to Pius XI, 20 November 1928, copy, ibid.; Redinger, *American Catholics and the Mexican Revolution*, 86; Ellis, "Dwight Morrow," 495–96.
85. Burke to Hanna, 28 January 1929, AASF, NCWC files.
86. [Burke, Interview with Morrow, Clark, Fumasoni-Biondi, and Montavon], 15 December 1928, ACUA, USCCB 10:145: Interview Book III.
87. Ibid.; [Burke, Interview with Clarke, Montavon, and Morrow], 18 December 1928, ACUA, USCCB 10:145: Interview Book III.
88. Burke to Hanna, 28 January 1929, AASF, NCWC files, draft enclosed.

Part III
Weathered

Chapter 18
Diplomacy

> The passion of our Lord in the Garden and on Calvary was the manifestation, the climax, the fulfillment of what was in His Heart from the beginning of His earthly life. Long before the altar of the Cross was the altar of His Heart. Therein, by the love which He bore us, He constantly immolated Himself. His immolation of self was His very life. To know that He came to do the Will of His Father, that to the Father He must win back the souls of men, was in itself a suffering and a passion.[1]

Rome and Mexico

In late November1928, Archbishop Pietro Fumasoni-Biondi had invited Father John Burke to accompany him to Rome and thence to the Holy Land in late winter and early spring of the coming year. The excursion was to be Dutch treat. The estimated cost was about $2,000 apiece (equivalent to $36,000 in 2024). Lacking such funds, Burke asked bishops of the Administrative Committee to help with his expenses. Archbishop Austin Dowling sent an additional $200 as pin money.[2]

Burke was still dealing with Mexico, but another trip south seemed remote. In late January 1929, Morrow returned from Florida where he met with President-Elect Herbert Hoover. Discouraged, he told Burke "he had done all he could do." Nor would Hoover give him the leeway Calvin Coolidge had. Morrow believed the Vatican was unwilling under any circumstances or with any guarantees to negotiate with Mexico. Burke insisted "emphatically" that all that had transpired was done in honesty. Rome was justified in asking guarantees and would certainly conclude the matter once they were received. Morrow said when he returned to Mexico in February, he would size up the situation and send word about the outlook.[3]

An unexpected breakthrough came when Morrow saw Emilio Portes Gil, who said many had asked him to settle the religious conflict. He knew the current status of negotiations and asked if Burke would come down immediately to continue them. Morrow saw Elías Calles, who wanted the same. The two had reason to seek a settlement. The government launched an all-out offensive against the Cristeros in Guadalajara, which only increased resistance and necessitated a 30 percent cut in government salaries to keep forces in the field.[4]

Undersecretary of State Reuben Clark informed Burke, who was taken by surprise. Already aware of the looming Roman trip, Clark considered it of secondary importance to the present opportunity. Burke consulted Fumasoni-Biondi, who just learned Rome wanted him back in the U.S. by April, nixing a Holy Land tour. He and Burke considered cancelling their trip, but feared doing so "would look like bad temper." As for Mexico, Burke told Dowling: "I'm willing to do anything but I don't see the worthwhileness of going unless the chances are stronger than appears of doing something effective. So I'll go East, not South."[5]

He so informed Clark. Burke recommended Morrow and Portes Gil follow up on steps already taken. He suggested the latter have Alberto José Pani Arteaga, Mexican ambassador to France, join Fumasoni-Biondi and him at the Vatican to work for a settlement. Or, Portes Gil might send Cardinal Pietro Gasparri the same letter Calles had prepared to give Archbishop Leopoldo Ruiz y Flores; Gasparri could reply with the letter Ruiz had prepared for Calles. Clark told Morrow that, while Burke was cautious about all this, "I think that Father Burke feels rather hopeful that he might be able to get something through while he is in Rome."[6]

Burke took ship from New York. While there he suffered one of his old attacks: "Evidently a high fever, certainly sore body, and an annoying heart." He had no idea what brought it on. He spent the next day in bed. By day of departure, the fever had almost gone. Dr. Mohan cleared him, and his brother James drove him to the ship. The first night found him no worse. The next day he felt much better, but did not say Mass until the day after. Of course, this "squall," as Burke called it, puzzled Fumasoni-Biondi, who could not understand what was going on with an apparently healthy man. Burke explained what it was like, "but understanding it would mean experimental knowledge," he told Grace Murray.[7]

Burke prided himself on being a good sailor. "In fact," he told Dowling, "I enjoy the sea and have no desire to reach port." Heavy seas caused the ship to roll greatly. Good tar that he was, Burke suffered no seasickness. Though accommodations were "gorgeous," Burke did not care for the formal dining, seated nightly at the captain's table in a dinner jacket. He preached the first Sunday aboard about restoration of the sovereignty of the pope, that is, the creation of the Vatican City State which had just occurred. The days were lazy and passed all too fast. Fumasoni-Biondi was good company and in high spirits. The two avoided shoptalk. "In the mornings and in the evenings when the moon weaves long golden threads on the moving waters (how's that!) I think of thee and I ask our Lord to bless and keep thee," Burke wrote to Lynch.[8]

The ship made landfall at Cape St. Vincent, Portugal, and thereafter remained within sight of land until arriving at Naples. Monsignor Francis Spellman of Boston, an ambitious functionary in the Secretariat of State, and Father Peter Guilday, Church historian at Catholic University, met them and whisked them to Rome. The following day, Fumasoni-Biondi gave Burke a Vatican tour and St. Peter's Basilica impressed him mightily. The two saw Gasparri at State where Burke discovered he was quite well known. The day ended with dinner at the home of Fumasoni-Biondi's sister.[9]

Wednesday brought a new round of visiting Vatican officials. That afternoon, Fumasoni-Biondi had an audience with the pope, which went quite well. The pontiff relented on their date of return. "We will go to the Holy Land!" the delegate exclaimed to Burke. It was "the most happy audience he had ever had."[10]

On 7 March, Burke met Pius XI privately in his personal library, with Spellman as interpreter. The pope greeted him as general secretary of the NCWC and Paulist priest. He was familiar and well pleased with the work of the "monsignor"—the form of address Pius used throughout. He doubly welcomed Burke to Rome because it was his first trip to the Eternal City. "To visit Rome for a first time is like opening for the first time a very interesting book," said the bibliophile pope. "That was the impression I had when I first visited Rome."[11]

Of course, Pius directed the entire conversation. He first spoke of the persecution of the Mexican Church. That country was "in tenebris [the dark night]," he said. It was impossible to discern the outcome. Pius was aware of Burke's conversations with Calles and knew all he had done for the Church there.[12]

He turned the conversation to the recent U.S. presidential election. He had followed it through Fumasoni-Biondi, who reported on the anti-Catholic animus that characterized it.[13] The pope asked Burke's thoughts on the Church's situation in its wake. Burke said the campaign attacked Catholicism. Pius spoke of the pamphlets, sent him by the delegate, which assaulted the Church and himself. Burke averred the ones against Pius were "often obscene and indescribable." He believed the Catholic community had a difficult course ahead. There was, however, a bright spot: some 10 million non-Catholics voted for Al Smith in an election about his religion. Pius said it was worthwhile to keep that in mind. Burke added his belief that since Protestantism was a dying religion, it sought sustenance in portraying itself as the sponsor of public morals.[14]

Pius wanted a prognosis on the Church under Hoover. Burke said it was not bright. Spellman explained that Hoover failed to make the one Catholic appointment expected to his cabinet: elevation of Assistant Attorney General William Donovan to attorney general. Burke thought, given the political structure in America, the situation called for united Catholic action. Absent that, Catholic power would dissipate. Pius stressed all Catholics and Catholic organizations must work together to show a "united front," or meet failure.[15]

He then brought up Catholic University and entered a long discourse about it. It was the only pontifical university in America. It must train those who would in turn train educated leaders and workers. It should nourish Catholic intellectual life. He stressed this point. Burke took the opportunity to remark that the NCSSS was affiliated with Catholic University and educated Catholic social workers on par with the highest technical training in the field. Pius praised the school and was adamant that as people widely denied or disregarded Christian truth, it was imperative men and women, especially physicians, receive thorough Catholic training in the interpretation and application of Christian values to their professions.[16]

Given Burke's expertise in publication, Pius considered him the person to ask about the Catholic press. Burke replied its condition was good; it had vastly improved in the previous decade owing largely to the NCWC News Service, whose operation he explained. The pope discussed the importance of a strong, well informed Catholic press.[17]

A related matter was defense of the faith and spread of Catholic truth. Although it was necessary to answer objections to the faith, that was only the lesser part of the work. "Catholic truth itself had a virtue and power all its own," said Pius. "The exposition of Catholic truth: the repetition of its content over and over again should be the habit of those who would seek to have Catholic truth win its further way." This must always be done with kindness, strength, and charity, and never with bitterness. These words resonated with Burke, who already lived by them. He thanked Pius for the timely words and informed him the CPA had recently adopted the irenic St. Francis de Sales as its patron.[18]

Pius brought up the Oregon School Law. Burke explained that the Court's unanimous decision had all but written the parental right over a child's education into the Constitution. When he said he had spent two years working on the matter, the pontiff replied, "I know you did," indicating he need say no more. Pius repeated the confidence he had in him.[19]

Pius ended the audience by wishing Burke well on the Holy Land tour. Burke had bought inexpensive rosaries and crucifixes as gifts and asked Pius to bless them. He had given them to Spellman for of fear dropping them in the pope's presence. Pius took one and examined it. As Burke noted, he "didn't seem to think much of them." He then blessed Burke's intentions and the man himself. The audience was his "most joyous and grateful memory of Rome."[20]

Burke and Fumasoni-Biondi left for Naples where they took ship for Alexandria, arriving three days later. They spent a day and a half in Cairo before boarding the train to Jerusalem. After debarking, the two found lodgings and went immediately to see Calvary, the Holy Sepulcher, and the Garden of Gethsemane. Next day, Palm Sunday, they returned to the garden, where the delegate said Mass in the chapel, after which Burke prayed divine office at the rock where Jesus prayed after the Last Supper. That afternoon, they visited the Sepulcher again. Burke entered and prayed for his deceased loved ones and his living friends that all "might know now and forever the risen life."[21]

On Monday, Burke said Mass at the Sepulcher. Afterward they drove down to the Dead Sea by way of Bethany and then up to Jericho and back around to Jerusalem. For two days, they toured the city some more. Burked climbed the Mount of Olives to view Jerusalem across the valley. He and the delegate saw the judgment seat of Pilate, the house of the visitation, and the Cenacle, site of the Last Supper. They could not enter into the Cenacle because Muslims controlled it. Although the latter permitted neither kneeling nor crossing oneself, "I prayed for you in a special way," Burke wrote to Lynch, "and for all the [St. Regis] Cenacle and its great work." Burke suffered another "squall," lasting through Holy Thursday and half of Good Friday. He fibbed to Murray, telling her, "All goes well: but it is very strenuous, if it is wonderful." More honestly, he confided to Lynch, "I have been well except once—but say nothing of it."[22]

Burke celebrated Easter by saying Mass at the Sepulcher. The next morning, he and the delegate traveled to Bethlehem where Burke offered Mass at the place of Jesus' birth. The following day, they left for Galilee and Nazareth to spend their final time there.[23]

After arrival, they ate supper and Burke went into the night. "I look out upon the stars of Nazareth," he wrote in his diary. "Mary looked upon the same and treasured the secrets of God in her heart. I think of His secrets to me and to Mary I speak of those I love." In the morning, he said Mass at the shrine of the Annunciation. After breakfast, he and the delegate headed to the Sea of Galilee. Stopping at Cana, Burke viewed the sea for the first time from the hills. "Farther shore looked a bit like Palisades of the Hudson," commented Burke. At Tiberias, they lunched. "Another heavy dinner. Ate some fish from the lake. Too much wine offered," he wrote. Afterward, they drove around the north end of the sea to Capernaum and then back to Nazareth.[24]

The next day, they departed for Haifa with a detour to Mount Tabor, where Christian tradition placed the Transfiguration of Jesus. The road to the top was quite treacherous. Fumasoni-Biondi said Mass in the church with Burke in attendance. In 67 A.D., more than thirty years after the Transfiguration, Jewish historian Josephus had built a walled fortress on the mountain during the rebellion against Rome, and his people made a valiant but unsuccessful stand there. While atop the mount, Burke penned a brief poem, which borrowed from *Macbeth* and tied together those two events: "Upon the fortress high in air / Where armies fought and lost and won / He stood erect in faithful prayer / Vested with glory like the sun." Because the trip up was so frightening, the delegate chose to walk back down. Thence, they drove to Mount Carmel and Haifa, ending their Holy Land tour.[25]

The trip back to Rome was circuitous and included a tour of Italy. They left Haifa by train for Cairo, thence to Alexandria where they took ship to Venice. They spent a week seeing the sites of Venice, Padua, Bologna, and Assisi. When they reached Rome on 16 April, the Mexican situation greeted them.[26]

In March, matters had worsened with outbreak of a fresh rebellion in the North under General José Gonzalo Escobar, an Obregonista. When the government shifted 35,000 crack troops from Guadalajara to face the new threat, the Cristeros launched a successful counteroffensive against the auxiliary forces remaining behind. Rather than link the Escobar revolt with the Cristeros, Portes Gill maintained an open stance toward the Church. After a conference with him on 19 March, Morrow sent a memorandum to William Montavon for transmittal to Burke in Rome. He reported Portes Gil was willing to pursue a settlement based on the Burke-Calles letters. Morrow had heard from Agustín Legorreta, president of Banco Nacional in Mexico City, and Sir Esmond Ovey, British ambassador to that country, that Gasparri would "warmly welcome" a Mexican envoy, though Morrow himself gravely doubted Portes Gil would send anyone. He proposed three avenues of approach: (a) Mexico send an envoy to the Vatican to negotiate; (b) the Vatican send an envoy to Mexico to negotiate; (c) Gasparri, in consultation with Burke, establish terms of a settlement in a letter to the Mexican foreign minister for acceptance by the government.[27]

In early April, Morrow received letters threatening his assassination. The U.S. government conducted an investigation that deemed the threats "serious" and reported they came from Catholic elements. Clark asked Montavon to have Church authorities condemn the action. Montavon arranged for Archbishop Ruiz and Bishop Pascual Díaz y Barreto to telegram Bishop Antonio Guizar y Valencia of Chihuahua "to declare in whatever way you can that plots of this kind are absolutely condemned by Christian morality." Both Clark and Arthur Lane considered the message inadequate. They sent a copy to Ambassador Henry Fletcher in Rome and suggested he speak with Burke about securing a stronger denunciation.[28]

Fletcher and Burke discussed the matter. Fletcher wired to State that Burke assured him Fumasoni-Biondi would cable Ruiz to broaden the denunciation and include an expression of thanks to Morrow for all he was doing on behalf of the Church. In fact, Burke cabled Montavon to ask if the situation demanded such a statement and from whom should it come. Montavon advised Fumasoni-Biondi should issue one without specific reference to plots against Morrow. State had not made the threats public, and in his view it was not the Church's role to do so. The message should express appreciation to Morrow. In the end, Burke and Fumasoni-Biondi decided against doing anything.[29]

With regard to Morrow's memorandum about restarting negotiations, Burke replied Rome was rife with good feeling and sincerity about a settlement. The Vatican wanted to pursue option "a": negotiations in Rome with a duly accredited envoy from Mexico, preferably Legorreta, who visited Gasparri in September 1928 and found Vatican authorities willing to negotiate personally and informally with a well disposed envoy. There should be no publicity on either side. If Portes Gil followed through, prospects were bright. Montavon relayed the message to Clark, who forwarded it to Morrow.[30]

In fact, Gasparri's willingness to negotiate was questionable. Walter Lippmann was in Rome the same time as Burke. After interviewing Gasparri, he reported to Morrow, "I got no further than being compelled to listen to a long and bitter harangue, in bad French, against our government for its favoritism to the enemies of the Church." Gasparri was concerned about the arms embargo against Cristeros. When Lippmann asked if it should be lifted, the cardinal was evasive. "But everything else he said, in manner and in substance," wrote Lippmann, "amounted to saying that he wanted to see the rebels armed and to have them overthrow the present government."[31] As it turned out, Morrow's option "b" was the one that would be followed.

On 23 April, Burke departed Rome for Paris where he was to meet his niece Elizabeth Salmon, a student at the University of Louvain. The two went to Lourdes, where they joined Fumasoni-Biondi and his sister. After two days, they returned to Paris, and Burke came down with another "squall," which laid him up for a night and day. On 8 May, he headed home.[32]

Burke reached the U.S. on 15 May 1929. "That trip certainly ironed some of the wrinkles out of your face," commented his sister, Mary. "I hope you feel the benefits of it for many days to come." Unfortunately, that was not to be. Burke contracted a cold just days before reaching port. Back in Washington, he learned the Vatican had appointed Archbishop Ruiz apostolic delegate to Mexico.[33]

A couple of days later, Clark summoned Burke to State to brief him on Mexico. Portes Gil publicly disclaimed the Church was linked to the Escobar rebellion. Furthermore, he said the government would never persecute any religion; Catholic clergy were free to resume worship whenever they wished, provided they respected the law. Ruiz sent word that men of good will, among whom he counted Portes Gil, could resolve the Church-state conflict. Ruiz asked him to reconsider the offensive legislation, and Portes Gil offered to discuss it. After briefing Burke, Clark phoned Morrow in Mexico City so he and Burke could speak directly. Morrow wanted Ruiz authorized to take immediate action. Given recent expressions of good will, Morrow recommended Ruiz write Portes Gil that the bishops would resume public worship if he issued a declaration offering the guarantees Calles made the previous June. Morrow said while Burke was away, Pius sent Father Edmund Walsh to Mexico to investigate the situation. Walsh's report echoed Morrow's recommendation. Legorreta too urged the Vatican to strike while the iron was hot. Burke said he would take the matter up with Ruiz.[34]

Legorreta informed Ruiz that Portes Gil welcomed his appointment as apostolic delegate and instructed Ambassador Manuel Télles to issue the necessary passport. The president would meet with Ruiz on 10 June. Apprising Burke, Ruiz asked him to have the American government send word south to emphasize the necessity of a just settlement. Ruiz said he would depart in early June and take Bishop Díaz with him.[35]

Burke went to see Dr. Marbury to get medicine for the persistent cold he was suffering. "He told me the cold was not much," Burke wrote Lynch, "but the heart muscle, whatever that is, had been overstrained and that I must rest it." Burke sought a second opinion with the same result. Marbury ordered him to bed where he was to lie quietly. He was not to say Mass, but was allowed to direct NCWC business.[36]

Burke was down only a couple days when he violated doctor's orders to host an important meeting about Mexico. Morrow was back for vacation and wanted to meet with Ruiz. In late May, Burke, Montavon, Ruiz, Morrow, and Lane gathered at the NCWC residence. Morrow briefly summarized events since Burke and Ruiz met with Calles. All parties in Mexico wanted a settlement, even the few Mexican bishops who previously opposed one. Morrow told Ruiz his upcoming meeting with Portes Gil afforded opportunity "to do for Mexico what has been needed for one hundred years."[37]

Ruiz said he had instructions from the Vatican. He was to ask Portes Gil for a "definite, explicit promise" to change Article 130 of the constitution because it denied corporate existence to the Church. The government must also agree to future conferences to entertain further changes to law and constitution. Unless a promise was forthcoming, Pius XI would not consent to the bishops' return. Morrow said to insist that Mexico repudiate its own constitution would not only endanger, but "kill the present opportunity." Mexico was approaching a political campaign. To make such a demand would throw the religious question into politics. Morrow believed it better to build on the present good will which would lead to an even better spirit and an ultimate willingness to adopt a constitutional adjustment that would do justice to the Church. "I would not be fair to you or to the Church if I did not tell you my judgment," Morrow told Ruiz. "I may be wrong: I hope I am. But in my judgment, if you insist upon this demand, if such are your orders, it would be better for you and the Church that you never go down on this trip. And as for me, I would much prefer to be in the Maine woods." Ruiz relented, agreeing to ask only for a promise that consideration be given to changing the constitution.[38]

The five discussed the letters exchanged between Burke and Calles and also one Ruiz would write. Morrow insisted if Ruiz went south without a well thought out plan, it would be a serious mistake. Burke noted Morrow politely but definitely and repeatedly asked Ruiz if he would like his company and assistance. "Not once did Ruiz express the wish that Morrow be there and give his help," commented Burke.[39]

Two days later, Morrow and Lane showed up unannounced in Burke's bedroom. "Under great stress and anxiety," Morrow said he was going back to Mexico. He hoped Ruiz would succeed, but if he did not, Morrow wanted to help pick up the pieces. He asked Burke if he had spoken with Ruiz. Burke said he had and Ruiz assured he would not insist on changes to the constitution as condition for return of the bishops. Morrow was glad

Díaz was accompanying Ruiz. He considered him "a stronger man, a clearer thinker." Burke noted "there were many silent spaces during this conference" and Lane said not a word. "Worried and bewildered," Morrow finally said goodbye "with rather unusual feeling," commented Burke.[40]

It was good Morrow returned to Mexico. Ruiz and Díaz met Portes Gil on 12 June. Portes Gil was prepared to renew the assurances given Burke a year earlier. The bishops accepted that as a basis, and both sides agreed to an exchange of statements. If those were mutually acceptable, and if Rome approved, they would be released to the press. Next day, Portes Gil presented a document virtually identical to Calles's letter to Burke; the two bishops presented nothing. Instead, they turned to a discussion of the anticlerical laws. The meeting foundered, and Morrow intervened by drafting statements for both parties. In summary these said (1) the government never intended to destroy the Church's identity, (2) it would register only priests appointed by a bishop, (3) religious instruction of children could take place in a church, (4) the government would periodically confer with the principal ecclesiastic about application of religious laws, and (5) clergy had the right to apply for modification of the constitution. Ruiz sent the statement to Rome, and Portes Gil took it under advisement. Within a week both sides agreed, and the statement was issued on 21 June 1929. Nine days later Mass was celebrated and church bells rang in Mexico City for the first time in three years.[41]

The Long Rest

Not until settlement of the Mexican situation did Burke inform Archbishop Hanna of his enforced rest: "I regret to report—as the war despatches [*sic*] used to say—that I have not enjoyed full health since my return from Europe." Bedridden for four weeks, Burke celebrated his birthday and anniversary of ordination on his back. "I never expected this siege," he wrote Murray. He explained his condition to his twenty-year-old niece, Kay, who said his detailed account had convinced her that his heart was in a bad way. "If not the heart then the head," she quipped. "However, I persevere in the hope that you'll regain your sanity as the days roll on. Just at present I don't know whether it is the head or the heart that makes you as you are." With the apostolic delegation just blocks away, Fumasoni-Biondi visited Burke nearly every day.[42]

In early July, Marbury allowed him outside every other day, but not to the office. Nor would he permit Burke to say Mass because of the intensity of the experience. Bishop Joseph Schrembs gently chided Burke: "You will have to learn how to take a real rest. You start off for a rest or a vacation, but the trouble is you take your work with you." Burke replied he was much improved, "If you saw me you would say I was looking very well and that I was not sick at all." In early August, Burke told Lynch he went to the office only three times since May, and then only for an hour each. His regimen of rest, correspondence, and direction of work by phone from home occupied his time.[43]

Yet, not completely so. Divine Office, a four-week cycle of psalmody and canticles repeated throughout the year, gave Burke a deep love of the Psalms. Because they were little known to the laity of his day, and their translation was less clear than it could be, he employed spare moments to translating them into English verse. He did so even while holding the dummy hand in bridge games with housemates after supper. He found the project "very profitable … spiritually." Burke explained to Murray, "It has helped to keep my thoughts on what one might call fundamental spirituality, the basic, deep seated, primary work that the soul must do under God before it can mount." His plan was to have his poetic translation published. He sent it to Paulist Father Theodore Peterson, an eminent Semitic scholar. As Mary Hawks later noted, Burke "expected criticism to be accepted objectively, with humility and would submit his own work to one he assigned as critic." Peterson viewed his translation with a critical eye. "I must do them over," Burke told Hawks.[44]

By October 1929, Marbury permitted Burke to go into the office every other day, but had curtailed hours of work so much that Burke averred he was "positively lazy." He had to spend more time in bed than he used to, though he was no longer bedridden. He complained that he no longer visited the few people he once did, and they did not understand why. Yet, his choice was either obey the doctor or rebel. Marbury now let him say Mass two or three times a week. When the NCCW held its annual convention in Washington, Burke gave a short address, which worked his heart pretty hard, but Marbury was pleased. So were listeners. Burke overheard staff of the Social Action Department discussing his speech. Someone said, "It cost Father Burke a great deal." Another answered, "Yes: but think of what he gave to us."[45]

Haiti

In fall 1929, a confluence of negative events caused popular unrest to surface in Haiti. First, the State Department canceled elections for delegates to a National Assembly scheduled for the coming January. President Louis Borno blamed it on the plotting of opposition parties. Simultaneously, the market for coffee, mainstay of the economy, collapsed, just as the occupation's policy of new taxes went into effect. Then, Dr. George Freeman, director of the Service Technique, cut scholarship payments to students at École Centrale d'Agriculture at Damien in order to offer grants to those at the new demonstration farm-schools. On Halloween, students at the École went on strike. A week later, their fellows at the schools of law and medicine joined in sympathy. Soon students at all schools, both public and private, were in the streets. The Haitian people supported them and turned to anti-American rioting.[46]

Burke reviewed the situation for the Administrative Committee in early November, especially regarding education. He recommended a memorandum on the matter be prepared and presented to Hoover, if possible in person. The committee authorized him to do so.[47]

On 27 November, the still-convalescing Burke went to the White House to discuss Haiti with Hoover. He explained the U.S. had been there since 1915 for the avowed purpose of "betterment of the Haitian people and the training of the Haitian people to govern themselves." Yet, the U.S. had "no intelligent plans" for doing so. It had permitted no elections since 1915. Borno appointed members to the Council of State, which in turn reelected him president in 1926. "The vicious circle is obvious," noted Burke. Occupation officials did nothing to promote the Haitian educational system. They paid Haitian teachers $5 per month ($90 in 2024), while they paid Freeman $15,000 a year ($270,000) and his assistants $5,000 annually ($90,000). Similarly, nothing was done to improve the judicial system, which was corrupt because of the pittance paid judges. It was even proposed that Americans take over the judiciary. "This is a very odd way to teach the Haitians to govern themselves," remarked Burke. "I respectfully submit that the situation is very serious and that we, as a nation, ought to take the matter seriously in hand and earnestly endeavor to promote the national well-being of Haiti." Asking for a memorandum on the matter, Hoover said he intended to send a commission to Haiti and wanted Burke to recommend a Catholic for it.[48]

On 7 December, Hoover asked Congress to fund a commission to investigate and make recommendations about American policy toward Haiti. Shortly thereafter, Burke suggested the Catholic commissioner should be Dr. Charles Fenwick, professor of political science at Bryn Mawr, who had a reputation in international law.[49]

At that moment, Burke fell victim to a new health issue. An abscess had developed on his rectum which he suffered for ten days. The condition was so severe he had to undergo surgery to correct it. His housemate, Father Ray McGowan, reported Burke would be back in the office in a week, but, in fact, New Year's Day 1930 found him in bed. No doubt, his already weakened condition prolonged his recovery. He reported the surgery had laid him up "altogether for a time." He was unable to return to work until mid-January.[50]

On 9 January, Morrow, now senator-elect of New Jersey, telephoned to say Democrat James Kerney, editor of the Trenton *Times*, wanted the Catholic appointment on the commission. Morrow and his political allies supported him, and Morrow already spoke to Undersecretary of State Joseph Cotton about it. He asked Burke to endorse Kerney. Replying he would give it consideration, Burke conferred with McGowan. McGowan advised remaining neutral about any Catholic commissioner in order to be free to take exception to the commission's findings if warranted. Burke agreed.[51]

He wrote, however, to Bishop John McMahon of Trenton to inquire about Kerney. Burke said it seemed likely Kerney stood good chance of being appointed to Hoover's commission. The government would probably be asking Burke's recommendation, so he wanted McMahon's advice.[52]

Before hearing back, Monsignor Maurice Spillane, vicar general of Trenton, showed up at the NCWC residence in Washington to pressure Burke to support Kerney. The convalescing Burke told Spillane he had "no personal interest in this matter." He would not support one Catholic against another. His sole purpose was to see a Catholic serve on the commission. He considered Fenwick eminently qualified and would not withdraw his name. He would also not object if Cotton or Hoover wished to appoint Kerney, and he would so inform them. Spillane asked if he could use Burke's phone to convey this information to Senator David Baird of New Jersey. When he got Baird on the line, he said Burke had withdrawn his endorsement of Fenwick and would support Kerney. After the call, Burke objected to his use of the word "withdraw," saying he would do no such thing.[53] Two days later, McMahon informed Burke that Kerney was a close friend and supporter of the late Woodrow Wilson and was a well educated, brilliant, and universally honored Catholic.[54]

On 20 January, Burke was well enough to leave the house and meet with Cotton. He reported his interview with Hoover and recommendation of Fenwick. He explained Morrow had asked him to recommend Kerney. Burke said his sole interest was ensuring a Catholic was on the commission because Haiti was a Catholic country. The appointment of either would meet the request of the NCWC. Cotton agreed a settlement of the Haitian problem must necessarily include consideration of the Catholicism of the Haitians, though Burke found him rather uninformed about the Catholic history of the country. He noted the previous day's *Washington Post* reported a black professor at Howard University had been suggested for the commission. Burke advised "it would be a mistake to regard the Haitian problem as a racial or colored problem: that the Haitians would at once resent such an inference." Cotton agreed. He also expressed strong opposition to continuance of the military administration of Haiti; it should be supplanted by civil administration.[55]

Burke wrote Archbishop George Caruana, internuncio to Haiti, for advice that might help in directing the commissioners. Caruana gave absolutely no guidance. He told Burke he had summoned Monsignor Pietro Cogliolo, chargé d'affaires at the internunciature, to join him at his headquarters in Havana. After consulting with Cogliolo, the two concluded "there was no question pending between the internuncio and the Haitian government." Burke commented to Dowling: "Literally true, and substantially false."[56]

Burke again saw Cotton, who informed him Hoover was about to appoint the commission. Kerney's selection was certain, and a second Catholic was to be named at the urging of Senator Felix Hébert of Rhode Island, who recommended appointment of Élie Vézina, a French-Canadian from his state who was a Francophone. "At once I thought of possible complications with the Canadian French trouble in Providence," Burke noted in a memorandum. He was concerned Vézina might be involved in the *Sentinelle* affair, a highly publicized display of Catholic resistance in Woonsocket, Rhode Island, aimed at maintaining traditional French-Canadian culture against seeming attempts by Bishop William Hickey to Americanize Francophones of his diocese. The Sentinellists were militant, even combative, taking their case to Rome, and when that failed, suing Hickey in civil court. The bishop excommunicated the leaders, suspended Sentinellist priests, and refused communion to Sentinellist followers. Appointment of a Catholic associated with that trouble to the commission would be unfortunate. Burke wanted to make sure Vézina had nothing to do with it. He thought Hébert would have been careful to select someone unconnected, but he needed certainty. Cotton said he would check with the senator.[57]

Thinking "no delay should be had on the matter," Burke told Montavon to telephone Hébert. His office sent word Burke could meet him on the Senate floor. Hébert assured him Vézina was not a Sentinellist. He had been careful in that regard so as not "to bring the President into any such controversy." He was certain Vézina must be a good Catholic because the pope recently made him a Knight of St. Gregory. Burke informed Cotton he had seen Hébert and all was well. In fact, Vézina was a leader of French-Canadian moderates who opposed the Sentinellists because of their tactics. He sympathized, however, with their stance that their national culture, French language, and Catholic religion were mutually interdependent, something that would give him unique ability among commissioners to understand how those same traits were interwoven in Haiti.[58]

On 7 February, Hoover announced the membership. The chairman was W. Cameron Forbes, former governor of the Philippines and expert on colonial matters. Serving with him were Henry P. Fletcher, diplomat with ambassadorial experience; William Allen White, editor of the Emporia, Kansas, *Gazette*; Vézina, knowledgeable on Haitian affairs; and Kerney. By this time, the commission's purpose was to find a graceful way to end the American occupation.[59]

To prep Kerney, Burke sent a letter reiterating much of what he said to Hoover. He cautioned Haiti was a poor country and "certain external things" might cause Kerney "to think the Haitians an inferior and barbarous people." Burke encouraged him "to look deeper." He explained the concordat with the Vatican. Whether or not Protestants on the commission liked the fact, it was "not a matter of religious opinion; it is a matter of justice." The U.S. pledged to uphold all Haitian treaties, and the concordat was one. Burke told Kerney military rule must be lifted. He argued education ought to be developed by Haitians, not the occupier. He asked Kerney to compare salaries of those in the Service Technique with those in the Haitian school system, which included Catholic schools. He should keep in mind salaries of both came from the Haitian treasury. Similarly, Burke spoke personally with Vézina to emphasize the government's obligation to honor the concordat. He had further data about Haiti sent to both before departure.[60]

McGowan recommended Burke send Montavon with the commission to help matters along. He had considerable foreign experience and could assist the Bretton bishops to interface effectively with the American commissioners. This was imperative because the Haitian hierarchy still thought the commission was simply to investigate the situation with a view to continued occupation. They had already met and agreed that, if called upon to testify, they would tell the commission the occupation gave no offense to the clergy, though certain adjustments needed to be made for enforcement of the concordat. The bishops needed to know the commission's new aim of finding a graceful way to end occupation. Burke felt the time was right for them to take a definite stand with Haitians against it. Fearful for some time that American officials might be reading communications between him and Haitian bishops, Burke agreed it was best to send Montavon, who could communicate viva voce with them. He appointed him as NCWC news representative in the small press corps authorized to travel with the commission. He thoroughly briefed and instructed his "reporter," whose primary task was to serve as advisor to the Haitian hierarchy and help it with the commission. Burke understood Montavon would have to exercise independent judgment on the scene.[61]

The commission and the little press corps sailed for Haiti in late February 1930. While at sea, commissioners read the material Burke provided the two Catholics. Montavon reported to Burke that the two newspaper men, Kerney and William Allen White, had partially won over Henry Fletcher "to their liberal, anti-imperialist position." Montavon found Cameron Forbes taciturn and inscrutable. The ship docked on Friday, 28 February, greeted by 6,000 well-wishers carrying placards denouncing the occupation.[62]

Immediately after debarkation, a delegation of Haitian journalists demanded the commission pledge to recommend restoration of self-government. The commission contacted Washington and awaited reply. The situation was tense through Saturday night. Commissioners won themselves goodwill on Sunday as Montavon, White, and Vézina participated in a prayer service and march organized by Haitian nationalists. When the procession reached commission headquarters, White brought cheers by blowing a kiss to an elderly black woman. As Montavon told Burke: "No speech making, no violence, no disorder, perfect discipline."[63]

Five days of anti-American testimony to the commission reinforced Haitian resentment. Montavon reported to Burke the inhabitants of the capital unanimously agreed Americans should leave. "I feel that the people of Port-au-Prince are in a dangerous mood," he explained. "Unless something is done quickly to relieve this situation there will be trouble." In his view, a provisional government should be formed to organize elections for representatives to a National Assembly "left wholly to the Haitians." The Assembly could reestablish constitutional government and elect a president; the U.S. should then reestablish normal diplomatic relations with Haiti. Montavon told Burke he was already helpful to the commission. Moreover, both he and Joseph-Marie Le Gouaze, coadjutor archbishop of Port-au-Prince, thought the hierarchy should stand with Haitians and distance itself from Borno and the occupation. Le Gouaze was deeply grateful to Burke for sending Montavon because of his thorough understanding of Haitian problems, "his very judicious counsels," and "the bond he has established between us and the members of the Commission."[64]

On 6 March, Archbishop Julien Conan of Port-au-Prince, following advice of Montavon and Le Gouaze, proclaimed his solidarity with Haitians. He read a statement to the commission declaring he and his clergy rejoiced that Hoover sent it to investigate "the present painful situation of Haiti and to recommend the means of bringing it to an end." Rightly proud of its independence, Haiti had suffered loss of it since 1915. Though foreigners, the clergy took "the greatest interest in the well-being of the country" and shared "its joys and its sorrows." They would sing solemn thanks to God at the occupation's end. Until then, they were one with Haitians in "their sufferings, their complaints, and their hopes." Every paper in Port-au-Prince carried the statement, which got favorable comment from nationalist journals around the country.[65] Burke was pleased Montavon encouraged the bishops in this matter. "It was the right line to pursue," he told him, "and I am very glad the Bishops did issue the statement."[66]

The commission concluded that Haiti should establish a provisional government, followed by elections to the National Assembly, and erect a formal government. It sent the recommendation in a wireless communique to Hoover. According to the commission's plan, the nationalist opposition would nominate Eugène Roy to succeed Borno. In April, the Council of State would elect Roy, who, after taking office in May, would call for elections to the National Assembly. The Assembly would elect a president to replace Roy and serve a full term. Borno agreed to the plan. Montavon cabled Burke to see officials in Washington, no doubt those at State and perhaps Hoover himself, to win support for it. Burke did and reported officials thought the commission was on the right track, though seemed to be acting "very quickly." "However, they say here they will support the action of the Commission." Hoover communicated his approval on 9 March.[67]

On that day, commissioners began a tour into the interior. Receiving word of Hoover's approval when they reached Hinche, they issued a formal announcement of the plan. Next morning, the devious Borno telegraphed a circular to all district prefects denying he made any agreement with the commission and insisting that whatever might be done must accord with the Haitian constitution. A nationalist leader telephoned this news to Vézina. Montavon translated the circular for the commissioners. They conferred by phone with James Dunn, their legal counsel in Port-au-Prince, and instructed High Commissioner John Russell to secure Borno's formal agreement. Not only did Borno refuse, he argued in the press the plan violated the constitution, which in fact it did. As Montavon explained it to Burke, Borno, perhaps in collusion with Russell, had gone along with the commission's plan so he could portray himself to the people as defender of the constitution against Hoover and the commission. Borno's action simply aggravated the unrest.[68]

At Cap Haïtien, the commission found nationalism even stronger than in Port-au-Prince. On behalf of the Catholics there, Bishop Jean-Marie Jan declared that, though he appreciated the good done by the U.S., his pastoral duty demanded he take the part of his unfortunate flock. "I cannot remain deaf to the voice of all the people who cry out their misery and sorrows," he said. "I cannot but take part in their sufferings, I cannot but sympathize with their just aspirations."[69] Borno was furious with the both Jan and Conan for their statements to the commission and declared if Monsignor Cogliolo were in the country he would have denounced the two for meddling in politics. The crafty Caruana, however, had outmaneuvered the president.[70]

When the commission returned to Port-au-Prince, it found itself at an impasse with Borno, who refused to budge. The day before the commission's departure, Montavon telegraphed Burke, "My chief here suggests you encourage highest authority there" to authorize immediate elimination of the Council of State and call elections as the "only means [to] avoid dangerous developments." The vague wording owed to Burke's fear the U.S. administration in Haiti was reading communications between the NCWC and the bishops. It seems either Forbes or possibly Archbishop Conan wanted Burke to see Hoover. Whether or not he did so is unknown. The situation in Haiti, however, was perilous. Montavon reported people there felt deceived, with the commission promising one thing and Borno upholding another. On the day of departure, "there was an ominous lack of any manifestation of any kind," Montavon told Burke. While thousands had come to welcome them, "not ten came to the wharf to wish them bon voyage." The State Department informed Borno the U.S. would offer him no military protection if he failed to follow the commission's plan.[71]

Montavon assured Burke that Kerney, Vézina, and White would vote as a bloc, and Fletcher would support them "against his will." In fact, those three hand-delivered to Burke the conclusions of the commission's report. It recommended Hoover recognize the provisional president of Haiti when elected, "provided the election is in accordance with the agreement reached by your Commission with President Borno and the leaders representing the opposition." When a new national legislature formally elected a president to a full term, the U.S. should recognize his government unless there was electoral fraud. Hoover should provide "for an increasingly rapid Haitianization of the services" carried out by the occupation. The U.S. ought to limit its involvement in Haiti strictly to matters included in the 1915 treaty (which excluded education). In selecting new American officials to be sent to Haiti, "the utmost care [should] be taken that only those free from strong racial antipathies should be preferred." The office of High

Commissioner should be abolished when the new government was in place, and a diplomatic minister should be sent to Haiti to replace Russell, assuming his duties and those of ambassador. The commission, however, considered immediate withdrawal of the Marines "inadvisable" and recommended a gradual process, mutually agreed upon. Burke praised the work of Montavon, Kerney, and Vézina, and told Helen Lynch, "This is an excellent step for the country and for the Church, and will probably save religious education in Haiti." On 28 March, Hoover announced his adoption of the commission's recommendations.[72]

Events proceeded apace. In April, the Haitian Council of State elected Roy temporary president. Two months later, he announced elections for delegates to the National Assembly to be held in October 1930.[73] Meanwhile, in July 1930, the State Department appointed Dana Munro new American minister to Haiti who would assume supervision of treaty officials. Two months later he and Burke had a long interview about the Church there. Burke explained that the papal internuncio was Vatican ambassador and stressed that education was the most important issue and the U.S. must honor both the Haitian constitution and the concordat.[74]

Endnotes to Chapter 18

1. Burke, *Christ in Us*, 45.
2. Burke to J. Murray, 27 November 1928, copy, ACUA, USCCB 10:152:31; Burke to J. Murray, 13 December 1928, copy, ibid.; Dowling to Burke, 4 and 5 February 1929, ibid., 10:152:9 (quote is from the letter of the second date); Burke to Dowling, 6 February 1929, copy, ibid.
3. [Burke, Interview with Clark, Morrow, and Montavon, 18 December 1928, ACUA, USCCB 10:145: Interview Book III; Burke to Hanna, 28 January 1929, AASF, NCWC files.
4. [Burke, Interview with Clark], 13 February 1929, ACUA, USCCB 10:145: Interview Book III; J. Meyer, *Cristero Rebellion*, 55–56; Bailey, *¡Viva Cristo Rey!*, 246; Sheerin, *Never Look Back*, 143.
5. [Burke, Interview with Clark], 13 February 1929, ACUA, USCCB 10:145: Interview Book III; Burke to Dowling, 15 February 1929, copy, ibid., 10:152:9.
6. [Burke, Interview with Clark], 15 February 1929, ACUA, USCCB 10:145: Interview Book III; Burke to Morrow, 15 February 1929, ASCACL, Morrow Papers 10:5:119; Clark to Morrow, 16 February 1929, ibid., 10:1:111.

7. Burke, Diary of Journey of 1929, Undated [18 through 22 February 1929], AP, Burke Papers, box 72; Burke to G. Murray, 3 March 1929, ibid., box 12.
8. Burke to Dowling, 16 February 1929, copy, ACUA, USCCB 10:152:9; Burke to Lynch, 28 February 1929, AP, Burke Papers, box 5; Peter R. d'Agostino, *Rome in America: Transnational Catholic Ideology from the Risorgimento to Fascism* (Chapel Hill: University of North Carolina Press, 2004), 197–206; Castagna, *Bridge Across the Ocean*, 109–11.
9. Burke, Diary of Journey of 1929, Second Monday [4 March 1929] and Tuesday [5 March], AP, Burke Papers, box 72; Burke to Lynch, 17 March 1929, ibid., box 5.
10. Burke, Diary of Journey of 1929, Wednesday [7 March 1929], AP, Burke Papers, box 72; Burke to Lynch, 17 March 1929, ibid., box 5.
11. Burke, Interview with Pius XI, 7 March 1929, ACUA, USCCB 10:153: Interview Book; Gerald P. Fogarty, S.J., "Francis J. Spellman: American and Roman," in Gerald P. Fogarty, ed., *Patterns of Episcopal Leadership* (New York: Macmillan Publishing Company, 1989), 216–18; John Cooney, *The American Pope: The Life and Times of Francis Cardinal Spellman* (New York: Times Books, 1984), 12–55.
12. Burke, Interview with Pius XI, 7 March 1929, ACUA, USCCB 10:153: Interview Book.
13. Report of the Apostolic Delegate to Cardinal Gasparri, 26 November 1928, full text in Massimo Faggioli, "The 1928 Presidential Campaign: Toward a Transatlantic and Institutional Approach to Catholic Histories," *American Catholic Studies* 126 (Summer 2015): 13 n. 28 and 15; Castagna, *Bridge across the Ocean*, 108, 109–12.
14. Burke, Interview with Pius XI, 7 March 1929, ACUA, USCCB 10:153: Interview Book; Faggioli, "1928 Presidential Campaign," 10–14.
15. Burke, Interview with Pius XI, 7 March 1929, ACUA, USCCB 10:153: Interview Book.
16. Ibid.
17. Ibid.
18. Ibid.
19. Ibid.
20. Ibid.; Burke to Lynch, 17 March 1929, AP, Burke Papers, box 5.
21. Burke, Diary of Journey of 1929, Friday through Sunday a week later [17 through 24 March 1929], AP, Burke Papers, box 72.
22. Ibid., Monday through Friday [25 through 29 March 1929]; Burke to G. Murray, Good Friday [29 March 1929], AP, Burke Papers, box 12; Burke to Lynch, Holy Saturday [30 March] 1929, ibid., box 5.
23. Burke, Diary of Journey of 1929, Easter through Tuesday [31 March] through Tuesday [2 April 1929], AP, Burke Papers, box 72.
24. Ibid., Tuesday and Wednesday [2 and 3 April 1929].

25. Ibid., Wednesday [3 April 1929].
26. Ibid., Friday through Tuesday a week later [5 through 16 May 1929]; H. H. Ben-Sasson, ed., *A History of the Jewish People*, trans. by George Weidenfeld and Nicholson Ltd. (Tel Aviv: Dvir Publishing House, 1969), 300–01.
27. Morrow to Clark, 19 March 1929, ASCACL, Morrow Papers 10:1:111; [Morrow], Memorandum for Mr. William F. Montavon, 19 March 1929, ACUA, USCCB 10:150:36; Bailey, *¡Viva Cristo Rey!*, 247; Rice, *Diplomatic Relations*, 169–71; Ellis, "Dwight Morrow," 497.
28. Montavon, Confidential Memorandum, 13 April 1929, with attachment Ruiz and Díaz to Antonio Guizar y Valencia, telegram, 12 April 1929, copy, ACUA, USCCB 10:145: Interview Book III.
29. Burke to Montavon, cable, 21 April 1929, ACUA, USCCB 10:145: Interview Book III; Montavon to Burke, cable, 22 April 1929, ibid.; Montavon, Confidential Memorandum, 20 April 1929, ibid.
30. Burke to Montavon, cables, 20 April 1929, two of same date, ACUA, USCCB 10:145: Interview Book III; Montavon to Burke, cable, 22 April 1929, ibid.; Montavon to Burke, Confidential Memorandum, 20 April 1929, ibid.; Agustín Legorreta to Luis Legorreta, 3 October 1928, enclosure with Morrow to Clark 16 October 1928, ASCACL, Morrow Papers 10:3:13; Morrow to Montavon, 1 May 1929, ibid., 10:3:96; Bailey, *¡Viva Cristo Rey!*, 247–48; Sheerin, *Never Look Back*, 145–46; Quirk, *Mexican Revolution*, 236; Ellis, "Dwight Morrow," 497; Rice, *Diplomatic Relations*, 172.
31. Lippmann to Morrow, 3 May 1929, ASCACL, Morrow Papers 10:3:20. Lippmann said the interview occurred in the third week of March.
32. Burke, Diary of Journey of 1929, Tuesday [23 April] through Wednesday two weeks later [8 May 1929], AP, Burke Papers, box 72.
33. Mary Burke to Burke, 22 May 1929, AP, Burke Papers, box 3; Burke to Hanna, 25 May 1929, AASF, NCWC files; Burke, [Interview with Clark], 21 May 1929, ACUA, USCCB 10:145: Interview Book III.
34. Burke, [Interview with Clark], 21 May 1929, ACUA, USCCB 10:145: Interview Book III; Morrow to Henry Stimson, 22 May 1929, copy, ibid.; A. Legorreta to Authorities in Rome, 9 May 1929, copy, ibid.; Redinger, *American Catholics and the Mexican Revolution*, 87–88; Ellis, "Dwight Morrow," 498–99; Gallagher, *Edmund A. Walsh*, 109–15.
35. Burke to Hanna, 25 May 1929, AASF, NCWC files.
36. Burke to Hanna, 21 June 1929, ACUA, USCCB 10:99:18.
37. [Burke, Interview with Lane, Morrow, Montavon, and Ruiz], 28 May 1929, ACUA, USCCB 10:145: Interview Book III; Redinger, *American Catholics and the Mexican Revolution*, 86–87; Reich, *Mexico's Hidden Revolution*, 20–21.
38. [Burke, Interview with Lane, Morrow, Montavon, and Ruiz], 28 May 1929, ACUA, USCCB 10:145: Interview Book III; Redinger, *American Catholics and the Mexican Revolution*, 86–87.

39. [Burke, Interview with Lane, Morrow, Montavon, and Ruiz], 28 May 1929, ACUA, USCCB 10:145: Interview Book III.
40. Burke, Interview with Morrow and Lane, Memorial Day [30 May] 1929, ACUA, USCCB 10:145: Interview Book IV.
41. Bailey, *¡Viva Cristo Rey!*, 259, 266–83; Quirk, *Mexican Revolution*, 240–45; Ellis, "Dwight Morrow," 502–03; Redinger, *American Catholics and the Mexican Revolution*, 87–88.
42. Burke to Hanna, 21 June 1929, copy, ACUA, USCCB 10:99:18; Burke to G. Murray, 24 June 1929, AP, Burke Papers, box 12; Burke to Lynch, 28 June 1929, ibid., box 5; Katherine "Kay" Salmon to Burke, 23 June 1929, ibid., box 3.
43. Burke to Lynch, 10 July 1929, AP, Burke Papers, box 5; Burke to Lynch, 10 August 1929, ibid.; Schrembs to Burke, 24 July 1929, ACUA, USCCB 10:153:8; Burke to Schrembs, 2 August 1929, copy, ibid.
44. Burke to G. Murray, 15 October 1929 and 9 February 1930, Paulist Archives, Burke Papers, box 12; Hawks, "Souvenir of Burke," 3 and 16; Malloy, "John Joseph Burke," 723; Sheerin, *Never Look Back*, 223.
45. Burke to Lynch, 10 October 1929, AP, Burke Papers, box 5.
46. Schmidt, *Occupation of Haiti*, 189–206; Trouillot, *Haiti*, 103; Pamphile, *La Croix et Le Glaive*, 137–39; Pamphile, *Clash of Cultures*, 124–34; Plummer, *Haiti and the United States*, 118–19; Arthur C. Millspaugh, *Haiti under American Control, 1915–1930* (Boston; World Peace Foundation, 1931), 176–79, 237–38.
47. Minutes of the Administrative Committee, 4 November 1929, ACUA, USCCB 10:64:5; Burke to Lynch, 28 June and 10 July 1929, AP, Burke Papers, box 5; Burke to G. Murray, 15 October 1929, ibid., box 12.
48. Burke, memorandum, 27 November 1929, ACUA, USCCB 10:39:13; Burke to Hoover, 6 November [*sic* for December] 1929, copy, with enclosure: A Short Memorandum on Haiti, ibid. (all quotes are here); Montavon, Memorandum #45, 11 January 1930, ibid.; Minutes of the Administrative Committee, 4 November 1929, ibid., 10:64:5; Schmidt, *Occupation of Haiti*, 182–83, 189–93; Pamphile, *Clash of Cultures*, 108–10. Burke was using figures from his visit to Haiti in 1924 (cf., Burke to James Kerney, 10 February 1930, copy, ACUA, USCCB 10:39:13). Pamphile indicates that in 1930 Freeman's salary was $10,000, while his assistants' were $7,000.
49. Burke to Hoover, 9 December 1929, ACUA, USCCB, 10:39:13; Schmidt, *Occupation of Haiti*, 201, 207–09; Pamphile, *Clash of Cultures*, 234–35; Pamphile, *La Croix et Le Glaive*, 139; Millspaugh, *Haiti under American Control*, 180–81, 238–39.
50. McGowan to Hanna, 17 December 1929, copy, ACUA, USCCB 10:99:18; McGowan to Conan, 14 January 1930, copy, ibid., 10:98:15; Burke to Caruana, 21 January 1930, copy, (quote is here), ibid., 10:39:13.

51. Burke, memorandum, 9 January 1930, ibid., 10:98:13; McGowan to Burke, 9 January 1930, ibid.
52. Burke to John McMahon, 9 January 1930, copy, ACUA, USCCB 10:98:13.
53. Montavon, Memorandum #45, 11 January 1930, ACUA, USCCB 10:39:13.
54. McMahon to Burke, 11 January 1930, ACUA, USCCB 10:98:13.
55. [Burke, Interview with Joseph Cotton], 20 January 1930, ACUA, USCCB 10:39:13.
56. Burke to Caruana, 21 January 1930, copy, ACUA, USCCB 10:39:13; Caruana to Burke, 6 February 1930, ibid.; Burke to Dowling, 27 March 1930, ibid., 10:152:9.
57. [Burke, Interview with Cotton], 6 February 1930, ACUA, USCCB 10:153: Interview Book; Richard S. Sorrell, "Sentinelle Affair (1924–1929)—Religion and Militant Survivance in Woonsocket, Rhode Island," *Rhode Island History* 36 (August 1977): 67–79; C. Stewart Doty, "'Monsieur Maurras est ici': French Fascism in Franco-American New England," *Journal of Contemporary History* 32 (October 1997): 534–35; Liptak, *Immigrants and Their Church*, 160–70.
58. [Burke, Interview with Cotton], 6 February 1930, ACUA, USCCB 10:153: Interview Book; Sorrell, "Sentinelle Affair," 73.
59. *Washington Post*, 8 February 1930; Montavon to Burke, Memorandum, 7 June 1930, ACUA, USCCB 10:39:20; Schmidt, *Occupation of Haiti*, 208; Pamphile, *Le Croix et Le Glaive*, 147; Pamphile, *Clash of Cultures*, 139; Millspaugh, *Haiti under American Control*, 183, 241.
60. Burke to James Kerney, 10 February 1930, copy, ACUA, USCCB 10:39:13; Burke to Caruana, 18 February 1930, copy, ibid.; Report of the General Secretary to the Administrative Committee, April 1930, ACUA, USCCB 10:62:10.
61. McGowan to Burke, 10 February 1930, ACUA, USCCB 10:98:13; Burke to J. Murray, 18 February 1930, copy, ibid.; Burke to Caruana, 18 February 1930, copy, ibid.; Conan to Burke, 7 January 1930, ibid., 10:98:15; Jules Pichon to Burke 8 January 1930, with enclosure, ibid.; Report of the General Secretary to the Administrative Committee, April 1930, ibid., 10:62:10.
62. Montavon to Burke, 3 February [*sic* for March] 1930, ACUA, 10:98:13; Report of the General Secretary to the Administrative Committee, April 1930, ACUA, USCCB 10:62:10; Schmidt, *Occupation of Haiti*, 208; Pamphile, *Clash of Cultures*, 136.
63. Quotation is from Montavon to Burke, 3 February [*sic* for March], 1930, ACUA, USCCB, 10:98:13; An Address Delivered by William F. Montavon, K.S.G., under the Auspices of the Catholic Study Club of Detroit, November 3, 1930, ASV, DAUS, V:74; Schmidt, *Occupation of Haiti*, p. 208; Pamphile, *La Croix et Le Glaive*, pp. 141–42.
64. Montavon to Burke, 5 March 1930, ACUA, USCCB 10:98:13; Joseph Le Gouaze to Burke, 3 March 1930, ACUA, USCCB 10:98:15.

65. Statement made by Archbishop Conan to the Full Forbes Commission on 6 March 1930, in French, ACUA, USCCB 10:98:13; Montavon to Press Department, cablegram, 6 March 1930, copy, ibid.; Montavon to Burke, memorandum, 21April 1930, ibid.
66. Burke to Montavon, 12 March 1930, copy, ACUA, USCCB 10:98:13.
67. Washington *Star*, 9 March 1930; Burke to Montavon, 12 March 1930, copy, ACUA, USCCB 10:98:13; Schmidt, *Occupation of Haiti*, 210–11; Millspaugh, *Haiti under American Control*, 184. Both Montavon and Burke were indefinite about whom they saw in the government because Burke suspected that U.S. officials in Haiti might be reading the correspondence among Montavon, the Haitian bishops, and himself (Report of the General Secretary to the Administrative Committee, April 1930), ACUA, USCCB 10:62:10.
68. *Washington Post*, 10 March 1930; Montavon to Burke, 16 March 1930, copy, ACUA, USCCB 10:98:13; *Constitution de 1918 de La République d'Haïti: Amendée par la Plébiscite des 10 et 11 Janvier 1928* (Port-au-Prince: Imprimerie du Service Technique, 1928), Titre III, Chapt. I, Sec. 3, Art. 42 and Sec. 5, Art. 107, and Titre VIII, Art. D; Schmidt, *Occupation of Haiti*, 211–12.
69. Montavon to NCWC Press Department, telegram, ACUA, USCCB 10:98:13; Déclaration de Monseineur Jan Évêque du Cap Haïtien a la Commission Présidentielle Amérique, 10 March 1930, ibid.
70. Conan to Burke, 16 April 1930, ACUA, USCCB 10:39:13; Caruana to Burke, 6 February 1930, ibid.; Montavon to Burke, Confidential Memorandum, 17 April 1930, ibid., 10:98:13.
71. Montavon to Burke, telegram, 15 March 1930, ACUA, USCCB 10:98:13; Montavon to Burke, 16 March 1930, ibid.; Burke, Report of the General Secretary, April 1930, ibid., 10:62:10; Schmidt, *Occupation of Haiti*, 212.
72. Montavon to Burke, 16 March 1930, ACUA, USCCB 10:98:13; Forbes Commission, Recommendations, 21 March 1930, ibid.; Burke to Lynch, 2 April 1930, AP, Burke Papers, box 5; Report of General Secretary, April 1930, ACUA, USCCB 10:62:10; Schmidt, *Occupation of Haiti*, 212–17; Pamphile, *Clash of Cultures*, 137–39; Millspaugh, *Haiti under American Control*, 184–87.
73. Montavon to Burke, Memorandum, 7 June 1930, ACUA 10:39:20; Pamphile, *Clash of Cultures*, 139.
74. [Burke, Interview with Dana Munro], 23 September 1930, ACUA, USCCB 10:39:13; Millspaugh, *Haiti under American Control*, 192.

Chapter 19
At Half Strength

> If mysticism, whatever else it may be, is at least communion and touch with God, the only true mysticism comes through the truth and faith of Jesus Christ, that faith which has been preserved for us by His own, His one Church. Outside of that faith and truth, there is no mystical life, any more than there is life without Christ. What share in His grace He grants to those who, without any fault, are outside His visible Church, no one can say. The mercies of God are uncovenanted. But in His evident and visible Providence, He has ordained but one way, and that way is Christ: and Christ is as visible today in His Church as He was when He walked upon the earth. That there are those who do not, or who will not, see and know, does not detract from the truth, nor the obligation: Christ was not less real because many who saw Him in the flesh did not or would not recognize and accept Him.... Through the Church we find Christ and through Christ are we one with God.[1]

Mexico

While dealing with Haiti, John Burke continued his efforts for Mexico—at half strength. Even though his heart was "behaving in quite a respectable manner," as he put it, Dr. Marbury kept him on a light schedule. "I am not allowed to do all I would," he wrote Grace Murray: "I suppose if I did I would have to rest again." His regimen called for morning rest and afternoon work in the office every other day. He could say Mass only two or three times a week and no more on Sundays at the NCSSS. Nor would Marbury permit him to take speaking engagements.[2]

With the settlement of 1929, cordial relations prevailed between Church and state in Mexico. In the presidential election that year, Pascual Ortiz Rubio won office. As president-elect, he paid a good-will visit to the U. S. In New York City, he told reporters the Church-state controversy was a closed issue: "As long as the Church … respects the provisions of the Constitution as it is doing now there will be no clouds in those skies." Archbishop Leopoldo Ruiz y Flores responded that success of the settlement owed to "mutual goodwill." Ortiz Rubio met in Washington with Burke, William Montavon, Dwight Morrow, and Arthur Lane. Burke explained that the modus vivendi was a welcome adjustment rather than a definitive solution of the Church-state problem. Such demanded alteration of the anticlerical articles of the constitution so that it could be itself. Ortiz Rubio wanted the same, but for the near future radicals in his party had tied his hands. If Catholics could "be patient and wait quietly," he thought after two years he could secure appropriate adjustments.[3]

Ortiz Rubio was inaugurated in February 1930, and on departure from the post-inaugural celebration, he and his wife were wounded in a failed assassination attempt. Lane telephoned Burke that rumor said the shooter was a Catholic. Certain religious articles and a Catholic prayer book were found on him. Lane said it was imperative to scotch any false impression before it spread through the country. He wanted Burke to meet with him and Cotton.[4]

When Burke told Archbishop Pietro Fumasoni-Biondi of State's anxiety at rumors of a Catholic plot, he bristled insisting the Church clearly discountenanced violence and revolution and distanced itself from the Mexican League for the Defense of Religious Liberty. Indeed, Ruiz had recently sent a confidential message in that regard to the Mexican hierarchy. Fumasoni-Biondi told Burke to give a copy to Cotton.[5]

Burke and Montavon saw Cotton and Lane. Lane thought Catholic authorities ought to issue a statement disavowing Church involvement. Burke disagreed, noting how often agitators used the cloak of religion for political purposes. The position of the Church would become weaker if every time such an outrage occurred, it denied responsibility. It would be better if Ruiz sent a message of sympathy to the injured president. Cotton agreed, averring Hoover himself had sent one. Burke said if Ruiz had not yet done so, he would ensure he did.[6]

Confirming that he had, Burke relayed word to Cotton. Next day, Lane left word for Burke that Reuben Clark, ambassador extraordinary and plenipotentiary to Mexico, saw Foreign Minister Genaro Estrada. Estrada said the government investigated the assassination attempt and concluded there was no religious motive behind it. The act was carried out by followers of José Vasconcelos, who ran against Ortiz Rubio in the fall.[7]

In April, Burke reported to the Administrative Committee that although "disquieting signs" were not absent in Mexico, "on the whole the work of the Church is going on fairly well." Ruiz just sent him a letter stating he interviewed the recovered Ortiz Rubio. "I had a very good conference with the man in question," said the archbishop, "and I confirm all your good impressions. I am hopeful."[8]

The NCCM and the "Catholic Hour"

From fall 1929 through March 1930, Burke oversaw the NCCM's launch of "The Catholic Hour." From its inception, the Men's Council had struggled to coordinate and motivate national Catholic manhood. Societies affiliated with the NCCM were, in Burke's view, fraternal in nature, serving their own members without a sense serving the common good. To Murray, he described the NCCM as "a one legged man without a crutch." "Some one must support him and help him swing his one good leg forward, if he is to make any progress," he wrote. "The weight on the assisting fellow is at times very heavy: he is tempted to throw off the cripple. But I guess it's all worth while. Some day through the miraculous favor of God and our own prayers the cripple may get two well coordinated legs, and walk manfully by himself." A halting step toward that was about to be taken as the NCCM mounted the public stage to defend the Church.[9]

Anti-Catholicism deepened through the 1920s and erupted in the 1928 presidential election. Soon thereafter, the NCCM turned to the new medium of radio communication. With the first station licensed in 1921, there were 618 throughout the nation in 1930. By that year, more than 13 million homes, over 40 percent, had a radio. At its annual convention in November 1928, the NCCM used radio for the first time in defense of Catholicism. It carried the address of Federal Judge William Cunningham who protested calumnies spread against the Church during the political campaign. The Men's Council received a number of positive responses from non-Catholics, indicating there was interest among them in learning more about the Church. So, the NCCM resolved to enter the field of apologetics.[10]

In March 1929, it established a bureau for such, which disseminated literature about the faith. It publicized and promoted the work of several local Catholic radio stations, including the Paulists' WLWL in New York City. In summer, NBC network offered the NCCM an hour gratis every Sunday. Burke considered it "an exceptional opportunity." With the approval of Bishop Joseph Schrembs, the Men's Council began preliminary work for broadcasts under two stipulations by Burke: the NCCM must interview and inform the managers of existing Catholic stations of its plan, and it must raise $50,000 ($900,000 in 2024) to defray cost of the first year's operation. The money would cover office rent at NCWC headquarters, salaries of a director and two assistants, program expenses, and stipends for speakers. In August, Charles Dolle, executive secretary of the NCCM, announced it would initiate a national radio program. At that point, NBC set down its own stipulations which would have "handicapped" airing a "full Catholic program." Broadcasts could contain no sermons, doctrinal instruction, or controversial matters. Burke told Dolle the Administrative Committee would not support "any broadcast if the talks were not to be Catholic and were not to voice Catholic principles and Catholic standards; unless we were in there as Catholics, there was no reason for our being there at all."[11]

When the NCCM informed Paulist station WLWL about the plan, Father John Harney, superior general, protested to Burke. He argued the program would "seriously injure" WLWL and may cause its demise. St. Paul the Apostle parish bore half the cost of the station; the other half was defrayed through an archdiocesan collection and a subsidy from the Catholic Missionary Union. The NCWC intended to recruit talented speakers and pay them a hefty stipend. The prestige of the NCWC would accompany its broadcast, thereby reducing the value of WLWL in the eyes of New York Catholics. The parish would either have to increase its outlay or let the station fail. Harney was sure the NCWC would "not wish to impale us on either of those horns." He believed this was "simply a clear-eyed reading" of the situation.[12]

Harney also offered a positive reason to scrap the project: "for the sake of the Church and of the Faith." The limitations NBC imposed on the broadcast robbed it of the freedom to proclaim the Catholic faith "*fully, clearly, convincingly.*" Instead, speakers would set forth "a thin, watery ... diluted and devitalized Catholicity" much like the Protestantism preached by its ministers. Harney considered the network's stipulations "a silken but a steel-strong muzzle."[13]

Burke replied the NCCM's plan placed him "in an embarrassing position." He had explained to Dolle the "pre-eminent" and pioneering effort of WLWL for the Catholic cause and encouraged him to explore having the Paulist station do a national broadcast. Burke considered Harney's objection "a very strong one" and sent copies of his letter to the Administrative Committee. Regarding restrictions imposed by NBC, Dolle protested them, and John Elwood, general manager of NBC, relaxed them. Burke spoke with Schrembs about it, and the bishop planned to go to New York to discuss matter with Cardinal Patrick Hayes. Burke asked that Harney be included in their conference.[14]

In October, Schrembs saw Hayes, who dismissed Harney's concerns and thought the NCCM should give the broadcast a try. Schrembs and Hayes's Auxiliary Bishop John Dunn met with Harney for "a long and amicable discussion." Dunn shared Harney's concerns. The three decided a practical solution would be to submit to Elwood two or three "high-class expositions of Catholic teaching on subjects of a controversial character" to get his reaction. The experiment went well. NBC even agreed Catholic stations around the country could carry the program at no cost other than the wire connection, thus eliminating the issue of competition.[15]

In March 1930, the NCCM launched the "Catholic Hour," a weekly broadcast at 6:00 P.M. Sunday evening over WEAF, an NBC station in New York City. Initially, twenty-two affiliates picked it up. Within two months, the number of stations grew to thirty-six and by year's end stood at more than fifty in all parts of the country. Programs were the Catholic contribution to the religious and spiritual life of America. Each week a distinguished layman or priest noted for scholarship and eloquence made an address. Scripts for the discourses were submitted weeks in advance for approval. Their purpose was to explain Catholic life and doctrine to the wider public in the spirit of St. Francis de Sales. Speaker for the Lenten series that launched the broadcast was Father Fulton J. Sheen, professor of apologetics at Catholic University. Each program also featured Catholic music, liturgical and otherwise, performed by the Paulist Choristers under direction of Father William Finn.[16]

After a half year, Burke pronounced the broadcast a success. The NCCM had received thousands of positive letters from non-Catholics, an eloquent testimony of their "open-mindedness." "Their declarations are kind, good-willed, complete," wrote Burke, "and demonstrate, first, the concern of the American people for religion and, second, their willingness to hear the claims of the Catholic Church presented by her own spokesmen." The "Catholic Hour" marked the most extensive use the Church had made of radio thus far.[17]

LIFE ON A SHORT LEASH

In February 1930, Burke explained to his spiritual daughters that his shortened work schedule and mandated rest cut into his ability to write them with any frequency. He had not, however, forgotten them in prayer, and they certainly did not forget him. Helen Lynch sent a Valentine reminiscent of a different occasion. "There was the blue bird recalling a certain Easter of years ago, and a dissatisfied editor," replied Burke; "and the blue bird was dejected." Burke himself was not dejected when in late February he was able to return to Manhattan and join Murray and Gertrude Delahunt in one of those romantic automobile rides along Riverside Drive. Unfortunately, the trip to Gotham had so sapped his strength that he sat in silence as they rode, physically incapable of speech. Back in Washington, he expressed to them the joy and gratitude he felt during the ride but was unable to utter at the time. "What one suffers, not alone in separation, but also in physical suffering, in the absences, makes deeper the appreciation," he told them. "Suffering draws me nearer to those I love: suffering, or rather the lack of strength, makes it impossible to say what one would say.... These thoughts were in the journey."[18]

In April, he made time to give Lynch his pascal blessing. "Blue birds or no blue birds, I'm sending you my special greetings for a glorious Easter," he wrote. He probably included this poem which he had just penned:

The light by which we see
Things as they seem to be
Comes from the glaring sun.
The light by which we know
Life's true, eternal flow
Comes from the Risen One.

During Easter season, he suffered more sick spells. Burke was puzzled by their cause. According to doctors, he had no "reserve strength." "The need of husbanding the strength makes me, outside of the work itself, lead a quiet life," he told Lynch, "and forbids me to travel much."[19]

Dr. Marbury did, however, let him travel for vacation in summer 1930. Burke and his sister Lizzie took a train to visit their brother Thomas at St. Mary's parish in San Francisco. More to Burke's liking was the return trip. He hated traveling by railroad when not for purposes of work. So, he and his sister booked first cabins on the S.S. *Virginia* from San Francisco to Los Angeles and thence via the Panama Canal to Havana and New York.[20]

While travel was permitted, public speaking was not. When in late summer Bishop Thomas Lillis of the Administrative Committee invited Burke to give a speech at the upcoming annual convention of the NCCM in Kansas City, Marbury said no. He told Burke the physical exertion of an address would undo much of the good gained. So, Burke replied he would attend the convention, but not speak. "The heart is not what it should be," he explained. "It is better. And I can carry the work here, but I cannot preach for any length of time and I am not yet in a condition to offer Mass every day." A month later, he told Murray he was still unable to say daily Mass. "Indeed that act seems to call for a great deal of effort," he said, "and that in turn 'depletes' me so to speak."[21]

Indeed it did. Mary Hawks later wrote that Burke's intensity in saying Mass left him so exhausted he would have "to sit down or even retire to his room." Doctors gave him the choice between Mass or work, which must have cost him dearly. When Hawks asked if he could say it with less intensity so as to be able to do so more often, he replied, "I cannot do differently," and fell silent for some minutes. Then, he told her the story about rushing through Mass as a young editor at *Catholic World*, only to have a grouchy older Paulist challenge him over breakfast about how quickly he went through the rite (see Chapter 3). "I never could do that again," he told her.[22]

The lengthy silence suggests Burke's careful weighing of what more he would say. It should be noted his anecdote did not answer Hawks's question. Saying Mass with less haste does not explain the intensity that sapped his strength. Clearly, Burke was loath to share what he experienced during Mass even with a spiritual daughter. It remains known only to him and God.

While Burke was prevented from public speaking, nothing kept him from issuing a press release when Hoover publicly slighted the Church. During the 1928 election, Hoover had failed to discountenance anti-Catholic attacks against Al Smith. He did advocate religious tolerance, but as Fumasoni-Biondi reported to the Vatican, "He never denounced, as he should, this campaign against the Catholic Church." For that reason, the delegate recommended against sending Hoover papal congratulations on winning office. In order that Pius XI might compliment him on his inauguration, Cardinal Pietro Gasparri asked the delegate to secure Hoover's congratulations on the Lateran Treaty (February 1929), establishing the Vatican City State. Hoover refused. As historian Massimo Faggioli notes, "The beginning of Hoover's presidency sent a clear non-conciliatory message to the Vatican, which perceived that the anti-Catholic stance of the political establishment in the United States was going to last."[23]

In early October 1930, Hoover sent "cordial greetings" to American Lutherans about to celebrate the 400th anniversary of the Augsburg Confession of Faith and the 413th anniversary of the Protestant Reformation. He hailed the Reformation as a signal event from which dated "so many of the changes in point of view from older conceptions both of religion and government." He went on to say the two events were "reflected in our national life and institutions, in religion through the predominant numbers of adherents to the Protestant faiths and in government through the principle of separation of church and state." He deemed it fitting the nation commemorate "the persons and events from which mighty forces have sprung."[24]

The message floored Burke. "Hoover has done what no President of the United States ever did," he wrote Murray. "He has declared that this country is founded upon Protestantism, upon the changes in religion which

Protestantism has introduced." Burke admitted it was commonly averred America was a Protestant country, but no chief executive ever publicly declared it so. He felt conscience-bound to protest because of the implication that to be an American one must be Protestant or at least sympathetic to those principles.[25]

He immediately drafted a rejoinder. Acknowledging the appropriateness of congratulating Lutherans on their civic work, Burke said Hoover's actual message clearly violated "the spirit if not the letter of his oath of office as President of the United States." It mattered little that it was "an insult to millions of Americans" or was inaccurate because Martin Luther was no champion of separation of Church and state. It mattered a great deal constitutionally that "the President of all the people, who is called by virtue of his office to respect the religious rights of all, congratulates one particular religious body on the changes it introduced from older conceptions of religion and government, and declares that we as a nation should commemorate the Protestant persons and events from which 'these mighty forces shaping our country have sprung.'" Anticipating the press would ask him for a statement, Burke sent copies of the draft to the Administrative Committee, which favored its release.[26]

When a reporter soon interviewed Burke, he issued the statement, sending it to all press services and to the principal dailies in major cities. Hoover's secretary, George Akerson, declared Burke's words "an injustice both to the President's own sentiments and the complete religious tolerance he has always felt and has always advocated both publicly and privately." Dr. Frederick H. Knubel, president of the United Lutheran Church in America, deplored Burke's objection to the message. On the other hand, the editor of the *New York Evening Post* considered it justified. So too did the editor of the New York *World*, who called the wording of Hoover's message "unfortunate and ill-considered." The Protestant *Christian Century* in Chicago believed Hoover made a misstep in issuing the greeting, but had intended no insult to Catholics as his prompt disavowal indicated.[27]

Burke certainly knew his protest would sharpen the religious issue, but probably did not foresee it would lead to personal attacks on himself and invective against the Church. He received some fifty letters from people around the country. Only fifteen were positive, mainly from Catholics. One

Catholic dissenter, May McDermott of Long Island, said Burke's attack on Hoover was "entirely uncalled for … childish and unnecessary." He read into Hoover's words a meaning not there. She thought he might be "looking for a little extra publicity." In any case, she felt the protest did harm. "Burke old man, you certainly are some big Irish ass to have criticized President Hoover," wrote Isaac Levy from Buffalo, who believed the nation would be better off if all "Irish Catholics & Kike Jews" were shipped back to their mother countries. He considered Catholic priests the "greatest inciters of bigotry." P.T.O. in Omaha sent Burke a two-page memo denouncing the beliefs of the "devil invented, devil inspired, devil empowered church of Rome." He derided the Catholic understanding of the Eucharist as "the rawest of raw cannibalism." The fruits of the Catholic Church were "hate and hatred, bigotry and intolerance, cruelty, torment and torture." Romanists would never change unless "converted by Divine grace to real Christianity." Burke saved all the letters without indication of how they affected him.[28]

When the Administrative Committee met in November, Burke reported that given his protest, there was distinct possibility he might be persona non grata at the White House. He was unsure how that might affect his relations with other government departments. The bishops needed to be aware of the potential effects.[29] In fact, Burke would not enter the White House again until a new administration.

He also brought up a matter touching his personal welfare. The work was "too much" for him, he said, though not in the sense of being overwhelmed. Too many problems "require[d] quiet, long-continued thought, conferences if possible—and I must say this is no longer possible for me, except on rare occasions." He urgently needed an assistant. He had attempted for two years to find one. Now, he no longer had the time or energy to do so. He asked the bishops' help. Hugh Boyle advised against an appeal to the hierarchy given the discretion necessary for selection. Moreover the decision rested with the committee. Burke noted the need of a priest to coordinate the Catholic Hour, which was then being handled by Father Karl Alter, director of the NCSSS. The overworked Alter needed relief, and Burke thought a search for a priest to assume charge of the Catholic Hour would afford opportunity to determine the qualifications of a candidate for executive secretary. The bishops authorized him to find such a man.[30]

Great Depression and Immigration

From spring 1930 through winter 1931, two works occupied Burke's half-strength and half-time: immigration and birth control. With the onset of the Great Depression, immigration restriction assumed new urgency. Unemployment almost tripled, from 1.55 million in late 1929 to 4.34 million during 1930. John Ryan published a pamphlet, asserting unemployment was a byproduct of the Depression's underlying cause: overproduction and underconsumption. Industry produced more goods than most could afford. The answer lay in higher wages for workers. "Money to buy goods must exist in the hands not merely of a few well-to-do, but of the masses," he wrote. "Increased power to consume must be extended to the only class that possesses in large measure the unsatisfied desire to consume." He advocated increasing wages while reducing the work week. Shorter hours would necessitate more employees, and higher wages would mean more people could afford to buy the goods produced. Essentially, Ryan was advocating a more equitable distribution of income.[31]

The federal government saw a different remedy to unemployment: halt immigration. In April 1930, Senator Hugo Black of Alabama sought to suspend it for five years except for foreign-born family members of American citizens. The measure narrowly failed. Later in the session, Hoover asked Congress to cut immigration quotas in half. When adjournment precluded that, he took executive action. In September, State announced it would enforce the "public charge" clause of the 1917 Immigration Act. That feature prevented American consuls from issuing visas to applicants who might become public wards after entering the U.S. Because the likelihood of an immigrant's finding work during the Depression was nil, the clause was the perfect device. With its implementation, immigration from Europe dropped 90 percent by December 1930.[32]

In November, Burke authored the American hierarchy's statement on unemployment. He lamented the "tragedy" of millions out of work, a calamity of human origin. "May God give the country His wisdom and grace," wrote Burke, "to throw off this yoke of suffering, unlike famine only in that men themselves inflict it in the midst of plenty." He thanked all who provided the unemployed food, clothing, and shelter. Yet, the situation demanded more than charity; "justice should be done." Burke viewed cycles of unemployment as "a sign of deep failure in our country." The nation needed a "change of heart" to distribute work and wealth so no one lacked security. He directed attention to Pope Leo XIII's encyclical *Rerum Novarum* (*Of New Things*, 1891) and the Bishops' Program of Social Reconstruction (1919). Quoting the latter, he declared a living wage was "only the *minimum* of justice." The bishops had called for capital to meet and go beyond that ethical pittance. Had their call been heeded, the nation would have prevented the calamity which now befell it. Again, quoting the program, Burke argued, "'The human and Christian, in contrast to the purely commercial and pagan, ethics of industry,' … will both cure our country of our present malady and prevent its cruel recurrence." Archbishop Edward Hanna, chairman of the Administrative Committee, was "delighted" with the document deeming it "excellent." Burke released it to the press the day before Thanksgiving.[33]

Still, the government's remedy was immigration restriction. In December 1930, Hoover told Congress enforcement of the "public charge" clause was a stopgap until it cut quotas. Senator David Reed quickly introduced a bill to suspend immigration for two years except for foreign wives and unmarried children of American citizens. Albert Johnson introduced its companion which excepted wives and unmarried children of both citizens and legal resident aliens. The NCWC learned Reed had omitted families of resident aliens because they were too few to matter. Statistics, however, revealed there were over 27,000 wives and children affected.[34]

Bruce Mohler brought Reed's bill to Burke's attention. Burke instructed him to attend the hearing on it. He was to say nothing against suspension of immigration because the bishops left that matter to governmental and economic authorities during this period of national crisis. The NCWC, however, "reserved the right to defend its traditional position that entire restriction of immigration was not advisable." He directed Mohler to object to the exclusion of families of resident aliens, which was also the position of other religious and charitable associations.[35]

In January 1931, Burke and Mohler saw Reed. Burke had no objection to his bill in the main, but wished to see the reunion of families made easier in it. He urged Reed to reconsider. Reed said he always favored uniting families whose fathers became citizens. He absolutely opposed doing so for a resident alien who would not become one. Mohler suggested perhaps the bill could admit families of men who came prior to the Immigration Act of 1924; those men had reason to believe their families could enter. Reed countered they had ample time to become citizens or begin that process, and excused himself for another appointment. At a loss about how to respond to such definiteness, Burke noted: "Altogether we made a sorry appearance. It is a mistake not to know a question fully when you begin to talk with one who does." He considered Reed's attitude evidence of the narrow view of a specialist. Like a train engineer with eyes fixed only on the track just ahead, Reed did not see the larger view.[36]

Secretary of State Henry Stimson, on the other hand, objected to Johnson's bill because it discriminated against "Nordic races" by halting all immigration except to reunify families, most of them from eastern and southern Europe. It would be fairer to reduce all quotas by 90 percent. Republican Thomas Jenkins of Ohio formulated such a bill, and the House Committee reported it. Democratic Representatives Edmund Cooke and Samuel Dickstein, both of New York, filed minority reports arguing the measure would end reunion of families.[37]

Burke authorized the Immigration Bureau to join with ten other national organizations, including the FCC, YWCA, and several Jewish agencies, in protesting against the measure. A letter endorsed by directors of the various bodies went to each member of the House. It argued no immigration bill should pass if it prevented or delayed reunion of husbands with wives and children because "the integrity of the family and the sanctity of the home" were American principles. Separation of family members caused immeasurable suffering. To claim their exclusion would help unemployed Americans was unfounded. Wives and children would not become competitors for jobs to any significant extent. Their exclusion also meant millions of dollars would be sent abroad for their support, money better spent to revive the home economy.[38]

When the House took up the bill two days before Congress expired, it turned a deaf ear, passing it without change. Reed got the Senate to place it on the calendar without going through committee. The protesting organizations sent senators the same letter they sent to representatives. When Reed tried to get the chamber to take up the bill, Catholic Senator David Walsh blocked it. Burke reported to the Administrative Committee the general attitude in Congress was "to limit immigration more and more."[39]

BIRTH CONTROL

While half-timer Burke dealt with immigration restriction, the issue of birth control reasserted itself. Since 1926, the NCWC had enjoyed a respite from it, but there had been no relief from propaganda. In April 1930, Burke told the Administrative Committee the campaign for birth control was making "inroads" in parts of the Catholic community. Although he and the NCWC tried to keep federal legislation Christian, "some of our own and even some priests" opposed the effort as "meddling in politics." Burke considered that notion indicative of "a defeatist attitude and policy ... essentially opposed to the spirit of the Catholic faith." He said the NCWC labored for "Christ and His Church." Catholics were not simply individuals, but were bound together in the Mystical Body "to restore the reign of Christ on earth." Laws constituted the "civic atmosphere" people breathed, for good or ill. To stand aloof from the legislative process was to permit removal of Christian standards from public life, opening the way for those favoring indifferentism, agnosticism, and atheism. Burke was not advocating entry into partisan politics, nor had the NCWC engaged in such. He said Catholics and their Church should do all in their power to keep laws as Christian as possible, whether or not they succeeded. That was one of "the great functions of the N.C.W.C."[40]

Within weeks, Congress had before it a birth control bill drafted by Margaret Sanger and her new organization, the National Committee on Federal Legislation for Birth Control (NCFLBC), headquartered in New York and chaired by herself. The bill amended both the tariff law and criminal code to permit postal dissemination of information about birth control produced by the medical profession as well as medicines and implements for contraception prescribed by licensed physicians. Agents of the NCFLBC carefully selected seventy-nine-year-old Senator Frederick Gillett of Massachusetts, destined for retirement, to introduce the bill because he would have nothing to lose. He did so and then neglected it.[41]

Indeed, the birth control movement had made headway. Sanger reported there were twenty-five clinics open around the country. By June 1930, four liberal religious bodies endorsed contraception for married couples: the Universalist General Convention, the American Unitarian Association, the New York East Conference of the Methodist Episcopal Church, and the Central Conference of American Rabbis. Two months later, the Lambeth Conference of Anglican Bishops gave qualified approval to contraception, and six months later the FCC blessed it. Patrick Ward reported to Burke the American Medical and American Bar Associations (AMA and ABA) believed traffic in contraceptives was uncontrollable under present law. It should be declassified as "obscene" because courts wrangled over what constituted obscenity, resulting in "very loose regulation of all matters relating to contraception." Both associations thought greater control over it might result from specific legislation about it and assigning enforcement to a special office in the Justice Department. Ward learned Cardinal Patrick Hayes of New York favored such action.[42]

In November 1930, Burke reported on Sanger's bill to the Administrative Committee. Referring obliquely to the AMA and ABA, he said "certain organizations" would stand against birth control if the NCWC were willing to remove the matter from the current obscenity clause and have it "classified under some other heading." He added that of the eighteen organizations that joined the NCWC in opposition in 1925, only five to date agreed to do it again. Burke asked for instructions. The members reiterated their stance that the NCWC "steadfastly … resist" with every available resource any change in the penal code regarding birth control.[43]

Meanwhile, Sanger geared up to push the bill in the lame-duck session. She created an Endorsement Committee of one thousand by soliciting from prominent individuals around the country consent to use their names as members. When she went to Washington, she learned to her amazement and chagrin that Gillett had done nothing. The measure lay dormant in the Judiciary Committee. Gillett told her that Chairman George Norris, who supported birth control, would appoint a good subcommittee for a hearing. Early in 1931, Sanger moved NCFLCB's headquarters from New York to Washington to place the issue of birth control, in the words of historian David Kennedy, squarely "on the forum of congressional politics." The committee promoted grassroots organization throughout the country to flood Congress with petitions and resolutions. Sanger's assistants in the capital, especially Hazel Moore, lobbied legislators and sounded out congressional support.[44]

In late January 1931, Ward informed Burke a subcommittee of Senators Gillett, William Borah of Idaho, and Sam Bratton of New Mexico would hold a hearing the following month. The hearing surprised Burke because Gillett had done nothing about the bill since introducing it, and there was no hint that Congress, in an already packed short session, had time to hold a hearing. Yet, Sanger and her people wanted publicity and succeeded in securing one.[45]

Ward, Montavon, Agnes Regan, and Margaret Lynch, assistant executive secretary of the NCCW, met to strategize. They wanted Burke to request time from Gillett for the opposition, a task he passed to Montavon. Ward secured twelve non-Catholic groups to appear, including five Protestant denominations. To lower the profile of Catholic opposition, the NCWC had the Sentinels of the Republic and its representative Ralph Burton manage opposition during the hearing. Burke carefully made sure there were witnesses to present economic, demographic, and medical arguments against. Because some NCFLBC propaganda referred to Gillett's measure as "Our Doctors' Bill," Burke got physician William Woodward, director of the AMA Legislative Bureau, to write Norris and each member of the Judiciary Committee to say the AMA had no part in drafting it or procuring its introduction, nor did it have an opinion.[46]

A week before the hearing, Burke and Montavon saw Bratton. Burke tried to impress on him what "a radical piece of legislation" the bill was, one with "far-reaching" implications for public morals. He advised against viewing Catholic opposition as simply based on Church teaching, but to see Catholic opponents also as American citizens defending what they considered essential to "America's well-being." Burke and Montavon added that birth control propagandists engineered the hearing. Bratton gave no indication of where he stood.[47]

The two gave him a memorandum on the subject. It argued that prior to the Comstock Act, every state had obscenity laws that were rendered porous by the U.S. mail. In 1873, that act added an obscenity clause to the federal penal code closing the postal loophole. Congress had not established "any new standard of morality," but extended the existing state ban into an area where states were incompetent to act. The Gillett bill intended to reopen that loophole. Yet, no state had weakened or abrogated its obscenity statute, "and therefore it seems there is no real popular demand for this legislation."[48]

Sanger opened the hearing stating the bill intended to empower women to regulate size of their families. The goal was for "motherhood to be a conscious and controlled function … and parenthood to be something other than the consequences of a reckless, careless shiftlessness." Supporters argued the legislation would promote eugenic control of population and reduce infant mortality, unemployment, poverty, and chance of war. Montavon presented the argument in the above memorandum and contended the bill opened wide the mails to information about and instruments for contraception. Other opponents argued doing so would be detrimental to public morals. Two doctors of wide experience and international repute said physicians had already the ethical duty and power to dispense contraceptive information and instruments in cases that called for it; the bill added nothing to that.[49]

Burke sent the Administrative Committee a report on the hearing. He was discouraged, not about the current showing, but about prospects in general. To meet the situation adequately, the NCWC must be able to support the Catholic position with "trained, capable, experienced" experts who could do so on the basis of ethics, medicine, population, and patriotism. Sanger and her committee had money for such specialists. "We can do nothing of this kind." Moreover, Burke noted the vast majority of doctors would not support the Catholic position. They insisted birth control be removed from obscenity laws. Christian traditions were "growing more flabby" among Americans, said Burke. He believed the Church should continue to uphold without compromise that birth control was intrinsically against natural law, but he refused to "hide" from himself the fact that doing so would be ineffective in keeping the penal code as it was.[50]

For her part, Sanger realized she had a formidable foe in the Church. She complained to a colleague that opponents instilled "terror and fear … in the minds of men." Sanger was furious at Catholic witnesses. "Dogmatists, harking back to the Dark Ages," she called them in her autobiography. They leveled the hoary arguments that hitherto thwarted advances in civilization: that birth control "was against nature, against God, against the Bible, against the country's best interests, and against morality." She concluded, "The appeal to intelligence was futile."[51]

The NCWC won the current round. Congress expired without the subcommittee reporting the bill. It would need to be reintroduced in the next Congress before it could come up again.[52] And so it would—with a curious twist.

ENDNOTES TO CHAPTER 19

1. Burke, *Christ in Us*, 128–29.
2. Burke to G. Murray, 9 February 1930, AP, Burke Papers, box 12; Burke to Lynch, 18 February 1930, ibid., box 5.
3. *New York Times*, 11 December 1929 (first quote is here); Burke, [Interview with Pascual Ortiz Rubio], 28 December 1929, ACUA, USCCB 10:145: Interview Book IV (second quote is here); Sheerin, *Never Look Back*, 157; Ruiz is quoted in Reich, *Mexico's Hidden Revolution*, 22–26; Redinger, *American Catholics and the Mexican Revolution*, 90.
4. Burke, [Memorandum], 6 February 1930, ACUA, USCCB 10:153: Interview Book; Juana Vásquez Gómez, *Dictionary of Mexican Rulers, 1325–1997* (Westport, Conn.: Greenwood Press, 1997), 121–22.
5. Burke, [Memorandum], 6 February 1930, ACUA, USCCB 10:153: Interview Book.
6. Ibid.
7. Burke, [Memorandum], 7 February 1930, ACUA, USCCB 10:153: Interview Book.
8. Burke, Report of the General Secretary, April 1930, ACUA, USCCB 10:62:10.
9. Burke to G. Murray, 9 February 1930, AP, Burke Papers, box 12; Burke, Report of the General Secretary, April 1930, ACUA, USCCB 10:62:10; Slawson, *Foundation of the NCWC*, 80–81, 96–100, 202–04, 228–31, 265–66.
10. "How to Combat Bigotry Concern of N.C.C.M. Convention," *NCWC Bulletin* 8 (December 1928): 18–19; "Archbishop McNicholas Denounces False Attacks on the Church," ibid., 23–24; "Judge Cunningham's Excellent Advice," ibid. 24; "Resolutions Adopted by the N.C.C.M. at Cincinnati Convention," ibid., 29; Charles F. Dolle, "Executive Secretary's Page," *NCWC Bulletin* 9 (January 1929): 22; *Historical Statistics*, 491; Hicks, *Republican Ascendancy*, 172–73; Harvey Green, *The Uncertainty of Everyday Life, 1915–1945* (New York: Harper Perennial, 1993), 189–90; David M. Kennedy, *Freedom from Fear: The American People in Depression and War, 1929–1945* (New York and Oxford: Oxford University Press, 1999), 228–29.
11. Burke to John Harney, 25 September 1929, ACUA, USCCB 10:110:13 (first and third quotes are here); Burke to Dolle, 2 October 1929, ibid. (second quote is here); Charles F. Dolle, "Developments in the N.C.C.M. Campaign of Apologetics," *NCWC Bulletin* 9 (February 1929): 16; Kerans, "Development of N.C.C.M. Apologetic Campaign," ibid. (March 1929): 29–30; Kerans, "N.C.C.M. Apologetic Campaign Making Progress," ibid. (April 1929): 20–21; Dolle, "N.C.C.M. Executive Secretary's Page," ibid. (August 1929): 26.

12. Harney to Burke, 20 September 1929, AP, Burke Papers, box 20; Burke to G. Murray, 9 February 1930, ibid., box 12; Harney to Burke, 25 September 1929, ACUA, USCCB 10:110:13 (quotes are here).
13. Harney to Burke, 25 September 1929, ACUA, USCCB 10:110:13 (emphasis in original).
14. Burke to Harney, 28 September 1929, copy, ACUA, USCCB 10:110:13.
15. Dolle to Burke, 1 October 1929; Schrembs to Burke, 3 October 1929; Harney to Burke, 16 October 1929—all in ACUA, USCCB 10:110:13.
16. Burke to Fumasoni-Biondi, 13 May 1930, copy, USCCB 10:30:5; "N. C. C. M. Inaugurates Weekly 'Catholic Hour,'" *NCWC Review* 12 (March 1930): 15; "Cardinal Hayes Explains Purpose of 'Catholic Hour,'" ibid. (April 1930): 6; "Catholic Radio Hour Evokes Widespread Response," ibid., 7–8; "Analysis of 1026 Commentaries on Catholic Radio Hour," ibid. (May 1930): 12.
17. Burke, "The Catholic Church on the Radio," *NCWC Review* 12 (October 1930): 20.
18. Burke to G. Murray, 9 February 1930, AP, Burke Papers, box 12; Burke to the Other Two [G. Murray and Delahunt], ibid.; Burke to Lynch, 15 February 1930, ibid., box 5.
19. Burke to Lynch 16 April and 27 May 1930, AP, Burke Papers, box 5; Burke, "Easter," 1930, ACUA, USCCB 10:72:24.
20. Passenger List: Panama Pacific Line, 23 August 1930, AP, Burke Papers, box 72.
21. Burke to Lillis, 17 September 1930, copy, ACUA, USCCB 10:152:20; Burke to G. Murray, 15 October 1930, AP, Burke Papers, box 12.
22. Hawks, "Souvenir of Burke," AP, Burke Papers, box 10; Unattributed Reminiscence, 1935, ibid., box 1 (quotations are from both).
23. Faggioli, "1928 Presidential Campaign," 13 n. 28 and 15; Castagna, *Bridge across the Ocean*, 108, 109–12.
24. *New York Times*, 10 October 1930.
25. Burke to Murray, 15 October 1930, AP, Burke Papers, box 12.
26. [Press Release], 13 October 1930, copy, ACUA, USCCB 10:122:31; Burke to Hanna, 10 October 1930, copy, ibid., 10:99:19.
27. [Press Release], 13 October 1930, with attached List of Papers Interview Delivered To, copy, ACUA, USCCB 10:122:31; *New York Sun*, 14 October 1930; *New York Evening Post*, 15 October 1930; New York *World*, 15 October 1930; Report of the General Secretary, November 1930, ACUA, USCCB 10:62:10.
28. Mary McDermott to Burke, 22 October 1930, ACUA, USCCB 10:122:30; Isaac Levy to Burke, 25 October 1930, ibid.; P.T.O., Memo on reading Priest Burke's statements, undated [October 1922], ibid.; Burke to G. Murray, 15 October 1930, AP, Burke Papers, box 12.
29. Minutes of the Administrative Committee, 10 November 1930, ACUA, USCCB 10:64:5.

30. Burke, Report of the General Secretary, November 1930, ACUA, USCCB 10:62:10; Minutes of the Administrative Committee, 10 November 1930, ibid., 10:64:5; "Rev. Karl J. Alter, of Toledo, Succeeds Dr. Kerby as Service School Head," *NCWC Bulletin* 11 (July 1929): 15.
31. "Unemployment—What Can Be Done About It?" *NCWC Review* 12 (February 1930): 22; *Historical Statistics*, 73; Kennedy, *Freedom from Fear*, 10–11, 34–42; Robert S. McElvaine, *The Great Depression: America, 1929–1941* (New York: Times Books, 1993), 25–50.
32. Department of State, Press Release, 10 September 1930, with Acting Secretary of State to President Hoover, 8 September 1930, ACUA, USCCB 10:42:3; Divine, *American Immigration Policy*, 78–79.
33. [Burke, Statement on Unemployment], 25 November 1930, ACUA, USCCB 10:64:29; "The Bishops' Program of Social Reconstruction, 12 February 1919," in Ellis, ed., *Documents of American Catholic History*, 594–95, 603; Hanna to Burke, telegram, 24 November 1930, ACUA, USCCB 10:99:19; Hanna to Burke, 28 November 1930, ibid. Earlier that month, the hierarchy gave authorization to issue the statement on its behalf.
34. Sara Weadick to Burke, 3 January 1930 [*sic* for 1931], ACUA, USCCB 10:42:3; Divine, *American Immigration Policy*, 78–80.
35. Burke, Memorandum Re Reed Immigration Bill, 13 December 1930, ACUA, USCCB 10:42:3; Divine, *American Immigration Policy*, 79–80.
36. [Burke, Memorandum of Interview with David Reed], 12 January 1931, ACUA, USCCB 10:42:3.
37. *Congressional Record*, 71st Cong., 3rd Sess., Vol. 74, Part 5, 4769, 5252; Divine, *American Immigration Policy*, 81–82.
38. Worth M. Tippy et al., including Mohler, to Representatives, 19 February 1931, copy, ACUA, USCCB 10:42:3.
39. FCC, NCWC, et al. to Nicholas Longworth, 2 March 1931, copy, ACUA, USCCB 10:42:3; Tippy et al. to Senators, 2 March 1931, copy, ibid.; Mohler to Burke, 4 March 1931, ibid.; Report of the General Secretary, April 1931, ibid., 10:62:11; *Congressional Record*, 71st Cong., 3rd Sess., Vol. 74, Part 5, 6575–79, 6738–44, 6720–21; Divine, *American Immigration Policy*, 82–84.
40. Burke, Report of the General Secretary, April 1930, ACUA, USCCB 10:62:10; Tentler, *Catholics and Contraception*, 56–62, 75–79; Sheerin, *Never Look Back*, 194–195.
41. S.4582, 26 May 1930, 71st Cong., 2nd Sess.; *Sanger Autobiography*, 417–19; Kennedy, *Birth Control*, 224–31; Baker, *Sanger: Life of* Passion, 204–05, 212–13; Chesler, *Woman of Valor*, 324–29. The bill reignited the feud between Sanger and Dennett who wanted the Comstock Act amended to permit literature about and the means of birth control to be accessed by everyone, not just those in the medical profession.

42. Circular from Sanger, undated [September 1930], copy, ACUA, USCCB 10:117:8; Note for Meeting of Administrative Committee, undated [September 1930], ibid.; Ward to Burke, 8 November 1930, ibid.; Chesler, *Woman of Valor*, 318; Tentler, *Catholics and Contraception*, 73; *Autobiography of Sanger*, 410–11.
43. Burke, Report of the General Secretary, November 1930, ACUA, USCCB 10:62:10; Minutes of the Administrative Committee, 10 November 1930, ibid., 10:64:5.
44. Circular from Sanger, undated [September 1930], copy, ACUA, USCCB 10:117:8; *Autobiography of Sanger*, 419–20; Kennedy, *Birth Control*, 230–33.
45. Ward to Burke, 28 January 1931, ACUA, USCCB 10:117:19; Burke to John Noll, 20 February 1931, copy, ibid.
46. Ward to Burke, 30 January 1931, ACUA, USCCB 10:117:19; Burke to William Woodward, 5 February 1931, copy; ibid.; Woodward to Burke, 7 February 1931, ibid.; Burke to Noll, 20 February 1931, ibid.; Woodward to George W. Norris, undated [February 1931], printed in *Birth Control: Hearings before a Subcommittee of the Committee on the Judiciary, United States Senate, Seventy-First Congress, Third Session, on S 4582, 13 February 1931* (Washington, D.C.: U.S. Government Printing Office, 1931), 30–31.
47. [Burke, Interview with Senator Bratton], 4 February 1931, copy, ACUA, USCCB 10:117:19; Burke to Albert Daeger, 4 February 1931, copy, ibid.
48. "NCWC Statement Concerning Senate Bill 4582, To Amend the Tariff Act and Penal Code To Permit Importation, Distribution, And Sale Of Contraceptive Literature and Instruments" in *Birth Control Hearing*, 77–80; also in ACUA, USCCB 10:117:19.
49. *Birth Control Hearing*, 1–76 (quote on p. 3); "Protests Registered Against Birth Control Bill," *NCWC Review* 13 (March 1931): 12–13.
50. Burke to Noll, 20 February 1931, copy, ACUA, USCCB 10:117:19. Burke sent copies of this letter to the committee (cf. Enclosure with Burke to Hanna, 21 February 1931, AASF, NCWC files).
51. Quoted in Chesler, *Woman of Valor*, 330 (first quote); *Autobiography of Sanger*, 421(remaining quotes).
52. Burke to Hanna, 8 March 1931, copy, ACUA, USCCB 10:99:19.

Chapter 20
Help at Last

> Calvary has no past, no future: Calvary is present. Jesus Christ is the same yesterday, today and the same forever.... With God, time is not nor are we, as God sees us, in time. God sees us not partially. He saw us before we were born: He sees us now: He will see us forever. But these tenses are the limitation of our vision and our existence. God sees us. God through Christ has made us one with Himself. God is all in all.[1]

Search for an Executive Secretary

With birth control legislation in abeyance until next Congress, John Burke returned to the search for an executive secretary, a quest compounded when Father Karl Alter, director of the NCSSS, was appointed bishop of Toledo. Burke now had two positions to fill. Fortunately, Alter was able to continue through the current academic year. In early May, Burke heard from Bishop Joseph Schrembs that Father Michael Ready, director of his Society for the Propagation of the Faith, might head the NCSSS. Burke invited him to Washington. After spending a day with Ready, Burke thought him a better fit as assistant general secretary and broached that idea. "I think he would do well," he commented in his diary. Schrembs was amenable.[2]

For directorship of the school, Burke eyed two priests of the New York archdiocese: Fathers Bryan McEntegarte and Edward Roberts Moore, both in Catholic Charities. He contacted Monsignor Robert Keegan, head of that organization, about releasing one or other to head the NCSSS. Considering them necessary to his operation, Keegan was unwilling to let either go, but he said he would not object if Cardinal Patrick Hayes sent one to Washington.[3]

In late May, Burke went first to New York to confer with Hayes and thence to Cleveland to finalize arrangements with Schrembs.[4] Grace Murray and Gertrude Delahunt met him at Jersey City. The train ride left him too drained to speak, so they sat silent on the ferry to Manhattan. When they reached the Cenacle, they conversed a little on the porch. "I think that talk cost me a dollar [$20 in 2024]," noted Burke. He retired to the garden guest house where he lodged. Completely exhausted, he told the caretaker he would not say Mass in the morning.[5]

Next day, Burke saw Hayes, who said his Catholic Charities just became fully functional and he must keep it so. After discussing how necessary McEntegarte and Moore were to the work, Hayes told Burke to speak with Keegan. If any of them were willing to go to D.C., Burke should let Hayes know and then he would have a definite question for decision. Yet, in saying goodbye, Hayes held out little hope, telling Burke he should pray for a new director.[6]

With Hayes's parting words, Burke experienced "a feeling of quite clean-cut loneliness." It was not a sense of aloneness; he experienced that since ordination, and it was never "loneliness" with him. The loneliness he felt resulted from the fact his beloved NCSSS was uncherished by and even unimportant to Hayes and others. They failed to appreciate how essential were trained Catholic social workers. "I seemed to be attempting a thing which the consecrated authorities of the Church seemed not to support, a thing outside the organization of the Church," wrote Burke. "Was I not wrong? Should I try to carry it? Is it God's will? Is it our Lord's wish. These thoughts didn't worry me. All I know is that for the time I felt alone—and alone with a coldness and an isolation that knows no warmth or comfort."[7]

"Quite sobered," Burke called on Delahunt at home, where he found it necessary to console her about a trouble she was having. Though it took a physical toll, Burke felt "gloriously repaid within" by thus sharing in "the love and joy of the Christ of Bethany [Luke 10:38–42 and John 11:1–44]." He noted wryly he and Delahunt then did what Jesus and the sisters Mary and Martha of Bethany never did: "We engaged a taxi and drove to Riverdale reminiscing some memories of other years."[8]

Next day, Burke met Keegan and pitched the importance of the NCSSS, "not only as a school but as an institution in the work of the church nationally and internationally." Keegan said he would speak with

McEntegarte and Moore, but held little hope. Burke considered the conversation helpful if only because it made the work of the NCWC and NCSSS better known.[9]

That evening he left New York empty-handed for Cleveland. He arrived next morning and went directly to speak with Schrembs about Ready. Schrembs thought Ready would do well. Burke would make the appointment on Schrembs's recommendation and the Administrative Committee would confirm it. The decision, though, was up to Ready. Schrembs summoned him and explained the assignment would be probationary because he might find he did not like the work or the committee might find him unsuitable. Burke would entrust him with elements little by little. Ready expressed his willingness. His title would be assistant general secretary. That night, Burke boarded a train for Washington praising God for his "unwarranted mercies."[10]

He shared the good news with Helen Lynch. Ready was "by all reports a capable and excellent priest." About his failure with Hayes, he had grown detached, even a bit humorous. "I was not successful in my appeal to New York," he told her. "My native city threw me down. I think Washington is too small for New Yorkers."[11]

For director of the NCSSS, Burke selected Father Francis Haas, professor of sociology at both St. Francis Seminary and Marquette University in Milwaukee. He held a doctorate in socio-economics from Catholic University, where he came under the influence of John Ryan. Haas was a champion of unionization and a living wage. Archbishop Samuel Stritch released him, and he took the helm of the school in July 1931.[12]

In late July and early August, Ready accompanied Burke west for two regional meetings of bishops, one in the ecclesiastical province of Portland and the other in the province of San Francisco. Afterward, Burke told Murray his new assistant benefitted from the experience. "He promises well," concluded Burke, who then left for rest at Homestead in Hot Springs.[13]

FEDERAL EDUCATION QUESTION

While Burke conducted searches, the education question came again to the fore. It had been sidetracked for two years by President Herbert Hoover, who at the urging of Ray Lyman Wilbur, whose Interior Department housed the Office of Education, appointed a National Advisory Committee on Education (NACE) to study the appropriate federal role in schooling. Neither Hoover nor Wilbur wanted a federal department of education.[14]

In April 1931, the NACE produced a draft report. Father George Johnson, director of the NCWC Department of Education and member of the NACE, shared a copy with Burke. Burke considered it "woefully lacking." The report claimed public schools trained character and prepared a person "to realize to the full his human potentialities." As a Catholic—as a citizen—Burke denied such schools could achieve either goal because they excluded religion. "Religious need and capability," free will "and the morality consequent on it," were "supreme factors" that fell beyond the pale of public education. Equally disturbing was the report's supposition there was "a definite, national life—a known and expressed 'soul' of America—for which education fits the individual citizen and moulds [*sic*] him." The report identified that soul with "American democracy." Burke's criticism of this contention was trenchant and went to the heart of the cultural conflict of the 1920s. "I think the report, in this matter, somewhat turned things upside down," he told Johnson. "The very meaning of democracy includes the note of change, the will of the people to decide. That there are certain fixed traditions of our national life is true," things like the Constitution, perpetuity of the union, universal suffrage, and checks balances. Yet, those emanated from the thinking of the people. "Education should be education," argued Burke "—and our democracy presupposes that in the hands of the people the destiny and government and soul of the nation may be left. This report rather supposes that all these are settled and known, and the purpose of education is to preserve them as they are."[15]

Burke saw the crux as maintenance and inculcation of traditional values and political mores versus change—or at least the possibility of change. Put another way, the issue was conformity versus pluralism, the former seeking to maintain the status quo, the latter expressing the will of different peoples to reshape the status quo for their benefit. In Burke's view, the purpose of schooling was not indoctrination, but education in the root sense of the word, namely, to lead out or liberate one from ignorance. The destiny of the nation and its government were secure in the hands of an educated citizenry.

Burke also correctly noted the report made a sustained argument against centralization of education. "Then to the reader's utter amazement," it concluded by recommending the creation of a federal department, after cataloging all the dangers of one. Burke believed the authors "surely" understood a secretary of education would be a political appointee. He also noted the report's admission that the current Office of Education could, empowered by proper legislation, do more to promote schooling. He hoped his comments would help Johnson at the moment of decision. In fact, Johnson recently proposed the NACE recommend making the Office of Education a free-standing bureau independent of every federal department.[16]

In June, the NACE steering committee considered the final draft of the report. Part I recounted the history of federal involvement in education and recommended federal grants on a per-capita basis with no strings attached. Johnson voted in favor of that part. Part II came out squarely for establishment of a department of education, but without any regulatory or executive responsibilities. Johnson and three colleagues voted against it, but went down to defeat, eleven to four. Shortly thereafter, he met with a special committee of bishops that Archbishop John McNicholas, chairman of the NCWC Department of Education, had appointed to advise him. Much to Johnson's surprise, the bishops ordered both him and Father Edward Pace, the other Catholic member of the NACE, to vote no on every issue at its plenary session.[17]

Johnson told Burke the bishops seemed to be acting out of some fear. This news worried Burke because if Johnson and Pace took an intransigently negative stand, there would be repercussions on all Church relations with the federal government. This so upset Burke that he spoke with Archbishop Pietro Fumasoni-Biondi, who told him he was duty-bound to express his views to McNicholas. This, he did in writing.[18]

While awaiting a reply, Burke heard from Johnson's new ordinary, Bishop Alter, who just took office and belonged to McNicholas's committee. Johnson had sent him a copy of the report and told him Burke's view of it. A new bishop, Alter did not know the hierarchy had gone on record as opposed to a department of education. Thus, the report impressed him favorably. He told Burke Catholics as citizens had an obligation to secure "such a form of Federal organization in the field of education as will truly advance the interests of our country." He asserted if Congress wished to establish a department like the one in the report, the Church could back it.[19]

Burke agreed Catholics had a civic responsibility to promote some form of federal agency for education, but not the one in the report. They should take a "positive stand" *against* a department. By that, Burke meant the Church should state if it were possible to have a department like the one proposed, lacking regulatory and executive functions, it would be a good thing. But it would "be practically impossible to keep a Federal Department within those limitations," contended Burke, "and ... inevitably a Federal Department, once established, would fall into the very faults and evils which the report ... itself condemns." He favored expansion of the Office of Education with its own separate budget. He encouraged Alter to help McNicholas and his committee to a more positive expression of its opposition, such as the one Burke outlined. Reluctantly, Alter admitted it might be a "far better strategy and perhaps safer" to favor an expansion of the Office of Education.[20]

Whether at Alter's urging or Burke's protestation—or both—McNicholas saw the wisdom of allowing Johnson and Pace to follow his advice. When the NACE met in October 1931 to vote on the report, it approved Part I recommending per-capita, regulation-free grants for education by a margin of forty-five to six, with both Johnson and Pace voting yes. Because neither man believed Congress would ever provide such a subsidy without strings attached, both felt safe in approving it. Thus, they took a positive stance toward federal education, regardless of their mental reservations. The proposal for a department was a different matter. The hierarchy opposed one at its last meeting. Too, if established, a department would undoubtedly administer the proposed federal aid and become the instrument of government control. So, the two cast dissenting ballots. The vote on Part II was thirty-eight in favor, eleven opposed, with two abstentions. In a final vote on whether to adopt or reject the report as a whole, the tally was forty-three to eight, with both Johnson and Pace joining representatives of vocational education and Negro education in voting no.[21]

The day before the hierarchy's convention in November, McNicholas told Burke several bishops thought it would be good to discover where Hoover stood regarding the report. The hierarchy did not want to publicly protest against the proposed department, but it might be necessary unless Hoover opposed the plan. Persona non grata with Hoover since the Lutheran debacle, Burke spoke with Ebert Burlew, Wilbur's administrative secretary. Reminding him the Catholic Church had consistently opposed a department because it would "trammel free thought among our people in its educational channels," Burke said if Hoover favored the NACE report, the bishops might have to issue a public protest, something they hoped to avoid because the public might attach political significance to such action. If assurance could be given otherwise, the air might be cleared. On the condition any word would remain confidential, Burlew promised to telephone Wilbur, who was in Texas. That evening Burlew told Burke that although Wilbur could not speak for Hoover, the matter would definitely be settled without creation of a department. Wilbur hoped Burke could forestall action by the hierarchy because public protest would only make his own opposition to the report more difficult.[22]

Burke immediately informed McNicholas who said if difficulties arose in the convention, he would telephone Burke for assistance. Burke then saw Cardinal Hayes, who considered Wilbur's assurance sufficient to prevent a protest. And so it was. When McNicholas made his report the next morning, the bishops accepted Wilbur's word. No protest was forthcoming and no further action contemplated.[23]

For Catholics, the best news came several days later. Archbishop Edward Hanna saw Hoover on NCWC business. During the conversation, Hoover indicated he would not follow the NACE's recommendation. Education and public welfare both properly belonged in the Interior, and he intended to reorganize government agencies accordingly.[24] In effect, the NACE report was a dead letter to be pigeonholed and forgotten by all but history.

MEXICO

While Burke dealt with education, there were troubling signs from Mexico. The modus vivendi had been functioning relatively smoothly under Pascual Ortiz Rubio, so much so that the exiled Archbishop Francisco Orozco y Jiménez decided to return to his diocese. Yet the government soon expelled him again, causing Burke to question Mexico's commitment to the agreement. In early February 1931, he reminded Reuben Clark, ambassador plenipotentiary, the modus vivendi stipulated that with the return of the bishops and the resumption of public worship, periodic discussions about altering the anticlerical articles in the constitution would occur. When Burke met with Ortiz Rubio, he agreed those articles needed change. "But nothing has been done," stated Burke. Archbishop Leopoldo Ruiz y Flores, the apostolic delegate, had publicly urged Mexican Catholics to cease opposition, yet the government did not abandon its antagonism to the Church. There was still active persecution in Tabasco. Unless the government did something positive, the situation would deteriorate. Burke confessed he did not know why he was writing, except his "heart [was] with Mexico" and he saw "little hope or cheer." "Surely the leaders must see the situation," he told Clark: "the men who really love Mexico must see it. Revolution will but bleed the country white. Revolution is disaster—for both sides."[25]

Desirous himself for resolution of the religious issue, Clark believed it would take "the proverbial patience of Job" to accomplish it. He recently lunched with Ruiz, Archbishop Pascual Díaz, and Father Wilfrid Parsons; all thought matters were going reasonably well, except in Tabasco. Ruiz said he had jokingly told Díaz he should marry the daughter of that state's governor to get the Church back on its feet there. Because there was dissatisfaction among clergy with the current situation, Ruiz polled the bishops about seeking changes to the anticlerical articles. A few replied the time was not ripe; the majority thought moderate changes should be sought; and a few wanted to acquire the same freedom for the Church as existed in the United States. Ruiz sent this information to the Vatican, which directed him to proceed with prudence. Clark encouraged the delegate to act accordingly.[26]

In March 1931, the Mexican Supreme Court ruled states could implement the anticlerical articles even if they interfered with the Church's internal life. Governor Sebastián Allende of Jalisco ordered enforcement of a previously unimplemented state law permitting only 250 priests to function there.[27]

In late April, Burke wrote again to Clark. Admitting need for "the patience of Job," he reiterated the modus vivendi's call for negotiations on the anticlerical articles. "I would not like the situation to drift in such a way as to bring about another crisis," said Burke. Díaz just visited and seemed hopeful. He told Burke Ruiz was consulting attorneys about a prudent course for change in the laws. Burke was convinced some Mexican leaders hated, even feared the Church, wanting to keep it "in bondage." "They cannot meet the problem of religious worship, religious education, by avoiding it or saying it must not exist," he argued. "It does and will exist. It is quite beyond their yes or no. More persistent than Banquo's ghost, it will appear time and time again." Lacking foresight to settle the conflict at its root, the rulers of Mexico were living in "a fool's paradise." Burke believed Clark had vision to see the situation. He thanked him for his "sympathetic and understanding mind."[28]

In June, Nelson Johnson of State's Mexican Division phoned Burke with news that Governor Adalberto Tejeda of Veracruz had limited the number of priests to one for every 100,000 people, a total of eleven clergymen. Bishop Rafael Guizar Valencia ordered all churches in the diocese closed. Burke arranged for Archbishop Pietro Fumasoni-Biondi to meet with Assistant Secretary Arthur Lane. After the conference, Fumasoni-Biondi told Burke Ruiz had spoken with Guizar and Bishop Jenero Méndez y del Río of Tehuantepec directing them to tell priests not to appear before local authorities because doing so would be tantamount to acceptance of the law. The clergy were not to leave their churches or rectories unless forced and then request an injunction against enforcement. As several other states followed suit, Ruiz publicly condemned resurgence of anticlericalism, but urged Catholics to petition peacefully for its halt.[29]

In November, Lane told Burke that Tejeda and Governor Tomás Garrido Canabal of Tabasco were both anticlerical fanatics and political masters of their states. He correctly noted, however, that federal officials in Mexico City were better disposed to the Church than those two.[30]

In what historian Peter Reich calls "a spectacular example of government tolerance," the Church went ahead with public celebration of the 400th anniversary of the apparition of Our Lady of Guadalupe to Indian Juan Diego in December 1531, a festival abetted by and participated in by government officials. Federal employees in the capital did not interfere, several cabinet members and numerous members of Congress participated, and Secretary of the Treasury Luis Montes de Oca reduced railroad rates for celebrants traveling to Mexico City. The public festivities, however, provoked backlash. Later that month, anticlericals in Congress pushed through a law limiting the Federal District to twenty-five priests. By year's end, every state except Morelos limited the number of clergymen.[31]

Twice, New York

Burke spent Christmas 1931 in Manhattan with family and friends. As was his wont, he penned a poem for the feast:

> This night, this hut, all secrets hold.
> Come, strengthening cup or chastening rod!
> My soul is justly over-bold
> Since Christ has brothered us in God.

He took the opportunity to see Murray's new apartment. "It is always a joy and a reward and a re-living in a way to go to New York," Burke wrote to her afterward: "I feel the happier for it." Yet, the short train ride back to Washington after the holidays exhausted him. "I was for a time very tired and even somewhat discouraged," he told her. "In the face of so much to do, it is a pity not to be able to do it." He had to rest "a great deal." He was puzzled that such short train trips exacted so much from him. He said his doctor placed him under even sterner discipline, which Burke considered "good."[32]

Despite fatigue, Burke could not escape some duties. "Mexico is in a bad way," he told Murray. On 11 January 1932, he went to see Undersecretary of State William R. Castle Jr. about it. The two had first met in 1928. Burke had deeply impressed him. "Father Burke ... by far the most important Roman Catholic in this country, has a rather wonderful, world-weary face," Castle penned in his diary. "He is obviously a man of great power and authority, very sure of himself, very adroit and clever. I should like him and at the same time be afraid of him. He could be ruthless in the pursuit of his purpose. He is rather the type of the great ecclesiastic of two or three hundred years ago who ran the political affairs of the Church, adaptable outwardly but steel underneath. I hope I shall see more of him because he is enormously interesting." Castle later explained why he feared and considered him dangerous: Burke was so adroit and persuasive Castle feared "he would make me promise something that I did not want to promise."[33]

Burke came for no promises this day. The two briefly discussed the religious situation in Mexico. Burke had recently spoken by phone with Ruiz who said the government might again exile certain bishops, but there would be no cessation of worship as had happened in the Cristero Rebellion. Castle deplored the renewed persecution and asked Burke to keep the department informed.[34]

Though the timing is uncertain, it seems shortly after this interview, Burke's health gave out. He developed some sort of urinary problem and his heart was giving trouble. Drs. Marbury and Lee sent him to New York for treatment and rest. While there, Burke "managed to remain hidden and unknown." Just where he stayed is a mystery. Not even his fellow Paulists knew he was there. The only ones in the know were Ready, whom Burke left in charge, and Iona McNulty, his secretary, who made daily trips to Manhattan to keep him abreast on large issues. Dr. Mohan gave Burke treatments for the urinary problem, and Dr. Bainton, quite possibly his childhood friend Dr. Joseph Bainton, confirmed Lee's diagnosis about the heart. "I'm idling my days," Burke wrote to William Kerby. "Not altogether but for the most part."[35]

In late January 1932, Burke interrupted his rest to see Lane who came to Manhattan to talk about Mexico. Burke said he suspected Elías Calles was behind the crackdown against priests as a way of validating his anticlerical credentials. Lane confirmed the persecution resulted from the Guadalupe celebration. At the festivities, Catholics cheered the name of Calles, whose wife contributed money to finance the fiesta. This caused members of the National Revolutionary Party (NRP) to accuse its "*Jefe Maximo* [supreme chief]" of betraying it in favor of the Church. Calles denied the charge. To prove his loyalty, he drafted and secured passage of the law reducing the number of priests in the Federal District.[36]

Burke returned to Washington sometime in April to find a letter from the Paulist superior general saying he had heard "vague rumors that you were quite ill, that you were in some N.Y. hospital etc." Burke explained he went there for treatment and rest without knowing how long his stay would last. It turned out to be longer than anticipated. "It helped me much to be away for a while," he wrote, "and also helped in the way of experience the new assistant, Father Ready." In an effort to salve the general, Burke said he was following his direction not to work as hard as he used to—adding honestly, "This also because I cannot."[37]

Financial Crisis

The Depression exacerbated a financial issue the NCWC had been dealing with since 1926. In that year, the War Council, which had been paying salaries of employees who worked for both organizations, closed its books. Its generosity had been making up for a shortfall in the NCWC's budget caused by bishops who underpaid or refused to pay their allotments to support it. In that year, the hierarchy reduced the budget from $200,000 to $185,000 ($3.5 to $3.2 million in 2024), forcing Burke in 1927 to reduce departmental services by a combined $30,000 because average annual intake from the bishops over the previous five years was only $161,000 ($2.8 million). For the next five years, the hierarchy maintained the budget at $185,000.[38]

In April 1932, the financial situation of the NCWC became acute. An examination of expenses revealed that to meet those of the previous fiscal year (1930–1931), Archbishop John Murray of St. Paul, treasurer, had been unable to collect $46,000 ($1 million) in allotments, necessitating his taking out a personal loan in that amount to cover the final quarter of the year. This condition was repeating itself in the current one (1931–1932), meaning another loan would be necessary. The committee ordered Burke to reduce expenses in each department by wage cuts of 10 percent for those earning $1,200 to $2,400 per year ($27,000 and $54,000 respectively) and 20 percent for those making more.[39]

In August 1932, Burke reported to Hanna that rather than cut salaries, departments had reduced their expenses by a combined $25,000 ($562,000), equivalent to the desired reduction in wages. That was the good news. The rest was bleak. Murray was finding it difficult to get bishops to pay their allotments, which left the NCWC unable to meet its expenses and salaries. The organization's current bills amounted to $4,720 ($106,200) with some overdue two months. When paydays approached, Burke had to write Murray to let him know the amount needed. Sometimes the check came at the last moment. Murray recently had to transfer the $46,000 loan from the New York bank to one in St. Paul at the cost of another $4,000, so the total amount of debt was $50,000 ($1.13 million) plus interest. Burke told Hanna that in the fiscal year just closed (1931–

1932) only $155,000 ($3.49 million) had been collected from the hierarchy. Given the situation, Burke acknowledged he must now cut salaries. He recommended a reduction of 5 percent for those making between $1,500 and $2,000 per year ($33,750 and $45,000, respectively) and 10 percent for those making more than $2,000. He wanted Hanna to order him in writing to do so. He also wanted desperately the archbishop's advice about the entire financial situation.[40]

Instead, Hanna called the Administrative Committee to meet in mid-September. Burke told Grace Murray he dreaded the session because he had no idea what the bishops might do. The NCWC was already understaffed. If the committee made drastic cuts, Burke hardly felt the organization could or should "make the claim of doing the work we claim to do."[41] Five of the seven bishops attended. The absence of minutes leaves it unclear what transpired. They seem to have done little more than apprise the apostolic delegate of the situation.[42]

In early October, Burke wrote Hanna that finances were "so critical and bewildering" he needed the archbishop's "immediate guidance." The previous payday, he had begged Murray for whatever he could give. The latter sent $8,000 ($180,000), which was $1,300 short of covering payroll alone. Burke wired him immediately, and Murray sent $1,300 more, "but I am sure he borrowed it," Burke told Hanna. He explained the NCWC had been unable for months to pay its bills amounting to $9,000 ($202,500); some were three and four months past due. The phone company was threatening to cut off service, there was no money for postage, and bill collectors were harassing the organization. Burke was keeping within budget, but the NCWC had received $38,000 ($855,000) less than allotted. The next payday was six days hence and there was no money. Burke had sent Ready to St. Paul to see Murray. The latter had suffered a physical breakdown and was confined to bed. "I can't press him on finances just now," wrote Burke. He thought Hanna should appoint another bishop to take over Murray's duties until he recovered. "Will you kindly advise me at once what to do," concluded Burke. "I will with great anxiety await your word."[43]

Aware of the NCWC's desperate financial straits, Fumasoni-Biondi summoned Burke. He told him both he and the pope considered the organization's work vitally important. The delegate felt obligated to speak out and thought he should issue a letter to the hierarchy about the situation. Burke wired Hanna for approval, and the latter willingly gave it.[44] Burke drafted a letter for the delegate's signature. Without detailing the critical monetary situation of the NCWC, Fumasoni-Biondi acknowledged the Great Depression left it with a serious lack of funds. Admitting every bishop now labored under financial burdens, he noted the annual convention of hierarchy and the business of the NCWC's departments were "a most important work for the entire Church of the country. In this I but voice the judgment of our Holy Father." The Administrative Committee too sent a letter of its own. Burke reported as a result of the two, money was coming in and the financial situation eased.[45]

When the Administrative Committee met prior the convention of the hierarchy, it decided to ask again for $185,000 ($4.16 million) for the coming year, but told Burke to limit expenditures to $151,000 ($3.4 million). The extra money would be used to begin paying off Murray's loan. The hierarchy approved the request.[46] It can hardly be doubted that the stress of the financial situation weighed heavily on Burke's health.

Birth Control

Just as the financial crisis began, Burke again faced the redoubtable Margaret Sanger and birth control. In April 1932, Representative Franklin Hancock of North Carolina reintroduced the NCFLBC bill in the House. To help promote it, Sanger hired retired Army Colonel J. Joseph Toy, a Catholic. He saw William Montavon to ask the attitude of the NCWC toward it. Montavon replied that because the bill was unchanged, the NCWC stood by its testimony at previous hearing on it. Toy agreed with much of what the NCWC had argued there and was trying to get Sanger to modify the bill. According to Toy, Montavon suggested that a rewrite with input from a Catholic physician might produce something the Church could support. Montavon later denied Toy's version of the meeting.[47]

Toy met with Father John Ryan and Dr. Joseph Mundell of Georgetown University, the NCWC consultant on medical matters. Ryan warned that Catholic involvement in rewriting the bill must be confidential. In any case, Mundell collaborated with Toy and Senator Henry Hatfield of West Virginia, whom Sanger chose because he was a physician and the former governor of that state. Her attorneys hoped that as a doctor, he might be able to offset religious and moral opposition with medical arguments. The revised bill removed from the criminal code and tariff laws all printed information, instruments, and medications to prevent conception for use by a licensed doctor, medical college, hospital, clinic, or druggist filling a prescription. Hatfield, who considered the measure "the most discouraging and disgusting bill he had ever worked on," reluctantly introduced it.[48]

In late April, Burke conferred with Montavon and directed him to dissuade the Committee on Ways and Means from holding a hearing on the Hancock bill. Montavon saw Charles Crisp of Georgia, acting chairman, who said he would leave the decision to the committeemen. In any case, he would limit a hearing to only the part of the bill applying to the tariff. In early May, Montavon reported to Burke the committee was receiving numerous letters and telegrams demanding a hearing and favorable action.[49]

Then came word that a subcommittee of the Senate Judiciary Committee scheduled a hearing on the Hatfield bill. Burke informed Hanna that Hatfield was noncommittal about his position toward it (in fact, he supported it only for eugenic purposes.) The subcommittee consisted of Senators Daniel Hastings of Delaware, Clarence Dill of Washington, and Warren Austin of Vermont. Burke and Ready had Regan mobilize the NCCW to protest to each member of the entire Judiciary Committee as well as to their individual representatives and senators. Burke and Ready contacted the bishops of the dioceses of subcommittee members to have their flocks do the same. Burke asked Schrembs to urge Frederick Kenkel of the German-American Central Verein to mobilize his constituents. "We have not much time and we have not the needed resources," Burke complained to Hanna. "There is little likelihood that the Bill will pass, but the champions of birth control are eager to have the public hearing because of the publicity it gives their cause."[50]

Burke placed Montavon in charge of organizing opposition at the hearing, which for tactical purposes had to be conducted by a third party to avoid accusation that antagonism was simply Catholic. Also, if opposition was under NCWC auspices, Protestant and Jewish opponents might be unwilling to appear. So, Burke secured the National Patriotic League and its representative Ralph Burton to introduce witnesses. Montavon had a hard time getting Hastings to give a date and time for the opposition. Burke thought his dilatoriness might owe less to prejudice against opponents than his desire to demonstrate he had "given every chance to the belligerent and publicity-seeking Birth Preventists [*sic*]." In fact, the subcommittee heard testimony from the protagonists before setting any date for the opposition.[51]

Sanger and her witnesses emphasized eugenics, economics, and maternal health. Their argument throughout was the need to keep population and poverty within limits, to reduce the workforce in light of mechanized production, to safeguard mothers, and to promote a better human stock. The religious issue was not absent from the session. Addressing moral and ethical aspects, Rabbi Edward Israel argued the religious beliefs of certain groups should not become law of the land in interference with what others considered perfectly ethical and indeed "a finer morality." Millions of people resented imposition of "ancient and medieval ideas upon a modern civilization." Israel averred there was evolutionary development in religious and moral thought, paralleling advances in "scientific thought and scientific knowledge." He declared, "Dogmatic religion will not concede these." For example, a certain faith resisted the idea that the earth revolved around the sun and fought the theory of evolutionary development. At the close of session, Hastings finally set a time for the opposition.[52]

The NCWC then received word the House Committee on Ways and Means would hold a hearing on the Hancock bill the same day the Senate subcommittee would hear opponents of the Hatfield bill. It was arranged for the opposition to appear before the subcommittee in the morning and testify before the House committee in the afternoon. At the Hatfield hearing, Catholic witnesses stressed social justice (a living wage) as the antidote to problems of labor and poverty, and argued the promiscuous effect a relaxation of the law would have on youth.[53]

While opponents testified against the Hatfield bill, Sanger and her people appeared at the House hearing on the Hancock one. There, Catholic committee member John McCormack, apparently at Burke's instigation, looked after the Church's interests while its representatives were in the other chamber. McCormack tried to corner Sanger into admission that continence through self-denial was an "affirmative" form birth control, but she dodged and parried. He then asked directly if birth control was "a means of affording self-satisfaction and preventing the consequences thereof by the use of artificial means." Her reply, "If you wish to put it that way." Her colleague Charlotte Perkins Gilman contended religious objectors were the foremost hindrance to passage of the bill, the Catholic Church in particular. Admitting its right to forbid adherents to use such means, she argued it had no right "to interfere with legislation of the country in the interests of a particular church."[54]

That afternoon, as opponents began to testify, Chairman Crisp halted proceedings so committee members could return to the House chamber for roll-call votes. His solution to proroguing the session was that the testimony opponents of the Hatfield bill gave that morning to the Senate subcommittee would be printed into the record of the House hearing as opposing testimony to the Hancock measure. Margaret Lynch brought this news to Burke, who quickly dictated a letter she hand-delivered to Montavon at the Capitol declaring it "impossible" to accept such an arrangement. He must insist on a special hearing. Crisp then agreed to let the opposition finish the next morning.[55]

Within a week the Ways and Means Committee reported the Hancock bill unfavorably. It pronounced the issue of birth control too controversial and considered it unwise for the House or the country to enter into a discussion of it. Montavon noted the report forestalled any attempt by the proponents to have the bill withdrawn from Ways and Means and referred to another committee. Several days later, he and Burke called on McCormack to thank him for "his attitude and work" on the Hancock bill. McCormack said he always referred to it as "the Race Suicide Bill." He averred the vast majority of committee members adamantly opposed it; most congressmen were "of wholesome mind" and appreciated receiving support for their view during hearings from people of "upright principles in public morals."[56]

To Hanna, Burke admitted "the only aggressive organized opposition" came from the Catholic Church. He said other entities had and would assist it, but doubted any would "take the initiative and positively" secure a hearing for antagonists. Burke lamented the NCWC's inability to handle the matter as it ought because it lacked funds. It was in no position to bring to Washington requisite experts on population, sterilization, and public health.[57]

That need soon became apparent. Senator Hastings agreed to hold a second closed subcommittee hearing in June on the Hatfield bill so Senator

Austin could hear firsthand from Dr. Bessie Moses, head of Sanger's birth control clinic in Baltimore, about the contraceptive devices she used that were unavailable to other physicians because of the criminal code. Burke had Montavon attend on behalf of the opposition. Near the end of a very technical session, Austin asked if Montavon would like to make a statement. Acknowledging he was unqualified, he said the NCWC would probably have someone appear before the subcommittee.[58]

Burke wrote to Bishop Charles White of Spokane, hometown of Senator Dill, a subcommittee member who refused to participate. Burke explained the NCWC had been asked to respond to technical testimony, but only "professional medical experts" could provide effective answer. Burke lacked money to summon one. The NCWC should have financial resources, he wrote, to call on those "who would help us prove that Christ is true King of all creation; that medical science and practical experience uphold and support the teachings of His Church." Having to deal with mechanical aspects of birth control was, for Burke, an "unpleasant and dirty task," the delving into "matters utterly repellant to Christian sense." He recalled, however, that "Christ emptied Himself and descended to our lowest depths that He might give hope to all."[59]

Burke decided to send Mary Hawks, president of the NCCW; Rita McGoldrick, head of the Catholic Alumnae Federation; and Dr. W. Gerry Morgan, dean of Georgetown's School of Medicine, to appear before the subcommittee. Unfortunately, Morgan was prevented from attending. McGoldrick produced copious evidence demonstrating widespread illegal trade in contraceptive information and devices. She argued the law should be tightened, not liberalized. Montavon remarked that birth control advocates advanced the same evidence to argue the Hatfield bill would curtail such abuses. He also told Burke Morgan's absence was "fatal" because it prevented presentation of technical evidence and from shoring up points McGoldrick made inadequately.[60]

Toward the end of July 1932, Dill resigned from the subcommittee, and no Democrat was willing to take his place. The rump subcommittee of Austin and Hastings was deadlocked. There the matter rested until the final session of Congress.[61]

When the Administrative Committee met in November, Burke reported the Hancock bill went down to defeat, but cautioned against overconfidence regarding the future. "We have, practically, been left alone as Catholics in our opposition to birth prevention," he told the committee. "Protestant churches and Protestant organizations will not, as a body, unite with us. There is grave danger that the question will be looked upon not as one of basic public morality, as a fundamental factor in our whole national life—but as a question solely of Catholic dogma." He recommended greater involvement of the laity as spokespersons on their own behalf in this matter. He urged, too, the necessity of securing more medical professionals behind the cause.[62]

In mid-January 1933, Senators Austin and Hastings sent a divided report to the Judiciary Committee. After recounting facts agreed upon, the two rendered opposing recommendations. Hastings saw nothing immoral in contraception and believed it would be beneficial for lower-class women. He urged the committee-of-the-whole to report the bill favorably. Austin recommended otherwise because of the damage already being done to labor and agriculture by the declining birth rate.[63]

Sanger and birth control advocates inundated the Senate committee with petitions to report the Hatfield bill. Hearing from two members of that body, Senators Thomas Walsh and Felix Hébert, there was no chance the committee would report the bill favorably, Burke responded with a quiet protest. He had Regan mobilize the NCCW and McGoldrick mobilize the Catholic Alumnae Federation in letter-writing campaigns to members of the committee. Because Sanger and her people sought publicity, he cautioned the two against any use of the press. The committee met on 13 February with eight members present to discuss the subcommittee report. With seven of eight balloting, the vote was four against and three in favor. The clerk then polled the entire membership. The final tally was nine opposed, six in favor, and two abstentions.[64]

MEXICO AGAIN

While Burke dealt with birth control, the situation in Mexico darkened. Through most of the year, President Ortiz Rubio had unsuccessfully struggled to right a faltering economy. Moreover, he ran afoul of many anticlericals and lost the support of Calles, who forced him to resign in September 1932. The Mexican Congress elected as interim president Abelardo Rodríguez, a former general who was then minister of war. Shortly after his inauguration, Pius XI issued the encyclical *Acerba Animi* (*With Pain at Heart*) which pointedly accused Mexico of not living up to the modus vivendi. The pope encouraged "Catholic laity to continue to protest with all their energy against such violation, using every legitimate means," even if the protest fell on deaf ears. He explained that priests who complied with the "iniquitous" and "impious" laws, while objecting to them, were not guilty of moral collusion with evil. Such men were essentially forced to submit "in order to avoid a greater evil": leaving the faithful without sacraments. Although Pius clearly favored peaceful protest against persecution, Rodríguez publicly declared the encyclical invited armed rebellion.[65]

The day after Rodríguez's declaration, Fumasoni-Biondi summoned Burke to say the Mexican Chamber of Deputies raised the question of demanding Rodríguez expel Archbishop Ruiz. Burke took the matter up with Castle. He said the encyclical was irenic. Pius's purpose was to hold priests in Mexico to observance of local laws even though he did not consider them just. Like Pius, Ruiz favored conciliation and observance of the laws. Burke feared deportation of Ruiz would leave in Mexico only those priests unwilling to follow the pope, those who wanted open resistance to the government. Believing Rodríguez had not seen the full text, Burke asked Castle to have Ambassador Clark urge him to await the entire document. Castle agreed. Four days later, he summoned Burke and read aloud a cable from Clark, who argued the Mexican Congress never ratified the modus vivendi, so it was not a binding agreement on Mexico. Moreover, the Mexican government had no power over state governments, which were free to limit the number of priests. Castle told Burke the Mexican government had the complete text of *Acerba* and already exiled Ruiz, who was now in Laredo. Castle had read the encyclical and "failed to see how the Mexican Government could interpret it other than a document of peaceful intent." Burke said there was nothing for the Mexican Church to do now except "beat time." It would not withdraw its priests and bishops as it had done in 1926. Yet local laws allowed too few clergy to function in an effective way.[66]

A little over a week later, Lane saw Burke to follow up on Ruiz's expulsion. He said State was informed through direct inquiry of Calles himself that there was no political reason behind it; the present government had nothing to fear politically. Lane believed that true. Burke thought otherwise.

He believed Calles said what he must to convince the U.S. that Mexico had a stable government. Burke argued facts failed to support that. The forced resignation of Ortiz Rubio; his replacement by a former general in direct contradiction of Calles's declaration that presidents should no longer be military men; the activities of Tejeda and Gonzalo Santos—all these suggested something of a crisis, of conflict within the Revolutionary Party necessitating the hand of a dictator. Lane upheld Clark's position that the modus vivendi was non-binding and the Mexican government had no power over states. Admitting the last bit, Burke countered the parties who entered into the modus vivendi never intended it to be submitted to the Mexican Congress: "It was an acceptance, a promise, an agreement by the Executive head of the nation." President Emilio Portes Gil had publicly acknowledged it; President Ortiz Rubio had acknowledged it in the presence of Burke, Montavon, Dwight Morrow, and Lane himself. "Did it mean nothing?" Lane reiterated Clark's position: the modus vivendi had no effect because the Mexican Congress had never ratified it.[67]

Burke considered the interview "significant" and telling. It signaled the U.S. government and its embassy in Mexico "abandoned and all but repudiated Morrow's policy and Morrow's line of action." As long as the administration in Mexico appeared stable, the U.S. had no further concern. Burke noted a subtle shift in Lane's attitude. Previously, he actively sympathized with the American Catholic Church's efforts to "secure something like justice" for the Mexican Church. He was not now unsympathetic, but that "active sympathy" was now "entirely absent."[68] Fortunately, it appeared likely there would be a change in American presidential administrations. Within a month, the nation elected Franklin D. Roosevelt, with a good deal of Catholic support.[69]

ENDNOTES TO CHAPTER 20

1. Burke, *Christ in Us*, 1.
2. Burke to Schrembs, 4 May 1931, copy, ACUA, USCCB 10:99:3; Schrembs to Burke, 9 May 1931, ibid.; Burke, Diary 1930–1931, 4, 5, and 15 May 1931, AP, Burke Papers, box 2.
3. Burke, Memorandum, 29 May to 1 June 1931, ACUA, USCCB 10:153: Interview Book.
4. Ibid.

5. Ibid.
6. Ibid.
7. Ibid.
8. Ibid.
9. Ibid.
10. Ibid.; Minutes of the Administrative Committee, 9 November 1931, ACUA, USCCB 10:64.
11. Burke to Lynch, 12 June 1931, AP, Burke Papers, box 5.
12. "Dr. Haas Heads National Catholic School of Social Service," *NCWC Review* 13 (August 1931): 22.
13. Burke to G. Murray, 16 August 1931, AP, Burke Papers, box 12; Burke to Kerby, 7 September 19331, ACUA, Kerby Papers 58:4:4.
14. Slawson, *Department of Education Battle*, 182, 213–25.
15. Burke to Johnson, 6 April 1931, ACUA, USCCB Department of Education 10:49:2.
16. Ibid.; Slawson, *Department of Education Battle*, 232–33.
17. Slawson, *Department of Education Battle*, 234–35.
18. Burke to Karl Alter, 20 July 1931, copy, ACUA, USCCB 10:100:8. Burke's correspondence with McNicholas cannot be located in either ACUA or in the AAC.
19. Alter to Burke, 16 July 1931, ACUA, ACUA, USCCB 10:100:8.
20. Burke to Alter, 20 July 1931, copy, ACUA, USCCB 10:100:8; Alter to Burke, 27 July 1931, ibid.
21. Pace to Mann, with corrections by John T. McNicholas, 11 September 1931, copy, ACUA, Vice Rector files; Johnson, Memorandum on the Department of Education, 3 October 1931, copy, ACUA, USCCB Department of Education 10:49:3; NACE, *Committee Findings and Recommendations*, 1:89, 99, 100.
22. Burke, Memorandum, 10 November 1931, ACUA, USCCB 10:153: Interview Book.
23. Ibid.; *Minutes of the Thirteenth Annual Meeting of the American Hierarchy, November 1931*, ACUA, USCCB Bound Volumes.
24. Burke, Interview with Hanna, 14 November 1931, ACUA, USCCB 10:153: Interview Book; Burke, Interview with Michael Ready, 18 November 1931, ibid.
25. Burke to Clark, 3 February 1931, copy, ACUA, USCCB 10:149:19; Redinger, *American Catholics and the Mexican Revolution*, 90.
26. Clark to Burke, 19 February 1931, with lengthy post script dated 28 February 1931, ACUA, USCCB 10:149:19.
27. Reich, *Mexico's Hidden Revolution*, 36.
28. Burke to Clark, 25 April 1931, copy, ACUA, USCCB 10:149:19.
29. Burke, Memorandum of Telephone Conversation with Nelson Johnson, 20

June 1931, ACUA, USCCB 10:145: Interview Book V; Redinger, *American Catholics and the Mexican Revolution*, 91; Reich, *Mexico's Hidden Revolution*, 36; Bailey, *¡Viva Cristo Rey!*, 294–95.

30. [Burke, Interview with Lane], 13 November 1931, ACUA, USCCB 10:145: Interview Book V.
31. Redinger, *American Catholics and the Mexican Revolution*, 91–92; Reich, *Mexico's Hidden Revolution*, 36–38; Bailey, *¡Viva Cristo Rey!*, 295.
32. Burke, untitled poem, Christmas 1931, ACUA, USCCB 10:72:24; Burke to G. Murray,13 January 1932, AP, Burke Papers, box 12.
33. Castle, 10 March 1928 and 4 November 1936, Diaries, HLHU.
34. [Burke, Interview with Castle], 11 January 1931, ACUA, USCCB 10:145: Interview Book V.
35. Burke to Kerby, 9 March 1932, ACUA, Kerby Papers 58:4:4; Burke to Harney, 13 April 1932, copy, AP, Burke Papers, box 20.
36. Lane to Burke, telegram, 19 January 1932, ACUA, USCCB 10:149:20; Burke to Lane, telegram, 19 January 1932, ibid.; [Burke, Interview with Lane], 22 January 1932, ibid., 10:145: Interview Book V; Redinger, *American Catholics and the Mexican Revolution*, 91–92; Reich, *Mexico's Hidden Revolution*, 37.
37. Burke to Kerby, 15 March 1932, ACUA, Kerby Papers 58:4:4; Harney to Burke, 11 April 1932, AP, Burke Papers, box 20; Burke to Harney, 13 April 1932, copy, ibid.
38. Dowling to Hanna, 30 August 1926, AASF, NCWC files, with enclosure List of Allotments and Payments to the NCWC 1920–1926; Burke to Hanna, 19 March 1927, copy, ACUA, USCCB 10:152:13; Minutes of the Administrative Committee, 14 and 16 September 1926, ibid., 10:64:4; *Minutes of the Eighth Annual Meeting of the Hierarchy, September 1926*, 14–15, ibid., 10 Bound Volumes; Burke to Dowling, 14 July 1927, copy, ACUA, USCCB 10:152:9; Burke to Dowling, 21 July 1927, copy, ibid.; Burke to E. Gibbons, 14 July 1927, copy, ibid., 10:103:27.
39. Minutes of the Administrative Committee, 6 April 1932, ACUA, USCCB 10:64:6; Lists of Allotments and Payments to the National Catholic Welfare Fund for 1920–1932 Inclusive, AASF, NCWC files.
40. Burke to Hanna, 3 August 1932, copy, ACUA, USCCB 10:152:13.
41. Burke to G. Murray, 11 September 1932, AP, Burke Papers, box 12.
42. Ibid.
43. Burke to Hanna, 9 October 1932, copy, ACUA, USCCB 10:152:13.
44. Burke, [Interview with Fumasoni-Biondi], 12 October 1932, ACUA, USCCB 10:152:1; Burke to Hanna, telegram, 13 October 1932, ibid., 10:152:13; Hanna to Burke, 17 October 1932, ibid., 10:99:20
45. Fumasoni-Biondi to the hierarchy, 20 October 1932, copy, 10:152:1; Burke to Emmet Walsh, 5 November 1932, copy, ACUA, USCCB 10:104:2.
46. Minutes of the Administrative Committee, 15 and 17 November 1932,

ACUA, USCCB 10:64:6; *Minutes of the Fourteenth Annual Meeting of the American Hierarchy, November 1932*, 19, ACUA, USCCB Bound Volumes.

47. Montavon to Ready, 13 April 1932, ACUA, USCCB 10:117:20; Chesler, *Woman of Valor*, 333, 552–53 n. 27 and 30; Kennedy, *Birth Control*, 236–37 n. 31.
48. H.R. 11082, 72nd Cong., 1st Session, 4 April 1932; S. 4436, 72nd Cong., 1st Session, 21 April 1932; Ready to John Swint, 4 May 1932, ACUA, USCCB 10:117:20; Baker, *Sanger: Life of* Passion, 204–05 (the quote is taken from here); *Autobiography of Sanger*, 423; Chesler, *Woman of Valor*, 330–35, 552–53 n. 27 and 30; Kennedy, *Birth Control*, 236–37 n. 31.
49. Montavon to Burke and Ready, Memorandum, 2 May 1931, ACUA, USCCB 10:117:20; Montavon to Burke, 4 May 1932, ibid.
50. Montovan to Burke, 4 May 1932; Ready to Swint, 4 May 1932; Regan to Affiliated Organizations, 5 May 1932; Montavon to Ready, 5 May 1932; Burke to Hanna, 6 May 1932, copy; Burke to Charles White, 6 May 1932, copy; Burke to Edmond FitzMaurice, 6 May 1932, copy; McNulty, Memorandum, 6 May 1932—all in ACUA, USCCB 10:117:20; *Birth Control: Hearings before a Subcommittee of the Committee on the Judiciary of the United States Senate, Seventy-Second Congress, First Session, on S. 4436, 12, 19, and 20 May* 1932 (Washington, D.C.: U.S. Government Printing Office, 1932), 1–3, hereinafter cited as *Birth Control, Senate Hearing, 1932*.
51. Montavon to Burke et al., Memoranda, 10 and 12 May 1932; Montavon to Daniel Hastings, 11 May 1932, copy; [Burke, Interview with Senator David Walsh], 12 May 1932; Burke to Hanna, 23 May, 1932, copy—all in ACUA, USCCB 10:117:20; Baker, *Sanger: Life of Passion*, 209–10.
52. *Birth Control, Senate Hearing, 1932*, 1–62 (quotes are on 19–21).
53. Ibid., 71–102, 114–19; Montavon to Burke et al., Memorandum, 16 May 1932, ACUA, USCCB 10:117:20.
54. *Birth Control: Hearings before the Committee on Ways and Means, U.S. House of Representatives, Seventy-Second Congress, First Session, H.R. 11082, 19 and 20 May 1932* (Washington, D.C.: U.S. Government Printing Office 1932), 1–66 (quotes are on 15 and 56); Baker, *Sanger: Life of Passion*, 208.
55. Burke to Montavon, 19 May 1932, copy, ACUA, USCCB 10:117:20; Burke to Hanna, 23 May 1932, copy, ibid.; *Birth Control, House Hearing, 1932*, 81.
56. Montavon to Burke et al., Memorandum, 28 May 1932, ACUA, USCCB 10:117:20; [Burke, Interview with John McCormack], ibid., 10:153: Interview Book.
57. Burke to Hanna, 23 May 1932, copy, ACUA, USCCB 10:117:20.
58. Montavon to Burke, 1 July 1932, ACUA, USCCB 10:117:20.
59. Burke to White, 27 June 1932, copy, ACUA, USCCB 10:117:20.
60. Montavon to Burke, 1 July 1932, ACUA, USCCB 10:117:20.
61. Montavon to Burke, 26 July 1932, ACUA, USCCB 10:117:20.

62. Burke, Report of the General Secretary, November 1932, ACUA, USCCB 10:62:14: Sheerin, *Never Look Back*, 195.
63. *United States Senate, Committee on the Judiciary, Report to Accompany S. 4436, 18 January 1933,* 10–11.
64. Regan to Burke, 30 January 1933, ACUA, USCCB 10:117:21; Regan to ten diocesan presidents, 31 January 1933, copy, ibid.; Burke to McGoldrick, telegram and letter, 31 January 1933, copies, ibid.; Montavon to Burke et al., Memorandum, 17 February 1933, ibid.; Report of the General Secretary, April 1933, ibid., 10:62:16.
65. *Acerba Animi*, 29 September 1932, http://w2.vatican.va/content/pius-xi/en/encyclicals/documents/hf_p-xi_enc_29091932_acerba-animi.html (accessed 23 Sept 2015); Reich, *Mexico's Hidden Revolution*, 38–39; Redinger, *American Catholics and the Mexican Revolution*, 10; Don M. Coerver et al., eds., *Mexico: An Encyclopedia of Contemporary Culture and History* (Santa Barbara: ABC-CLIO, 2004), s.v. "Rodríguez, Abelardo."
66. [Burke, Interviews with Castle], 3 and 7 October 1932, ACUA, USCCB 10:145: Interview Book V; Message from Ambassador Clark of 6 October, with reference to Father Burke's message of 5 October, ibid., 10:149:20; Castle, 8 October 1932, Diaries, HLHU.
67. Burke, [Interview with Lane], 16 October 1932, ACUA, USCCB 10:145: Interview Book V.
68. Ibid.
69. George Q. Flynn, *American Catholics and the Roosevelt Presidency, 1932–36* (Lexington: University of Kentucky Press, 1968), 1–21; Castagna, *Bridge across the Ocean*, 113–17.

Chapter 21
Changing of the Guards

> Christ Himself comes to us disguised in the garments of the poor, the wretched, the fallen. To give to them is to give to Christ Himself: to relieve them is to relieve Christ. He Himself has said: "As long as you did it to one of these My least brethren, you did it to me" (Matt. 25:40). By thus identifying himself with the lowest He has given hope to every one of us, for none is outside Him. His gospel changed all human society and made the strong the servants of the weak. To that gospel humanity owes the expression of its highest, its unselfish traits. Yet by our service of social welfare we are ceaselessly working to the end that there be no poor or needy. That we should do so is justified by the commandment of Christ and by His self-identification with the poor.[1]

Russian Recognition: Part I

Since the Bolshevik Revolution in 1917, the U.S. refused diplomatic recognition to the Soviet Union. That nation embodied totalitarian, atheistic communism, which was antithetical to American democracy and laissez-faire capitalism, and through the Third Communist International (Comintern) promoted worldwide revolution to spread the communist system. The entire Soviet program was anathema to American Catholics. During the Depression, however, elements of the labor movement sympathized with it, while industry hoped for increased trade through diplomatic recognition of Russia. During the 1932 presidential campaign, Democratic candidate Franklin Roosevelt sidestepped the issue by saying domestic concerns were so all-consuming he had no time to inform himself on the issue of

Russian recognition. Evidence indicates he opposed the policy of non-recognition and dodged the issue to avoid alienating his sizable Catholic support. After winning the campaign, it became increasingly clear that Roosevelt favored recognition.[2]

In January 1933, John Burke notified the Administrative Committee it was "quite certain" Roosevelt would recognize Russia. His dealings with State taught him that the morals and religion of a nation played no part in a decision about granting it recognition, which was "purely a civil matter." Burke acknowledged Catholic instinct recoiled at giving it to Russia, and a great number of coreligionists and some diocesan newspapers would decry it. He wanted to be prepared for the issue when it arose, so he polled the members for advice.[3]

The only bishop to consider publicly opposing recognition was Hugh Boyle, who would take that step only if it suggested approval of Soviet internal conduct. Two others were disgusted the U.S. would consider recognition. Bishop Joseph Schrembs thought it almost suicidal: "Here is a nation that is plotting to destroy our government, and we are going to give it recognition. I cannot see it." The other, Archbishop John McNicholas, saw the issue as money (new markets) over "international justice and honesty." He thought absent a protest, Hanna should issue a statement regretting "that a nation can be arrayed against God, can wage a diabolical war against religion, can have as its avowed purpose the subversion of the very foundations of other nations, and yet be recognized for no other reason than 'a mess of pottage.'"[4]

Burke considered Archbishop John Murray's view the most thoughtful. He wanted to avoid a public stand, but use every arm of the NCWC to fight recognition. Headquarters should urge every senator and congressman to pressure officials of the incoming administration against granting it. The NCWC should argue there was "no justification in fact or in law for such action." Although the Soviet government appeared stable, the principles on which it rested "must by their very nature tend to disintegration of the government." It kept its people under its thumb through "terrorism which is the antithesis of orderly government." Inevitably this would lead to revolution once people were "aroused to the point of preferring death to slavery." The NCWC should argue that the Comintern itself evidenced Russia's inability to fulfill its international obligations; it sought the overthrow of legitimate governments. "You might as well argue the propriety of admitting Al Capone and his gang to your private home," wrote Murray. He thought the Administrative Committee ought to meet.[5]

Burke reminded him that to mobilize NCWC resources, he needed "definite direction from the Administrative Committee" about the stand to take. This set Burke off on a disquisition about the annual convention of bishops. He lamented the hierarchy's habit of listening to reports and approving them without thoughtful discussion of the important problems they raised. The hierarchy left those to the Administrative Committee, when in fact they were problems the bishops as a whole should resolve. The hierarchy needed to grapple with important "matters that concern the external well-being of the Church in this country" and decide a stance, argued Burke. It was then the Administrative Committee's duty to implement it. Instead, the hierarchy increasingly focused on concerns internal to the Church, leaving external affairs to the committee.[6] In his view, the NCWC should be the voice of the Church on public matters.

After reviewing responses, Burke reported they indicated the committee as a whole ought to discuss the question at its April meeting. Burke learned that, in addition to the hoped-for monetary benefit of exports to the Soviet Union, the government was seeking better relations with Russia as a counterbalance to Japanese expansion in Asia and the Pacific.[7]

While Burke polled the Administrative Committee, the Vatican asked Archbishop Pietro Fumasoni-Biondi to canvas the hierarchy on Russian recognition. With his elevation to the cardinalate, that task now fell to Monsignor Paolo Marella, chargé d'affaires of the delegation. Burke sent Marella the letters from his poll, remarking they should not be "considered in any sense of the word as final, or even as very deliberate."[8]

Rome

Over the years, Fumasoni-Biondi and Burke had grown close, so the Administrative Committee asked him to represent it at the consistory in Rome whereat the delegate would receive the red hat. Little more than a week before Burke's departure, tragedy struck his family. His brother, James, had a seizure that hospitalized him. Burke told Helen Lynch James was physically in poor shape and worse, "his memory seems to have gone." The family was quite anxious. Burke remained in New York two days, until there was nothing more to be done. He thought of foregoing the trip to Rome, but explained to Lynch his promise to the Administrative Committee that he would represent it at the consistory, "and I must go."[9]

Burke, Agnes Regan, and Bruce Mohler sailed on 1 March 1933. Burke came down with "a heavy cold" just before departure and had to struggle the first night with a berth too short for his six-foot-three frame. He was abed all next day, except while stewards lengthened the berth. That night, his fever rose to 103 degrees, and the cold turned into one of his "squalls." The night watchman treated him, but the fever did not break until the following evening. Burke spent the day after resting in his berth. The next morning, Sunday, he said public Mass in the salon which "proved a physical trial," though he recovered by evening. Burke gradually regained strength, though he admitted to Lynch he had not gotten all the rest he would have wished. He told Grace Murray he was unable to focus on the trip because he could not get James out of his head and heart. He was not worried about arrangements for him because their brother Thomas was handling them, "but I do feel for and with James," he wrote.[10]

The ship reached Cherbourg on 8 March. Burke's party arrived in Paris at noon and then boarded a train that night for Rome, a journey lasting eleven hours. He lodged at the Grand Hotel and spent the first several days making necessary visits to Vatican offices. He congratulated Archbishop Amleto Cicognani on his appointment as new apostolic delegate to the U.S. Burke noted he was quite proficient in English, was a hard worker, and would do well. More encouraging, Cicognani knew much about the work of the NCWC. Physically, Burke was very careful not to overdo it, which was "always a discipline" for him: he slept late every morning, napped again in the afternoon, and stayed in his room after supper almost every night. At times, he felt "exhausted to the limit," but rest restored him.[11]

On 13 March, he witnessed the pontiff bestow a red biretta on each new cardinal. The following day came the formal ceremony in St. Peter's Basilica where Burke was seated with families of those being elevated. Fumasoni-Biondi was grateful and pleased he was present as representative of the NCWC. Each new cardinal approached the pontiff, and Pius placed a broad-brimmed cardinal's hat on his head. The man descended and received a fraternal kiss from his fellow cardinals. The pope blessed all and departed.[12]

On 15 March, Burke met Pius privately, with Monsignor Moses Elias as interpreter. Pius gave a "gracious" welcome, and Burke explained he came to thank him in the name of the Administrative Committee for the honor conferred "on our Apostolic Delegate." The two conversed about the encyclicals *Casti Conubii* (*Of Chaste Marriage*, 1930) and *Quadragesimo Anno* (*Forty Years After*, 1931). Burke told of their being publicly read over the air as the cable of each came in, their publication in Catholic and secular press, and their effect. Pius spoke about the Roosevelt administration and its attitude toward the Church, which was more open and sympathetic than Hoover's. The pope knew Roosevelt appointed two Catholics to cabinet posts: James Farley as postmaster general and Thomas Walsh as attorney general. When asked about economic conditions in America, Burke said he believed Roosevelt's emergency measures would be short-term, but there would be "radical changes" regarding laws governing banking, stock speculation, taxes, and more. He stressed the increasing power of the federal government "and took the opportunity of showing how even more than ever the N.C.W.C. was absolutely necessary and that the Church in the U.S. would be at a loss without it." Pius agreed "very explicitly" and repeated several times its necessity, its work, and its permanency. He was confident the U.S. would weather the financial storm and soon emerge from it. Toward the end of the audience, he addressed Burke personally, praising his work and that of the NCWC. Pius gave his blessing to Burke, all those he had in mind, and all his intentions.[13]

On Sunday, Burke said Mass in his hotel sitting room. Later he went to the Vatican State Department where he met with Monsignor Alfredo Ottaviani, deputy secretary, to discuss a new English translation of *Quadragesimo Anno*. Roman Jesuits had done the official one transmitted to the U.S., but it contained inaccuracies. The NCWC drafted a revised text, which Burke brought with him, to supplant the original. After much discussion, Ottaviani finally agreed to the substitution if Burke could get Jesuit Superior General Vlodomir Ledochowski, to accept it.[14]

Burke then had a long conversation with Archbishop Giuseppe Pizzardo, secretary of the Congregation for Extraordinary Affairs. The two conversed about Mexico. Burke found him knowledgeable about the situation of the Church there. Vatican officials seemed to blame the U.S. for the fact that Mexico did not enjoy full religious liberty, that somehow it "could make

Mexico walk in the path of justice if the U.S. wanted to do it." With regard to Russia, Pizzardo strongly opposed diplomatic recognition. He said the Soviet Union was financially bankrupt, tottering on the brink of collapse. He believed recognition by the U.S. would only prop it up.[15]

The following day, Burke received an unexpected visit from William Adams Brown, a member of the Committee of Six whom he had not seen in twelve years. Brown was "manifestly overjoyed" at their meeting. He stepped back to look at Burke to see if and how he had changed. Brown commented his hair had thinned and greyed, and his face showed he had passed through trials. He could tell Burke no longer had "the vigor and energy" he did on the committee. Burke replied, "I had had, and did have, a hard task."[16]

Brown said he was preparing a book for Protestants about how helpful the Catholic Church could be to them. Deploring the ravages of individualism present in Protestantism, he hoped his coreligionists would return to the "founders" (Martin Luther, John Calvin, and Ulrich Zwingli), who never intended other than organized religion and who would perhaps never have left the Catholic Church if things had been different. Brown said there was an increasing hunger among Protestants for supernatural religion. He begged Burke to tell him what would decrease the curse of naturalism. Burke answered only belief in Christ as savior, and peoples' oneness with him and with one another. He asked Brown if Protestants still believed in the divinity of Christ. He replied they did, except such as were purely "local" like the Congregationalists. Burke noted that American Protestants ceased taking public stands on moral issues like birth control. While never entering politics, the NCWC endeavored to imbue legislation with Christian principles. Burke knew of no Protestant body that did, viewing legislation as a political matter, not a Christian one. The two men conversed about "the failure to hold to, to defend, to expound Xtian principles in the actual life and labor of the day." Brown hoped to write a book that would. Brown saw the nation as "drifting into doubt and denial of fundamental Christian truth and principles." Burke told him his book might save Protestants "from further bewilderment and disaster and lead them some distance at last back 'to the faith that saves.'"[17]

Later, Burke mused: "I cannot put in words the interest shown by Dr. Brown, whether it was in meeting me again or in what I said, but time and again his eyes grew moist and he was visibly affected. Dr. Brown does not know what he wants nor what he wants to do. He dreams his dream but the clouds of Prot[estantism] surround him and it is hard to let the light to come through.... It is significant that in Rome we met and in Rome we had this heart to heart talk."[18]

At the time, Burke himself was working on a book of meditations titled *Christ in Us*. They were the fruit of his fifty-nine-year life in Christ and summed up its meaning: the incarnation of Jesus united all creation and every human being in himself and with his Father, sweeping the Christian into life in the Trinity, a totally unmerited gift. The Holy Spirit moved each Christian with the same love that moved Jesus, the very "life of God in us, the bond of life between God and us, by which He gives to us His life." Life in Christ meant realizing one is loved so much by God that one in turn fell so much in love with God—a love "more truly God's than [one's] own"— as to become as selfless as God Himself. Christians were visible members of the Mystical Body of Christ, actively sharing and participating in his salvific mission, despite their faults and failures.[19]

Soon after meeting Brown, Burke saw Ledochowski about the translation of *Quadragesimo Anno*. The general said the NCWC was free to publish its own translation. Burke insisted on the value of only one official English version. Finally, Ledochowski agreed to a single text. Burke left a copy of the revision for Jesuit translators to review. He then informed Ottaviani of the general's decision and said Ledochowski would be in touch.[20]

On the final evening in Rome, Burke dined in his sitting room with Fumasoni-Biondi, Regan, Mohler, and Monsignor Francis Hyland, secretary of the apostolic delegation in the U.S. The new cardinal was happy to be permanently situated in his native city. He felt honored by the dignity bestowed on him. He also realized the "comparatively easier days of the Delegation ... had passed" and that he faced a "greater burden" than ever before as new prefect of Propaganda Fide and a member of four other congregations. This gathering on the eve of separation was happy, "yet all was deeply touched by sadness," wrote Burke. After supper, he and Fumasoni-Biondi went into Burke's bedroom where they privately bade each other farewell "after ten years of labors and a friendship that will last into eternity."[21]

The following morning, Burke boarded a train for Genoa, where he took ship on the fabled S.S. *Rex*, current Blue Riband holder for westward crossings of the Atlantic. He reached New York at the end of the month and was back at his desk in early April.[22]

FINANCIAL CRISIS AGAIN

On Burke's return, the most pressing problem facing him was finances, which had again reached crisis proportions. Just before his arrival, Michael Ready had had to ask Archbishop Murray for $5,000 ($120,000 in 2024) to meet the mid-month payroll. Headquarters had only $2,900 on hand. Murray sent $1,900 with instructions to pay all only 50 percent of their salary. He then sent a second check directing Ready to pay only 50 percent again at the end of the month. Because funds were still insufficient to meet even that second payment, Ready asked Frank Hall of the Press Department to collect subscription fees for the News Service. Those receipts helped, but the beleaguered Ready told Hanna, "From present indications, I don't think we shall have enough money to meet even the fifty percent basis." He did not know what to do.[23]

On his second day back at work, Burke wrote Hanna that the financial situation was "enough to take the heart out of one" and required the "immediate and definite attention of the Administrative Committee." Burke "earnestly" begged him to attend its meeting later in the month because matters were "so critical" his presence was "imperative." The committee needed to take action and let all at headquarters know what the future held.[24]

Burke's report at that meeting led with finances, which were "more than critical." He reminded the bishops that five months earlier they reduced the budget by $25,000 ($600,000). He read them a memorandum from Charles McMahon, the longest-serving staff member, which illustrated "the generous spirit" of the workers. McMahon said he and his colleagues were willing to make "whatever sacrifices necessary." They believed that given Roosevelt's many initiatives, the NCWC was "more necessary than ever before to the well-being of the Catholic Church." The bishops asked for Burke's recommendation. He advised reducing the annual salaries of employees by a total of $22,000 ($528,000). This would require a 10 percent reduction for those earning $3,000 ($72,000) or less, provided it would bring no one below $1,200 ($28,000); it would require a 20 percent reduction for those earning more than $3,000. The committee so ordered it, effective 1 May.[25]

The committee considered closing the Immigration Bureau, but found that work too important to Catholic interests. It then discussed the deficit caused by publication of *Catholic Action*. Bishop John Noll, publisher of the *Catholic Digest* and *Our Sunday Visitor*, offered to take it over at a savings of $9,000 a year. The chairman of each department agreed to discuss with his personnel further savings that might be made. Expressing "the mind" of the committee, Bishop Thomas Lillis cautioned against "anything that would spell the end of the work."[26]

By 10 May, Burke had completed a "just revision" of salaries, which "required a good deal of thought," taking into consideration years of service and the importance of a person's assignment. He sent a list detailing the reduced salary of each of employees for the department chair's approval. Burke recommended holding off on the acceptance of Noll's offer about *Catholic Action* until he could make a more detailed examination of its effect. He noted that if the NCWC outsourced the printing and mailing of the magazine to Noll, it would also have to turn over all subscription fees. Burke had yet to determine which option would be least detrimental to NCWC finances. In the end, the NCWC kept control of the journal. Explaining the financial situation to Helen Lynch, Burke wrote: "I fear the bottom has been reached. Much more reducing and we will not be able to do the work at all. As it is, the reductions make our work pitiably hard."[27]

Birth Control: Puerto Rico

While dealing with the financial crisis, Burke faced birth control legislation in Puerto Rico. In January 1932, Herbert Hoover appointed James Beverley governor general of the island. Beverley decided to confront its overpopulation. In his inaugural address he stressed the necessity of birth control. Again, in his annual report to Washington in September, he declared the populace was too large for the country to sustain and proposed three partial solutions: new industry to increase employment, out-migration, and contraception. In November, the Birth Control League of Puerto Rico opened its first clinic in San Juan.[28]

In March 1933, Dr. Leopoldo Figueroa, member of the Puerto Rican Chamber of Representatives, introduced a bill authorizing the public health commissioner to license birth control clinics to dispense information about and devices for contraception. He sent a copy to Beverley for comment, with a cover letter stating the legislation was a response to his expressed interest in the matter. Beverley replied the bill was "in excellent form" and contained "proper restrictions," which seemed limited to a prohibition against abortion. When *El Mundo* published both letters, Bishop Edwin Vincent Byrne of San Juan protested to Beverley objecting to lending the prestige of his office to the bill. Byrne asked the NCWC's help.[29]

Burke and William Montavon went on consecutive days to protest Beverley's endorsement first to John McDuffie of Alabama, chairman of the House Committee on Insular Affairs, and then to Millard Tydings of Maryland, chairman of the Senate counterpart. Burke argued that as a representative of the U.S. president, Beverley lent his influence to one side of Puerto Rican legislation. He averred it was Beverley's duty to uphold the known policies of the U.S. government. In the previous Congress, both houses went on record as opposed to any change in the obscenity law. Both McDuffie and Tydings agreed that Beverley exceeded his powers and both recommended Burke see the secretaries of State and War.[30]

Burke and Montavon saw Secretary of War George Dern, whose department had charge of insular affairs. Burke reviewed the history of the issue, detailed in a memorandum about it. He argued Beverley should stand for legislation in harmony with American law. He explained the economic history of the island. Prior to American takeover, it had consisted of small farmers. American corporations came in, bought up the land, drove the people into the cities, "created slums: made them practically industrial slaves." Burke argued the proper way to assist Puerto Rico "was to help the people to regain their land—not to cut them off by birth control." Though soon to see Roosevelt, he would not bring the matter up if Dern took action. Promising to read Burke's memorandum, Dern told him Beverley would soon be replaced.[31]

Before the month was out, the Puerto Rican legislature tabled the bill, and Roosevelt appointed Robert Hayes Gore, a Catholic, governor of the island. Shortly thereafter, Burke met with Gore, who knew little of Puerto Rico's history. Burke explained at length Beverley's attempt to promote birth control legislation on the plea of overpopulation. The real problem, argued Burke, was that American sugar interests had deprived Puerto Ricans of their landholdings. "The people … needed a chance to return to the land," said Burke, "—to have a portion of it as their own." He found Gore "eager" and "right-intentioned" about his new post.[32]

Introductions

In April 1933, entering the West Wing for the first time since the Lutheran debacle, Burke introduced himself to Roosevelt. "Memories crowded in," wrote Burke. Greeting him with "warmth and energy," Roosevelt said he needed no introduction because he already knew of his good work. Burke said the NCWC would gladly advance the president's efforts when it was for the public good. Roosevelt averred there were two matters with which the Church might help. First was a growing sentiment that the federal government ought to give "financial aid, money, a dole" to those in need. Roosevelt absolutely opposed the idea. The federal government should give aid, "but it should always be in the form of work." Otherwise, a person lost his dignity. Roosevelt wanted the Church to back him on this. Burke replied the Administrative Committee always opposed the establishment of new federal departments and had repeatedly expressed the conviction that federal aid should be given through the states. Roosevelt agreed. Experience taught him that federal aid tended to make local communities "careless and indifferent."[33]

He said he also wanted the Church's help in urging people back to the land. The concentration of population in cities needed to be lessened. He wanted to encourage country life, and the building of small churches in rural areas would be a boon to that. Burke told him the NCWC's Rural Life Bureau was in perfect accord with his thinking. The two men discussed the project at some length. At the conclusion, Roosevelt said he would be happy to see Burke at any time. Memorializing the conversation, Burke commented: "After a while, one questions whether the [president's] energy is sustained by serious thought or not. Indeed, I fear Roosevelt may grow tired of thinking: or believe he has thought enough, when he has thought too little. He proposes large questions: but one fears he hardly knows the depths of their roots."[34]

Two months later, Burke accompanied Archbishop Cicognani to introduce him to Roosevelt. When previous presidents had met with the delegate, it was in the West Wing. On this occasion, Roosevelt received Cicognani in the White House itself. He arranged that no newsmen or photographers were present. Roosevelt greeted the new delegate saying, "Of course, I wouldn't say this publicly, but I hope the day will soon come when I will be able to welcome you as an Ambassador." Cicognani replied the U.S. once had an official representative to the Vatican. The president hoped it would have one again soon.[35]

Roosevelt said there would be times he needed to communicate with the pope. He did not care to send dispatches through any of the four American cardinals, but would be glad to do so through Cicognani. Cicognani said he would happily be of service. Roosevelt commented on the effect papal encyclicals were having on the nation and noted that he quoted from *Quadragesimo Anno* in his campaign. He said the nation would do all in its power to prevent further war between Japan and China as well as to prevent one in Europe. Roosevelt explained that anti-Catholic bigotry, especially in the 1928 campaign, was 90 percent ignorance. His time recuperating from polio in Warm Springs, Georgia, had convinced him of that. He encouraged Cicognini to do what he could to increase the number of priests in the South and West where they were sparse. For his part, Cicognani spoke favorably about the appointments of Gore and Frank Walsh as governors of Puerto Rico and the Philippines, respectively. Roosevelt averred both were capable men and added with a laugh, "I told Governor Gore not to make any speeches favoring birth control." He believed the cure for economic woes in Puerto Rico was to have the people return to small landholding. He instructed Gore to have the large sugar interests give some of their land to families so each might have perhaps an acre apiece.[36]

Burke considered the way Roosevelt received Cicognani "unusual, significant, and I think a manner used only for the special representative of other governments." Cicognani himself reported to Rome on the distinctive manner in which Roosevelt met him.[37] Whether or not it portended more, the changing of the guards was complete. The new president had been inaugurated and Burke had met him. Likewise, the new delegate took up his post and paid respects to him. Church and state were under new administrations.

Russian Recognition: Part II

While Burke was in Rome, Marella took his advice that the answers of the NCWC's administrative bishops on Russian recognition lacked focus. So, he created a survey of three questions: Would recognition of the Soviet Union have an adverse effect on social, moral, and religious life? If yes, should the bishops publicly oppose recognition? Third, would a pastoral of the hierarchy on the dangers of communism be valuable? He sent the questionnaire to the Administrative Committee, the four cardinals, and to five other bishops. He received fifteen replies. With one abstention, they split evenly, seven saying recognition would have an adverse effect and seven no. None wanted a public protest. Eleven favored a pastoral and four opposed. Marella shared the information with Burke on his return. Curiously, Marella sent the Vatican a slanted report, suggesting the majority of respondents took a pragmatic view of recognition and opposed issuance of a joint pastoral letter. When the Administrative Committee met, Burke said their responses to his inquiry in January showed all opposed recognition and none endorsed public protest. It directed Burke to apprise Cicognani of its mind.[38]

In late July, Undersecretary of State William Phillips summoned Burke to explain that recognition had nothing to do with the religious or moral position of the Russian government. The reasons for withholding it no longer prevailed. Russia disavowed official connection with the Comintern and claimed to have ceased working through it. The Soviet Union was broke; it lacked money to push communist propaganda. Therefore the theory of "an enemy state" no longer held water. Likewise the repudiation of Czarist war debts to the U.S. was a dead letter. All debtor nations quit repayment of their war loans. Nor were trade advantages the reason for recognition; no informed person would grant credit to Russia in its present condition.[39]

Burke asked Phillips why the government wanted to extend recognition. He gave no reply. Burke persisted to no effect. He suspected Phillips knew the reasons, but was not at liberty to speak. He also suspected the administration was prepared to recognize Russia. He noted the government's policy of the past dozen years withheld it. "To change now," averred Burke, "would require some special explanation to the American people." He said the Administrative Committee strongly opposed it, but would make no public protest. The Soviet Union officially espoused communist theories; it denied God's existence and sought to destroy religion. Recognition would give the impression the administration was uninterested in principles as long as the Soviet government was stable. Such thinking indicated "the material and not the spiritual was the ultimate test." Burke said he had not divulged the Administrative Committee's view to Roosevelt because he did not wish to "tax his time." Phillips said he would make it known to him. Burke pressed the matter. He urged that if Roosevelt recognized Russia, some official explanation go out that recognition was not endorsement of the religious and moral principles of the Soviet Union. Noncommittal, Phillips said he would relay Burke's views to Roosevelt.[40]

When the press reported recognition was very likely, Burke reiterated to Phillips that the Administrative Committee considered it "a grave mistake," one that "would do unwarranted injury to the institutions of our own country." Soviet denial of religion and religious liberty undermined the basis "accepted by all civilized nations for centuries as the common standards of private, family and public morals." Burke argued the U.S. had "a moral responsibility" to discountenance a nation that repudiated "accepted standards and principles of civilization." The committee "respectfully and urgently" asked that, if Roosevelt went ahead, he publicly declare his reason for doing so was solely the stability of the Soviet government. Recognition constituted no endorsement of the Soviet system. Phillips asked Burke to put his views in writing.[41]

Burke sent them in a letter. Phillips thanked him for expressing them "so fully and frankly," no doubt because it provided ammunition for his boss Secretary of State Cordell Hull, one of the few cabinet members opposed to Russian recognition. Phillips reported that Hull had "taken note of its contents" and assured Burke it would be given to Roosevelt. In October 1933, Roosevelt addressed the Catholic Charities Congress in New York City. He stated in part that Americans firmly believed "that spiritual values count in the long run more than material values." He said those who "sought by edict to eliminate the right of mankind to believe in God and to practice that belief" always discovered they were vainly trying to eradicate "an inherent, essential, undying quality, and indeed necessity, of the human race." Burke could not say if these remarks resulted from his letter, but they were a clear repudiation of Soviet principles. At this point, Cicognani and the apostolic delegation took charge of the matter.[42]

Within a week, Roosevelt made overtures to Russia about recognition. He met with Jesuit Edmund Walsh, one of the staunchest Catholic critics of it, to say he would insist on religious liberty and freedom of worship. Roosevelt asked Walsh to inquire about Rome's position. Papal Secretary of State Eugenio Pacelli informed Cicognani that Walsh must insist on a written commitment that the Soviets would stop religious persecution, halt anti-religious propaganda, and release those imprisoned for their faith. It must commit itself to freedom of conscience and worship. Roosevelt promised to do what he could. In the end, he was able to secure those two freedoms only for American citizens visiting or resident in the Soviet Union. When all was said and done, most Catholic commentators viewed that concession by Russia as a step forward.[43]

New Deal

In accepting the Democratic nomination, Roosevelt promised those Americans dealt a bad hand, "a new deal … a call to arms" in a "crusade to restore America to its own people." He had no program in mind other than improvisation and experimentation. While Burke was in Rome, Roosevelt launched his New Deal. The initiative that touched Burke most personally was creation of the Civilian Conservation Corps (CCC) aimed at unemployment relief. It called for enlisting 250,000 young men ages eighteen to twenty-five to work in national parks, forestry, soil conservation, road-building, and dam construction. The men would earn $30 per month ($720 in 2024), $25 of which they must send home. They would live in work camps constructed by the War Department and receive room and board. Military officers would serve as camp commandants with responsibility for all aspects of life, including religious services.[44]

Burke found himself reprising his World War I role as agent for securing chaplains. In April, he saw Major General Hugh Drum, deputy chief of staff and a Catholic. Drum said the Department of Labor would select recruits, the Department of Interior would assign them to various areas, and the Department of Agriculture would determine work to be done. The War Department would have charge of camps and would afford assistance for religious services. The government decided to establish 1,250 camps around the country, each with 200 men.[45]

The CCC presented Burke with a challenge. The army's suggested plan placed religious services under the Army chief of chaplains, who would call to active duty chaplains in the Army Reserve. The CCC had nine corps areas, each under a corps commander and corps chaplain. The chaplain assigned reservists to camps. There were not, however, enough Catholic reservists to serve the number of Catholics, and most were now older and pastors of parishes they would be reluctant to leave. Given that, Burke needed to resurrect something like the old camp pastors of World War I. For that reason, he wanted religious services placed under camp commandants. Thus, when it was necessary for a local priest to conduct services, the commandant would not have to clear it with the corps chaplain first. Burke sent Henry Caravati of the NCCM to see Colonel Duncan Major Jr., acting assistant chief of staff, about the matter. Major was willing to scrap the Army's plan in favor of whatever the NCWC believed would suit its needs.[46]

At Burke's aegis, the Army was willing to commission local priests recommended by their bishops as reserve chaplains in their corps areas. Burke, however, could not guarantee that a chaplain would serve exclusively in the bishop's diocese because each corps area covered several states. Burke also got Roosevelt to agree that the Army pay a travel expense of 5 cents per mile (about $1.20) to local priests who provided volunteer services in camps. The president also instructed commandants whose camps were nearby a parish to transport Catholic boys by truck to Sunday Mass. Robert Fechner, director of the CCC, agreed to permit local priests to reside permanently in camps when necessary. Such resident clergy would receive room and board, and Burke was working to secure them a minimum salary of $30 per month.[47]

In his apparent eagerness to be of help, Roosevelt got ahead of himself. In December, Burke received word the Army refused to permit any ministers except reserve chaplains in camps. The service of any others would require personal authorization by the president. Burke and Michael Ready saw Roosevelt to say the number of such chaplains was insufficient and could never offer the level of ministry necessary. Burke asked Roosevelt to authorize bishops with camps in their dioceses to appoint priests to minister in them at $30 a month and mileage. Roosevelt admitted he initially favored that plan, adding that if it were a question of only one denomination it would be easy. He could not deal with ministers of every denomination demanding the same treatment as Catholics. As a workaround, Burke described how the Committee of Six had handled it and recommended appointment of a committee of three: a Catholic, a Protestant, and a Jew. Roosevelt liked the idea. He said he would appoint such a committee to include both the chief of chaplains and the director of the CCC.[48]

At Roosevelt's request, Fechner and his assistant James McEntee met with Burke, Ready, and representatives of the Jewish faith and Protestant denominations. After a two-hour discussion, Fechner asked each religious group to submit a memorandum regarding the number of civilian clergymen needed for the work. Based on available statistics, the NCWC estimated the number of civilian Catholic clergy necessary at 250. Burke informed the Administrative Committee, "We cannot say that the result of this conference was very promising."[49] Only time would tell.

While the CCC was the most popular New Deal initiative, the one viewed as most Catholic was the National Industrial Recovery Act (NIRA). It established the National Recovery Administration (NRA) to oversee industrial and trade associations in adopting and implementing voluntary codes of fair competition governing all aspects of business from production through marketing, including wages, work conditions, and pricing. It also provided for collective bargaining of labor. Catholics saw these features as harmonious with, if not drawn from, *Quadragesimo Anno*. Codes of fair competition were a step toward social justice.[50]

Burke waxed eloquent about the "Spiritual Significance of the N.R.A." in a statement written for Bishop Schrembs, who wanted to herald the popular legislation. Taking as a starting point Roosevelt's remark to Catholic Charities that "spiritual values" counted more than "material values," Burke saw the NRA as a call to the American people to meet that law's stipulations with their spiritual power and the virtue of truthfulness. Without that, the NRA would fail. That law helped make clear in practical terms the nature of social justice. Yet, it took spiritual power to render it real. The owner, manufacturer, or employer was "a human being—a spiritual being" with a conscience and heart. He must not exploit his workers, impoverishing them to enrich himself. Similarly, wrote Burke, "The man who labors must give conscientious service for there is more in labor than mere hours of time or physical effort, because labor is human." Burke argued only spiritual motivation and the power of generosity, sacrifice, and love would make the NRA work. The NRA also implied another virtue: hope. "The N.R.A. not only asks us to be hopeful," wrote Burke: "it expresses our hope.... The N.R.A. is a cooperative effort built upon this foundation—the worthiness and hopefulness of the American people." He admitted the law was not perfect and may or may not succeed. Yet, the virtue of hope would sustain and give courage to frame other better measures if necessary. "We have 'screwed our courage to the sticking place,'" concluded Burke, "and we will not fail."[51]

There was considerable concern, however, in certain Catholic quarters about whether their hospitals, churches, schools, and colleges were subject to NRA codes. Burke inquired and reported to the Administrative Committee that Catholic educational institutions were exempt from any code. Other Church institutions or agencies which engaged in business would remain exempt as long as they maintained nonprofit status and did not compete in the open market.[52]

Burke enunciated a decidedly Catholic understanding of the causes of the Depression and remedies for it. The roots of the crisis lay in materialism and greed, which led to concentration of power in corporations, monopolies, and lobbies, and which blinded people to true morality and social justice—indeed to fundamental human rights. Big industry and capitalism were lords. "Money, not man, has been the supreme consideration and justifying end." The divorce of religion from education and economics not only nurtured the evils, but had led to erosion of moral standards and the desacralization of marriage and home, evident in the birth control movement. "Economic conditions especially are advanced as justification of what is in reality a criminal marital life," wrote Burke. "The new paganism of our day has begotten this propaganda." Moreover, concentration of wealth in the hands of a few had "all but crushed agriculture" and spawned widespread unemployment in cities.[53]

The remedy was restoration of the authority of Christ, Christian morality, and natural law, matters derided as "medieval." Burke called for study of the apostolic letters and encyclicals of Leo XIII, Benedict XV, and Pius XI, living representatives of "Christ upon earth." The fruits of study should be applied to questions of the day, and Burke named thirty-five of them, such as the injustices of corporations, absentee control, and price fixing; the need for consumers' cooperatives, labor unions, honest banking, fair price, etc. Reform of the social order would result from wise exercise of the vote to elect "competent, conscientious men of high moral principles." Furthermore, Catholics must battle for the rights of workingmen, cooperation between capital and labor, morality in corporations, and tax reform. All of this must be carried out in the spirit of the gospel and through prayer.[54]

The Administrative Committee considered Burke's draft in November 1932. Archbishop McNicholas made adjustments. He recast the segment on restoring the authority of Christ, but left most of the remainder untouched. In June 1933, the committee issued the statement as its own in pamphlet form as *A Statement on the Present Crisis*.[55]

Finances, Catholic Action, Motion Pictures, and Resignation

In early October 1933, Burke warned Hanna the NCWC's continuing financial deterioration was "affecting and imperilling [*sic*] the work." From May through September, each payday found the organization facing bills and salaries averaging $7,800 more than it had on hand. Every two weeks Burke had to badger Archbishop Murray for money to meet payroll and bills. The prelate "generously" complied, though Burke was certain he had to borrow each time. Sometimes he was unable to send the required amount as happened the payday just passed. Burke sent some sixty-five employees home without full wages. Bill collectors were at the NCWC's door. He noted Murray's $50,000 debt of the previous year had risen to $75,000 and might reach $100,000 ($2.4 million in 2024) by the time the hierarchy met in November. As the situation currently stood, the NCWC owed bills in the amount of $2,426, with a mid-October payroll of $4,272 and another $1,025 still due on September salaries. It had only $1,313 in the bank. "I think the outlook for the next year," concluded Burke, "will be very, very doubtful."[56]

Also doubtful was Burke's health. By mid-October 1933, he was too worn out to work and confined himself to bed. Paying him a visit, Dr. Marbury predicted "the 'reserve' will come back in a few days," but it did not.

Burke suffered a severe attack of neuritis which laid him up for five weeks. The ailment was crippling and painful. On eve of the Administrative Committee's meeting in November, the fifty-eight-year-old Burke wrote his letter of resignation, explaining his repeated illnesses and weakened condition convinced him he was unable to fulfill his duties. Nor did he want to become a burden to the Paulists, which would likely happen if he continued at NCWC. "With the greatest and keenest regret," he urged Hanna and the committee to accept his departure.[57]

The committee met at the invalid Burke's home so he could give the first part of his report. For some time, Burke had pondered the nature of the NCWC and its relation to Catholic Action, the papal initiative calling for lay participation in the apostolate of the hierarchy to bring Catholic principles to play in every aspect of life. The NCWC's purview was the Church's external life, not its internal life. The latter belonged by canon law to local ordinaries or to provincial, plenary, and general councils. In recent years, however, the hierarchy's annual convention found internal matters of more interest, but they diverted the NCWC from its real purpose. The convention was a voluntary association of the hierarchy offering opportunity to establish insofar as possible a common approach to civic and social issues based on Catholic principles and the interests of the Church. The NCWC went so far as to proclaim itself the embodiment of Catholic Action in the U.S.: the laity acting under the aegis of the hierarchy. Indeed, Catholic Action was the organic Mystical Body of Christ in society.[58]

What troubled Burke were the many "national" Catholic organizations and movements like the League of Social Justice, the National Conference of Catholic Charities, and national sodalities, which were not under the hierarchy or its executive arm: the Administrative Committee. Burke was not disparaging the work of such organizations, but the fundamental issue was their incorporation into Catholic Action which, in his view, the NCWC epitomized. Burke admitted it had not always functioned in the orderly way demanded by Catholic Action. Yet, he believed all national Catholic bodies must be affiliated with the NCWC to bring them under the guidance of the hierarchy. "I know that I am proposing a very large matter," said Burke, "but I feel that I should put before you some of the actual difficulties and problems and to ask your guidance." The committee directed him to try to prevent further multiplication of organizations.[59]

It then adjourned to reconvene without Burke at headquarters, where Hanna presented his letter of resignation. Archbishop Murray moved refusal of its acceptance and requested instead Burke "take the vacation necessary to recover his health." The committee concurred.[60]

There would be no vacation in the short term. Burke's attack of neuritis continued into December and incapacitated his right arm, leaving him unable to write. By 11 December, the severest pain had passed, but he remained unable to work. "I am still in the house," he wrote left-handed to Lynch, "for the arm is quite helpless."[61]

After refusing Burke's resignation, the committee turned its attention to the sad state of motion pictures. In late 1927, Jason Joy, head of the MPPDA's Studio Relations Committee, had issued a production code called the "Don'ts and Be Carefuls." The code's purpose was to guide producers in making decent pictures through a list of things to avoid and others calling for ginger handling. Unfortunately, studios honored the "Don'ts and Be Carefuls" more in the breach than in the observance. In late 1929, with input from several Catholics, Jesuit Daniel Lord turned them into the two-part Hollywood Production Code of 1930. The first section expanded on the "Don'ts and Be Carefuls"; the second set forth the moral principles underpinning the first. Cardinal George Mundelein of Chicago provided the leverage to have Hollywood accept them.[62] The code enjoyed initial success despite the fact it had no teeth. As box-office receipts declined, however, the industry once again turned to sex and violence to boost viewership. Catholics hoped the new NRA Code of Fair Competition for the Motion Picture Industry would include the Production Code of 1930, thereby giving the latter the force of law. Instead, Article VII of the NRA code simply pledged producers "to maintain right moral standards" established in "the regulations promulgated by and within the industry."[63]

The Administrative Committee appointed Archbishop McNicholas and Bishops John Cantwell, John Noll, and Hugh Boyle to a special committee to propose remedies for the evils of the motion pictures. When the hierarchy met two days later, it blessed their appointment and ordered that the proposed remedies "be ratified by the body of Bishops." Without notifying Burke, Cantwell asked Mary Hearn, a wealthy Los Angeles Catholic, to contact him. She chaired a Motion Picture Committee of well-heeled Catholic women schooled in the craft of movie-making. She told Burke that through the good will of the Academy of Motion Picture Arts and Sciences, her committee previewed new releases. She proposed to condense the reports of its members and send them to Burke for publication in *Catholic Action*. She enclosed a list of pictures, some recommended for family and others condemned as unfit.[64]

The letter and list caught Burke off guard. He had no idea why he received it. He wrote to McNicholas and Cantwell there was no warrant or authority to publish it. Doing so would lend NCWC sanction to the films recommended, which the producers and exhibitors would exploit. Moreover, Frank Hall, director of the Press Department, told him one of the recommended films, *Roman Scandals*, had been condemned by the secular press "for its scantily clad women and one rather pronounced shimmy dance." The day the list arrived, Burke received a protest against that movie with enclosed "pictures of quite naked and sensually appealing women." Thinking the photos might simply be advertising and the film contained no such images, he asked a priest and laywoman, both experienced, to view *Roman Scandal*. They reported the movie was "excessive in its exhibitions of undressed women, and the sensual appeal of half-clad women." The questionable dance was "thoroughly suggestive." Burke told McNicholas he thought Hearn's committee ought to publish the list on its own authority and responsibility.[65]

Burke then turned to the matter of Catholic Action and the NCWC. Rather than have the Bishops Committee on Motion Pictures establish a new, special organization for the betterment of films, Burke urged McNicholas to use the NCCW with its diocesan councils, many of which already had special committees on motion pictures. These councils were under authority and guidance of the local bishop and were directed by priests. Such would also be in keeping with Catholic Action. Burke reminded McNicholas the Administrative Committee directed avoidance of further proliferation of organizations.[66]

In late January 1934, Burke went to rest at Homestead in Hot Springs where he stayed in one of the private cottages until a snowfall iced over the path up to the hotel making it too dangerous to traverse for meals. So, he moved into a room in the lodge. He remained there until mid-February when his money ran out. The quiet and rest helped, but not enough. Back in Washington, he wrote to Lynch, "The few days have shown me I couldn't take up the work again—not yet." He planned to go west as the guest of Hanna in San Francisco where his brother Thomas was stationed.[67]

The trip was "long and tiresome" because he traveled on railroad passes that neither permitted him to take express trains nor go by direct route. Thomas met him and took him to Hanna's residence. For the sake of rest, Burke insisted Hanna keep secret his presence in the city. Burke's health was still tenuous. He wrote to Grace Murray, "The [right] arm has never come entirely around again: it is still weak: still catches me now and then." His strength refused to return in any appreciable measure. To be sure, rest restored it some, but any action quickly depleted it. He lacked the physical stamina to return to work, especially with staff cuts due to financial constraints that only increased the burden on himself. Problems of the NCWC weighed on him, and he felt "lost" thinking of them. Nor could he stop thinking about whether or not to insist on his resignation. Thomas was sympathetic to that idea, but Burke could not get Hanna to understand. He did enjoy one day of respite from all the worry. "I sailed on the bay in a private yacht and really one didn't care what else was happening or would happen," he told Murray. "To me that's a new attitude and I begin to ask myself if I'm in my right or at least my normal mind. It is warm here: the sun has shone all day and I could stay here for a long, long time."[68]

Ten days later, Burke reported to her that he "loafed a great deal" and finally got his mind off the NCWC. He went every day to visit his fellow Paulists at St. Mary's parish. "It's years since I had so much Paulist life," he told her. He and Thomas were of a mind he must resign. When John informed Hanna, the archbishop said the Administrative Committee would not accept it. Burke could not get him to understand the situation. He told Murray Hanna "doesn't give serious thought to it." For her part, she was happy to learn he was "loafing" and pleased he finally let go of NCWC troubles. She was certain rest, relaxation, and an abundance of sleep would give him clarity and enable him "to make a right decision."[69]

In early April, Burke returned to Washington having "made up my mind so definitely and finally" to resign. He already decided what he would do after leaving the NCWC—though he left no record what it was—and arranged for storage of his books. Shortly before the Administrative Committee met, he gave Hanna his second letter of resignation, which explained his strength and health had not returned in the measure necessary for him to fulfill the duties of general secretary as they should be. Burke gave three months' notice to enable the committee to find a replacement. He deeply regretted leaving the work, but believed it "imperative" the NCWC have a man at its helm who need not worry about health and could devote his entire energy to the task. Hanna discouraged him from presenting it, but Burke insisted. When the bishops convened, Hanna began reading the letter aloud without introduction or warning. The startled Burke got up and left the room.[70]

The committee sent Archbishop Murray and Bishop Thomas Lillis to confer with him. They asked he withdraw his resignation. Refusing, he elaborated on his reasons. They countered that the committee wanted him to take a ten-month vacation. Burke replied it would change nothing; he "was physically handicapped and always would be." The NCWC should have an able-bodied general secretary at its head. The pair said the committee could think of no one to replace him. Burke objected that when he became chairman of the CSWA, he had to learn on the job; his successor must to do likewise. The two insisted he stay. Burke was equally insistent on leaving. He said that for the past five years he was generally able to say Mass only once a week. He wanted to offer it daily and have some relief. They said he could come and go to the office as he pleased and take whatever vacations he needed. They simply wanted benefit of his judgment. "We are not asking much of you," said Murray: "you have to live somewhere and we're making it as easy as we can, but we ask you to continue as General Secretary." Burke gave in. The two reported back the conditions under which he would remain. The committee accepted them and tabled his letter of resignation.[71]

Following the meeting, Burke informed Lynch and Murray what happened. "After all my prayers and resolve it so ends," he told Lynch. "I am disappointed. I do not see altogether how I am to carry on—but I will have to study that out." He told Murray, "It has been hard for me to realize that I am to hold the job," which now required "a rearrangement of thought and attitude." He explained that, in light of the concessions the bishops offered, "I could not refuse … unless I were actually dying. So I'm still General Secretary NCWC." It was "evidently God's will" that he stay in the job. "I had prayed for months, and I *thought* His will was otherwise," he told her. "But I was wrong." When Burke explained his decision to Drs. Marbury and Mohan, both agreed it was best he remain, "even to work but little."[72]

Endnotes to Chapter 21

1. Burke, *Christ in Us*, 47.
2. Flynn, *Catholics and Roosevelt*, 122–32; Gribble, *Archbishop for the People*, 228–30; McNamara, *Catholic Cold War*, 61–64, 70–79; Castagna, *Bridge across the Ocean*, 126–30; Herring, *Colony to Super Power*, 495–96; H. W. Brands, *Traitor to His Class: The Privileged Life and Radical Presidency of Franklin Delano Roosevelt* (New York: Anchor Books, 2008), 438.
3. Burke to Hanna, 30 January 1933, circular to committee, ACUA, USCCB 10:99:21; McNamara, *Catholic Cold War*, 80–81.
4. Boyle to Burke, 3 February 1933; Noll to Burke, 3 February 1933; Schrembs to Burke, 3 February 1933; McNicholas to Burke 7 February 1933; Hanna to Burke, 11 February 1933—all in ACUA, USCCB 10:25:21.
5. McNicholas to Burke, 3 February 1933, ACUA, USCCB 10:25:21.
6. Burke to J. Murray, 6 February 1933, ACUA, USCCB 10:25:21.
7. Burke to J. Murray, circular, 27 February 1933, copy, ACUA, USCCB 10:25:21; Burke to Hanna, circular, 28 February 1933, copy, ACUA, USCCB 10:99:21; Herring, *Colony to Super Power*, 496; Brands, *Traitor to His Class*, 438.
8. Burke to Marella, 27 February 1933, ACUA, USCCB 10:25:21; Burke to Hanna, 22 February 1933, AASF, NCWC files; "Elevated to the Cardinalate," *Catholic Action* 15 (March 1933): 4; Castagna, *Bridge across the Ocean*, 130.
9. Burke to Lynch, 24 February 1933, AP, Burke Papers, box 5.
10. Burke, Diary of 1933 Trip, 2 and 5 March 1933, AP, Burke Papers, box 72; Burke to G. Murray, 6 March 1933, ibid., box 12; Burke to Lynch, 6 March 1933, ibid., box 5.
11. Burke, Diary of 1933 Trip, 13 March 1933, AP, Burke Papers, box 72; Burke to Hanna, 4 April 1933, copy, ACUA, USCCB 10:99:21. Until 19 March, the diary is an absolute jumble. Burke himself noted in it that "by this time this diary is confused as to exact dates" because he had no time to write at night.
12. Burke, Diary of 1933 Trip, 13 March 1933, AP, Burke Papers, box 72; Burke to Hanna, 4 April 1933, copy, ACUA, USCCB 10:99:21.
13. Burke, Diary of 1933 Trip, 15 March 1933, AP, Burke Papers, box 72.
14. Burke, Diary of 1933 Trip, 19 March 1933, AP, Burke Papers, box 72; Burke to Hanna, 4 April 1933, copy, ACUA, USCCB 10:99:21.
15. Burke, Diary of 1933 Trip, 19 March 1933, AP, Burke Papers, box 72.
16. Ibid., 20 March 1933.
17. Ibid. Two years later, Adams published *The Church, Catholic and Protestant: A Study of Differences That Matter* (New York: C. Scribner's Sons, 1935).
18. Ibid.

19. John J. Burke, C.S.P., *Christ in Us: Meditations* (Philadelphia: The Dolphin Press, 1934), 1, 5 (quotations are here), 26–28, 52–57, 59–60, 62–65, 67, 77–78, 112–13, 133–37, 159–62, 166–71.
20. Burke to Hanna, 4 April 1933, copy, ACUA, USCCB 10:99:21.
21. Burke, Diary of 1933 Trip, 21 and 22 March, AP, Burke Papers, box 72 (final quote is here); Burke to Hanna, 4 April 1933, copy, ACUA, USCCB 10:99:21 (other quotes are here).
22. Burke to Kerby, 18 March 1933, ACUA, Kerby Papers, 58:1:3; Burke to Hanna, 4 April 1933, copy, ACUA, USCCB 10:99:21.
23. Ready to Hanna, 18 March 1933, copy, ACUA, USCCB 10:99:21; Ready to Burke, 1 April 1933, ibid., 10:125:10.
24. Burke to Hanna, 4 April 1933, copy, ACUA, USCCB 10:99:21.
25. Burke, Report of the General Secretary, April 1933, ACUA, USCCB 10:62:16; Minutes of the Administrative Committee, 25 April 1933, ibid., 10:64:7.
26. Minutes of the Administrative Committee, 25 April 1933, ACUA, USCCB 10:64:7.
27. Burke to Hanna, 10 May 1933, copy, ACUA, USCCB 10:99:21; Burke to Lynch, 14 May 1933, AP, Burke Papers, box 5. The former was a circular.
28. *New York Times*, 26 September 1932; Ramírez de Arellano and Seipp, *Colonialism, Catholicism, and Contraception*, 27–29.
29. The letters are reproduced in Burke to George Dern, 7 April 1933, exhibit #2 in Burke, Report of the General Secretary, April 1933, ACUA, USCCB 10:62:17.
30. Burke, Interview with John McDuffie, 4 April 1933, USCCB 10:153: Interview Book; Burke, Interview with Millard Tydings, 5 April 1933, ibid.
31. Burke, Interview with George Dern, 7 April 1933, USCCB 10:153: Interview Book; Burke to George Dern, 7 April 1933, exhibit #2 in Burke, Report of the General Secretary, April 1933, ACUA, USCCB 10:62:17.
32. Minutes of the Administrative Committee, 25 April 1933, ACUA, USCCB 10:64:7; Burke, Interview with Robert Gore, 26 April 1933, ibid., 10:153: Interview Book.
33. Burke, An Interesting Morning, or, Meeting Another President, 13 April 1933, ACUA, USCCB 10:153: Interview Book. On FDR's attitude toward doles, see Brands, *Traitor to His Class*, 420–23.
34. Burke, An Interesting Morning, or, Meeting Another President, 13 April 1933, ACUA, USCCB 10:153: Interview Book; Jeffrey Marlett, *Saving the Heartland: Catholic Missionaries in Rural America* (DeKalb: Northern Illinois University Press, 2002), 10–51; Edward S. Shapiro, "Catholic Agrarian Thought and the New Deal," *Catholic Historical Review* 65 (October 1979): 583–99; Brands, *Traitor to His Class*, 11–13, 106–08; Kennedy, *Freedom from Fear*, 200–01; McElvaine, *Great Depression*, 117–18.

35. Burke, The Ceremony of Reception, [12 June 1933], ACUA, USCCB 10:153: Interview Book; Burke, [Interview between Franklin D. Roosevelt and Amleto Cicognani], 12 June 1933, ibid.; Castagna, *Bridge Across the Ocean*, 140.
36. Burke, [Interview between Franklin D. Roosevelt and Amleto Cicognani], 12 June 1933, ibid.; Castagna, *Bridge Across the Ocean*, 140–41, 142–43.
37. Burke, The Ceremony of Reception, [12 June 1933], ACUA, USCCB 10:153: Interview Book; Castagna, *Bridge Across the Ocean*, 140.
38. Marella circular to Select Bishops, 10 March 1933, copy, with fifteen responses, ACUA, USCCB 10:25:21; Minutes of the Administrative Committee, 25 April 1933, ibid. 10:64:7; Castagna, *Bridge across the Ocean*, 130–31.
39. Burke, Interview with William Phillips, 27 July 1933, ACUA, USCCB 10:153: Interview Book.
40. Ibid.
41. Burke to Phillips, 30 September 1933, copy, ACUA, USCCB 10:25:21; Burke to Hanna, 5 October 1933, copy, ibid., 10:99:21.
42. Quoted in Burke to Hanna, 5 October 1933, copy (a circular), ACUA, USCCB 10:99:21; Minutes of the Administrative Committee, 13 November 1933, ibid., 10:64:7; Castagna, *Bridge across the Ocean*, 131.
43. Department of State, *Establishment of Diplomatic Relations with the Union of Soviet Socialist Republics* (Washington, D.C.: U.S. Government Printing Office, 1933), 5–11; Flynn, *Catholics and Roosevelt*, 135–49; Castagna, *Bridge across the Ocean*, 131–33; Herring, *Colony to Super Power*, 495–96.
44. Brands, *Traitor to His Class*, 209, 251–53; Kennedy, *Freedom from Fear* 144 and 154; Anthony J. Badger, *The New Deal: The Depression Years, 1933–1940* (New York: Noonday Press, 1989), 6–7; James T. Patterson, *America in the Twentieth Century: A History*, 3rd ed. (New York: Harcourt Brace Jovanovich, Inc., 1989), 211; George Moss, *America in the Twentieth Century* (Englewood Cliffs, N.J.: Prentice Hall, 1989), 143.
45. Burke, Interview with Hugh Drum, 12 April 1933, ACUA, USCCB 10:153: Interview Book; Henry Caravati, Memorandum on Reforestation Camps, undated [April 1933], exhibit 25 in Burke, Report of the General Secretary, April 1933, ACUA, USCCB 10:62:17.
46. Burke, Report of the General Secretary, April 1933, with exhibit 25: Caravati, Memorandum, ACUA, USCCB 10:62:17; Brigadier James McKinley to Burke, 13 May 1933, ibid., 10:129:1; Colonel Julian E. Yates, circular, 15 May 1933, copy, ibid.
47. Burke, circular to hierarchy, 12 September 1933 and Burke to Amleto Cicognani, 27 October 1922, both exhibit 2 in Burke, Report of the General Secretary, November 1933, ACUA, USCCB 10:62;19.
48. Burke, Interview with Roosevelt, 19 December 1933, ACUA, USCCB 10:153: Interview Book.
49. James McEntee to Burke, 5 February 1934, ACUA, USCCB 10:129:2; Ready

to Robert Fechner, 14 February 1934, copy, ibid.; Burke to Fechner, telegram, 16 February 1934, ibid.; Burke, Report of the General Secretary, April 1934, ibid., 10:62:20.

50. Kennedy, *Freedom from Fear*, 151–52; Brands, *Traitor to His Class*, 371–87; Flynn, *Catholics and Roosevelt*, 78–102; David O'Brien, *Public Catholicism* (New York: Macmillan Publish Company, 1989), 171–72; Badger, *New Deal*, 73–80; William E. Leuchtenburg, *Franklin E. Roosevelt and the New Deal, 1932–1940* (New York: Harper Colophon, 1963), 57–58.
51. [Burke], "Spiritual Significance of N.R.A.," ACUA, USCCB 10:125:10.
52. Burke, Report of the General Secretary, November 1933, ACUA, USCCB 10:62:18.
53. Bishops of the Administrative Committee of the National Catholic Welfare Conference, *A Statement on the Present Crisis* (Washington, D.C.: National Catholic Welfare Conference, 1933), 1–23.
54. Ibid., 24–47.
55. Minutes of the Administrative Committee, 15 November 1932, ACUA, USCCB 10:64:6; *Minutes of the Fourteenth Annual Convention of the Hierarchy, November 1932*, 18, ibid., USCC Bound Volumes; "Statement on the Present Crisis: A Digest by Patrick Ward," *Catholic Action* 15 (July 1933): 9–12.
56. Burke to Hanna, 3 October 1933, copy; Ready to Burke, 10 May, 9 June, 18 July, 21 August, 9 and 19 September, and 6 October 1933, ibid., 10:125:10; Ed Gannon to Burke, 25 July 1933—all in ACUA, USCCB 10:99:21.
57. Burke to G. Murray, 21 October 1933, AP, Burke Papers, box 12; Burke to Lynch, 22 October 1933, ibid., box 5; Burke to Cicognani, 9 November 1933, ACUA, USCCB 10:127:20; Burke to Hanna, 12 November 1933, ibid., 10:152:2.
58. Burke, Report of the General Secretary, November 1933, ACUA, USCCB 10:62:18; Minutes of the Administrative Committee, 13 November 1933, ACUA, USCCB 10:64:7; Burke, Memorandum on Proposed Committees, undated [November 1930], copy, ibid., 10:152:13; Charles A. McMahon, "The Meaning of Catholic Action," *Catholic Action* 14 (January 1932): 7–8; Joseph Rummel, "Doctrine of the Mystical Body," ibid., 15 (October 1933): 5–6; Pius XI, *Non Abbiamo Bisogno* [*We Have No Need*], 29 June 1931; Una M. Cadegan, "Guardians of Democracy or Cultural Storm Troopers? American Catholicism and the Control of Popular Media, 1934–1966," *Catholic Historical Review* 87 (April 2001): 256–57.
59. Burke, Report of the General Secretary, November 1933, ACUA, USCCB 10:62:18; Minutes of the Administrative Committee, 13 November 1933, ACUA, USCCB 10:64:7.
60. Minutes of the Administrative Committee, 16 November 1933, ACUA, USCCB 10:64:7.

61. Burke to Harney, 4 December 1933, copy, AP, Burke Papers, box 20; Burke to Lynch, 11 December 1933, ibid., box 5.
62. Pollard, *Sex and Violence*, 50–52; Tropiano, *Obscene, Indecent, Immoral*, 32–33, 269–85 (both parts of the code are reproduced here); Walsh, *Sin and Censorship*, 46–49, 54–65; Miller, *Censored Hollywood*, 39–41; Black, *Hollywood Censored*, 33; Couvaris, "Hollywood, Main Street, and Church," 593–94; Thomas Doherty, *Hollywood's Censor* 20–46; Black, *Hollywood Censored*, 34–44.
63. National Recovery Administration, *Code of Fair Competition for the Motion Picture Industry as Approved on 27 November 1933 by President Roosevelt* (Washington, D.C.: U.S. Government Printing Office, 1933), 255; Walsh, *Sin and Censorship*, 78; Black, *Hollywood Censored*, 156–62.
64. Mary Hearn to Burke, 8 January 1934, ACUA, USCCB 10:30:27; *Minutes of the Annual Meeting of the Hierarchy, November 1933*, 14, ACUA, USCCB Bound Volumes; John J. Cantwell, "Priests and the Motion Picture Industry," *Ecclesiastical Review* 90 (February 1934): 136–46 (emphasis in original); "Members of the Hierarchy Meet in Annual Session," *Catholic Action* 15 (December 1933): 7; Walsh, *Sin and Censorship*, 87–88; Black, *Hollywood Censored*, 163.
65. Burke to McNicholas, 15 January 1934, copy (first quote is here), ACUA, USCCB 10:30:27; Burke to Cantwell, 23 January 1934, copy (remaining quotes are here), ibid.
66. Burke to McNicholas, 15 January 1934, copy, ACUA, USCCB 10:30:27
67. Burke to Kerby, 2 February 1934, ACUA, Kerby Papers 58:4:7; Burke to Lynch, 17 and 22 February 1934, AP, Burke Papers, box 5.
68. Burke to G. Murray, 10 March 1934, AP, Burke Papers, box 12; Burke to Lynch, 11 March 1934, ibid., box 5.
69. Burke to G. Murray, 20 March 1934, AP, Burke Papers, box 12; G. Murray to Burke, 26 March 1934, ibid.
70. Burke to Hanna, undated [early April 1934], ACUA, USCCB 10:152:2 (second quote is here); Burke, [Memorandum], 29 April 1934, ibid.; Burke to G. Murray, 19 April 1934, AP, Burke Papers, box 12 (first quote is here).
71. Burke, [Memorandum], 29 April 1934, ACUA, USCCB 10:152:2; Minutes of the Administrative Committee, 10 April 1934, ibid., 10:64:7; Burke to Lynch, 11 April 1934, AP, Burke Papers, box 5.
72. Burke to Lynch, 11 April 1934, AP, Burke Papers, box 5; Burke to G. Murray, 13 and 19 April 1934, ibid., box 12.

Chapter 22
Little Rest for the Weary

> The Holy Spirit does all things in order. We think of Him moving where he listeth (John 3:8). But He moves not, nor moves us, aimlessly. He never moves a human creature simply to have that creature do this or that good act. The act to which He would inspire is not to be separated from the work of God and His Divine Son Jesus Christ. The Holy Spirit urges to that act that the whole creation may witness to the glory of the God-Man, Jesus Christ, and that His kingdom, His Body, be one and visible before the eyes of men. Otherwise, there is no visible Christ: no known acceptance of Christ.[1]

Motion Pictures: Legion of Decency

In spring 1934, Archbishop John McNicholas's Committee on Motion Pictures decided to recruit a Legion of Decency consisting of Catholics and others who condemned "vile and unwholesome moving pictures." Members would sign a pledge to "arouse public interest" against immoral movies and view only those inoffensive to "decency and Christian morality." McNicholas read it to the Administrative Committee, which approved. It ordered Burke to publish no lists of recommended or non-recommended pictures. McNicholas then asked for consideration of two bills Wright Patman of Texas introduced into Congress, one establishing a federal commission for censorship of films and the other eliminating block booking, a practice whereby motion-picture studios compelled theaters to purchase and screen a set of films, some worthy and others of questionable morals or worth. The committee directed Burke to postpone action on both until McNicholas's committee met in June.[2]

The committee's nebulous relation to the NCWC troubled Burke. He believed all national organizations should fall under purview of the Administrative Committee. It became an issue when Father Michael Ready informed him of McNicholas's intention to appoint a priest as agent of the "Motion Picture Committee, N.C.W.C." with headquarters in New York, identifying the committee with the Welfare Conference when in fact there was no connection. Burke dashed off a letter urging McNicholas to stop: "Such a plan would bring disorder, if not disruption, into the whole work of the N.C.W.C." When the committee was appointed, Cantwell had begged Burke to ensure it became part of the NCWC. Burke told him he had no authority to do so. That conversation clearly indicated Cantwell's mind on the matter. He told McNicholas it was "inconceivable" for the committee to be part of the NCWC unless it reported to the Administrative Committee. An agent acting independently would necessarily lead to confusion. The press would report that Father so and so of the Motion Picture Committee of the NCWC said the committee did this or that. Meanwhile the Administrative Committee would know nothing about it. "Unless the Administrative Committee is the center of unity there is no unity," wrote Burke, "there is no common action." He begged pardon if he was "overemphatic." He believed McNicholas shared his concern and explained, "I really write to you for my comfort."[3]

The comfort proved cold; the committee went its independent way. It decided on a nationwide drive to clean up movies modeled on action taken by Bishop Philip Scher of Monterey–Fresno. Scher notified managers of studio-owned theaters about the Legion of Decency's campaign against immoral movies. Acknowledging the managers' hands were tied by block booking, Scher urged them to pressure producers for decent films. Catholic Joseph Breen, director of Studio Relations for the MPPDA, reported Scher's action caused a stir in Hollywood. Breen sent Cantwell the names and addresses of theater managers in every diocese. McNicholas's committee sent them to local bishops with a sample letter modeled on Scher's.[4]

The committee never intended to boycott the industry, only to bring pressure on it. In late May, however, Cardinal Dennis Dougherty demanded Catholics in his archdiocese boycott under pain of sin the 500 theaters in his jurisdiction. His action put the Legion of Decency on the public map. It also forced Will Hays, president of the MPPDA, to negotiate with

McNicholas's committee when it met in June 1934. MPPDA agents offered to establish a new Production Code Administration (PCA) under Breen, who would have power to approve every script before filming began, with a hefty fine for violations. In return, Hays hoped to get McNicholas to halt the Legion of Decency. The committee accepted the deal, but kept the Legion active to hold the industry honest. Dougherty continued his boycott, while Cardinal William O'Connell threatened to establish his own review committee. Moreover, the archdiocese of Chicago, the diocese of Detroit, and Father Daniel Lord were each publishing three different lists of approved or condemned pictures. As historian Frank Walsh points out, "Movie makers wondered who really spoke for the Church"—Burke's very fear.[5]

In July, Burke put his thoughts on paper. The record showed, he noted correctly, that the Administrative Committee appointed the Committee on Motion Pictures, which the hierarchy sanctioned to investigate immoral movies and propose remedies to be ratified by the bishops in annual convention. Instead, the committee drew up a pledge and launched the Legion of Decency. Proper procedure called for the committee to report its findings first to the Administrative Committee for approval. Yet, at its recent meeting, McNicholas simply reported his committee formulated a pledge and would meet in June. Burke had no quibble with the administrative bishops' appointing special committees, but those should be under and report to the Administrative Committee and work through the NCWC. The matter of motion pictures raised large questions and demanded unity of plan. These larger issues, noted Burke, were being lost "in the present crusade" and demanded "more than advertising and ballyhoo." For instance, the NRA code for the movie industry did not address the evils of distribution and monopoly. The NCWC Legal Department had means to deal effectively with the code and congressional legislation. The News Service was the "logical source" for dissemination of information to the press. "The use of these present facilities," concluded Burke, "would be certainly much more economical than establishing a new office or employing a special personnel." Burke gave a copy of this memorandum to Archbishop Amleto Cicognani.[6]

In October, President Franklin Roosevelt sent Sol Rosenblatt, NRA code administrator for the movie industry, to the NCWC for help in ending Dougherty's boycott. Rosenblatt said attendance at theaters in Philadelphia had dropped 20 to 30 percent, causing wage cuts and layoffs in theater staff, slightly more than half of whom were Catholics. The AFL appealed to Roosevelt to do something to get Dougherty to end the standoff. Michael Ready said he would bring the matter to Burke. Burke had no authority to do anything except refer it to McNicholas. He drafted a letter to him explaining the situation and offering assistance.[7]

Burke showed the draft to Cicognani, who said it was a matter for McNicholas's committee and he would not interfere. Burke should tell Roosevelt he referred it to that committee which would bring it to the hierarchy at its convention next month. Burke asked if Cicognani thought Dougherty would agree to follow the committee's decision and if it could compel him to comply. He answered, "We will see." His auditor, Monsignor Egidio Vagnozzi, laughed, saying Dougherty would never obey it. Burke thought Dougherty ought to declare at least his condition for lifting the boycott. Cicognani answered he had: "Hollywood must clean up." Burke reminded him the committee accepted the creation of the PCA, but Dougherty refused to go along with it. To everything, the delegate replied: "Hollywood must clean up"; "we shall see." Burke asked if it was right to deprive so many employees of their livelihoods. Cicognani said doing good always entailed harm. He informed Burke that Breen had seen Dougherty and assured him his course of action—absolute boycott—was the only one feared by producers. Burke opined the Church was taking "a dangerous position" with an absolute boycott against the nation's third largest industry, especially since the Committee on Motion Pictures already approved the PCA. Roosevelt showed great respect and regard for Catholic authorities, and Burke thought the Church "should be considerate of that." Cicognani told him to say nothing to Roosevelt about their having discussed the matter.[8]

When the hierarchy met in November, McNicholas brought some order to a chaotic situation by securing passage of six resolutions, one of them a half-bow to Burke. The bishops agreed the Chicago list of motion pictures would be the official one. This list ranked movies as "approved," "objectionable in part" (suitable only for adults), and "condemned." Archbishop Michael Curley was to appoint a priest in Washington as secretary of the Committee on Motion Pictures under joint supervision of the committee and Burke. All those pledged to the Legion of Decency would publicly renew their commitment in December. A national committee of priests and laymen would be established to "criticize fearlessly and constructively, moving pictures which are objectionable from a moral point of view." Every bishop would appoint a permanent council of the Legion of Decency in his diocese. Finally, the movie industry would be warned that if it failed to maintain decent standards, the hierarchy would impose an absolute, week-long boycott of motion pictures.[9]

FEDERAL AID FOR EDUCATION

While Burke was convalescing in winter 1933–1934, Commissioner of Education George Zook established an advisory committee to consider federal aid for Depression-ravaged schools, particularly in the South. A subcommittee drafted a legislative plan emphasizing "the necessity for, and desirability of" aid to education in the amount of $400 million ($9.2 billion in 2024) in the coming year. The advisory committee invited Father George Johnson of the NCWC Department of Education to its next session. Speaking unofficially, Johnson said the Church opposed federal control of education and therefore opposed federal aid which would lead to that. If, however, Congress determined emergency aid was warranted, the funds should go to a non-governmental committee with Catholic representation to allot the money to children and their parents without regard to the schools attended. The committee listened in stunned, volatile silence at this frank call for Catholic inclusion in federal aid. Fortunately, two prominent non-Catholic members argued that unless Catholic schools were included, Congress would not enact the legislation. The committee felt it could not recommend aid to Catholic schools, but would eliminate the word "public" from every mention of schools in its report.[10]

In March, Catholic John Douglass, chairman of the House Committee on Education, informed Johnson that Zook presented a draft bill authorizing an appropriation of $75 million ($1.73 billion) in emergency aid. To distribute funds, it recommended a Federal Emergency School Board consisting of the commissioner, the director of the Federal Emergency Relief Administration (FERA), and a third member appointed by Roosevelt. Allotments would be based on need and entail no federal control. A subcommittee chaired by Douglass would finalize the bill and submit it to Roosevelt and the full committee for comment. Johnson told Douglass the language should be broad enough to permit Catholic schools to receive aid, which should go to individual states and be dispensed by state commissions. Douglass said he would convey that to the subcommittee and the president. Ready asked the Administrative Committee for advice.[11]

Burke, who was then in San Francisco, drafted Hanna's reply. It said the NCWC should secure "definite assurance" from the House committee that it would recommend no legislation unless it permitted states to dispense federal funds to parochial schools. Absent such a promise, headquarters should notify the hierarchy of the proposed legislation and urge bishops to protest "against the injustice of not including the right of the state, if the state so judges, to give of this Federal aid to Catholic schools." NCWC staff should have no more conferences with either the committee or the commissioner until it received such assurance. "I fear that in this as in other matters," wrote Burke, "we may be led on until it is almost too late to make a protest." He said the Administrative Committee would take up the matter at its meeting in April.[12] Five other bishops responded, four arguing Catholic schools should have a share in the funds, and the fifth deferring comment until the committee met.[13]

Johnson saw the House subcommittee in early April. The members explained if Congress authorized emergency aid to schools in the current year, it would have to do so again in the next, and that would open the door to permanent federal aid, which they opposed. The members wanted to withhold action until pressure became too great to withstand. Johnson asked if aid would be given to Catholic schools. The members were willing to include language stating nothing in the bill should be construed as preventing states from dispensing federal money to non-public, tuition-free schools. The last-mentioned ruled out parochial schools. When the Administrative Committee met a week later, it reviewed the situation and directed Burke to inform Roosevelt personally of its opposition.[14]

Burke told Roosevelt the committee emphatically opposed appropriating $75 million for education, but would not do so publicly lest it be misconstrued as antagonism to public schools, which they supported. The bishops were certain a grant would open the way to larger, permanent subsidies. Some proponents planned to secure yearly subventions of $500 million ($11.5 billion in 2024). If that happened, federal control of public education would become a reality. Roosevelt cut him off: "Father Burke, you know that I am opposed to all and every kind of centralization of education and all Federal financial aid to education. I learned my lesson from my experience in New York State." Roosevelt said he recently told Harry Hopkins, director of the FERA, the only federal funds to be available for education were those of his Relief Administration. He instructed Hopkins to keep such grants at about $17 million annually ($390 million), most of it for relief of indigent teachers. Roosevelt "expressed himself very strongly and decisively" against federalization of education. Burke reported this to Hanna.[15]

Shortly thereafter, Douglass informed Burke the House strongly favored aid to education, so his committee must report something. It drafted a bill appropriating $75 million for one year. The FERA would, in cooperation with the commissioner, allocate money to states for maintenance of primary and secondary schools. Section 5 nixed federal power to control instruction or administration; section 6 stipulated nothing in the act should "be construed to prevent the distribution of funds … to privately owned free-standing tuition schools in need." The committee would report it, and Douglass wanted the NCWC to approve it. Burke sent it to the Administrative Committee and asked for direction.[16]

Within a week all members replied. Under no circumstances was the NCWC either to support or oppose the bill publicly. Headquarters was to try to have section 6 made more positive and specific. Meanwhile, the House committee reported the bill favorably. Burke asked Johnson to inform Douglass of the Administrative Committee's decision. Douglass said it was impossible to get stronger wording in section 6. With the bill before the House, change could come only by amendment from the floor. Attempting such would focus debate on that section and probably result in its deletion. Douglass believed his committee established a precedent by its unanimous recommendation of a measure that allowed private schools to share in federal funds. Reporting this back to the Administrative Committee, Burke noted the NEA intended to have the bill amended. In any case, it seemed a moot point. Roosevelt was sending Congress a bill to appropriate $1.322 billion for relief ($30 billion in 2024). Burke said this measure would take precedence over all other House legislation. The only chance the Douglass bill had was as an amendment to Roosevelt's. In the end, the House did nothing for education.[17]

BIRTH CONTROL

Also during Burke's convalescence in winter 1934, birth control resurfaced. In late spring the previous year, Margaret Sanger had Senator Daniel Hastings and Representative Walter Pierce of Oregon reintroduce the so-called Doctors' Bill of 1932. The Judiciary Committees of House and Senate scheduled separate hearings on the measure.[18]

Since the last bout with Sanger, a development in medical science occurred with repercussions on the Catholic position. Nineteenth-century physicians argued there was a period in the menstrual cycle when conception was unlikely. In the 1920s, physicians calculated the time frame of that safe period. In late 1932, Chicago physician Leo Latz, a Catholic, popularized using this safe period to avoid conception in his book *The Rhythm of Sterility and Fertility in Women*. Cardinal George Mundelein gave it "ecclesiastical approbation." Father John A. O'Brien promoted the "rhythm method" in *Our Sunday Visitor* and in *Legitimate Birth Control*.[19]

The most novel aspect of the House hearing was the attention given this method. Dr. Joseph Mundell, who had cooperated in writing the Doctors' Bill, was now present to argue against it. He explained the period of fertility lasted no more than nine or ten days and could be calculated with "almost mathematical precision." He argued mechanical and chemical contraceptives, if used over time, were hazardous to a woman's health. So, there was no need for the present bill to legalize them. His implication was that women who needed to avoid pregnancy for health reasons, could do so through continence in their fertile period.[20]

At the end of the hearing, Sanger offered a rebuttal to arguments of the opposition. She averred that though it seemed proponents and opponents were at polar opposites, they were not far apart. The bill had been drafted in consultation with Mundell, who came recommended by the NCWC. She directed attention to Latz's book *Rhythm*, which had "ecclesiastical approval" and was highly recommended by Catholic journals. "Now it comes down to a safe device or a safe period," concluded Sanger, "and that is just about where both sides are now."[21]

At the hearing before a Senate subcommittee, Dr. Prentiss Willson, president of the D.C. Medical Society, favored the Doctors' Bill over the rhythm method. He asked senators which method of contraception was more likely to endanger the morals of youth: Sanger's, which required consultation with a doctor, the sizing and fitting of a contraceptive device, the purchase of additional supplies from a druggist, and time, opportunity, and privacy for their application; or, rhythm, which could be applied immediately by any high-school girl on the backseat of a car on a remote country road who could do mental arithmetic?[22]

Not long after Burke's return from San Francisco, the Senate Judiciary Committee reported the Doctors' Bill favorably. Its chairman was Catholic Senator Henry Ashurst of Arizona, and two coreligionists were members: Felix Hébert and Patrick McCarron of Nevada. At the end of April, Burke telephoned Ashurst about the bill's chances. Defending himself by stating he voted against reporting it, Ashurst told Burke the Senate favored it by a margin of three to one. Astonished, Burke asked if telegraphic protests to senators might alter the situation. Ashurst said senators received scores daily and added, "A Senator having once made up his mind never changes it." Burke asked if they based decisions on principle. Ashurst replied they "were sick of the Birth Control bill: it had been so often before them, they just wanted to get rid of it." Burke suggested they could do so by killing it. He reminded Ashurst this was the first time such a bill had come before the full Senate. Ashurst admitted he had not polled his colleagues, so his estimate of a three to one margin might be mistaken. He also acknowledged protests could do no harm and might even do some good.[23]

So, Burke and Agnes Regan mounted a protest. They had branches of the NCCW and NCCM wire opposition to their senators. Burke himself asked Patrick Scanlan, editor of the Brooklyn *Tablet*, to urge readers to protest to New York Senators Robert Wagner and Royal Copeland on moral, economic, and population grounds. Scanlan should also encourage physicians to object on professional basis. "Of course, I think, as Miss Regan and I sit here," wrote Burke during a lull, "that we are two simpletons, for after 'Rhythm,' the Catholic cause has no bright outlook."[24] Clearly, he believed it undercut Catholic objections to birth control.

In May, the bill came before the Senate which was operating under the unanimous consent rule, that is, only one senator need object to prevent a bill's passage. When the measure was called, Catholic Senator David Walsh objected to it and the chamber passed it over. Several days later, an angry Walsh telephoned William Montavon to say that since his objection, he received abusive communications denying his was the Catholic position because the three Catholics on the committee neither filed a minority report against the bill nor objected to it on the floor. Walsh wanted the NCWC to pressure them into open opposition. He suggested the News Service poll committee members and release a story to the Catholic press, including that the only opposition thus far came non-Catholic Senator David Reed and Catholic David Walsh. Montavon told Burke a "very indignant" Walsh apparently wanted to shame his coreligionists into action.[25]

Burke had Frank Hall of the Press Department canvass the committee. His people met with about half the members, who were evenly split for and against the measure. Montavon learned from Hébert's office that Walsh objected on the floor before Hébert could. In fact, all three Catholic members voted against the bill in committee.[26]

Burke and Montavon went to see Walsh. Still fuming, he wanted to know if the NCWC really backed anything. "You backed up non-recognition of Russia and you gave up that cause: you opposed this Birth Control Bill—do you still oppose it?" He hammered away at Burke so he could not get a word in edgewise. Finally able, he explained the Administrative Committee protested against recognition of Russia privately to Roosevelt rather than publicly. He explained the actions of the NCWC regarding birth control. Walsh argued if it did its job properly, there would have been a minority report from the Catholics on the committee, which would have sealed the bill's fate. The Senate could not have calendared it for unanimous consent as "an uncontested measure." Walsh expected little from his friend Ashurst because he was not well versed in Catholic teaching. But, Hébert had no excuse. He did not even object when it came up for consideration. Walsh asserted without his intervention, the bill would be law.[27]

The bill's demise seemed a Pyrrhic victory. Like Burke, Ready believed injection of rhythm into the equation "destroyed the force" of Catholic arguments. It also opened the question of whether the Church itself was advocating contraception. Ready informed Jesuit Ignatius Cox, chaplain of the Guild of Catholic Physicians, that there was a case pending in the Post Office as to whether mailing books and other printed material about rhythm violated the law. In November, Burke told the Administrative Committee the Customs Service was also considering the book's legality. An agent recently confiscated a copy of *Rhythm*. Moreover, it was giving clerical circles pause about the lure of materialism and non-procreative sex.[28]

So concerned was the Administrative Committee it issued a letter to the hierarchy that open discussion and advocacy of rhythm was "unwarranted." In 1880, the sacred penitentiary in Rome warned confessors to be circumspect in advising married persons on this issue. "If the confessor in the sacred tribunal must be cautious in suggesting this means, certainly writers of popular books and pamphlets who give indiscriminate instruction on this delicate subject disregard the caution imposed by the Holy See." The letter went out on 22 December 1934 and for the most part had the desired effect of abating Catholic publications about rhythm.[29]

Three weeks after the Doctors' Bill died on the Senate floor, the NCWC faced birth control in Puerto Rico in connection with economic reconstruction. Puerto Ricans' love of children and large families became a demographic problem in the colonial economy dominated by corporate sugar interests. There were neither enough jobs nor was there enough domestically produced food to support growing population. Neo-Malthusians sought to remedy the situation through birth control. Puerto Rican nationalists countered with calls for a return to traditions of motherhood, Hispanic culture, and Catholicism. They romanticized the image of Puerto Rican women with abundant children, reproducing both indigenous people and their traditional culture in the same act.[30] The Catholic Church joined nationalists in opposing contraception not only on moral grounds, but also on grounds of social justice and culture: the right of people to land ownership or a living wage capable of enabling them to have and support in comfort a family the size they desired.

In March, Eleanor Roosevelt and Assistant Secretary of Agriculture Rexford Tugwell visited the island on separate fact-finding missions. Tugwell reported to President Roosevelt the need for a more equitable distribution of resources, diversification of the economy, and reduction of population. Noting Puerto Ricans loved children and loved having them, Tugwell believed out-migration would be necessary until people became conscious that an improved standard of living depended on population control.[31]

The president told Tugwell he wanted to increase small landholding devoted to food production. It was also necessary to decrease the number of poor through birth control, a measure whose "dysgenic probabilities" left Tugwell "cold." Roosevelt authorized the Puerto Rican Policy Commission (PRPC) to study the situation and formulate a plan. The commission had the Chardón Plan, named after chairman Carlos Chardón, in Roosevelt's hands by mid-June. It called for governmental purchase of the best, most productive sugar lands and their transfer to peasant cane growers. Parcels vacated by the latter were to be distributed to the landless for the production of food. Population was to be reduced by emigration, though the plan did recognize that a long-term solution to overpopulation must include "a scientific scheme for birth control."[32]

When American papers carried news of the plan, Burke saw Brigadier General Creed Cox, chief of Insular Affairs, to discover the truth of the reports. Cox explained there was yet no definite program. Chardón's commission was developing it, but finalization rested with the FERA, the Agricultural Adjustment Administration, and the Public Works Administration. Burke explained any recommendation of birth control would evoke strong opposition from Bishops Edwin Byrne of San Juan and Aloysius Willinger of Ponce as well as constitute a "public insult" to the vast majority of Puerto Ricans.[33]

Briefing Byrne and Willinger, Burke recommended against protest until more definite information was available. He drew up a memorandum for Roosevelt. Recounting steps taken thus far, Burke noted Dorothy Bourne, whose husband James directed the Puerto Rican Emergency Relief Administration (PRERA), was "a public advocate of birth control" and held a position in the Puerto Rican government. Burke considered it "almost unthinkable" the Rehabilitation Program would "recommend birth control." Contraception "directly and explicitly" violated laws of the U.S. It was irrelevant that Puerto Ricans were developing the plan; American officials would finalize it, thereby opening themselves to impeachment. Furthermore, Puerto Rico was bound to respect laws of the U.S. Burke argued that the monopoly of sugar corporations on agricultural property produced overcrowding and slums. The answer was "a more equitable distribution" of land. He left a copy of the memorandum with Roosevelt's secretary Marvin McIntyre.[34]

McIntyre communicated it to Roosevelt who was vacationing in the Caribbean. Roosevelt authorized Burke to issue a public statement that the reconstruction plan for Puerto Rico would make no mention of birth control. Roosevelt made this clear on the island itself. Byrne sat at Roosevelt's table at a banquet held in his honor. When the president of the Puerto Rican Senate brought up birth control, Roosevelt stated nothing should be done in that regard which violated Catholic teaching, the faith of practically all islanders. Similarly, Willinger cited Roosevelt's published remark from that banquet: "The Government will not countenance any legislation that tends to offend the conscience of the good people of Puerto Rico."[35] While these official protestations were comforting, they would not prevent the unofficial promotion of contraception.

"THE RADIO PRIEST"

Father Charles E. Coughlin, popular "radio priest" and pastor of the Shrine of the Little Flower (St. Thérèse of Lisieux) in Royal Oak, Michigan, began broadcasting in 1926 and quickly became a sensation. He established the Radio League of the Little Flower, essentially a mail list to raise funds. In 1932, Detroit Mayor Frank Murphy introduced him to Roosevelt who was running for president. Coughlin became a supporter, though not yet over the radio. After Roosevelt's inauguration, Coughlin broadcast it was "Roosevelt or ruin!" averring "the New Deal is Christ's Deal!" Believing bankers and financiers caused the Depression by tight money policies, he encouraged Roosevelt to inflate the price of gold and later to remonetize silver.[36]

The silver proposal prompted Roosevelt to seek Burke's help. After discussing education with him in April, Roosevelt suddenly turned from charming to serious. He said Coughlin urged him to purchase silver to raise its value from 43 points to 62. The Treasury did, but value rose only 2 points. Secretary Henry Morgenthau published a list of silver investors, showing the Radio League of the Little Flower held twenty contracts for 500,000 ounces. The *New York Herald-Tribune* ran the story with a statement by Coughlin's secretary Amy Collins that she "invested" $20,000 ($460,000 in 2024) of league funds on Roosevelt's "promise that he would raise the price of American goods to the 1926 level." "Father Burke," said Roosevelt, "I never gave any word to anybody." He noted $20,000 would have bought only 50,000 ounces, which meant Collins purchased the 500,000 ounces on margin, putting10 percent down and borrowing the rest. "This," said Roosevelt, "is speculation, and not investment." Collins and Coughlin hoped silver's price would rise so they could sell at a profit. Roosevelt alleged that some of the invested money came from parish funds, which was untrue. He added Coughlin stirred up antisemitism, even attacking the Jewish Morgenthau as a tool of Wall Street for revealing the Radio League's purchase. Burke noted Roosevelt was deeply concerned that Coughlin had taken advantage of him and used "his word" for speculation. Burke said he would "inform the proper authorities." He memorialized the conversation and gave it to Cicognani.[37]

While Roosevelt vacationed in the Caribbean, he asked McIntyre to see Burke about Coughlin. McIntyre showed him a stack of papers identifying stations that carried Coughlin's broadcasts, mainly in the East and Midwest. McIntyre said he received word that in the coming broadcast season, Coughlin would "take off the lid," particularly in bitter attacks against Jews. Burke asked for evidence of the antisemitism. McIntyre agreed that was proper.[38] Nothing indicates he supplied Burke with proof. Still, the two interviews gave Burke cause to put his thoughts on paper. If Coughlin intended to attack Jews, Burke could see no reason why he should not be permitted to do so—"permitted in the sense of allowing him to take all the rope he wants for his own hanging." Church authorities had plenty of evidence about "the temper and character" of Coughlin. If they deemed proper, they could take action against him. Yet, Burke thought it "unbecoming" of Roosevelt to use the Church to silence him. He wondered why the eagerness to have it do that. Roosevelt once encouraged Coughlin as a loyal, public supporter because his listeners believed he had the confidence of the administration. If he no longer did, the administration should publicly repudiate him. Burke concluded, "I do not think we should be party to the Administration's purposes." Roosevelt's conversations with him about Coughlin posed "great danger, and likelihood of great misunderstanding."[39] Indeed, Coughlin grew disillusioned with the New Deal. In the months following, he became more critical of Roosevelt's policies.[40]

New Deal

Meanwhile, Burke handled new and old business arising from the New Deal. When Roosevelt spoke with him about Coughlin, he also shared the idea of a comprehensive insurance plan that would become Social Security. He envisioned an all-inclusive program covering health, accident, workmen's compensation, maternity, and old age. Both employer and employee would contribute funds to it. Burke said the scheme was "a great common social obligation." Every charitable organization that collected donations for a cause had an obligation not only to engage in relief work but to return to society funds they gathered from it. Burke thought the plan should ask them to contribute half to one percent of their collections to the social insurance fund. Roosevelt wanted Burke to consider the concept and offer suggestions.[41]

At the end of June, Roosevelt issued Executive Order 6757 establishing both the Committee on Economic Security and the Advisory Council on Economic Security to study and recommend proposals to promote greater economic security of individuals. Although he asked Burke his suggestions, Burke understood the request to mean Roosevelt wanted advice of the administrative bishops. He circularized the Administrative Committee about Roosevelt's idea of a comprehensive plan covering an "individual from the cradle to the grave."[42]

Four of seven bishops replied. The responses split evenly: two for and two opposed. Bishops John Noll and Joseph Schrembs supported the idea, the former "in a general way" and the latter cautiously effusive. Schrembs commented the scheme was the very thing "Catholic political economists … have been preaching" for years. The important thing was making it work, which would be impossible unless the government was willing "to reach into the pockets of the very rich." Because the scheme was so far-reaching, only the government could administer it, which entailed dangers of bureaucracy, red tape, political graft, and racketeering.[43]

Bishop Hugh Boyle and Archbishop John Murray opposed it. The latter considered it "the most demoralizing proposition ever presented to the people of the United States." Considering the scheme "unwise," Boyle went into specifics. He believed it would have "a deadening effect" on individuals, increasing the number of "ne'er-do-wells." Presciently, he predicted a fund so large as the one to be amassed would be "a temptation in times of crisis." In wartime, for instance, Congress would raid and exhaust the fund no matter how "sacred" it was to be. Nor would it relieve citizens of the obligation to support the elderly and afflicted because even present relief money proved insufficient. As alternatives, Boyle suggested corporations be limited to earning a reasonable profit, that government establish a minimum wage, and joint-stock corporations gradually disappear in favor of "cooperative groups … in which the laborer may have some of the fruits which now go to capital, as well as a wage for his labor."[44]

When the Administrative Committee met, Burke recounted his conversation with Roosevelt and presented the views of the four respondents. Discussion led the committee to accept in principle the government's obligation to safeguard the aged and underprivileged. The bishops, however, wanted to ensure the plan in no way handicapped or precluded private charitable institutions and that it included stipulations upholding individual responsibility.[45]

That afternoon, Burke saw Roosevelt to inform him of the committee's thoughts. The bishops, he said, were "most solicitous" that the legislation contain provisions to protect personal initiative as well as personal, municipal, and state responsibility. Moreover, it should respect the right of spontaneous charity and do no injustice to existing fraternal insurance organizations like the Knights of Columbus. Finally, it should diminish in no way the rights of private hospitals, charitable organizations, and protective agencies. Roosevelt assured Burke he would take every care to see that was done.[46]

While dealing with social security, Burke finally resolved the matter of nonmilitary chaplains for the CCC. In early June, the government agreed to permit such ministers and pay them $30 a month with 5 cents per mile for travel. It authorized 250 chaplaincies for the Catholic Church. Army regulations required priests to say Mass at least once a week and attend to all sick calls for Catholics in camp. They need not make calls themselves, but must arrange to have them answered immediately by a substitute. When Burke informed Cicognani of the news, he was quite pleased, saying, "Father Burke, all this is owing to you and to the respect in which the President holds you." Burke was "profoundly grateful." "Next to going out personally in the ministry to these boys," he wrote to Helen Lynch, "is to enable others to go out."[47]

When two months passed with no such order forthcoming, Burke saw Army Chief of Staff General Douglas McArthur, who thought the matter had been settled. Burke explained no order had gone out to corps commanders to pay civilian chaplains. McArthur said the Army left the number of priests and their payment to the CCC. The latter would appoint chaplains, and the corps commander would then authorize the CCC to pay them. McArthur referred Burke to James McEntee, assistant director of the CCC. The whole situation seemed confused to Burke. On his way out, he visited General Hugh Drum, who showed him the order described by McArthur, which needed only the signature of Robert Fechner, director of the CCC, who was out of town.[48]

Burke saw McEntee about the order and was assured everything would be all right. Burke told him there were already problems. He notified bishops around the country that money was available and the steps they should take to notify area commanders to authorize payment. As it stood, commanders knew nothing and could do nothing. McEntee said priests would receive back pay from their start date. Burke complained that would create misunderstanding and unnecessary paperwork. In the end, McEntee agreed to sign the order as soon as it came.[49]

It took more than a week to cut through the bureaucratic red tape. On 14 August, Drum called Burke to say the order would go out that day. He was relying on Burke to provide the number of civilian chaplains the bishops in each corps would supply. Burke assured him as soon as the CCC sent him the number for each location, his people would contact bishops and provide the CCC with the information to register the priests and forward their papers to the War Department. He delegated oversight to Ready. By November, the Church had 131 priests in the program representing forty dioceses.[50]

MEXICO

While handling the foregoing, Burke addressed again the persecution in Mexico. By 1934, thirteen Mexican states closed all churches or nearly so. Moreover, the NRP adopted a Six Year Plan as its platform for the upcoming presidential election wherein the party pledged to build 12,000 schools by 1940. These would be under government direction, socialist in character, and devoid of religious instruction. Elías Calles, *jefe máximo* (supreme chief) of the NRP, approved the nomination of Lázaro Cárdenas for president. The latter publicly promised: "I shall not permit the clergy to intervene in any manner in the education of the people."[51]

At home, Burke faced an altered diplomatic situation. In his inaugural address, Roosevelt committed himself "to the policy of the good neighbor."[52] Its implication became clear when Secretary of State Cordell Hull signed a formal convention at the International Conference of American States declaring "no state has the right to intervene in the internal or external affairs of another." Burke understood this policy ruled out any formal government action regarding the persecution in Mexico. He thought, however, Roosevelt might be willing "to use his good offices" on behalf of the Mexican Church, though he would "have to be very careful what he does and how he does it." Roosevelt selected for Mexican ambassador his old boss, former Secretary of the Navy Josephus Daniels, whom Burke considered "a rather simple man: altogether uninformed about Mexico" and lacking "initiative."[53]

In June, Monsignor Egidio Vagnozzi told Burke the Vatican wanted Cicognani to submit a plan of action regarding Mexico; Cicognani wanted Burke to formulate it. Burke outlined his ideas for Vagnozzi. He would first see Roosevelt, provided Daniels and Hull approved. Roosevelt would have Daniels informally offer his good offices to help resolve the Church-state conflict, with suggestions about how this might be done. Nothing more would be done until after the Mexican election on 1 July. Burke would then urge Roosevelt to have Daniels request the incoming administration permit exiled Apostolic Delegate Leopoldo Ruiz y Flores to return to Mexico and exiled Archbishop Francisco Orozco y Jiménez to return to his see. If the Mexican government refused to allow Ruiz to return as delegate, then Daniels should ask if he could return to his diocese as ordinary, with the understanding that within three months of his return, the Vatican would appoint a new delegate. Burke thought the new delegate ought to be an Italian, "well experienced, of firmness, and of a judicial turn of mind." Vagnozzi liked the plan. Burke wanted Cicognani to get Vatican permission for him to pursue that line. He wanted no actual approval for any of it because he wanted negotiations to seem fluid, so he could tell Roosevelt he "had reason to feel that these things were worth while considering, and … they had a great chance of being accepted if the Mexican Government would agree." Vagnozzi said he would try to shape the report to Rome accordingly.[54]

Within a week, burdens of the previous several months took their toll on Burke. "Indeed the days have been heavy upon me," he told Grace Murray, "and ... I began to feel something of the old exhaustion." He spent Friday in bed. "The trouble is," he told her, "the whole work here is heavy and the problems do come up to me. I suppose I take them too seriously, but I can hardly help that." He explained Mexico was again in his "hands," and he saw no escape because he knew the problem best. "I know as no one else does what it will mean for me," he wrote. Cicognani would report Burke's plan to the Vatican, and he dreaded the reply, but would "have to accept" if it meant renewed involvement with Mexico. Burke asked Lynch for her prayers. "I may have added burdens soon considering the situation there," he explained, "and I do not feel that I have the strength to cope with them. However I am hardly free in the matter."[55]

In mid-August, Burke left for vacation. Archbishop Murray thanked him for "being good enough" to himself to take the time off he was "supposed to be enjoying ever since last April." He went to Shimmo Hills on Nantucket Island with his sister Lizzie and his housekeeper Frances Boyle. They stayed at Corscaden, "a small house, very near the water and out of town and quite by itself." It was situated on the bay directly across from the harbor's mouth. During the first week, Burke went about "too actively" and ended "badly laid up." His heart failed him and landed him in bed. By 1 September he was better and determinedly less active. He explained to Lynch, "I just rest, but that is blessed." Lizzie departed in early September, and his older sister Mary joined him two days later. By mid-month, Shimmo Hills was deserted. He wrote Lynch, "I have been through the week out on the moors and they hold voices for me." He told her one of the joys of the place was "the hours I may spend with our Blessed Lord." He recommended Corscaden house to his friend William Kerby: "It is quiet: you have the water: the harbor calm—the ocean restless, the far stretching moors, and the exceptionally blue of heaven." He and Mary remained there until the 25th, "called back as of old: this time by the Mexican question."[56]

At issue was the storm of Catholic protest over Daniels's injudicious praise of Calles's declaration on education. Shortly after Cárdenas's election, the *jefe máximo* demanded the hostile influence of clergy and conservatives be expunged from the schools. "We must now enter into and take possession of the minds of the children, the minds of the young," he declared, "because they do belong and should belong to the Revolution." Having seen only a brief extract of the declaration—one shorn of its anticlerical context—Daniels thought it accorded with the best North American tradition. "General Calles sees, as Jefferson saw, that no people can be both free and ignorant," he told Americans visiting the embassy. "... Calles issued a challenge that goes to the very root of the settlement of all the problems of tomorrow when he said: 'We must enter and take possession of the mind of childhood, the mind of youth.'" Catholics in both countries roundly denounced him for endorsing the educational program.[57]

Back at Washington, Burke saw Cicognani about Mexico. Because Vagnozzi never formalized his plan, the two discussed the situation for two hours, formulating a new one as they went. Cicognani took copious notes. The first step called for Burke to see Roosevelt about Mexico with a view to lessening the persecution. The second would be for Montavon to write a brief pamphlet explaining the reasons for the Church's protest against the present Mexican administration. The third was issuance of a pastoral letter by the Mexican bishops requesting their government rescind laws denying religious and education freedom. The fourth was to have the government accept an Italian apostolic delegate to Mexico. Finally, the present delegate, Archbishop Ruiz, must take definite responsibility for the Church there. Cicognani said Ruiz had deferred to him about Mexico. Burke insisted Ruiz must take it in hand. Cicognani said the Vatican wanted Burke to handle affairs regarding the U.S. government. Burke begged to be excused, but two days later Cicognani told him a cable from Rome indicated Pius XI explicitly requested Burke assume this representation. "You," said the delegate, "are the soul of this work of solving the Mexican situation in the United States." Burke was not sanguine about possibilities. "Mexico is again demanding my attention," he wrote Lynch. "I think a man might give his whole time to that problem—and yet not get very far in beneficial results." He did not report his Vatican assignment to the Administrative Committee until a year later.[58]

In October, Burke told Roosevelt of the pope's desire for a peaceful settlement of the Church-state conflict. Admitting the NPR's economic goals were laudable, Burke held its educational program was "godless, and indeed positively atheistic." He argued pursuit of such by a bordering country ought gravely to concern the U.S. The government's lack of interest caused American Catholics to believe the administration gave "tacit approval" to

Mexico. Intended or not, Daniels's endorsement of its educational program confirmed that belief. It was reprehensible and exceeded his portfolio.[59]

Skeptical about a persecution, Roosevelt apparently thought the Mexican Church opposed universal schooling, which the NRP was determined to promote; he wanted proof Mexico actually tried to destroy religion. Burke pointed to parts of the Six Year Plan, Article 3 of the constitution outlawing religious schools and instruction, and decrease in the number of priests permitted to function. He averred Mexico seemed determined to drive bishops and clergy out and confiscate all Church property. Burke said he would provide documentation. Relenting, Roosevelt said something ought to be done and asked Burke's recommendation. He replied the administration should issue a statement explaining that while it favored extension of education to all, it could not support schooling that was anti-religious. "I think such a statement ought to be made," said Roosevelt. "I think it should be issued from Mexico City." He wanted to discuss it with Undersecretary William Phillips, who had charge of State for the absent Hull. Burke asked if Roosevelt would approve his speaking with Phillips about it. Happy to let him, Roosevelt suddenly blurted: "Father Burke, I think we can go farther than this. I think I should informally send a message to Calles … saying that I think if the Mexican Government proceeds with a programme of exiling the Bishops and priests and introducing an atheistic programme, Mexico would make of itself a spectacle before the civilized world." "Would you do that, Mr. President?" asked Burke. "Yes, I will do it informally," Roosevelt replied.[60]

As Burke departed, he turned to ask FDR what he should tell reporters about their topic of conversation. Roosevelt told him to say nothing about Mexico. Burke suggested that their discussion was about the CCC. "Good," replied FDR, and called out, "Father Burke, tell the Bishops the camps are to last for a long time and will be increased, and I want them to take care of the boys."[61] Despite their effort to cover tracks, the press figured out the truth of Burke's visit to Roosevelt, with unfortunate consequences.

Burke saw Phillips, who agreed an explanatory statement about education should be issued, and they almost reached accord on wording. Two days later, however, Phillips phoned Burke with word from Mexico City that a further statement by Daniels about his speech "would not only be inadvisable but would intensify the present Mexican Government's warfare against religion," the last thing Roosevelt wanted. Phillips stressed the "importance and definiteness of the advice received." He asked if Burke was satisfied. He said the refusal to issue a statement was a disappointment, but he trusted Roosevelt's judgment. Phillips's emphatic explanation signaled to Burke that further apologies by Daniels would cause Calles to demand his recall, which would mean severance of diplomatic relations.[62]

Burke told Cicognani the bad news. The delegate was "very disappointed." He asked if it meant the American government was "closed" to influencing Mexico. Burke said not insofar as good will went. He stressed any American influence must be of good will only. If the Mexican government thought the U.S. was trying to compel it, it would resist. Burke deplored publicity about his visit to Roosevelt. Word of it, he believed, reached Calles, who was determined to fight the Church "to the bitter end." Burke told Cicognani that the *jefe* now knew the American government was prepared to issue an explanation that would rob him of the support of Daniels's speech. At least "that was something," noted Burke. Cicognani was unimpressed. Burke heard how defensive his comment sounded, which of course it was.[63]

While dealing with Mexico, he received an emotional blow: Lynch was being transferred to the Cenacle in Boston. "I read the letter and it shocked me," he wrote to her. "I knew it might be; but one knows that death may be—and yet the shock is there nor does foreknowledge ease it." He felt the trauma even as he wrote. He acknowledged it would take him time to adjust "and indeed accept." Of course, he accepted the news "in principle ... but it were a poor fidelity and love and affection that can change its 'localities' and all they mean without struggle and pain and suffering.... Sincerity always asks its price." He identified her with his birthplace New York, to which he remained deeply rooted. He said in his "more serious thoughts," he never felt he left that city or the Paulist house there. He always felt he was "on loan" in Washington and would return there. "The years of exile have been so many that I have forgotten at times the exile," he wrote, "and the work so strenuous that it calls for all I have." He always thought of his trips to New York "as going to the Cenacle and to you." "It was no lack of perfection in St. Teresa," he wrote, "that she yearned to go back to Avila." In times of critical illness, he always thought he would end up in New York and she would be at the Cenacle. After baring his feelings, he chose to dwell on her twenty-two years in the convent and her life with Christ there. She would carry that with her to Boston and continue the work with "the yearning and determination to boast—'I live; no, not I, but Christ lives in me [Gal. 2:20].'"[64]

With this emotional hurt in his heart, Burke took another run at the Mexican problem in a memorandum to Roosevelt. He noted the Mexican government exiled many of its citizens—clerical and otherwise—"delivering" them to the U.S. Though the situation resulted from the religious problem, an untouchable internal matter, Burke pointed to the resentment this policy would surely engender in Americans, Catholic and non-, as the number of exiles grew, resulting in problems for State and the Immigration Bureau. The memorandum included a sample note Roosevelt might send. It disavowed any desire to interfere in Mexico's internal affairs, but when those had repercussions on the U.S., its government hoped to be permitted to speak "informally." Such was now the case as exiles streamed across the border causing embarrassment to the American government. Without entering into the merits of the Church-state controversy, the U.S. respectfully asked if it would be possible to settle it. The U.S. wanted no part in the settlement; that was between the Church and Mexico.[65]

The Administrative Committee met and approved the memorandum and authorized Burke to present it to Roosevelt in its name. He saw Roosevelt that afternoon and told him the Mexican government was driving many Catholics into exile in the U.S. He considered it "the right" and "the grave obligation" of the government to address the matter "informally" with Mexico. He gave the president the memorandum. Roosevelt read it. "I think this might be done," he said; "but I think this is putting it in too mild and gentlemanly a way. If I were Ambassador to Mexico, I would speak very plainly to the Mexican Government." Roosevelt explained he was going away for a few days, but he wanted to take some action. Hull would be back in town the next afternoon, and the president would speak with him about it.[66] Apparently, the secretary of State dissuaded him from doing anything.

ENDNOTES TO CHAPTER 22

1. Burke, *Christ in Us*, 167–68.
2. Pledge of the Legion of Decency, ACUA, USCCB 10:125:30; McNicholas to hierarchy, 4 April 1934, copy, ibid.; Burke, Report of the General Secretary,

April 1934, ibid., 10:62:20; Minutes of the Administrative Committee, 10 April 1934, ibid., 10:64:7; NCWC News Service, 16 April 1934; Walsh, *Sin and Censorship*, 92–93; Black, *Hollywood Censored*, 163; Couvares, "Hollywood, Main Street, and Church," 596–97; Jowett, *Film*, 199–201.

3. Burke to McNicholas, 8 May 1934, copy, ACUA, USCCB 10:30:27.
4. McNicholas et al. to hierarchy, undated [spring 1934], copy, ACUA, USCCB 10:30:27; Walsh, *Sin and Censorship*, 93–94.
5. Walsh, *Sin and Censorship*, 95–105; Black, *Hollywood Censored*, 179–83.
6. Burke, Memorandum, 10 July 1934, ACUA, USCCB 10:152:5.
7. Burke to McNicholas, 24 October 1934, copy, exhibit #3 in Burke, Report of the General Secretary, ACUA, USCCB 10:62:23.
8. Burke, Memorandum, 25 October 1934, ACUA, USCCB 10:153: Interview Book.
9. *Minutes of the Sixteenth Annual Meeting of the Hierarchy, November 1934*, 17–22, ACUA, USCCB Bound Volumes; Walsh, *Sin and Censorship*, 118–28.
10. James N. Rule to Johnson, 16 November 1933, ACUA, USCCB Legal Department 10:50:11; Tentative Recommendations for the Subcommittee on Legislative Plan, undated [winter 1933], ibid.; Montavon to E. Walsh, 1 December 1933, copy, ibid.; Johnson to Hanna, 1 February 1934, AASF, NCWC files.
11. Ready to Hanna, 24 March 1934, AASF, NCWC files.
12. Hanna to Ready, 2 April 1934, copy, ACUA, USCCB 10:116; draft of same in Burke's hand, undated [March 1934], AASF, NCWC files.
13. Murray to Ready, 28 March 1934, copy; Peterson to Ready, 28 March 1934, copy; Boyle to Ready, 28 March 1934, copy; E. Walsh to Ready, 3 April 1934, copy; Schrembs to Ready, 9 April 1934, copy—all in ACUA, USCCB 10:11:6.
14. Butler to Ready and Johnson, 28 March 1934, ACUA, USCCB 10:11:6; Burke, Report of the General Secretary, April 1934, ibid.,10:62:20; Minutes of the Administrative Committee, 11 April 1934, ibid., 10:64:7.
15. Burke, [Interview with Roosevelt], 30 April 1934, ACUA, USCCB 10:153: Interview Book; Burke, Memorandum of the line on which I will speak to the Chief Executive, undated [April 1934], ibid., 10:123:1; Ambrose A. Clegg Jr., "Federal Aid to Education: A Study of the Interest of Church and Labor Groups in Proposals for Federal Aid to Elementary and Secondary Schools,1890–1945," (Ph.D. diss., University of North Carolina, 1963), 89–93; Frank J. Munger and Richard F. Fenno, *National Politics and Federal Aid to Education* (Syracuse: University of Syracuse Press, 1962), 6; Gilbert E. Smith, *The Limits of Reform: Politics and Federal Aid to Education 1937–1950* (New York: Garland Publishing, Inc., 1982), 1–9, 24–36.
16. Burke to Hanna (a circular), 7 May 1934, with enclosure, copies, AASF, NCWC files.

17. Burke to Hanna, 15 May 1934, AASF, NCWC files; H.R. 9544, 73rd Cong., 2nd Sess.; House Committee on Education, Report to Accompany H.R. 9544, 73rd Cong., 2nd Sess.; *Chicago Daily Tribune*, 12 May 1934; Burke, Report of the General Secretary, November 1934, ACUA, USCCB 10:62:22.
18. H.R. 5978, 73rd Cong., 1st Sess.; S. 1841, 73rd Cong., 1st Sess.
19. Tentler, *Catholics and Contraception*, 106–111; Chesler, *Woman of Valor*, 321–23; Sheerin, *Never Look Back*, 197.
20. *Birth Control: Hearings before the Committee on the Judiciary, House of Representatives, Seventy-Third Congress, Second Session, on H.R. 5978, 18 and 19 January 1934* (Washington, D.C.: U.S. Government Printing Office, 1934), 144; Kennedy, *Birth Control*, 239; Chesler, *Woman of Valor*, 344–45; Autobiography *of Sanger*, 424–26.
21. *Birth Control: Hearings*, 231–32; *Autobiography of Sanger*, 425–26.
22. *Birth Control: Hearings*, 37–38.
23. [Burke, Memorandum], 28 April 1934, ACUA, USCCB 10:153: Interview Book.
24. [Burke, Memorandum], 29 April 1934, ACUA, USCCB 10:153: Interview Book; Burke to Patrick Scanlan, 29 April 1929, copy, ibid., 10:117:11.
25. Montavon to Burke, 17 May 1934, ACUA, USCCB 10:117:21.
26. Hall to Burke, 21 May 1934 and Montavon to Burke, 21 May 1934—both in ACUA, USCCB 10:117:21.
27. [Burke, Memorandum], 22 May 1934, ACUA, USCCB 10:153: Interview Book.
28. Burke, Report of the General Secretary, November 1934, ACUA, USCCB 10:62:22/23; Ready to Ignatius Cox, 16 February 1934, ibid., 10:117:11; Tentler, *Catholics and Contraception*, 111–14.
29. Minutes of the Administrative Committee, 13 November 1934, ACUA, USCCB 10:64:7; Burke, draft, November 1934, ibid., 10:117:11; Hanna to the hierarchy, 22 December 1934, copy, ibid.; Tentler, *Catholics and Contraception*, 116–18.
30. Laura Briggs, *Race, Sex, Science and U.S. Imperialism in Puerto Rico* (Berkeley and Los Angeles: University of California Press, 2002), 74–102.
31. Rexford Guy Tugwell, *The Stricken Land: The Story of Puerto Rico* (Garden City, N.Y.: Doubleday & Company, Inc., 1947), 34–35; Ramiréz de Arellano and Seipp, *Colonialism, Catholicism, and Contraception*, 30–35; James L. Dietz, *Economic History of Puerto Rico: Institutional Change and Capitalist Development* (Princeton: Princeton University Press, 1986), 149–50.
32. Tugwell, *Stricken Land*, 35–36; Ramírez de Arellano and Seipp, *Colonialism, Catholicism, and Contraception*, 35–37; Diets, *Economic History of Puerto Rico*, 151–56; Alaya and Bernabe, *Puerto Rico in the American Century*, 100–01.
33. [Burke, Interview with Creed Cox], 10 July 1934, ACUA, USCCB 10:117:17.

34. Burke to Byrne, 10 July 1934, copy, ACUA, USCCB 10:117:17; Burke to Willinger, 10 July 1934, copy, ibid.; [Burke, Memorandum], 14 July 1934, copy, ibid.; Ramiréz de Arellano and Seipp, *Colonialism, Catholicism, and Contraception*, 31–32.
35. Byrne to Burke, 18 July 1934, ACUA, USCCB 10:117:17; Willinger to Burke, 31 July 1934 (emphasis in original), ibid.; Burke, Report of the General Secretary, November 1934, ibid., 10:62:22/23; Burke to Hanna, 3 February 1934, AASF, NCWC files; Brands, *Traitor to His Class*, 408; A. W. Maldonado, *Luis Muñoz Marín: Puerto Rico's Democratic Revolution* (San Juan: Editorial Universidad de Puerto Rico, 2006), 127–28.
36. Alan Brinkly, *Voices of Protest: Huey Long, Father Coughlin & the Great Depression* (New York: Vintage Books, 1983), 89–112; Charles J. Tull, *Father Coughlin and the New Deal* (Syracuse: Syracuse University Press, 1965), 122, 40–44; Sheldon Marcus, *Father Coughlin: The Tumultuous Life of the Priest of the Little Flower* (Boston: Little, Brown and Company, 1973), 23–44; Leslie Woodcock Tentler, *Seasons of Grace: A History of the Catholic Archdiocese of Detroit* (Detroit: Wayne State University Press, 1990), 322–23; Brands, *Traitor to His Class*, 401.
37. Burke, [Interview with Roosevelt], 30 April 1934, ACUA, USCCB 10:153: Interview Book; Burke to Cicognani, 30 April 1934, copy, ibid., 10:16:1; *New York Herald-Tribune*, 29 April 1934; Brands, *Traitor to His Class*, 401–02; Earl Boyea, "The Reverend Charles Coughlin and the Church: The Gallagher Years, 1930–1937," *Catholic Historical Review* 81 (April 1995): 215–16; Marcus, *Father Coughlin*, 58–70; Chip Berlet and Matthew N. Lyons, *Right-Wing Populism in America: Too Close for Comfort* (New York: Guilford Press, 2000), 140–41.
38. Burke, [Interview with Marvin McIntyre], 6 July 1934, ACUA, USCCB 10:153: Interview Book.
39. Ibid.
40. Brinkley, *Voices of Protest*, 124–27.
41. Burke, [Interview with Roosevelt], 30 April 1934, ACUA, USCCB 10:153: Interview Book; Brands, *Traitor to His Class*, 412–13.
42. Franklin Roosevelt, Executive Order No. 6757, ACUA, USCCB 10:89:25; Burke circular to Administrative Committee, 10 July 1934, copy, ibid.
43. Noll to Burke, 21 July 1934, exhibit #2 of Report of the General Secretary, November 1934, ACUA, USCCB 10:62:23/24; Schrembs to Burke, 7 August 1934, ibid., 10:89:25.
44. Boyle to Burke, 31 July 1934, ACUA, USCCB 10:89:25; J. Murray to Burke, 13 August 1934, ibid.
45. Burke, Report of the General Secretary, November 1934, ACUA, USCCB 10:62:24; Minutes of the Administrative Committee, 12 November 1934, ibid., 10:64:7; Press Release, 10 November 1934, ibid., 10:89:25; Burke to Hanna, 30 January 1935, AASF, NCWC files.

46. Burke, [Interview with Roosevelt], 12 November 1934, ACUA, USCCB 10:145: Interview Book V.
47. Burke to G. Murray, 9 June 1934, AP, Burke Papers, box 12 (first quote is here); Burke to Lynch, 12 June 1934, ibid. (remaining quotes are here); Burke to Hanna, 14 and 28 July 1934, AASF, NCWC files.
48. Burke, [Interview with McArthur, Drum, and Moses], 6 August 1934, ACUA, USCCB 10:153: Interview Book.
49. Burke, [Interview with McEntee], 6 August 1934, ACUA, USCCB 10:153: Interview Book.
50. Burke, [Telephone Interview with Drum], 14 August 1934, ACUA, USCCB 10:153: Interview Book; Burke, Report of the General Secretary, November 1934, ACUA, USCCB 10:62:23.
51. Quoted in E. David Cronan, "American Catholics and Mexican Anticlericalism, 1933–1936," *Mississippi Valley Historical Review*, 45 (September 1958): 205–06 (the quotation appears on 206); E. David Cronan, *Josephus Daniels: In Mexico* (Madison: University of Wisconsin Press, 1960), 88–89; Reich, *Mexico's Hidden Revolution*, 45–50; Lyle C. Brown, "Mexican Church-State Relations, 1933–1940," *Journal of Church and State*, 6 (Spring 1964): 202–05; Nathaniel and Sylvia Weyl, *The Reconquest of Mexico: The Years of Lázaro Cárdenas* (London; Oxford University Press, 1939), 111–21; John W. F. Dulles, *Yesterday in Mexico: A Chronicle of the Revolution, 1919–1936* (Austin: University of Texas Press, 1961), 567–68; Charles C. Cumberland, *Mexico: The Struggle for Modernity* (London: Oxford University Press, 1968), 283–89.
52. Franklin Delano Roosevelt, *The Public Papers and Addresses of Franklin Delano Roosevelt*, 5 Vols. (New York: Random House, 1938), 1:14.
53. Burke, [Memorandum of Phone Conversation with Hayes], 23 May 1933, ACUA, USCCB 10:145: Interview Book V; Burke, [Memorandum], 14 May 1934, ibid.; *Rights and Duties of States: Convention between the United States of America and Other American Republics* (Washington, D.C.: U.S. Government Printing Office, 1935); J. Lloyd Mecham, *The United States and Inter-American Security, 1889–1960* (Austin: University of Texas Press, 1961), 112–16; Federico G. Gil, *Latin American–United States Relations* (New York: Harcourt Brace Jovanovich, 1971), pp. 155–59; Herring, *Colony to Superpower*, 497, 499–500.
54. Burke, [Interview with Vagnozzi], 1 June 1934, ACUA, USCCB 10:145: Interview Book V.
55. Burke to G. Murray, 9 June 1934, AP, Burke Papers, box 12; Burke to Lynch, 12 June 1934, ibid., box 5.
56. J. Murray to Burke, 13 August 1934, ACUA, USCCB 10:89:25; Burke to Lynch, 5 September 1934, AP, Burke Papers, box 5; Burke to Lynch, undated [probably 17 September 1934], ibid.; Burke to Kerby, 1 and 24 September, ACUA, Kerby Papers 58:4:7.

57. Quoted in Cronan, "Mexican Anticlericalism," 206–13 (quotes are on 206 and 207); Cronon, *Josephus Daniels*, 90–96; Flynn, *Catholics and Roosevelt*, 153–56; Redinger, *American Catholics and the Mexican Revolution*, 123–25. For the ambassador's explanation, see Josephus Daniels, *Shirt-Sleeve Diplomat* (Chapel Hill, 1947), 181–82.
58. Burke to Lynch, 12 October 1934, AP, Burke Papers, box 5; Burke, [Interview with Cicognani], 29 September and 1 October 1934, ACUA, USCCB 10:145: Interview Book V; Programme for the Conduct of the Mexican Situation, 15 October 1934, copy, ibid., 10:150:8; Burke, Report of the General Secretary, November 1935, ibid., 10:62:26; Sheerin, *Never Look Back*, 161.
59. Burke, [Interview with Roosevelt], 22 October 1934, ACUA, USCCB 10:145: Interview Book V; Sheerin, *Never Look Back*, 161–62.
60. Burke, [Interview with Roosevelt], 22 October 1934, ACUA, USCCB 10:145: Interview Book V; Sheerin, *Never Look Back*, 162–63.
61. Burke, [Interview with Roosevelt], 22 October 1934, ACUA, USCCB 10:145: Interview Book V.
62. Burke, [Telephone Conversation with Phillips], 27 October 1934, ACUA, USCCB 10:145: Interview Book V; Burke, Report of the General Secretary, ibid., 10:62:22 (quotes are from both); Memorandum by William Phillips, 27 October 1934, NA, State Department 812.404/1307 1/2; Redinger, *American Catholics and the Mexican Revolution*, 93–94.
63. Burke, [Interview with Cicognani], 27 October 1934, ACUA, USCCB 10:145: Interview Book V.
64. Burke to Lynch, 2 November 1934, AP, Burke Papers, box 5.
65. Burke, Statement left with President Roosevelt, 12 November 1934, ACUA, USCCB 10:145: Interview Book V; Sheerin, *Never Look Back*, 163–64.
66. Burke, [Interview with Roosevelt], 12 November 1934, ACUA, USCCB 10:145: Interview Book V.

Chapter 23

"The Labor Is Heavy"

> With a real personal love, I personally must live in Jesus Christ.... He has taken me into Himself and is ever the loved One of my heart.... To set out upon this mission, to keep to it, in spite of miserable and repeated failures, will give the soul the satisfaction for activity and accomplishment in life which is its native hunger. Life is not as a consequence stripped of its hard, daily tasks, its temptations, its rebellious desires, its depression and its failures—but Power has lifted us far above our own strength. That Power gives a greater spontaneity: eagerness: willingness, than the most absorbing of human loves, for it embraces all human love. It gives a greater initial force: a yearning for true love and the satisfaction thereof. It never leaves us weary: but ever comforted. It reveals our supernatural dignity. It unfolds our great part in life and it makes life greater than loss or suffering or death.[1]

Mexico: A Rivalry Revisited Yet Again

The New Year 1935 faced John Burke immediately with Mexico. Without consulting the NCWC, the Knights of Columbus adopted a resolution demanding Roosevelt warn that country unless it ended the persecution "forthwith, further recognition of the Mexican Government will be withdrawn and diplomatic relations ... will be severed." When they found Secretary of State Cordell Hull sympathetic but noncommittal, they met with Senator David Walsh and nine others who favored a resolution calling for investigating conditions in Mexico with a view to severance of diplomatic relations.[2]

Informing Burke that the Knights were introducing the resolution in the Senate, Daniel Callahan asked him to appear at a hearing to supply facts about the persecution. Burke "offered at once" to do so, but cautioned he could not endorse it without authorization. Callahan promised him its text for transmittal to the Administrative Committee.[3] Thus, a situation strikingly similar to the Boylan resolution of 1926 was developing.

William Borah of Idaho, foremost isolationist in the Senate, introduced the Knights' resolution shorn of the threat to sever diplomatic relations. It demanded Mexico "cease denying fundamental and inalienable rights to ... our nationals" resident there and authorized hearings to determine a policy that would best "serve the cause of tolerance and religious freedom."[4]

The Mexican embassy issued a statement denying any persecution, noting clergymen who obeyed Mexican laws ministered unmolested. Burke issued a press release insisting Mexico did persecute its citizens for religion. His rejoinder catalogued measures enacted against the Church and religion. With regard to clergy, he noted there were only 334 priests for a population of 15 million; legal restraints prohibited 3,500 others from functioning.[5]

The *New York Times* feared the resolution was likely "to inflame the religious warfare" and lead to new charges against the Mexican clergy. It hoped the Senate would disregard it. Some below the border felt the same. *El Hombre Libre* (*The Freeman*), a paper sympathetic to the Catholic cause, begged Borah to let Mexicans handle the situation. Archbishop Pascual Díaz of Mexico City urged the State Department to oppose the resolution.[6]

Given its altered wording, Burke informed Callahan the NCWC had no evidence to support its claim that Mexico abridged religious rights of American residents. He sent the administrative bishops copies of the resolution, the *Times* editorial, and his rejoinder to the Mexican embassy, with an appeal for instructions. "The situation here is not an easy one," he told them. If he appeared at the hearing with data on the persecution, the Foreign Relations Committee would ask whom he represented and if they favored the measure. Burke needed to know if the board wanted him to endorse it. "If the ... resolution is to be understood as being also the mind of the Bishops," he cautioned, "the Bishops of this country may be criticized as having taken or supported political action of our government in an international affair."[7]

Within days, eight committeemen responded, five voting members and three non-voting assistant bishops. Although a few were sympathetic, none wanted Burke to endorse the resolution, and several thought that if subpoenaed, he should make it clear the Knights acted without consulting the NCWC.[8]

The bishops also expressed varying degrees of irritation with the Knights. Most felt they were the tail that wagged the dog. Joseph Rummel considered their acting without approval of the NCWC another illustration of "well intentioned" but "disorganized procedure" whose "results become extremely embarrassing to those who are burdened with definite and ultimate responsibility for the Church." He wanted the Supreme Board notified "its independent action [was] causing the Administrative Committee … great embarrassment." The Knights should be warned "against any similar procedure in the future."[9]

Meanwhile, Archbishop Michael Curley wired Hanna that "national backing" was needed for the Borah resolution and asked him to have the committee offer the senator support in the name of the NCWC. Shortly thereafter, Callahan told Burke to prepare evidence immediately. He confidentially told Callahan the Administrative Committee refused to support the resolution. Callahan said if the Foreign Relations Committee knew that, it would kill the resolution. Burke gently explained the Knights should have checked with the NCWC before charging ahead. Callahan asked if he could tell Walsh the bishops' decision. Burke replied that the senator had no right to the information.[10]

Burke informed the ailing Hanna's coadjutor Archbishop John Mitty of the conversation. "The situation is difficult," he wrote, "and plainly shows the unhappy results of divided action." The Knights placed themselves squarely behind the Borah resolution. If the NCWC were forced to state it opposed the measure, "it would publicly look like cleavage in the Catholic body." The division between the NCWC and Knights also compromised Burke's ability to represent the bishops before the government. If he visited Roosevelt or State, reporters would ask if the NCWC supported the resolution. Unless he wholeheartedly answered yes, they would grow suspicious and publish it was opposed.[11]

Burke told Helen Lynch the Mexican issue "engaged [him] daily, calling on all the physical and mental (if I have any) strength I have." Most difficult was trying to eliminate differences and unify Catholics behind a common effort. "The labor is heavy," he told her. He explained to Grace Murray all

American Catholics opposed the persecution, but lacked "unity of policy in fighting it." The situation was "deplorable and heart breaking." The effort was defeated by Catholics' "apparent inability to act together under the definite leadership of the Bishops."[12]

Meanwhile, Walsh solicited views of three Administrative Committeemen. Suspecting he wrote to more, Burke believed he was trying to win their individual support for the resolution. He recommended the committee either meet soon or explain to the hierarchy their refusal to support it. Like Walsh, Supreme Advocate Luke Hart attempted an end run around the committee. He secured letters of endorsement from the bishops of El Paso, San Antonio, and Santa Fe. He asked Archbishop Leopoldo Ruiz y Flores to write all U.S. bishops encouraging them to send letters in support. Ruiz gladly complied.[13]

Rumors of the Administrative Committee's decision were abroad. Walsh told Curley of "apparently authentic" reports that State knew the NCWC did not support the resolution. "It is difficult for us to believe this is possible," wrote Walsh. "United support would remove the result entirely from the realm of doubt." Hanna then informed Curley of the committee's opposition and asked him to keep the news "in strict confidence." Curley sarcastically replied there was nothing secret about it; he already heard "from Official Headquarters (not 1312 Massachusetts Avenue [NCWC headquarters])" State had been apprised of the decision. Obviously, official headquarters was Walsh, symbolizing those on the correct side of the issue.[14]

At the same time Hanna wrote Curley, he sent Burke his letter of resignation for presentation to the committee and the hierarchy. He cited the "growing infirmities of age" and his desire "to retire from all active work."[15] His sudden withdrawal lent added urgency to the need for a special meeting of the committee.

In early March, Roosevelt sent Frank Murphy to ask Burke what action the president might take with Mexico. Burke explained he twice urged him to issue a statement to its government to which he agreed. Murphy said Roosevelt intended to send a private, personal one. Murphy had urged him to do it publicly. Burke agreed. Murphy hinted Burke might help frame a message and offered to do what he could.[16]

When the Administrative Committee held a special session to discuss Mexico, it elected Thomas Lillis acting chairman. Burke reported on the interview with Murphy and said the Borah resolution would probably fail to clear the Foreign Relations Committee. The bishops officially declined to approve it, but had no objection to Catholic organizations' supporting it. For the time being, they opted not to send the hierarchy an explanation of their decision.[17]

Burke met Murphy who informed him Hull convinced Roosevelt to send no message to Mexico, public or private. Hull feared any note would offend its government and cause resentment among Protestants at home. Burke "believed more firmly than ever" Roosevelt "owed it to the country" to defend freedom of worship. Murphy said a public or private note was out of the question. The only solution was a back-channel conference like the one between Burke and Elías Calles. Burke explained the active support the Coolidge administration gave to that effort. The good will of Roosevelt's, he said, would go a long way. Instead, Roosevelt "was practically leaving the situation" up the American Catholic church.[18]

Two days later, Catholic Postmaster General James Farley summoned Burke to inquire about the misunderstanding concerning Roosevelt and Mexico. Burke recounted the history of persecution from 1926 to his meeting with Roosevelt, who agreed to issue a statement. Burke believed such public utterance was in keeping with the Good Neighbor Policy. Like Murphy, Farley spoke about having an American priest meet with Lázaro Cárdenas. Burke said it could be done only with the good will of the administration. He offered to draft several versions of a note Roosevelt might send. The two met again a week and a half later, but little came of it.[19]

Although opposed to an official note, Hull himself intervened informally. He told Mexican ambassador Francisco Castillo Nájera that American Catholics bitterly denounced him because of his inaction on Mexico. To ease the pressure on him, he was certain Nájera's government would "give thought and attention to the question of avoiding or minimizing any utterances or actions … calculated to feed the agitation and violent utterances … in the United States." Pledging full cooperation, Nájera deplored the situation on both sides of the border and expressed hope it might change within a few months.[20]

Nájera intended to do something to bring that about. In mid-April he told Assistant Secretary of State Sumner Welles he intended to beg Calles and Cárdenas to reduce opposition to the Church. He even had a plan of action. With the approval of the two leaders, he would have Archbishop Pascual Díaz petition the Supreme Court against the actions of state governors who prohibited many or all clergy to function. The court, packed by Cárdenas, would assuredly rule in favor of the petition. This would be a first step.[21]

When Welles asked Burke what he thought of the plan, he injected a note of realism. Unless authorized by the bishops whose dioceses were affected by the policy, Díaz had no right to make such petition. In Burke's view, the plan, "however favorable it may outwardly appear, done in a disorderly way will only increase the disorder of a situation already disorderly enough." He recommended Díaz get approval of the bishops and even the pope. Both Cicognani and the Administrative Committee concurred.[22]

Meanwhile, Curley made a blistering attack on the Roosevelt administration for blocking the Borah resolution. He then trained his sights on Burke for engineering the modus vivendi of 1929. "Let our gentle, sacerdotal diplomats stay at home," declared Curley, because they were no match for clever Mexican politicians, who "built nests in their ears." Calles maneuvered Burke into having the Cristeros lay down arms in return for a promise the Church would suffer no more. In Curley's view, the six years thereafter were the bloodiest yet. He said Mexicans held Burke's name in "malediction."[23] The speech was uncalled for and unfair. It demonstrated, however, that Curley considered the modus vivendi a mistake and blamed Burke for it.

The Administrative Committee met in April. In light of Curley's attack on Burke, it directed him and Bishop John Noll to prepare a statement explaining that he had acted on behalf of the Vatican in negotiating the modus vivendi. They were to present it in person to Cicognani for use as he deemed fit. At last, the committee followed Burke's advice and issued two statements: one to the press recounting the NCWC's efforts in the present crisis, the other to the hierarchy explaining the reasons for the board's recent decisions. The committee also ordered Burke to see Roosevelt.[24]

Roosevelt met with him in the White House probably to avoid the press. Burke reminded the president of the memorandum he had given him in November 1934. Because he had done nothing, Catholics were growing more indignant and intolerant of inaction. Roosevelt said he gave the matter much thought and wanted to do something, but had no idea what to do. He was very firm on the last point. Burke insisted he was obligated to take some action. Roosevelt thought of advising the Vatican to send someone to Mexico to negotiate. Burke told him he could use his good offices to encourage Mexico to accept a new apostolic delegate, preferably a foreigner, to begin negotiations. Roosevelt "positively assured" Burke he would ask Nájera to have his government do that.[25]

For months, Burke had been husbanding strength, taking care to get a "good deal of rest" so that he was up to the work. Yet, Murray predicted his health would not hold, and it did not. After seeing Roosevelt, he was forced "to lie up." Burke told her the preparations for the meeting and the sessions themselves were "too much" for him. He did nothing for two days thereafter and then went to bed for two more. His physician saw him and concluded Burke was worn out. "I knew it any way," he wrote to Murray. "Rest alone gives me relief from the tire."[26]

Meanwhile, Roosevelt and Welles met Nájera. The president explained he was "speaking informally," but wanted to express his anxiety at the Mexican government's denial of religious liberty—a principle he held dear—which caused unrest in the U.S. He asked if the time was ripe to relax strictures on religious liberty and negotiate with the Church. Nájera said he and his government were moving in that direction. He recounted his plan to have Díaz petition the court to permit priests to function unhampered. Primed by Burke, Roosevelt asked if the government might recognize an apostolic delegate from the Vatican. Such a man should be foreign-born—dissociated from Mexican interests. It was the only practical solution that would offer security and understanding for the future. Nájera agreed and would urge the idea in his upcoming trip to Mexico. He thought Cárdenas and Portes Gil would be receptive, but was unsure of Calles. He was certain, however, all three would reject a foreigner for that post. They would insist on a Mexican and urge the selection of Díaz. Roosevelt thought that a mistake and tried to win Nájera over. Nájera stressed his government would accept only a Mexican. Afterward, Welles filled Burke in on the details.[27]

For their part, the Knights resolutely pursued their policy. Believing the Foreign Relations Committee would report the Borah resolution if Roosevelt withdrew opposition, Supreme Knight Martin Carmody asked for a conference. Roosevelt failed to reply. Carmody sent him another letter recounting the facts of the persecution and urging he cease opposing a Senate investigation and speak out on behalf of Mexican Catholics.[28]

Marvin McIntyre told Burke he thought Roosevelt should meet with Carmody. Roosevelt wanted to tell him the steps he had taken. Burke considered it "very inadvisable" to extend "confidences" any further than presently existed. It was best to wait until Nájera reported back. Roosevelt should tell Carmody only that he gave "earnest attention" to Mexico and was unfree to say anything more definite. McIntyre said that was the advice he had given. Burke opined Roosevelt should have met the Knights back in February and it was good he intended to now. They were doing zealous work. Yet, he repeated it would be "entirely inadvisable" to reveal anything that was going on if there was to be successful conclusion to matters.[29]

Nájera's visit to Mexico coincided with a dramatic political crisis there: the open break between Calles and Cárdenas over serious ideological differences. The two made counter declarations. With the army loyal, Cárdenas asked his cabinet to resign and appointed a new *jefe maximo* of the NPR, Portes Gil, the man who had concluded the 1929 modus vivendi.[30] Nájera conferred with both men. Cárdenas favored reopening churches and freedom of worship in accord with state laws, provided "the political situation made it possible." Portes Gil, a confirmed moderate, desired a reasonable solution of the religious question. He thought a settlement might be possible if negotiated by Mexicans without foreign interference. For that reason, he favored appointment of a Mexican apostolic delegate to replace the exiled Ruiz. His choice was Díaz. Portes Gil warned, however, any pressure from the Vatican or Church in the U.S.—or in any other country for that matter—would delay, if not render impossible, detente.[31]

On return to Washington, Nájera reported these conversations to Welles. He said churches in Colima had reopened and those in Querétaro would soon follow. In Mexico City, more priests functioned than the law permitted, and orderly Catholic demonstrations went unmolested. The federal government intended to promote these policies in other states, though the process might take time in Tabasco and Sonora where two ardently anti-Catholic governors remained in control.[32]

Welles informed both Roosevelt and Burke of developments. This was timely news. The Vatican had just asked Cicognani to double as apostolic delegate to Mexico. Burke told him that would be "most inadvisable." Mexico had always resented U.S. interference in its affairs. It was "proud enough" to want its own delegate, one appointed to and resident in Mexico. Moreover, the U.S. government would view such appointment unfavorably. Burke told Welles that in accord with Portes Gil's wish, he advised Cicognani to urge the Vatican to work for appointment of a Mexican national. Burke asked to meet informally with Nájera. Welles said he had offered to host a conference at his own home, but Nájera demurred because of NCWC pamphlets attacking the Mexican government. So, Roosevelt appointed Welles his "personal … 'unrepresentative' representative" to act as a go-between the two.[33]

Unaware of these happenings, the Knights sent Roosevelt a lengthy letter of protest. The president responded by meeting with their Special Committee on Mexican Affairs in July. He opened with "things are very much better down there." Carmody countered with the many ways Mexico was still persecuting the Church. American Catholics were perplexed by the indifference of their government because it protested persecution of other faiths in other countries. Roosevelt replied Mexico suffered an exaggerated form of a worldwide trend away from religion. There was also matter of the Good Neighbor Policy. He said passage of the Borah resolution would exacerbate the persecution. He told of his effort to have Mexico accept an Italian apostolic delegate, something it refused to do. Only a delegate of Mexican origin would meet its approval. Luke Hart urged him to withdraw his opposition to the resolution claiming its passage would result in Cárdenas's fall and might lead to adoption of a new constitution. Roosevelt defended his policy, repeatedly stating he was in close touch with Rome, Cicognani, the Hierarchy, the NCWC, and "particularly with Father John Burke." This failed to impress Hart, who noted Burke negotiated the unsatisfactory modus vivendi of 1929. No similar arrangement would do. "That is as much as you can get and it is all that you are going to get for another fifty years," retorted a prophetic Roosevelt. Carmody suggested that a statement by him on conditions in Mexico might help. Roosevelt agreed and offered to do so in his next public address.[34]

Over the next two months, Mexico negotiated with the Vatican via Burke, Welles, and Nájera for appointment of a native-born apostolic delegate.[35] These dealings were hard work, fruitless, and took their toll on Burke.

He wrote to Lynch they presented "very trying situations" and confessed he did not "always 'interiorly' keep up," that is, attend to his inner spiritual life. Even so, he felt the effective power of Jesus within him. He hoped this was not "presumption" on his part. "But unless I did it in Him, through Him and for Him," wrote Burke, "I could not do it at all." He found it "a great joy" to labor so for the Lord and at times thought Christ honored him "with some shadow of participation in His sufferings and His sacrifice."[36] The issue of a delegate was on hold for another month while Welles vacationed.

On 2 October 1935, Roosevelt fulfilled his promise to the Knights. In a speech vetted by Burke and delivered at San Diego, twenty miles north of the border, he declared: "Our national determination to keep free of foreign wars and foreign entanglements cannot prevent us from feeling deep concern when ideals and principles that we have cherished are challenged. In the United States we regard it as axiomatic that every person shall enjoy the free exercise of his religion according to the dictates of his conscience.... It is true that policies that may be pursued under flags other than our own are beyond our jurisdiction. Yet in our inner individual lives we can never be indifferent." The NCWC News Service touted the speech as a "notable declaration" and, like many papers, interpreted Roosevelt's remarks as directed at Mexico. The Knights, however, believed he broke faith with them. Hart felt the NCWC had "become a mere apologist for the President" with regard to his Mexican policy.[37]

On Halloween, Cicognani informed Burke the Vatican doubted any Mexican bishop could command obedience of the nation's hierarchy. Moreover, because of the family, social, and governmental connections of most of bishops, Rome asked for reconsideration of a foreign-born delegate who could negotiate with it as objective arbiter. It had in mind Archbishop Guglielmo Piani, apostolic delegate to the Philippines, and suggested he reside in Texas, Cuba, or Puerto Rico and direct the Mexican Church from there. Without mentioning Piani by name, Burke informed Welles and asked him to have Nájera insist on preference for a foreign-born delegate. Nájera did so. Cárdenas and Portes Gil regretted inability to accept a foreign-born delegate. Burke told Welles he thought the Mexican government was making a mistake.[38] There, the matter rested until the New Year.

The Mexican situation did receive attention at the annual convention of the hierarchy in November. Lillis confidentially reported Roosevelt urged

Mexico to grant religious liberty. Mexican officials promised it would in states where freedom was denied. His report carefully avoided mention of negotiations concerning appointment of a new delegate to Mexico.[39] On behalf of Ruiz, Archbishop Arthur Drossaerts of San Antonio appealed for the hierarchy's help to establish a seminary for Mexicans in the U.S., thereby aiding Mexican bishops to circumvent confiscatory laws. A committee of three prelates—Curley (chairman), Drossaerts, and Francis Kelley—was appointed to study feasibility. On learning membership of the committee, the Knights interpreted it as "a clear indication that our position has the support of the Bishops."[40]

REORGANIZATION OF THE NCWC

Although Mexico was Burke's major preoccupation in 1935, a proposed reorganization of the NCWC was the issue most alarming because of its potential to distort his vision of how the American Catholic Church should function. At the hierarchy's convention in 1934, Archbishop John McNicholas suggested forming episcopal committees on various matters to meet for two days prior to the convention, which would consider the conclusions of the various groups. He also urged devising a scheme whereby each year two bishops retired from the Administrative Committee. The hierarchy appointed a reorganization committee under Mitty to devise a plan embodying McNicholas's suggestions. Mitty's group was to present its plan to the Administrative Committee for approval at its April meeting in 1935.[41]

Burke had hoped to meet Mitty in San Francisco in February of that year to discuss the history and function of the NCWC, but lacked money for the trip. Mitty asked him for a copy of the NCWC's constitution. Burke replied it had none. Its factual constitution consisted of the decisions of the hierarchy at its first convention which established the NCWC, the Administrative Committee, and the various departments. The hierarchy defined the work of the Administrative Committee and elected its members. They elected their own officers and the chairman of each department.[42]

Burke sent Mitty a lengthy letter explaining that a few bishops opposed creating the NCWC because it would be an "imperium in imperio [a power within a power]," that is, it would take the place of a canonical plenary council whose decisions had force of law. Burke stressed the NCWC was a voluntary organization and no bishop was bound by its decisions. The Administrative Committee generally opposed presenting "conclusions" to the annual convention, even though many bishops wished it would. The committee believed it preferable to furnish data and "let every Bishop attending understand that he is free to discuss the matter from the beginning." Indeed, many issues were "liquid," and the hierarchy might not want to decide, leaving itself free to change direction. The Administrative Committee refused to place on the agenda any issue affecting the internal life of the Church or canon law. Finally, the function of headquarters was to serve the Administrative Committee and the chairmen of the departments.[43]

Burke explained that on his appointment as general secretary, the administrative bishops made clear "they were the Administrative Committee, elected as such by the general body of Bishops: that all things would clear through them: be directed by them: that they would be the means and channel of unified Catholic action." Burke argued all committees should be responsible to and report to the Administrative Committee. Otherwise, matters would be "haphazard" at best. He thought the idea of having a number of bishops' committees on various subjects was "excellent," if their work was coordinated through the Administrative Committee.[44]

Mitty thought members of Administrative Committee should live near Washington so they could meet more often without inconvenience. While favoring the idea, Burke cautioned that having all members elected from one region might give the wrong impression and likely would be unacceptable to the hierarchy. Perhaps four of the seven voting members might live in proximity to Washington and constitute an "executive committee," which would meet monthly at headquarters to direct things more closely.[45]

Meanwhile, Mitty sent Burke an outline of proposed changes for critique. It created two divisions within the NCWC: one, the Administrative Committee and its departments; the other, a set of episcopal committees. The first would be expanded to ten voting members, and those chosen to chair departments would each select a bishop from the hierarchy to assist him. All would become the Administrative Board. Its elected members would serve no more than five years, with the two longest-serving rotating off the committee each year. The second division would consist of some fifteen episcopal committees, the five current standing ones and ten new ones (including the Committee on Motion Pictures) each with a specific interest.

Every bishop in the hierarchy, except those on the Board, would volunteer for a committee without time limit on service. Committees would meet during the year and for two days prior to the annual convention. At that meeting, the chairman of each would present conclusions for approval.[46]

Burke considered the new committees "excellent," with the caution that any contemplated public pronouncement go first to the Administrative Committee, not for approval, but to ensure it was in accord with previous pronouncements and policies. He repeated his caution regarding "conclusions." Burke considered the annual convention something of a "final tribunal" and, as such, should "seldom … give definite conclusions." He believed the hierarchy should maintain its "privilege to be a deliberative body" which directed the Administrative Committee and held it responsible. In every case, it should clear for presentation to the convention the recommendations of all other committees. Burke noted the expansion of committees would require more staff at headquarters. Mitty was in complete accord.[47]

When the Administrative Committee took up this plan in spring 1935, the ailing Mitty was absent. McNicholas read the plan to members, who discussed it for a day. They favored expansion of the Administrative Committee and viewed "cordially" the idea of having every bishop serve on one of the fifteen others. The idea of having committees submit reports to the Administrative Committee caused considerable debate, with McNicholas opposed and Burke decidedly in favor. Because the matter was so important, the committee asked Lillis to call a special meeting for July devoted solely to reorganization. Burke sent Mitty an account of the discussion, and he heartily favored Burke's position.[48]

In July, the committee met in Chicago. On the trip there, Burke fretted that if the NCWC were radically altered, his convictions might compel him to resign. Uppermost for him was the requirement of the fifteen committees to report to the Administrative Board. Ten bishops attended, all six voting members and four assistant bishops. Their deliberation included a "historical and documentary review of the NCWC since its beginning," with the evidentiary record supplied by Burke's secretary Iona McNulty. As Burke explained to Grace Murray, "the review revealed a consistent, well-jointed structure: we had built better than we knew." The members accepted the expansion of the Administrative Board. On the critical issue of having committees report to it, there were nine in favor and McNicholas opposed. After much discussion, he finally yielded. In the end, members retained only the six present standing committees which were to coordinate with the Administrative Board and refer reports to it antecedent to their printing. The hierarchy was free to appoint more standing committees as it deemed necessary, which would also report to the Board.[49]

Birth Control

As Burke dealt with reorganization and Mexico, he faced birth control. Although the Administrative Committee's circular in December 1934 was generally successful in quelling publications about rhythm, an exception was Monsignor Theodore Ryan's *The Wheel of Life*, popularizing it. Ryan asked his Bishop Gerald Shaughnessy of Seattle for an imprimatur, but was denied. Ryan proceeded without it, using a local company to have the *Wheel* printed and distributed in Seattle, Tacoma, and across the border in Vancouver, British Columbia. Shaughnessy convinced the company to withdraw it and warned Burke that Ryan was on his way to Benziger Press to secure national distribution and would continue on to Washington, D.C., to have the FERA offer the *Wheel* to those on relief rolls.[50]

When Burke so advised Alfred Benziger, he replied Ryan had already seen him and received his refusal because his own bishop opposed publishing or distributing anything about rhythm.[51] Burke also warned Harry Hopkins that individuals or publishing houses might approach him to have the FERA distribute material about Catholic teaching on birth prevention. Hopkins should contact Burke if a request came so he could advise about whether the information had Church approval. Responding for Hopkins, Assistant Director Aubrey Williams said it was not within the FERA's "province" to distribute such literature. Its policy was "to administer relief solely on the basis of need."[52]

When Congress opened in January 1935, Margaret Sanger had Walter Pierce and Daniel Hastings reintroduce the Doctors' Bill. In anticipation of hearings, Burke directed William Montavon to see Father David McCauley, regent of Georgetown's School of Medicine, and Dr. Eugene Whitmore, chief pathologist in the school, about organizing a committee "entirely independent of the NCWC" to handle the portion of the hearing against birth control. Whitmore believed the position of opponents would be strengthened by clearly defining the difference between use of contraceptives and practice of self-restraint in rhythm as well as explaining the moral principles involved.[53]

The urgency to establish the new committee lessened when the House Committee on the Judiciary made short work of the bill, voting fifteen to eight in early February against reporting it. The situation in the Senate went similarly. Its counterpart assigned the bill to a subcommittee, which decided no hearing was necessary in light of the extensive one held the previous year. It referred the bill back to the whole Judiciary Committee, which voted nine to six against reporting it.[54]

Sanger and Pierce then blindsided the NCWC. On behalf of Postmaster General Farley, Representative John Higgins of Massachusetts introduced a bill to strengthen penalties for violations of the Comstock Act. At a hearing on 4 April before a House subcommittee on the Post Office and Post Roads, Pierce urged amending it to include language of the Doctors' Bill exempting medical professionals from the criminal code, in essence making an end run around the Judiciary Committee. Sanger told the subcommittee the Comstock Act was "menacing" to the medical profession. She also pointed out the Post Office permitted sending *Rhythm* through the mail, but not scientific writings on birth control.[55]

When Burke learned of the maneuver, he complained to Representative James Mead, chairman of the postal committee, that the NCWC received no notice of the hearing and therefore had no opportunity to be present. Although the NCWC had no position regarding the substance of the Higgins bill, it had a very definite one on the Pierce amendment. Burke referred Mead to statements NCWC agents made against the Doctors' Bill before House and Senate subcommittees in 1934. Mead told Burke the subcommittee chairman was arranging another session to accommodate the NCWC.[56]

Monsignor John Ryan, Agnes Regan, and Edward Heffron of the NCCM appeared at the session to oppose the amendment. Ryan argued against birth control on the basis of population. He also made the moral case for a distinction between contraception and rhythm. Both Regan and Heffron emphasized natural law and the purpose of sexual intercourse: procreation. Regan stressed the immorality of using "artificial," "mechanical," and "chemical" means of birth control. Heffron contended the "positive frustration" of sexual intercourse through such means was not to be confused with "continence," as advocates of birth control sometimes argued. In the end, the subcommittee deferred action on the legislation.[57]

While countering birth control on the domestic front, Burke faced it again regarding Puerto Rico. After previously promising him contraception would have no role in economic reconstruction of the island, Roosevelt removed federal oversight of Puerto Rico, the Virgin Islands, and Hawaii from the War Department and placed them in the Interior under the direction of Dr. Ernest Gruening, an ardent promoter of birth control. Gruening supported James and Dorothy Bourne's use of the PRERA to foster contraception. The Bournes were Hyde Park neighbors and friends of the Roosevelts.[58]

In December 1934, Dorothy, who collaborated with her husband in the PRERA, instructed Ana Alfonso Colón, Catholic district director of social work in Ponce, to establish a new maternity health center and enroll women for instruction in birth control using an apparatus manufactured in Puerto Rico with federal money from the PRERA and materials shipped from the United States. When Colón refused, Dorothy told her she would be transferred. Before steps could be taken, Colón went on maternity leave. On her return in February 1935, James said he did not want her because she would interfere with his experiment. Colón informed Bishop Aloysius Willinger, who asked her to get affidavits in support of her allegations. She visited a maternity center and discovered it promoted artificial means of contraception. Willinger sent Dorothy a letter asking if the information was true. She replied educational work regarding maternal health was in accord with Catholic teaching. She added, however, that "other information" approved by doctors and given for health reasons was being provided "to *persons who have no religious scruples against receiving such information.*"[59]

In March, Colón flew to Washington to complain to Burke and the NCWC. She reported the Bournes were fostering birth control and said people were afraid to speak against the program for fear of loss of federal relief money and because the couple were friends of the Roosevelts.[60]

Burke wrote to Stephen Early, Roosevelt's principal spokesman. He enclosed two memoranda, one outlining Colón's accusations and the other recounting the president's promise. Stating "something very definite ought to be done, and done at once," he asked to meet Early to stress "the importance and gravity of this situation." The memo about Roosevelt's promise made clear the action Burke desired: removal of the Bournes for violation of the federal penal code. Without responding, Early gave the material to Roosevelt.[61]

The following day, Regan and Colón interviewed Dr. Jacob Baker of the FERA. According to Regan's account, Baker admitted birth control was an integral part of reconstruction in Puerto Rico. The only objection came from a small group of "highly intellectual Catholic women," not the mass of Puerto Rican womanhood. Next day, Father Michael Ready and Eugene Butler saw Baker to confirm what Regan and Colón reported. Baker denied all, saying Colón's allegations were "colored by her disgruntled attitude to her superiors" and her uncertain status with the PRERA. He claimed the only means of birth control promoted in Puerto Rico was rhythm. Back at headquarters, Ready, Butler, Regan, and Colón discussed the matter at length. As a result, Ready sent a telegram to Willinger asking for affidavit evidence that the PRERA was conducting a program of birth control.[62]

Willinger had none. He had asked Colón to get it, but she left for Washington before doing so. He acknowledged her resentment over her treatment by the Bournes, but she must not "throw her defense upon the Church." Willinger said rumors and accusations were rife about promotion of birth control by artificial means. He enclosed a copy of Dorothy's reply to his own query, with the comment Ready could "readily judge the lady's attitude." As historian Thomas Mathews points out, the official line of the U.S. government was nothing should be done in Puerto Rico that gave offense to the Catholic church; unofficially, those in charge tackled the population problem from all angles.[63]

In April, Roosevelt replied to Burke's letter to Early. He took Burke's protest at once to Hopkins, who said he would investigate. If allegations proved true, Hopkins would "take summary action" to halt use of artificial means. Roosevelt learned Bishop Edwin Byrne of San Juan highly commended work of the PRERA and asked Burke to contact him about this matter.[64]

Burke sent Byrne a copy of Roosevelt's letter and explained it came in reply to his definite charge that the Bournes and the PRERA were disseminating birth control information and devices. His action was prompted by Colón's allegations, which he considered "exaggerated: prejudiced, and in some cases imaginative." However, enough other evidence reached him to convince him of the truth of the matter. Burke suspected the Bournes were using *Rhythm* to convince Puerto Ricans the Church permitted birth control and then providing them with "actual effective methods of contraception." Recalling Byrne's telling him the previous year that Roosevelt assured birth control would not be permitted in Puerto Rico, Burke asked him to write a letter that he might take to the president.[65]

Byrne did so, noting Roosevelt's public declaration at a state dinner that his administration would not favor enforcing birth control in Puerto Rico because the island was Catholic. It now pained Byrne to report his conviction that the PRERA was disseminating information about birth control and even instruments for that purpose. Dorothy Bourne was actively working in that regard. The unfortunate "general impression," wrote Byrne, was that Eleanor Roosevelt, who visited the island in 1934, was "using her influence or the influence of her position, to favor Birth Control in Puerto Rico." Byrne said it was his duty to oppose and expose this work of the PRERA. He regretted having to bring it to the president's attention. Burke delivered the letter to Roosevelt.[66]

Roosevelt replied to Byrne that his administration was not enforcing birth control on the island. James Bourne assured him the PRERA was neither promoting nor disseminating information or instruments for contraception. Any advice being given was in accord with the Catholic position on rhythm. Roosevelt stressed overpopulation was an "extremely serious" problem there. The administration had definite plans for economic reconstruction of the island that would put many unemployed to work. Yet, the population was growing at such a rate even the contemplated industrialization and emigration would not be able to meet it. Roosevelt welcomed any recommendations Byrne might have to alleviate the problem.[67]

Meanwhile, both Byrne and Willinger told Burke the Chardón plan was going forward, with its statement that "a scientific scheme of birth control should be part of any far-sighted policy for Puerto Rico." Byrne warned Gruening against imposing birth control on the island. Both bishops urged Burke to do everything in his power to have the offensive language eliminated. Burke sent Butler to Gruening about keeping that passage out of the official reconstruction plan. Gruening assured Butler no official plan had yet been formulated. When the official program was developed, it would make no mention of birth control.[68]

McIntyre came to see Burke with the same news. The final program for Puerto Rico had yet to be approved. It would "absolutely" not include any mention of birth control. Burke explained his anxiety that Roosevelt previously gave him assurances and then came word to the contrary from Byrne and Willinger. McIntyre was definite on the matter.[69]

Burke relayed the information to both bishops. He explained that after Colón's visit, he considered sending a priest to Puerto Rico to investigate firsthand and secure affidavits. As events unfolded, he considered that unnecessary. Now, after McIntyre's visit, Burke discussed the idea with Ready and Father Mariano Vassallo, Byrne's secretary who was then in Washington. The three agreed it would be good to send Father Raymond McGowan to Puerto Rico under joint auspices of the NCWC and the two bishops to investigate. Burke ran the plan by Cicognani, who approved.[70]

Byrne sent Burke a copy of Roosevelt's letter. Burke felt Roosevelt's request that Byrne offer recommendations made McGowan's investigation the more appropriate. McGowan spent late summer and early fall 1935 on the island. He interviewed social workers in and out of the PRERA who confirmed the agency encouraged artificial contraception. Toward the end of his investigation, McGowan gave Gruening, who was then director of the Puerto Rican Reconstruction Administration (PRRA), a memorandum detailing all he learned. Gruening had Dorothy Bourne respond. McGowan sent Burke a copy of her reply noting she admitted the charges regarding artificial birth control.[71] At the November meeting of the Administrative Board, Burke reported that although definitive information was difficult to ascertain, it seemed Roosevelt took steps to halt the spread of birth control information in Puerto Rico. Yet Burke was no fool. He added individual federal officials "wish to do the right thing; that is, to operate in Puerto Rico according to the laws of the United States. On the other hand, certain officials of PRERA—and these officials seem to be tolerated by the federal government here—are bent on promoting birth control through their opportunities of social work in Puerto Rico."[72]

NEW DEAL

When the Administrative Committee held its special session in March on Mexico, it also considered the social security bill, whose old-age insurance feature relied on a payroll tax which applied to clergy and religious. Archbishop John Murray recommended informing Congress that dioceses already had arrangements for their elderly priests as did religious communities for their members. The bishops authorized Burke to make such representations.[73]

After the meeting, Burke thought it might be good to send a letter to the hierarchy about the meaning and purpose of the bill. He drafted one for Lillis's signature. It noted the legislation had three ends: old-age insurance for those over sixty-five; special aid to needy mothers, their children, and crippled children; and unemployment insurance. The letter explained the first feature would be funded by a payroll tax; the other two relied on federal and state funds. The bill's definitions of employer and employee would likely subject all assistant pastors to the payroll tax. Burke doubted this was the sponsors' intention. The Administrative Committee instructed headquarters to secure an exemption on grounds that dioceses and religious communities were corporate, moral persons responsible for their members. When the committee approved the draft, Burke sent it. At the end of April, he informed the committee members that religious, charitable, and educational institutions were exempt from the payroll feature and thereby excluded from old-age benefits.[74]

While protective of charitable institutions, the NCWC was solicitous for Catholic schools. In January 1935, Roosevelt sought passage of the Emergency Relief Appropriation Act amounting to $5 billion ($112.5 billion in 2024), legislation he dubbed "the Big Bill." The measure earmarked $40 million ($900 million) for aid to public schools. Burke and the NCWC got Congress to alter wording to apply the appropriation "for assistance for educational, clerical and professional persons," thereby opening possibility of aid to private and parochial schools. Congress also increased the amount from $40 million to $300 million ($6.75 billion). With that boost, Commissioner of Education John W. Studebaker and associations like the NEA lobbied for the U.S. Office of Education to control the fund. On behalf of the Administrative Committee, Burke wrote Roosevelt against granting Studebaker that power. He argued such "action would be construed as a tendency at least toward federal control of education." He further pointed out Herbert Hoover's NACE had studied the issues of a department of education and federal aid. Its report spoke forcefully against consolidation of federal educational activities. Burke quoted both the report and the act establishing the Office of Education, confining its function to collection of facts and statistics. Nothing in the office's portfolio authorized it to disburse funds. Roosevelt replied that Burke's letter presented "very clearly a point of view that will be taken into consideration in determining this matter."[75]

So it was. When Burke saw him about Mexico in early May, Roosevelt brought up the Big Bill. He told Burke Studebaker and others in the Office of Education besieged him about giving them control of the entire $300 million. Speaking confidentially, he said he would never do that, adding, "As long as I am President, I will be absolutely opposed to the nationalization of education." Roosevelt repeated his experience in New York. He declared he would not allow the $300 million to be used for control of education or even education itself. The furthest he would go was to use some for relief of needy teachers and perhaps for development of physical training. None would ever be used for educational purposes. He made that very clear to Studebaker.[76]

While tending to these new initiatives, Burke monitored priests for the CCC. In April he reported to the Administrative Board the NCWC had placed 189 "civilian contract chaplains" representing sixty-two dioceses in a number of the 1,640 conservation camps. Priests received $30 a month plus mileage. Plans called for increasing the CCC to 600,000 young men. The Department of Agriculture planned to put 400,000 to work in soil conservation. Burke asked if the committee wanted the present program of volunteer chaplains continued with a possible increase in the Catholic quota of such clergymen. It directed him to work for an extension and a higher number of priests.[77]

When Burke saw Roosevelt about the CCC, the president said the unit of young men in each camp would remain 200. So, there would be many more camps throughout the country. He wanted Burke to inform bishops to prepare for appointment of more priests. He was very interested in the religious care and welfare of the men. Burke told him of the 189 contract chaplains already at work and of the Church's quota of 250. Roosevelt said if a higher quota was required, Burke need only speak with Robert Fechner of the CCC.[78]

By July 1935, Catholic use of contract chaplains came under attack by Protestant clergy, who refused to accept the $30 subsidy and insisted all chaplains should be unpaid volunteers. Burke explained the situation to the hierarchy via circular. He contended it was impossible to give adequate care simply through volunteers because of the difference in ministry offered by priests and Protestant ministers. Three types of chaplains worked in camps: regular and reserve Army chaplains; volunteer clergymen in the vicinity of camps who were reimbursed five cents a mile; and contract clergymen subsidized at $30 a month and five cents a mile. Burke told bishops the NCWC assured CCC authorities that "great numbers of priests in the vicinity of the camps" would serve the young men voluntarily for mileage, so it was important to be able to show Catholic care was not limited to contract chaplains. He asked bishops to fill out a questionnaire about the number of their contract and volunteer chaplains as well as the number of their churches that provided religious care to men transported to them. It also asked the number of young men prepared for first communion or confirmation as well as the number of converts and those under instruction in the faith.[79]

In November, Burke reported the CCC numbered 600,000 young men and camps nearly doubled from 1,640 in April to 2,879. There were 225 priests serving as contract chaplains. For the most part, dioceses were doing good work bringing religiously indifferent young men back to practice of the faith. For example, during a six-month period, twelve dioceses reported 730 prepared for first communion, 269 prepared for confirmation, 369 under instruction in the faith, and 204 converts. Burke considered this a remarkable record because the camps in question were in sparsely populated, almost inaccessible areas.[80]

Equal to the spiritual care of men in the CCC was humanitarian care for a certain class of immigrants. As already seen, the congressional answer to unemployment was closing the door on newcomers and deportation of many already within. In 1935, Democratic Representative John Kerr of North Carolina sought amendment of the deportation laws to grant the Secretary of Labor the discretion to permit certain deportable aliens of good moral character to remain in the country. Sara Weadick appeared for the NCWC at the hearing to support the measure. She pled for aliens who arrived as infants and grew up knowing only the English language and American culture. It was inhumane to send them to a country they never saw, whose tongue they spoke not, and where they had no kin or friends. "Deportation in such a case is frequently tantamount to banishment," she explained. "Such a punishment has often been considered unthinkable with civilized countries but de facto such a punishment at times results from the application of our deportation laws as they now stand." Weadick spoke harshly of those who opposed the amendment because they thought it gave the secretary power to harbor criminals who broke the nation's immigration laws. She considered the contention a gross misrepresentation by those who "seem to be constitutionally unable to consider aliens as human beings."[81]

A month later, the House committee amended the bill by adding a 50 percent reduction in all immigration quotas. The amendment caused Burke to vent his frustration at restrictionists and the stinginess of a capitalist system that denied workers a living wage. He told Bruce Mohler to file a statement declaring the NCWC stood by Weadick's testimony. Moreover, it took "emphatic exception to this unexpected and unlooked for amendment." When Congress first considered the quota system, he wrote, it argued a reduction in immigration would help the labor and employment situation of the country. "As a matter of fact, it has not helped the situation at all," declared Burke. Furthermore, the human being, considered economically, was a source of wealth. The nation's immigration policy went against all economic laws. "We are not going to have any more employment," bristled Burke, "until we get a better distribution of wealth."[82] He obviously had had it with wrongheaded solutions to the country's economic problems.

ENDNOTES TO CHAPTER 23

1. Burke, *Christ in Us*, 134–35.
2. Resolutions Adopted by the Supreme Board of Directors of the Knights of Columbus at Its Meeting January 13th, 1935, at the Waldorf Astoria, New York City, FDRL, OF 28; *New York Times*, January 21 and 22, 1935; Kauffman, *Faith and Fraternalism*, 300–301; Redinger, *American Catholics and the Mexican Revolution*, 125–26.
3. Burke, [Interview with Callahan], 22 January 1935, ACUA, USCCB 10:145: Interview Book VI; Callahan to Luke Hart, 22 January 1935, AKC, SC–11–2–83.
4. The entire text is given in *New York Times*, 1 February 1935; Burke, [Interview with Callahan], 1 February 1935, ACUA, USCCB 10:145: Interview Book VI.
5. Statement by Father John J. Burke, C.S.P., General Secretary of the National Catholic Welfare Conference, 1 February 1935, copy, enclosure with Burke

to Hanna, 2 February 1935, AASF, NCWC files; *New York Times*, 1 February 1935; Redinger, *American Catholics and the Mexican Revolution*, 95.

6. *New York Times*, 2 February 1935; Cronan, "Mexican Anticlericalism," 217, and *Josephus Daniels*, 100.
7. Burke to Hanna, 2 February 1935, AASF, NCWC files; Redinger, *American Catholics and the Mexican Revolution*, 95–96. In fact, several Protestant organizations had already gone on record as opposed to the resolution, and the Scottish Rite Masons of the Southern Jurisdiction were lining up against it (Burke to Hanna, February 2, 1935), AASF, NCWC files; Cronan, "Mexican Anticlericalism," 216–17, and *Josephus Daniels*, 100–01; Flynn, *Catholics and Roosevelt*, 159.
8. Mitty, writing for Hanna, to Burke, 5 February 1934, copy; J. Murray to Burke, 4 February 1935, copy; Lillis to Burke, 5 and 7 February 1935, copies; John Peterson to Burke, 2 and undated February 1935, copies; Edward Mooney to Burke, 5 February 1935, copy; Noll to Burke, 1 and 6 February 1935, copies; Rummel to Burke, 5 February 1935, copy; Francis Keough to Burke, 10 February 1935, copy—all in AASF, NCWC files.
9. Noll to Burke, 1 February 1935, copy, AASF, NCWC files; Rummel to Burke, 5 February 1935, copy, ibid.
10. Michael Curley to Hanna, telegram, 11 February 1935, AASF, NCWC files; Burke, [Interview with Callahan], 25 February 1935, ACUA, USCCB 10:145: Interview Book VI; Burke to Mitty, 2 March 1935, AASF, NCWC files.
11. Burke to Mitty, 2 March 1935, AASF, NCWC files; Mitty to Burke, March 6, 1935, copy, ibid.; Gribble, *Archbishop for the People*, 279.
12. Burke to Lynch, 21 February 1935, AP, Burke Papers, box 5; Burke to G. Murray, 8 March 1935, ibid., box 12.
13. D. I. Walsh to Hanna, 25 February 1935, ACUA, USCCB 10:99:22; Burke to Mitty, 2 March 1935; AASF, NCWC files; Hart to Matthew Mahorner, 14 March 1935, copy, AKC, SC–11–2–104; Arthur Drossaerts to Carmody, 12 March 1935, copy, ibid., SC–11–2–95; Anthony Schuler to Carmody,16 March 1935, copy, ibid., SC–11–2–69; Rudolph Gerken to Carmody, 11 April 1935, copy, ibid., SC–11–2–71; Hart to Ruiz, 20 March 1935, copy, ibid., SC–11–2–115; Ruiz to Hart, 25 March and 6 April 1935, ibid.; Kauffman, *Faith and Fraternalism*, 303.
14. D. I. Walsh to Curley, 23 February 1935, AAB-AASMSU, W131; Hanna to Curley, March 6, 1935, ibid., H227; Curley to Hanna, March 9, 1935, copy, ibid., H228.
15. Hanna to Burke, 5 March 1935, ACUA, USCCB 10:99:22; Burke to J. Murray, 6 March 1935, copy, ibid., 10:152:30; Gribble, *Archbishop for the People*, 278–81. For a discussion of the reasons for Hanna's retirement, see the last mentioned, 283–89.

16. Burke, [Interview with Frank Murphy], 8 March 1935, ACUA, USCCB 10:145: Interview Book VI; Redinger, *American Catholics and the Mexican Revolution*, 96.
17. Minutes of the Administrative Committee, 12 March 1935, ACUA, USCCB 10:64:7.
18. Burke, [Interview with Murphy], 20 March 1935, ACUA, USCCB 10:145: Interview Book VI.
19. Burke, [Interview with James Farley] 22 March 1935, ACUA, USCCB 10:145: Interview Book VI; Burke, Report of the General Secretary, April 1935, ibid., 10:62:24; Minutes of the Administrative Committee, 30 April 1935, ibid., 10:64:7.
20. Memorandum of Conversation between Secretary Hull and the Mexican Ambassador, Señor Dr. Francisco Castillo Nájera, 5 March 1935, NA, State Department 812.404/1604.
21. Burke, Report of the General Secretary, April 1935, ACUA, USCCB 10:62:24; Burke to Sumner Welles, 23 April 1935, printed in ibid.; Minutes of the Administrative Committee, 30 April 1935 ACUA, USCCB 10:64:7. On the packing of the court, see Dulles, *Yesterday in Mexico*, 606–07; William Cameron Townsend, *Lázaro Cárdenas: Mexican Democrat* (Ann Arbor: University of Michigan Press, 1952), 99–100.
22. Burke, Report of the General Secretary, April 1935, ACUA, USCCB 10:62:24; Burke to Sumner Welles, 23 April 1935, printed in ibid.; Minutes of the Administrative Committee, 30 April 1935 ACUA, USCCB 10:64:7. The quotation is taken from the letter, which elaborated on Burke's response during the interview with Welles.
23. *Baltimore Catholic Review*, 29 March and 19 April 1935.
24. Minutes of the Administrative Committee, 30 April 1935, ACUA, USCCB 10:64:7.
25. Burke, [Interview with Roosevelt], 2 May 1935, ACUA, USCCB 10:145: Interview Book VI.
26. Burke to G. Murray, 8 March and 7 May 1935, AP, Burke Papers, box 12 (quotes are from the second); Burke to Lynch, 24 May 1935, ibid., box 5.
27. Burke, [Interview with Welles], 15 May 1935, ACUA, USCCB 10:145: Interview Book VI.
28. Carmody to Roosevelt, 22 April and 3 May 1935, FDRL, OF 28; Hart to Ruiz y Flores, 20 March 1935, AKC, SC–11–2–115.
29. Burke, [Interview with McIntyre], 6 June 1934, ACUA, USCCB 10:145: Interview Book VI.
30. Charles H. Weston, Jr., "The Political Legacy of Lazaro Cardenas," *Americas*, 39 (January 1983): 383–405; Weyl, *Reconquest of Mexico*, 122–68; Townsend, *Lázaro Cárdenas*, 85–92, 105–16; Albert L. Michaels, "The Cardenas-Calles Break," in James W. Wilkie and Michaels, eds., *Revolution in Mexico: Years of*

Upheaval, 1911–1940 (New York, 1969), pp. 219-221; Michaels, "The Modification of the Anti-clerical Nationalism of the Mexican Revolution by General Lázaro Cárdenas and Its Relationship to the Church-State Detente in Mexico," *Americas*, 26 (July 1969): 35–41; Dulles, *Yesterday in Mexico*, 629–43.

31. Conversation [between Welles and Nájera], June 25, 1935, enclosure with Welles to Roosevelt, June 25, 1935, FDRL, PSF Mexico; a copy of the Conversation is also in NA, State Department 812.00/30227; Report of General Secretary, November 1935, copy, ACUA, USCCB 10:62:26; Minutes of the Administrative Committee, 3 July 1935, ACUA, USCCB 10:64:7.
32. Conversation [between Welles and Nájera], 25 June 1935, enclosure with Welles to Roosevelt, 25 June 1935, FDRL, PSF Mexico; Burke, [Interview with Welles], 25 June 1935, ACUA, USCCB 10:145: Interview Book VI.
33. Burke to Cicognani, 20 June 1935, ACUA, USCCB 10:150:9; Conversation [between Welles and Castillo Nájera], June 25, 1935, enclosure with Welles to Roosevelt, 25 June 1935, FDRL, PSF Mexico; Burke, [Interview with Welles], 25 June 1935, ACUA, USCCB 10:145: Interview Book VI; Burke, Report of the General Secretary, November 1935, copy, ibid., 10:62:26.
34. [Hart], Memorandum re Conference between President Roosevelt and Knights of Columbus Committee on Mexican Affairs, 8 July 1935, AKC, SC–11–2–19; Hart to Ruiz, 10 July 1935, copy, ibid., SC–11–2–115; Hart to Noll, 11 July 1935, copy, ibid., SC–11–2–69; Hart to Kelley, 13 July 1935, copy, ibid., SC–11–2–124 Kauffman, *Faith and Fraternalism*, 304–05; Redinger, *American Catholics and the Mexican Revolution*, 131–32.
35. Burke, [Interviews with Welles], 12, 19, 21 and 30 July, ACUA, USCCB 10:145: Interview Book VI; Burke, [Interview with Welles], 27 July 1935, ibid., 10:153: Interview Book; Burke, Diary, 1 August [1935], AP, Burke Papers, box 70; Report of General Secretary, November 1935, copy, ACUA, USCCB 10:62:26; Welles to Roosevelt, 2 July 1935, FDRL, PSF State Department.
36. Burke to Lynch, 17 October 1935, AP, Burke Papers, box 5.
37. Quoted in NCWC News Service, 7 October 1935; Hart to the NCWC, 12 October 1935, copy, AKC, SC–11–2–100; Kauffman, *Faith and Fraternalism*, 306–307; Redinger, *American Catholics and the Mexican Revolution*, 96 and 133; Flynn, *Catholics and Roosevelt*, 166–67.
38. Burke, [Memorandum], 19 September 1935, ACUA, USCCB 10:145: Interview Book VI; Burke, [Interviews with Welles], 7 and 11 October 1935, ibid.; Burke, [Interviews with Cicognani and Welles], 31 October 1935, ibid.; Burke, [Interview with Welles], 4 November 1935, ibid.
39. Report of General Secretary, November 1935, containing confidential report of administrative chairman to the hierarchy, copy, ACUA, USCCB 10:62:26; Minutes of the Administrative Committee, 11 November 1935, ibid., 10:64:7.

40. *Minutes of the Seventeenth Annual Meeting of the American Hierarchy, November 1935*, 25–26, ACUA, USCCB Bound Volumes; Hart to Parsons, 30 November 1935, copy, AKC, SC–11–2–114.
41. *Minutes of the Sixteenth Annual Meeting of the American Hierarchy, November 1934*, 28–30, ACUA, USCCB Bound Volumes.
42. Mitty to Burke, 15 February 1935, copy, AASF, NCWC files; Burke to Mitty, 10 March and 2 April 1935, ibid.
43. Burke to Mitty, 2 April 1935, AASF, NCWC files.
44. Ibid.
45. Ibid.
46. Mitty to Burke, 1 April 1935, copy, AASF, NCWC files; Suggestions for the National Catholic Welfare Conference, undated, ibid.
47. Burke to Mitty, 10 April 1935, AASF, NCWC files; Mitty to Burke, 15 April 1935, copy, ibid.
48. Minutes of the Administrative Committee, 1 and 2 May 1935, ACUA, USCCB 10:64:7; Burke to Mitty, 3 May 1935, AASF, NCWC files; Mitty to Burke, 10 May 1935, copy, ibid.
49. Minutes of the Administrative Committee, 3 July 1935, ACUA, USCCB 10:64:7; Burke to G. Murray, 8 July 1935, AP, Burke Papers, box 12; Burke to Mitty, 21 July and 12 August 1935, AASF, NCWC files.
50. Gerald Shaughnessy to Burke, 29 December 1934 and 14 February 1935, ACUA, USCCB 10:117:11; Tentler, *Catholics and Contraception*, 117.
51. Burke to Alfred Benziger, 21 February 1935, copy, ACUA, USCCB 10:117:11; Benziger to Burke, 25 February 1935, ibid.
52. Burke to Harry Hopkins, 18 February 1935, copy, ACUA, USCCB 10:117:11; Aubrey Williams to Burke, 27 February 1934, ibid.
53. H.R. 2000, 74th Cong., 1st Sess; S. 600, 74th Cong., 1st Sess.; Montavon to Burke, 11 February 1935, ACUA, USCCB 10:117:22; Burke to Butler, 10 April 1935, copy, ibid.; *Autobiography of Sanger*, 427.
54. Montavon to Burke et al., 22 and 28 January 1935, ACUA, USCCB 10:117:22; Butler to Burke et al., 18 February 1935, ibid.; Burke to Hanna, 7 and 27 February 1935, AASF, NCWC files; Chesler, *Woman of Valor*, 352.
55. *Offenses against the Postal Service: Hearings before Subcommittee No. 8 of the Committee on the Post Office and Post Roads, Seventy-Fourth Congress, First Session, 8 March, 4 April, and 10 April 1935* (Washington, D.C.: U.S. Government Printing Office, 1935), 7, 9, 42–43, 45, and 47; Chesler, *Woman of Valor*, 352.
56. Burke to James Mead, 5 April 1935, copy, ACUA, USCCB 10:117:22; Mead to Burke, 8 April 1935, ibid.
57. *Offenses against the Postal Service: Hearings*, 68–83; Montavon to Burke, 28 May 1935, ACUA, USCCB 10:117:22.

58. *Many Battles: The Autobiography of Ernest Gruening* (New York: Liveright, 1973), 180–81; Ramírez de Arellano and Seipp, *Colonialism, Catholicism, and Contraception*, 37.
59. [Burke, Memorandum], 1 April 1935, ACUA, USCCB 10:117:17; Willinger to Dorothy Bourne, undated [March 1935] copy, ibid.; D. Bourne to Willinger,16 March 1935, copy, (emphasis in original), ibid.; Ramírez de Arellano and Seipp, *Colonialism, Catholicism, and Contraception*, 37–38.
60. [Burke, Memorandum], 1 April 1935, ACUA, USCCB 10:117:17; Ramírez de Arellano and Seipp, *Colonialism, Catholicism, and Contraception*, 38; Thomas G. Mathews, *Puerto Rican Politics and the New Deal* (Gainesville: University of Florida Press, 1960), 221.
61. Burke to Stephen Early, 1 April 1935, with enclosures, ACUA, USCCB 10:117:17; Mathews, *Puerto Rican Politics*, 221.
62. [Regan], Mrs. Colón's Interview with Jacob Baker, 2 April 1935, ACUA, USCCB 10:117:17; Ready, [Interview with Baker], 5 April 1935, ibid.; Mathews, *Puerto Rican Politics*, 221–22.
63. Willinger to Ready, 4 April 1935, ACUA, USCCB 10:117:17; Mathews, *Puerto Rican Politics*, 221; Nieves, *The Catholic Church in Puerto Rico*, 135–36.
64. Roosevelt to Burke, 23 April 1935, ACUA, USCCB 10:123:1.
65. Burke to Byrne, 26 April 1935, ACUA, USCCB 10:117:17.
66. Byrne to Roosevelt, 3 May 1935, copy, ACUA, USCCB 10:123:1; Burke to Roosevelt, 11 May 1935, copy, ibid.
67. Roosevelt to Byrne, 31 May 1935, copy, ACUA, USCCB 10:123:1.
68. Byrne to Burke, 3 June 1935, ACUA, USCCB 10:117:17; Willinger to Burke, 4 June 1935, ibid; Burke, [Interview with Butler], 5 June 1935, ibid.
69. Burke, [Interview with McIntyre], 6 June 1935, ACUA, USCCB 10:145: Interview Book VI.
70. Burke to Byrne, 7 June 1935, copy, ACUA, USCCB 10:117:17; Burke to Willinger, 7 June 1935, copy, ibid.
71. Byrne to Burke, 12 June 1935; Burke to Byrne, 23 June 1935, copy; McGowan to Burke, undated [September 1935]; McGowan to Burke, 17 October 1935, with Memorandum on Puerto Rico with Comments of Mrs. Bourne—all in ACUA, 10:117:17; *Many Battles: Autobiography of Gruening*, 188.
72. Burke, Report of the General Secretary, November 1935, ACUA, USCCB 10:62:26.
73. Minutes of the Administrative Committee, 12 March 1935, ACUA, USCCB 10:64:7.
74. Burke to J. Murray, 15 March 1935, copy, with enclosed draft, ACUA, USCCB 10:89:25; Lillis to the hierarchy, 1 April 1935, ibid.; Burke, Report of the General Secretary, April 1935, ibid., 10:62:24.

75. Burke to Roosevelt, 12 April 1935, copy, ACUA, USCCB 10:123:1; Roosevelt to Burke, 26 April 1935, ibid.; Kennedy, *Freedom From Fear*, 249–53; Leuchtenburg, *Roosevelt and the New Deal*, 124–28; Brands, *Traitor to His Class*, 420–23.
76. Burke, [Interview with Roosevelt], 2 May 1935, ACUA, USCCB 10:145: Interview Book VI.
77. Burke, Report of the General Secretary, April 1935, ACUA, USCCB 10:62:24; Minutes of the Administrative Committee, 2 May 1935, ibid., 10:64:7.
78. Burke, [Interview with Roosevelt], 2 May 1935, ACUA, USCCB 10:145: Interview Book VI.
79. Burke to the hierarchy, 9 July 1935, copy, exhibit #17 in Report of the General Secretary, November 1935, ACUA, USCCB 10:62:27.
80. Burke, Report of the General Secretary, November 1935, ACUA, USCCB 10:62:26.
81. *Congressional Record*, 74th Cong., 1st Sess., Vol. 79, Part 4, 3918; *Hearings before the Committee on Immigration and Naturalization, House of Representatives, Seventy-Fourth Congress, First Session, on H.R. 6795, 9, 10, and 11 April 1935* (Washington, D.C.: U.S. Government Printing Office, 1935), 1–3, 162–65.
82. Burke, Memorandum, 8 May 1925, ACUA, USCCB 10:42:3.

Chapter 24
"I Had Often Thought Our Lord Would Long since Have Taken Me to Himself"

> When all else is said; when that silence comes which destroys false values and reveals true ones; when the noise of this world dies; when learning has uttered its last wisdom and human invention found its greatest wonder, the soul will still realize that most blessed is the message of human service, of selfless love uttered by those who are holy in the holiness of Christ. If humanity had not saints, it would seek to create them for its hope and consolation. Our thirst is to know that our life—that all life—is worth while; that it is not the defeat but the crowning of love.[1]

MEXICO

In early 1936, John Burke had a brush with episcopal firebrands over Mexico. The special committee to study feasibility of a Mexican seminary in the U.S. immediately overstepped its mandate. Archbishop Michael Curley and Bishop Francis Kelley undertook incorporating it as the Catholic Bishops' Commission for Mexican Relief. Its purpose would be to raise money for relief and support of Mexico's clergy and laity, for support of "Seminaries, Colleges, Schools, Institutions, and other agencies," and for assistance to Mexicans "in their efforts to obtain the rights of conscience and freedom of religion."[2]

Meanwhile, Apostolic Delegate Amleto Cicognani told Burke a cable arrived stating that given Mexico's resistance to a foreign apostolic delegate, the Vatican now agreed to appoint a Mexican one, but only if the Mexican government gave guarantees. Rome was concerned because the government had promised to fulfill the modus vivendi of 1929 but had not. So, Rome considered the modus vivendi "a dead letter."[3]

Burke argued otherwise. He told Cicognani the mission given him by the Vatican in 1928 was to have Mexico recognize the corporate nature of the Church, permit a delegate to live and function in Mexico, and acknowledge that only a bishop could appoint and remove pastors. The government currently recognized the rights of bishops and had admitted an apostolic delegate and permitted him to function. Burke agreed Mexico had by no means lived up fully to the agreement, but it contradicted fact to say the modus vivendi was "a dead letter." This information was news to Cicognani. He told Burke to continue work with the State Department.[4]

Two days later, Egidio Vagnozzi told Burke the wording in that cable was either the pope's or represented his immediate directions. Vagnozzi read aloud another letter Cicognani received in response to his query regarding the Vatican's attitude toward insurrection by Mexican Catholics. It said the Church plainly sought peace and was against armed rebellion. It would insist on obedience to constituted authority. When, however, authority became tyrannical, the Church could not condemn citizens who sought by arms to destroy tyranny, provided rebellion would not cause worse conditions than previously existed. In support, the letter quoted at length from the *Summa Theologiae* of St. Thomas Aquinas. Vagnozzi told Burke: "You see the situation is now in the hands of the Jesuits. They have shown their power. The Holy Father is not really informed of the situation or the facts."[5]

Hearing this qualified support of armed rebellion, Burke felt like quitting work for the Mexican Church altogether. Vagnozzi insisted he keep with it. When Burke asked the guarantees he was to secure, Vagnozzi said the Vatican was mum, adding even if Burke got guarantees, Rome might deem them insufficient. "We (the Apostolic Delegation) had opened the door for them (the Holy See) to make a great step toward settlement," said Vagnozzi: "yet they won't recognize the open door." Burke said he would do what was asked, but under no circumstance would he "lend [himself] to deceit of any kind." He said the Vatican's "delay, procrastination, requests … favorable answers secured, then the very requests not acted upon," gave the impression the pope was "jockeying for position over small matters" while missing the big picture. He had always tried to present the Vatican "in the highest light, the worthiest way." His vivid impression was the government's sense of the "vacillating, wavering, unforceful and indefinite character of our conversations." Vagnozzi was unsurprised. Not only did he agree, but expressed his own criticism of the present Vatican Secretariat of State. Cardinal Eugenio Pacelli, its head, knew little about special matters like Mexico; Archbishop Giuseppe Pizzardo, secretary of Extraordinary Ecclesiastical Affairs, was "incapable."[6]

Burke committed his dispirited thoughts to paper. The Vatican had seen Mexico drive out Elías Calles and knew the stability of the Cárdenas government. He got Roosevelt to urge an easing of the persecution and accept a new apostolic delegate. Now, the Vatican wanted guarantees. Burke echoed Vagnozzi, "We opened the door as the Holy See requested, and the Holy See won't use the open door." It was evident advocates of "physical force," those who wanted no compromise, who publicly opposed Roosevelt, now had the ear of the Vatican. He saw the hands of Curley, Kelley, and those with them behind the altered attitude. Kelley had assured Burke the committee on a Mexican seminary would simply collect funds for one. Yet, Kelley, a Republican and member of the Administrative Board, was at present incorporating the committee without the board's knowledge or permission and was working with Republican William Borah on Mexico. Borah was running for president, causing Burke to wonder if Kelley sent word to Rome that if elected, Borah would insist Mexico grant religious liberty to Catholics or face the consequences? "And have those who have the power to speak for the Holy Father been working with these through misinformation and misguidance in which money has already played its part?" wondered Burke. "Prayer is very helpful," he concluded.[7]

The Vatican soon clarified the guarantees. Burke told Sumner Welles the Holy See identified two Mexican candidates for delegate in Mexico; it wanted certainty the one appointed would be permitted to fulfill his mission and not be exiled. Welles agreed to proceed on that line. It was time for the Mexican government to let Ambassador Francisco Nájera meet directly with himself, Burke, and Cicognani.[8]

Welles turned the conversation to Curley and Kelley's just-incorporated Commission on Mexican Relief. It opened a headquarters in New York City and hired Joseph Moore, a fundraiser. Welles was concerned about its purpose to aid Mexicans in their struggle for religious freedom. He assumed the NCWC had approved it. Burke said this was the first he heard that the incorporation was now a fact. He assured Welles neither Cicognani nor the Administrative Board knew of it and he should not view it as done with their approval. "The moment was more than embarrassing for me," confided Burke in a memorandum. "Do not the officials sometimes think that I am playing a game: that it is very strange I do not know certain facts?"[9]

Burke saw Vagnozzi to say he seriously questioned if he could continue as general secretary. He felt he was being forced to play a double game with U.S. officials. In his negotiations, he always represented the Vatican as above politics, straightforward, and honest. With any appearance to the contrary, "the prestige and estimate of the Holy See would be lowered." Vagnozzi said Cicognani must get clarification about who could speak authoritatively for the Vatican on Mexico. Vagnozzi had in hand a letter from Pacelli to Archbishop Leopoldo Ruiz y Flores stating no one could. "Am I acting just as representative of the Administrative Board, N.C.W.C.?" wondered Burke. "If I am acting as representative also of the Apostolic Delegate here—what right has he to authorize me so to act?"[10]

Later that day, Burke informed Cicognani about the incorporation. He became quite agitated and asked Burke to send him the minutes of the hierarchy's convention regarding appointment of the seminary committee and secure a copy of the articles of incorporation. Cicognani was emphatic in his denunciation of Curley and Kelley: "The former was not honest: the latter had no brains."[11]

To the Vatican, Cicognani stressed that great injury would redound on the Church in both the U.S. and Mexico if Rome no longer authorized him to speak in its name on the matter. It would be tantamount to telling the U.S. government its efforts to this point were negligible and the Vatican no longer wanted its help.[12]

Burke apprised the Administrative Board of the incorporation. The board telephoned Kelley, who claimed Moore arranged it. Denying knowledge of the charter's contents, Kelley promised to have it voided. Instead, he challenged the accuracy of the minutes of the annual convention which defined the seminary committee's portfolio, a challenge supported by Curley. News of the board's attitude sent Curley's blood pressure sky-high. He publicly announced establishment of the commission and its approval by the pope, and took to his sickbed.[13]

When the board met in February, Burke presented a telegram from Curley resigning from the commission and announcing his "withdrawal from the NCWC." The board then confronted Kelley with overwhelming evidence that the committee's portfolio was limited to a feasibility study. Suspecting "there was and there is a colored person in the wood-pile though I have not seen him to name him," Kelley agreed to void the incorporation and release Moore. Working thereafter within the confines of the original mandate, the special committee made its report and received permission to proceed with plans for a Mexican seminary on U.S. soil, eventually establishing one near Las Vegas, New Mexico.[14]

Meanwhile, Ambassador Nájera worked with his government on wording a guarantee about the appointment of a new delegate. By mid-month, he was ready to present it to Cicognani when negotiations suddenly collapsed. Inexplicably, Cárdenas now interpreted the Mexican Hierarchy's pastoral letter of September 1935 on education as an attack on the government. When Welles informed Burke, the latter said wording in the pastoral was conditional: "If education of such and such kind were obligatory ... etc." He had no idea if the bishops intended the letter as an assault. Moreover, Burke protested as "a gross injustice" the recent expulsion of Archbishop Pedro Vera y Zuria from his home because it was national property. Vera was to be appointed the new delegate. Welles thought with passage of a little time, he could renew negotiations about guarantees. Regarding Vera's eviction, he needed to investigate.[15]

While awaiting further word, Burke stressed to Welles what was at stake for himself in negotiations. If he accepted guarantees as trustworthy and Mexico reneged on them, his position as negotiator would be ruined. The Vatican would no longer trust his advice, "and rightly so." Given recent developments, the guarantees ought to cover the right of religious education and a proper understanding of the nationalization of property. In Burke's view, the right of eminent domain included the concomitant responsibility to use property for the purpose intended. He insisted that any guarantees must be "definite and trust worthy [*sic*]."[16]

At the end of March, no doubt motivated in part by politics, Roosevelt directed Ambassador Josephus Daniels to see Cárdenas about granting a fuller measure of religious liberty. Daniels did so with both "anxiety and emphasis." Cárdenas admitted his own desire to grant such liberty, but was opposed by many state governments. He wanted the issue settled so the government could focus on key matters of agriculture, industry, and foreign capital. Informed by Welles, Burke thought the news important, but noted the omission of any mention of education. He stressed again the need for an apostolic delegate in Mexico.[17]

In mid-May, Cicognani told Burke the Vatican intended to send Archbishop Guglielmo Piani into Mexico incognito to investigate and report on conditions there. Burke said it was a bad idea. The Vatican should send Piani openly and with permission from Mexico. Rome had nothing to hide. If a clandestine mission were discovered, Mexico would make political capital of it. Burke did not think it would consent to such a visit, but was convinced his was "the only course." Cicognani asked him to try to secure the approval.[18]

Burke explained the Vatican's intention to Welles. He wanted permission from Mexico for a man to enter on a fact-finding mission. If it agreed, it must say nothing publicly. Welles thought it "most advisable" and would present the idea to Nájera. He asked Burke whom he had in mind. He replied he was not free to divulge the name.[19] Next day, he told Welles he withheld the identity because he did not wish to expose the Vatican to the "unnecessary affront" of having Mexico refuse him entry. "Well, Father Burke, I don't think the question of revealing the name is in issue now," said Welles. He already informed Nájera, who supported the idea, name unknown.[20]

In June, Welles told Burke Mexico would issue the visa and keep the mission secret. Welles would arrange for Piani to meet with Nájera. Burke informed Cicognani, who said Piani would speak with Nájera in a "kindly way." Burke advised that "while it be kindly, it be not too kindly, nor as if we were indebted to the Mexican Government for a favor." When they met with Piani, Burke insisted he wear secular clothes in Mexico, say Mass privately, and swear to secrecy any bishop or priest with whom he spoke. Welles informed Roosevelt that Piani's mission was to investigate conditions of the Church in Mexico, secure unity of the bishops, and reestablish discipline among the clergy. Piani agreed to make no public statements in either the U.S. or Mexico and was to refrain from speaking about politics with the bishops. Later that month, Father Michael Ready escorted him to the border.[21]

The duration of Piani's visit is unknown. He was back in Washington by October. Burke read his report and was permitted to communicate parts to the Administrative Board. The Mexican bishops, with only two or three exceptions, warned "any public threat of intervention or public interference on the part of the United States in Mexico would not only be inadvisable but would be injurious to the Church in Mexico." They appreciated the NCWC's role in having the U.S. exert informal influence to ease the situation, noted Burke, and wanted the effort continued. This was vindication of the NCWC's course and implicit repudiation of the Borah resolution. The bishops also asked its help in having the Mexican government allow them to return to their dioceses. This meant all prelates, not only exiles in the U.S., but the nearly dozen detained in Mexico City. Burke began negotiations for this with Welles and Najera.[22]

Legion of Decency

Back in 1934, the hierarchy had chosen the Chicago list of motion pictures as guide for the Legion of Decency. Immediately, clergy and laity criticized it for its severity. It condemned pictures that passed the scrutiny of Catholic Joseph Breen, head of the Production Code Administration, and gave rise to an alternate, more lenient list out of the archdiocese of New York. The rivalry caused recrimination, threatening to fracture the fledgling Legion.[23]

At its 1935 convention, the hierarchy directed the Administrative Board to study the feasibility of establishing a movie-review board in New York. The NCWC would pay the board's expenses and its News Service would publish the official list of ratings to be known as the National Legion of Decency. Until it was up and functioning, the Chicago list would continue at NCWC expense. The Administrative Board directed the Committee on Motion Pictures to establish the new review board. The ratings were to be negatively worded, that is, instead of "recommended for children," the wording should be "not objectionable for children." Cardinal Patrick Hayes would appoint a priest to interface with board and NCWC. The National Legion of Decency list would appear without identification with the NCWC.[24]

In January 1936, Bishop Noll informed the Administrative Board that Martin Quigley's *Motion Picture Herald* carried an item stating the Motion

Picture Bureau of the International Federation of Catholic Alumnae would likely become the review board for the National Legion of Decency. Catholic papers inquired of the NCWC News Service about the accuracy of the report. Archbishop Edward Mooney, chairman, directed Burke to ascertain from McNicholas the steps taken thus far regarding selection of a review board and a priest to oversee it.[25]

Burke politely requested an update on progress. Three weeks lapsed without a reply. In the meantime, word came from Father Edward Moore in New York that the archdiocesan Legion of Decency would send the list of films directly to Catholic papers. Burke informed Moore the Administrative Board directed the News Service to release it. Then, Cardinal Hayes appointed Father Joseph Daly, a psychologist, as executive secretary of the National Legion of Decency. Daly issued a press release announcing a new rating system: "A-1 Unobjectionable for General Patronage; A-2 Unobjectionable for Adults; B Objectionable in Part; C Condemned." Burke considered all the above actions "very serious" because they countered decisions of the Administrative Board and caused the News Service to issue statements contradicting others it made. He so informed Mooney. When the board met in February, McNicholas explained Hayes personally selected the new rating classifications. The board obligingly deferred to him.[26]

McNicholas then presented for approval a statement by the Committee on Motion Pictures. It said the Legion of Decency had carefully considered congressional legislation to secure clean movies by outlawing block booking. Doing so, however, posed "grave danger of political censorship." The Legion preferred to secure wholesome films through public opinion and public pressure. Admitting block booking had a moral dimension—the forced screening of salacious films—the Legion urged support of exhibitors who opposed it through protests and legal actions against producers. After lengthy discussion, chairman Mooney saw no connection between outlawing block booking and federal censorship. Refusing to adopt the statement as its own, the board felt it could not object if the committee chose to release it, which it did.[27]

Shortly after the meeting, a House subcommittee opened hearings on the Pettengill bill to outlaw block booking. Agnes Regan presented a resolution the NCCW unanimously adopted three years running which condemned indecent films, suggestive advertising, and the practice of block booking. She said the NCCW supported the bill.[28]

McNicholas telegraphed Burke his hope that Regan's statement had not given the impression she spoke "for the hierarchy, the Episcopal Committee, or the Catholic Body." He told Burke to have the Legion of Decency statement submitted to the hearing. Burke replied Regan "did not in any way claim to speak for anybody except the NCCW." She stated the resolution had the approval of Bishop Noll, chairman of the Lay Activities Department. Burke presented the Legion's statement to the hearing. "I need not say," he wrote, "it seems to me regrettable that there is not some way to secure a unity of action in such matters."[29] Burke learned that movie producers rejoiced at the statement because it indicated the Legion of Decency opposed legislative restriction on the industry, including the Pettengill bill.[30]

The situation worsened. McNicholas telegraphed Burke he was sending Daly to the hearing "to make clear" the part about block booking in the committee's statement.[31] Daly's appearance was an unmitigated disaster. He opened remarks by saying he represented the Committee on Motion Pictures which "is alone able to speak authoritatively for the 22,000,000 Catholics in the United States on matters involving the morality of motion pictures and is exclusively authorized to dictate the policies and practices to be followed by the Catholic people in the United States in the campaign for wholesome motion pictures." The Legion of Decency believed the best way to secure clean movies was through public pressure on producers, therefore it opposed the Pettengill bill. When congressmen countered many bishops and Catholic societies favored outlawing block booking, Daly insisted the committee and the Legion spoke for all Catholics. The *Washington Post* ran a story on his testimony under the title "Decency Legion Opposes Block Booking Curbs."[32]

Burke sent Mooney the *Post* article and a transcript of Daly's testimony, noting his claim that the committee had "authority to dictate to all Catholics ... on the betterment of moving pictures," a statement which was "not Catholic." The authority of a local bishop "may not be set aside in this way." Burke averred that when the hierarchy felt compelled to speak publicly on a matter, "the recognized agency" for doing so was the Administrative Board. He felt conscience-bound to say actions like the committee's and Daly's were "going to break down the worthwhileness of any expression from the Bishops of this country on any matter of general public concern in the eyes of Senators, Congressmen and Government officials generally."[33]

Mooney found the situation "indeed, disturbing." He told Burke that when McNicholas proposed the statement, he had no idea it would be used against the Pettengill bill. Nor was he entirely sure that Noll, a member of the Committee on Motion Pictures, understood McNicholas's intention. He had just met with McNicholas, who said nothing about having Burke present the statement to the hearing. Part of the problem was Daly himself, "a rather forward young man … who is rather impressed with the importance of his position, and does not hesitate to step boldly into print or into speech." Mooney recommended Burke meet with McNicholas to bring home the importance of having Daly in contact with him and headquarters to "be kept in line with the general policy of the N.C.W.C."[34]

Burke saw McNicholas in mid-April. The important part of their conversation was Burke's advice to hold a meeting of the Committee on Motion Pictures as soon as possible to frame a few fundamental resolutions, including one specifying that no official of the committee was authorized to make any statement in its name without "explicit," prior approval.[35]

BIRTH CONTROL

Although Margaret Sanger sailed to Asia in fall 1935 to promote birth control there, her NCFLBC remained active. In January 1936, it persuaded Senator Royal Copeland of New York to introduce a modified version of the Doctors' Bill. It exempted from the Comstock Act information and devices "intended solely for the prevention of contraception." Away in Nassau, Cardinal Hayes, a friend of Copeland, instructed Monsignor Robert Keegan to inform the latter how "greatly disturbed" Hayes was by this action. Copeland replied "a group of constituents" convinced him the bill would make it legal for only physicians, prescription druggists, and medical schools to receive such information. The senator argued it was better for those professionals to have accurate knowledge of the subject than a "bootlegged" variety. He was certain once Hayes read the bill he would see it guarded against spread of birth control information to the public. Keegan sent Copeland's letter and his bill to both Burke and Hayes.[36]

When the Administrative Board met in February, the bishops saw great danger in further discussion of rhythm because proponents of birth control never failed to cite it in defense of their own position. The bishops believed non-Catholics found it difficult to understand the difference between abstinence and the use of artificial means of contraception. Burke had the Legal Department offer analysis of Copeland's measure. It considered the bill "as objectionable, and perhaps even more objectionable," than previous ones.[37]

After the meeting, Burke wrote Keegan that Copeland's reply was "evasive." Enforcement of obscenity laws was already lax and growing more so. Rather than improve enforcement, the bill would provide a physician with a new defense "based on his 'intention' as to the sole use" of the information or device he dispensed. Burke said the "constituents" referenced by Copeland were in fact the NCFLBC. He was certain Copeland knew his action would be offensive to a much larger group of constituents. He "deliberately chose" to alienate Catholics in order to please the NCFLBC. His sponsorship made him known in Congress as a supporter of Sanger. Further proof of the purpose of the bill was that Representative Percy Gassaway of Oklahoma would introduce its companion measure in the House. Gassaway publicly advocated birth control and sterilization.[38]

Keegan paraphrased parts of Burke's letter and directly copied others into his reply to Copeland. The chastened senator responded if he knew then what he knew now, he would never have introduced the bill. He added if he had no other reason to oppose it, the fact that Gassaway would introduce the companion bill was reason enough. Copeland assured Keegan the legislation would not pass and he would not reintroduce it in the next Congress.[39]

While dealing with birth control on the home front, Burke met it indirectly again in Puerto Rico. In late January, he received a letter from Bishop Edwin Byrne informing him Dorothy Bourne was in transit to Washington as guest of the White House. Her mission was establishment of a Department of Social Welfare on the island with herself or one of her lieutenants at its head as presidentially appointed commissioner. Given her promotion of birth control there, Byrne asked Burke to protest to Roosevelt against her appointment. The proposed department should have a Catholic at its head.[40]

Burke did so in a letter which included the pertinent passage from Byrne's about appointment of a Catholic. "I know, from many reliable sources, well-versed in the Puerto Rican matter," Burke added, "that the request is fully warranted, and that great injury would be done to the people of Puerto Rico were such an appointment to be made." Diplomatically assuring Burke that Byrne's objection would be taken into account, Roosevelt explained that if a department was established, the appointment of its head belonged to the governor, unless the enacting legislation gave it to the president. In defense of Bourne, Roosevelt commented on "her fine service in the relief of the needy and the improvement of social conditions," adding "she is, as you know, high minded and conscientious and an indefatigable worker." If the appointment became his, Roosevelt would take Burke's "suggestions" into consideration.[41]

Burke read Roosevelt's letter to the Administrative Board. The bishops supported the protest and directed Burke to make their support known to FDR. He wrote Roosevelt that Byrne and Willinger objected to Bourne because she was "out of sympathy with the religious and ethical views of the vast majority of Puerto Ricans." He noted that the administrative bishops authorized him to convey "their unanimous support of the petition of Bishop Byrne and to express their gratitude that you would favor it." Burke reported to Byrne the actions taken and urged him, especially in light of Roosevelt's letter, to enter his own protest against Bourne's appointment directly to Puerto Rican authorities.[42]

In fact, it was not Bourne who needed to be feared, but Dr. Ernest Gruening, director of the PRRA. An admirer of Sanger and firm believer in birth control, he and his general counsel, Francis Michael Shea, a Catholic advocate of contraception, established friendly relations with Byrne. They wanted to establish maternal health clinics to distribute information about and devices for birth control. The bishop initially opposed the idea, but at Gruening's insistence agreed "to look the other way," provided there was no publicity. The actual scale of the project soon caused Byrne to withdraw support. The matter became public in the U.S., and Roosevelt's reelection campaign called a halt to the clinics shortly before the balloting in 1936.[43]

FATHER COUGHLIN AND THE 1936 ELECTION: PRELUDE

In mid-summer 1936, Father Charles Coughlin came to Burke's attention. Once an unabashed supporter of Roosevelt and the New Deal, Coughlin had grown ambivalent and then in November 1935 openly broke from him. In June 1936, he formed the Union Party with William Lemke of North Dakota its presidential candidate. Dr. Francis Townsend of California, another Roosevelt critic, backed Coughlin and held a national convention in Cleveland to endorse the Union Party ticket. Coughlin delivered the closing speech in which he denounced Roosevelt as a "double-crosser" and a "great betrayer and liar."[44]

Because Coughlin's public utterances were often taken as the Catholic view, Burke sent Mooney a letter: "This thought came to me very strongly," he wrote. "Some Catholic authority ought for the sake of the Catholic record state at once that the Catholic Church utterly disapproves of anyone, be he priest or layman, who terms the Chief Executive 'a liar.'" Burke suggested Mooney give a short interview to the Associated Press.[45]

Before Mooney could, Bishop Michael Gallagher, Coughlin's ordinary, gave a statement to the press. Though supportive of and typically reticent about his priest, he said Coughlin "should have had more respect for the Executive," but stressed he had not rebuked him. Burke telephoned Mooney to say although Gallagher's statement was "not all that might be desired," it was "certainly good" that he made one, and it precluded the necessity of Mooney's doing so.[46] In fact, Gallagher telephoned Coughlin and told him to apologize. The Vatican, too, through Cicognani, informed him such was in order at once. Coughlin publicly apologized on 23 July, explaining he had gotten carried away in heat of the rhetorical moment.[47]

Roosevelt summoned Burke to meet him in the White House after close of business. They met in his private study, and he had Burke sit next to him on the sofa. Marguerite "Missy" Le Hand, Rossevelt's personal secretary and known by intimates to be his lover, served refreshments and remained with them. After distracted conversational wanderings, Roosevelt said, "Father Burke, don't you worry about Father Coughlin, for I am not worrying." Burke expressed regret about the indignity of the remarks in Cleveland. "I didn't mind Father Coughlin calling me a liar," replied Roosevelt: "but I do mind his reference to my father and to my father's attitude towards me." Burke said he was unaware Coughlin said anything about his father. Surprised, Roosevelt explained that in a different address, Coughlin said Roosevelt's father had so little trust in him, he excluded him by will from management of his estate. "Now the fact is," averred Roosevelt, "I was eighteen years of age when my father died; therefore a minor, and being a minor could not legally take charge of my father's estate.... I was named in my father's will as executor and took and fulfilled that office when I was twenty-one." He said no more, except he believed Coughlin was misled. Thinking it time to leave, Burke sought to excuse himself. He asked Roosevelt to convey his "good wishes" to wife Eleanor, but Roosevelt's thoughts seemed far, far away. Le Hand accompanied Burke out. He noted, "She stopped to shake hands with me, and I thought there was a pressure of gratitude in her clasp."[48]

In memorializing the conversation, Burke wrote it seemed "Roosevelt's soul was suffering and in his suffering he had asked me to come." He seemed "hurt: wounded." There could have been much which caused the suffering, the greater part, however, "seemed to be the words of Father Coughlin." "It is the more striking that, while it was a priest who hurt him," concluded Burke, "he sends for a priest who may give him some measure of healing."[49]

A Daughter and a Death

In early May 1936, Burke wrote to Helen Lynch, who had not heard from him "since the blue birds came" at Easter. Indeed, there had been little time to do anything other than was what "immediately imperative." The work was "varied ... important, and generally exacting," though all in all it went well. "Clouds gather and darken: the sky is overcast, and then mercifully the light shines through," explained Burke. "Our Lord is considerate beyond words. In any case it is happiness working for Him: being permitted to labor a little for Him: helping as long as one may His own saving mission in this world. So my heart is very, very grateful." Throughout all that labor, Burke maintained good health "by resting, and by discipline."[50]

Death, however, was on his mind. He told Lynch a story he considered "worth retelling." A Catholic doctor in the suburbs was about to make a house call in early evening. His four-year-old daughter asked to accompany him. As they drove west, the sun was about to set. The girl chatted endlessly about this and that. Suddenly, she asked, "Daddy, where does the sun go?" He told her it went back to God. She asked what He did with it. The doctor explained since people did not need the sun while they slept, God gave it to those in Japan and China. "Then, He gives it back to us in the morning." The girl asked if the sun died. Dad said it did, that is, it went back to God. She asked, "When does a person die?" Her father replied, "Oh, not till one is very old." She asked, "Am I very old?" "No, you are not old at all," came the reply. "Are you old, Daddy?" she asked. "Well, I'm not very young: I'm getting old," he told her. "Well, daddy, I want to die before you die because I want you to carry me back to God."[51]

A month later, Burke celebrated his sixty-first birthday. "My years are many as I count them," he wrote Lynch, "and I had often thought our Lord would long since have taken me to himself." He told her Jesus left him on earth so that he might improve his ways and do penance for his sins. "With added mercy, He permits me to do something for his added glory—for His Church." It was probably with this letter Burke sent her the poem "M * * *" by Abram J. Ryan, poet priest of the south, with slight adjustment to apply it to her.

When I am dead, and all will soon forget
My words, and face, and ways —
I, somehow, think I'll walk beside thee yet
Adown thy after days.

I die first, and you will see my grave;
But child! you must not cry;
For my dead hand will brightest blessings wave
O'er you from yonder sky....

For — from the first — your soul was dear to mine,
And dearer it became,
Until my soul, in every prayer, would twine
Thy name — my child! thy name....

You came to me in girlhood; as your guide
I watched your spirit's ways;
We walked God's holy valleys side by side,
And so went on the days.

And so went on the years —'tis ~~five~~ 30 and more;
Your soul is fairer now;
A light as of a sunset on a shore
Is falling on my brow —

Is falling, soon to fade; when I am dead
Think this, my child, of me:
I never said — I never could have said —
Ungentle words to thee....

'Tis better far that I should go before,
And you awhile should stay;
But I will wait upon the golden shore
To meet my child some day....

I guide you here — I go before you there;
But here or there — I know —
Whether the roses, or the thorny crown you wear
I'll watch where'er you go,

And wait until you come; when I am dead
Think, sometimes, child, of this:
You must not weep — follow where I led,
I wait for you in bliss.

Fr. A. Ryan
As J.J.B. would have said
to H.M.L.[52]

Later that month, Burke made his annual retreat at the Convent of the Sacred Heart in Noroton, Connecticut. On return to Washington, he found his friend and mentor, William Kerby, in a bad way. For nearly two years he declined in health with heart trouble and high blood pressure, but no one thought him in danger of death. Burke saw him on 17 July. His friend was tired and weak, but the two conversed for quite a long time. A few days later, Kerby slipped into unconsciousness and remained so until death on the twenty-seventh. "You know what he was to me for many, many years,"

Burke wrote Lynch, "and as the years grew, so grew my indebtedness.... The rectitude of his life was such that I feel he will receive his reward at once and be received by our Lord and Saviour Jesus Christ." Burke penned a brief poem in Kerby's honor, concluding: "Night took thee the way of death / Friend, my friend without stain / When I am free by the Spirit's breath / God will end my pain."[53]

Burke wrote a tribute to Kerby's life and spirit for publication in the *Ecclesiastical Review.* "It cost me much," he explained to Grace Murray, "and one would rather say those things to one whom he loved than to the general public. I miss and will miss Dr. Kerby very much. To me something has dropped out of the work." Burke then told her of his recent, "rather serious" interview with Roosevelt about Coughlin, and said he had fallen a bit under the weather and felt so tired he could work no more. "So all in all," he confessed to Murray, "I decided to arise and like Abraham go into another land [Gen. 12: 2 and 4]." He left for Homestead in Hot Springs, Virginia, where he took residence in his favorite cottage. He recalled the poem "Bagley Wood" by Lionel Johnson wherein the poet wrote that patriarch "Abraham looking at the stars 'found God through reverence.'" "One sees the stars here, as you know," he told Murray. For most of the first week, Burke did nothing but sleep and rest. He was surprised one day by the young black serving boy who tended his cottage. As the lad left, he said, "Remember me in your meditations to-day." Where, wondered Burke, did he get that word "meditations"? The climb up the hill twice a day for meals began to prove too strenuous for him. After about a week and a half, he left the cottage for a room in the hotel itself. By 1 September, he was back at his desk in Washington.[54]

Prelacy

Three days after Burke's return to the capital, Cicognani returned from Rome and summoned him to ask, "If the Holy Father wished you to be a prelate, would you accept?" Burke answered he would do whatever the pope wished. "You are a prelate," said the delegate handing him a papal document. Because it was a fait accompli, Burke could not refuse. The honor was quite unusual, for popes rarely made a member of a religious community a monsignor. In fact, Burke was the first in America to become one.

Burke told his sister Lizzie he would now have to wear "the red or purple or whatever color the cassock and cape, etc. etc." He could still wear the Paulist cassock in his house, but, he told Lynch, "It shatters my hopes of dying a simple Paulist priest." He informed his superior general, Father John Harney, "an honor came to me in such a way as to leave me no freedom of choice."[55]

Harney was pleased the pope rewarded Burke for his faithful service, all the more because the recognition came unhoped for and unasked, "through the spontaneous appreciation of others." Several years earlier, Vatican friends urged Harney to seek a prelacy or bishopric for a Paulist. "Their main point," he told Burke, "was that in conjunction with the 'Decretum Laudis' [Decree of Praise] it would strengthen our position at home and abroad, for it would be new proof of the Holy See's satisfaction with our aims and work." Obviously, the Paulists were still suspect for their alleged part in the Americanist crisis of the 1890s. Bestowal of papal honors carried papal approval. Harney had refused the advice. "To me the praise and honor that an individual or community gets by fishing for them are not of great value," he wrote. Confessing embarrassment and discomfort at the publicity, Burke said his consolation was "that the honor will reflect credit on the Paulist Community."[56]

The investiture ceremony occurred on 21 September at the Shrine of the Immaculate Conception on the campus of Catholic University. Cicognani officiated, Monsignor Michael Ready read the papal decree, and Archbishop Mooney preached the sermon. A banquet in Burke's honor followed the service.[57]

Later, Harney informed Burke that not one Paulist thought a prelacy "fitting or adequate" reward for his "long and faithful work." He all but said the pope should have made Burke a bishop. Burke thanked him for the words, but explained he had always been "outspokenly against any honor of any kind." He could have had a bishopric "simply by expressing the wish." Indeed, authorities had asked if he would be willing to accept one. His answer was a resounding no. "This, my personal attitude, has been and is … fully known by the ecclesiastical authorities," he told Harney. "I have held to it, not alone because of my personal convictions of the consecration of myself as a Paulist, to a religious life where I would be just one among many, but also because I felt from the beginning that the General

Secretary of N.C.W.C. should never be 'elevated' but should always remain a priest." The work of general secretary "was to be for the whole Church of the country," not for gaining personal promotion or winning honors. Moreover, the NCWC was the work of the hierarchy, and to make that more evident, "the General Secretary must be and should remain just a priest." Finally, in Burke's view, honoring an organization's chief executive weakened an institution, for his successor must be honored in the same way, "and a man will be appointed to be so honored." "The tradition should be established that a man will do the work for the sake of the work itself," he concluded. "That tradition I sought to establish." All things considered, he believed a domestic prelacy was more than he deserved.[58]

Father Coughlin and the 1936 Election: Denouement

On return from a routine visit to Rome, Bishop Gallagher said neither pope nor other officials ever discussed Coughlin with him. Coughlin was an outstanding churchman whose voice was listened to by millions. "It's the voice of God," he declared, "that comes to you from this great orator of Royal Oak." *L'Osservatore Romano*, however, reported Gallagher's words failed to accord with truth because the bishop "knew too well what was said to him thereto."[59]

Soon thereafter, Burke received a letter from Archbishop John Mitty asking the Vatican's attitude regarding Coughlin, who was to speak in the San Francisco area. Burke sent a confidential letter to be shared with no one. He said the item in *L'Osservatore* was accurate. Pius XI told Gallagher, although respectful of freedom of speech, he deplored Coughlin's abusive language toward Roosevelt. While in Rome, Cicognani spoke with Pius about it and was since authorized to state publicly that the Roman paper was correct. He felt no pronouncement was necessary unless Gallagher again claimed otherwise. Burke believed Gallagher had not lied; he suspected Pius told him not to make public what he had said about Coughlin.[60]

Burke added the situation was "very delicate as well as very serious." The Vatican wanted it clearly understood it would never interfere in American politics. Still, it wondered why American bishops took no action against Coughlin, permitting the matter to fester. The bishops best knew conditions in America, and action on their part would be viewed "as 'native.'" Burke said unless they acted, Vatican officials felt they may have to issue something more definite than was in *L'Osservatore*. If it came to that, their statement would be as kind and considerate of American sensibilities as it could. "I for one," wrote Burke, "earnestly hope the word will not have to be said by the Holy See."[61]

Burke said many believed when Coughlin spoke somewhere, he had permission of the bishop. "The unregulated activities of Father Coughlin," lamented Burke, "the impossibility of keeping apart the 'citizen' and the priest—are sowing seeds that will greatly injure the name and the work of the Catholic Church in the United States." He reported the NCWC was already beginning to hear from sympathetic congressmen, who voted for legislation it favored, that "the Church harbors and apparently supports one who defames them and their record of public service." Burke concluded that the situation was "far more serious than the Bishops seem to realize." Mitty agreed, replying he was "disturbed" so many eastern ones remained silent.[62]

He did not have long to wait for some to find their voice. Emboldened by Gallagher's continued support, Coughlin spoke in Cincinnati, archiepiscopal seat of McNicholas, in late September. Asserting Roosevelt was "anti-God," he advocated "use of bullets when any upstart dictator in the United States succeeds in making a one-party government and when the ballot is useless." McNicholas had enough. He issued a pronouncement stating Coughlin was "morally in error" for inciting rebellion against conditions that did not exist. Upstate in Cleveland, Bishop Joseph Schrembs said Coughlin's calling Roosevelt "anti-God" was "a harsh statement, not justified by the facts." His use of the phrase "'bullets and ballots' was unfortunate in view of the fact that we haven't reached the stage he was talking about."[63]

Burke sent Mitty copies of their statements and reiterated that Pius wanted Coughlin handled by the American bishops. Burke opposed any corporate action by the hierarchy because it would appear it was pronouncing judgment on one of its brothers, Gallagher. "But if a number of Bishops publicly state their own mind and direction for their own diocese," wrote Burke, "the effect will be orderly and fruitful." He believed it "beyond question" this course of action be followed. He was leaving for New York to confer about the matter with Mooney.[64]

Undeterred by rebukes from McNicholas and Schrembs, and undaunted by press reports that the Vatican was contemplating issuing "a stronger 'warning,'" Coughlin went to Philadelphia where he repeated to a crowd of 20,000 Roosvelt was "anti-God" and averred he would not "disdain the use of bullets for preservation of our liberties." Cicognani finally took action, informing Gallagher the article in *L'Osservatore* was official.[65]

With Coughlin berating Roosevelt, Father John Ryan came to the president's defense. Given the election year, the Administrative Board directed Burke to inform every department head and staff member no one was to "take any public part in politics, nor lend any of the services of the National Catholic Welfare Conference or any of its Departments to politics or to the platform or candidate of any political party." Burke distributed the directive.[66]

In early fall, the Democratic National Committee sought Ryan's help to counter Coughlin. Ryan allowed himself to be persuaded. In October, he delivered a national radio address. At one point in his far-ranging speech, he spoke directly to the interests of laborers, Coughlin's principal supporters. He said Coughlin was 50 percent wrong about economic problems and 90 percent wrong about monetary solutions. If any of his remedies were implemented, they would prove disastrous to the American people. He begged the working class not to abandon Roosevelt.[67]

Two nights later a "quite angry and emphatic" Mooney telephoned Burke that bishops would protest Ryan's action. Burke argued the NCWC could not be implicated because of the "very definite instructions" he sent staff. Mooney agreed those gave it cover, but was livid at Ryan's thoughtlessness regarding his position in the Social Action Department and how his address involved the NCWC. He wanted Ryan to resign. Burke noted Ryan never informed him of his intention. The first he heard was from Monsignor Joseph Corrigan, rector of Catholic University, just hours before the speech. Burke argued the consequences of forcing Ryan's resignation would be "worse" than those of his disobedience. It would appear the bishops sided with Coughlin in opposition to Roosevelt. When Mooney was unmoved, Burke asked to speak with Ryan and Bishop Edwin O'Hara, chairman of Social Action, before any action was taken.[68]

He confronted Ryan about his violation of the directive. Ryan denied traducing it; the order did not preclude personal activity. This was splitting hairs and reminiscent of the 1924 election. Burke emphasized how "inadvisable" it was to speak under the auspices of the Democratic National Committee. Mooney thought Ryan should resign. Burke argued against that. Ryan explained that at the beginning of the address, he specifically stated he was speaking on his own authority and not on behalf of the NCWC. He said he felt conscience-bound to discountenance the impression that Coughlin spoke for the Church. He believed he did the right thing and would resign if the board asked.[69]

Burke spoke with Noll who thought Ryan should never have made the speech. Like Burke, he considered it "most inadvisable" to ask for or permit Ryan's resignation at the time. O'Hara later telephoned Burke that he believed Ryan had the right to speak as he did, not with the authority of the NCWC, but as a citizen.[70]

Mooney asked Burke to draft a letter to the Administrative Board explaining the situation. Burke found the task difficult in the sense that he wished to make it "as objective as possible." So, his letter kept to facts, beginning with the directive against political activity, Ryan's disobedience, Burke's defense of him, and no mention at all about resignation. Burke concluded by asking each bishop if he considered the matter closed or if further action was required. Mooney thought the letter asked the right questions, which could be taken up when the board met in November after the election. "Then we can discuss it without any of the embarrassments that are connected with it in view of the actual political situation," he wrote.[71]

VISIT OF CARDINAL PACELLI

On 30 September, word came to Cicognani that Cardinal Pacelli, Vatican secretary of state, would visit the U.S. Rome left unmentioned that the trip was a back-channel effort, disguised as a private vacation, to explore some form of diplomatic relations between the U.S. and the Vatican. James Farley and Joseph P. Kennedy, prominent Massachusetts Democrat and father of the future president, approached Roosevelt and found him receptive. Kennedy so informed Bishop Francis Spellman, auxiliary of Boston, who was a close friend of Pacelli. Spellman himself arranged the entire trip.[72]

On learning news of the visit, Cicognani asked Burke about the protocol for arranging a meeting with Roosevelt. Burke explained Pacelli should express his wish to see the president. Cicognani would then arrange a meeting through the NCWC. Burke and Cicognani would accompany the cardinal to the interview. Mooney too asked Burke's advice about what to do. Burke counseled waiting until Pacelli was in Washington with Cicognani; then, Mooney should come down to pay his respects as chairman of the board.[73]

On 8 October, Pacelli arrived in New York City. Accompanied by Spellman, he visited Boston, New York, Philadelphia, and Baltimore. Burke and Cicognani waited anxiously for a request to meet with Roosevelt. While the delegate was with Pacelli in Baltimore, he even explained the protocol for getting one. Meanwhile, Burke arranged for Pacelli to visit Mount Vernon and the tombs of George and Martha Washington. He arrived at the capital on 21 October. At that point, Burke learned Pacelli would not be seeing Roosevelt on this trip to Washington, but would return after the election to meet him. On the evening of Pacelli's arrival, Burke dined with him at the apostolic delegation.[74]

The next day, Pacelli visited Catholic University where he spoke. He went to NCWC headquarters to converse about Welfare Conference affairs with Burke and Cicognani. Later, Burke introduced him to the staff whom the cardinal greeted individually. Burke accompanied him to the National Press Club for a luncheon in his honor attended by 450 newsmen. If they hoped to learn the reason of his visit, they were disappointed. Pacelli simply praised the professionalism of American journalists and offered a message of world peace. Burke considered the event "the most important public part" of Pacelli's visit, one that Spellman recommended passing up, advice causing Burke to consider him a not very "capable guide." After the luncheon, Pacelli left for Mount Vernon and thereafter Georgetown University. He and Spellman returned to New York. On 25 October, they flew to Chicago to begin an extended tour of the country.[75]

The following morning, Cicognani told Burke Pacelli just phoned that he would not be returning to Washington; he would meet Roosevelt at Hyde Park after the election. "Of course, this is unthinkable," wrote Burke. "And of course, the Apostolic Delegate is convinced that all this has been prearranged: that the invitation was solicited, that Hyde Park was asked for, by Bishop Spellman." So it was. Burke told Mooney that Spellman's action and Pacelli's acceptance of it did "a grave injury to the welfare and standing of the Catholic Church in this country." Although not a diplomat recognized by the U.S., Cicognani had a position of "dignity and responsibility" before its government. Pacelli should not meet with Roosevelt without the delegate present. Moreover, "this virtual putting aside" of the NCWC was unwise. For Spellman "to assume all this responsibility," and "be abetted in it" by the Vatican secretary of state, showed callous indifference to the representative organization of the hierarchy. "Sentiment of friendship," concluded Burke, "should not be allowed to guide the objective interests of the Church which are above all friendship."[76]

Of course, without knowledge of the ulterior purpose of Pacelli's visit, Burke was left to judge events by their surface appearance. Still, there was validity to his complaint. Spellman himself belatedly realized the slight against the pope's official representative to the American hierarchy and attempted to rectify it. At the eleventh hour, he unsuccessfully sought to have Cicognani invited to Hyde Park. In the end, Spellman's diary made no mention of diplomatic relations as a topic of conversation. For months thereafter, he pursued the subject with Roosevelt's son, James. The president, however, seems to have preferred dealing with his friend, Cardinal George Mundelein of Chicago.[77]

Burke filled in Grace Murray about Pacelli's visit to Washington, adding there were "some problems still" concerning it—an allusion to Spellman's machinations—which he would relate to her in person. Murray had been concerned about Burke's health and urged him to see his heart specialist Dr. Lee. Burke had a checkup just days before writing. Lee wanted him to reduce his work and gave him new directions about his digitalis. The doctor said his heart was in good condition and his blood pressure was better than usual. Burke was grateful because the number of problems he faced was "a tax on the brain."[78]

While Pacelli and Spellman traveled, Mooney tried to arrange for the Administrative Board to host a dinner for the cardinal just before his meeting with Roosevelt at Hyde Park. When Burke went into the office on Friday, 30 October, he considered the tightness of Pacelli's schedule and the previous commitments of bishops on the board. He did not see how a dinner could be squeezed in. Burke, however, dashed off a note to Mooney suggesting the advisability of having the board go ahead and offer to hold a luncheon or dinner anyway either in New York or Washington; the gesture would serve as evidence of good will. It was mid-afternoon when Burke finished the letter. He had not eaten lunch and was feeling unwell. He gave the draft to his secretary Iona McNulty. Usually, he had someone ride home with him, but he went alone. As was his custom, he entered his residence through the NCSSS and greeted one or two of its members.[79]

Within minutes of entering his room at about 3:00 P.M., he summoned housekeeper Frances Boyle, who found him lying on his bed. Telling her to remain calm, Burke said he had pain around his heart and asked her to call Dr. Lee. After doing so, she watched him for a moment as he looked at her in silence. She then hurried to phone Ready at the NCWC. Returning, she cupped Burke's face in her hands and said, "Father, you are not leaving." Before either physician or priest arrived, he was dead of a heart attack at age sixty-one. The headline of the next day's early edition of *Washington Post*, released the night of his death at 10:00 P.M., read: "FATHER BURKE DIES AT HOME."[80]

Endnotes to Chapter 24

1. Burke, *Christ in Us*, 47–48.
2. Curley to Kelley, 2 November 1935, copy, AAB-AASMSU, K247 (the minutes of the foundational meeting). The articles of incorporation are quoted in full in both the Minutes of the Administrative Board, 13 January 1936, ACUA, USCCB 10:64:8, and in *New York Times*, 2 February1936. Gaffey, *Francis Clement Kelley*, 2:92–93; Spalding, *Premier See*, 352.
3. Burke, [Interview with Cicognani], 2 and 3 January 1936, ACUA, USCCB 10:145: Interview Book VII.
4. Ibid.
5. Burke, [Interview with Vagnozzi], 6 January 1936, ACUA, USCCB 10:145: Interview Book VII.
6. Ibid.
7. Burke, "Is the Following Wild Imagination?" 6 January 1936, ACUA, USCCB 10:145: Interview Book VII.
8. Burke, [Interview with Welles], 8 January 1936, ACUA, USCCB 10:145: Interview Book VII.
9. Ibid.; Gaffey, *Francis Clement Kelley*, 2:93.
10. Burke, [Interview with Vagnozzi], 9 January 1936, ACUA, USCCB 10:145: Interview Book VII.
11. Ibid.
12. Burke, [Interview with Vagnozzi], 14 January 1936, ACUA, USCCB 10:145: Interview Book VII.
13. Minutes of the Administrative Board, 13 January and 25 February 1936, ACUA, USCCB 10:64:8; Gaffey, *Francis Clement Kelley*, 2:93–94, 390 n. 93.; Spalding, *Premier See*, 352; *New York Times*, 2 February 1936.

14. Minutes of the Administrative Board, 25 and 26 February 1936, ACUA, USCCB 10:64:8 (containing telegram Curley to Burke, 24 February 1936, quoted in full); Kelley to Curley, 4 and 13 March 1936, AAB-AASMSU, K260 and K261; Curley to Kelley, 25 March 1936, copy, ibid., K264; Gaffey, *Francis Clement Kelley*, 2:94–98; Spalding, *Premier See*, 352.
15. Burke, [Interview with Welles], 24 February 1936, ACUA, USCCB 10:145: Interview Book VII.
16. Burke, [Interview with Welles], 10 March 1936, ACUA, USCCB 10:145: Interview Book VII; Burke to Clark, 25 April 1931, ibid., 10:149:19 (for Burke's understanding of eminent domain and nationalization of property); "Our Common Catholic Interests: NCWC Pamphlets Add New Facts on Persecution of Church in Mexico," *Catholic Action* 17 (November 1935): 3–4.
17. Burke, [Interviews with Welles], 1 April and 4 May 1936, ACUA, USCCB 10:145: Interview Book VII.
18. Burke, [Interview with Cicognani], 22 May 1936, ACUA, USCCB 10:145: Interview Book VII.
19. Burke, [Interview with Welles], 22 May 1936, ACUA, USCCB 10:145: Interview Book VII.
20. Burke, [Interview with Welles], 26 May 1936, ACUA, USCCB 10:145: Interview Book VII.
21. Conversation [between Welles and Nájera], 2 June 1936, NA, State Department 812.404/1895; Welles to Roosevelt, 17 June 1936, FDRL, PSF Mexico; Burke, [Interviews with Welles, Cicognani, and Piani], 5 June 1936, ACUA, USCCB 10:145: Interview Book VII.
22. Report of General Secretary, November 1936, ACUA, USCCB 10:62:26; Matters to be submitted to Meeting of Visiting Committee, Administrative Board, National Catholic Welfare Conference, Monday, 21 September1936, copy, ibid.; Burke, [Interview with Welles], 15 October 1936, ibid., 10:145: Interview Book VII.
23. Walsh, *Sin and Censorship*, 128–34; Black, *Hollywood Censored*, 198–220.
24. *Minutes of the Seventeenth Annual Convention of the Hierarchy, November 1935*, 9–14, ACUA, Bound Volumes; Minutes of the Administrative Board, 14 November 1935, ibid., 10:64:7; Walsh, *Sin and Censorship*, 134; Black, *Hollywood Censored*, 220–21.
25. Minutes of the Visiting Committee of the Administrative Board, 13 January 1936, ACUA, USCCB 10:64:8; Walsh, *Sin and Censorship*, 96.
26. Burke to McNicholas, 17 January 1936, copy, ACUA, USCCB 10:30:28; Burke to Mooney, 6 February 1936, copy, ibid., 10:140:4; Burke, Report of the General Secretary, February 1936, ibid., 10:62:29; Minutes of the Administrative Board, 25 and 26 February 1936, ibid., 10:64:8; Walsh, *Sin and Censorship*, 135; Black, *Hollywood Censored*, 221.
27. Bishops' Statement on Legion of Decency Sent Out for Release Week of 2

March 1936, ACUA, USCCB 10:30:28; Minutes of the Administrative Board, 25 and 26 February 1936, ibid., 10:64:8; Burke to Mooney, 26 March 1936, copy, ibid., 10:30:28; Mooney to Burke, 31 March 1936, ibid., 10:140:4; *Washington Herald*, 28 February 1936; *Washington Post*, 28 February 1936.

28. H.R. 6472, 74th Cong., 1st Sess.; *Motion-Picture Films: Hearing before a Subcommittee of the House Committee on Interstate and Foreign Commerce, Seventy-Fourth Congress, Second Session, 9, 10, 11, 16, 17, 23, 24, 25, and 26 March 1936* (Washington, D.C.: U.S. Government Printing Office, 1936), 155–57.
29. McNicholas to Burke, telegram, 10 March 1936, ACUA, USCCB 10:30:28; Burke to McNicholas, 11 March 1936, copy, ibid.
30. Montavon to Burke, 12 March 1936, ACUA, USCCB 10:125:31.
31. McNicholas to Noll, telegram, 13 March 1936 (with Noll's handwritten note), ACUA, USCCB 10:30:28; McNicholas to Burke, telegram, 14 March 1936, ibid.
32. *Motion-Picture Films: Hearing*, 226–35; *Washington Post*, 18 March 1936.
33. Burke to Mooney, 26 March 1936, copy, ACUA, USCCB 10:30:28.
34. Mooney to Burke, 31 March 1936, ACUA, USCCB 10:140:4.
35. Burke to McNicholas, 24 April 1936, ACUA, USCCB 10:30:28.
36. S. 4000, 74th Cong., 2nd Sess.; Robert Keegan to Royal Copeland, 14 February 1936, copy, ACUA, USCCB 10:117:13; Copeland to Keegan, 18 February 1936, copy, ibid.; Keegan to Burke, 20 February 1936, ibid.; Chesler, *Woman of Valor*, 361–67.
37. Burke, Confidential Report of the Administrative Board, NCWC, to the Cardinals, Archbishops, and Bishops of the United States, undated [March 1936], ACUA, USCCB 10:4:140; Montavon to Burke, 3 March 1936, ibid., 10:117:13.
38. Burke to Keegan, 5 March 1936, ACUA, USCCB 10:117:13; *Offenses against the Postal Service: Hearings*, 39.
39. Keegan to Copeland, 6 March 1936, copy, ACUA, USCCB 10:117:13; Copeland to Keegan, 9 March 1935, copy, ibid.
40. Byrne to Burke, 25 January 1936, ACUA, USCCB 10:137:2; Byrne to McGowan, 30 January 1936, copy, ibid.
41. Burke to Roosevelt, 5 February 1936, copy, ACUA, USCCB 10:137:2; Roosevelt to Burke, 17 February 1936, ibid., 10:123:1.
42. Burke, Report of the General Secretary, February 1936, ACUA, USCCB 10:62:29; Minutes of the Administrative Board, 25 February 1936, ibid., 10:64:8; Burke to Roosevelt, 3 March 1936, copy, ibid., 10:123:1; Burke to Byrne, 7 March 1936, copy, ibid., 10:137:2.
43. *Many Battles: Autobiography of Gruening*, 103–06, 200–01; Ramírez de Arellano and Seipp, *Colonialism, Catholicism, and Contraception*, 42–44.
44. *New York Times*, 17 July 1936; Brinkley, *Voices of Protest*, 124–42, 252–56;

Marcus, *Father Coughlin*, 111–19; Tull, *Coughlin and the New Deal*, 134; Flynn, *Catholics and Roosevelt*, 202–04.

45. Burke to Mooney, 17 July 1936, copy, ACUA, USCCB 10:16:1.
46. *New York Times*, 20 July 1936; Burke by telephone to Mooney, 19 July 1936, ACUA, USCCB 10:16:1; Boyea, "Coughlin and the Church," 221; Marcus, *Father Coughlin*, 120.
47. Marcus, *Father Coughlin*, 111–19.
48. Burke, [Interview with Roosevelt], 10 August 1936, ACUA, USCCB 10:153:1 (there are three different versions of this interview, each with more details about the content); Brands, *Traitor to His Class*, 179–80.
49. Burke, [Interview with Roosevelt], 10 August 1936, ACUA, USCCB 10:153:1.
50. Burke to Lynch, 6 May 1936, AP, Burke Papers, box 5.
51. Ibid.
52. "M * * *," undated [probably June 1936] (the insertion of 30 is his), AP, Burke Papers, box 5; Abram J. Ryan, *Poems: Patriotic, Religious, Miscellaneous* (Baltimore: John B. Piet & Co., 1884), 259–62.
53. Burke to Lynch 28 June and 27 July 1936, AP, Burke Papers, box 5; "To W.J.K," 28 July 1936, ibid., box 12.
54. Burke to G. Murray, 20 and 26 August 1936, AP, Burke Papers, box 12; Burke to Lynch, 22 August 1936, ibid., box 5; John J. Burke, "The Right Reverend William J. Kerby—An Appreciation, 1870–1936," *Ecclesiastical Review* 95 (September 1936): 25–33.
55. Burke to Harney, 5 September 1936, AP, Superior General Papers of John Harney; Burke to E. Burke, 4 September 1936, ibid., Burke Papers, box 3.
56. Harney to Burke, 7 September 1936, AP, Superior General Papers of John Harney; Burke to Harney, undated [8 September 1936], ibid.
57. NCWC News Service, 22 September 1936.
58. Harney to Burke, 25 September 1936, AP, Superior General Papers of Harney; Burke to Harney, 26 September 1936, ibid.
59. *New York Sun*, 3 September 1936; *Washington Post*, 4 September 1936; Enrico Pucci, Cable, NCWC News Service, 3 September 1936.
60. Mitty to Burke, 17 September 1936, copy, AASF, NCWC files; Burke to Mitty, personal and confidential, 23 September 1936, ibid.
61. Burke to Mitty, personal and confidential, 23 September 1936, AASF, NCWC files.
62. Ibid.
63. Washington *Evening Star*, 25 September 1936; *Washington Post*, 25 September 1936; Statement of Archbishop McNicholas Regarding Father Coughlin's Address in Cincinnati, 24 September 1936, AASF, NCWC files; *New York Herald Tribune*, 27 September 1936; Karen G. Kechaver, "Coughlin and Cleveland" (Master's Thesis: John Carroll University, 2009), 26.

64. Burke to Mitty, 29 September 1936, AASF, NCWC files.
65. Washington *Evening Star*, 25 September 1936; *Washington Post*, 25 September 1936; *New York Times*, 27 September 1936; Boyea, "Coughlin and the Church," 222; Tentler, *Seasons of Grace*, 327–28.
66. Burke to J. A. Ryan, 3 March 1936, copy, ACUA, USCCB 10:5:29.
67. Broderick, *Reverend New Dealer*, 225–26.
68. Burke, [Telephone Interview with Mooney], 11 October 1936, ACUA, USCCB 10:153: Interview Book.
69. Burke, [Interview with J. A. Ryan], 12 October 1936, ACUA, USCCB 10:153: Interview Book.
70. Burke to Mooney, 12 October 1936, copy, ACUA, USCCB 10:140:4.
71. Burke to Mooney, 13 October 1936, copy, with enclosure: Burke to Administrative Board, draft, ACUA, USCCB 10:140:4.
72. Castagna, *Bridge Across the Ocean*, 139–47; Fogarty, *The Vatican and the American Hierarchy*, 248–49; Fogarty, "Francis J. Spellman," 219–20; Cooney, *American Pope*, 65–66.
73. Burke, [Telephone Interview with Mooney], 11 October 1936, ACUA, USCCB 10:153: Interview Book; Burke to Mooney, 26 October 1936, copy, ibid., 10:152:27; Fogarty, "Francis J. Spellman,"220; Sheerin, *Never Look Back*, 217–18.
74. Burke to Lynch, 21 October 1936, AP, Burke Papers, box 5; Burke to Mooney, 26 October 1936, copy, ACUA, USCCB 10:152:27; Castagna, *Bridge Across the Ocean*, 147–48.
75. Burke to Mooney, 24 October 1936, copy, ACUA, USCCB 10:140:4; Burke to G. Murray, 26 October 1936, AP, Burke Papers, box 12; "Our Common Interests: His Eminence, Cardinal Pacelli, Papal Secretary of State, Welcome Visitor to the U.S.," *Catholic Action* 18 (November 1936): 3–4; Castagna, *Bridge Across the Ocean*, 147–48.
76. Burke to Mooney, 26 October 1936, copy, ACUA, USCCB 10:152:27; Fogarty, *The Vatican and the American Hierarchy*, 248.
77. Fogarty, "Francis J. Spellman," 220–21.
78. Burke to Lynch, 21 October 1936, AP, Burke Papers, box 4; Burke to G. Murray, 26 October 1936, ibid., box 12.
79. Burke to Mooney, 30 October 1936, copy, ACUA, USCCB 10:140:4; Bruce Mohler to Ella Mohler, 1 November 1936, ibid., Bruce Mohler Papers 141:8:6; McNulty to Tanner, 6 May 1964, ibid., USCCB 10:72:24.
80. Bruce Mohler to Ella Mohler, 1 November 1936, ACUA, Bruce Mohler Papers 141:8:6; *Washington Times*, 30 October 1936; New York *Catholic News*, 7 November 1936; McNulty to Tanner, 6 May 1964, ACUA, USCCB 10:72:24; Malloy, "John Joseph Burke," 725; Sheerin, *Never Look Back*, 239.

Epilogue

The sudden death of Monsignor John Burke was a shock. His secretary Iona McNulty telegraphed news to Helen Lynch. "I have tried all through the years to prepare myself for this hour," wrote Lynch to a friend, "—but I must confess I have done it badly because I find myself in deepest grief. Nearly thirty-two years of close association and friendship establishes bonds." She consoled herself with the timing of his death. "To die in harness—at 3 o'clock on Friday—in the very shadow of the Feasts of All Saints and All Souls—should be to us a heavenly sign that the Lord has claimed His own for everlasting happiness." She considered Burke's recent investiture as monsignor his Mount Tabor, with a voice from the overshadowing cloud proclaiming, "This is my beloved son, in whom I am well pleased" (Matt. 17:5).[1]

The evening of Burke's passing, Franklin Roosevelt issued a statement: "A powerful spiritual force has been lost to our national life in the passing of Mgr. Burke. I personally mourn the loss of an old and dear friend." Two days later, Bruce Mohler told his mother everyone at the NCWC was stunned. "In fact we are still in a daze," he said. "Just cannot realize it is true."[2]

The day following Burke's death, the editor of the *Washington Star* wrote his life was proof of the might of Christianity "in the materialistic modern world." "Such men as Monsignor John J. Burke are not accidents," he declared. They were explicable only in terms of the power of religion, for no other force could motivate such zeal, enthusiasm, and devotion: selfless service to God and humanity. The editor rightly saw Burke dedicated his public life to teaching "the applicability of Christ's philosophy of love and righteousness to contemporary problems." Many Protestants would join Catholics in mourning his passing. "They loved him for the gentleness of his manner, the charity of his mind and the elemental justice of his heart," said the editor. "He was a noble character, illuminated by a light which is eternal and cannot be dimmed." The city of Washington would remember him "with gratitude and affection always."[3] Of course, this last sentiment never saw fulfillment.

When the NCWC announced Burke's death, telegrams and letters of condolence streamed in from around the nation and parts of the globe, from prelates, priests, and lay persons, Catholic and non-Catholic alike. "Now he is dead, few of us can trust ourselves to write temperately of the qualities of head and heart that made Monsignor Burke wise in counsel and beloved by everyone who had even slight contact with him," commented Bishop Hugh Boyle. Indeed, praise for the man was lavish. "His loss at this critical period seems irreparable," remarked Archbishop John McNicholas. "He ever kept before him the best interest of the Church and the general welfare of his country.... He was anxious that the non-Catholic world realize that his Church had the solution of nearly all our modern problems in her moral principles." Wrote Archbishop John Mitty: "[Burke] was animated by a supreme love for the Church as the Mystical Body of Christ and gave himself unreservedly to her service in every way possible.... This country has lost one of its noblest priests and that loss is irreparable." According to Bishop Edwin O'Hara, Burke's signal gift was his breadth of vision. "I think that his peculiar and permanent contribution to the service of the Church arose from his capacity to view the work of the Church as a whole," said O'Hara. "Difficult problems concerning every phase of Catholic thought and action engaged his attention, but he was not confused by the multiplicity of seeming conflict, for he had a deep understanding of the relations of the members of the Mystic Body to Christ, the Head."[4]

Kind words from those outside the Catholic fold were equally lavish. Sumner Welles wrote: "In addition to all of his other rare and fine qualities, he was a statesman of an unusual breadth of vision. I feel that the American people have suffered an irreparable loss." "I found him wise in counsel and noble in spirit and holy in life," remarked Josephus Daniels. "His face reflected the beauty of the religion of Christ Who was his Exemplar. He was wise beyond human wisdom." Perhaps Raymond Fosdick offered the highest tribute:

> I cannot think of him in any detached fashion, because he was a close friend. During the war, he was a pillar of strength in

> Washington and what we would have done without his counsel and sound common sense I cannot imagine. He had a completely honest mind and a capacity for cool judgment and impersonal appraisal that was exceedingly rare. Back of this talent lay human qualities that were broad and deep—a sensitive sympathy, a love of people for their own sakes, and a sense of humor....
>
> In recent years it has not been my fortune to see him as often as I wished, but it was reassuring to know that a man like Father Burke was alive in the world and that the ties of human affairs were, to some extent at least, being influenced by his inspiring personality. The world is poorer because he is gone.[5]

The picture of Burke that emerges is of a man who lived in and with Christ in his own life. Deeply loyal to the Church, he believed the principles of Catholicism alone held the answer to national problems, and he sought to impart that truth to his fellow citizens. His vision was broad, and his sense of the Mystical Body of Christ enabled him to view the operations of the Church as a whole and to understand the importance and function of the various members. He blended love of Church with love of country, both of which he drew together in the NCWC, the organization he came to symbolize and embody.

On 3 November, Archbishop Amleto Cicognani celebrated the solemn funeral Mass at the National Shrine of the Immaculate Conception, where little more than a month earlier Burke was robed as a monsignor. Present were fifteen bishops and archbishops and hundreds of priests, nuns, and laity. Bishop Boyle, the longest sitting member of the Administrative Board, delivered the sermon. He described Burke as "a unique compound of the mystic, the priest, and the skillful man of affairs." Boyle said Burke internalized his priesthood. He took "very literally" the words of St. Paul: "I live. Now not I, but Christ liveth in me [Gal. 2:20]." His sense of the Mystical Body of Christ "was a consuming passion." The spirit that moved Burke was not the spirit of the time. He eschewed expediency and opportunism for permanent solutions to problems and the secure end of conflicts. Boyle declared Burke would not "abandon" the work of the NCWC. "His life has changed," he said. "It is not destroyed." He would pray for and assist, "in such ways as are permitted him," those who carried on the work.[6]

Burke's body was taken by train to New York where the next day his brother Thomas celebrated a second solemn Mass in St. Paul the Apostle church. Father Edward Mullaly preached the sermon, which recounted Burke's priestly career. Mullaly was one of the few who commented on the toll the work took from him. "I have wondered how, during the past six or eight years, Father Burke ... was even able to carry on his tasks," said Mullaly. "I have sat with him at times when it seemed to me that he must fall from fatigue. But he had pledged himself to his God, his Church, and his Country, and right ready was he to die in their service."[7]

At the end of November, Sara Murphy, who worked at the Chaplain's Aid Association after years of service with Burke at *Catholic World*, wrote Lynch that at St. Paul's, there had been a procession of Burke's secretaries, but her thoughts turned to the one "who had been nearest to him, and who could not be there." Like Mullaly, she understood Burke wore himself out "in his work for the Church and for souls." It was good Lynch had not seen him "in his physical aspect." "It was just as though I had been looking at a strange man," wrote Murphy. "He must have been sick for a very long time, ... for his face was so pale, his eyes so large, everything distorted." McNulty sent the employees at Chaplain's Aid a photo of Burke in his monsignor's robes. The image was "of a man we do not know," remarked Murphy. She was happy Lynch still had her memories of him in health. "Do not all those carefree days come back to you, when I flew in and out of the Catholic World offices, and we were so merry?" she asked. "And you and I were so jealous of each other, and Father Burke kept up the fiction through sheer playfulness?" Murphy said his life had grown "so much more serious" as time passed. He did not seem the same person: "I am sure that when I recalled some of the happy times of long ago with Miss McNulty, she must have felt that she did not know that man." He bore the burden of the American Church on his shoulders, "and it took all the joy of life from him," wrote Murphy. "Or perhaps it was that it was wearing him out and he would not spare himself."[8]

Though considering herself a "worldling," she told Lynch she and those at Chaplains Aid felt Burke was still interested in them and would continue to guide and direct them, a feeling stronger now than when he was alive. Lynch noted in the margin: "Yes. So have I." "I have him canonized already," proclaimed Murphy, a process requiring miracles. She recounted a "silly" incident the Sunday after Burke's death because she believed Lynch would understand. Murphy was terribly upset by it as she and her sister closed their summer home in New Jersey. Thoughts of him filled her all day. As she carried a bundle of blankets to the first floor, she lost footing at the top of the stairs and tumbled the full flight crashing her head against the wall at the bottom. Her ankle was sprained and swollen. As she fell, she thought, "This is my finish." Next morning, she did not see how she could make the trip to New York City. She limped with a cane to the train station. "In a few hours I was quite all right," she wrote, "—not a bruise, not a headache, the ankle perfectly normal.... So that is my miracle! I felt Father Burke was right there to save me." She believed him a saint. "A modern saint," she said, "without the quietude of the old saints, but ready to fight, full of indignation, where God's glory was being disregarded. Aren't you glad of those years beside him?"[9]

Another of Burke's spiritual daughters, Mary Hawks, reminiscing years later, set down her memories of him. At the close, she noted Boyle's remark that Burke was "a combination of priest, mystic and man of affairs." "If, indeed, one may speak of these three phases or facets of his personality," she wrote, "it must be with a realization of their complete integration—the man of affairs was wholly directed by the priest-mystic. In this spiritual fact lay the power and success of his work." She quoted the French Church historian, Henri Daniel-Rops: "With the great mystics there is no separation between practical action and transcendent knowledge." Without claiming Burke was a great mystic, she did recognize in him that "essential unity." "His prayer was Christ centered and his work Christ directed," she concluded. "In disconcerting silences, which few understood [like the one about his intensity at Mass], he passed from the thing of the moment to the Source of all knowing, the Light of all doing. Christ was his Master during the working hours of the day, his 'yoke-fellow' in the wakeful suffering hours of the night. Not to know this is never to have known him at all."[10]

ENDNOTES TO EPILOGUE

1. Lynch to Brother Joe, 31 October 1936, AP, Burke Papers, box 6.
2. *Washington Post*, 31 October 1936; Mohler to Ella Mohler, 1 November 1936, ACRC, Mohler Papers 141:8:6.

3. *Washington Star*, 31 October 1936.
4. "Universal Praise for Monsignor Burke," *Catholic Action* 18 (December 1936): 40–46 *passim*.
5. Ibid.
6. NCWC News Service, 3 November 1936; "Father Burke's Distinguished Career," *Catholic Action* 18 (December 1936): 7; "A Bishop Speaks for the Hierarchy," ibid., 9–10; Sheerin, *Never Look Back*, 239–40.
7. "Burke's Distinguished Career," 7; Mullaly, "Eulogy," *Catholic Action* 18 (December 1936): 10–11 and 13.
8. Sara Murphy to Lynch, 30 November 1936, AP, Burke Papers, box 6.
9. Ibid.
10. Hawks, "Souvenir of Burke," AP, Burke Papers, box 10.

Index